The System for Graphics for the PC

SYSTAT, Inc.

References

SAS is a trademark of SAS Institute, Inc.
MS-DOS is a trademark of the Microsoft Corporation.
SYSTAT is a trademark of SYSTAT, Inc.
Lotus 1-2-3 is a trademark of Lotus Development Corporation
dBase is a trademark of Ashton-Tate, Inc.
McDonald's is a trademark of McDonald's, Inc.

SYSTAT, Inc.
1800 Sherman Avenue
Evanston, IL 60201

(312) 864-5670

The proper citation for this manual is:

Wilkinson, Leland. SYGRAPH. Evanston, IL: SYSTAT, Inc. 1988.

Copyright Notice

Second Edition, January, 1989.

PREFACE

SYGRAPH was supposed to be a supplementary module for SYSTAT with high resolution versions of the basic graphs in that statistical package. As I programmed during the last year, I could not resist adding a new graph each time I saw it published. Consequently, the release was delayed more than I wished.

If you are a statistician or researcher familiar with the techniques in this package, I hope you will find them useful for your work. If not, I hope this might be an opportunity for you to learn about the research on human perception of graphics, good graphic design, and state-of-the-art statistical graphics. At the same time, I hope it can be an opportunity for me to learn about the kinds of graphs you need so that I can revise SYGRAPH to include them. As with the statistical package SYSTAT, I have made it difficult for you to do some things which I and experts in the field of statistical graphics consider bad practice, but you are welcome to lobby for new techniques. Often, I am wrong. My goal in writing SYGRAPH is to create a package which can plot every well-designed graph appearing in journals like *Science*, *Scientific American*, and *Harvard Business Review*. I haven't entirely succeeded, but you can help to realize this goal.

Bill Cleveland, John Hartigan, and Paul Tukey influenced much of this work, although not always in directions they might have anticipated or approved. Neil Polhemus, author of *Statgraphics*, kept me to a high standard. Our two packages contrast and will always appeal to somewhat different groups of users, but Neil's work inspires me because he programs what he loves and it shows.

Many SYSTAT users suggested graphics for this package. I would like to be able to blame them for the delays, but every addition made it a better package. I cannot name them all here, but I hope by including the procedures they suggested I will have thanked them.

This package could not have been produced without the assistance of SYSTAT staff. Eve Goldman directed production and marketing. Mark Bjerknes helped with design and wrote the entire Macintosh interface. David Koepke helped me with design and algorithms. Chris Soderquist provided numerous examples. Leah Dorsey, Tom Wassink, and Mark Coward communicated with users. Jon Goldman and Stephanie Shishko assisted with document preparation. I thank all the other members of the SYSTAT staff who endured this long development process.

Leland Wilkinson
Evanston, IL
January, 1988

SYSTAT, Inc.

TABLE OF CONTENTS

SYSTAT, Inc.

CHAPTER SUMMARIES

PART 1 Introduction

Chapter 1 Tutorial
This chapter gets you started.

Chapter 2 Cognitive Science and Graphic Design
This chapter introduces you to the theory and methods of designing useful graphs.

PART 2 Reference

Chapter 1 General Commands
This chapter summarizes the general, control, and graphics commands in SYGRAPH.

Chapter 2 BAR
This chapter introduces bar graphs.

Chapter 3 BOX
This chapter presents schematic (box) plots.

Chapter 3 CPLOT
This chapter covers category plots, which are graphs of continuous against categorical variables. Typical examples are line graphs, dot plots, and star plots.

Chapter 4 DENSITY
This chapter involves histograms, frequency polygons, and other displays of the density of a variable.

Chapter 5 DRAW
This chapter presents drawing tools for annotating graphs.

Chapter 6 ICON
This chapter covers a variety of graphical symbols for displaying multivariate data, such as Chernoff's FACES, profiles, Fourier blobs, and stars.

Chapter 7 MAP
This chapter shows you how to draw geographical and other types of maps.

Chapter 8 PIE
This chapter serves pies.

Chapter 9 PLOT
This chapter covers XY and three-dimensional plots of continuous variables. Scatterplots, function plots, polar graphs, and line graphs are included.

Chapter 10 PPLOT
This chapter involves probability plots for a variety of probability distributions.

Chapter 11 QPLOT
This chapter discusses quantile plots for empirical distributions.

Chapter 12 SPLOM
This chapter describes scatterplot matrices or casement plots.

Chapter 13 STEM
This chapter covers stem-and-leaf diagrams.

Chapter 14 WRITE
This chapter shows you how to write text on your graphs in various fonts.

PART 3 Advanced Applications

Chapter 1 Two-Dimensional Plots
This chapter gives examples for constructing more complex two-dimensional displays.

Chapter 2 Three-Dimensional Plots
This chapter covers advanced examples of three-dimensional displays.

SYGRAPH Installation

This section describes how to install SYGRAPH and its drivers on your system and how to select the options appropriate to your particular configuration. You can install SYGRAPH automatically or manually on either a hard disk or two-floppy system.

We recommend using INSTALL, the automatic installation program. It prompts you for all necessary information, copies all program files to your hard disk, selects the correct drivers for your hardware, and automatically modifies your AUTOEXEC.BAT and CONFIG.SYS files after making backup copies of them.

Here is an outline of this section:

I. Backup Your Disks!
II. Automatic Installation
III. Manual Installation
IV. It's All Installed, Is Everything Ready to Go?
V. Saving RAM
VI. Sample CONFIG.SYS and AUTOEXEC.BAT Files
VII. Two Monitor Configuration
VIII. Graphing without a Graphics Monitor
IX. Common Installation Problems
X. Common Usage Questions

The manual also contains the following appendices which will help you choose and configure the drivers for your devices:

Appendix C.......Emulation modes supported by common output devices (look here if we do not have a specific driver for your device).
Appendix D.......Driver files by Driver Disk number.
Appendix E.........Driver files by output device.
Appendix F.........Supplemental drivers available from SYSTAT.
Appendix G........Hardware specific configuration notes—check to see if any apply to your devices.
Appendix H........Saving SYGRAPH graphs to a file.
Appendix I..........Saving metafiles

Backup Your Disks!

Before you install SYGRAPH you must backup your disks! Make a copy of each SYGRAPH disk using either the COPY or DISKCOPY command in DOS and then put the backups in a safe place.

Automatic Installation

The INSTALL program copies SYGRAPH to your system simply and safely. It is fully menu driven, prompting you for information and choosing and installing appropriate drivers for your hardware. SYGRAPH program files come in a compressed format, and INSTALL automatically unpacks them and copies them to the location of your choice.

INSTALL modifies two of your system files, CONFIG.SYS and AUTOEXEC.BAT (if you do not have these files, INSTALL creates them). Before modifying them it makes backup copies named CONFIG.BA*n* and AUTOEXEC.BA*n* where *n* is the number of the backup. If you still get worried, however, you can quit INSTALL at any step in the procedure. When you have completed the installation procedure, proceed to the section, "It's All Installed—Is Everything Ready to Go?," to check if installation was successful.

INSTALL asks the following questions, so be ready to answer them:

From Which Drive Will SYGRAPH Be Installed?

INSTALL needs to know which drive you will be inserting program disks into. This will usually be the A: drive. INSTALL reads the files from this drive and copies them to the destination drive (which you also specify).

For floppy disk installation you must have two disk drives, at least one of which is high density. The high density drive will be the destination drive. Choose the low density drive in response to this question.

What Is Your Startup (Boot) Disk?

INSTALL modifies two files, CONFIG.SYS and AUTOEXEC.BAT, which are located on your startup or boot disk (the first disk your computer reads when you turn it on). INSTALL needs you to tell it which disk this is. For hard drive systems, the startup disk is typically drive C:. For floppy systems, your boot disk is the disk that you insert in drive A: before you start your machine.

Where Do You Want SYGRAPH Installed?

Where do you want to put SYGRAPH? We recommend the default selection of the \SYSTAT subdirectory on your C: drive. If you specify a new subdirectory, INSTALL will automatically create it. With floppy installation, you must select your high density drive.

Note: do not confuse this with the first question. That asks where the computer will read the program files from, while this asks where it will write them to.

Where Do You Want the Driver Files Installed?

Where do you want to put your drivers? They are not usually stored in the same subdirectory as your program files. We recommend the default location of the \DRIVERS subdirectory on your C: drive. If you specify a new subdirectory, INSTALL will automatically create it.

Where is the File DATA.DEF?

DATA.DEF is a file which must be in your SYSTAT subdirectory (or on your boot disk) in order for SYGRAPH to run. If you have purchased SYGRAPH by itself, DATA.DEF is on the EDIT disk. If you have purchased SYGRAPH with the SYSTAT statistical package, DATA.DEF is on the DATA disk. If you are updating from a previous version of SYSTAT, use the copy of DATA.DEF that came with that version.

You can (and should) use INSTALL each time you add another piece of hardware to your system. This will make certain that the appropriate drivers are installed and that your system is configured correctly.

INSTALL will ask your permission before it overwrites any existing files. If, for example, you install more than once, INSTALL will ask you if you want to overwrite the file GSSCGI.SYS (it is okay to do this). If you do not want to overwrite a file, type "N", return to the main menu, and either move that file or tell INSTALL to copy files to a different subdirectory.

To start INSTALL, do the following:

- Place the disk labelled INSTALL in either drive A: or B:.
- Type:

```
>A:          (or B:, depending where the disk is)
>INSTALL
```

- Choose SYGRAPH installation at the first prompt and follow the subsequent instructions.

Manual Installation

This section explains how to install SYGRAPH manually onto a hard disk. Explanation for installing on a two-floppy system is given below. When you have completed the installation procedure, proceed to the next section, "It's All Installed—Is Everything Ready to Go?," to check if installation was successful.

There are four steps in hard disk installation:

- Copy SYGRAPH and other files to the hard disk
- Select and copy device drivers
- Modify CONFIG.SYS and AUTOEXEC.BAT files
- Reboot your machine

Copy SYGRAPH and Other Files to the Hard Disk

The SYGRAPH module is shipped to you in a compressed format in a file called SYGRAPHI.EXE. To unpack the file and copy it to your hard disk, do the following:

- Make a \SYSTAT subdirectory, if one does not already exist, by typing from your C: prompt:

  ```
  >MD  \SYSTAT
  ```

- Change to the SYSTAT subdirectory by typing:

  ```
  >CD  \SYSTAT
  ```

- Insert the SYGRAPH program disk into drive A: and type:

  ```
  >A:SYGRAPHI
  ```

  This command both unpacks and copies the SYGRAPH program to the current subdirectory (\SYSTAT). Once unpacked, the name of the program changes to SYGRAPH.EXE.

- Insert the disk containing the file DATA.DEF into drive A: and type:

  ```
  >COPY  A:DATA.DEF
  ```

  If you have purchased SYGRAPH by itself, DATA.DEF is on the EDIT disk. If you have purchased SYGRAPH with the SYSTAT statistical package, DATA.DEF is on the DATA disk. If you are updating from a previous version of SYSTAT, use the copy of DATA.DEF that came with that version.

- Insert the SYGRAPH FONTS disk into drive A: and type:

  ```
  >COPY  A:*.*
  ```

Select and Copy Device Drivers

SYGRAPH will operate a wide variety of output devices. Each output device, whether it be a monitor, printer, or plotter, communicates with your computer through a file called a device driver. There is a unique driver for each output device (for monitors, the drivers are specific to the graphics card as opposed to the monitor itself).

SYGRAPH provides many device drivers. Appendix E at the back of this manual lists output devices, the drivers which run those devices, and the DRIVERS DISK that contains a specific device. If your device is not listed in Appendix E, look to Appendix C. This is a list of emulation modes for many devices. Your device may emulate another for which SYGRAPH provides a driver. You must copy one driver for each output device *and the driver GSSCGI.SYS (on DRIVER DISK 2)* to your hard disk as follows:

- Make a \DRIVERS subdirectory, if one does not already exist, by typing from your C: prompt:

```
>MD  \DRIVERS
```

- Change to the DRIVERS subdirectory by typing:

```
>CD  \DRIVERS
```

- Insert DRIVERS DISK 2 into drive A: and type:

```
>COPY  A:GSSCGI.SYS
```

- Insert consecutively the appropriate DRIVERS DISKs for your devices into drive A: and each time type:

```
>COPY  A:<filename>
```

where <filename> is the name of the device driver.

Modify CONFIG.SYS

CONFIG.SYS is a text file located on your boot disk (C:\ for most hard drives) in which you can control certain system parameters and configurations. You can edit and create CONFIG.SYS with almost any word processor or text editor. Remember always to save it as a text or non-document file.

Modify CONFIG.SYS as follows:

- Add one DEVICE statement corresponding to each driver file that you copied into your \DRIVERS subdirectory:

  ```
  >DEVICE=C:\DRIVERS\<filename>
  ```

  where <filename> is the name of the driver.

Note: The DEVICE statement for the GSSCGI.SYS driver must be the last device statement in CONFIG.SYS.

For example, if you have an HP Plotter and an IBMEGA monitor which require the drivers HPGLPLTR.SYS and IBMEGA.SYS, you would add these DEVICE statements to CONFIG.SYS:

```
DEVICE=C:\DRIVERS\HPGLPLTR.SYS
DEVICE=C:\DRIVERS\IBMEGA.SYS
DEVICE=C:\DRIVERS\GSSCGI.SYS
```

- Add a FILES and a BUFFERS statement to CONFIG.SYS:

  ```
  FILES=20
  BUFFERS=16
  ```

Do not put spaces in any of these statements. When you are done, save CONFIG.SYS as a text only file into your root directory.

Modify AUTOEXEC.BAT

AUTOEXEC.BAT is similar to CONFIG.SYS. It is a text file located in your root directory in which you can enter environmental commands that the computer will read when you start it up. You create and edit AUTOEXEC.BAT in the same manner as CONFIG.SYS.

Modify AUTOEXEC.BAT as follows:

- Appendix G lists required AUTOEXEC.BAT commands for specific output devices. You will add at least one command to AUTOEXEC.BAT for each device you operate. Notice that for many devices there are optional commands which you can add to AUTOEXEC.BAT.

  For example, for the IBMEGA monitor and HP plotter mentioned above, you would add these lines to AUTOEXEC.BAT:

  ```
  SET  DISPLAY=IBMEGA
  SET  PLOTTER=HPGLPLTR
  ```

  No AUTOEXEC.BAT statement is required for the GSSCGI.SYS driver.

- Create or modify the PATH command. PATH is a DOS command that tells the computer which subdirectories to search for executable files. Modifying it will enable you to run SYGRAPH from subdirectories other than \SYSTAT. If AUTOEXEC.BAT does not contain a PATH command, add the line:

```
SET   PATH=C:\SYSTAT
```

  If a PATH command exists, add ;C:\SYSTAT to the end. For example, if your PATH reads PATH=C:\DOS, append \SYSTAT to produce:

```
SET   PATH=C:\DOS;C:\SYSTAT
```

When you are done, save AUTOEXEC.BAT as a text file in your root directory.

Reboot Your Machine

Your computer reads CONFIG.SYS and AUTOEXEC.BAT when it starts up, so you must reboot in order for the changes you have just made to take effect. Reboot by pressing the Control, Alt, and Delete keys simultaneously.

Manual Two-Floppy System Installation

SYGRAPH can run on a two-floppy drive system. At least one of the floppy drives must be high density. The steps for floppy installation are similar to those for hard disk installation:

- Format a boot disk
- Copy SYGRAPH to a disk
- Select and copy device drivers
- Modify CONFIG.SYS and AUTOEXEC.BAT files
- Reboot your machine

After completing installation, proceed to the next section, "It's all Installed—Is Everything Ready to Go?" to see if installation was successful.

Format a Boot Disk

To run SYGRAPH, you will need to start your computer with a boot disk configured specifically for SYGRAPH. This disk receives a special format and contains the CONFIG.SYS, AUTOEXEC.BAT, DATA.DEF, and other files.

To make this boot disk, do the following:

- Insert your DOS system disk (your current boot disk) in drive A:.

■ Insert a blank disk into drive B: and type:

```
>A:
>FORMAT  B:/S
```

■ Copy CONFIG.SYS and AUTOEXEC.BAT to the disk in drive B: by typing:

```
>COPY  CONFIG.SYS  B:
>COPY  AUTOEXEC.BAT  B:
```

If these files are not on the disk in the A: drive, find the disk that contains them, insert it in the A: drive, and enter the same commands. If you do not have either of these files, you can make them in a word processor (the contents of CONFIG.SYS and AUTOEXEC.BAT are discussed below).

■ Insert the disk containing the file DATA.DEF into drive A: and type:

```
>COPY  DATA.DEF  B:
```

If you have purchased SYGRAPH by itself, DATA.DEF is on the EDIT disk. If you have purchased SYGRAPH with the SYSTAT statistical package, DATA.DEF is on the DATA disk. If you are updating from a previous version of SYSTAT, use the copy of DATA.DEF that came with that version.

■ Insert the SYGRAPH FONTS disk into drive A: and type:

```
>COPY  *.*  B:
```

Select and Copy Device Drivers

SYGRAPH will operate a wide variety of output devices. Each output device, whether it be a monitor, printer, or plotter, communicates with your computer through a file called a device driver. There is a unique driver for each output device (for monitors, the drivers are specific to the graphics card as opposed to the monitor itself).

SYGRAPH provides many device drivers. Appendix E at the back of this manual lists output devices, the drivers which run those devices, and the DRIVERS DISK that contains a specific device. If your device is not listed in Appendix E, look to Appendix C. This lists emulation modes for many devices. Your device may emulate another for which SYGRAPH provides a driver. You must copy one driver for each output device *and the driver GSSCGI.SYS (on DRIVER DISK 2)* to your SYGRAPH boot disk as follows:

■ Insert DRIVERS DISK 2 into drive A: and type:

```
>COPY  GSSCGI.SYS  B:
```

- Insert consecutively the appropriate DRIVERS DISKs for your devices into drive A: and each time type:

```
>COPY  <filename>  B:
```

  where <filename> is the name of the device driver.

Copy SYGRAPH to a Disk

The SYGRAPH module is shipped to you in a compressed format in a file called SYGRAPHI.EXE. When it is unpacked, it will fit only on a high density disk with at least 440K free. To unpack SYGRAPH, do the following:

- Insert a high density disk into drive A: (your high density drive).

- Insert the SYGRAPH program disk into drive B: and type:

```
>A:
>B:SYGRAPHI
```

  This command both unpacks and copies the SYGRAPH program to the disk in the A drive. Once unpacked, the name of the program changes to SYGRAPH.EXE.

Modify CONFIG.SYS

CONFIG.SYS is a text file on your boot disk in which you can set certain system parameters and configurations. You can edit and create CONFIG.SYS with almost any word processor or text editor. Remember always to save it as a text or non-document file.

Modify CONFIG.SYS as follows:

- Add one DEVICE statement corresponding to each driver file that you copied onto your SYGRAPH boot disk:

```
>DEVICE=\<filename>
```

  where <filename> is the name of the driver.

Note: The DEVICE statement for the GSSCGI.SYS driver must be the last device statement in CONFIG.SYS.

For example, if you have an HP Plotter and an IBMEGA monitor which require the drivers HPGLPLTR.SYS and IBMEGA.SYS, you would add these DEVICE statements to CONFIG.SYS:

```
DEVICE=\HPGLPLTR.SYS
DEVICE=\IBMEGA.SYS
DEVICE=\GSSCGI.SYS
```

- Add a FILES and a BUFFERS statement to CONFIG.SYS:

```
FILES=20
BUFFERS=16
```

Do not put spaces in any of these statements. When you are done, save CONFIG.SYS as a text only file.

Modify AUTOEXEC.BAT

AUTOEXEC.BAT is similar to CONFIG.SYS. It is a text file on your boot disk in which you can enter environmental commands that the computer reads when you start it up. You create and edit AUTOEXEC.BAT in the same manner as CONFIG.SYS.

Modify AUTOEXEC.BAT as follows:

- Appendix G lists required AUTOEXEC.BAT commands for specific output devices. You must add at least one command to AUTOEXEC.BAT for each device you operate. Notice that for many devices there are optional commands which you can add to AUTOEXEC.BAT.

  For example, for the IBMEGA monitor and HP Plotter mentioned above, you would add these lines to AUTOEXEC.BAT:

  ```
  SET  DISPLAY=IBMEGA
  SET  PLOTTER=HPGLPLTR
  ```

  No AUTOEXEC.BAT statement is required for the GSSCGI.SYS driver.

- Create or modify the PATH command. PATH is a DOS command that tells the computer which drives and subdirectories to search for executable files. Your PATH command should read:

  ```
  SET  PATH=A:;B:
  ```

When you are done, save AUTOEXEC.BAT as a text file in your root directory.

Reboot Your Machine

Your computer reads CONFIG.SYS and AUTOEXEC.BAT when it starts up, so you must reboot in order for the changes you have just made to take effect. Put your new SYGRAPH boot disk in drive A: and reboot by pressing the Control, Alt, and Delete keys simultaneously.

It's All Installed—Is Everything Ready to Go?

Remember that in order for the changes you have made to AUTOEXEC.BAT and CONFIG.SYS to take effect, you must reboot your machine.

To make sure that your drivers are installed correctly, run the test program CGITEST.EXE located on DRIVER DISK 3. CGITEST.EXE is automatically copied onto hard drive systems by INSTALL. You can copy it manually by inserting DRIVERS DISK 3 into drive A:, logging into the \SYSTAT subdirectory on your C drive, and typing:

```
>COPY   A:CGITEST.EXE
```

To run CGITEST from the hard disk, type:

```
>CGITEST
```

at the DOS prompt.

To run the program from a floppy drive, insert DRIVERS DISK 3 into drive A: and type:

```
>A:CGITEST
```

The program will present 20 pages of graphics to the device specified in the SET DISPLAY command in AUTOEXEC.BAT. If *any* graphics appear on your screen, your system is correctly configured. If the test program does not execute successfully, retrace the installation steps to discover any possible errors. After fixing them, reboot your system and try CGITEST again.

NOTE: Testing an output device other than a display is ***very*** *time consuming. Test other output devices directly from SYGRAPH by directing output to the device and plotting a graph.*

Saving RAM

The required driver for all machines, GSSCGI.SYS, consumes approximately 50K of RAM. Each time you start your machine, this memory is reserved for SYGRAPH. The program DRIVERS.EXE, located on DRIVERS DISK 3, allows you to remove GSSCGI.SYS from memory when you are not using SYGRAPH. This is called the Transient Mode.

To use DRIVERS.EXE, do the following:

- Add "/T" to the DEVICE=GSSCGI.SYS statement in CONFIG.SYS so that the statement reads:

  ```
  DEVICE=GSSCGI.SYS  /T
  ```

  The statement must look exactly like that—no spaces except for the one before /T.

- To obtain graphic output from SYGRAPH when using transient mode, you must execute the program DRIVERS.EXE. DRIVERS.EXE is automatically copied to your hard drive if you use the INSTALL program. To copy DRIVERS.EXE manually to your hard drive, insert DRIVERS DISK 3 into the A: drive and type:

  ```
  >CD\SYSTAT
  >COPY  A:DRIVERS.EXE
  ```

  To execute the program, type:

  ```
  >DRIVERS
  ```

  To run DRIVERS.EXE from a floppy drive, insert DRIVERS DISK 3 into the B: drive and type:

  ```
  >B:DRIVERS
  ```

- To remove GSSCGI.SYS from memory, type:

  ```
  >DRIVERS  /R
  ```

  If you are running from a floppy drive, put DRIVERS DISK 3 into the B: drive and type:

  ```
  >B:DRIVERS  /R
  ```

When you load GSSCGI.SYS into memory the computer displays the following message:

```
Transient GSS*CGI loaded and initialized.
```

When you remove it from memory, the computer responds:

```
Transient GSS*CGI removed.
```

If you include the /T option in CONFIG.SYS but do not execute DRIVERS.EXE, you will not be able to produce graphical output from SYGRAPH.

Sample CONFIG.SYS and AUTOEXEC.BAT Files

This section offers several common CONFIG.SYS and AUTOEXEC.BAT file combinations for hard disk systems.

- IBM Color Graphics Card/Epson FX-80 Printer

CONFIG.SYS

```
DEVICE=C:\DRIVERS\IBMCO.SYS
DEVICE=C:\DRIVERS\EPSONX.SYS
DEVICE=C:\DRIVERS\GSSCGI.SYS
FILES=20
BUFFERS=16
```

AUTOEXEC.BAT

```
SET DISPLAY=IBMCO
SET PRINTER=EPSONX
```

- IBM Enhanced Graphics Adapter/HP Plotter

CONFIG.SYS

```
DEVICE=C:\DRIVERS\HPGLPLTR.SYS
DEVICE=C:\DRIVERS\IBMEGA.SYS
DEVICE=C:\DRIVERS\GSSCGI.SYS
FILES=20
BUFFERS=16
```

AUTOEXEC.BAT

```
SET DISPLAY=IBMEGA
SET PLOTTER=HPGLPLTR
MODE COM1:9600,N,8,1,P
```

- Compaq III/LaserJet+

CONFIG.SYS

```
DEVICE=C:\DRIVERS\COMPAQ3.SYS
DEVICE=C:\DRIVERS\LASERJET.SYS
DEVICE=C:\DRIVERS\GSSCGI.SYS
FILES=20
BUFFERS=16
```

AUTOEXEC.BAT

```
SET DISPLAY=COMPAQ3
SET PRINTER=LASERJET
MODE COM1:9600,N,8,1,P
```

Two Monitor Configurations

If you have two monitors, you can configure your hardware so that you can enter commands on one screen and have graphics printed to the other. SYGRAPH commands will be written to your primary monitor and graphics will be written to the "first" graphics monitor that SYGRAPH "sees". You will have to refer to your graphics card documentation to configure your system to use two monitors.

Graphing without a Graphics Monitor

You can produce graphics on a printer or plotter without having a graphics monitor in one of two ways. First, you can install SYGRAPH (with or without the automatic INSTALL program) and each time you enter the SYGRAPH program, type:

```
OUTPUT = PRINTER     (or OUTPUT = PLOTTER)
```

prior to plotting any graphs.

Alternatively, you can redirect output by changing one command in AUTOEXEC.BAT. After you install SYGRAPH, there will be one of two lines in your AUTOEXEC.BAT file:

```
SET PRINTER=<device name>   or,
SET PLOTTER=<device name>
```

Simply change the line to:

```
SET DISPLAY=<device name>
```

and reset your system. Now each time you start SYGRAPH, output will be directed to your output device.

Common Installation Problems

The following is a list of the most common installation problems.

PROBLEM:

When I execute any command to produce output within SYGRAPH nothing happens.

SOURCE 1 (There are many possible sources for this problem):

The driver for your output device is not installed correctly. Be certain that each line required by SYGRAPH in your CONFIG.SYS and AUTOEXEC.BAT is in uppercase.

SOURCE 2:

Other drivers or commands in your CONFIG.SYS file are taking up RAM. SYGRAPH and its drivers require much RAM. If SYGRAPH does not have enough RAM to operate, it will not produce graphical output. Remove from your CONFIG.SYS file anything not associated with SYGRAPH, reboot your machine, and try running SYGRAPH again. You may want to create a separate CONFIG.SYS that you boot your computer with before you use SYGRAPH.

SOURCE 3:

Remove all memory resident programs (disk caching software included).

SOURCE 4:

Plotters and any device on a communications port require that you issue a DOS MODE command prior to starting SYGRAPH. If your device, for example, is connected to COM1, issue the command:

```
>MODE   COM1:96,N,8,1,P
```

For COM2, issue the command:

```
>MODE   COM2:96,N,8,1,P
```

You can also add these commands to your AUTOEXEC.BAT file so that your computer will read them every time it starts up.

SOURCE 5:

Compaq DOS Version 3.1 has bugs that prevent SYGRAPH from producing hardcopy output. You will need a later version of DOS to get around this problem.

SOURCE 6:

If you have another program that uses the SYGRAPH drivers (e.g., Sigma Plot), be certain that you do not use the /G switches with the DEVICE statements in your CONFIG.SYS file. The /G switch loads multiple drivers into RAM and does not leave SYGRAPH enough free RAM to run properly.

SOURCE 7:

If you are using a LaserJet printer, be sure that you are using the correct port. If you do not have output with LPT1, for example, try COM1. This will usually solve any LaserJet problems. Remember SYGRAPH requires your printer to have 2 megabytes of RAM for you to obtain a full page of 300 DPI graphics. If you have less RAM use the SET RESOLUTION command discussed in Appendix E.

SOURCE 8:

If you have installed SYGRAPH manually, check your SET and DEVICE commands. SET commands in AUTOEXEC.BAT that refer to a port cannot identify the colon associated with the port. For example,

```
SET  EPSONX=LPT1:
```

is not correct, and should be

```
SET  EPSONX=LPT1
```

DEVICE commands in CONFIG.SYS must specify the full path to the driver file.

PROBLEM:

Upon booting my machine the following message appears

`BAD OR MISSING` *`text output`*

SOURCE:

One of two things is wrong. First, you may have misspelled the DEVICE command in CONFIG.SYS. Second, you may not have copied the necessary drivers into your root directory.

PROBLEM:

Upon booting my machine the following message appears:

```
Unrecognized command in CONFIG.SYS
```

SOURCE:

You have misspelled a DEVICE command in your file CONFIG.SYS.

PROBLEM:

I cannot use more than several colors on one graph.

SOURCE:

Your monitor is limited in the number of colors it can have on the screen at one time. Refer to Appendix G for information about the number of colors your hardware can support.

PROBLEM:

The message

```
Out of environment space
```

appears when I start my system.

SOURCE:

There are two possible solutions to solving this problem. First, you can reduce the environment space required by your AUTOEXEC.BAT file commands. Reduce the number of SET commands or reduce the size of your DOS path. Second, you may be able to increase the environment space for your system. If you own a Microsoft compiler, you can use the SETENV utility to allocate more environment space.

Or, if you have DOS 3.2 (or higher), you can use the DOS SHELL command to increase environment space (refer to your DOS documentation for details). SHELL must be the first command in your CONFIG.SYS file. Here is an example:

```
SHELL=C:\COMMAND.COM  1e:1024  /p
```

See your DOS manual for more complete instructions.

PROBLEM:

I have poor graphics resolution on my color monitor.

SOURCE:

Some configurations allow you to choose between higher resolution or multiple colors. If you want the highest resolution possible you cannot use multiple color graphics. Refer to Appendix G for information regarding the resolution and color options supported by your monitor.

Common Usage Questions

Continuing a Command Line Past 80 Columns

Often it will be necessary to have commands longer than one line. In order to continue a command statement onto the next line, type a comma as the last character (before the 80th column), then press the Return key. A single command can be extended on as many lines as needed.

Printing Output

Use the OUTPUT @ command to direct any subsequent output to your printer.

Viewing a SYGRAPH Data File

Use the CASELIST command in the DATA module. This option will print the values for all or selected variables in a SYGRAPH file. The REPEAT command will allow you to list a specified number of cases.

FEDIT Doesn't Work

If the editor does not work properly, you may have a display that FEDIT does not recognize. FEDIT supports the following monitors:

- Monochrome display adaptor
- Color Graphics adaptor (CGA)
- EGA (including 43-line mode)
- VGA

Unable to Read Files

If you get the message::

```
***ERROR***YOU ARE TRYING TO READ AN EMPTY OR
NONEXISTENT FILE
```

you may have misspelled the filename or the file may be located in a directory other than the current directory.

You can access a file in another directory by enclosing the complete path and file name in quotes. The following command would access SYGRAPH.SYS in the DATAFILE directory:

```
USE   '\SYSTAT\DATAFILE\SYGRAPH.SYS'
```

Unable to SORT or SAVE

If you receive the message:

```
There has been a system I/O error opening,
closing, reading from or writing to a file or
device. SYSTAT cannot recover.
```

you may need to add FILES=20 to your CONFIG.SYS file. CONFIG.SYS should be located in your root directory or on your boot disk. You should add this line to your existing CONFIG.SYS file, or create a new file. Once you have added the line, reboot your machine and try, try again.

Device driver doesn't work

Try a different display mode for the driver (e.g., for EGA monitors try SET EGA=HR4 in your AUTOEXEC.BAT file). Not all "EGA compatible" boards are compatible at the same level. Try a lower resolution compatible driver (e.g. CGA driver with an EGA board).

How can I overlay plots in SYGRAPH?

See the BEGIN...END commands in the SYGRAPH manual.

Part 1
Chapter 1
TUTORIAL

Is SYGRAPH for you?

This is a very unusual graphics package. As you can see by leafing through the illustrations in this manual, SYGRAPH can draw many different types of technical and business graphics. If all you want in a graphics package is to produce simple bar and pie charts for meetings or newsletters, then this package is a lot more than you need. Of course, SYGRAPH can produce bar and pie charts, but you can get other programs to do them in less time and for less money.

SYGRAPH is unusual in another way. Most graphics packages use icon based, screen paint, or mouse driven interfaces. With these programs, you can drag symbols around the screen and make slight adjustments in lines and fonts without redrawing a graph. These interfaces are especially valuable for making single graphs on a small amount of data. SYGRAPH, on the other hand, uses commands instead of menus and icons. There are several reasons for this. First, SYGRAPH can produce extremely complex displays through overlaying sets of commands. These commands can be read from batch files, so that you can make similar graphs on different data with only minor modifications. Second, SYGRAPH is a graphics database. It includes commands for selecting subsets out of large statistical files and it interfaces directly to other statistical and database packages. Finally, SYGRAPH includes intelligent scaling, positioning, and plotting routines. Variable labels, for example, will not collide or overlap with each other when large numbers of categories are plotted. Plotting scales and cutpoints need not be selected from menus. They are chosen automatically via sophisticated statistical analyses of the data being plotted. Thus, many plots which would require numerous menu selections in other graphics packages can be accomplished with a single command. The commands in SYGRAPH were designed so that you should never have to "touch up" a graph.

If SYGRAPH sounds right for you, then you should continue with the tutorial. If not, then please contact SYSTAT immediately. We prefer to have customers who understand and appreciate the specific capabilities of our software. We don't want a single copy of SYGRAPH to sit on the shelf unused.

Making a Bar Graph

Let's make some graphs right away. We'll start with a bar graph because it is typical of many of the types of graphs you can do with SYGRAPH. I assume you have followed the installation instructions which came with your SYGRAPH program disks and now can invoke SYGRAPH by typing its name from your operating system or clicking its icon on your desktop. I have prepared a file called US.SYS, which contains data about the 48 continental United States in 1970. I am not discriminating against Alaska and Hawaii. For several reasons, our tutorial will be simpler by leaving them out at this time. I have chosen 1970 instead of 1980 (the most recent census) because of some interesting features in these data.

The statistics in this file are from various sources documenting state statistics for the year ending in 1970 (*U.S. Statistical Abstract, 1970*; *The World Almanac, 1971*). POPDEN is people per square mile. PERSON is F.B.I. reported incidences, per 100,000 people, of personal crimes (murder, rape, robbery, assault). PROPERTY is incidences, per 100,000 people, of property crimes (burglary, larceny, autotheft). INCOME is per-capita income. SUMMER is average summer temperature and WINTER is average winter temperature. RAIN is average inches of rainfall per year. Two additional variables used in some of the analyses are not listed here. They are LABLAT (latitude in degrees of the center of each state) and LABLON (longitude of the center).

Figure 1

Vital Statistics for Continental United States in 1970

STATE$	REGION$	POPDEN	PERSON	PROPERTY	INCOME	SUMMER	WINTER	RAIN
ME	New England	32	21	588	3054	69	22	43
NH	New England	80	14	556	3471	70	22	39
VT	New England	47	19	608	3247	69	16	33
MA	New England	719	51	1181	4156	74	30	43
RI	New England	879	51	1355	3858	70	32	40
CT	New England	613	43	1106	4595	72	30	46
NY	Mid Atlantic	376	169	1374	4442	74	28	35
NJ	Mid Atlantic	941	70	1096	4241	75	35	42
PA	Mid Atlantic	259	53	645	3659	76	32	41
OH	Great Lakes	257	71	1097	3738	74	31	37
IN	Great Lakes	142	56	1027	3687	75	29	39
IL	Great Lakes	196	117	1104	4285	76	26	33
MI	Great Lakes	154	144	1644	3994	75	27	31
WI	Great Lakes	80	21	872	3632	69	19	30
MN	Plains	48	38	1017	3635	73	12	25
IA	Plains	50	21	808	3549	74	20	33
MO	Plains	67	101	1266	3458	78	32	35
ND	Plains	9	9	557	3012	72	10	15
SD	Plains	9	23	654	3027	75	17	15
NE	Plains	19	46	790	3609	79	23	28
KS	Plains	27	51	1147	3488	81	32	28
DE	Southeast	273	82	1312	4107	76	34	45
MD	Southeast	392	156	1339	4073	77	35	43
VA	Southeast	114	65	1028	3307	79	41	45
WV	Southeast	71	31	418	2603	76	35	39
NC	Southeast	101	93	758	2888	79	42	43
SC	Southeast	83	71	930	2607	81	50	49
GA	Southeast	77	75	1026	3071	79	45	47
FL	Southeast	123	125	1607	3525	82	66	49
KY	South	79	55	754	2847	78	36	41
TN	South	93	69	707	2808	81	40	45
AL	South	66	74	704	2582	82	51	59
MS	South	46	45	374	2218	82	49	50
AR	South	36	56	735	2488	82	41	49
LA	South	79	103	968	2781	82	55	60
OK	South	36	51	927	3047	83	37	31
TX	South	42	90	1243	3259	83	53	35
MT	Mountain	5	28	924	3130	68	19	11
ID	Mountain	8	31	1011	2953	75	29	11
WY	Mountain	3	28	953	3353	70	26	15
CO	Mountain	21	89	1654	3604	73	29	15
NM	Mountain	8	73	1314	2897	79	36	10
AZ	Mountain	15	93	1848	3372	90	50	7
UT	Mountain	13	34	1355	2997	77	28	14
NV	Mountain	4	100	1789	4458	71	28	8
WA	Pacific	50	55	1552	3848	68	29	33
OR	Pacific	21	64	1477	3573	68	39	40
CA	Pacific	126	119	1955	4290	68	52	16

Let's look at a simple bar graph of income by region. Make sure you are inside SYGRAPH and then type:

```
USE US
```

You should see the names of all of the above variables on your screen. There will be some additional variables which we will use later. If you get an error message instead, such as:

```
***ERROR***
YOU ARE TRYING TO READ AN EMPTY FILE
```

then the file US.SYS is not on your disk and in your directory. Exit the SYGRAPH module by typing QUIT and review the installation instructions in the **READ ME FIRST** brochure which came with your program.

Now, to produce a bar graph, simply type:

```
BAR  INCOME*REGION$
```

Press the Enter or Return key after the dollar sign. The dollar sign ($) indicates that the variable (REGION$) contains characters instead of numbers.

If you typed the command correctly, you should see on your screen the graph in Figure 2. Notice that SYGRAPH automatically chooses scale values and angles the value labels to fit on the lower scale. The axes are labeled with the variables you chose (INCOME and REGION$). We will see later how to change all these details to suit your preferences. Every aspect of the graph in Figure 2 can be modified. The important thing to notice is that everything is done automatically when you don't want to bother with details.

Notice that in our data there are several states in each REGION and only one bar on the graph. SYGRAPH computes the mean (average) of the value of INCOME in each REGION in order to plot a bar. If there is only one value in the dataset corresponding to each bar, then you will see that as the height of the bar.

Figure 2 is labeled at the top with the command which you typed to produce the graph (**BAR INCOME*REGION$**). I will do this in every figure in this manual so that you can reproduce the graph exactly by looking only at the figure. SYGRAPH, of course, does not reproduce the command itself on the figure.

Figure 2

```
BAR  INCOME*REGION$
```

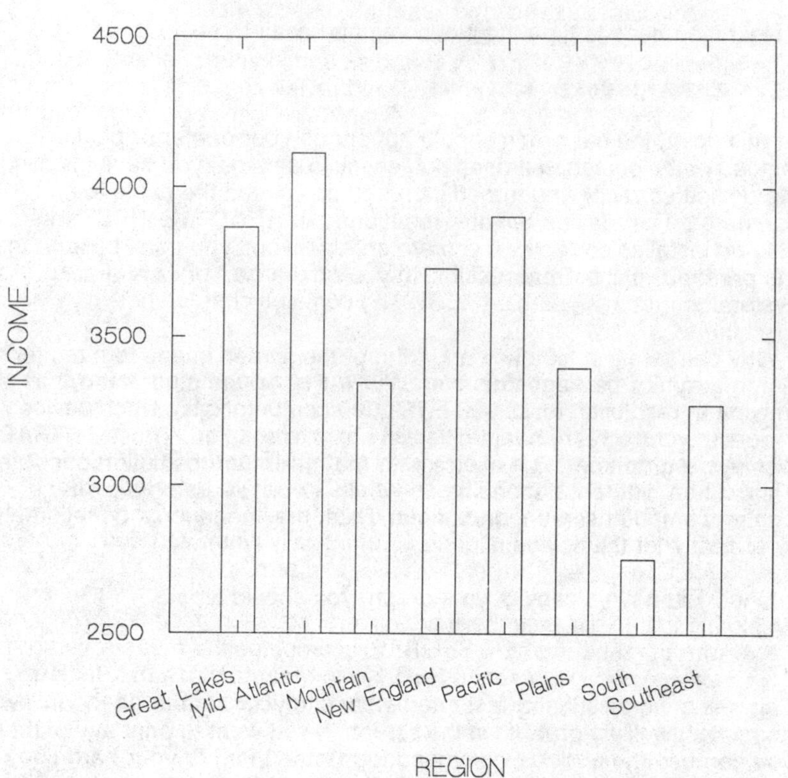

Making a Hard Copy of Your Graph

Let's make a hard copy of your graph. First, you must type

```
OUTPUT=PRINTER   (or OUTPUT=@)
```

or

```
OUTPUT=PLOTTER
```

depending on whether you have installed a printer or plotter as your output device. If you do not know which is installed, refer to the **READ ME FIRST** brochure which came with SYGRAPH.

Next, you need to type the plot command again:

```
BAR  INCOME*REGION$
```

At this point, the bar graph should appear on your printer or plotter instead of the screen. If it does not, check to see that you have installed the device correctly and turned it on and connected the cable to the computer. The "device drivers" mentioned in **READ ME FIRST** must also be installed correctly. If you are on a network, you must be sure that the printer or plotter is accessible to you on the network's operating system.

Why can't we just hit a key and "dump" the screen image to a printer? Some graphics packages do this. SYGRAPH, on the other hand, has a maximum resolution of 32,000 by 32,000 points (pixels). Each device, including your screen, has a different actual resolution. Thus, SYGRAPH displays a graph on each device with the maximum resolution possible. This will be different depending on whether you are using a plotter, printer, computer screen, or camera. Thus, the image must be tailored specifically for the device.

Once you have a copy of your graph, you should type:

```
OUTPUT=DISPLAY   (or OUTPUT=*)
```

This will bring all subsequent graphs back to your screen. In the following examples, we'll try graphs on the screen. If you want to print any of them, you can use the `OUTPUT` command to reroute them to your hard-copy device.

Changing the Size of Your Graph

What if you want to modify the size of your graph? Each SYGRAPH command has an option to make a graph any size. We do this by adding the option after the command on the same line, e.g.

```
BAR  INCOME*REGION$/HEIGHT=3IN,WIDTH=4IN
```

If you want to work in centimeters instead of inches, just type **CM** instead of **IN** after the numbers you use for **HEIGHT** and **WIDTH**. You may choose any values for the size of your graph, as long as it fits on the device you are using.

Figure 3 shows the result of this command. Notice that the labels are automatically rescaled to fit the new graph size. This command is longer than the last one. It just fits on one line. If you run out of room and need to continue on an additional line to complete the command, just type a comma at the end of the line, press the Return or Enter key, and continue typing the remainder of the command on the next line or lines.

Figure 3

```
BAR   INCOME*REGION$/HEIGHT=3IN,WIDTH=4IN
```

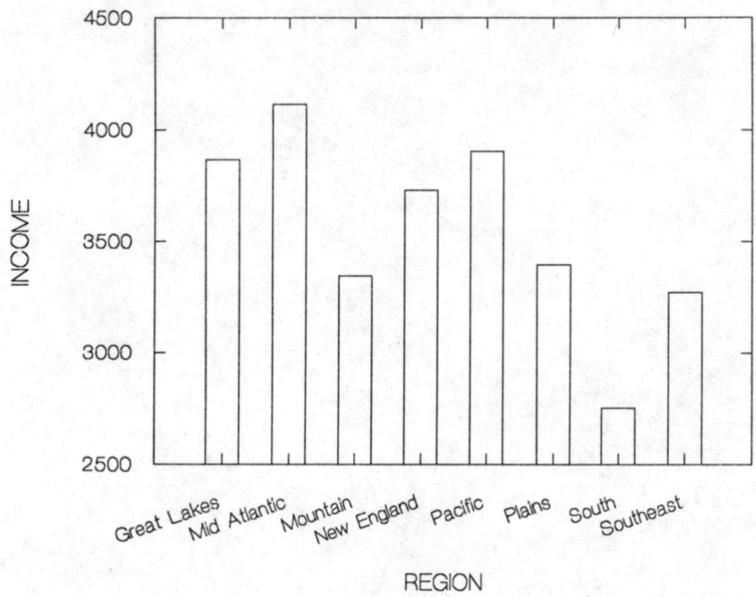

Changing the Axes on your Graph

You may not want four axes, like a box, around your bar graph. There is an option which works like the **HEIGHT** and **WIDTH** options to control the number of axes plotted. For example, if you want only one axis at the bottom of the graph, just type:

```
BAR   INCOME*REGION$/AXES=1
```

Figure 4 shows the result. Notice that only the bottom axis is drawn. Normally, SYGRAPH draws four axes on a bar graph. These are numbered from 1 to 4 clockwise beginning at the bottom axis. The **AXES** option causes SYGRAPH to draw up to and including the number of axes specified. Thus, **AXES=2** produces axes on the bottom and left side.

If you want to draw only one of these four axes, use a negative number with the **AXES** option. For example, **AXES=-4** will draw an axis only on the right side of the graph. Of course, **AXES=1** and **AXES=-1** are equivalent.

Figure 4

```
BAR INCOME*REGION$/AXES=1
```

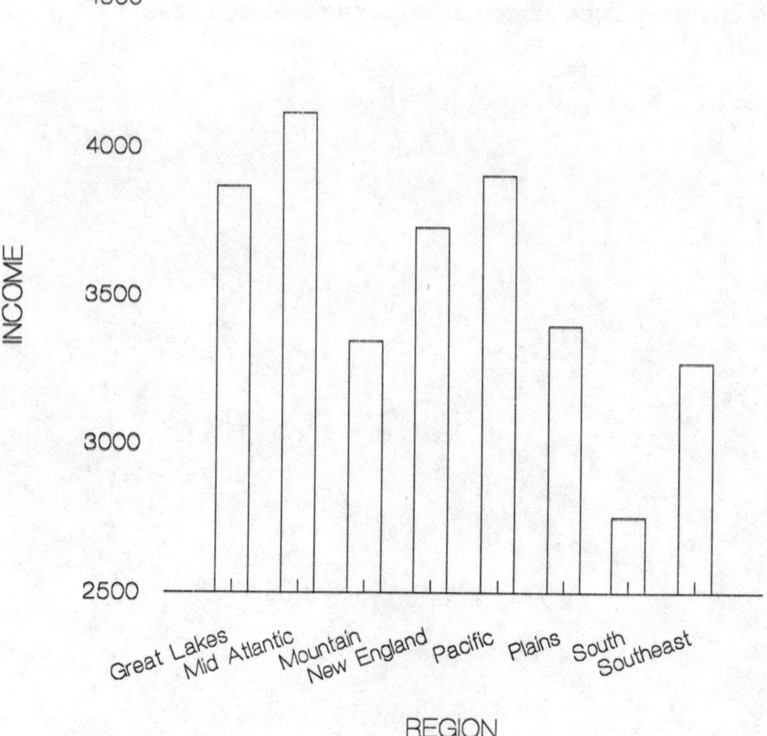

Changing Scales

You may have noticed that the scale values for INCOME were printed even though the left side axis was omitted when we used the option **AXES=1**. You can manipulate the scale values separately with the **SCALE** option. It works exactly like the **AXES** option except that only the scale values or labels are affected. Keep in mind that the **AXES** and **SCALE** options work independently.

Figure 5 shows the **AXES** and **SCALE** options used together. In this example, we have produced a simple graph with no axes (**AXES=0**) and a scale on the bottom and left side (**SCALE=2**). To get an idea of how **AXES** and **SCALE** work together, you should try some other combinations, such as:

```
BAR  INCOME*REGION$/AXES=1,SCALE=-4
```

or

```
BAR  INCOME*REGION$/AXES=-2,SCALE=2
```

Figure 5

```
BAR   INCOME*REGION$/AXES=0,SCALE=2
```

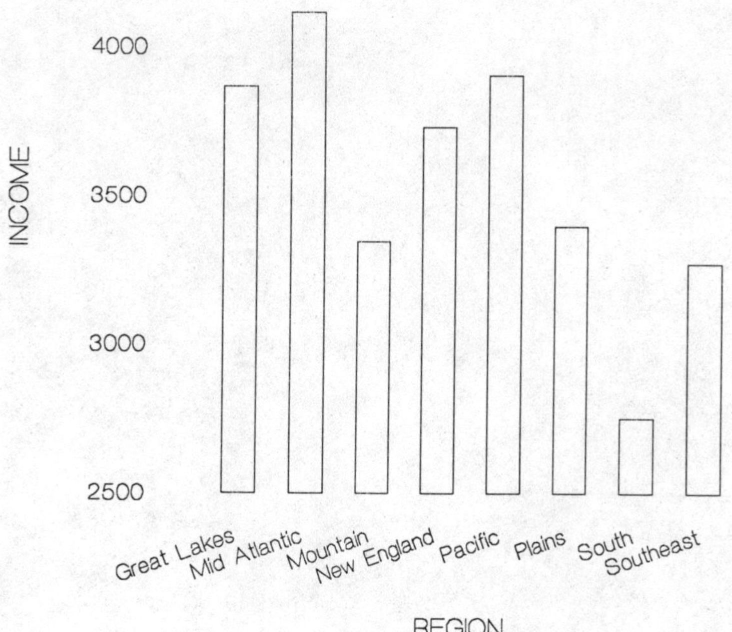

Labeling Axes

You may not want to use the names of the variables to label the axes. Sometimes longer labels are necessary to make a clear graph. There is an option on all SYGRAPH commands to do this for both the X (**XLABEL**) and Y (**YLABEL**) axis. Figure 6 shows an example. The material to be included in the label is surrounded by quotation marks (") or apostrophes ('). In this figure, we have combined all the options so far.

If there are quotation marks (") in your text, then you should surround the text with apostrophes (') and if there are apostrophes, surround the text with quotes. Here are examples:

```
BAR   INCOME*REGION$/XLABEL="Regions"

BAR   INCOME*REGION$/XLABEL='"Regions"'
```

Notice that I typed a comma at the end of each line but the last. This is how to continue commands on additional lines.

Figure 6

```
BAR INCOME*REGION$,
  /AXES=0,SCALE=2,
   XLABEL='Census Region',
   YLABEL='Per Capita Income'
```

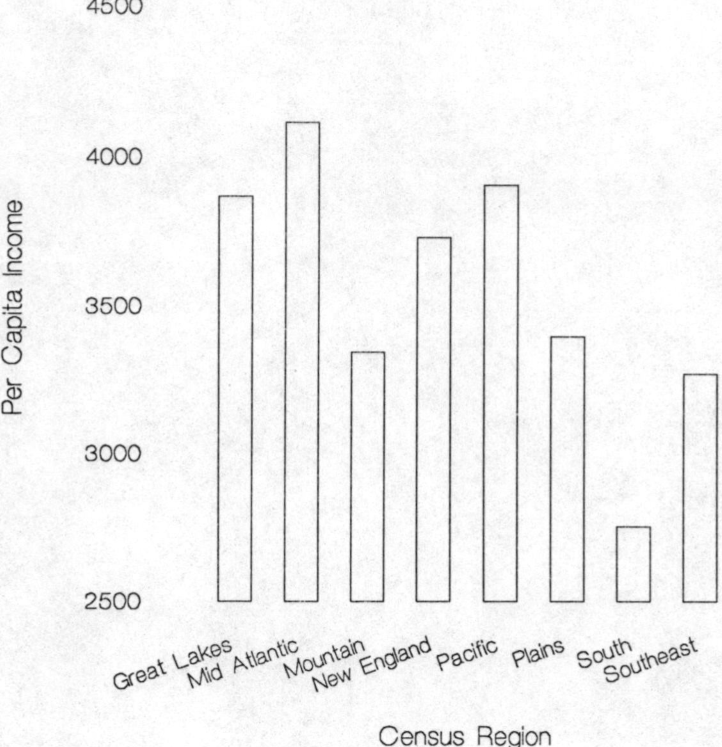

Modifying the Limits of a Scale

Notice that our bar graph has a minimum income of $2500 and a maximum of $4500. SYGRAPH chooses this range based on the data. It searches for round numbers below and above the minimum and maximum values in the data, respectively. You may want to modify these values in order to standardize your graph on a different scale. Each type of graph in SYGRAPH has a **MIN** and **MAX** option to govern these values. When there is only one scale possible in a graph, you need type only **MIN** or **MAX** to specify these values. When there is more than one scale, you must specify the scale separately for each axis. Normally, the horizontal axis is called X and the vertical axis is called Y. Therefore, for these graphs, the options are **XMIN**, **XMAX**, **YMIN**, and **YMAX**. Figure 7 shows an example for our bar graph. We have used **YMIN=0** for the INCOME axis. Since we have not specified **YMAX**, the maximum value for the scale will be chosen from the data.

Figure 7

```
BAR  INCOME*REGION$/YMIN=0
```

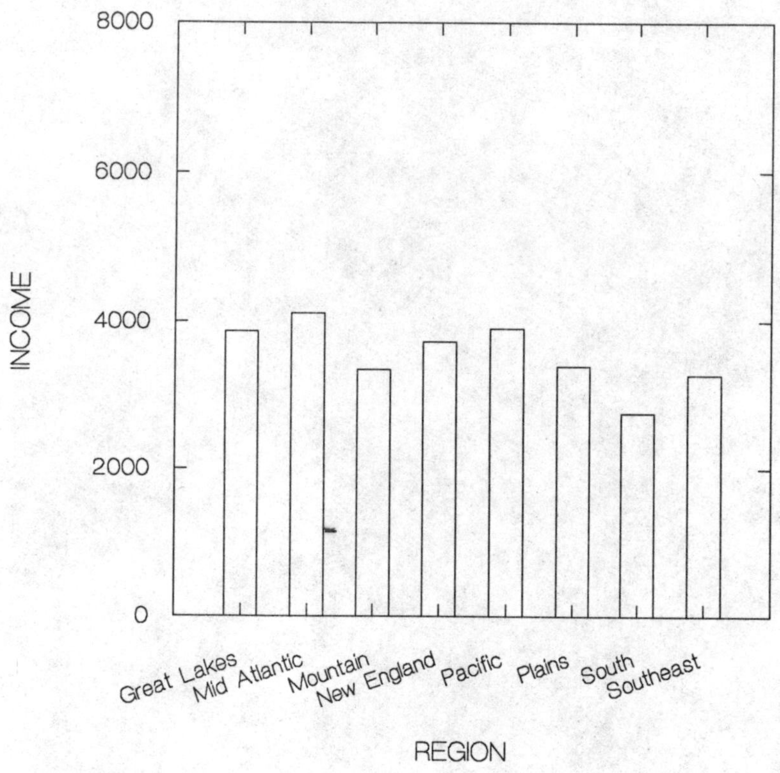

Modifying the Tick Marks on a Scale

You can change the number of tick marks on a graph with the `TICK` options. First of all, SYGRAPH chooses a number of tick marks which will produce round numbers and a pleasing display which fills the frame. Sometimes you might want fewer or more tick marks. To do this, add the `TICK` option. Figure 8 shows a graph with 8 tick marks on the vertical (Y) axis instead of the 4 chosen by SYGRAPH. Usually, you will have difficulty choosing a number of tick marks which produces a better display than that chosen by SYGRAPH, but having this option can help you when the data are unusual. There is no limit on the number of ticks, but if you choose too many the scale values will overlap.

Figure 8

```
BAR   INCOME*REGION$/YMIN=0,TICK=8
```

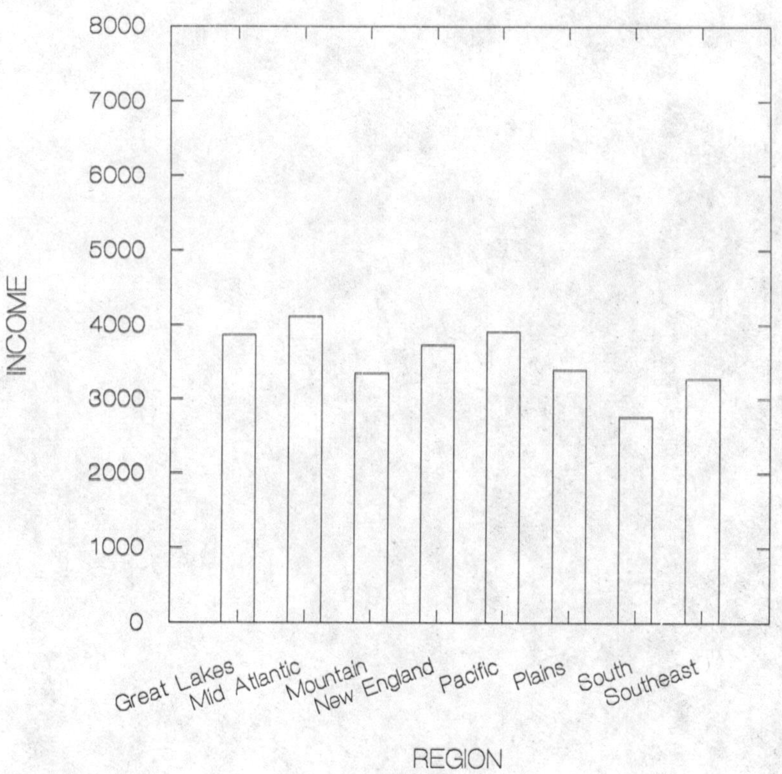

Pip Marks

You can also make finer tick marks between those with scale values. These are called pip marks in SYGRAPH. For example, if you want to put 4 pip marks between each tick on our bar chart, add the option `PIP=4`. This will make a break at each $500 interval on the graph. Figure 9 shows an example. You can choose any number of pip marks for any axis.

Figure 9

```
BAR  INCOME*REGION$/YMIN=0,PIP=4
```

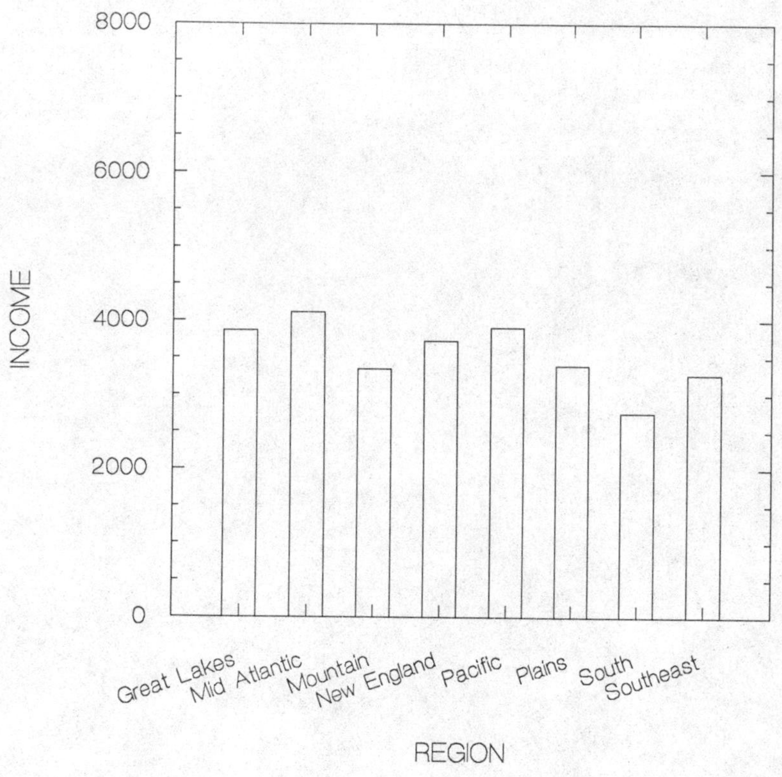

Ticks Inside or Outside

You can place tick and pip marks inside or outside the frame of a graph. Normally, SYGRAPH places tick marks inside the frame. If you add the option `STICK`, they will be placed sticking out. Figure 10 shows our bar graph with the tick marks placed out. We also include pip marks as in Figure 9.

Figure 10

```
BAR   INCOME*REGION$/YMIN=0,PIP=4,STICK
```

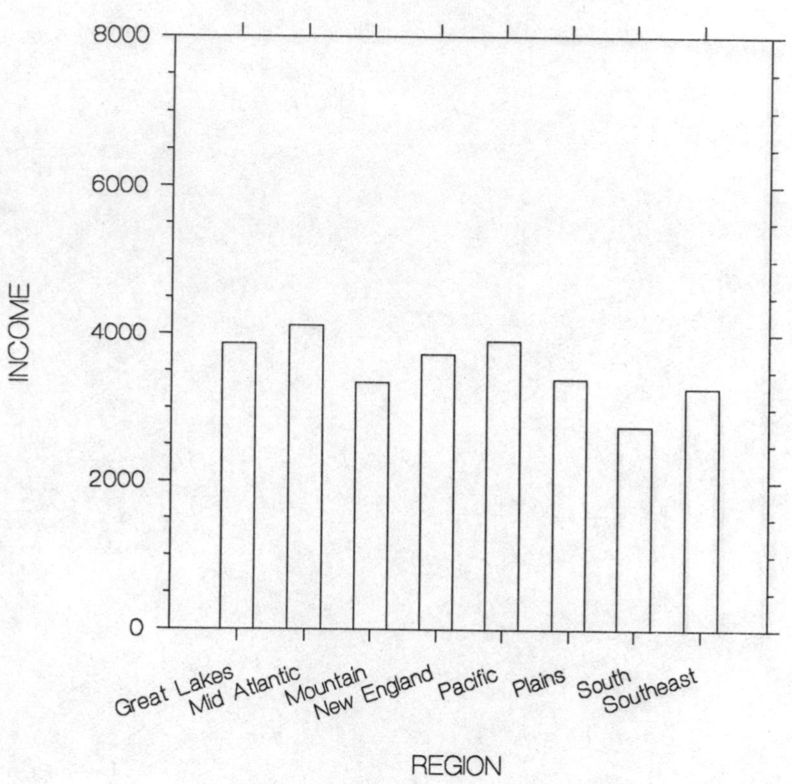

Reversing a Scale

Now we're going to do something goofy. We're going to reverse the scale on the vertical (Y) axis to make an upside down bar graph. To reverse a scale, simply add the **XREV** or **YREV** option to your SYGRAPH command. Figure 11 shows the result of this operation.

Why would you want to do this? Maybe you like upside down graphs. Some of us are glass-half-full/empty, yin/yang,head/toe kind of people. Others like to do special graphs which require reversing scales. Age-sex pyramid graphs and back-to-back histograms are two examples which require reversed scales for half the graph. You can take a look at some of these graphs in the more advanced examples later. Just remember, any graph with one or more scales which make sense reversed can be reversed in SYGRAPH.

Figure 11

```
BAR  INCOME*REGION$/YMIN=0,YREV
```

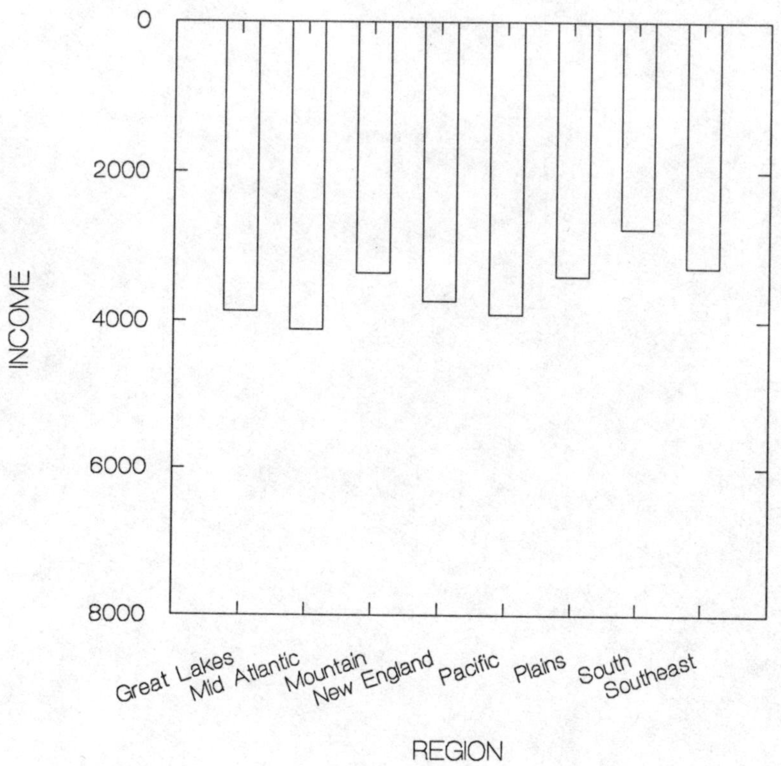

Transposing a Graph

Bar graphs are normally vertical. Why not make them horizontal? For most graphs in SYGRAPH, there is a simple option to transpose your graph so that it is sideways. Figure 12 shows an example of this. In many ways, it is more pleasing than the previous graphs because it has a simple numerical scale at the bottom, clear labeling of the bars on the side, and otherwise clean features. Because the default for bar graphs is **SCALE=2**, we do not need to add that option.

You must remember this. **TRANS** affects everything in a graph. **XLABEL** becomes **YLABEL** and so on. In other words, specify a graph as you would ordinarily and then add the **TRANS** option. Everything will be transposed appropriately, including the labels and scales.

Figure 12

```
BAR   INCOME*REGION$/TRANS,AXES=1,YMIN=0
```

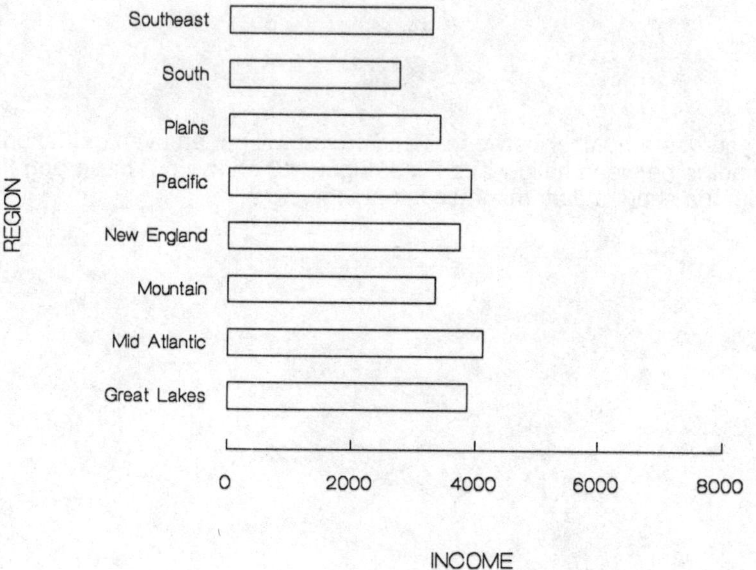

Filling a Graph

You can fill bars, symbols, or other fillable features in a graph with the **FILL** option. The option works this way:

```
BAR   INCOME*REGION$/FILL=1
```

The number you choose after **"FILL="** determines the type of fill pattern. Here are the possibilities:

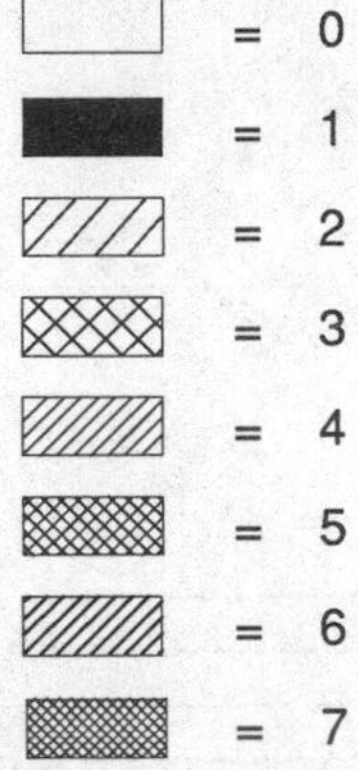

If you use a number between 0 and 1, you will get an even gradation of shading between hollow and filled. Figure 13 shows our bar graph filled with the shaded pattern to accentuate the bars.

Figure 13

```
BAR   INCOME*REGION$/FILL=7
```

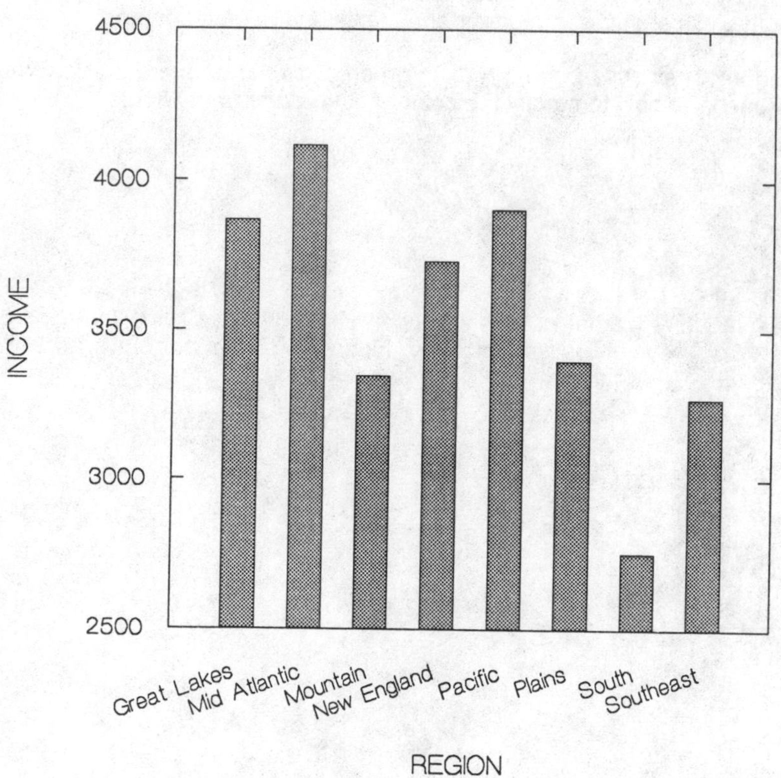

Coloring a Graph

You can choose different colors for a graph the same way you specified fill patterns. Choose either a name or a wavelength in nanometers Possible colors and their approximate nanometer wavelengths are: **RED** (615), **ORANGE** (590), **YELLOW** (575), **GREEN** (505), **BLUE** (480), **VIOLET** (450). You may also name **BLACK**, **WHITE**, **GRAY**, and **BROWN**. The option works this way:

```
BAR   INCOME*REGION$/COLOR=RED
```

Your graphics device must support color for this to work, of course. If your graphics device supports color mixing (e.g. a CRT or color camera), then you can specify color more continuously in nanometers wavelength, e.g. **COLOR=543**. SYGRAPH will hold brightness and saturation constant. If you do not know anything about color perception and the use of colors in graphs, you should read further about color in the next chapter.

Figure 14 shows our bar graph in green. Only the bars are green. We will see later how to modify the color of other parts of the figure.

Figure 14

```
BAR   INCOME*REGION$/COLOR=GREEN,FILL=1
```

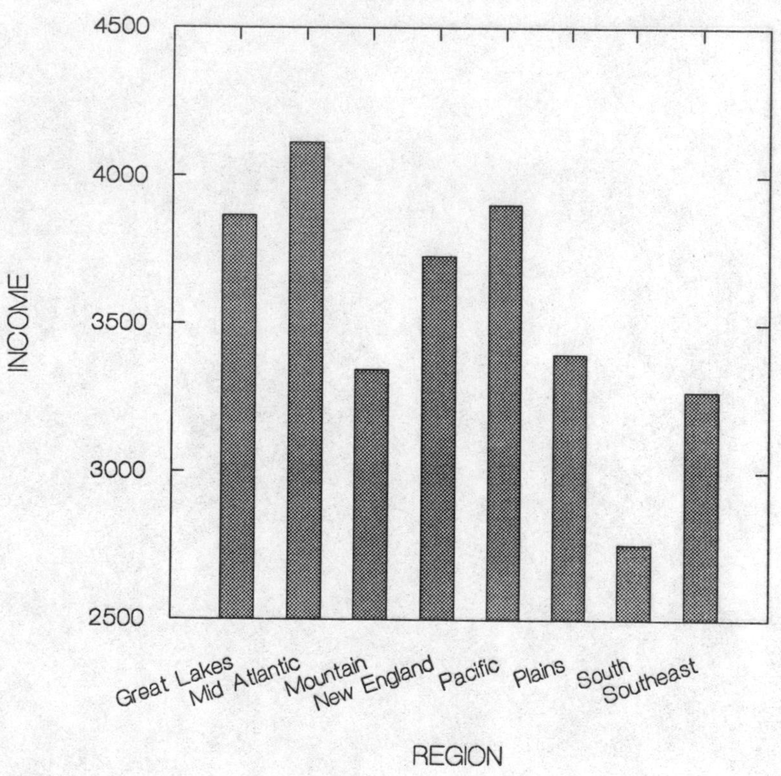

Making a Pie Chart

We've used the bar chart to illustrate many of the standard options to SYGRAPH commands. Now let's try another command to make a different graph. The pie chart is one of the most common methods for displaying portions of a whole. To display relative proportions of total per-capita income, we can use the **PIE** command the same way we used **BAR**. Figure 15 shows the result.

Many of the options we have tried with bar graphs work also with pie charts. We will not try them here, however. You can try a few. Obviously, options like **TRANS**, **AXES**, **SCALE**, and **TICK** are meaningless. Others can have curious results. You can use the **HEIGHT** and **WIDTH** options to control the size of a pie chart, for example. But if you make **HEIGHT** different than **WIDTH**, you will get an oval instead of a circular pie.

Figure 15

```
PIE  INCOME*REGION$
```

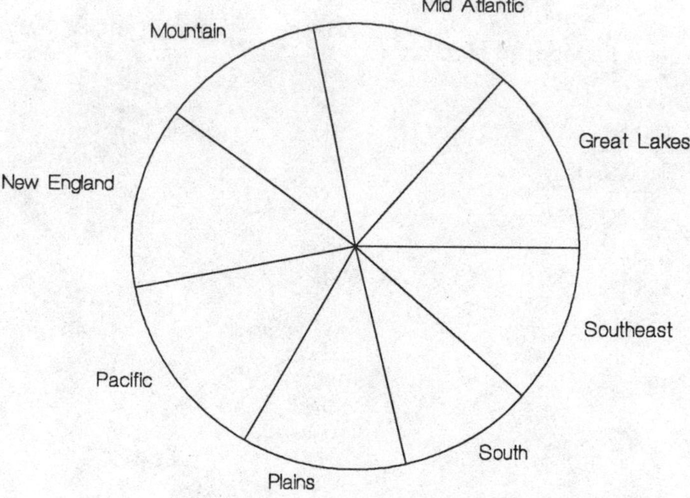

Graphing a Scatterplot

One of the most common statistical displays is the two-way data plot called a **scatterplot**. These are easy to do in SYGRAPH with the **PLOT** command. The syntax of the **PLOT** command is similar to that of **BAR** and **PIE**. Let's consider another variable in addition to income and region of the country. Population density might be related to income because of differences between urban and rural economies. Figure 16 shows this plot. Notice that we simply have to type:

```
PLOT  INCOME*POPDEN
```

to get it.

The **PLOT** command has most of the options we reviewed with **BAR**. For example, **HEIGHT**, **WIDTH** and all the axis and scale options apply to **PLOT** in the same way they do to **BAR**. Some other options, like **TRANS**, are inapplicable because you can type:

```
PLOT  POPDEN*INCOME
```

to get a transposed plot.

Figure 16

PLOT INCOME*POPDEN

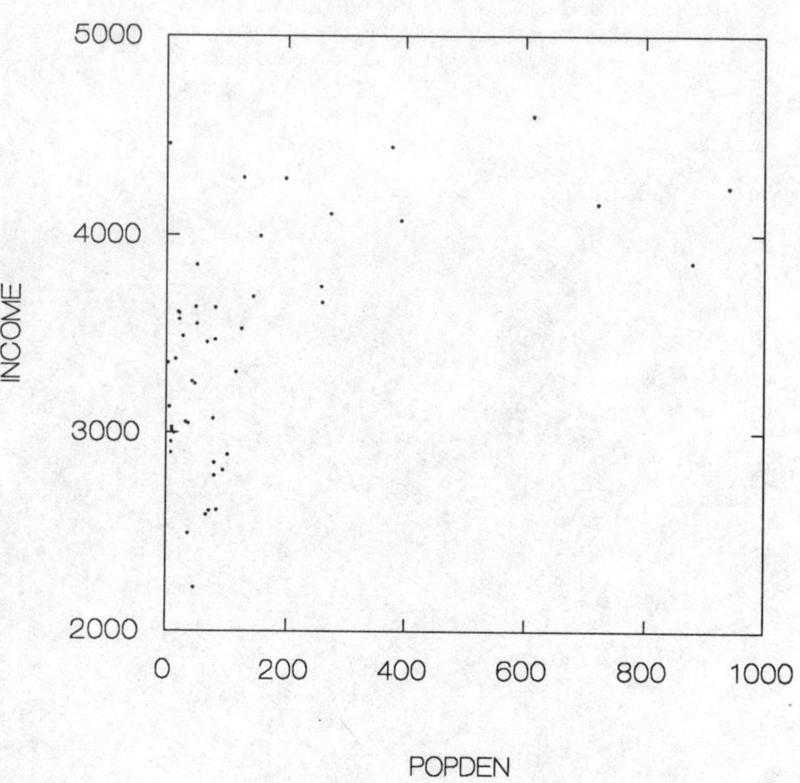

Smoothing a Scatterplot

The points appear to follow a curve rather than a straight line relating INCOME to POPDEN. Let's allow SYGRAPH to fit a curve through the data without our making any presuppositions about its form. To do this, repeat the `PLOT` command with a `SMOOTH=LOWESS` option. This option implements LOWESS, a robust smoothing algorithm developed by Bill Cleveland at Bell Telephone Laboratories.

Figure 17 shows the result of this smoothing. Notice that, despite local jagged features the line is curved. The exact form of a plausible function relating INCOME to POPDEN is not unambiguous, but we might say a log or square root function is plausible. Both of these functions are steeper for smaller values of POPDEN than for larger.

Figure 17

```
PLOT   INCOME*POPDEN/SMOOTH=LOWESS
```

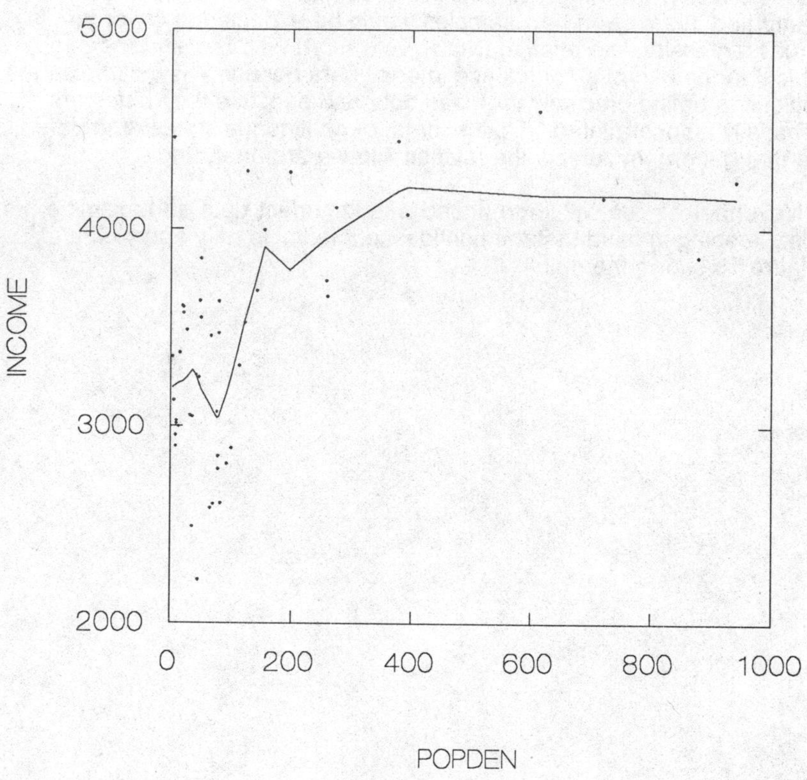

Transforming a Plot Scale

Let's try a logarithmic function. SYGRAPH will allow you to log the vertical or horizontal scale on any base log (e.g. 2 or 3 or 10). The base of the log won't affect the appearance of the plot, but for most data, base 10 is easiest to understand. We're going to log the X axis (POPDEN), which will squeeze together large values of population density more than small. This option (`XLOG=10`) should straighten our line.

Instead of smoothing by `LOWESS` this time, let's fit a regression line by using the option `SMOOTH=LINEAR`. This smoothing method fits a line through the points such that the sum of the squared vertical deviations of each point from the line is as small as possible. In addition, we will request a confidence interval on the fitted line. By choosing a value of .95 (`CONFI=.95`), we will get an interval such that 95 out of 100 intervals computed this way on new samples would be expected to cover the "true" regression line relating INCOME to POPDEN. Statisticians might object to the use of a confidence interval here because new samples are difficult to define precisely for these data and because the values are "spatially autocorrelated." That is, data for contiguous states are related, so that geography affects the relationship we are analyzing.

Nevertheless, we will forge ahead with imperfect data and examine our plot, keeping in mind that the confidence interval is only approximate. Figure 18 shows the result.

Figure 18

```
PLOT   INCOME*POPDEN/SMOOTH=LINEAR,CONFI=.95,XLOG=10
```

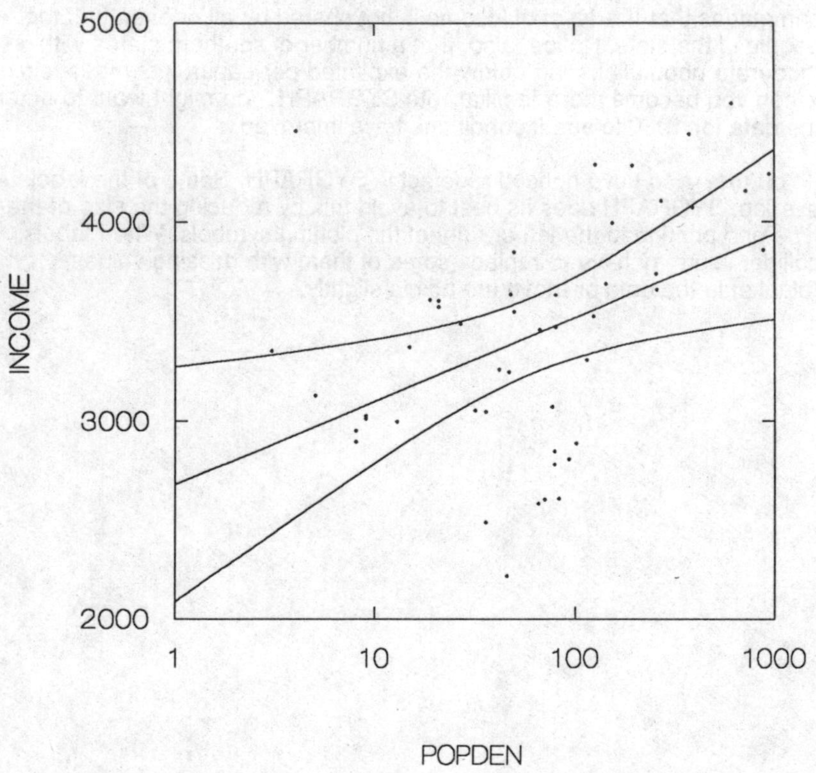

Labeling Points in a Scatterplot

Some of the points in the plot are far from the fitted line. In fact, another condition for the confidence interval to be valid is that the points cluster in an even band along the line. Clearly, it would be valuable to identify the points which fit poorly. This is easy to do with the `LABEL` option. Let's use the two letter post-office abbreviation of the state names to label the points. These are stored in the character variable STATE$. This time, we will leave out the confidence interval and just plot the line. Figure 19 shows the result.

Notice in the figure that Nevada has an extremely low population density and extremely high per-capita income. I need not go into the explanation for this except, perhaps, for those not familiar with U.S. social customs. It is also an interesting reminder of the pitfalls of statistical summaries that this level of income is not shared by all or even half the people in the state. Notice, also, that a number of southern states with moderate populations lag below the expected per-capita income levels. When you become more familiar with SYGRAPH, you might want to enter the data for 1980 to see if conditions have improved.

You may also have noticed a defect in SYGRAPH. Some of the labels overlap. SYGRAPH does its best to avoid this by reducing the size of the type and printing to the left or right of the plotting symbols. When labels collide, you may have to replace some of them with missing values (blanks) in the data or move the points slightly.

Figure 19

```
PLOT INCOME*POPDEN,
/SMOOTH=LINEAR,XLOG=10,LABEL=STATE$
```

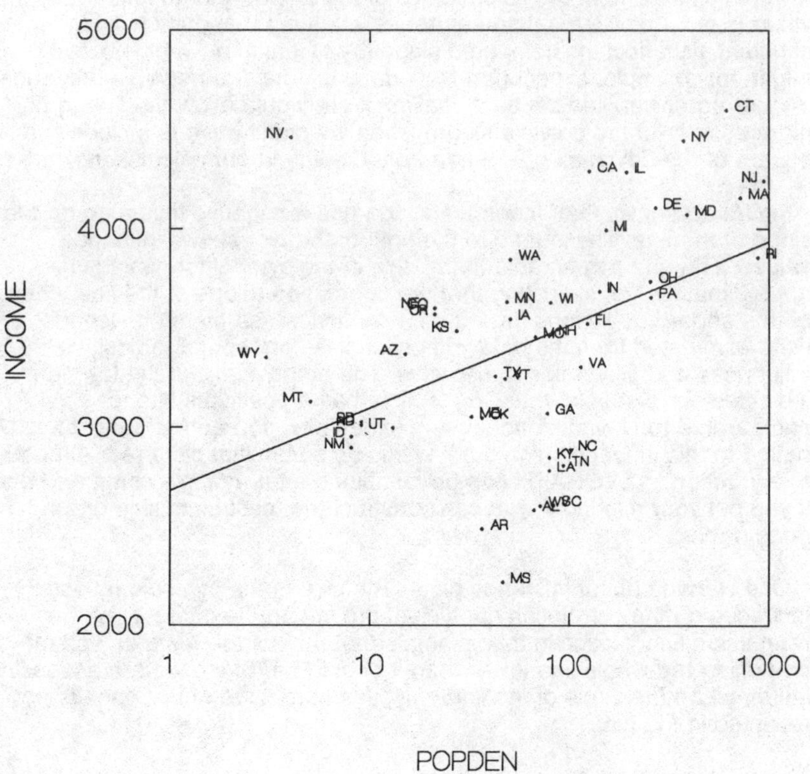

Influence Plots

Let's try an exotic plot at this point. You may not understand everything about it, but it gives you a chance to see how statisticians diagnose problems with a graphical summary. As I mentioned earlier, the confidence interval we computed is somewhat questionable with these data, partly because Nevada and the southern states fall outside an even band we might expect. The graph in Figure 20 displays the influence of each point on a certain aspect of the fitted line, namely its slope.

If we standardize INCOME and the log of POPDEN such that their standard deviations (spread) are the same, then the slope of possible lines relating the two variables would vary between -1 and +1. The influence of a point measures how much the slope would vary if the point were eliminated from the calculations of the slope. A large influence value (say, .4 or -.3) would mean that eliminating that point would substantially affect the computed slope (by as much as .4 or -.3). We might, for example, expect that Nevada would have a negative influence on the regression line because leaving it out would allow the line to tilt more steeply (more positive slope) when we didn't have to include the square of the deviation of Nevada from the line in our calculations.

Figure 20 shows that, indeed, Nevada has a negative influence on the slope of the line. The legend to the right of the plot shows influence values. The one comparable to the size of the symbol for Nevada is approximately .05, indicating that the correlation (slope of the line when both standard deviations are equal) would increase by .05 if Nevada were eliminated from the data. Empty circles correspond to positive influences and filled ones to negative. The empty circle at the top right indicates, for example, that Connecticut has a positive influence comparable to Nevada's negative. Incidentally, you can add the `LABEL` option to this influence plot, but it would be somewhat cluttered. Almost every option in SYGRAPH can be combined after a single command and if you put your mind to it, you can construct the most confusing graph imaginable.

One warning about influence plots. The size of the symbols reflects influence on the correlation coefficient but not on the intercept of the regression line. Notice in this example that the southern states appear to be pulling the whole line lower than it should be. Since we are assessing influence on the slope of the line only, this other type of influence is not reflected in the plot.

Figure 20

```
PLOT   INCOME*POPDEN/XLOG=10,INFLUENCE
```

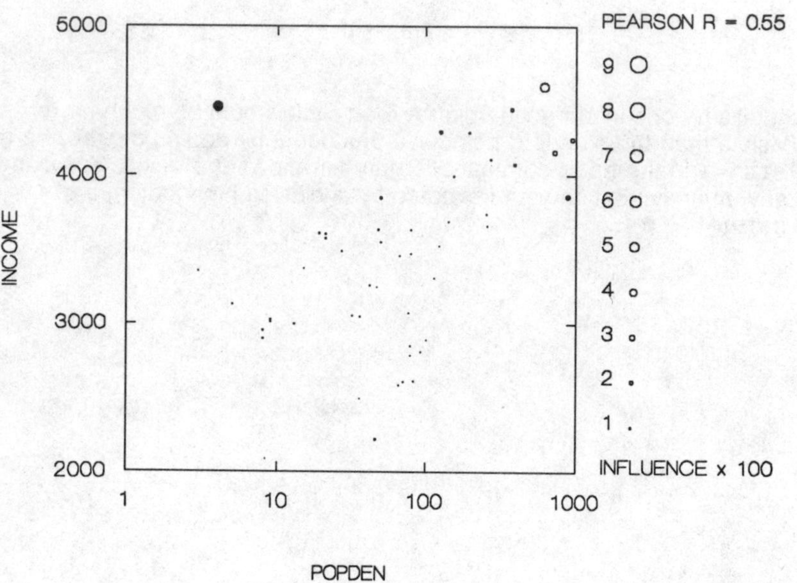

Plotting Symbols

So far, we have been using the default plotting symbol, a small point. You may have noticed that a different symbol, a circle, was used in the influence plot. You can choose a number of symbols as alternatives. Here are the possibilities:

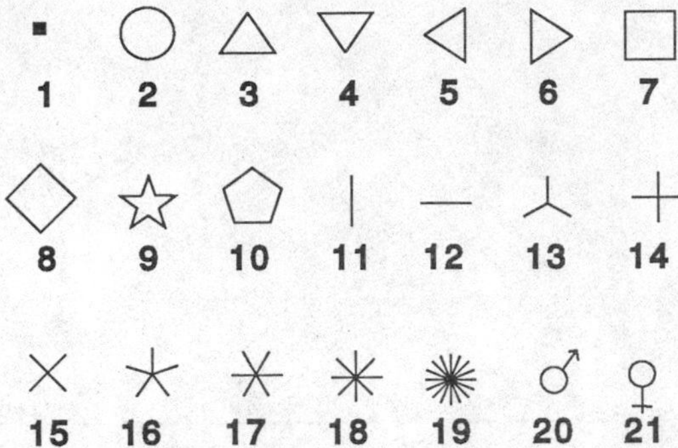

Let's try one in our scatterplot. A filled circle would be much more visible than the standard point. We produce it by adding `SYMBOL=2` and `FILL=1` to the `PLOT` command. Figure 21 shows the result. You can use any other symbol on your keyboard by enclosing it in quotes, e.g. `SYMBOL='#"`.

Figure 21

```
PLOT   INCOME*POPDEN/XLOG=10,SYMBOL=2,FILL=1
```

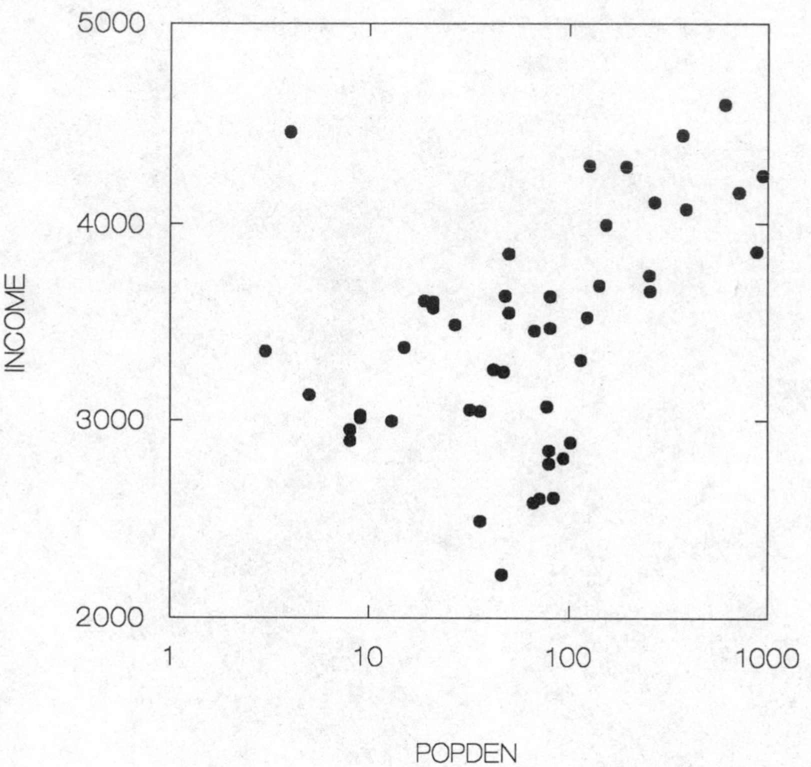

Symbols from Data Values

You can also choose your symbols from a data file. This way, you can use a different plotting symbol for each case or group of cases. Figure 22 shows a plot of the first letter of each state at the latitude (LABLAT) and longitude (LABLON) of each state. In order to make the map correspond roughly to a Mercator projection, I've scaled the size of the axes to make the plot rectangular.

This plotting symbol option is handy for denoting subgroups. For example, you could have a character variable in your file with one symbol for males and another for females. This way, the plot symbols would reveal the distribution of gender across the plotting space.

Figure 22

```
PLOT  LABLAT*LABLON,
     /SYMBOL=STATE$,HEIGHT=3IN,WIDTH=4IN
```

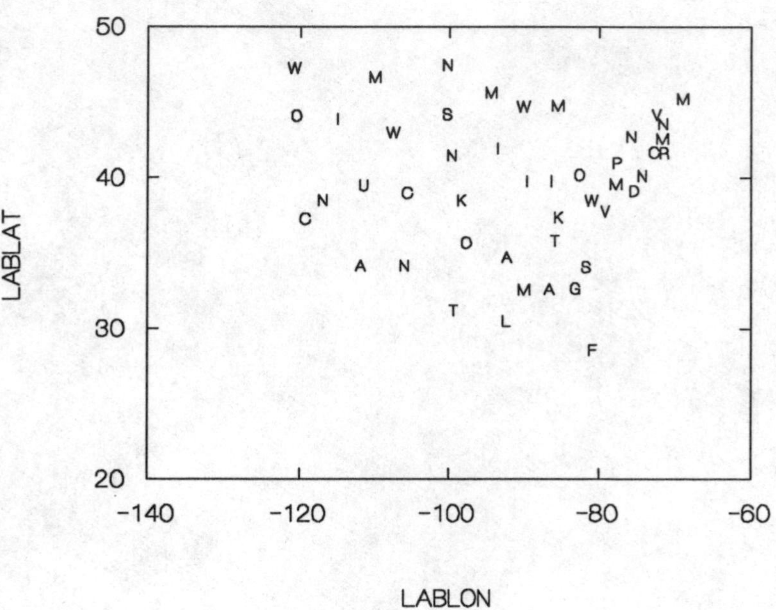

Varying Symbol Sizes

You can make your plotting symbols smaller or larger by using the `SIZE` option. `SIZE=1` is the standard size we have been using. If you use another number for `SIZE`, then you will get a symbol that many times the size of the standard symbol. `SIZE=.5`, for example, produces symbols half the size of the standard one. `SIZE=2.3` makes them 2.3 times as large. If a symbol has a size less than .001, it is not plotted at all. This is handy for plotting axes in special positions or drawing lines without symbols. We'll take advantage of this feature later.

Figure 23 shows a scatterplot with symbols half again as large as usual.

Figure 23

```
PLOT PERSON*PROPERTY,
 /SYMBOL=10,SIZE=1.5
```

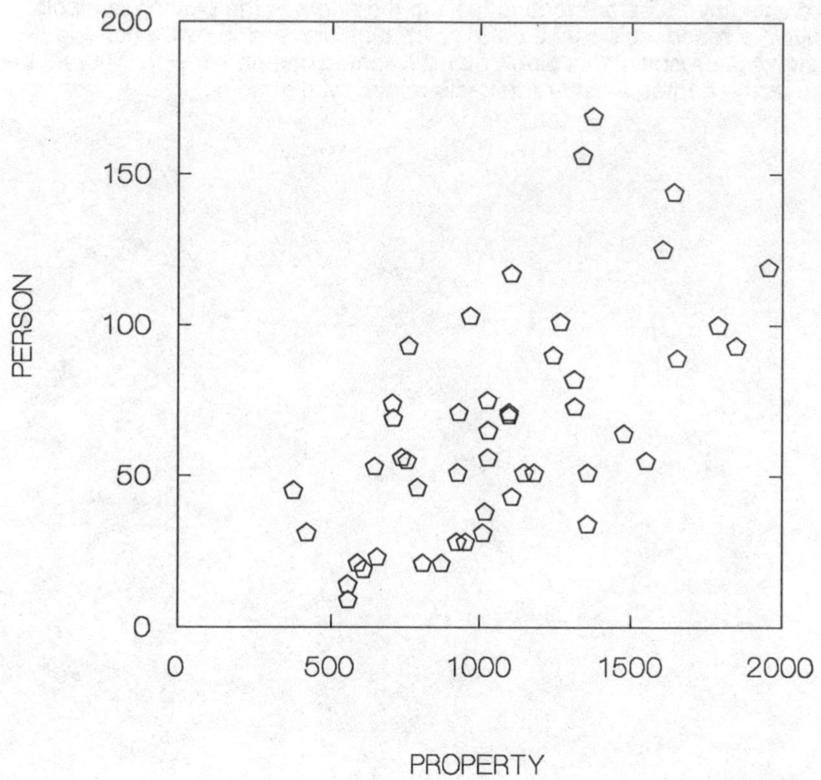

Varying Symbol Sizes

You can use a variable to control the size of plotting symbols. This way, you can use one scatterplot to represent three variables. SYGRAPH uses the value of the variable you specify to determine the diameter of the plotting symbol. Keep in mind, however, that viewers are more likely to notice area rather than diameter when judging the size of many symbols. For this reason, you should usually use the*square root* of your controlling variable to determine the size of plotting symbols with area, such as circles and squares.

Here is an example. I used the DATA module to square root the value of RAIN (average annual rainfall):

```
LET  RAI=SQR(RAIN/30)
```

I divided by 30 before rooting to keep the areas of the plotting symbols within a reasonable range on the plot, thus preventing overlaps. Figure shows the result of this plot. You may want to compare it with Figure 3 in the **MAP** chapter, which represents rainfall with shading.

Figure 24

```
PLOT  LABLAT*LABLON,
    /SYMBOL=2,SIZE=RAI,HEIGHT=3IN,WIDTH=4IN
```

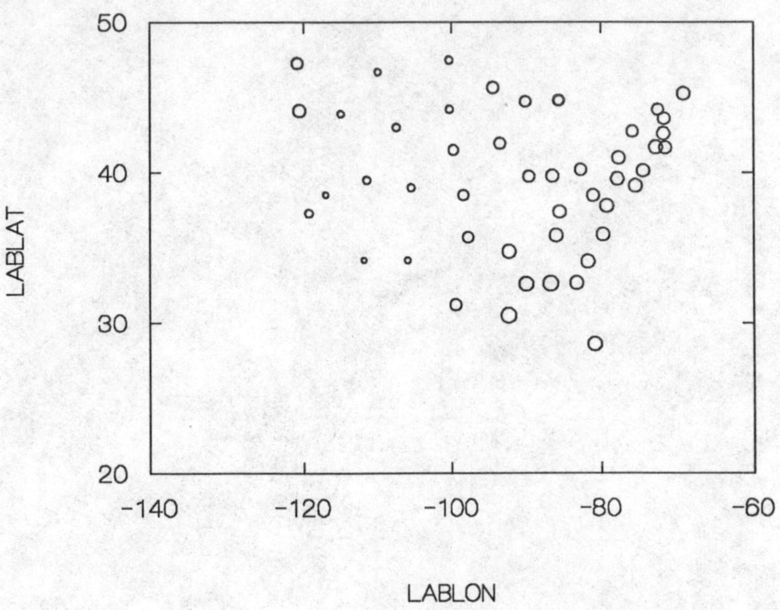

Grid Marks

Sometimes you may want a grid on your graph to allow closer visual inspection. This is easy to do with the **GRID** option. You can add vertical (**GRID=1**), horizontal (**GRID=2**), or crossed (**GRID=3**) grid lines to a plot this way.

Figure 25 shows an example of this using the per-capita income data. I've added a lot of options to make a more attractive graph and to review how they can be combined. I've put pip marks in for the logarithms to show the relative scaling. Do you see why **XPIP=9** instead of 10? If not, just count along the scale. The bold numbers correspond to the tick marks and the light ones to the pips.

1,2,3,4,5,6,7,8,9,**10**,20,30,40,50,60,70,80,90,**100**,200,300. . .

In case you didn't know it already, this plot is called a **semilog plot** because one scale is logged. In addition, I've labeled the plot to make it more meaningful.

Figure 25

```
PLOT  INCOME*POPDEN,
    /XLOG=10,SYMBOL=2,GRID=3,XPIP=9,YPIP=10,
     XLABEL='Log  of  Population  Per  Square  Mile',
     YLABEL='Per  Capita  Income'
```

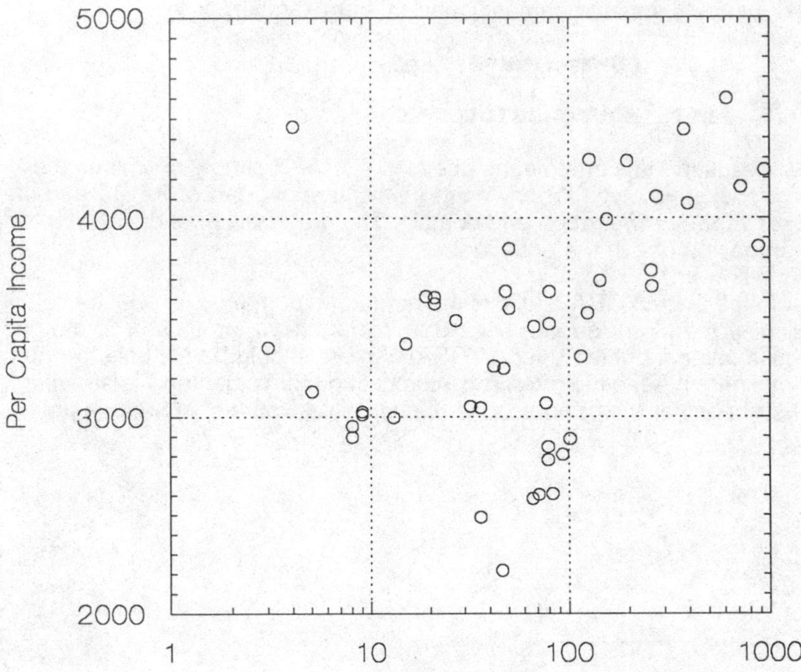

Plotting Mathematical Functions

SYGRAPH will plot functions without any data. This feature is handy for students of algebra, calculus, and analysis. Scientists will also find it useful for superimposing theoretical functions on their data plots. Just type the function you want plotted, e.g.

```
PLOT Y=X*X*X
```
or,

```
PLOT  Y=X^3
```

These two expressions are equivalent. Both are written in a language called BASIC. If you know BASIC, then any standard numerical BASIC function can be plotted. If you don't know BASIC, you can examine the additional examples in this manual or any introduction to BASIC. You can use any variable names you wish. For example,

```
PLOT   CUBE=LINE^3
```
and,

```
PLOT   SOUP=BOUILLON^3
```

will result in the same plot as above. SYGRAPH simply examines the expression you type for any names which are not part of BASIC and then uses them for the range and domain. The graph will be labeled with the names you use in the equation.

Notice that SYGRAPH picks the range and domain over which to display the plot. You can use **XMIN**, **XMAX**, **YMIN**, and **YMAX** to change these values, but the ones SYGRAPH picks should be suitable for many functions. It does the picking by computing trial values and examining their behavior (first and second numerical derivatives) at various points.

Figure 26

`PLOT Y=X^3`

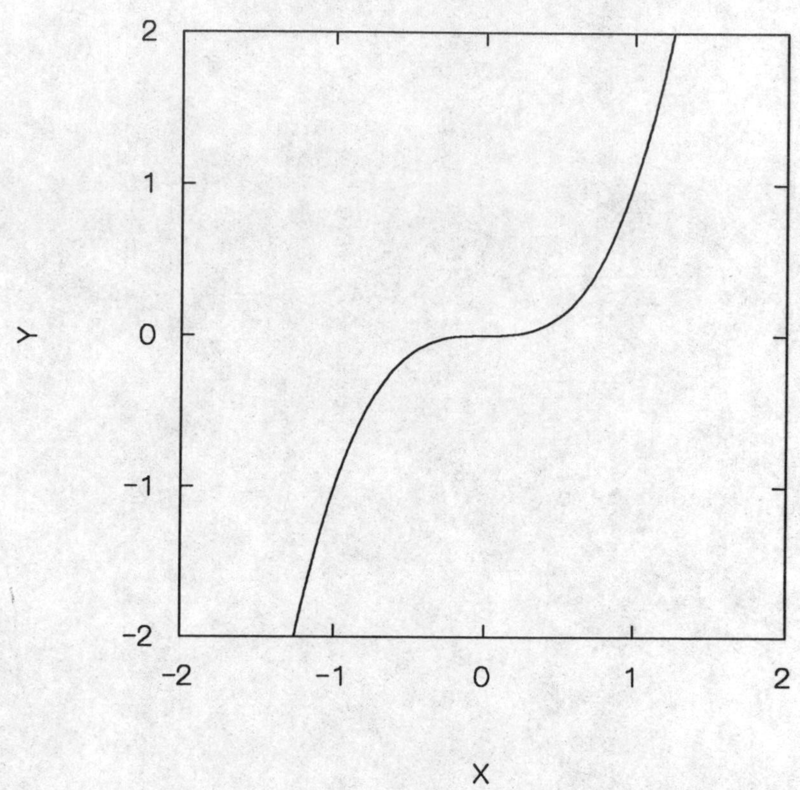

Three Dimensional Data Plots

You can do 3-D plots simply by adding one more variable to the **PLOT** command, e.g.:

```
PLOT  Z*Y*X
```

Figure 27 shows an example for our income data. We're plotting INCOME against LABLAT and LABLON, so that the XY plane is like a map of the U.S. and the vertical (Z) axis is income. I've added one other feature to the plot so that you can see it better. This is the option **SPIKE**, which causes a line to be dropped to the XY plane from each point.

You should be able to see the southern states in the foreground with lower per-capita income and the northwest and northeast with higher.

Figure 27

```
PLOT   INCOME*LABLAT*LABLON/SYMBOL=2,SPIKE
```

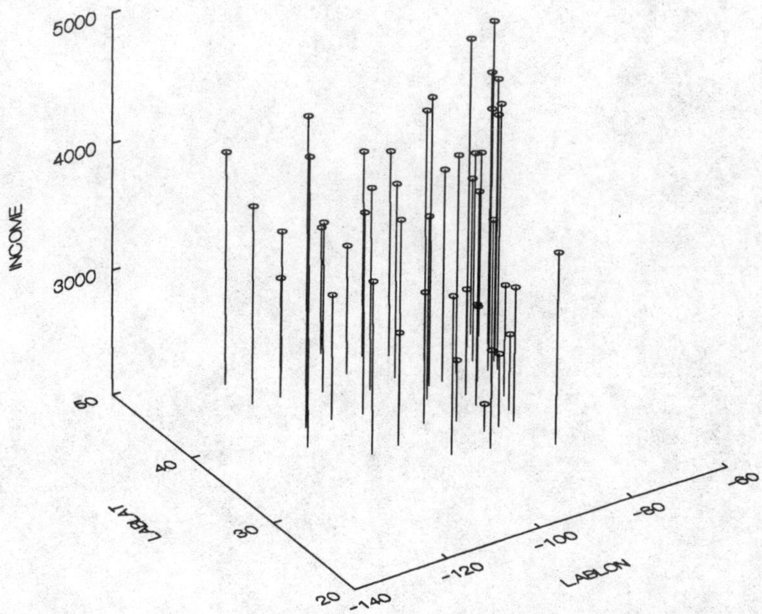

Three Dimensional Function Plots

Here's a simple three dimensional function plot. All we do is add another variable to our equation. Figure 28 shows a saddle function. I've added one option, **HIDE**, which you usually want. It slows things down a bit, but it causes portions of the surface in the background to be hidden behind portions in the foreground:

```
PLOT  Z=X^2-Y^2!HIDE
```

One thing might look peculiar to you here: the exclamation point (!). We need to use this to separate options when you type functions because the usual slash (/) is a divide sign (/) in BASIC.

Figure 28

```
PLOT  Z=X^2-Y^2!HIDE
```

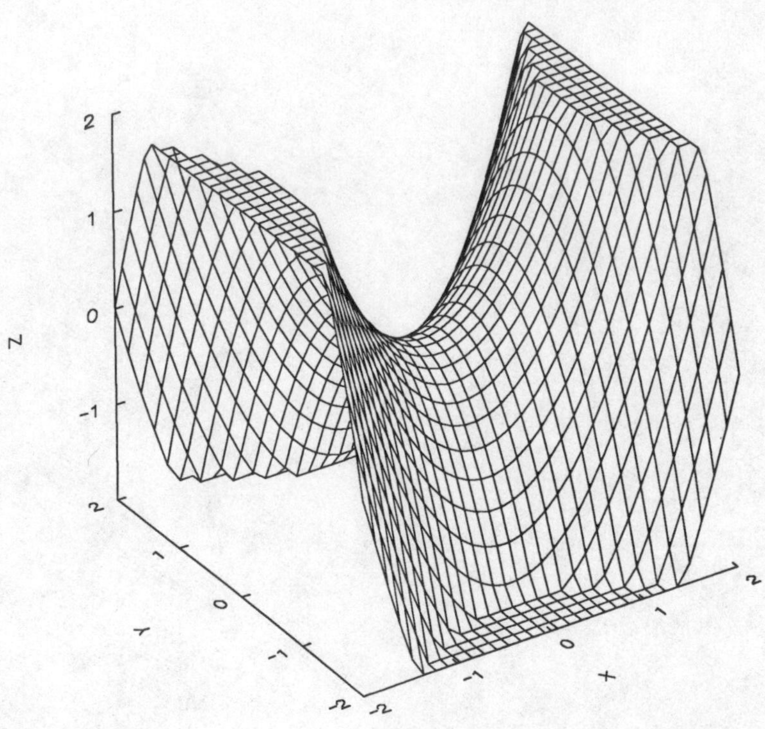

I Could Go On But I Think You're Getting the Idea

There is no way I'm going to be able to show you every feature of SYGRAPH in a tutorial. The important thing is to get a feel for how the program is organized. At this point, you should turn off your machine and go to bed. Tomorrow, you should begin with the next chapter. If you're really impatient, you can skip the next chapter and go directly to the reference section. If you do, you will miss all the pearls of wisdom you'll need to make well designed graphs. You'll use SYGRAPH to make a bunch of chart-junk and sully our reputation. Were there world enough and time . . .

Chapter 2

Cognitive Science and Graphic Design

This chapter has nothing to do with SYGRAPH. It has everything to do with graphics. If you are anxious to start using SYGRAPH, you can skip this chapter and go directly to the reference section. If you do skip, I hope you will return to read this sometime, because this chapter is about how to design good graphs.

The Function of Quantitative Graphics

Graphics can have many functions. They can entertain. They can persuade. The function of *quantitative* graphics, however, is to inform. By presenting graphics to others, we are attempting to communicate information through a wide and complex channel: the human visual system. In communicating this information, we may entertain or persuade or do other things, but if we distort the information underlying our graphics, we have failed.

Many designers of quantitative graphics confuse these functions or subordinate informing to other goals. Sometimes this is intentional, as in graphic propaganda, but often it is inadvertent, as in popular newspaper graphs which distort their message with bright colors and "perspective" views.

If we think of quantitative graphics as a mode of information processing, then we can use the tools of cognitive psychology to evaluate displays. In this chapter, I will cover the basics of visual information processing, principals of graphic design, and then conclude with examples of good and bad graphs. If you want to read more in this area, you should look at Frisby (1980), Haber and Hershenson (1980), Levine and Shefner (1981), Spoehr and Lehmkuhle (1982), Tufte (1983), Chambers, Cleveland, Kleiner & Tukey (1983), and Cleveland (1985).

Visual Information Processing

The visual system can be represented by several abstract components. Figure 1 shows schematically these components. The **graphic image** is the composite of physical aspects which contains the information we are communicating. It may originate on paper, on a computer screen, or in another medium. For our purposes, the image is the set of critical features which stimulate the retina to fire its neurons such that the remainder of the visual system in the brain can process the information.

Iconic memory is the first component of memorization. Cells in the retina fire neural impulses when they absorb a quantity of photons from a light stimulus. They continue to fire for a short time after the stimulation ceases and thus serve as a brief store for the image itself.

Short term memory holds essential features of the stimulus so that it can be integrated into the framework of long term memory. A famous study by George Miller (1956) and others since have indicated that short term memory can hold at least four, and perhaps as many as seven or eight "chunks" of information. These "chunks" can be made up of other chunks from long term memory, so that short term memory can be used to build up arbitrarily complex constructs. This is why I have used two arrows between short and long term memory to indicate feedback. Some psychologists who have worked in verbal learning claim that short term memory is *acoustical*, meaning that information is rehearsed subvocally until it can be integrated into long term memory. Others, such as Shepard (1978) and Kosslyn (1980), have shown that visual perceptual units can be stored in short term memory as well. In either case, perceptual chunking in short term memory allows time for long term memory encoding to occur. This time appears to be 20 seconds or so for each chunk of information.

Long term memory contains the permanently remembered information from the perceived graph. I use "permanently" advisedly, since there is no compelling evidence to show that we ever forget anything once it is encoded into long term memory (assuming no physiological damage from toxins like alcohol or other physical deterioration associated with aging). Forgetting is more likely a failure to draw connections between associated information stored in memory. "Forgotten" information can often be recovered by a careful reconstruction of associated information, experiences, and sensations.

Figure 1

Abstract Representation of the Visual System

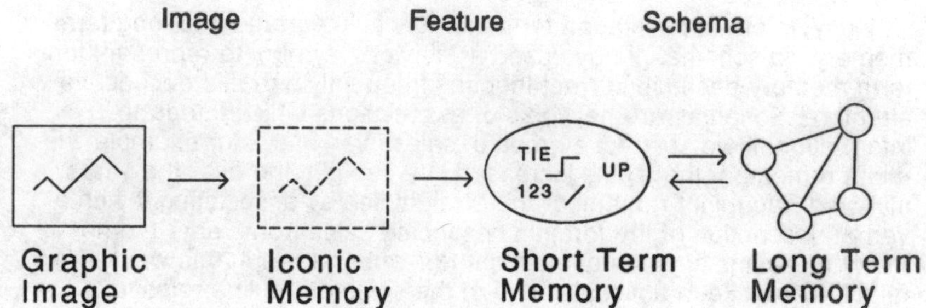

Above the diagram, I have indicated components of the information which are processed at each stage. Information passed from the graphic image to iconic memory depends on the optical quality of the image. If a graph has poor contrast and fuzzy lines, for example, critical aspects will not register in the iconic store. Knowing this, we should attempt to keep graphic images clean, with high contrast and crisp delineation. If we are using colors, we should avoid faint pastels, muddy tones, and other low intensity shades.

Features of an image are transmitted from the iconic store to short term memory. If a graph is cluttered with a large number of features (e.g. 15 curves), we know that this information cannot be held in short term memory following a few seconds look at the graph. Knowing this, we should limit the essential features in one graph to a manageable number unless we expect our viewers to spend considerable time processing the information.

Finally, information in short term memory is integrated into long term memory via schemas. I have used a "network" symbol to represent long term memory because current theories frequently use this descriptive structure. Schemas are networks of associations which integrate information. If we abstract a graph of sales over years, for example, we might remember that sales increased in a straight line over the years involved. We might remember this straight line by associating it with a verbal description of the formula describing sales from years (some mathematicians and actuaries might remember a graph this way). We might instead keep a visual image of the slope of the line relative to the frame around the graph and associate this image with remembered values of the axes (e.g. "millions of sales in the 1960's").

Psychologists disagree on exactly how information is stored in long term memory. There is evidence that information can be stored as a set of linked propositions and other evidence that it can be stored as linked icons, or visual mental representations. We need not resolve this controversy in order to decide how to use graphic designs, however. In either case, we should realize that the information in a graph will be stored most effectively if it can be associated with other information. Unusual scales, break points in graphs, puzzling anchor points for data values, all may interfere with the process of storing the fundamental information in a graph, e.g. the change in one variable relative to another.

The Psychophysics of Perception

We have seen a representation of the path from graphic image to long term memory. While this structure has implications for the design of good graphs, we still need to understand how images are perceived. The visual system, like our other sensory systems encodes information in various forms. Perhaps because quantitative graphs are relatively recent visual icons in human history, we process them with the same tools we use to perceive three-dimensional scenes and two-dimensional pictures. Sometimes these tools cause us to distort the very information we are attempting to perceive accurately.

The Power Law

Early in the nineteenth century, Weber noticed that the increment in stimulation required to produce a just noticeable difference between two stimuli was proportional to the size of the stimuli. The bigger (more intense) were the stimuli, the bigger was the difference needed to notice a difference between the two. For example, we can easily see two objects separated on our desk. We have more trouble discriminating two objects a quarter mile from our desk if they are separated by the same distance.

Not long after Weber's discovery, Fechner derived a scale for sensation. Assuming that Weber's just noticeable differences in sensation were equivalent at all levels of stimulation, Fechner computed a logarithmic function relating the magnitude of sensation (S) to the intensity of stimulation (I). In Fechner's function sensation increases logarithmically with stimulation, so that differences in sensation are produced by the same ratios of stimulation:

$$S = k \log(I)$$

In the 1950's, Stevens (following the work of Plateau in the 1800's) proposed a power function for sensation instead of Fechner's logarithmic curve. Using a wide variety of stimuli, Stevens fit his data with a power function:

$$S = k I^p$$

There is still some controversy whether Stevens' or Fechner's curves describe perceptual data and even the possibility that both are correct under different experimental conditions. Figure 2 shows both curves for a typical application. The important thing to notice is the downward curvature of both. In practical terms, increasing the size of symbols on a graph will not increase the *perceived* size in the same increments. Increasing the darkness of a filled area will not increase the perceived darkness in the same increments. This downward bias should make us wary of using area, darkness, and volume in graphs when we can use other modes of representing quantitative variation which are less susceptible to these distortions.

Stevens and his associates measured a wide variety of auditory, visual, and tactile stimuli. For our purposes, it is most useful to note that the value of the exponent in the power function varies across types of graphical stimuli. For length judgments, it has ranged from .9 to 1.1; for area, from .6 to .9; for volume, from .5 to .8 (Baird, 1970; Cleveland, 1985).

The lower part of Figure 2 illustrates this perceptual bias. In which pair of circles (A, B, or C) is the right circle twice the area of the left? What about the densities on the right? Which is twice as dark as its partner? I drew each pair using a different exponent in the Stevens power function to modify what would otherwise be twice the area of the circle on the left or twice the density of the rectangle on the left. Pair A has an exponent of 1.0, pair B has .95 and pair C has .90. The answer, then, is that the right circle in pair A is twice the area of the circle on the left and the right rectangle in pair A is twice as dark as the one on the left.

These examples should alert you to the dangers of using area and shading to represent numerical quantities. One solution might be to adjust areas, shadings, and other features in a graph to fit the psychometric functions derived from perceptual experiments. This would be easy to do in a computerized graphing package. We shall see, however, that there are usually alternative ways to represent quantitative variation without resorting to shading, area, or other features governed by exceptionally flat psychometric functions.

Figure 2

Power (Stevens) and Log (Fechner) Curves Relating Stimulus Intensity and Magnitude of Sensation (Circle Areas and Densities Follow Power Law)

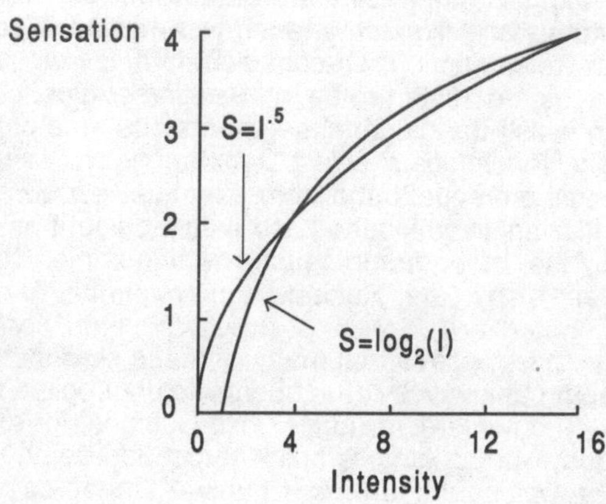

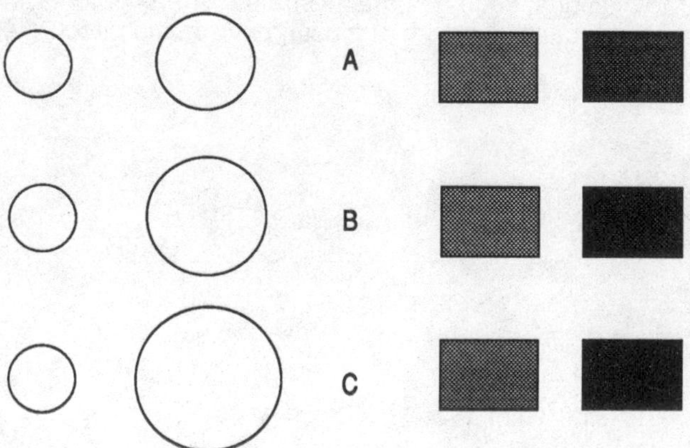

Visual Illusions

PICTURE: *a representation in two dimensions of something wearisome in three.* (Ambrose Bierce, *The Devil's Dictionary*)

Pictures have a dual reality (Haber & Hershenson, 1980). We live in a three-dimensional world in which pictures are two-dimensional, yet pictures can represent three-dimensional objects. Consequently, our perception of graphs (pictures) is influenced by the tools we have for perceiving three-dimensional space. Sometimes, these tools interfere with accurate perception of a graph.

Figure 3 shows some of the well known two-dimensional illusions. The first (A) is the horizontal-vertical illusion in which two equal line segments are distorted by relative orientation. The second (B) is the Muller-Lyer, in which equal line segments are distorted by intersecting angles. C is the Poggendorf illusion, in which the diagonal segments line on a common line but are displaced by the verticals. D is a Delboeuf figure, in which the sizes of the center circles are equal but distorted by their surrounds. Finally, E is a Ponzo illusion, in which the perceived sizes of two equal circles are distorted by the the surrounding perspective angle. Coren and Girgus (1978) document many other illusions.

Gregory (1969) and others believe that many of these illusions evoke three-dimensional depth cues which are inappropriately applied in two-dimensional contexts. The Muller-Lyer and Ponzo illusions, for example, distort size judgments by surrounding stimuli with pseudo depth cues which are angular. The Delboeuf figure may involve "tunnel" cues which are used in three dimensional processing. These features make it difficult to judge absolute size in two dimensions because we are accustomed to using depth cues for three-dimensional size judgments.

Whatever the explanation for these illusions, we should keep in mind that judgments involving angles and figure-ground relations (such as in illusion D) in graphs will often be biased. If we can find alternatives to angle representations, such as parallel straight line segments, we will often be more successful in communicating information accurately.

Figure 3

Visual Illusions

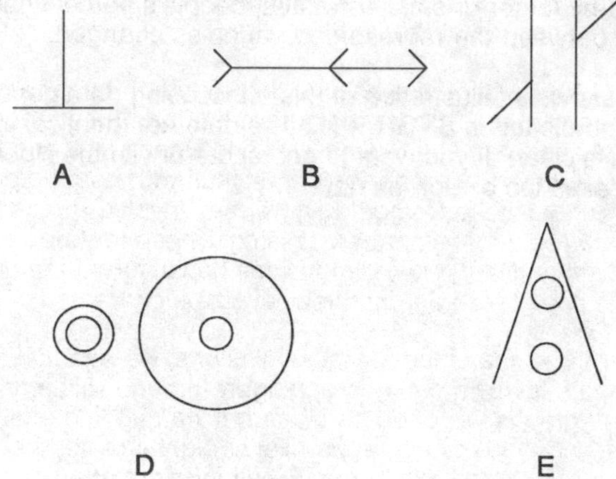

Gestalt Psychology and Figure-Ground Separation

Gestalt psychologists proposed early in this century that "the whole is more than the sum of its parts. In graphical terms, this means that elements in a graph look different when viewed alone than when viewed in context of the entire graph. The Gestalt psychologists showed, for example, than when objects are placed near each other, they are perceived as part of an integral pattern. Furthermore, similar objects in an overall display tend to be perceived as part of a unified pattern. Other features of objects, such as symmetry and continuity, affect how we perceive them when they are embedded in more general patterns. This perceptual organization is not always inherent in the retinal image. We impose organization on the image in order to process it.

A closely related phenomenon is the figure-ground effect. Objects can be framed or placed against a background in ways which change their appearance. An object which contrasts with its background, for example, will tend to look more integrated. One interesting example of this effect in graphical perception has been found by Cleveland, Diaconis, and McGill (1982). They showed that when point clouds of scatterplots are surrounded by larger or smaller frames, people's perceptions of the correlation between the represented variables changed.

Figure 4 shows an illustration of this effect using data generated by SYSTAT and plotted in SYGRAPH. The data are identical in both plots. The lesson is clear. If you want to get tenure or win the Nobel Prize, make your axes too big for the data.

Figure 4

The Top Scatterplot Looks More Correlated

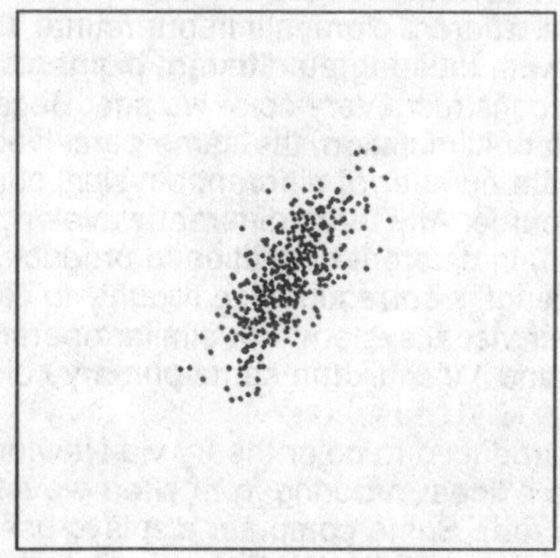

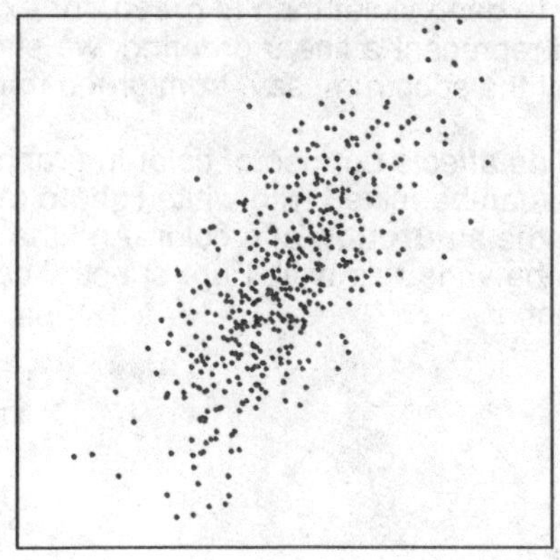

The Perception of Color

Color is one of the most popular media in computer graphics. Unfortunately, it is one of the most difficult to use effectively. We want graphs to look pretty, so we choose color to represent scales or categories. In doing so, we often overlook the complexities in the perception of color.

Color is not a physical characteristic of objects or light. It is purely a psychological phenomenon, a "fabrication of the visual system" (Levine & Shefner, 1981). The colors we see are the summation of stimulation by light photons of three different pigments in our retina. The firings of neurons associated with these three different pigments are integrated in the visual system to construct every color we see. Because perceived color is a summation of stimulation, the same perceived color can be produced by an infinite number of different physical characteristics in an object and/or light source. Any three different wavelengths of light can be added (or subtracted) in different quantities to produce the entire visible spectrum, but wavelengths corresponding roughly to RED, GREEN, and BLUE are used in our visual system. For similar operating reasons, color computer terminals and TV's mix the same primary colors.

Most of us were introduced to color theory via Newton's spectrum, which appears to be a linear ordering from short wavelengths (deep violet) to long (deep red). Some computer displays use this spectrum to represent dimensions (e.g. COOL-WARM temperature, or LOW-HIGH altitude). Because of the way our visual system sums wavelengths, however, we do not perceive the spectrum linearly. We perceive it as an open circle or horseshoe, with deep red and deep violet at each end of the opening and green at the opposite closed portion. Deep red is judged more similar to deep violet than to green, for example. Thus, if we want to use color to represent a linear ordering, we should probably choose a segment of the spectrum, say, from green to red.

Another complication affects our use of color in graphics. A spectral color of a given **hue** can be mixed with white light to make it appear pale. This mixture affects the **saturation** of a color. And the energy of a color, its **brightness**, can be varied as well. Pure spectral colors do not appear equally vivid or bright.

Colors are best used to represent categories instead of scales. We might use red symbols for an experimental group and green for a control, for example. The perception of color categories is innate, cross-cultural and not dependent on language. Infants, for example, show clear boundaries between perceived colors (Bornstein, Kessen, & Weiskopf, 1976). When using colors for category definition in a graph, it is a good idea to choose contrasting colors (e.g. RED-GREEN, or RED-YELLOW-GREEN-BLUE) to enhance these boundary discriminations.

Colors can create visual illusions. A gray patch against a green background will appear reddish, for example. You may have noticed a similar contrast effect after working at a green computer screen. The world looks pink when you look away from the screen. Colors also affect area judgments. In three dimensions, a blue disk will look more distant than a red disk of the same size, controlling for saturation and brightness. In two dimensions, a red area will look larger than a blue, probably because of a three-dimensional illusion. Cleveland and McGill (1983), for example, found that people judged red areas on maps as larger than blue. Durrett (1987) contains several informative papers on the use of color for computer graphics.

Graphic Design

We can apply psychological principles to the design of graphs and we can supplement them with aesthetic principles. Cleveland (1985) integrated both areas in a landmark book. After a survey of statistical and psychological research, including some of his own, Cleveland derived an approximate ordering of graphical features from most to least accurate in representing quantitative variation. Figure 5 presents this hierarchy.

The criterion for constructing this hierarchy is the linear agreement between quantitative information presented graphically to subjects and the actual values underlying the graphical representation. In a variety of experiments, tasks involving modes higher up in the hierarchy were performed more accurately than tasks lower. Thus we should, all other things being equal, prefer a bar chart to a pie chart for presenting comparative information because a bar chart provides a common scale and a pie chart involves angle judgments. Simkin and Hastie (1987) have found exceptions to this rule when proportional judgments are involved, but Cleveland's basic hierarchy has proved useful in practice.

Sometimes we have no choice. Time series plots, scatterplots, and mathematical functions often require angle judgments because slope is intrinsically angular relative to a horizontal or vertical orientation. In these cases, experimental evidence indicates it is important to choose scales which make the physical slope of the graphed function as close to 45 degrees as possible (Cleveland & McGill, 1988).

Bertin (1983) and Tufte (1983) have written about graphics more from a design point of view. Both stress economy and simple graphic icons. Although both speak of maximizing the information in a graph, we should qualify this rule with what we know about the visual system. In graphs intended for a glance, such as in a slide presentation, Mies Van der Rohe's dictum "Less is More" is a better rule. If a graph contains too many visual modes, its information is unlikely to make its way into long term memory. On the other hand, if we are presenting graphs in a publication, we can tolerate a high degree of complexity provided components of the graph can be processed in "chunks" to make their way through short term to long term memory. By now, you should see that there is no simple rule which discriminates good and bad graphics. The appropriateness of a graph depends on the conditions in which it is presented and the information to be communicated.

Figure 5

Cleveland Graphic Tasks Hierarchy

BETTER

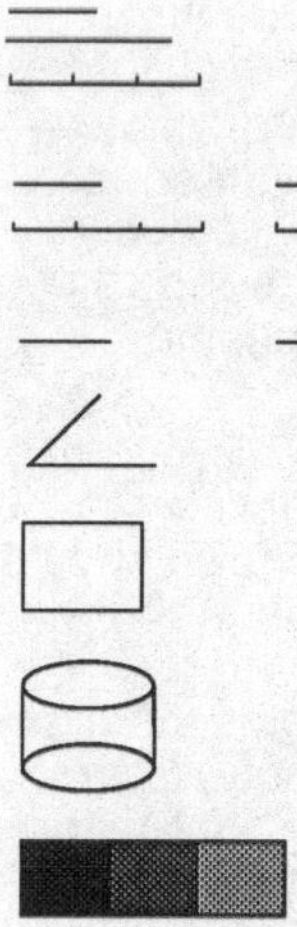

1. Position along a common scale
2. Position along identical, nonaligned scales
3. Length
4. Angle - Slope
5. Area
6. Volume
7. Color hue - Color saturation - Density

WORSE

Some Examples

A few examples should illustrate the psychological and design principles we have seen. In the following figures, I have contrasted two alternative graphs of the same information. The upper graph is less effective in communicating the information than the lower.

Perspective mania

Figure 6 illustrates a three-dimensional bar graph. These perspective bar charts are popular in business programs. I cannot think of a single instance in which a perspective bar graph should be used for any application. Like all perspective plots, the depth information is confusing and gives rise to several visual illusions. The actual height of the bars is difficult to establish. Some users ruin the plot further by adding color coding to the bars which enhances the pseudo perspective illusions.

The lower graphs in the figure are less glamorous but more effective. If you wish to compare trends between the two grouping variables, the line graph in the middle of the figure is particularly useful. It is easy to see where the profiles are parallel and their heights and values are easily identified on the common scale. If you are more interested in highlighting differences at each comparison point, then the multi-value bar chart at the bottom of the figure is more suitable. Here, the graphic focus is on each pair of bars, facilitating individual comparisons. Finally, you should consider a dot plot (Cleveland,1985), which can be done with the `CPLOT` command in SYGRAPH. Dot plots are similar to bar graphs but they do not connect the data points to a base the way bars do.

You may have noticed that SYGRAPH has a full assortment of 3-D graphs. I had to make *some* concession to the marketplace. Nevertheless, before you use them, you should consider 2-D alternatives.

Figure 6

Three Dimensional Bars versus Lines

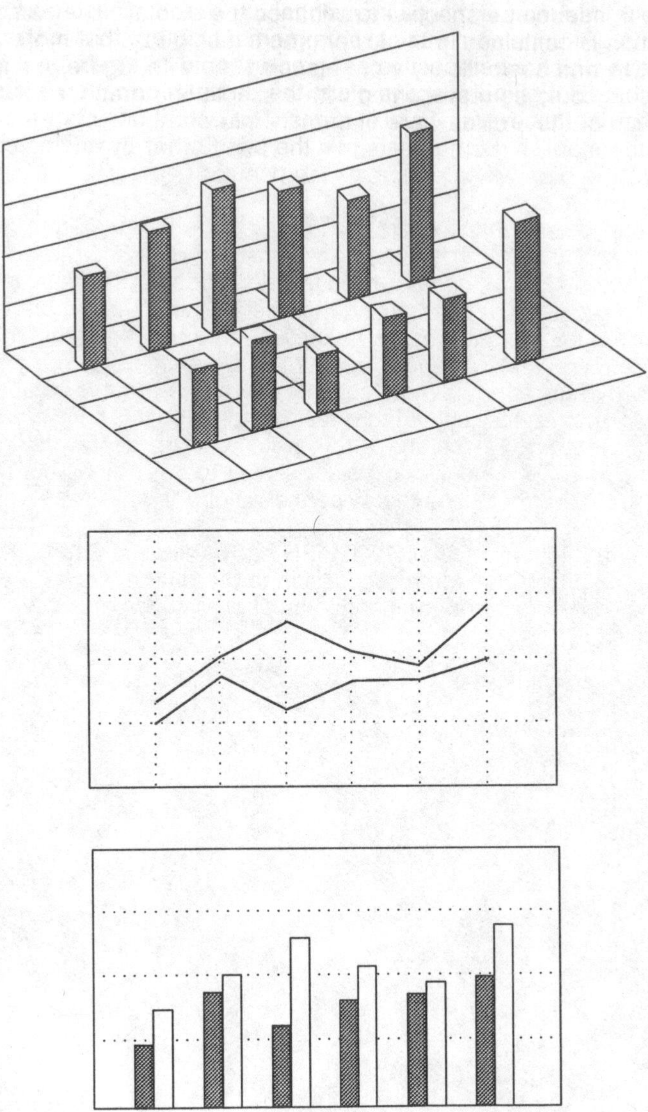

Pseudo Perspective Bar Chart

A nasty relative of the perspective bar chart is the pseudo perspective bar chart. Illustrators frequently feel the need to make two dimensional bars look like blocks or skyscrapers. Doing so makes it difficult to reference the top of the bar against a scale. It is never clear whether the "front" or "back" of the bar is intended to be the height indicator. Figure 7 shows an example of this type of graph. The upper figure is a double bar graph with pseudo perspective to enhance the display. The same information is contained in the lower graph: less glitzy, but more informative and aesthetically more pleasing. As with Figure 6, this information could be represented with a simple line graph, especially if parallelism of the profiles were of primary interest.

Figure 7
Pseudo Perspective Bars versus Two Dimensional Bars

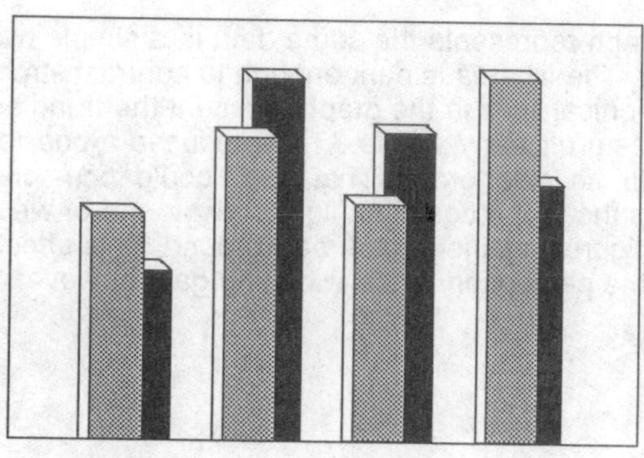

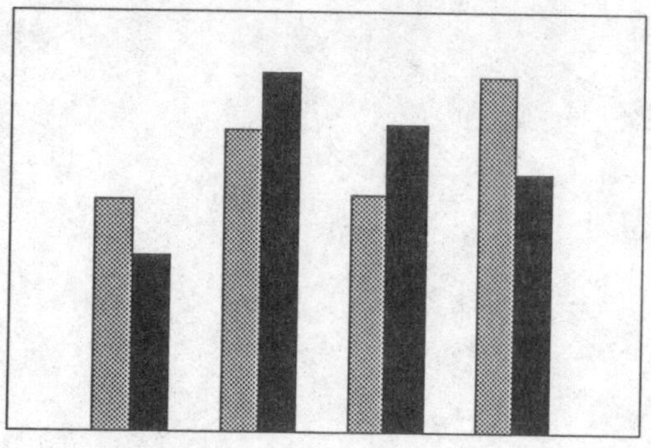

Pseudo Perspective Line Graphs

The graph in the next figure was adapted from a chart of grain production in China and the Soviet Union featured in a leading national newspaper. The point of the accompanying article was to highlight the widening gap between Soviet and Chinese grain production. Although the graph shows production on the vertical axis against years on the horizontal, it does little to make the point. First of all, the pseudo three-dimensional perspective makes it difficult for us to line up the two trends. Shifting the upper trend to the left to simulate perspective ruins the calibration of the horizontal scale. Secondly, the uneven shading across the graph enhances our depth perception by making foreground darker than background, but it ruins our focus on the widening gap, which is the purpose of the graph and article.

The lower graph represents the same data in a simple two-dimensional filled line chart. The fill area is dark enough to contrast strongly with the background. Vertical lines in the graph segment the trend so that year to year differences are clearly visible. I have induced a possible figure-ground effect in the lower graph. That is, we could focus on the central dark portion as the figure against a light background or we could view the white bars as figures against a dark background. This effect does not interfere with the perception of the widening gap, however.

Figure 8

Pseudo Perspective Line Graph vs. Filled Line Graph

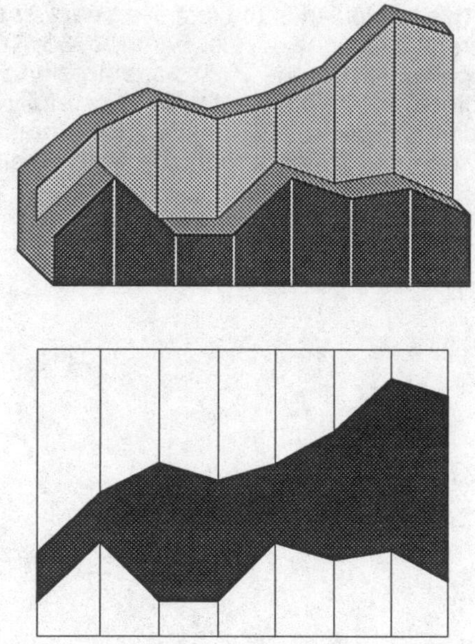

Perspective Pie Charts

Pie charts are among the most abused of graphics icons. A favorite among business packages is the three-dimensional pie chart. These floating platters appear frequently in newspapers, TV graphics, and textbooks. They incorporate nearly every visual illusion we have discussed. Figure 8 shows an example of a 3-D versus a regular pie chart of the same information. The upper figure includes some of the texturing which is popular in these displays and which further distorts the proportional area information. The shading on the side of the pie makes the area judgments even more difficult. Finally, removing the slice impedes anchoring judgments, in which we must mentally superimpose one slice on another in order to compare their magnitudes. Pulling slices out of 3-D or 2-D pies is never as effective as shading or coloring the slice in its proper place in the pie, as I have done in the lower figure. Coloring and shading pies can enhance their attractiveness, but if you are interested in accurate judgments, keep them empty. Both shading and coloring interfere with size judgments.

Pie charts have been ridiculed in the last five years or so by many statisticians and graphic designers. (e.g. Bertin, 1983; Tufte, 1983). There are many studies going back to the 1920's attempting to show that bar charts are more effective than pie charts. More carefully designed recent studies (e.g. Simkin and Hastie, 1987) have shown that pie charts can be more effective than bar charts for proportion-of-the-whole judgments.

Figure 8
Three-dimensional vs. Two-dimensional Pie Chart

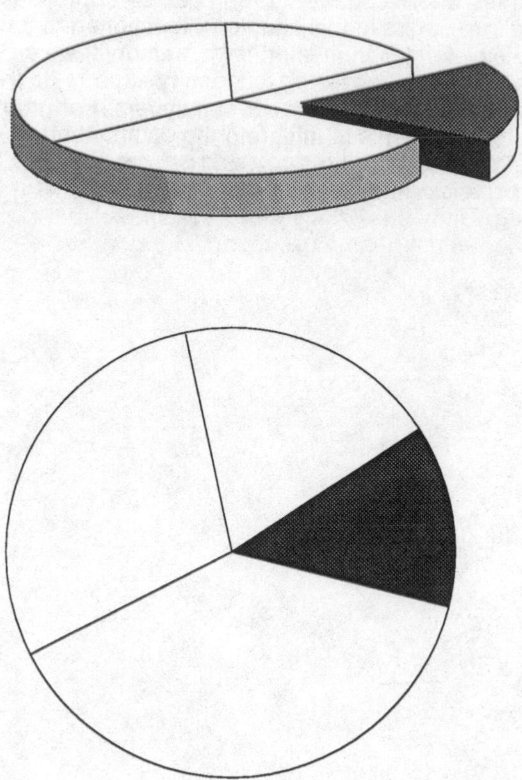

Information Overload

You can put too much information in a graph intended for a glance. Tufte (1983) and Bertin (1983) recommend a high ratio of "data" to "ink" in order to discourage distracting irrelevant features, but this principle can backfire if pushed to the extreme. Figure 9 shows a graph I adapted from an advertisement showing off all the bells and whistles of a new computer graphics package. The graph was being used in a slide presentation. A composite graph of this sort is like "integrated" software - the pieces work tolerably but the whole is an intimidating mess. In trying to cram too much information into a single panel of a display, the designer of this graph compromised the individual choices. I haven't got an effective alternative to this graph. Several independent graphs would be the logical choice.

There are times when a complex graph can be appropriate - even in a slide presentation. Earlier in this chapter, I mentioned that we can "chunk" complex information in short term memory if we can find simple rules and analogies for processing it. Memory experts do this when they memorize thousands of digits of random numbers. For graphs, the best way to facilitate chunking is to integrate the components in an ordered arrangement. You can see the **ICON** and **SPLOM** chapters below for examples of complex graphs which can nevertheless be memorized after careful viewing.

Figure 9
An Excessively Complicated Graph

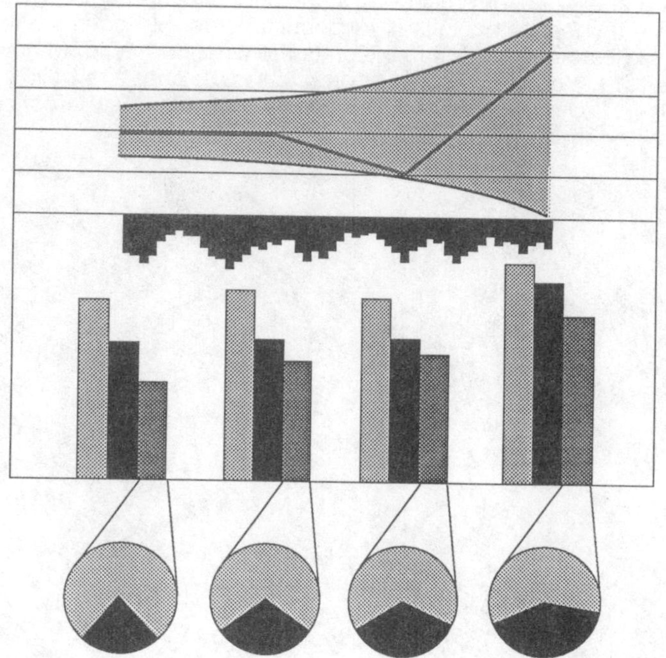

Part 2
Chapter 1

General Commands

Input Data

SYGRAPH accepts data directly from SYSTAT files. Use the SYSTAT Editor to create these files. Data can also be transferred to SYSTAT files from other programs in the DATA module.

SYGRAPH Commands are:

Graphics	General	Controls
BAR	BY	COLOR
BOX	HELP	DEPTH
CPLOT	NOTE	EYE
DRAW	OUTPUT	FACET
DENSITY	QUIT	FORMAT
ICON	SELECT	ORIGIN
MAP	SUBMIT	THICK
PIE	USE	TYPE
PLOT	WEIGHT	SCALE
PPLOT		SEPARATE
QPLOT		WAY
SPLOM		
STEM		
WRITE		

Syntax of Commands:

SYGRAPH commands work like simple sentences without concluding periods:

```
BAR  HARBOR
PLOT  SUMMER*WINTER
PLOT  Y=LOG(X)
STEM  SUN,MOON,
      TIDE
```

The last example spans two lines. To continue on an additional line, just add a comma at the end of the first line. You can span any number of lines this way. Sometimes you may want to add options to these commands by separating them with a slash (or exclamation point if you are using a formula):

```
BAR  TENDER  /  COLOR=RED
PIE  FACED  /  HEIGHT=5IN,WIDTH=5IN
PLOT  Y=LOG(X)  !  AXES=2
```

We can denote these commands more generally with a few symbols. Angle brackets (<>) enclose words which stand for other words. Square brackets (`[]`) enclose optional words. If you are using data from a file, for example, the general command syntax is:

```
<COMMAND>  [<VARIABLE>,<VARIABLE>]  /  <OPTIONS>
```

If you are using a formula with the **PLOT** command, the syntax is:

```
PLOT  <FORMULA>  !  <OPTIONS>
```

The exclamation point is used as a separator for formulas because the usual slash (/) would look like a divide sign in a formula.

If you use a command without giving variable names, then all numerical variables in the data file you are using will be processed. With the US file, for example, the following two commands are equivalent because all the numerical variables are included:

```
PIE
PIE  PERSON,PROPERTY,INCOME,POPDEN,
      SUMMER,WINTER,RAIN
```

You can denote ranges of variables with a dash (-) this way:

```
BAR  ITEM1-ITEM21,ITEM61
```

Most SYGRAPH commands will produce a separate graph for each variable you name this way. Some commands (e.g. **BAR**, **BOX**, **PLOT**, **SPLOM**) can produce a single graph with many variables. You need to check the individual reference chapters to see some examples.

Graphics Commands:

`BAR:`	This command plots frequencies of a categorical variable, or a continuous variable against a categorical variable.
`BOX:`	This command shows the distribution of a continuous variable by itself or against a categorical variable.
`CPLOT:`	This command plots a continuous variable against a categorical variable.
`DRAW:`	This command draws lines, arrows, boxes, and ovals.
`DENSITY:`	This command portrays the distribution of a continuous numerical variable.
`ICON:`	This command draws Chernoff's faces, Fourier blobs, star plots, rectangles, and other icons to represent cases in a multivariate dataset.
`MAP:`	This command draws geographical maps.
`PIE:`	This command draws pie charts.
`PLOT:`	This command produces two- and three-way plots of continuous numerical variables.
`PPLOT:`	This command compares a continuous variable to a probability distribution.
`QPLOT:`	This command compares the values of a continuous variable to its fractiles (e.g. percentiles). It also compares the fractiles of two variables against each other.
`SPLOM:`	This command displays many continuous variables against many continuous variables in a connected panel of plots. Its name refers to its appearance, namely a matrix of scatterplots, or scatterplot matrix.
`STEM:`	This command displays the distribution of a continuous variable.
`WRITE:`	This command writes text.

A Taxonomy of Graphics Commands

Graphical data are usually of two types, continuous and categorical. Continuous data come from a scale of values which can be any real number from minus to plus infinity. Categorical data may be numbers or characters, but their distinguishing feature is that they fall into a relatively small number of unordered discrete categories. You may plot continuous data on categorical graphs in SYGRAPH, but if there are too many values, the graphs will be uninterpretable. Doing a bar chart of income, for example, would be impractical unless you split income into a small number of separate categories.

The following table summarizes the types of graphs available for various combinations of these types of data. There is no best graph for every purpose, but you should try the recommended graphs first.

	VARIABLES		
DATA	**One**	**Two**	**Many**
Categorical	BAR CPLOT PIE		
Continuous	BOX DENSITY MAP PPLOT QPLOT STEM	MAP PLOT QPLOT SPLOM	ICON MAP PLOT QPLOT SPLOM
Mixed	BAR CPLOT PIE	BAR BOX CPLOT	BAR CPLOT

The following pages show examples of each of these commands. Notice that some of the commands are capable of producing a variety of plots.

Figure 1

BAR

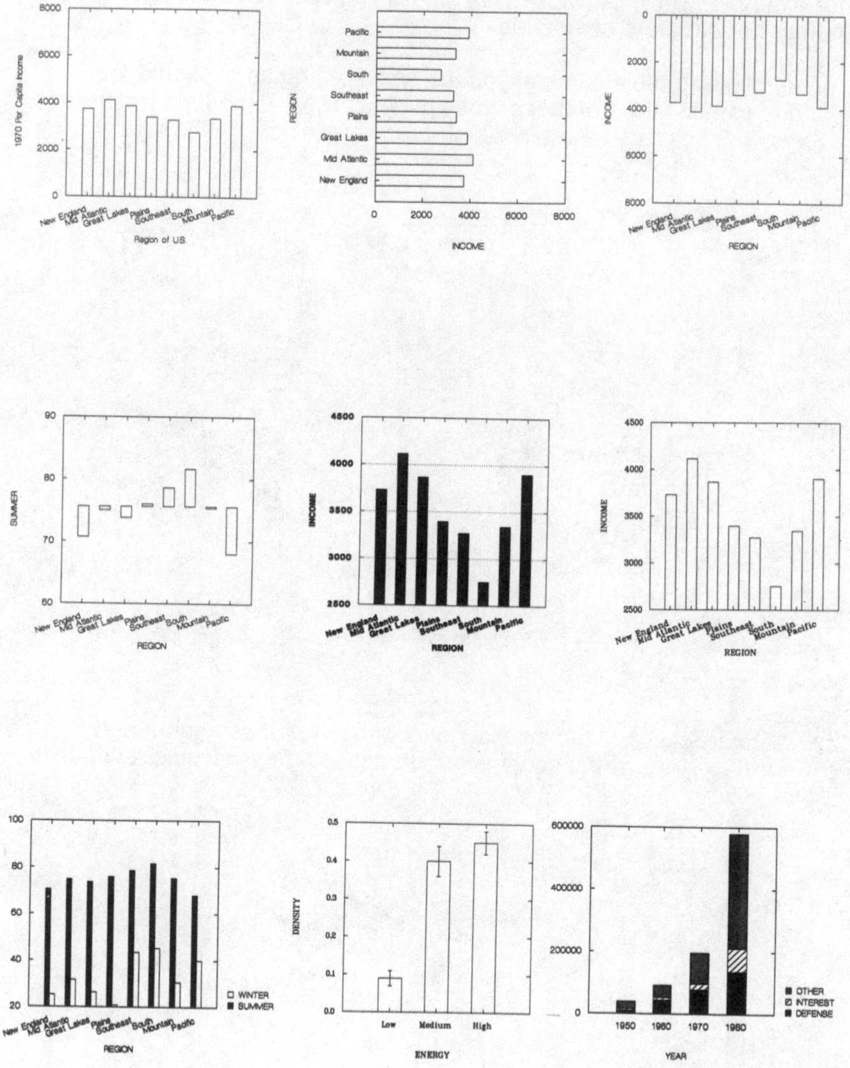

Figure 2

BOX

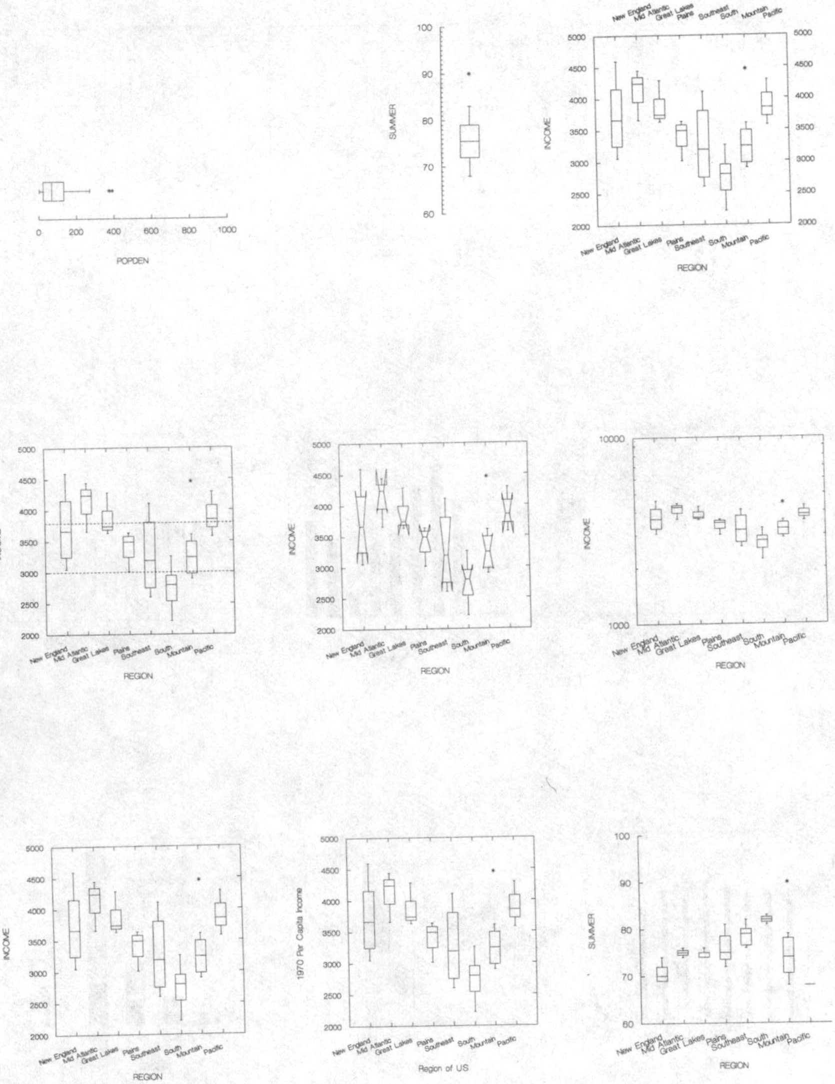

Figure 3

CPLOT

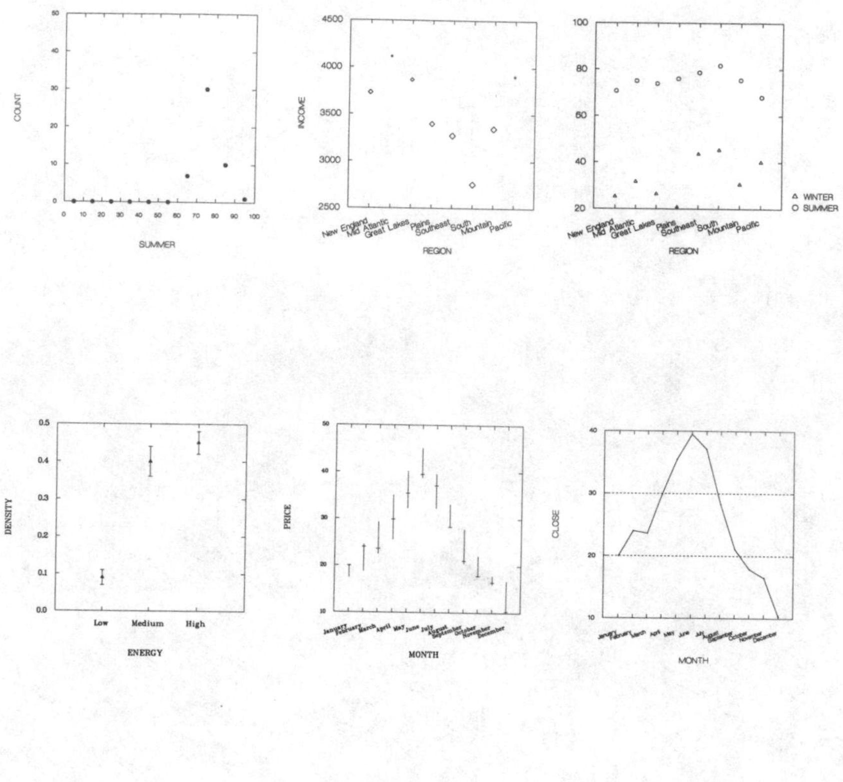

Figure 4

DENSITY

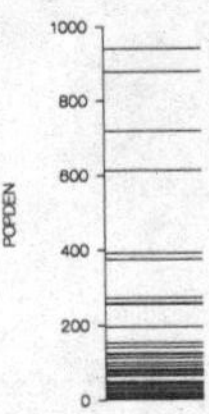

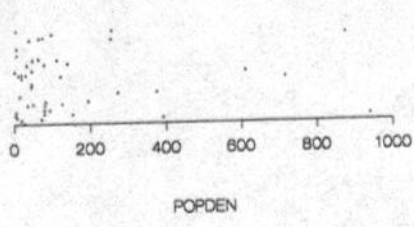

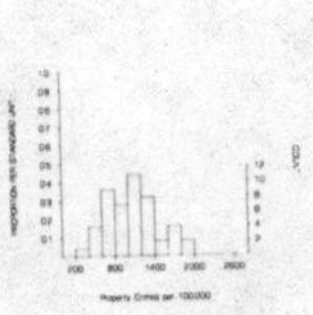

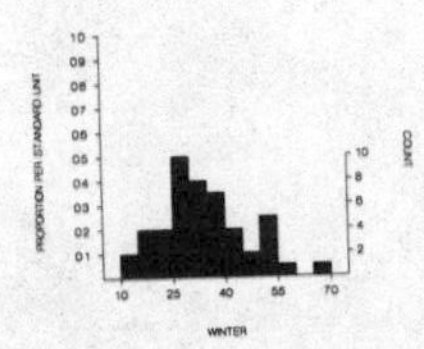

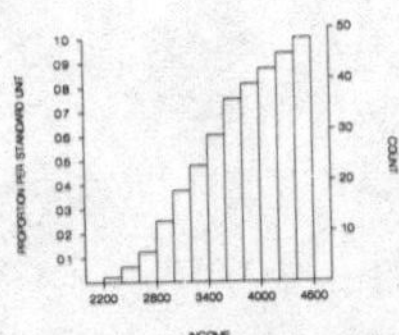

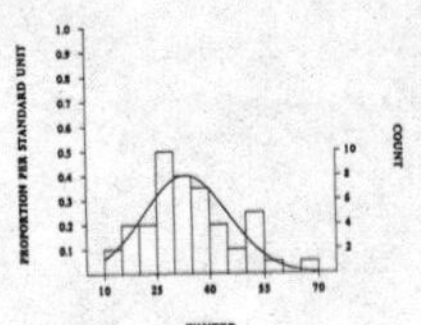

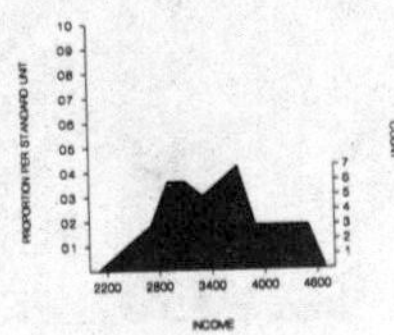

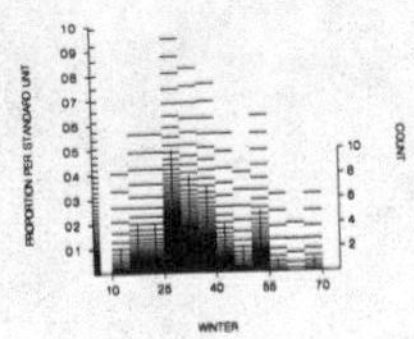

Figure 5

DRAW

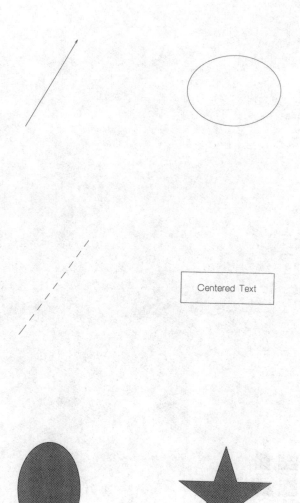

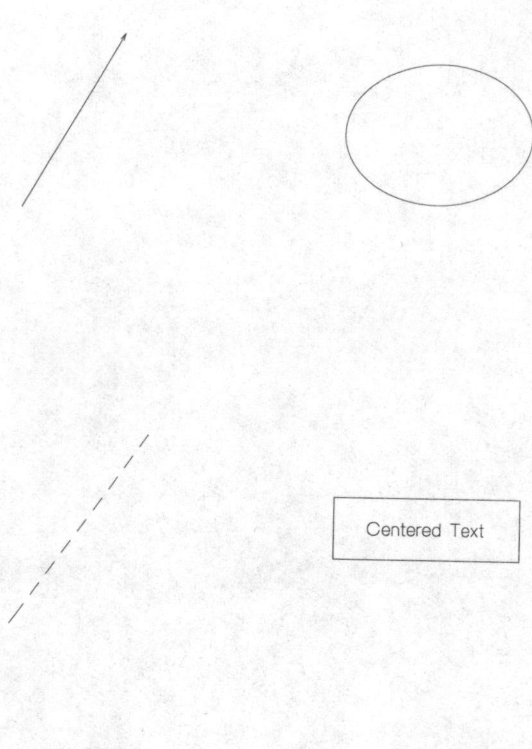

Figure 6

ICON

Socio-Demo-Metero-Mumbo-Jumbo

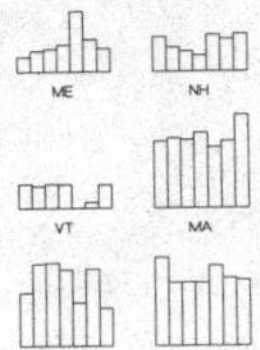

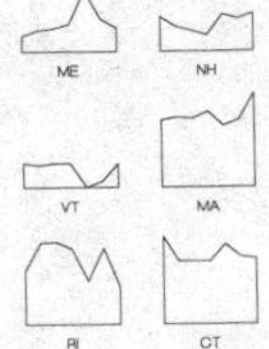

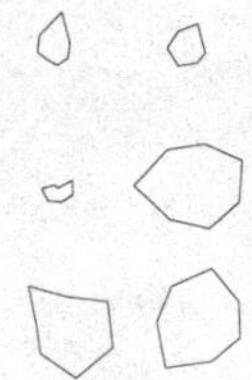

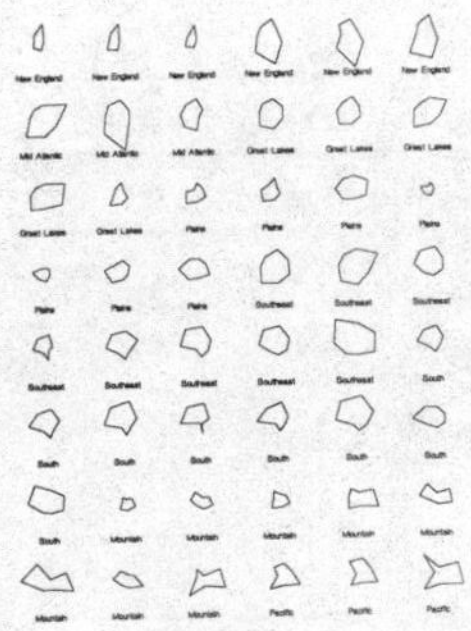

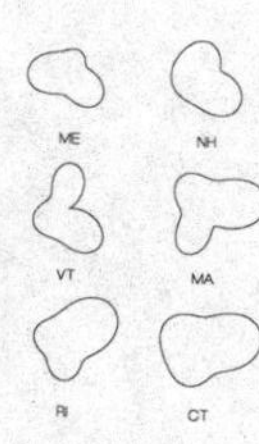

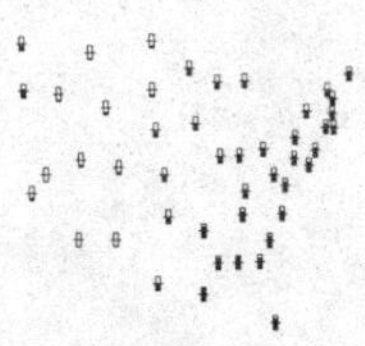

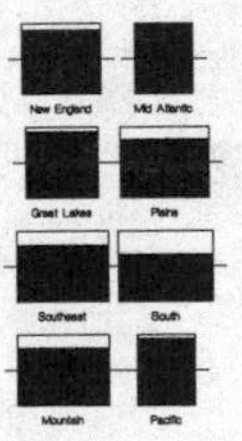

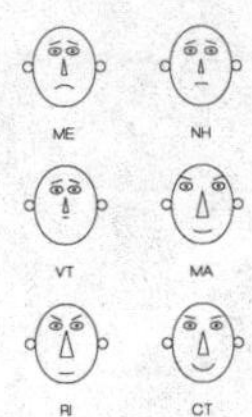

Figure 7

MAP

Figure 8

PIE

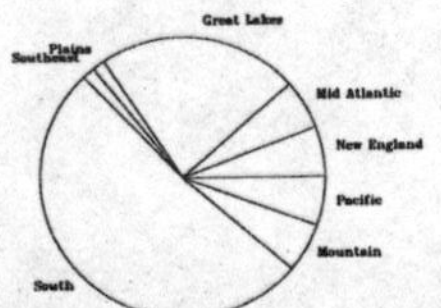

Great Lakes
Plains
Southeast
Mid Atlantic
New England
Pacific
Mountain
South

Great Lakes
Mid Atlantic
New England
Plains
Southeast
Pacific
South
Mountain

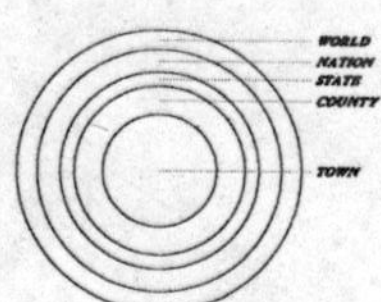

WORLD
NATION
STATE
COUNTY
TOWN

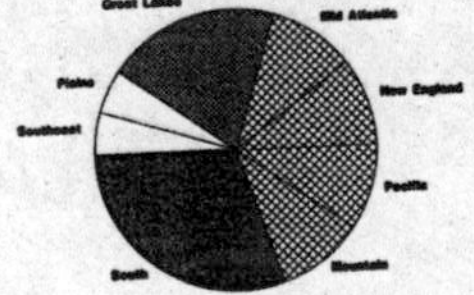

Great Lakes
Mid Atlantic
New England
Plains
Southeast
Pacific
South
Mountain

Figure 9

PLOT

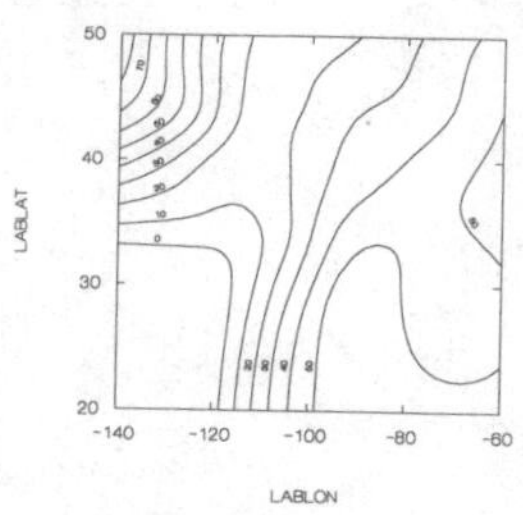

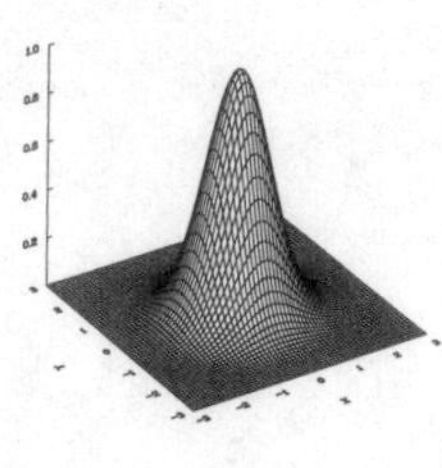

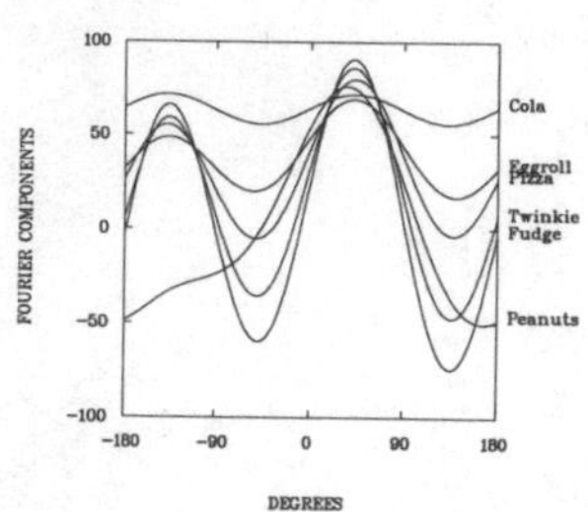

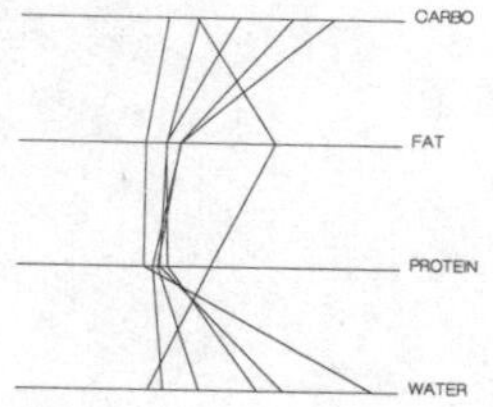

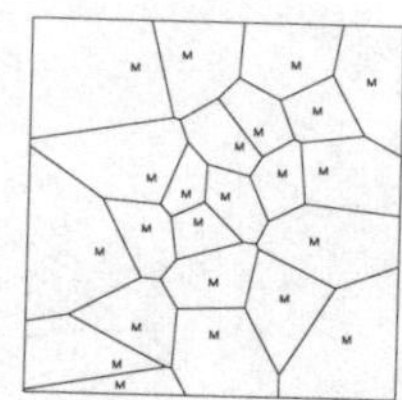

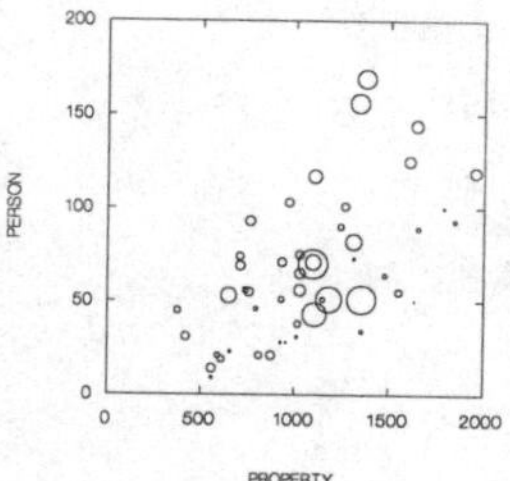

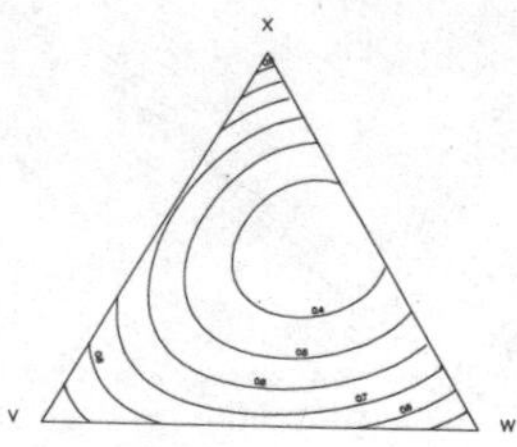

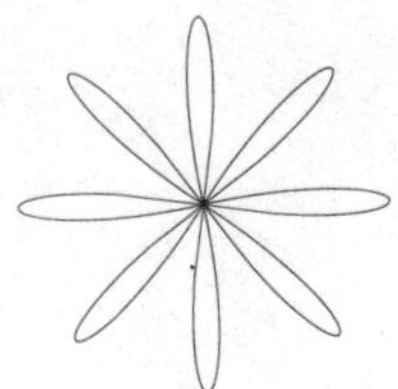

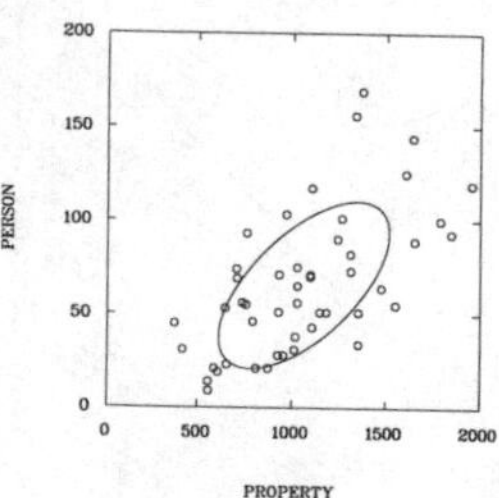

Figure 10

PPLOT

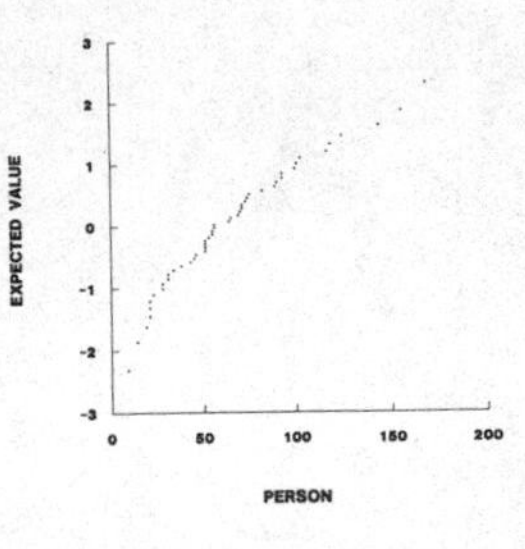

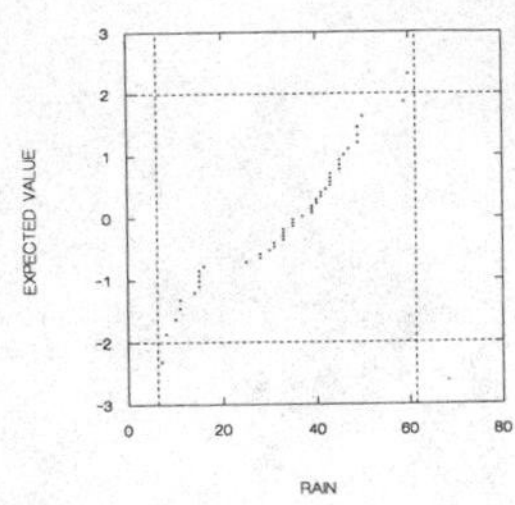

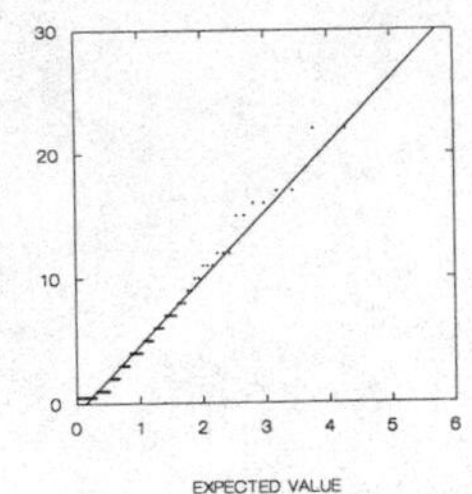

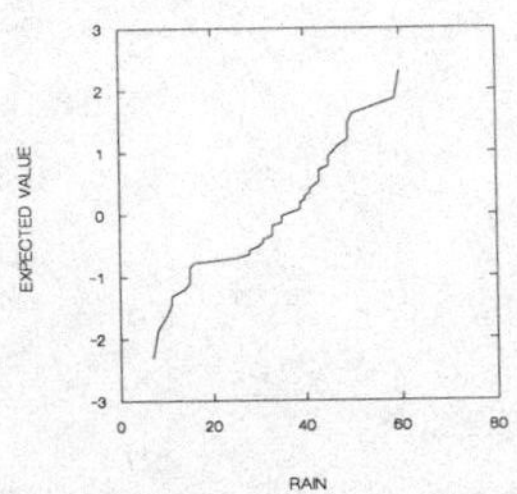

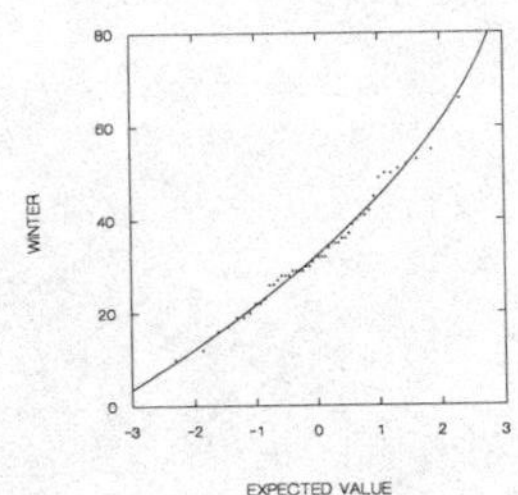

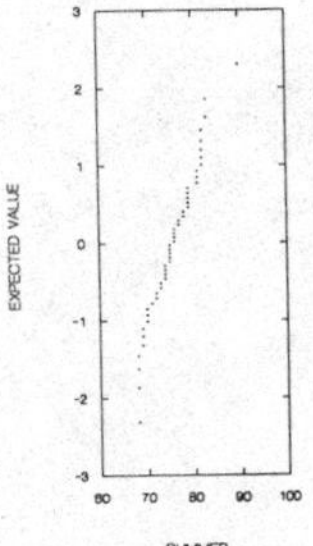

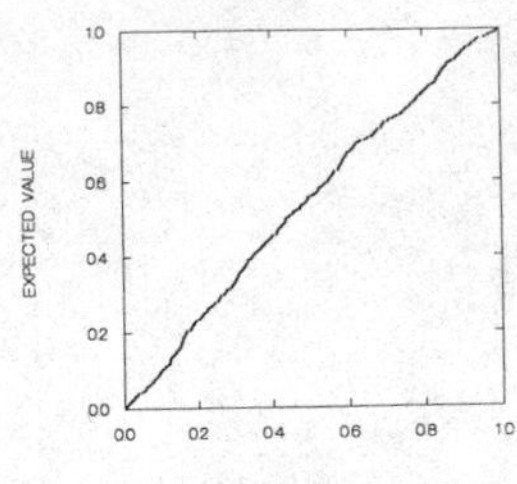

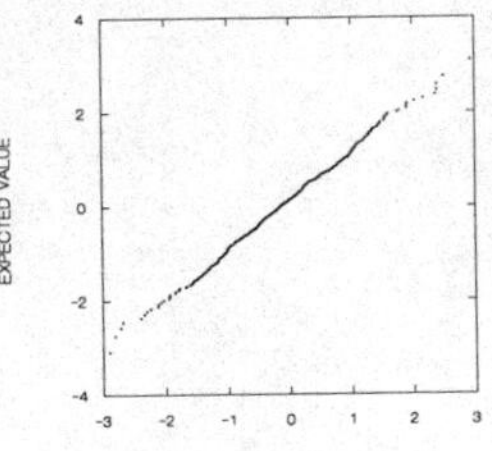

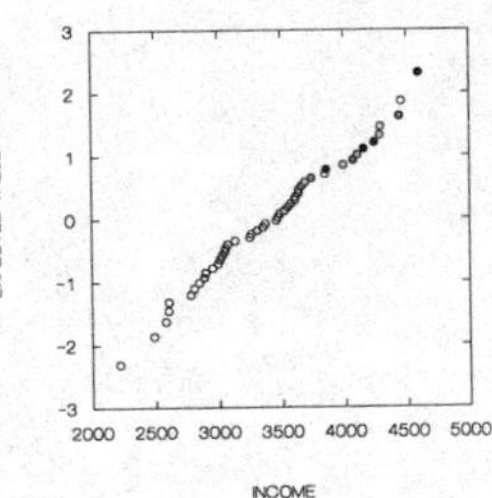

Figure 11

QPLOT

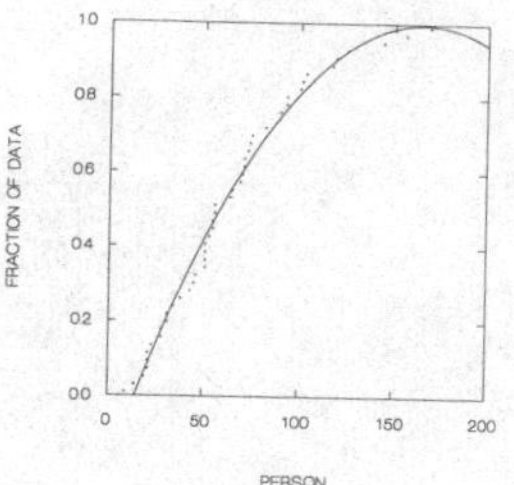

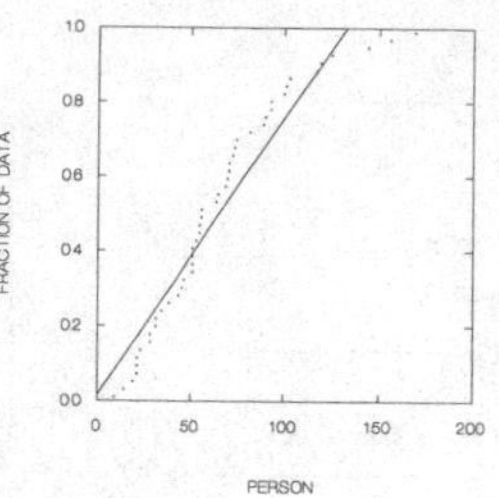

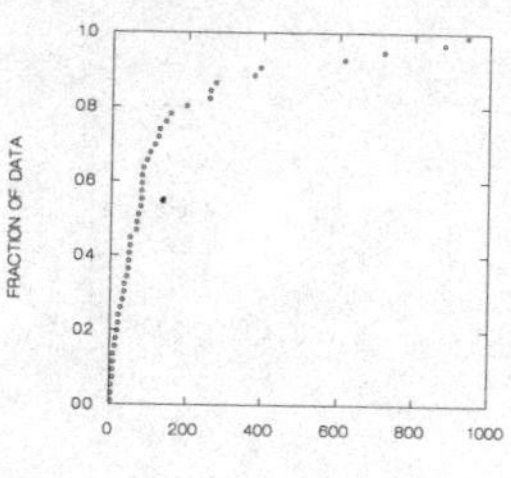

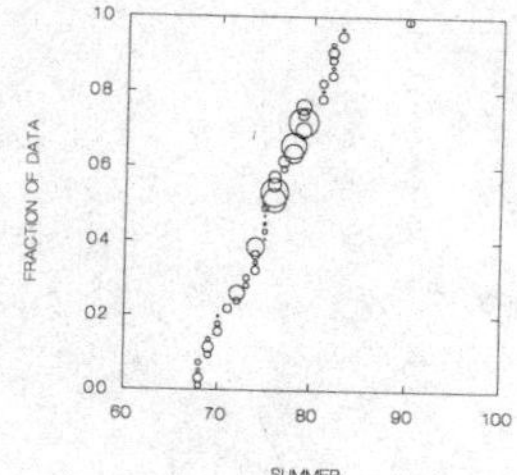

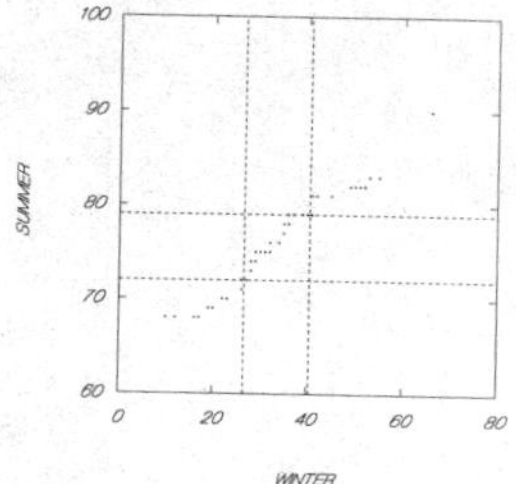

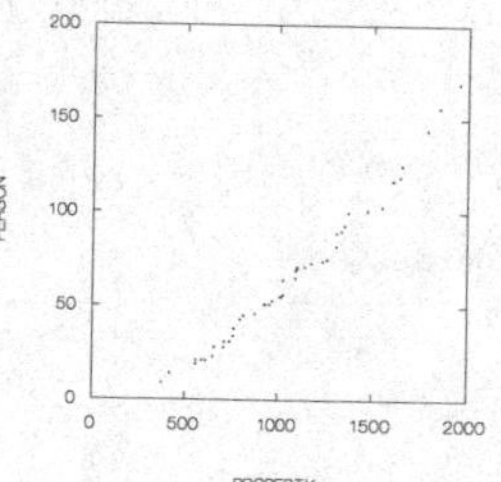

Figure 12

SPLOM

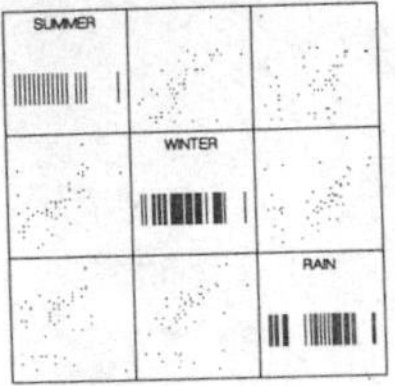

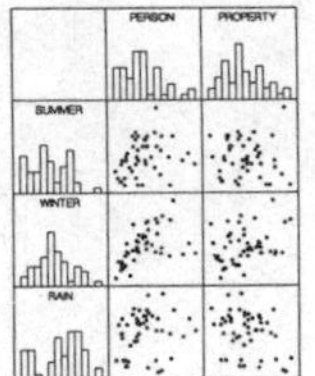

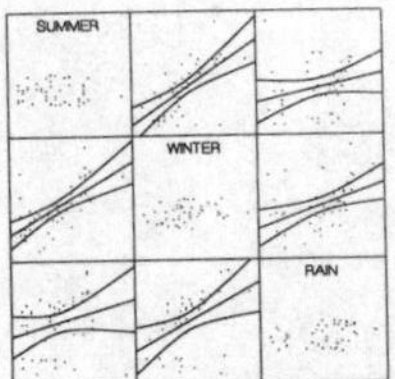

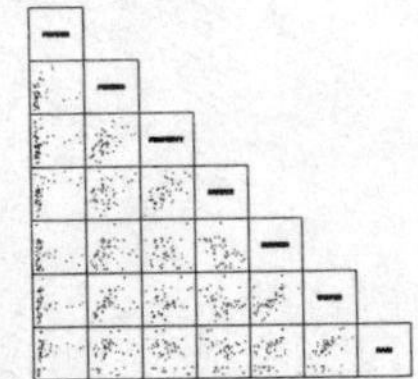

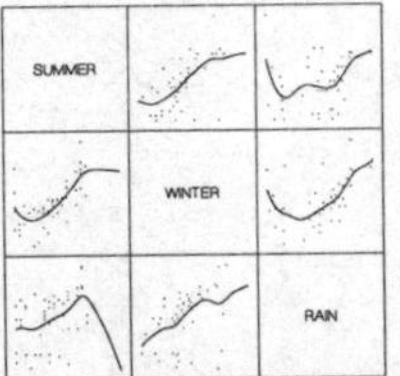

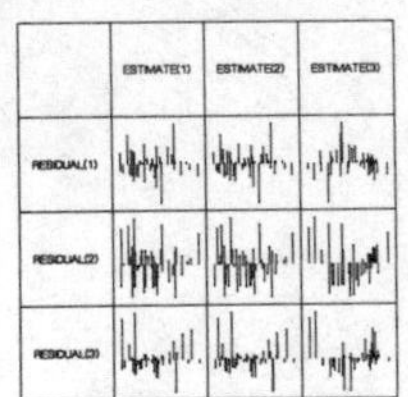

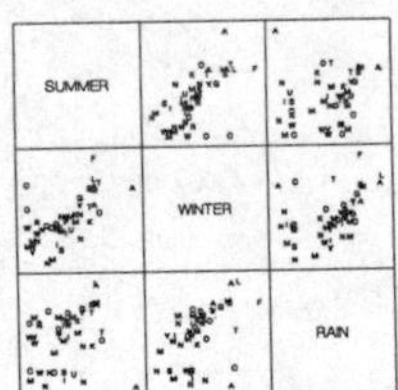

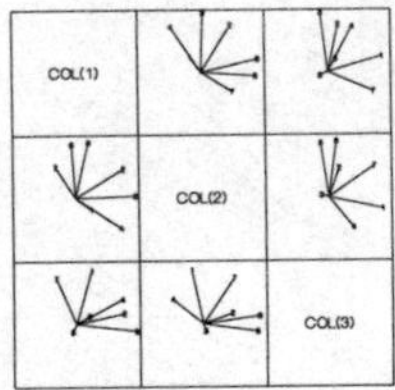

Figure 13

STEM

```
0    0000000111
0H   222333
0    444455
0M   667777
0    8889
1    01
1H   22
1    45
1
1    9
2
2
2    55
2    7
     ***OUTSIDE VALUES***
3    79
6    1
7    1
8    7
9    4
```

```
68   0000
69   000
70   000
71   0
72H  00
73   00
74   0000
75M  00000
76   0000
77   00
78   00
79H  00000
80
81   000
82   00000
83   00
     ***OUTSIDE VALUES***
90   0
```

Figure 14

WRITE

LOVE, a temporary insanity cured by marriage

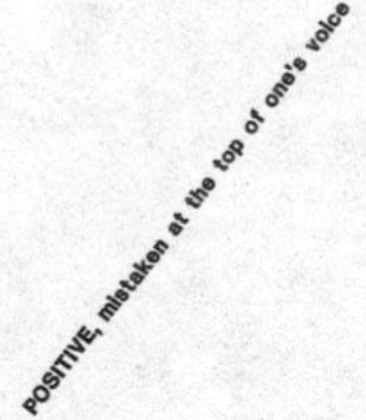

POSITIVE, mistaken at the top of one's voice

TRICHINOSIS, the pig's reply to pork chops

ALONE, in bad company

General Commands:

These commands affect graphics processing.

BEGIN: This command begins a graph. It is needed when you are plotting several graphs on the same page or screen. Here is an example:

```
BEGIN
PLOT  Y=X
PLOT  Y=X^2
END
```

Notice that you need an **END** statement (see below) to complete the block of commands. With this construction, both plots will be superimposed. The **BEGIN-END** block can be used only if you **SUBMIT** a file or a block of commands from the full screen **FEDIT** editor (see below). The Advanced Applications chapters in Part 3 below illustrate what you can do with **BEGIN-END** blocks of graphics commands.

BY: This command produces multiple graphs stratified by a variable or combination of variables. For example, you can produce scatterplots of two variables (A and B) stratified by a third (**GROUP**) in just two commands:

```
BY  GROUP
PLOT  A*B
```

The **BY** command works with all graphs. The data must be sorted in the order of the **BY** variable(s). Use the **SORT** command in the **DATA** module if your data are not already sorted. To turn off the **BY** command, type **BY** alone.

END: This command marks the end of a block of commands which are to be plotted on a single screen or page. See the **BEGIN** command above for more information.

FEDIT: This command gives you the full screen text editor to review, edit, and resubmit commands or text. This command is not available on Macintosh systems.

HELP: This command gives you the syntax of any command. Type **HELP** to get a list of all commands, and **HELP** followed by the name of a command to get further information about a specific command.

NOTE: This command writes a comment on your output (not on the graph). Type **NOTE** *"comment"* where comment is a string of text. If you need quotation marks in your comment, then type **NOTE** *'comment in "quotes" here'*. Either quotes or apostrophes can be used to set off comments.

OUTPUT: This command routes output to various destinations. Type:

```
OUTPUT=DISPLAY      (or OUTPUT=*)
OUTPUT=PRINTER      (or OUTPUT=@)
OUTPUT=PLOTTER
OUTPUT=CAMERA
```

to route graphic output to a device. You must have an appropriate device attached to your computer and device drivers to run your device. Almost always, you will have a **DISPLAY** device, such as a graphics window or high resolution screen, but this is not absolutely necessary. The **PRINTER** device is usually a dot-matrix or laser printer printers with some computers. **PLOTTER** is for a pen plotter. **CAMERA** is for a camera slide making device.

QUIT: Cease, desist, stop, bail-out.

SELECT: This command works like **BY**, except only one group is selected. For example, if you have a character variable denoting Census region in a file, you can select a subgroup as follows:

```
SELECT  REGION$='New  England'
PLOT  INCOME*POPDEN
```

SUBMIT: This command submits a file of commands to SYGRAPH. It is handy for constructing complex graphs which you need to do over and over again. Type **SUBMIT** *myfile*, where *myfile*.cmd is the name of an ASCII character file containing a list of SYGRAPH commands.

USE: This command opens a SYSTAT file for graphing. Type **USE** *myfile* , where *myfile.sys* is the name of a SYGRAPH or SYSTAT data file.

WEIGHT: This command weights the number of cases in a file by an additional variable. It is useful for working with aggregate data. For example, if you have several people with the same measurement, you can use a variable called COUNT to denote this and let the graph reflect these weights:

```
WEIGHT=COUNT
BAR  AGE
```

Control Commands:

These commands control graphics attributes or settings.

COLOR: This command sets background, foreground, graph ,and label color. Available colors are : **RED**, **ORANGE**, **YELLOW**, **GREEN**, **BLUE**, **VIOLET**, **BLACK**, **WHITE**, **GRAY**, and **BROWN**. The option has the following forms:

```
COLOR  BACK=RED
COLOR  FORE=YELLOW
COLOR  GRAPH=GREEN
COLOR  LABEL=BLUE
```

Instead of using a color name, you can use a number to indicate wavelength in nanometers, e.g.:

```
COLOR  BACK=550
```

The colors you specify will apply to all subsequent graphs until you modify them with another **COLOR** command. To modify more than one color aspect (background, foreground, etc.), you must put all of them together in a single **COLOR** command, e.g.:

```
COLOR  FORE=RED,BACK=BLUE
```

DEPTH: This command controls the position of a plane along a facet (see **FACET** command below). The depth of a plane is normally set at the rear of the usual 3-D plotting frame, which is equivalent to typing **DEPTH=50** (see the figure following the **FACET** command below). You can move it to any other position by typing a positive number, e.g. **DEPTH=***x* , where *x* is a real number in inches, centimeters, or percent of the display window. For example, type **DEPTH=3IN** to move the depth in 3 inches. Type **DEPTH=3CM** to move the depth by 3 centimeters. If you omit **IN** or **CM** after the numbers, they will refer to percent of the display window. **DEPTH=3** or **DEPTH=3%** would mean 3 percent depth. Type **DEPTH** without any number (**DEPTH**) to return it to its default value. See Figure 15 below for some examples.

EYE: This command sets the point of view for three dimensional plotting. Think of a 3-D plot as a cube floating in a three dimensional space. Each edge of the cube is one unit. The lower left hand corner of the cube is the origin. The viewing coordinates of your eye as you float in space looking at the cube are specified by the **EYE** command. If you say, for example, **EYE=-1,-1,1** you will be looking at the cube from the southwest upper corner. The default (usual) setting is **EYE=-8,-12,8**. To return the point of view to this original setting, type **EYE** with no arguments. You can set your point of view anywhere, but in some positions you will get curious results. For example, if you put your eye inside the cube (e.g. **EYE=.5,.5,.5**), you will see your data or equations distorted from inside. If you put your eye under the cube (e.g. **EYE=-1,-1,-6**), some of the labels will be backwards in true perspective.

FACET: Graphs are plotted inside a unit square (or cube for three-dimensional graphs). You can place any two-dimensional graph in 3-D perspective, however, with the **FACET** command. Ordinarily, you would use this command to produce complex three-dimensional graphics by overlaying separate two-dimensional plots in perspective. Use this command sparingly and wisely, however. For almost every three-dimensional graph, there is a clearer, simpler two-dimensional graph of the same data. Figure 15 shows the orientation of each facet. **FACET=XY** (or **YX**) puts the plane on the XY axes (perpendicular to Z). **FACET=YZ** (or **ZY**) plots on the YZ axes (perpendicular to X). **FACET=XZ** (or **ZX**) plots on the **XZ** axes (perpendicular to Y). See the **DEPTH** command above for how to vary the position of the plane along the facet axis. If you want to turn off the **FACET** command after using it, just type **FACET** to return to two-dimensional graphics. Figure 15 shows the commands used to produce this figure. They are documented elsewhere in this reference section.

Figure 15

Facets

```
FACET=XY
DEPTH=0
DRAW  BOX/HEIGHT=3IN,WIDTH=3IN,FILL=5
TYPE=SWISS
DRAW  BOX/HEIGHT=3IN,WID=3IN,ZHEIGHT=3IN
FACET=YZ
DEPTH=3IN
WRITE  'YZ',
  /HEIGHT=1IN,WIDTH=1IN,X=1.5IN,Y=1IN,CENTER
FACET=XZ
DEPTH=3IN
WRITE  'XZ',
  /HEIGHT=1IN,WIDTH=1IN,X=1.5IN,Y=1IN,CENTER
FACET=XY
DEPTH=3IN
WRITE  'XY',
 /HEIGHT=1IN,WIDTH=1IN,X=1.5IN,Y=1.5IN,CENTER
```

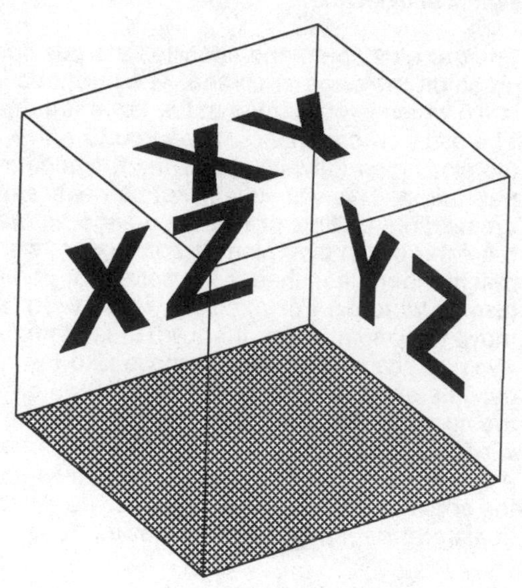

FORMAT: The **FORMAT** command regulates the number of digits printed to the right of the decimal point in graphs. GRAPH usually chooses the best number of digits for a given set of data. If you give GRAPH unusual ranges or cutpoints, however, it can print many superfluous digits to represent cutpoints exactly because GRAPH uses high precision arithmetic. Sometimes, it will do the opposite and print too few digits to represent the numbers reasonably. For example, the numbers

.33333 .66667 1.00000

might print as

```
.3          .7          1.0
```

respectively. This will look odd to a viewer who does not realize that the numbers have been rounded. In these rare cases, you can type **FORMAT=2** or another small number to print a few additional digits.

In the case where too many digits are printed, e.g.

```
.0000001      .2000001      .4000001
```

you can type **FORMAT=1** to cut the values back to the significant decimal.

ORIGIN: The **ORIGIN** command specifies the position of an entire graph on the page or screen. The normal origin for graphs is 0,0 which is positioned at the lower left of the axis frame. The **ORIGIN** command allows you to move a graph around the plotting window by specifying the coordinates of the new origin. This will usually not be necessary unless you are plotting multiple graphs on a page. In that case, you can reset the origin by typing **ORIGIN=***x*,*y* , where *x* and *y* are real numbers in inches, centimeters, or percent of the display window. For example, type **ORIGIN=3IN,4IN** to move the origin to the right by 3 inches and up 4 inches. Type **ORIGIN=3CM,4CM** to move it to the right by 3 centimeters and up 4 centimeters. If you omit **IN** or **CM** after the numbers, they will refer to percent of the display window. **ORIGIN=3,4** would mean 3 percent to the right and 4 percent up. You can use negative numbers to shift the origin to the left or below 0,0. If you do so, the labels for some graphs may run off the viewing area.

PEN: This command sets the speed of a plotter pen between 1 (one percent of full speed) and 100 (full speed). This allows you to slow down fast plotters to make more finely drawn lines. An example is **PEN=50**. If you type **PEN** with no number, it will reset to the default value of 100. The setting remains in effect until you type another **PEN** command.

SEPAR: This command does **color separations**. Just name a color and SYGRAPH will plot only that color in a particular graph. Here is an example for a three-color graph (black, red, blue):

```
COLOR   GRAPH=BLACK,LABEL=BLACK
SEPARATE  BLACK
PLOT   A,B*C/COLOR=RED,BLUE
SEPARATE  RED
PLOT   A,B*C/COLOR=RED,BLUE
SEPARATE  BLUE
PLOT   A,B*C/COLOR=RED,BLUE
```

If you do not use **COLOR GRAPH=BLACK, LABEL=BLACK**(see **COLOR** command above), the axes and other black portions of the graph will be included in every separation. For black-and-white originals, you may need to add **FILL=1** (solid fill) to color areas so that they will be solid black for clear photo-reproduction.

THICK: This option sets the thickness of lines in a graph. The standard value is **THICK=1**. Higher values will make lines twice as thick (**THICK=2**) and so on. If you want to make graphs for slide presentations and overheads, you might want to consider **THICK=7** or so. Decimal values are allowed (e.g. **THICK=2.5**). If you set line thickness greater than 5, labels and scale values will be automatically enlarged to keep them in proportion to line widths. If you use a large enough value (**THICK=10**), you can make a graph that looks like the ones you did in kindergarten with a thick crayon. Page 261 shows a graph with **THICK=7**.

TYPE: This option specifies the typeface for your graph. The following options are available:

TYPE=STROKE
TYPE=SWISS
TYPE=BRITISH
TYPE=HERSHEY
TYPE=GREEK

For examples of these type faces, see the **WRITE** command later in this chapter and Appendix A.

SCALE: This command rescales graphs to a specified size. **SCALE=100,100** is the usual option (100 percent of the display window on both the X and Y axes). Like **ORIGIN**, you can use inches (**IN**) or centimeters (**CM**) after the X and Y scale numbers, but it is simpler to stay with percentages. For example, **SCALE=50,50** halves the size of a graph. If you make the X and Y scales different, your graph will be expanded or contracted differently on the horizontal and vertical axes. This will affect all features of the graph, including the lettering. Consequently, you should usually keep X and Y the same when altering the size of graphs. If you want to produce rectangular graphs, use the **HEIGHT** and **WIDTH** options of the specific commands (see below).

WAY: This option governs the orientation of the graph in the frame. **WAY=TALL** is the standard option. **WAY=WIDE** turns the graph sideways so that you can fit it on a different shaped page. If you are combining SYGRAPH graphs with text, you probably won't need this command because other programs can reorient the page after you have completely set it up. Furthermore, there is a page orientation option in the printer dialog of the file menu on some computers which serves the same purpose. The **WAY** command, however, turns even the screen image sideways.

Options Used in Most Graphs (Modifying the Standard Graph)

Most graph commands in GRAPH have standard options. All graphs, for example, are produced in a unit square or unit cube. Tick marks are usually oriented inside the square frame. Scale ranges are chosen automatically according to the limits of the input data. The following commands, for example, will each produce a complete graph.

```
BAR  SOAP
PLOT  Y*X
PLOT  Y=SIN(X)
SPLOM
BOX
```

Often, you may wish to modify these standard square graphs to be different shapes, have different numbers of axes, types of tick marks, grids, and so on. Most of the graphics commands have a standard set of options which control these modifications. These options are chosen by placing them after a command and separating them with a slash, e.g.:

```
PLOT  AGE*WEIGHT/STICK
```

If you are typing an equation, you need to use an exclamation point (!) instead of a slash (/) because a slash is a divide sign in equations:

```
PLOT  Y=X!STICK
```

The names of options are consistent across commands. **HEIGHT**, for example, means the same thing for all commands. When graphs have more than one numerical axis, some options may be preceded by an **X**, **Y**, or **Z** to denote the axis. In the **PLOT** command, for example, **LABEL** is called **XLABEL**, **YLABEL**, and **ZLABEL** depending on the axis.

Here are the most frequent options:

AXES: The number of axes on a graph are specified with the **AXES** option. If **AXES=0**, no axes are placed on a graph. This option is useful for overlaying several graphs in two or three dimensions. **AXES=1** plots only the horizontal (X) axis. **AXES=2** plots the horizontal and vertical (X and Y) axes. **AXES=3** plots the horizontal, vertical, and top axes, and **AXES=4** plots all four axes like a box surrounding the graph. Most 2-D graphs have **AXES=4** (four axes) as the default. Three-dimensional graphs have up to 12 axes to cover all edges of a cube. For 3-D graphs, **AXES=3** is the default. The most popular combinations are 3, 5, 7, 9, and 12. **AXES=9**, for example, provides a horizontal plane plus two vertical panels in the background. Of the labeled options, **AXES=3** is least likely to collide with plotted points. If you use a negative number (e.g. **AXES=-2**), then only the numbered axis will be drawn. **AXES** and **SCALE** operate independently. If you set one without setting the others, you may get weird results, like scales without axes.

Figure 16

Axis Options

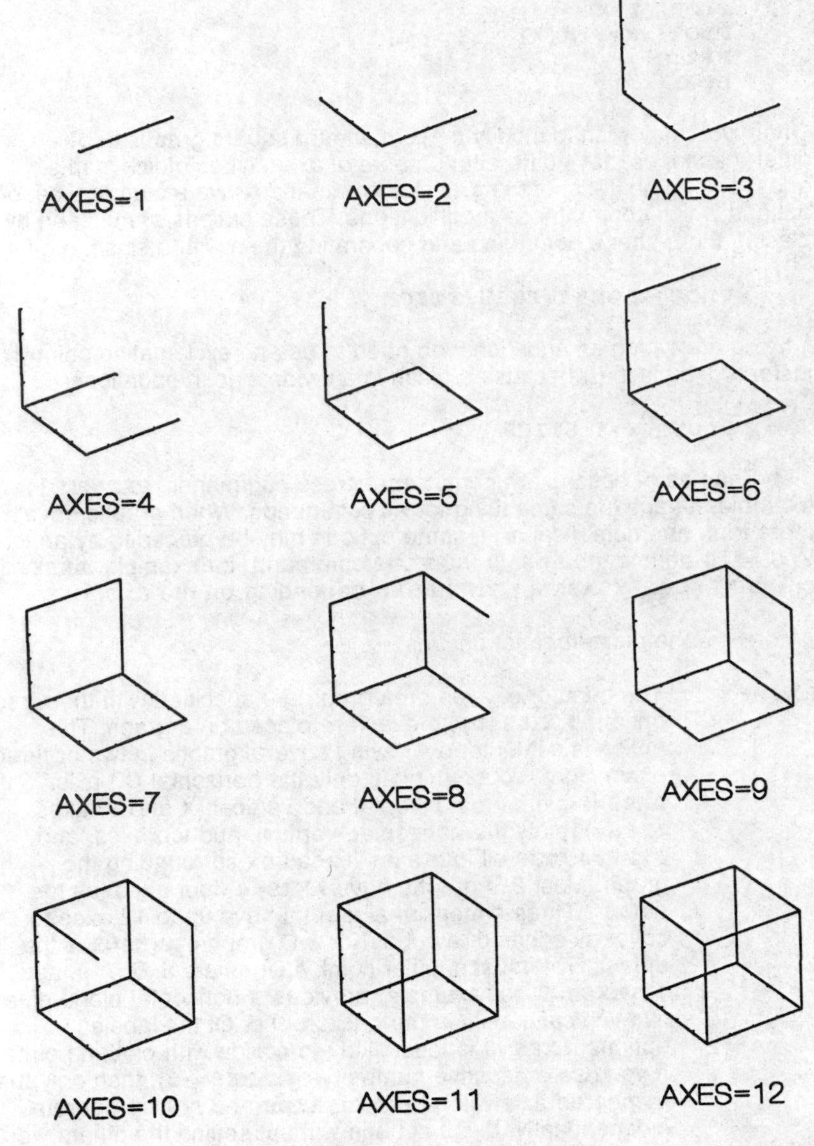

ERROR: You can add error bars to many plots with the **ERROR** and **ERROR1** options. Error bars are lines with tick marks denoting the size of standard errors or standard deviations in a plot. The **ERROR** options work with point plots, character plots, and bar graphs. **ERROR** produces symmetric error bars while **ERROR1** produces one-sided error bars. For example:

```
PLOT   RESPONSE*DOSE/ERROR=STD
```

makes error bars around each point plotted against DOSE using the variable STD to determine the length of the bar. The overall size of the bar is twice the value of STD. As with the **SIZE** option, you must be careful to scale STD correctly or your error bars will run off the graph.

HEIGHT: This option controls the vertical size of a graph. For example, **HEIGHT=3IN** will make a graph 3 inches high. You can specify the height of a graph in inches (**IN**), centimeters (**CM**), or percentage of the window size. **HEIGHT=25** makes a graph 25 percent of the window size in height.

LABEL: This option adds a label to an axis. It works like this:

```
XLABEL='Dosage'
YLABEL='Response  Level'
ZLABEL='Altitude'
```

LINE: The **LINE** option connects plotting symbols with lines. If the data are in order, the **LINE** option will produce a line graph. The **LINE** option connects points as they are plotted, however, so unordered data will plot like a messy spider web if you use the **LINE** option. Time series graphs are especially suited for the **LINE** option because the observations are in time order and connecting them with lines produces a time series trace line. See the specific command chapters for further information on the types of lines (solid, dotted, etc.) available.

PIP: This option controls the number of pip marks between tick marks. Pip marks are half-sized tick marks. **XPIP=10**, for example, puts 10 pip marks between ticks on the X axis.

REV: This option reverses the direction of an axis. For instance, if your axis runs from 0 to 100, the **REV** option will make it run from 100 to 0. All the plotted points or function will be reversed. This option is useful for reflecting values.

SCALE: The **SCALE** option works like **AXES** to determine which scale values are to be printed. See the **AXES** option above in this chapter to see how the axes and scales are numbered. If the number is negative, then only the numbered scale will be drawn. Although **AXES** and **SCALE** work the same way, they are entirely independent. You should usually specify both the same way if you use either so that axes will be drawn with their proper scale values, unless you wish to produce special effects like axes without scales or scales without axes.

SIZE: The **SIZE** option regulates the size of plotting symbols. The default size is 1. If you wish points plotted with symbols twice as large as usual, type **SIZE=2** after the specific plotting command. Sizes can be any real number, but if you make it too large, you will fill the entire graph window with one symbol. For example, **SIZE=3.5** makes plotting symbols three and a half times the regular size. To plot lines with no symbols, choose **SIZE=0** with the **LINE** option. You can also use a variable to determine the size of each plotting symbol. Just type **SIZE=***variable*, where *variable* is the name of a numerical variable. Remember, there is no limit to **SIZE**, so if your graph has variables which are too large (such as 100), the plotting symbols can completely occlude the plot. One other caveat. Representing a variable by size of plotting character can introduce visual distortions. Cleveland, Harris, and McGill (1982) have shown that circle sizes on maps are not perceived on a linear scale. Like other psychological stimuli, the perceptual mapping involves a power function. For most symbols, you should make size a function of the *square root* of a variable because the area of a symbol is proportional to the square of its width.

SMOOTH: This option chooses various methods for smoothing data in a graph. For example, a linear regression line can be fitted to a graph by adding the option **SMOOTH=LINEAR**. There are many smoothing options and these vary by type of graph. See the specific types of graphs below for more information.

SORT/ SNORT: This option allows you to plot levels of a categorical variable in either sorted or unsorted order. The default is **SORT**: if you plot a categorical variable in a bar chart, box plot, categorical plot (cplot), or pie chart, SYGRAPH automatically arranges the levels of that variable in ascending numeric or character order. If you select **SNORT**, SYGRAPH arranges the categories in the order in which they appear in the file.

STICK: This option forces tick marks to face outside the frame. The numbers on the axes will be automatically adjusted to accommodate the tick marks.

SYMBOL: Many of the graphical procedures in SYGRAPH allow special symbols. The **SYMBOL** option lets you select symbols. You can select any character by typing **SYMBOL='@'**, where @ is any printable character. For example, **SYMBOL='*'** will use asterisks as a plotting symbol.

If you are plotting several variables against another, you can specify a different symbol for each. Here is an example:

```
PLOT  SUMMER,WINTER*RAIN/SYMBOL='S','W'
```

The values of SUMMER will be plotted with an S and those of WINTER with a W.

Sometimes you can choose the values of a variable to label a plot. In these cases, you can add the option **SYMBOL=***label$*, where *label$* is a character variable. The first letter of the character variable will be used as the plotting symbol.

Finally, you can choose plotting symbols by number. For example, **SYMBOL=2** uses a circle as a plotting symbol. The next figure shows the 21 plotting symbols available in all type faces. Numbers above 21 (up to 128) may produce different symbols in different type faces. See Appendix A for more information on the different type faces. To fill a symbol with solid or hatched pattern, use the **FILL** option.

Figure 17

Plot Symbols

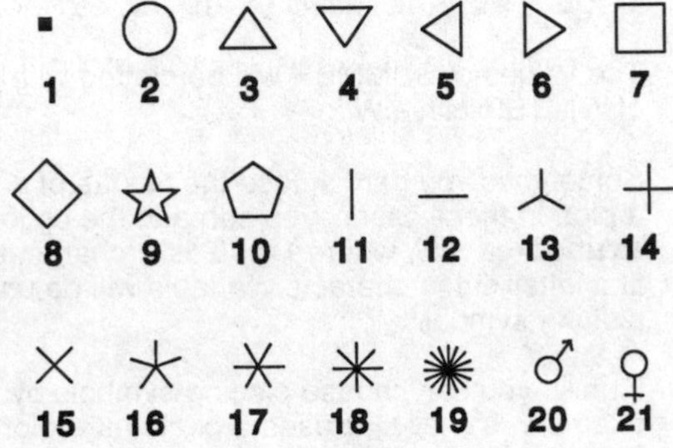

TICK: This option controls the number of tick marks on a graph. **TICK=4**, for example, puts 4 tick marks along an axis. If you do not use this option, SYGRAPH will choose the number for you.

TITLE: This option places a title at the top center of your graph. It works exactly like the **LABEL** option above.

TRANS: Many graphs can be transposed, or flipped over so that the vertical axis becomes the horizontal and the horizontal vertical. You can do this by adding the **TRANS** option. Bar charts, for example, print vertically by default. They can be made horizontal by a command like the following:

```
BAR   SALES*YEAR/TRANS
```

WIDTH: This option works like **HEIGHT** to control the horizontal size of a graph. Use **IN**, **CM**, or no suffix after the number to specify the metric as inches, centimeters, or percent of window size, respectively. For example, **WIDTH=3CM** will produce a graph 3 centimeters wide.

Additional options
Each graph type has additional options. These will be discussed in the relevant sections below.

Making Graphs with GRAPH Commands

The remaining chapters cover the graphics commands in SYGRAPH. Some commands, like **PLOT**, produce many different types of graphs, so their sections are longer.

Chapter 2

BAR

A bar chart plots both counts of categories and continuous against categorical variables. With the BWIDTH option, you can also divide a continuous variable into categories for plotting. Because lengths of bars are easy to compare, the bar chart is an effective display for counts and positive data. SYGRAPH produces a variety of bar charts, both horizontal and vertical.

SYGRAPH automaticaly sorts the levels (categories) of categorical variables in ascending numeric or character order. If you want the categories arranged according to the order they appear in your data file, use the **SNORT** option (see below).

Simple Bar Chart (Bar Chart of Counts)

The **BAR** command will produce a bar graph of counts in categories by a simple command. To tally counts of states in each Census region from the US file, for example, just type:

```
BAR  REGION$
```

SYGRAPH will read the file and tally duplicate values. The printed bar graph will show the counts of cases for each region in the file.

If you have already tallied a variable, you can produce a bar chart directly from the counts. Suppose your file looks like the following. Instead of 48 cases with duplicates, you have only 8 cases with a COUNT variable indicating duplicates.

REGION$	COUNT
New England	6
Mid Atlantic	3
Great Lakes	5
Plains	7
Southeast	8
South	8
Mountain	8
Pacific	3

To produce the same bar chart, you can type:

```
WEIGHT=COUNT
BAR  REGION$
```

You can also use a numerical categorical variable (such as REGION) to specify groups. With this, however, the values of the categories will be displayed as numbers.

Notice that SYGRAPH often prints the labels for the bars at a slant. If there is not enough room to print the labels horizontally, SYGRAPH will automatically make this adjustment. Furthermore, if there are more than 10 categories on the horizontal axis, SYGRAPH will shrink the size of the lettering to fit the labels on the scale. You can do a bar graph on up to 200 categories, but you will need an ultra high resolution device to display clearly the labels for that many categories.

Figure 1

`BAR REGION$`

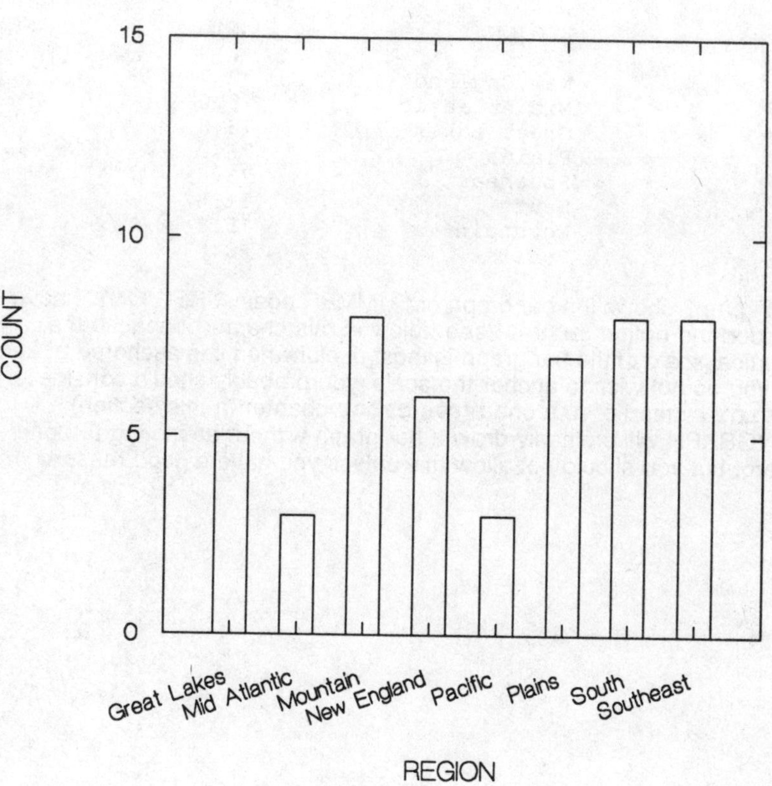

Two-way Bar Chart (Bar Chart of Means)

If you wish to produce a bar graph of a continuous variable against categories, use the **BAR** command with two arguments, e.g.:

```
BAR  INCOME*REGION$
```

SYGRAPH plots the *average* value of the continuous variable, excluding missing values, for each subgroup of the categorical variable. The command:

```
BAR  SUMMER*REGION$
```

computes and plots the following average summer temperatures

REGION$	SUMMER
New England	70.7
Mid Atlantic	75.0
Great Lakes	73.8
Plains	76.0
Southeast	78.6
South	81.6
Mountain	75.4
Pacific	68.0

Figure 2 shows the bar graph of SUMMER against REGION$. I have added the option **YMIN=0** (see below in this chapter) because the vertical scale of the bar graph is most useful when it is anchored at zero. If you do not wish to anchor the scale, you probably should consider a **CPLOT** instead of **BAR** chart (see **CPLOT** chapter in this section). SYGRAPH will ordinarily draw a bar graph without anchoring the bars at zero, but you should not allow this unless you have a good reason.

Figure 2

```
BAR   SUMMER*REGION$/YMIN=0
```

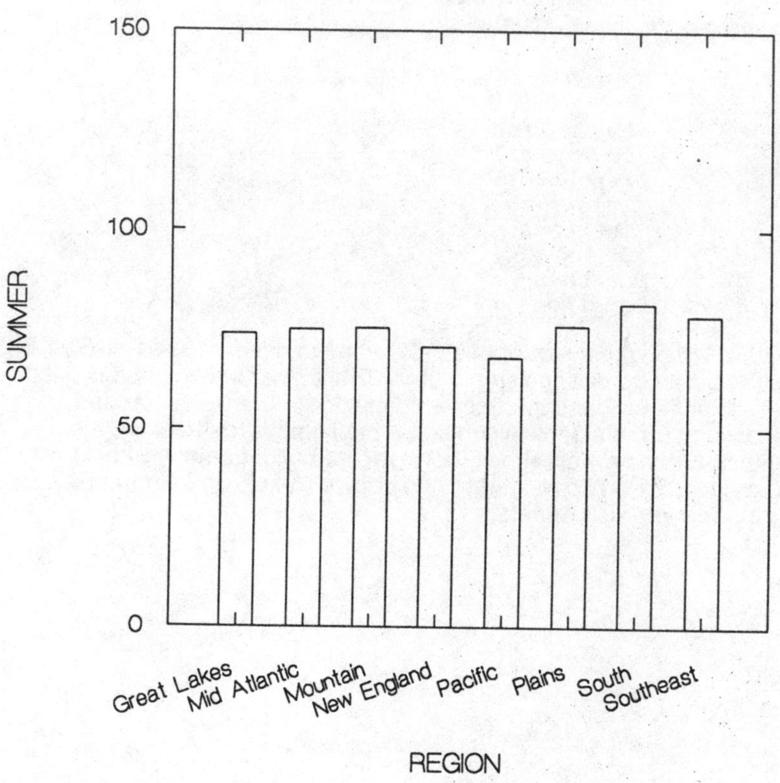

Multi-Valued Bar Charts

You can tabulate up to 12 continuous variables against a categorical variable. SYGRAPH computes the average of each continuous variable within subgroups of the categorical variable. Here is an example of three variables (A,B,C) against a fourth (D$):

```
BAR  A,B,C*D$
```

Each variable on the left is placed on a common vertical scale against the categories on the horizontal scale. From this command:

```
BAR  SUMMER,WINTER*REGION$
```

SYGRAPH computes the average summer and winter temperatures for each region in the US dataset:

REGION$	SUMMER	WINTER
New England	70.7	25.3
Mid Atlantic	75.0	31.7
Great Lakes	73.8	26.4
Plains	76.0	20.9
Southeast	78.6	43.5
South	81.6	45.3
Mountain	75.4	30.6
Pacific	68.0	40.0

Figure 3 shows the plot of this data. I have added **FILL=7,4** (see **FILL** option below) to distinguish the bars. The left bar in each pair is filled with pattern number 7 and the right with number 4. I have also added **YMIN=0** to force a zero minimum on the vertical scale. Since the temperatures are Fahrenheit, however, you might object. Should we use 32 degrees? Perhaps a category plot (see **CPLOT** chapter in this section) might be more appropriate.

Figure 3

```
BAR   SUMMER,WINTER*REGION$/FILL=7,4,YMIN=0
```

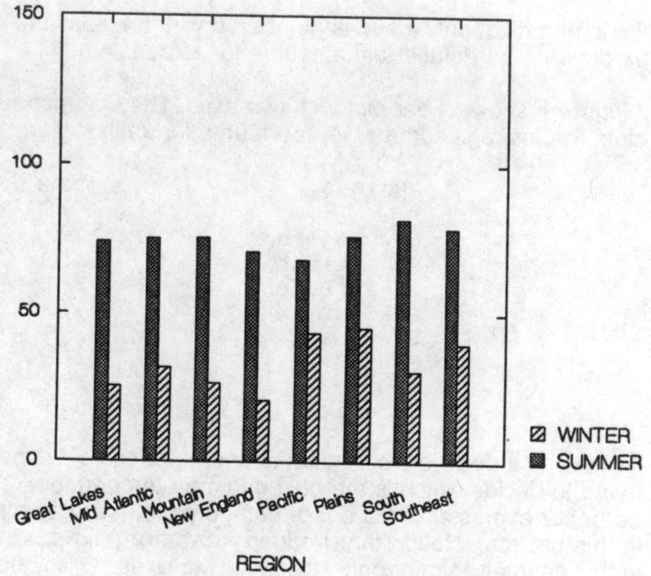

AXES *(Number of Axes)*

The **AXES** option controls the number of axes drawn in a bar graph. Its syntax is:

```
AXES=n
```

where *n* is an integer from 0 to 4. If *n* is 0, no axes will be drawn. If *n* is an integer from 1 to 4, all axes from 1 to *n* will be drawn. Axes are numbered from 1 to 4 clockwise, beginning with the bottom axis:

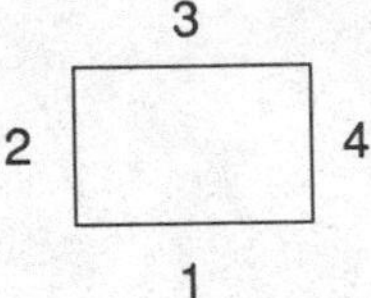

If *n* is negative, only the axis numbered with the absolute value of *n* will be drawn. The default (usual) value for **AXES** is 4.

Figure 4 shows a bar plot with two axes. The command computes and plots the average summer temperatures for each region:

REGION$	SUMMER
New England	70.7
Mid Atlantic	75.0
Great Lakes	73.8
Plains	76.0
Southeast	78.6
South	81.6
Mountain	75.4
Pacific	68.0

I haven't anchored the vertical temperature scale. I'm getting sick of trying to decide which is the best origin for temperature. This graph would be better expressed as a dot or category plot (see **CPLOT** chapter below in this section). Notice that I added **SCALE=2** (see **SCALE** option below in this chapter) to print only scales for two axes. This is optional since 2 scales is the default.

Figure 4

```
BAR   SUMMER*REGION$/AXES=2,SCALE=2
```

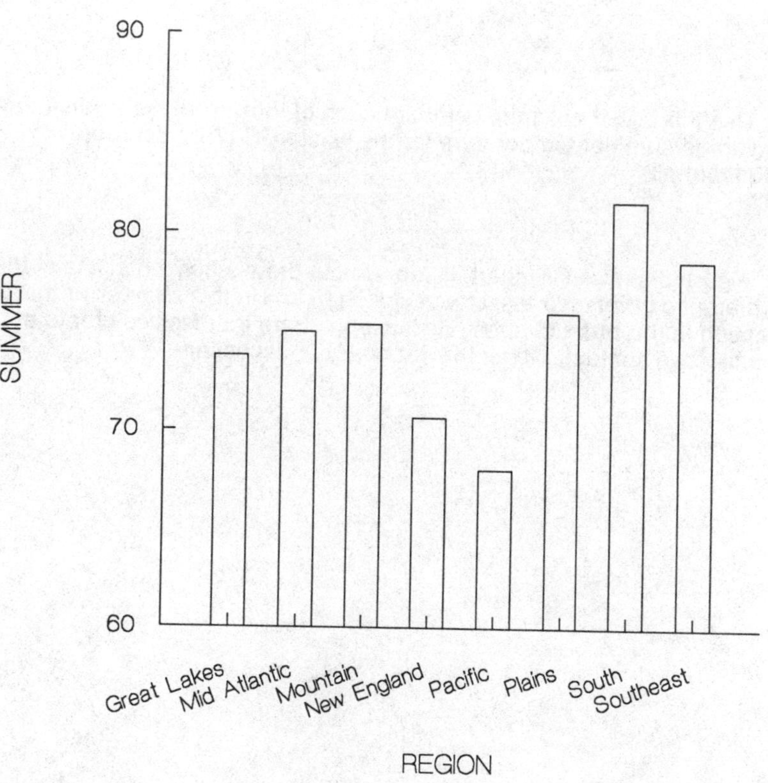

BASE *(Anchored Bars)*

The **BASE** option anchors bars at a selected level. This feature is useful for profit-loss charts and other graphs which compare a variable against a standard level. The command below computes and plots these average summer temperatures.

REGION$	SUMMER
New England	70.7
Mid Atlantic	75.0
Great Lakes	73.8
Plains	76.0
Southeast	78.6
South	81.6
Mountain	75.4
Pacific	68.0

Use the BASE option to compare each of these regions against the average summer temperature for the whole US (75.6 degrees Fahrenheit):

```
BAR  SUMMER*REGION$/BASE=75.6
```

Figure 5 shows this chart. If you want to draw a horizontal line at the reference point, see the **LIMIT** option below in this chapter or the **LINE** option in the **DRAW** chapter. Because the bars themselves create a subjective contour, I think this is usually unnecessary.

Figure 5

```
BAR  SUMMER*REGION$/BASE=75.6
```

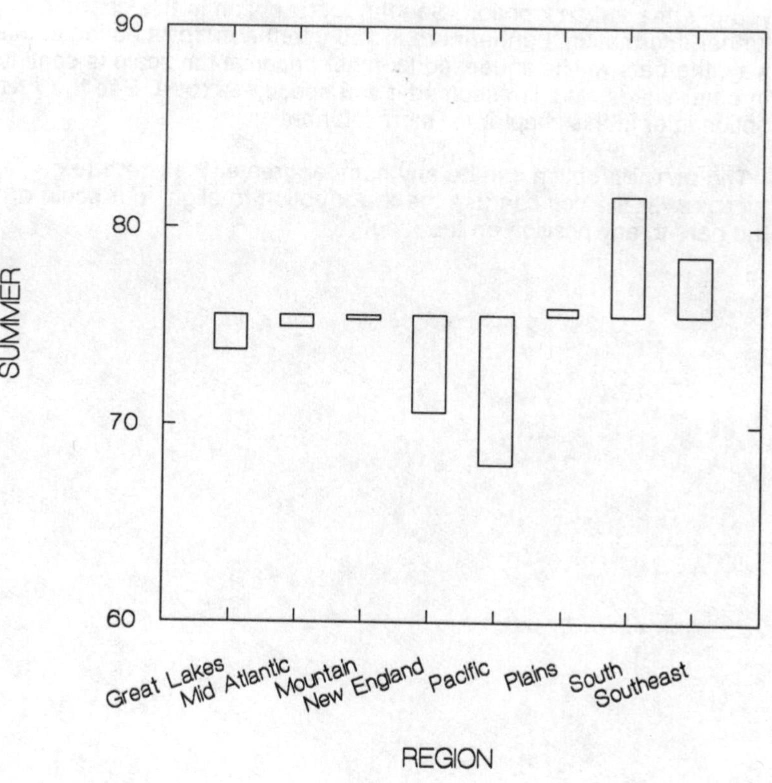

BWIDTH *(Cutpoints for Numerical Data)*

If you want to plot a bar graph on a continuous variable (like INCOME), you can use the **BWIDTH** option to break the variable at evenly spaced cutpoints. In this case, the **BAR** command will not plot a single bar for each separate data value. Instead, the data on the continuous variable will be binned into separate bars defined by cutpoints on the continuous variable. This works for simple and two-way bar charts. For example, the following command collects the 48 states in the US dataset into temperature groups at each 10 degree increment:

```
BAR   SUMMER/XMIN=0,BWIDTH=10
```

You *must* specify the minimum value for the bars (**XMIN=0** in this case) if you use the **BWIDTH** option. See the **XMIN** option in this chapter for further information. Furthermore, if you use the **BWIDTH** option in this way, the bars will be squeezed together because the scale is continuous. In other words, **FAT** is assumed if you specify **BWIDTH**. See the **FAT** option later in this chapter for more information.

The **BWIDTH** option can be any number greater than zero (e.g. **BWIDTH=3.5**). You can use the **XMAX** option to align your scale or force the bars to any position on the range.

Figure 6

`BAR SUMMER/XMIN=0,BWIDTH=10`

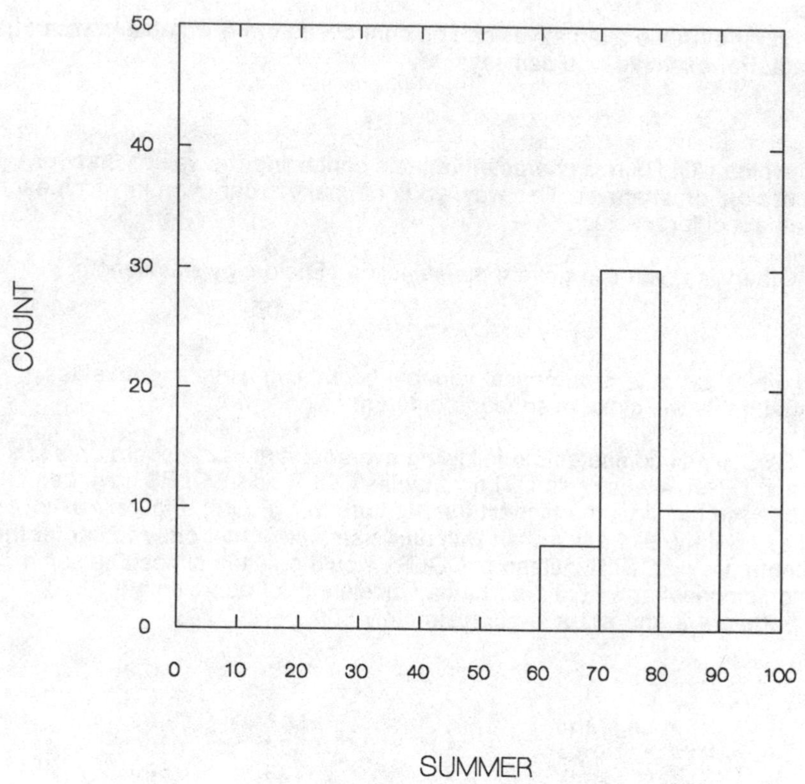

COLOR *(Setting Color of Bars)*

You can choose a color for your bars with the **COLOR** option. Choose either a name or a wavelength in nanometers. Possible colors and their approximate nanometer wavelengths are: **RED** (615), **ORANGE** (590), **YELLOW** (575), **GREEN** (505), **BLUE** (480), **VIOLET** (450). You may also name **BLACK**, **WHITE**, **GRAY**, and **BROWN**.The following command will make all bars in the graph red:

```
BAR   REGION$/COLOR=RED
```

You can also specify color in nanometers wavelength. The following example will make all the bars greenish:

```
BAR   REGION$/COLOR=540
```

Either of these alternatives can be controlled from a variable in your data. For example, you can say:

```
BAR   REGION$/COLOR=COLR$
```

in which COLR$ is a character variable containing the values '**RED**' or '**YELLOW**' or whatever. This way, you can make a bar chart in which each bar is a different color.

Otherwise, you can govern the selection of colors by wavelength:

```
BAR   REGION$/COLOR=COLR
```

in which **COLR** is a numerical variable containing wavelength values. Again, this will make every bar a different color.

SYGRAPH computes the following average summer temperatures for each U.S. Census region. The variables COLR and COLR$ have been added to highlight the highest temperature bar (South). Figure 7 uses these data to plot a bar chart with blue bars, except for one red bar for the South. Using COLR instead of COLR$ would result in almost the same plot, since what we call **RED** has a wavelength of approximately 600 nanometers and **BLUE** is approximately 500.

REGION$	SUMMER	COLR$	COLR
New England	70.7	BLUE	500
Mid Atlantic	75.0	BLUE	500
Great Lakes	73.8	BLUE	500
Plains	76.0	BLUE	500
Southeast	78.6	BLUE	500
South	81.6	RED	600
Mountain	75.4	BLUE	500
Pacific	68.0	BLUE	500

Figure 7

```
BAR   SUMMER*REGION$/COLOR=COLR$,FILL=1
```

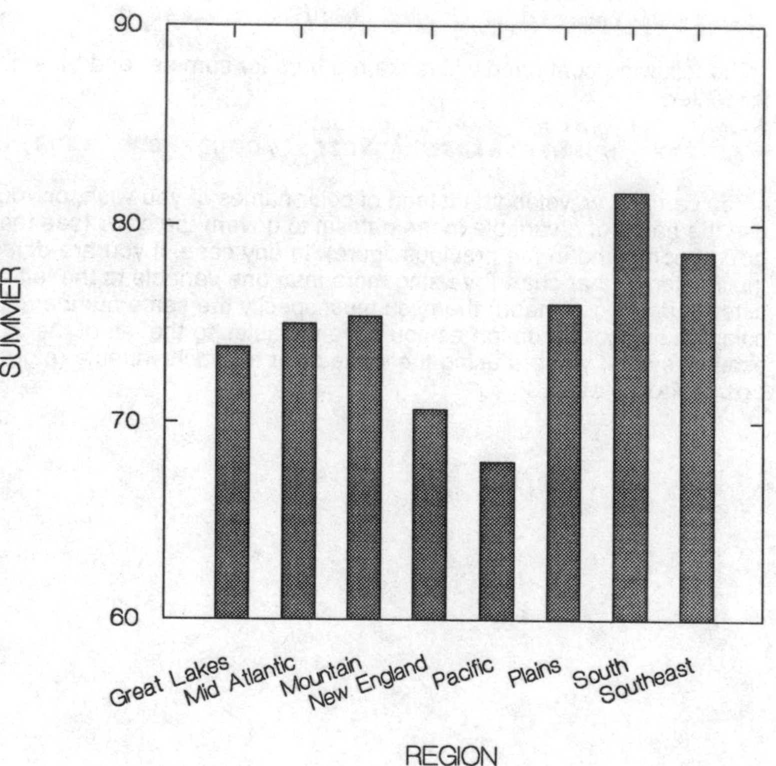

COLOR *(Multi-colored bar charts)*

You can make bar charts with a different color for each dependent variable. SYGRAPH computes the following means for SUMMER and WINTER by REGION$:

REGION$	SUMMER	WINTER
New England	70.7	25.3
Mid Atlantic	75.0	31.7
Great Lakes	73.8	26.4
Plains	76.0	20.9
Southeast	78.6	43.5
South	81.6	45.3
Mountain	75.4	30.6
Pacific	68.0	40.0

The following command will make red bars for summer and blue bars for winter:

```
BAR   SUMMER,WINTER*REGION$/COLOR=RED,BLUE
```

You can use wavelength instead of color names, if you wish, or you can use the name of a variable in the dataset to govern the color (see the **COLOR** command in the previous figure). In any case, if you are doing a multi-category bar chart (by using more than one variable to the left of the asterisk in the command) then you must specify the same number of colors in the **COLOR** option as you have variables to the left of the asterisk even if you are using the same color for each variable (e.g. **COLOR=RED,RED**).

Figure 8

```
BAR   SUMMER,WINTER*REGION$/
        COLOR=RED,BLUE,FILL=1,1,SNORT
```

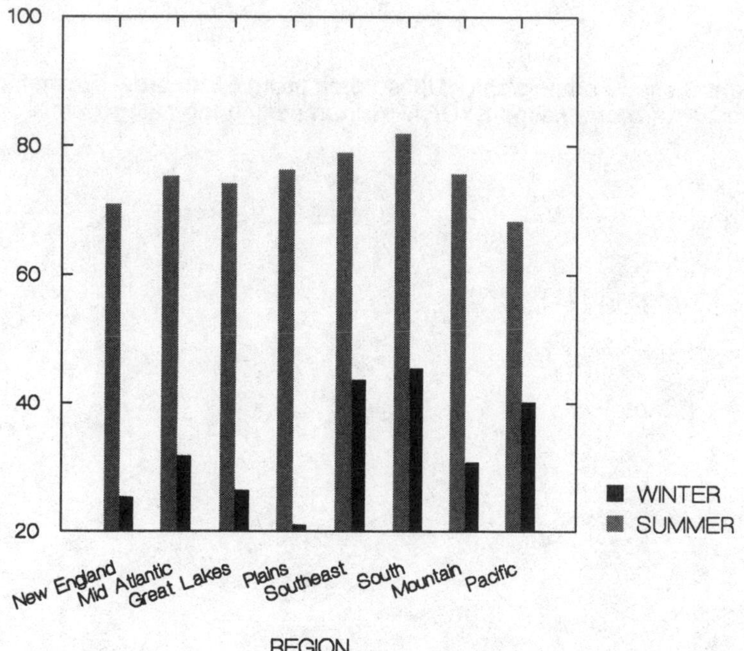

ERROR/ERROR1 *(Symmetric and One-Sided Error Bars)*

You can use an additional variable to represent errors in a bar graph. The **ERROR** option works just as it does with the **CPLOT** and **PLOT** commands. It draws symmetric error bars around the top of each bar. The variable used for the error bars should have a value equal to one half the length of each error bar it specifies.

You can draw one-sided error bars with the **ERROR1** option. If the variable you assign to **ERROR1** is positive, the error bar will face upward. If it is negative, the bar will face downward.

Suppose we have the following data:

DENSITY	SE	ENERGY$
.09	.03	LOW
.40	.04	MEDIUM
.45	.02	HIGH

Figure 9 shows a bar graph of these data using SE to draw symmetric error bars (**SNORT** keeps SYGRAPH from sorting the categories).

Figure 9

```
TYPE=HERSHEY
BAR   DENSITY*ENERGY$/ERROR=SE,SNORT
```

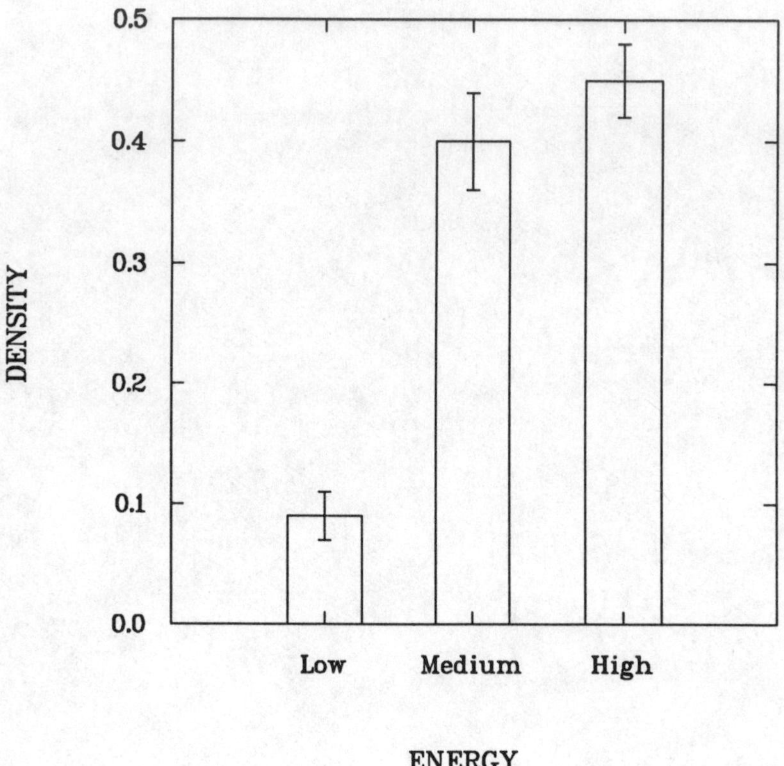

FAT *(Fat Bars)*

Bar graphs are easiest to discern when the bars are separated by a space. Occasionally, however, you may want to squeeze them together. This is done with the **FAT** option. Figure 10 shows an example of this option.

Figure 10

```
BAR   SUMMER*REGION$/FAT
```

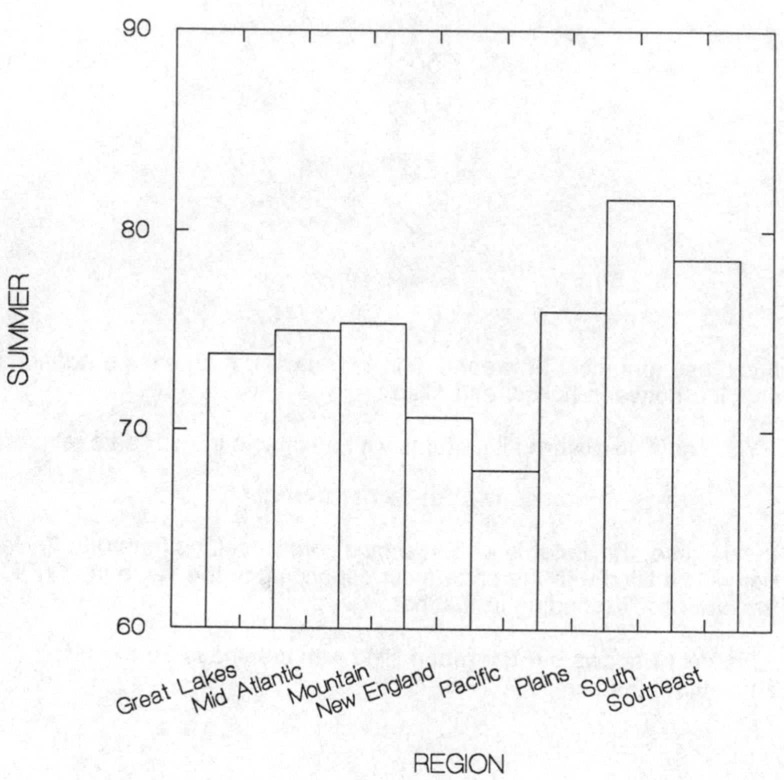

FILL *(Filling bars)*

You can fill bars with different patterns. The **FILL** option works this way:

```
BAR  INCOME*REGION$/FILL=1
```

The number you choose after "**FILL=**" determines the type of fill pattern. Here are the possibilities:

hollow	= 0
solid	= 1
wide diagonal hatch	= 2
crosshatch	= 3
diagonal hatch	= 4
fine crosshatch	= 5
diagonal hatch	= 6
fine dense pattern	= 7

If you use a number between 0 and 1, you will get an even gradation of shading between hollow and filled.

You can also govern fill patterns with a variable in your dataset:

```
BAR  INCOME*REGION$/FILL=MYFIL
```

In this case, the variable MYFIL should contain values from 0 to 7. Each bar will be filled with the pattern corresponding to the value in MYFIL for the case corresponding to that bar.

Figure 11 shows our bar graph filled with the shaded pattern to accentuate the bars.

Figure 11

```
BAR   INCOME*REGION$/FILL=7
```

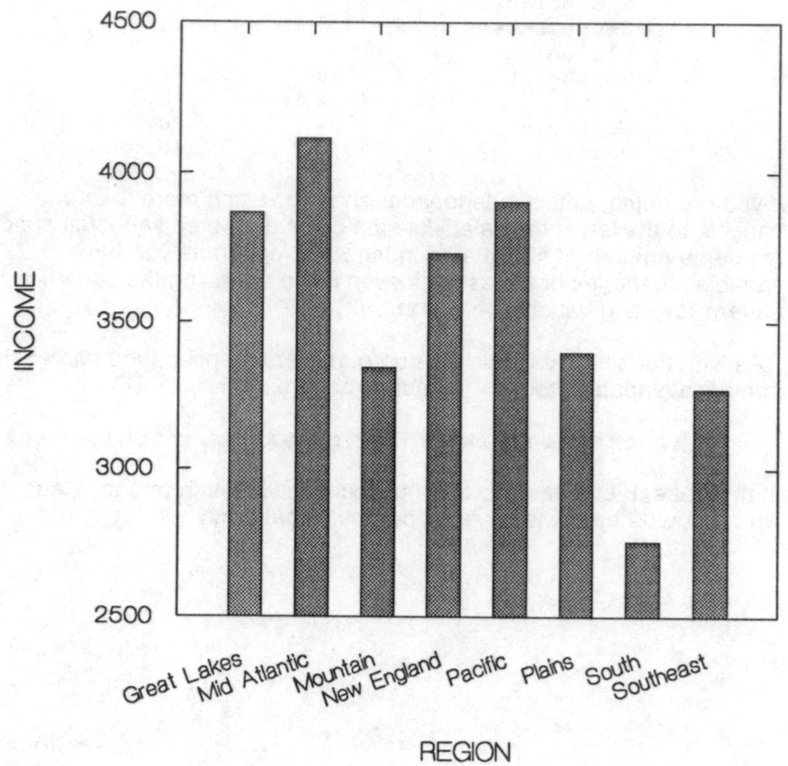

FILL *(Multi-filled bar charts)*

You can make bar charts with a different fill pattern for each dependent variable. The following command will make solid bars for summer and hollow bars for winter:

```
BAR   SUMMER,WINTER*REGION$/FILL=1,0
```

SYGRAPH computes and plots these averages of SUMMER and WINTER for each subgroup of REGION$:

REGION$	SUMMER	WINTER
New England	70.7	25.3
Mid Atlantic	75.0	31.7
Great Lakes	73.8	26.4
Plains	76.0	20.9
Southeast	78.6	43.5
South	81.6	45.3
Mountain	75.4	30.6
Pacific	68.0	40.0

If you are doing a multi-category bar chart (by using more than one variable to the left of the asterisk in the command) then you must specify the same number of fill patterns in the **FILL** option as you have variables to the left of the asterisk even if you are using the same fill pattern for each variable (e.g. **FILL=2,2**).

As with the single variable version of the **FILL** option, you can specify numerical variables to govern your fill patterns:

```
BAR   SUMMER,WINTER*REGION$/FILL=FILL1,FILL2
```

In this case, FILL1 and FILL2 should contain values from 0 to 7, each of which would determine for each bar the fill pattern.

Figure 12

```
BAR   SUMMER,WINTER*REGION$/FILL=1,0
```

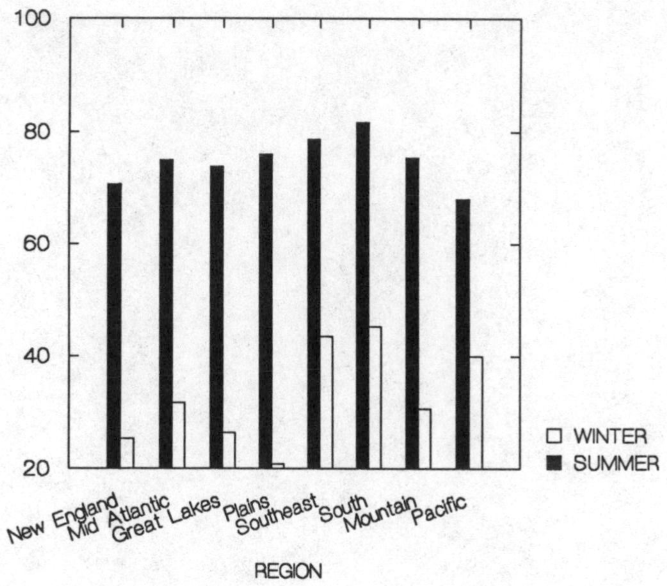

GRID *(Grid Marks)*

You can add grid marks to bar charts with the **GRID** option. The possible values are:

`GRID=1`	*(vertical grid marks)*
`GRID=2`	*(horizontal grid marks)*
`GRID=3`	*(horizontal and vertical grid marks)*

For bar charts, you probably want only **GRID=2**. Furthermore, if you use a grid, you should use solid bars (see the **FILL** option in this chapter) to hide the grid marks behind the bars. The example in Figure 13 does this (**SNORT** keeps SYGRAPH from sorting the categories).

Figure 13

```
TYPE=SWISS
BAR   INCOME*REGION$/FILL=1,GRID=2,SNORT
```

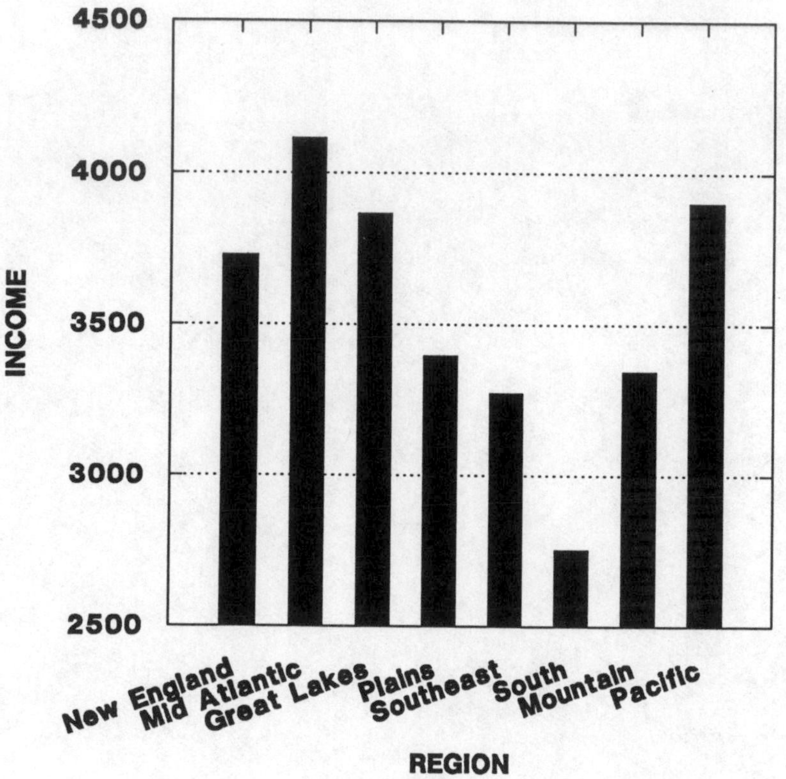

HEIGHT *(Physical Height of Plot)*

You can control the physical height of your bar graph with the **HEIGHT** option. It works like this:

```
HEIGHT=50%      (or HEIGHT=50)
HEIGHT=4IN
HEIGHT=10CM
```

The first example specifies percent of display height. The second specifies inches, and the third centimeters.

When you use the **HEIGHT** option, you probably also want to use **WIDTH**, which works exactly the same way (see below in this chapter). The following graph shows how to use them together.

Figure 14

```
BAR   INCOME*REGION$/HEIGHT=3IN,WIDTH=4IN
```

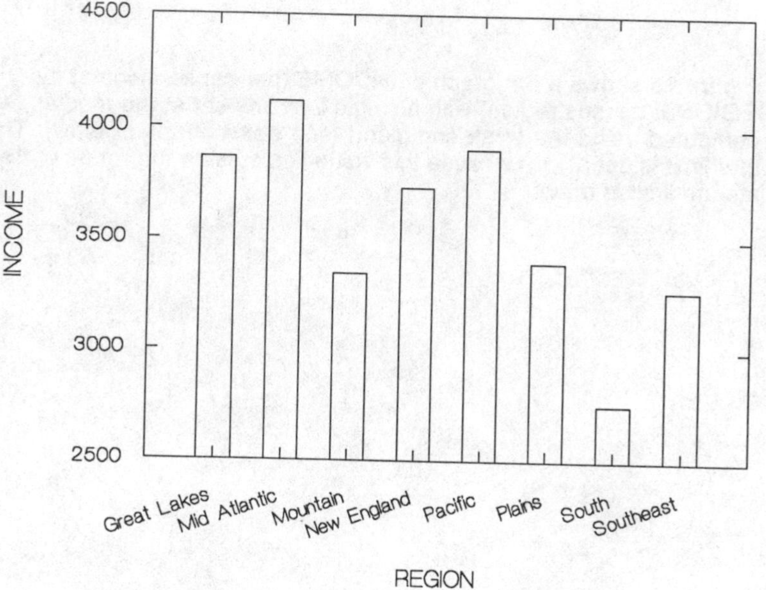

LIMIT *(Control Limits)*

You can add dashed lines to mark limits on the numerical axis of a bar graph. **Quality control charts**, for example, mark upper and lower limits on an axis to indicate permissible bounds for a production process. Axis limits can be used in other applications to mark simultaneous standard errors. The **LIMIT** option works this way:

```
BAR  X/LIMIT=3,8                                  or,
BAR  Y*X$/LIMIT=.43,24.5
```

The first example places limits on counts, since there is only a grouping variable. The second example plots a continuous against a categorical variable. Notice that you must specify two numbers for the limit (upper and lower). They need not be in order. Limits will not be plotted for numbers outside the extremes of the specified axes. Thus, if you want to plot only one limit (dashed line) on your axis, type something like this:

```
BAR  X/LIMIT=2,-9999
```

Figure 15 shows a bar graph of INCOME (per-capita income) by REGION$ (census region) with a single limit line set at the median, which I computed using the **STEM** command (see **STEM** chapter below). The other limit is set at -1. Because this value lies outside the range of the data, no limit is drawn.

Figure 15

```
BAR INCOME*REGION$/LIMIT=-1,3464.5,YMIN=0
```

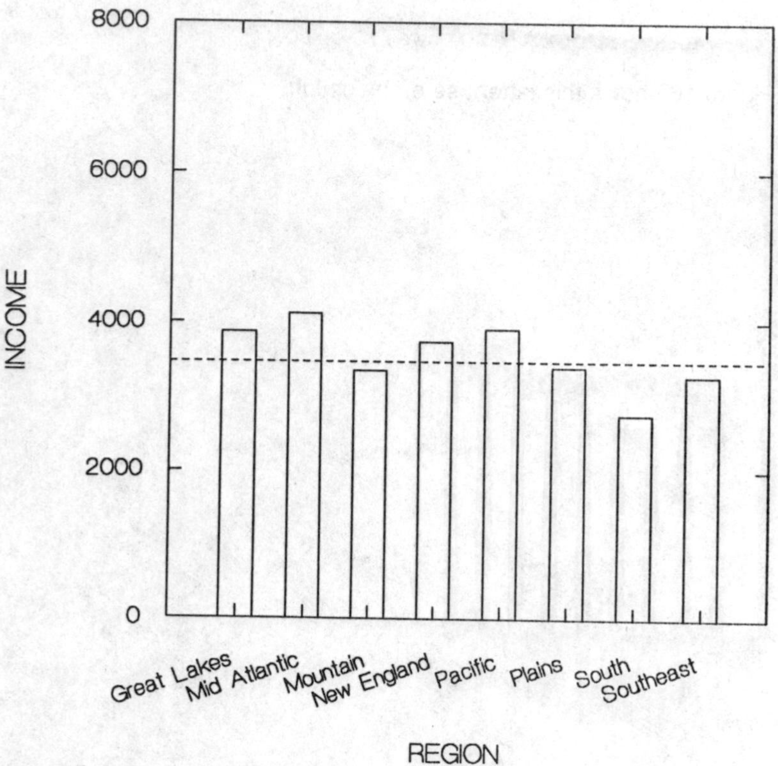

LOG *(Logging Data)*
You can log the vertical scale of your bar graph with the **LOG** command. Logs may be computed to any base, e.g. **LOG=2**, **LOG=3**, **LOG=10**, **LOG=.5**. Natural logarithms will be computed if you use **LOG** with no argument, i.e. **LOG**. Only round number log bases (e.g. 0.5, 2, 3,10) will result in round number tick values, however.

LOG works with any form of the **BAR** command. The following command, for example, will log frequencies:

```
BAR  REGION$/LOG=10
```

The following logs INCOME.

```
BAR  INCOME*REGION$/LOG=10
```

Figure 16 shows this latter use of the option.

Figure 16

```
BAR   INCOME*REGION$/LOG=10
```

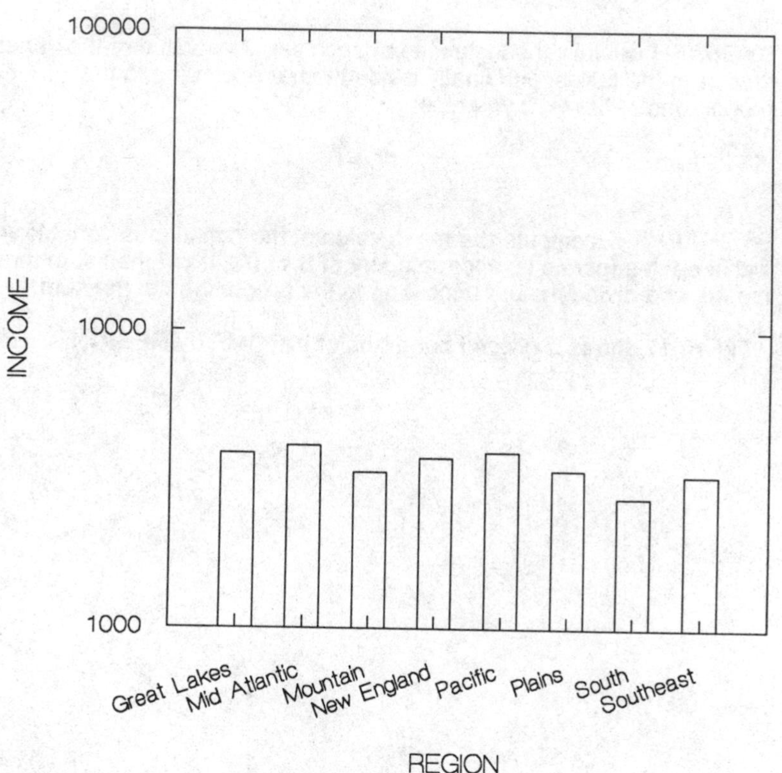

PERCENT *(Percentage, or Divided Bar Graphs)*

If you have data which are percents of wholes, you can use a pie or ring chart (see `PIE` chapter below). Otherwise, you can do a divided bar chart. I'm not sure which chart is better, since the experimental evidence favoring one or the other is scant and mixed (e.g. Simkin and Hastie, 1987). In any case, the divided bar graph is like unrolling a pie chart into a soldier's service bars.

As with the pie graph, the percentage bar graph can be produced several ways. If you type:

```
BAR  B/PERCENT          or,
BAR  B$/PERCENT
```

SYGRAPH will tally the instances of each separate value of the variable, then sum the tallies, and finally divide the bar according to the proportions of tallies. If you type:

```
BAR  A*B                or,
BAR  A*B$
```

SYGRAPH will compute the mean value of the continuous variable A within each separate level or category of B or B$. It will then sum these means and divide the bar according to the proportions of the sum.

Figure 17 shows a divided bar graph of INCOME by REGION.

Figure 17

```
BAR   INCOME*REGION$/PERCENT
```

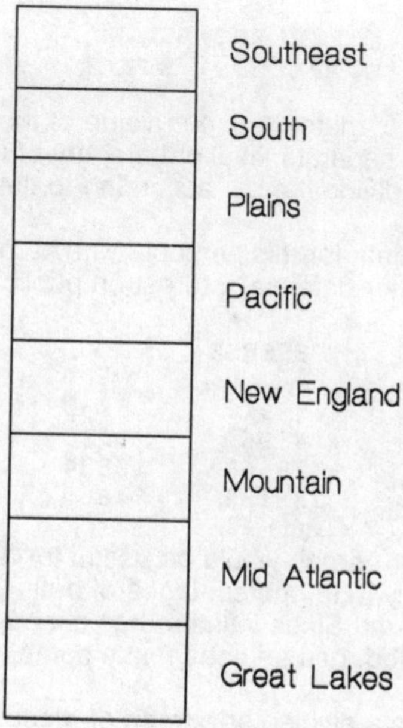

Southeast

South

Plains

Pacific

New England

Mountain

Mid Atlantic

Great Lakes

PERCENT *(Multi-variable Percentage, or Divided Bar Graphs)*

If you have more than one variable to apportion in a percentage bar graph, you can do it in a multi-variable percentage graph. This graph is like placing several divided bar graphs next to each other (see Figure 16). Almost always, you want to use the **STACK** option as well (see below in this chapter). Otherwise, the percentages will be placed alongside one another instead of dividing a single bar.

As with the pie graph, the multi-variable percentage bar graph can be produced several ways. If you type:

```
BAR  A,B/PERCENT,STACK          or,
BAR  A$,B$/PERCENT,STACK
```

SYGRAPH will tally the instances of each separate value of the variables, then sum the tallies, and finally divide the bars according to the proportions of tallies. If you type:

```
BAR  A,B*C/PERCENT,STACK        or,
BAR  A,B*C$/PERCENT,STACK
```

SYGRAPH will compute the mean value of the continuous variables A and B within each separate level or category of C or C$. It will then sum these means and divide the bar according to the proportions of the sum.

Here are some data for this purpose. They are U.S. expenditures in millions of dollars for defense, interest on public debt, and all other.

YEAR$	DEFENSE	INTEREST	OTHER
1950	9919	5750	23875
1960	43969	9180	39075
1970	78368	19304	98972
1980	136138	74860	368013

The percentage bar graph would be useful for these data if we are interested primarily in the percentages of outlays in each year rather than the absolute amount. Since inflation has changed the meaning of these dollars in this period, percentages make some sense.

Figure 18 shows a divided bar graph of these data. Compare this graph to the graph of the same data using the **STACK** option without **PERCENT** below. You may also want to consider the **FAT** option (see below in this chapter) for this graph. I have used **FILL** to distinguish the areas.

Figure 18

```
BAR   DEFENSE,INTEREST,OTHER*YEAR$,
 /STACK,FILL=1,2,7,PERCENT
```

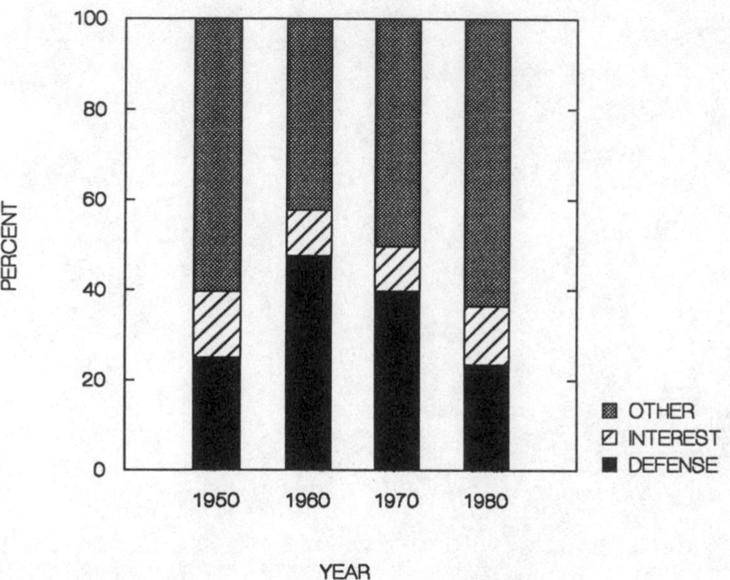

PIP *(Pip Marks)*

Pip marks are half sized tick marks. SYGRAPH normally omits pip marks from bar charts. The `PIP` option adds them. Just specify the number you want. Figure 19 shows an example with 10 pip marks. I have added `YMIN=0` (see below in this chapter) to force the bottom of the vertical axis to be 0.

Figure 19

```
BAR  INCOME*REGION$/YMIN=0,PIP=10
```

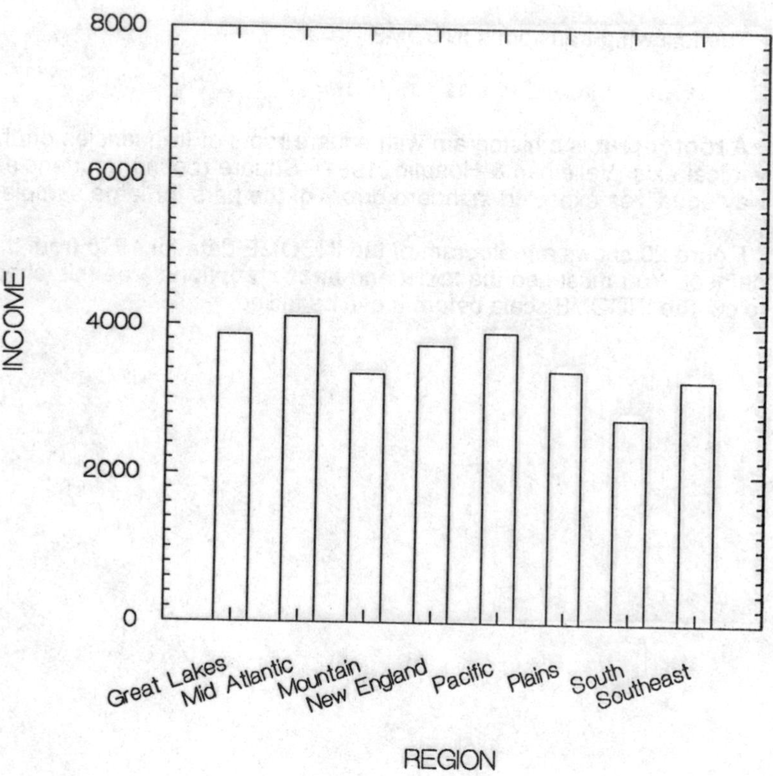

POW *(Powering Data)*

You can power the vertical scale of your bar graph with the **POW** command. Powers may be computed to any exponent, e.g. **POW=.5** (square root), **POW=.33333** (cube root), **POW=-1** (inverse), **POW=2**. Square roots will be computed if you use **POW** with no argument, i.e. **POW**. Some exponents (e.g. 3) will produce non-integer tick marks. **POW** is implemented in SYGRAPH only for positive data. Negative values will be deleted.

POW works with any form of the **BAR** command. The following command, for example, will transform frequencies:

```
BAR  REGION$/POW=.5
```

The following transforms INCOME.

```
BAR  INCOME*REGION$/POW=.5
```

A **rootogram** is a histogram with square roots of frequencies on the vertical axis (Velleman & Hoaglin, 1981). Square rooting frequencies this way equalizes expected standard errors of the bars for large samples.

Figure 20 shows a rootogram of the INCOME data for 1970 from the US dataset. You must use the **XMIN** and **BWIDTH** options (see this chapter) to cut the INCOME scale before it can be tallied.

Figure 20

```
BAR   INCOME/POW=.5,XMIN=2000,BWIDTH=500,FILL=5
```

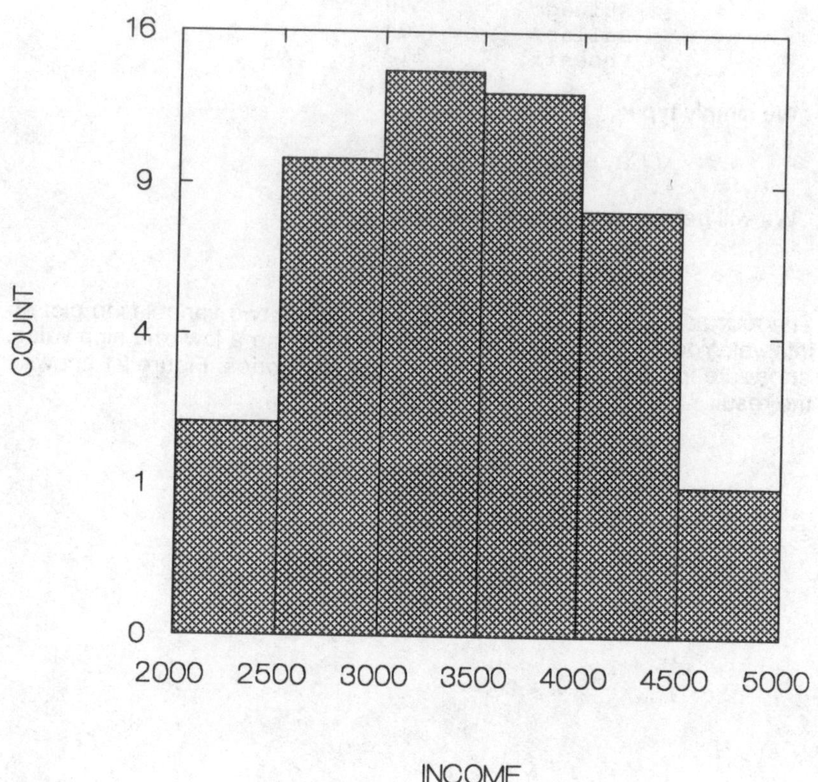

RANGE *(Range Bar Charts)*

You can use the **BAR** command to represent ranges of variables against a categorical variable. The following data consist of record low and high July temperatures for eight U.S. cities in 1983. We can plot the range of temperatures by city with the **RANGE** option.

CITY$	HIGH	LOW
Los Angeles	86	62
Miami	90	71
New York	91	59
Seattle	91	50
Denver	97	55
Chicago	99	47
Dallas	104	64
Phoenix	112	68

We simply type:

```
BAR  LOW,HIGH*CITY$/RANGE
```

We will get the same result if we type:

```
BAR  HIGH,LOW*CITY$/RANGE
```

The **RANGE** option causes SYGRAPH to use the two variables to plot an interval. You must use only two variables to define a low and high value. **SNORT** keeps SYGRAPH from sorting the categories. Figure 21 shows the result.

Figure 21

```
BAR   LOW,HIGH*CITY$/RANGE,SNORT
```

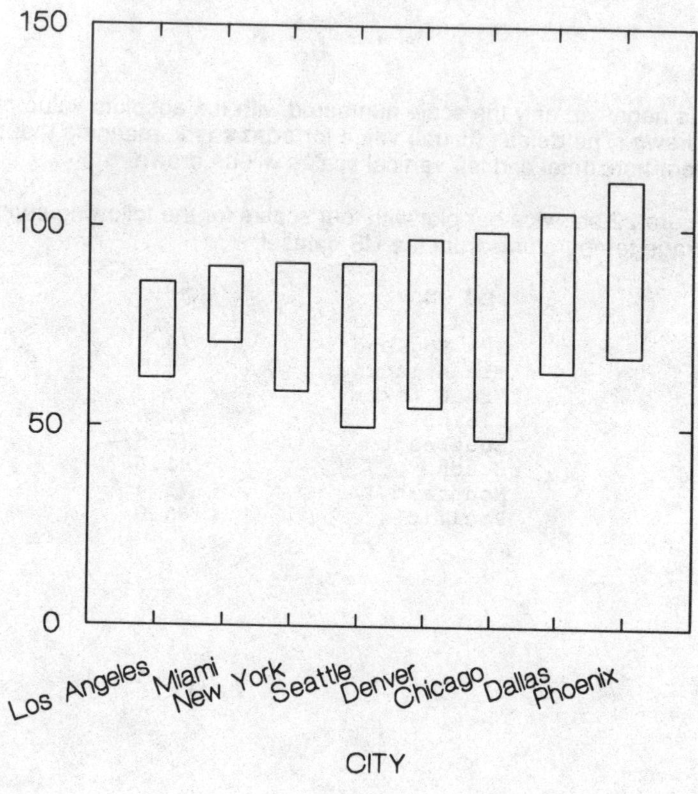

SCALE *(Number of Scales)*

Scales are the numbers which label the tick marks on an axis. The **SCALE** option controls the number of scales drawn in a bar graph. Its syntax is:

```
SCALE=n
```

where *n* is an integer from 0 to 4. If *n* is 0, no scales will be drawn. If *n* is an integer from 1 to 4, all scales from 1 to *n* will be drawn. Scales are numbered from 1 to 4 clockwise, beginning with the bottom axis:

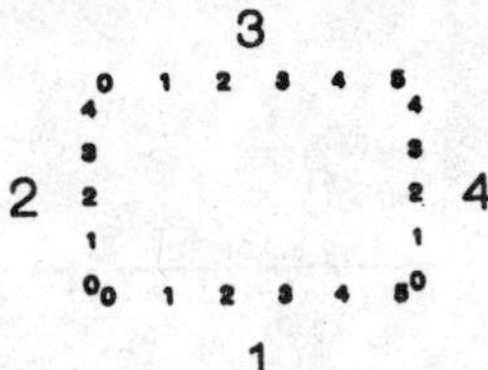

If *n* is negative, only the scale numbered with the absolute value of *n* will be drawn. The default (usual) value for **SCALE** is 2, meaning that the bottom horizontal and left vertical scales will be drawn.

Figure 22 shows a bar plot with four scales for the following summer average temperatures from the US dataset.

REGION$	SUMMER
New England	70.7
Mid Atlantic	75.0
Great Lakes	73.8
Plains	76.0
Southeast	78.6
South	81.6
Mountain	75.4
Pacific	68.0

Figure 22

```
BAR  SUMMER*REGION$/SCALE=4
```

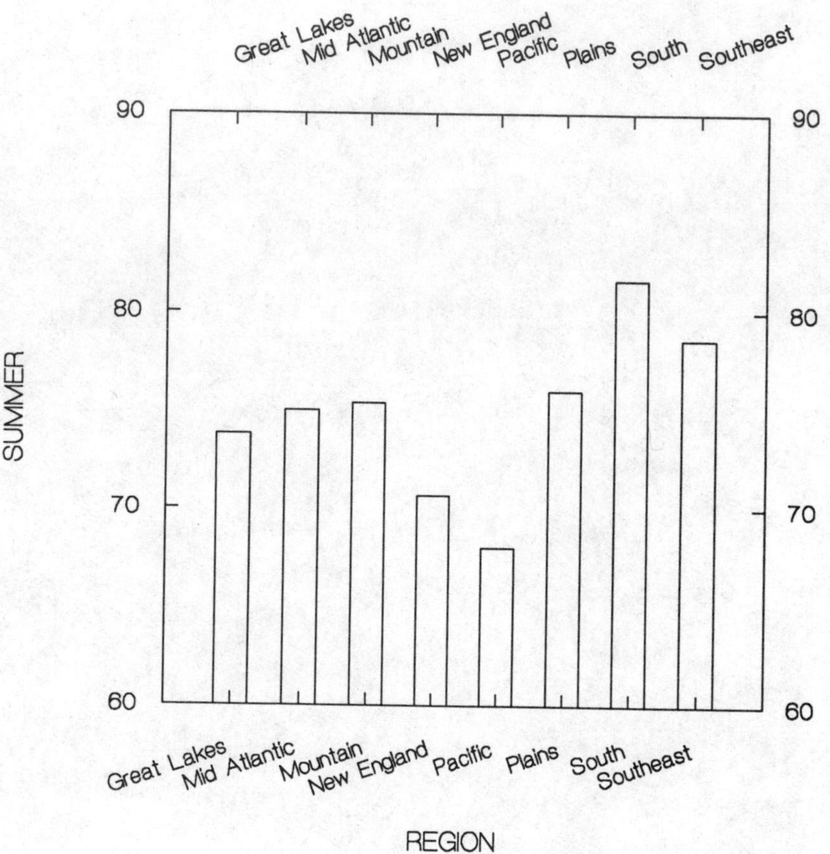

SORT/SNORT *(Sorting Categories)*

SYGRAPH automatically sorts the levels (categories) of categorical variables in ascending numeric or character order. If you want the categories arranged according to the order they appear in your data file, use the **SNORT** option. Figure 23 shows an example of this option. Compare the bottom scale with that in other figures in this chapter to see how **SNORT** works.

Figure 23

```
BAR   SUMMER*REGION$/SNORT
```

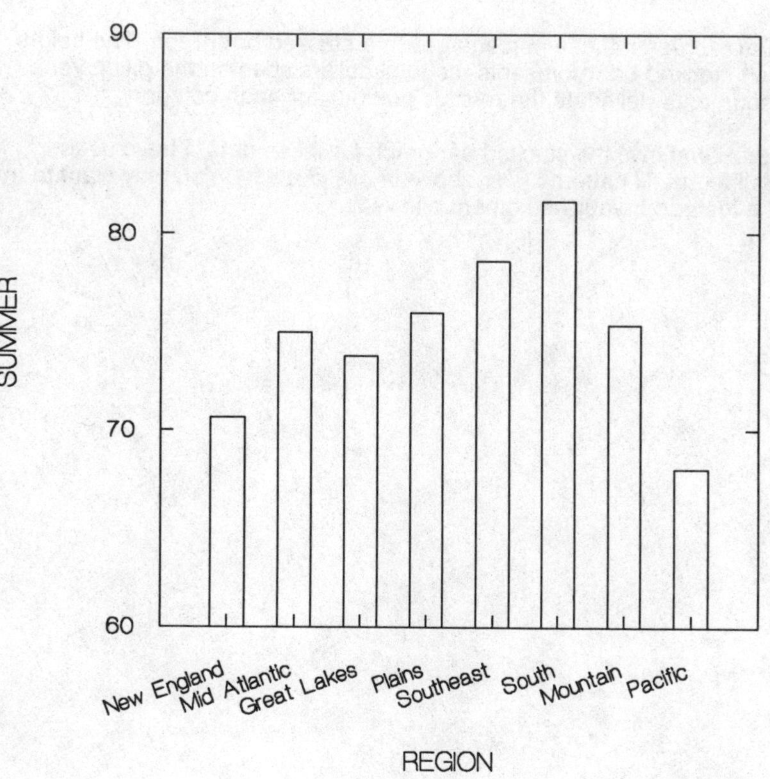

STACK *(Stacked Bars)*

A stacked bar chart works like a multi-valued bar chart (see beginning of this chapter) except that the bars for each category are stacked on top of each other instead of being placed side by side. As with the multi-valued charts, you can stack up to 12 different variables. These charts are most useful for comparing segments of a single variable over several categories, such as budget information. I used the following data to illustrate the **PERCENT** option above in this chapter. There are millions of dollars in U.S. budget outlays.

YEAR$	DEFENSE	INTEREST	OTHER
1950	9919	5750	23875
1960	43969	9180	39075
1970	78368	19304	98972
1980	136138	74860	368013

We can represent these percentages in a stacked bar graph. The height of each stacked bar represents the total dollars spent in the given year. The segments delineate the relative portions for each category.

Figure 24 shows the stacked bar graph for these data. I have used three different fill patterns (see above in this chapter). You may want to try **COLOR** instead if your equipment allows it.

Figure 24

```
BAR   DEFENSE,INTEREST,OTHER*YEAR$
   /STACK,FILL=1,2,7
```

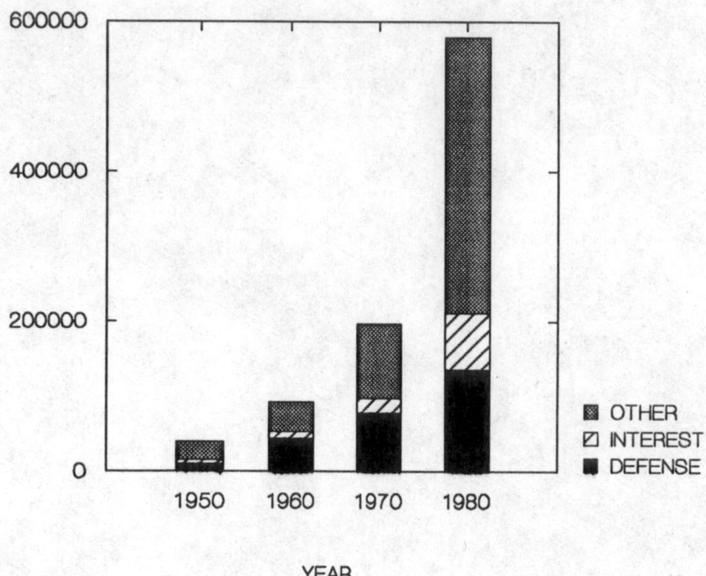

STICK *(Tick Marks Outside Frame)*
SYGRAPH normally places tick marks inside the frame. If you wish tick marks outside the frame, use the **STICK** option.

Figure 25 shows an example of a bar graph with tick marks outside the frame.

Figure 25

```
BAR   SUMMER*REGION$/STICK
```

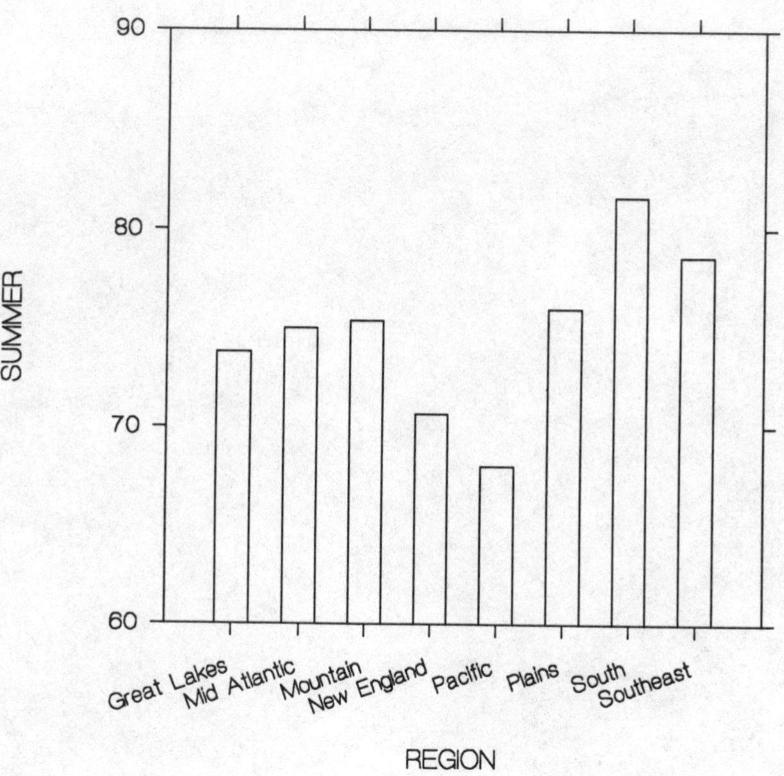

TICK *(Number of Tick Marks)*

SYGRAPH examines your data to determine how many tick marks to use on the vertical axis of a bar graph. If you wish to modify this value, use the `TICK` option with a number. For example, `TICK=8` will force the vertical axis to have 8 tick marks. SYGRAPH will attempt to find minimum and maximum values for the scale such that the tick mark numbers are round. If it fails, you can control the values with the `YMIN` and `YMAX` options as well.

Figure 26 shows an example of a bar graph with 10 tick marks. Notice that SYGRAPH automatically adjusts the size of the scale values when there are more tick marks. I have added `YMIN=0` (See below in this chapter) to force the minimum value of INCOME to 0.

Figure 26

```
BAR   INCOME*REGION$/TICK=10,YMIN=0
```

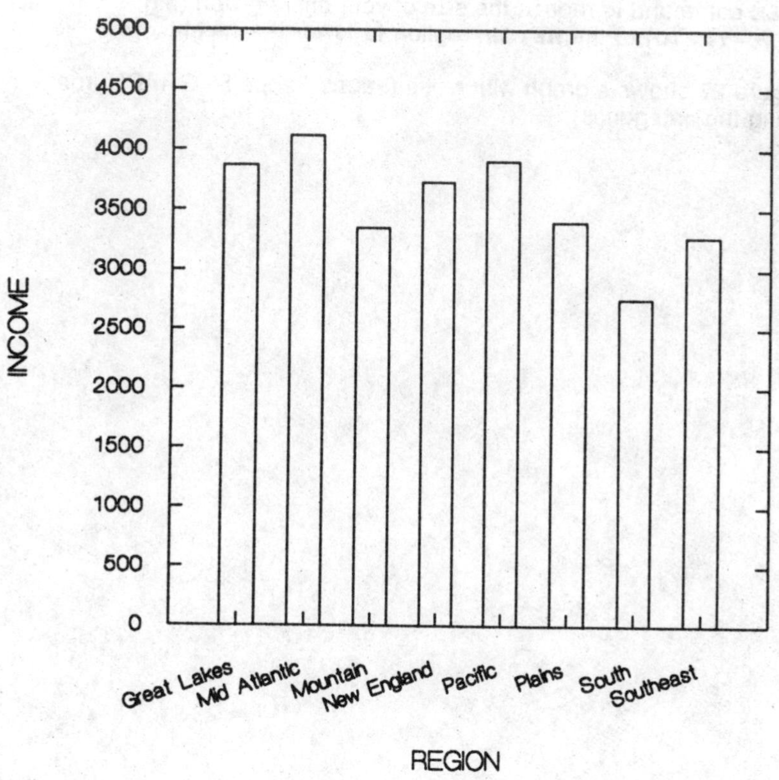

TITLE *(Graph Title)*

You can place a title at the top center of your graph with the **TITLE** option:

```
TITLE='Worldwide Sales in U.S. Dollars'
TITLE="Roger's Fraudulent Experiment"
TITLE='Perceived variation in "Impact"'
```

The text must be surrounded by quotes (") or apostrophes ('). If your text includes apostrophes, as in the second example, surround it with quotes. If it includes quotes, as in the third example, surround it with apostrophes.

On some display devices the title will run off the top of the page because the standard display window is chosen to make the labels and graph as large as possible. If this happens, you will have to use the **SCALE** command to reduce the size of your entire graph (e.g. **SCALE=70,70**) or the **HEIGHT** option to lower the height.

Figure 27 shows a graph with a title (**SNORT** keeps SYGRAPH from sorting the categories).

Figure 27

```
TYPE=HERSHEY
BAR  INCOME*REGION$/SNORT,
   TITLE='Average Income within Region'
```

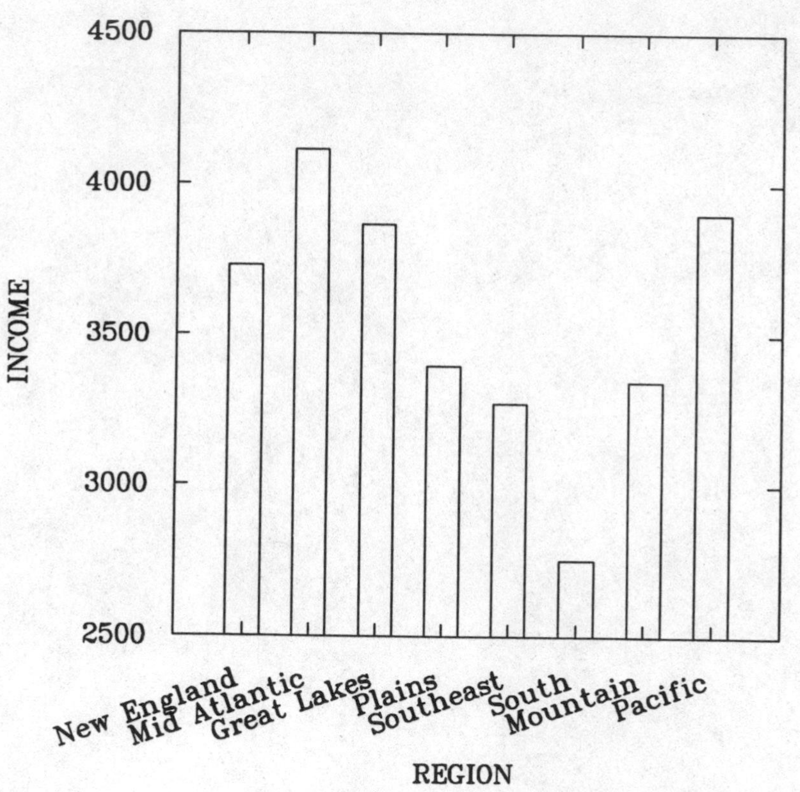

TRANS *(Transposing a Bar Graph)*

Bar graphs normally have vertical bars. You can make your bars horizontal by transposing the entire graph, labels and all. To do this, just add the option **TRANS** to the **BAR** command.

TRANS affects everything in a graph. **XLABEL** becomes **YLABEL**, **XTICK** becomes **YTICK**, and so on. In other words, specify a graph as you would ordinarily and then add the **TRANS** option. Everything will be transposed appropriately, including the labels and scales.

Figure 28 shows an example of a transposed bar graph. I have added **YMIN=0** to make the origin of the INCOME scale 0. **SNORT** keeps SYGRAPH from sorting the categories.

Figure 28

```
BAR   INCOME*REGION$/YMIN=0,TRANS,SNORT
```

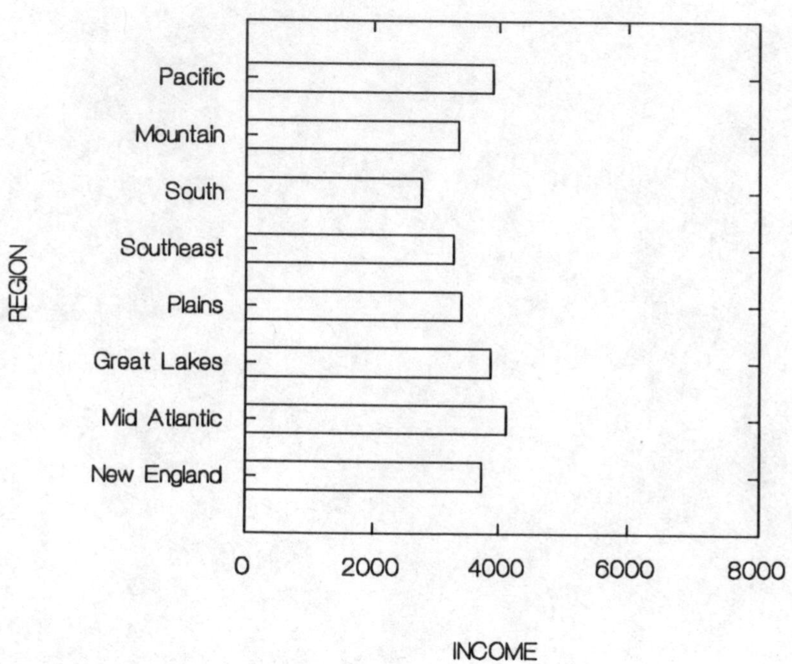

WIDTH *(Physical Width of Plot)*

You can control the physical width of your bar graph with the **WIDTH** option. It works like this:

```
WIDTH=50%        (or WIDTH=50)
WIDTH=4IN
WIDTH=10CM
```

The first example specifies percent of display width. The second specifies inches, and the third centimeters.

When you use the **WIDTH** option, you probably also want to use **HEIGHT**, which works exactly the same way (see above in this chapter). The following graph shows how to use them together.

Figure 29

```
BAR   INCOME*REGION$/HEIGHT=3IN,WIDTH=4IN
```

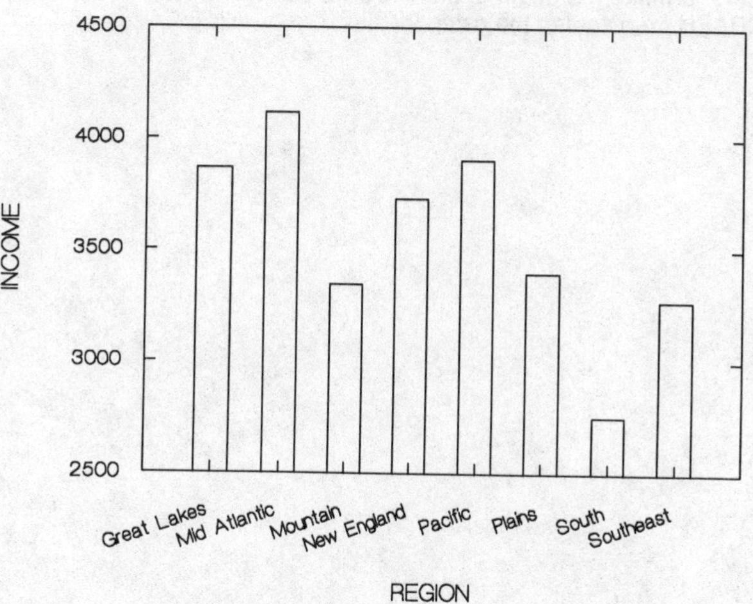

XLABEL,YLABEL *(Labeling a Bar Graph)*

Bar graphs are usually labeled with the names of the variables you use in the **BAR** command. If you want different labels, use the **XLABEL** and/or **YLABEL** command, e.g.:

```
XLABEL='Proportion of Variance'
YLABEL='Per Capita Income'
XLABEL="Peter's Portion"
XLABEL='Proportion of "Widgets" Bid'
YLABEL=' '
```

The label text must be surrounded by quotes (") or apostrophes ('). If your text includes apostrophes, as in the third example, surround it with quotes. If it includes quotes, as in the fourth example, surround it with apostrophes. The last example shows how to remove labels from your graph. Just assign a blank (' ') to your label.

Figure 30 shows an example of a relabeled bar graph. I have added **YMIN=0** to make the origin of the INCOME scale 0. **SNORT** keeps SYGRAPH from sorting the categories.

Figure 30

```
BAR  INCOME*REGION$
  /YMIN=0,SNORT,
   YLABEL='1970 Per Capita Income',
   XLABEL='Region of U.S.'
```

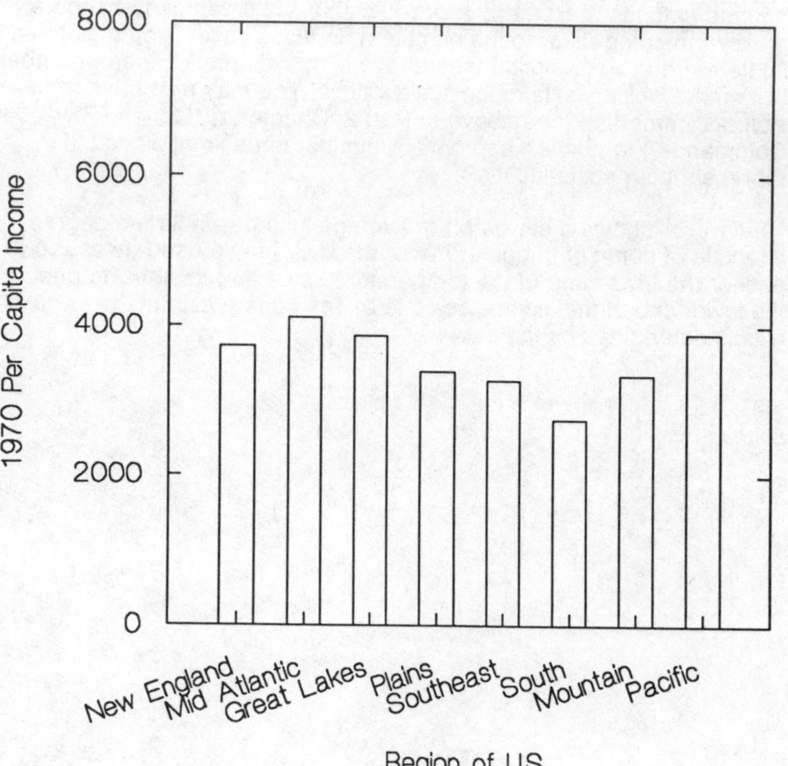

XMIN,YMIN,XMAX,YMAX *(Data Limits)*

SYGRAPH usually determines minimum and maximum scale values from the data in your file. If you wish to override this feature, use the **MIN/MAX** options. **YMIN** and **YMAX** control the lower and upper limits of the vertical scale. **XMIN** and **XMAX** do the same for the horizontal scale. Since the horizontal scale is categorical, however, you can use **XMIN** and/or **XMAX** only together with the **BWIDTH** option (see above in this chapter), which cuts a continuous variable into categories to make the horizontal scale.

If you set the **MIN** and **MAX** options inside the range of your data, you will zoom in to get a closer view, but you will eliminate certain data values from your plot. SYGRAPH will warn you when this happens.

Some settings of **MIN** and **MAX** will cause scale values to become messy (not integers or round numbers). In these cases, you may have to fiddle with the **TICK** option (see above in this chapter) to get a number of tick marks which yields round scale values. You may also have to use the **FORMAT** command (see above in Part 2, Chapter 1, "General Commands") to print an appropriate number of decimal places to represent your scale values.

Figure 31 shows a bar graph of average income within ten degree intervals of summer temperature for the U.S. I have used **XMIN=30** to anchor the lower end of the temperature scale and **YMIN=0** to anchor the lower end of the income scale to 0. The upper value of the vertical axis is determined by the data.

Figure 31

```
BAR   INCOME*SUMMER/YMIN=0,XMIN=30,
         BWIDTH=10,STICK,FAT
```

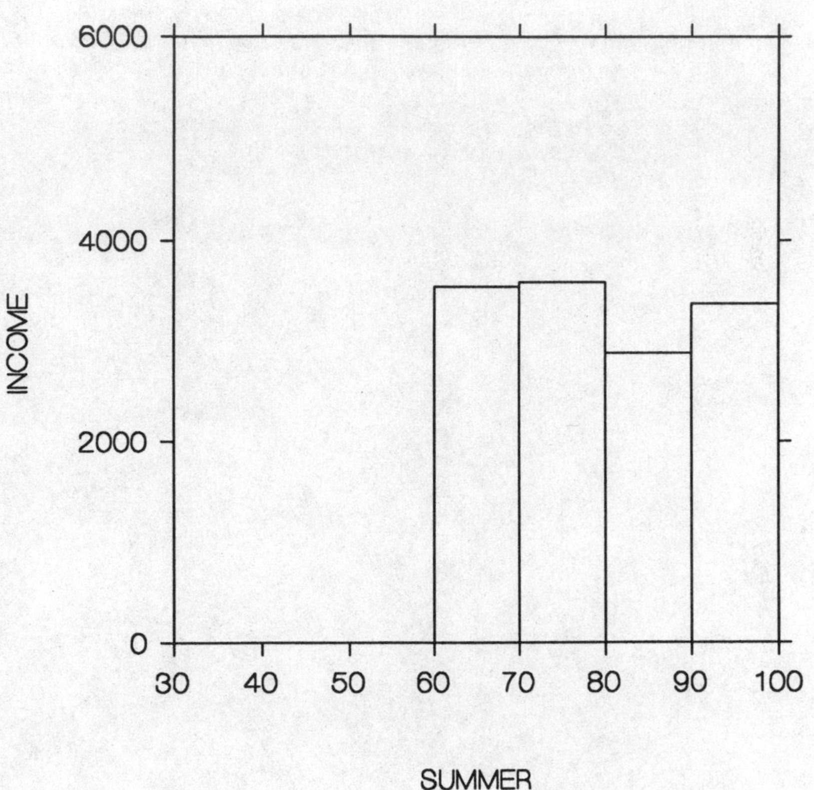

XREV,YREV *(Reversing the Axes)*

You can reverse the horizontal axis with the **XREV** option. In addition, you can reverse the vertical axis and thus make bars hang upside down with the **YREV** option. This may seem odd at first, but in the Advanced Applications section below you can see some applications which make sense. Together with **TRANS** (see below in this chapter), this option can be used to make back-to-back or dual bar graphs.

Figure 32 shows an example of a reversed scale. I have added **YMIN=0** to make the top of the INCOME scale 0. **SNORT** keeps SYGRAPH from sorting the categories.

Figure 32

```
BAR   INCOME*REGION$/YMIN=0,YREV,SNORT
```

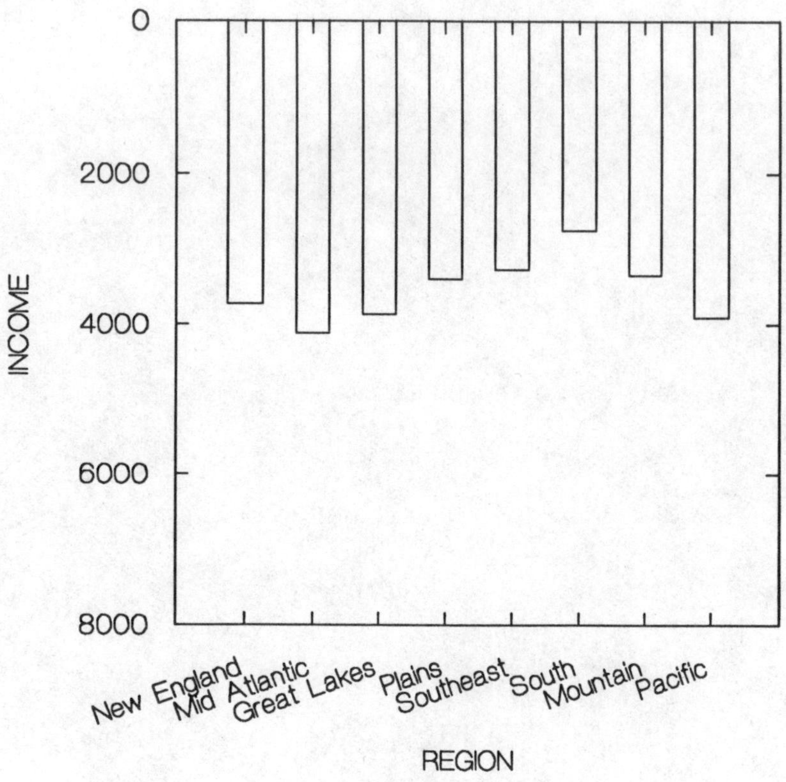

Chapter 3

BOX

Box plots provide a simple graphical summary of a batch of data. Tukey (1977) originally presented these as **schematic plots**. Velleman and Hoaglin (1981) introduced box plots to non-technical users and demonstrated their power for a range of data.

SYGRAPH offers both single and multi-way box plots. Single plots display the distribution of a single variable and multi-way plots show the distribution of a single variable stratified across the levels of a grouping variable. These latter plots can be especially useful for illustrating the results of an experiment or survey data on multiple groups. As in other SYGRAPH procedures, the **BOX** command offers numerous options for scaling and annotating box plots for presentation graphics.

Single Box Plots

The **BOX** command produces a single box plot aligned on a scale. Figure 1 shows this simple example using POPDEN (population density per square mile) from the US dataset. The median of the batch is marked by the center vertical line. The lower and upper hinges comprise the edges of the central box. While the median splits the ordered batch of numbers in half, the hinges split the remaining halves in half again.

To understand the remainder of the box plot, we need some definitions. The **Hspread** is comparable to the interquartile range or midrange. It is the absolute value of the difference between the values of the two hinges.

The **inner fences** are defined as follows:

lower fence = lower hinge - (1.5Hspread)
upper fence = upper hinge + (1.5Hspread)

The **outer fences** are defined as follows:

lower fence = lower hinge - (3Hspread)
upper fence = upper hinge + (3Hspread)

Values outside the inner fences are plotted with asterisks. Values outside the outer fences are plotted with empty circles.

You can use the **MIN** and **MAX** options (see below in this chapter) to control the scale on which the boxes are plotted.

Figure 1

```
BOX  POPDEN
```

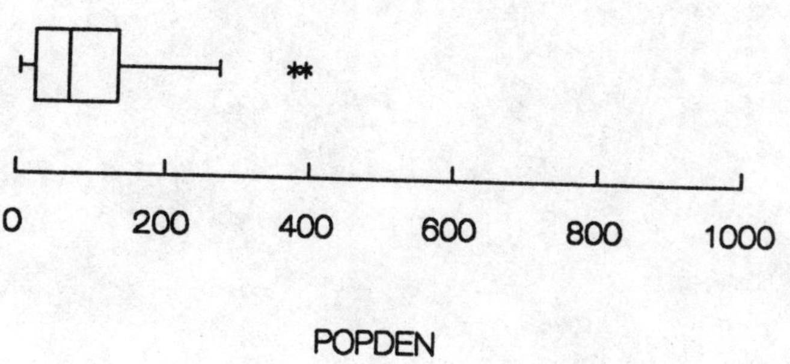

Grouped Box Plots

To plot several box plots against a common scale, we use a syntax resembling the **CPLOT** command (see **CPLOT** chapter). After all, the two-way grouped box plot is itself a category plot. Here is an example:

```
BOX  AGE*GROUP$
```

If you use a numerical grouping variable, only integers will be printed.

Here is an example using INCOME (per-capita income) by census region from the US file (**SNORT** keeps SYGRAPH from sorting the categories).

Figure 2

```
BOX   INCOME*REGION$/SNORT
```

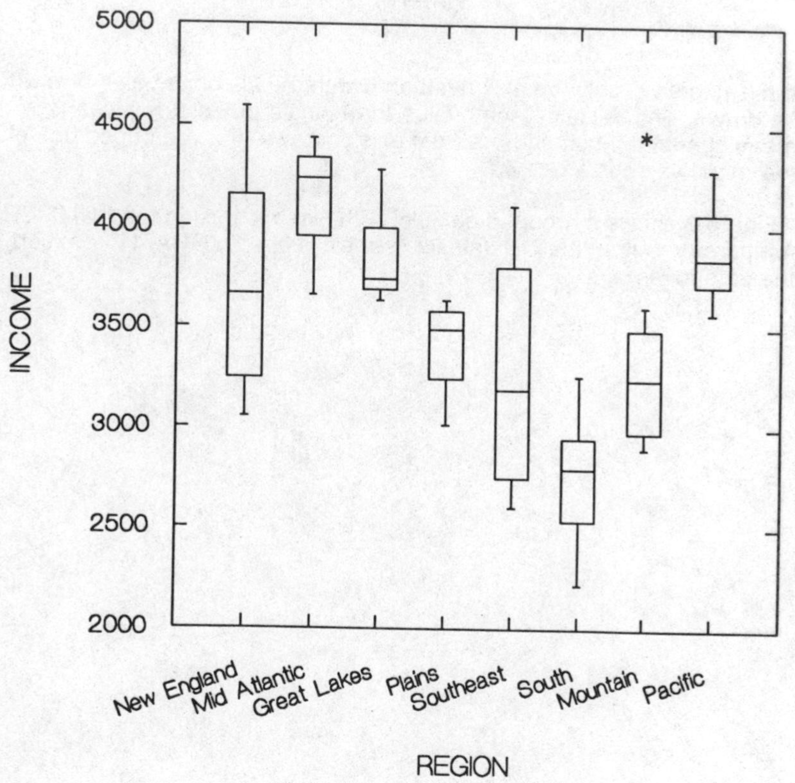

AXES *(Number of Axes)*

The **AXES** option controls the number of axes drawn in a box plot. Its syntax is:

```
AXES=n
```

where *n* is an integer from 0 to 4. If *n* is 0, no axes will be drawn. If *n* is an integer from 1 to 4, all axes from 1 to *n* will be drawn. Axes are numbered from 1 to 4 clockwise, beginning with the bottom axis:

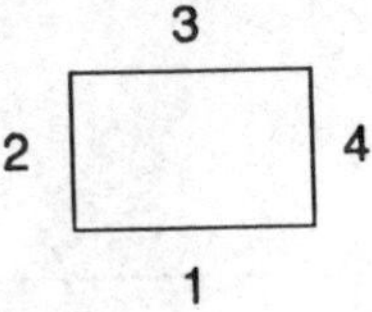

If *n* is negative, only the axis numbered with the absolute value of *n* will be drawn. The default (usual) value for a single box plot is **AXES=1**, meaning that the bottom horizontal axis is drawn. For a grouped box plot, the usual value is **AXES=4**.

Figure 3 shows a grouped box plot with two axes using the SUMMER temperatures from the US dataset (**SNORT** keeps SYGRAPH from sorting the categories).

Figure 3

```
BOX   SUMMER*REGION$/AXES=2,SNORT
```

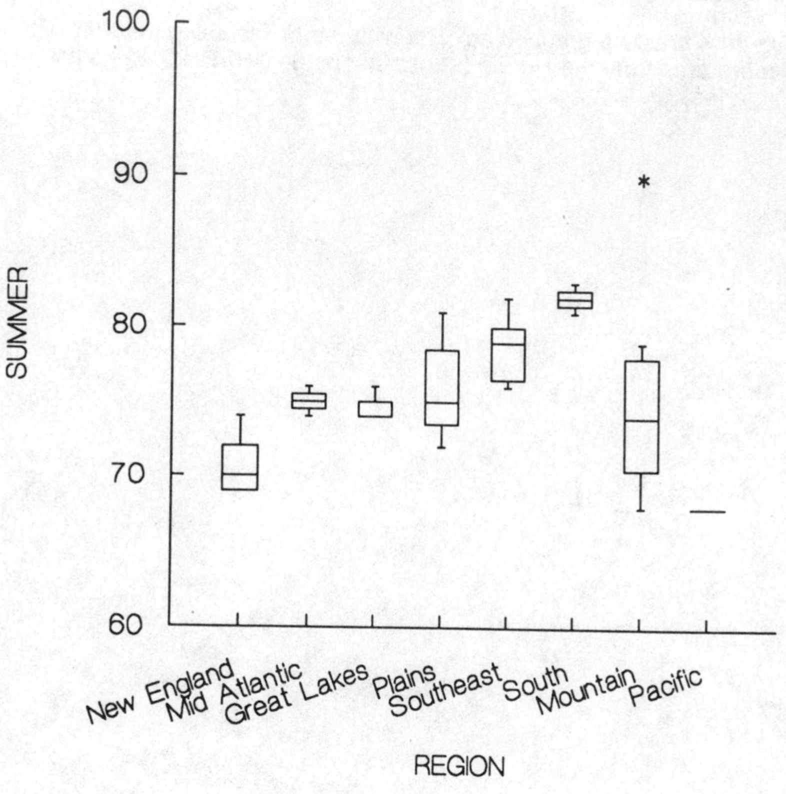

COLOR *(Setting Color of Boxes)*

You can choose a color for your boxes with the **COLOR** option. Choose either a name or a wavelength in nanometers. Possible colors and their approximate nanometer wavelengths are: **RED** (615), **ORANGE** (590), **YELLOW** (575), **GREEN** (505), **BLUE** (480), **VIOLET** (450). You may also name **BLACK**, **WHITE**, **GRAY**, and **BROWN**. The following command will make all boxes in the graph red:

```
BOX  INCOME*REGION$/COLOR=RED
```

You can also specify color in nanometers wavelength. The following example will make all the boxes greenish:

```
BOX  INCOME*REGION$/COLOR=540
```

Figure 4 shows a grouped box plot with red boxes using the WINTER temperatures from the US file (**SNORT** keeps SYGRAPH from sorting the categories).

Figure 4

```
BOX  WINTER*REGION$/COLOR=RED,SNORT
```

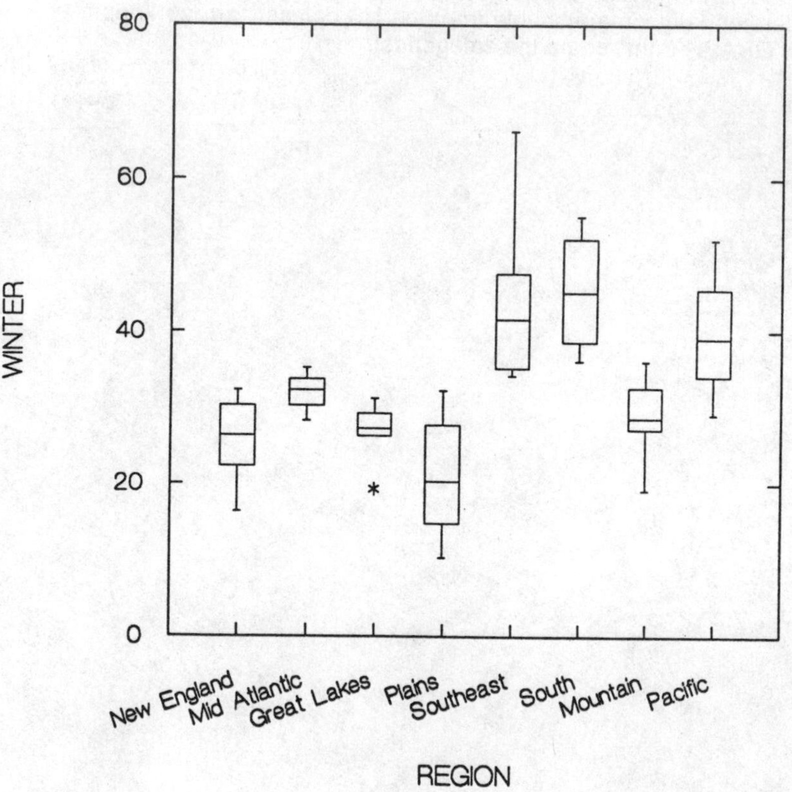

HEIGHT *(Physical Height of Box Plot)*

You can control the physical height of your box plot with the **HEIGHT** option. It works like this:

```
HEIGHT=50%      (or HEIGHT=50)
HEIGHT=4IN
HEIGHT=10CM
```

The first example specifies percent of display height. The second specifies inches, and the third centimeters.

When you use the **HEIGHT** option, you probably also want to use **WIDTH**, which works exactly the same way (see below in this chapter). The following graph shows how to use them together on the INCOME (per-capita income) variable from the US dataset (**SNORT** keeps SYGRAPH from sorting the categories).

Figure 5

```
BOX   INCOME*REGION$/HEIGHT=3IN,WIDTH=4IN,SNORT
```

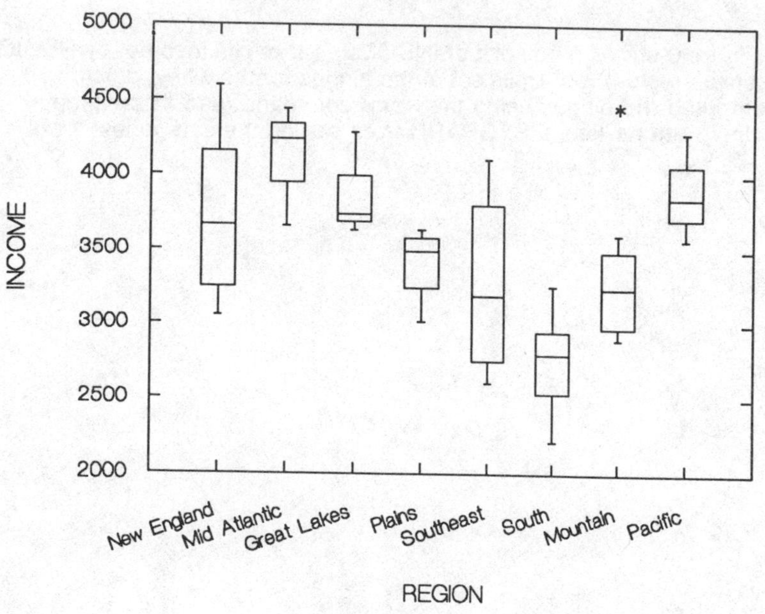

LIMIT *(Control Limits)*

You can add dashed lines to mark limits on the numerical axis of a box plot. **Quality control charts**, for example, mark upper and lower limits on an axis to indicate permissible bounds for a production process. Axis limits can be used in other applications to mark simultaneous standard errors. The **LIMIT** option works this way:

```
BOX X / LIMIT=3,8                          or,
BOX Y*X$ / LIMIT=.43,24.5
```

The first example places limits on a single box plot. You might use this device to overlay standard deviations or a mean on a box plot. The second example places limits on a two-way box plot. It is especially suited to quality control applications.

Limits will not be plotted for numbers outside the extremes of the specified axis. Thus, if you want to plot only one limit (dashed line) on your axis, type something like this:

```
BOX X / LIMIT=2,-9999
```

Figure 6 shows a box plot of INCOME (per-capita income) by REGION$ (census region) with limits set at the hinges for the whole batch. I computed the hinges using the **STEM** command (see **STEM** chapter below). **SNORT** keeps SYGRAPH from sorting the categories.

Figure 6

```
BOX  INCOME*REGION$/LIMIT=3004.5,3793,SNORT
```

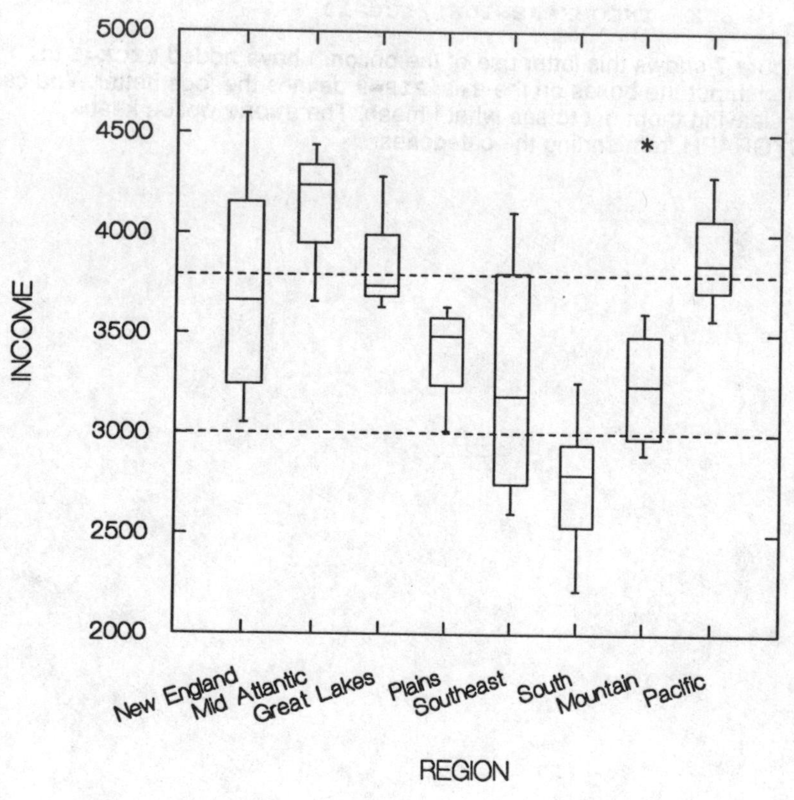

LOG *(Logging Data)*

You can log the scale of your box plot with the **LOG** command. Logs may be computed to any base, e.g. **LOG=2, LOG=3, LOG=10, LOG=.5**. Natural logarithms will be computed if you use **LOG** with no argument, i.e. **LOG**. Only round number log bases (e.g. 0.5, 2, 3,10) will result in round number tick values, however.

LOG works with any form of the **BOX** command. The following command, for example, will log one variable:

```
BOX  INCOME/LOG=10
```

The following logs INCOME in each REGION:

```
BOX  INCOME*REGION$/LOG=10
```

Figure 7 shows this latter use of the option. I have added **TICK=1** to stretch out the boxes on the axis. **PIP=9** defines the logs better. You can try leaving them out to see what I mean. The **SNORT** option keeps SYGRAPH from sorting the categories.

Figure 7

```
BOX   INCOME*REGION$/LOG=10,TICK=1,PIP=9,SNORT
```

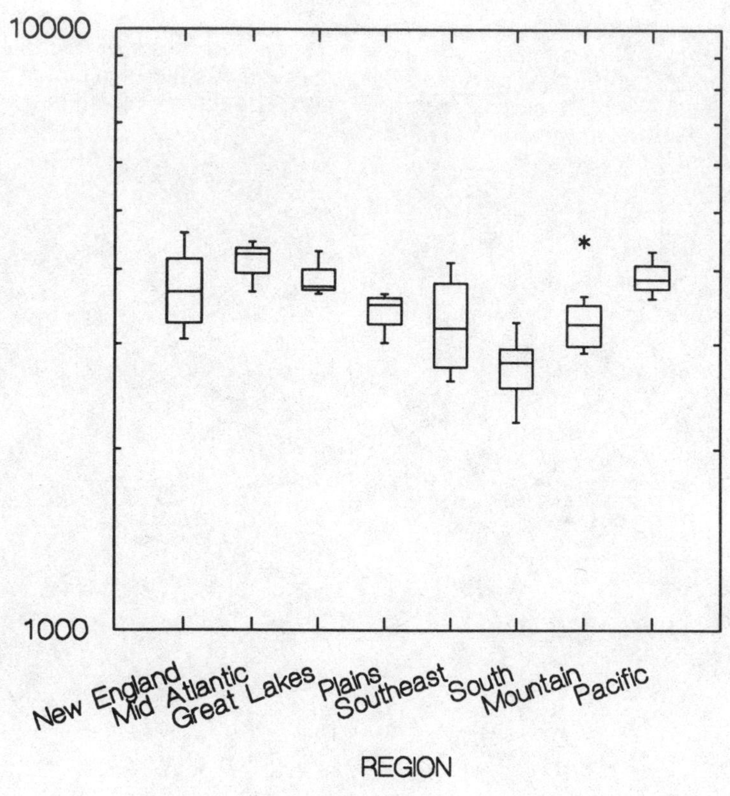

MAX *(Maximum Scale Value)*

You can limit the upper end of your box plot scale with the **MAX** option. Usually, you should use this with the **MIN** option, which regulates the lower end of the scale.

Figure 8 shows both options on the RAIN (annual inches rainfall) variable from the US dataset.

Figure 8

```
BOX   RAIN/MIN=0,MAX=100
```

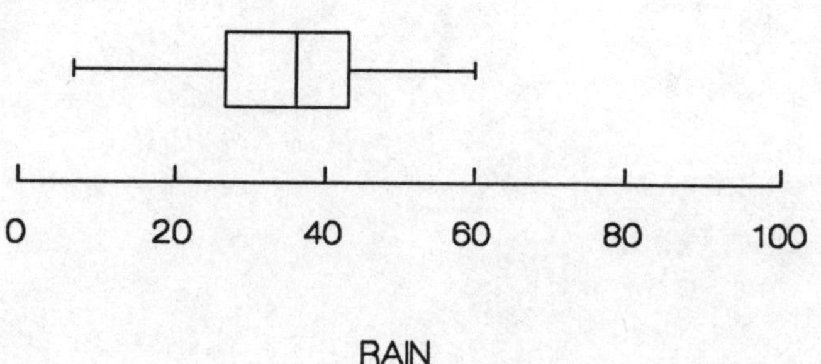

MIN *(Minimum Scale Value)*

You can limit the lower end of your box plot scale with the **MIN** option. Usually, you should use this with the **MAX** option, which regulates the upper end of the scale. This feature is useful for placing a number of different box plots on the same scale when they are not grouped by a common variable.

Figure 9 shows both options on the INCOME (per-capita income) variable from the US dataset.

Figure 9

```
BOX   INCOME/MIN=0,MAX=5000
```

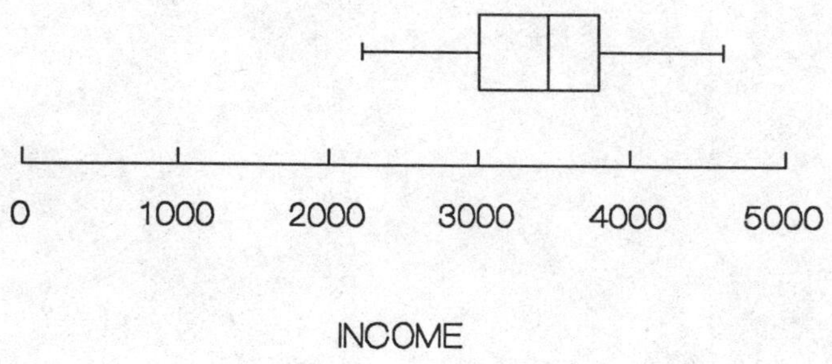

NOTCH *(Notched Box Plots)*

McGill, Tukey, and Larsen (1978) implemented simultaneous confidence intervals on the median of several groups in a box plot. If the intervals around two medians do not overlap, one can be confident at about the 95% level that the two population medians are different. You can do this plot in SYGRAPH by adding the `NOTCH` option.

Figure 10 shows a notched box plot of INCOME (per-capita income) by REGION for the 1970 US dataset. The boxes are notched at the median and return to full width at the lower and upper confidence interval values. Notice that some of the outer confidence limits extend beyond the hinges (the horizontal lines on either side of the narrow median line). This is unaesthetic, but it adheres to Tukey and McGill's original standard for the plot. In SYSTAT, these confidence limits are denoted by parentheses.

The notches are especially handy for judging differences between groups. Note, for example, that the South had a significantly lower income than New England, but not significantly lower than the Mountain states.

Figure 10

```
BOX INCOME*REGION$/NOTCH, SNORT
```

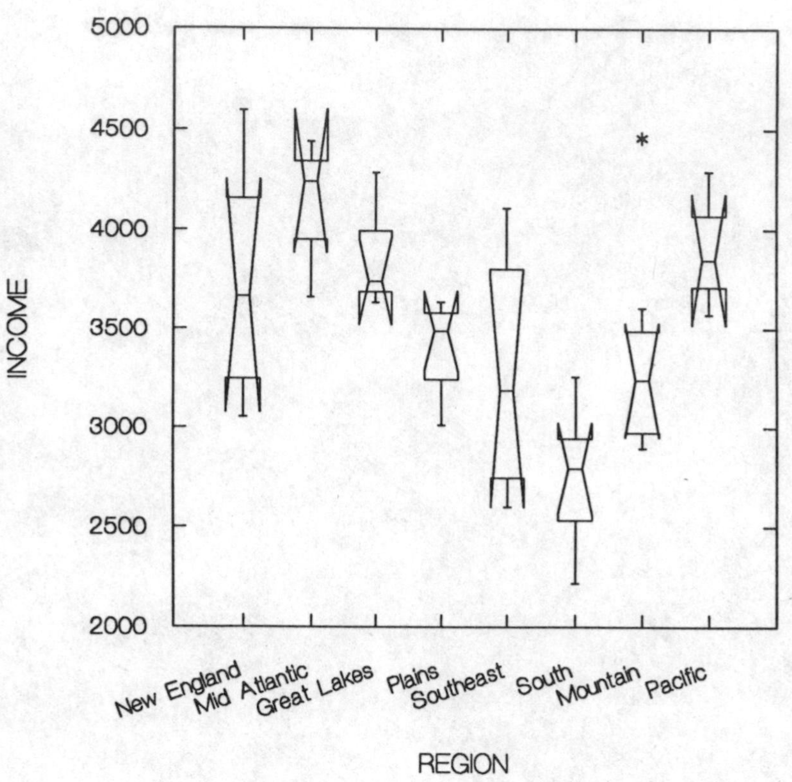

PIP *(Pip Marks)*

Pip marks are half sized tick marks. SYGRAPH normally omits pip marks from box plots. The `PIP` option adds them. Just specify the number you want. Figure 19 shows an example with 10 pip marks. I have transposed the plot for fun.

Figure 11

```
BOX   SUMMER/TRANS,PIP=10
```

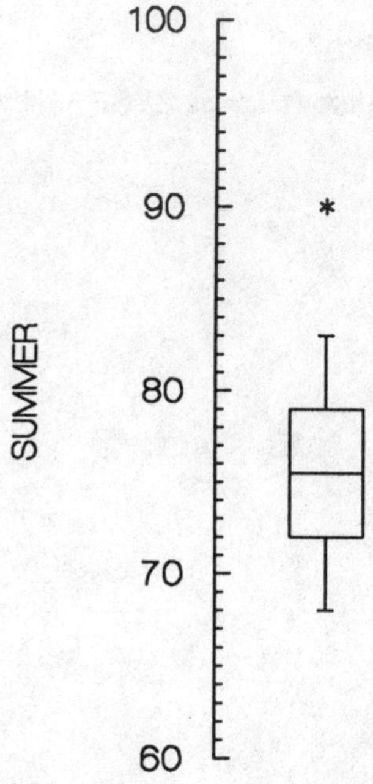

POW *(Powering Data)*

You can power the scale of your box plot with the **POW** command. Powers may be computed to any exponent, e.g. **POW=.5** (square root), **POW=.33333** (cube root), **POW=-1** (inverse), **POW=2**. Square roots will be computed if you use **POW** with no argument, i.e. **POW**. Some exponents (e.g. 3) will produce non-integer tick marks. **POW** is implemented in SYGRAPH only for positive data. Negative values will be deleted.

POW works with any form of the **BOX** command. The following command, for example, will transform a single box plot:

```
BOX  INCOME/POW=.5
```

The following transforms INCOME for all regions.

```
BOX  INCOME*REGION$/POW=.5
```

Figure 12 shows the latter example (**SNORT** keeps SYGRAPH from sorting the categories).

Figure 12

```
BOX   INCOME*REGION$/POW=.5,SNORT
```

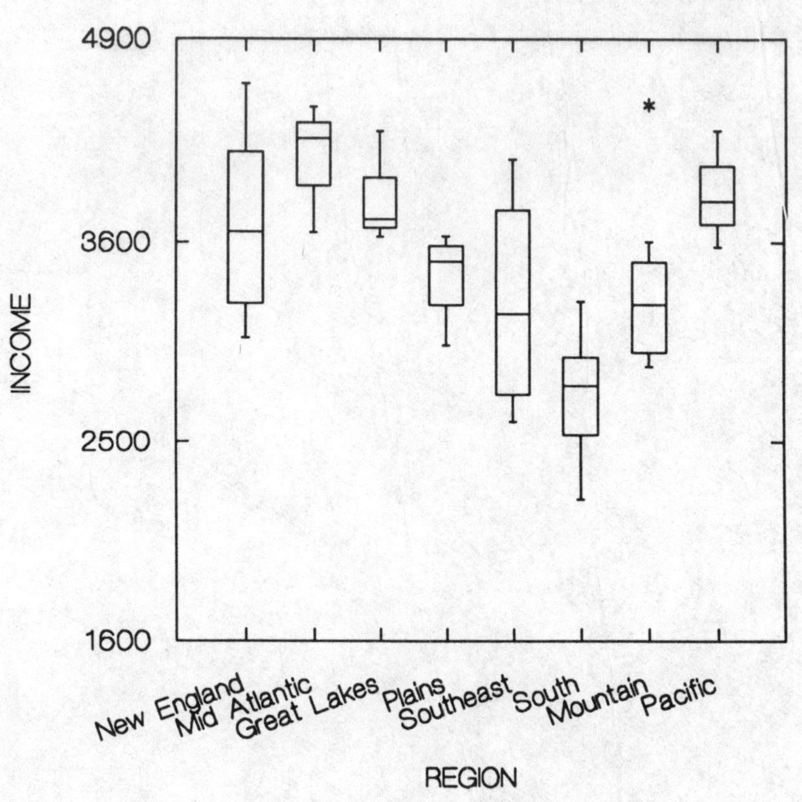

REV *(Reversing the Axis)*

You can reverse the box plot axis with the **REV** option. For a single box plot, this reverses the scale. For a grouped box plot, this reverses the vertical scale. Together with the **TRANS** option (see below in this chapter), you can use **REV** to construct side by side box and grouped box plots.

Figure 13 shows an example of a reversed scale (**SNORT** keeps SYGRAPH from sorting the categories).

Figure 13

```
BOX  INCOME*REGION$/REV,SNORT
```

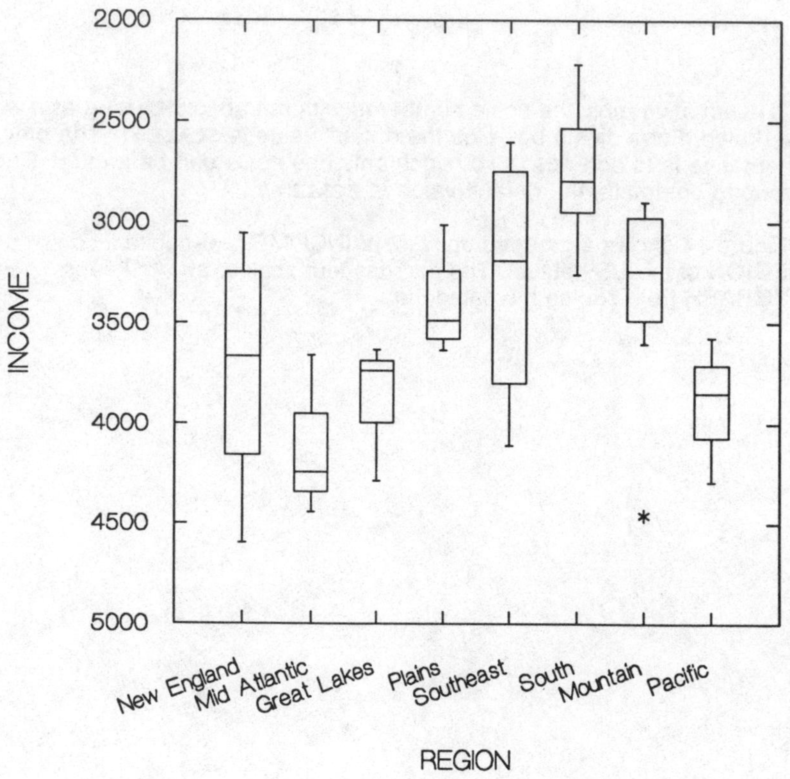

SCALE *(Number of Scales)*

Scales are the numbers which label the tick marks on an axis. The **SCALE** option controls the number of scales drawn in a box plot. Its syntax is:

```
SCALE=n
```

where *n* is an integer from 0 to 4. If *n* is 0, no scales will be drawn. If *n* is an integer from 1 to 4, all scales from 1 to *n* will be drawn. Scales are numbered from 1 to 4 clockwise, beginning with the bottom axis:

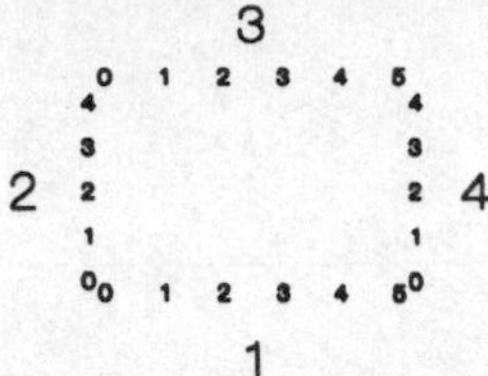

If *n* is negative, only the scale numbered with the absolute value of *n* will be drawn. For a single box plot, the default value is **SCALE=1**. The only alternative is to add **SCALE=0**, since only one scale can be printed. For grouped box plots, the default value is **SCALE=2**.

Figure 14 shows a grouped box plot of INCOME (per-capita income) by REGION of the US dataset. The plot has four scales. **SNORT** keeps SYGRAPH from sorting the categories.

Figure 14

```
BOX   INCOME*REGION$/SCALE=4,SNORT
```

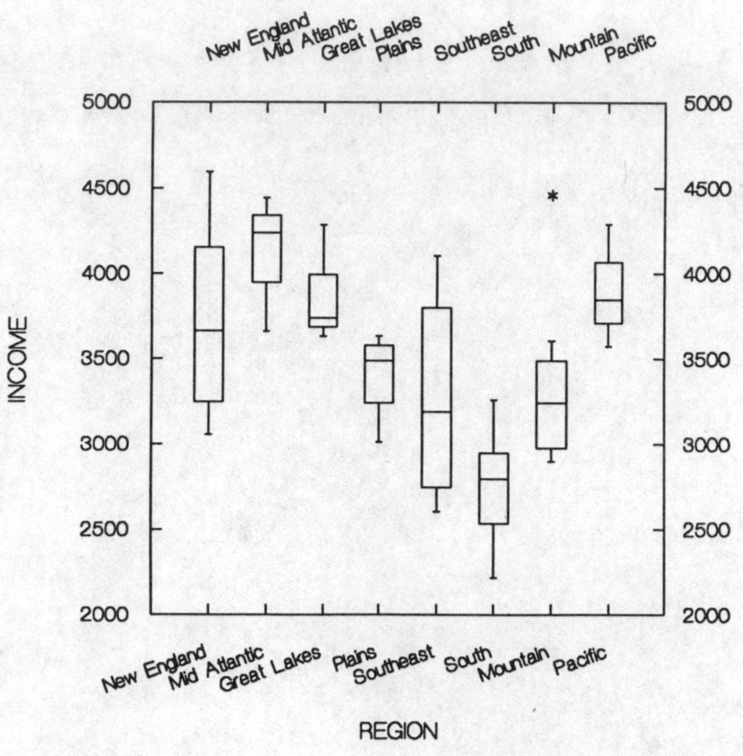

SORT/SNORT *(Sorting Categories)*

SYGRAPH automatically sorts the levels (categories) of categorical variables in ascending numeric or character order. If you want the categories arranged according to the order they appear in your data file, use the **SNORT** option. Figure 15 shows an example using the SORT option. Compare the bottom scale with that in other figures in this chapter to see how **SORT** and **SNORT** work.

Figure 15

```
BOX   INCOME*REGION$/SORT
```

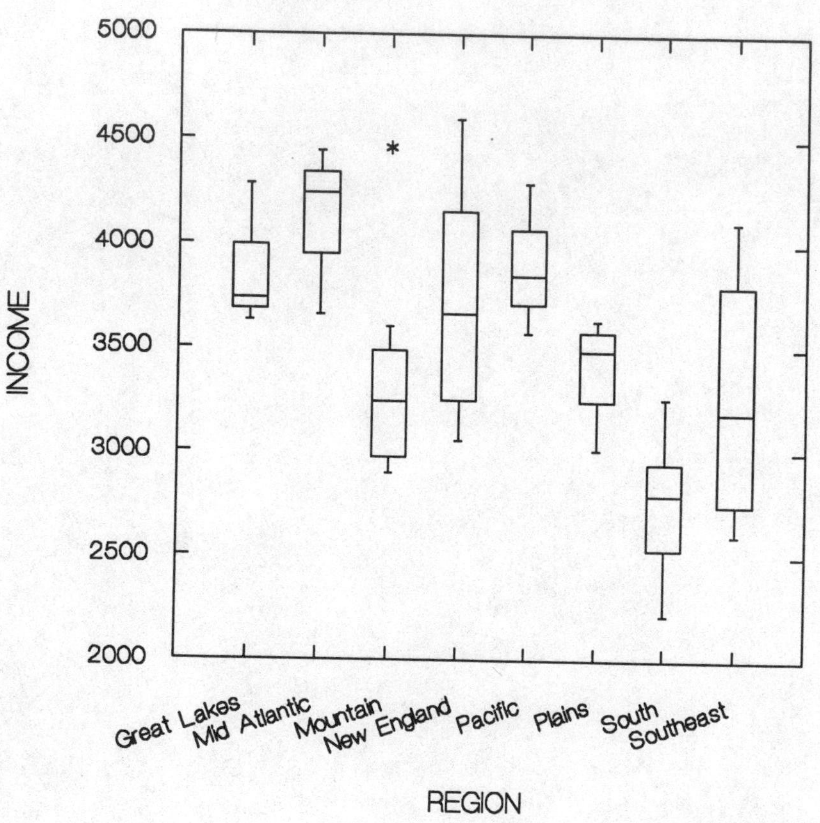

STICK *(Tick Marks Outside Frame)*

SYGRAPH normally places tick marks inside the frame. If you wish tick marks outside the frame, use the **STICK** option.

Figure 16 shows an example of a box plot with tick marks outside the frame using the RAIN variable (annual rainfall from the US file). **SNORT** keeps SYGRAPH from sorting the categories.

Figure 16

```
BOX   RAIN*REGION$/STICK,SNORT
```

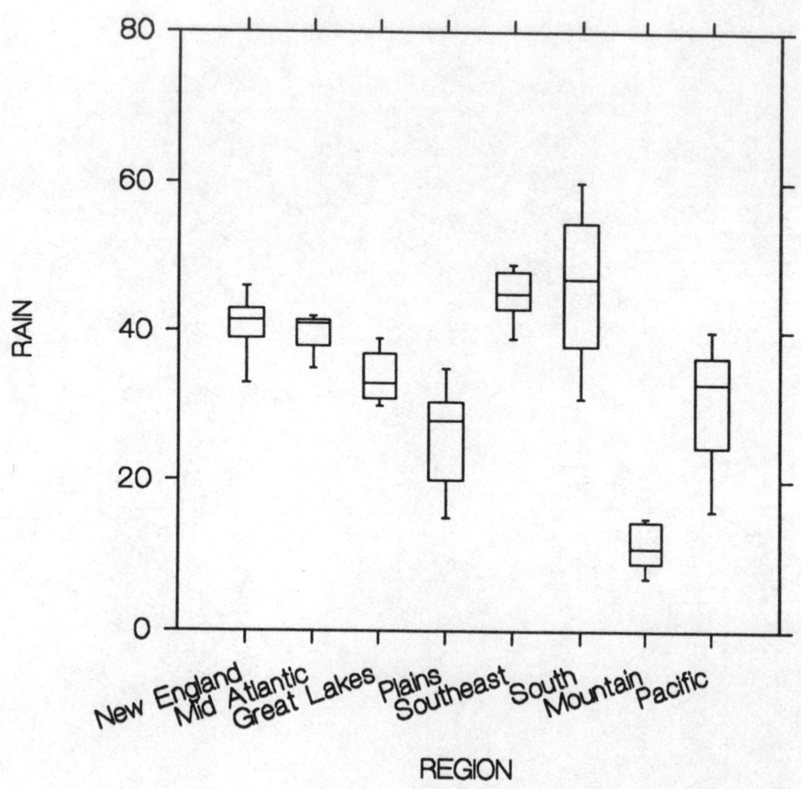

TICK *(Number of Tick Marks)*

SYGRAPH examines your data to determine how many tick marks to use on the axis of a box plot. If you wish to modify this value, use the `TICK` option with a number. For example, `TICK=8` will force the axis to have 8 tick marks. SYGRAPH will attempt to find minimum and maximum values for the scale such that the tick mark numbers are round. If it fails, you can control the values with the `MIN` and `MAX` options as well (see above in this chapter).

Figure 17 shows an example of a box plot with 6 tick marks. Notice that SYGRAPH automatically adjusts the size of the scale values when there are more tick marks. `SNORT` keeps SYGRAPH from sorting the categories.

Figure 17

```
BOX   INCOME*REGION$/TICK=6,SNORT
```

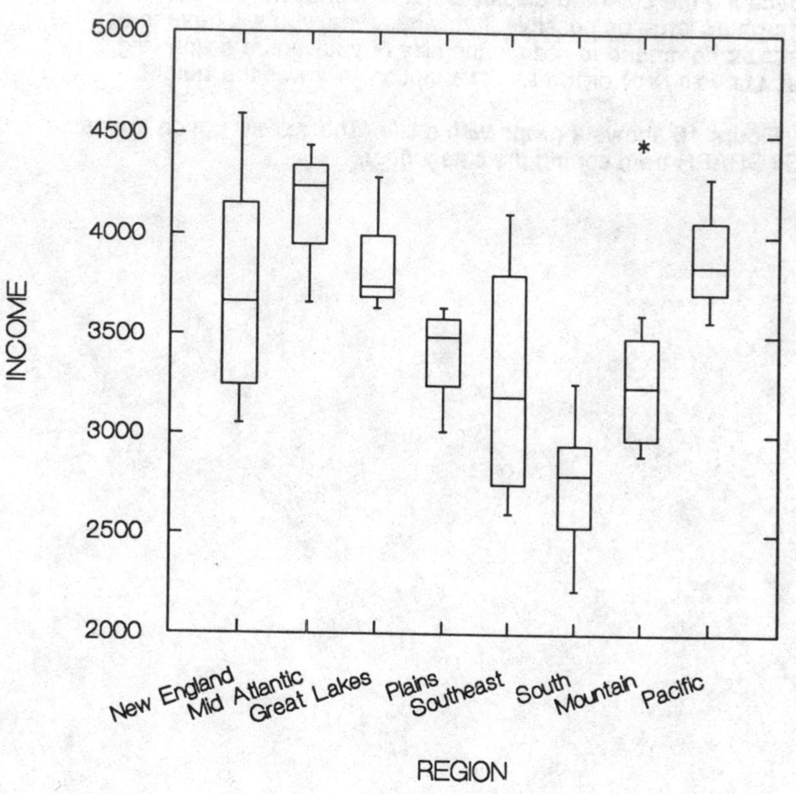

TITLE *(Graph Title)*

You can place a title at the top center of your graph with the **TITLE** option:

```
TITLE='Worldwide  Sales  in  U.S.  Dollars'
TITLE="Roger's  Fraudulent  Experiment"
TITLE='Perceived  variation  in  "Impact"'
```

The text must be surrounded by quotes (") or apostrophes ('). If your text includes apostrophes, as in the second example, surround it with quotes. If it includes quotes, as in the third example, surround it with apostrophes.

On some display devices the title will run off the top of the page because the standard display window is chosen to make the labels and graph as large as possible. If this happens, you will have to use the **SCALE** command to reduce the size of your entire graph (e.g. **SCALE=70,70**) or the **HEIGHT** option to lower the height.

Figure 18 shows a graph with a title (The **SNORT** option keeps SYGRAPH from sorting the categories).

Figure 18

```
TYPE=BRITISH/ITALIC
BOX  INCOME*REGION$,
   /SNORT,TITLE='Income  within  Region'
```

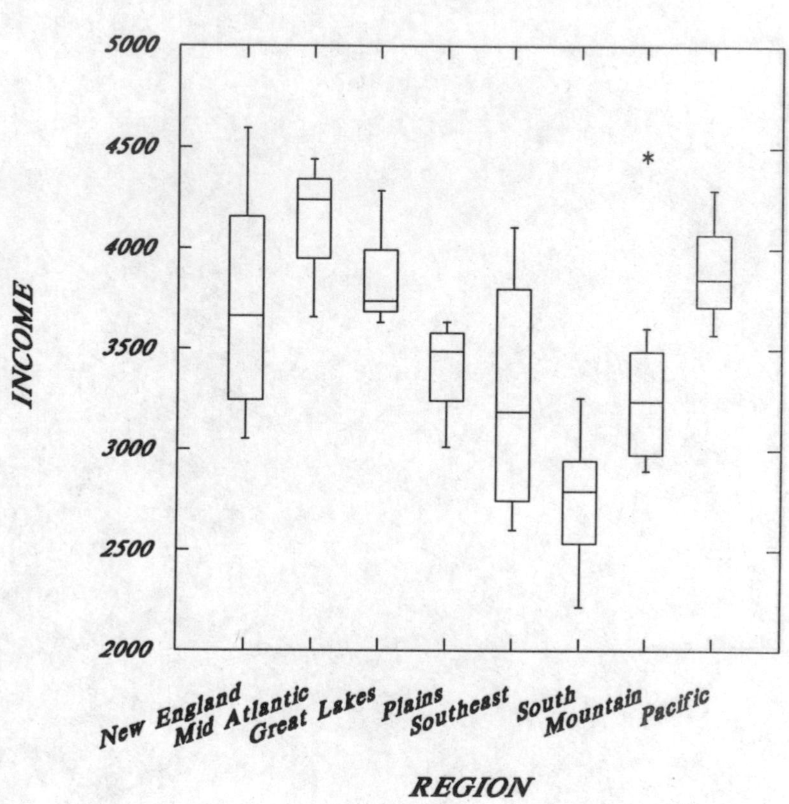

TRANS *(Transposing a Box Plot)*
You can transpose your entire box plot, labels and all. To do this, just add the option **TRANS** to the **BOX** command.

TRANS affects everything in a graph. **XLABEL** becomes **YLABEL**, **XTICK** becomes **YTICK**, and so on. In other words, specify a graph as you would ordinarily and then add the **TRANS** option. Everything will be transposed appropriately, including the labels and scales.

Figure 19 shows an example of a transposed box plot (**SNORT** keeps SYGRAPH from sorting the categories).

Figure 19

`BOX INCOME*REGION$/TRANS,SNORT`

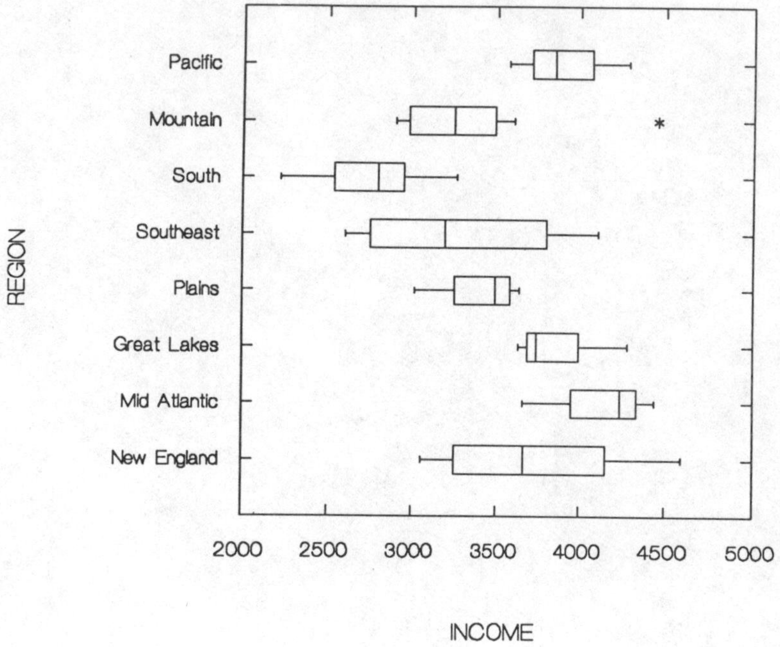

WIDTH *(Physical Width of Plot)*

You can control the physical width of your box plot with the `WIDTH` option. It works like this:

```
WIDTH=50%        (or WIDTH=50 )
WIDTH=4IN
WIDTH=10CM
```

The first example specifies percent of display width. The second specifies inches, and the third centimeters.

When you use the `WIDTH` option, you probably also want to use `HEIGHT`, which works exactly the same way (see above in this chapter). The following graph shows how to use them together (`SNORT` keeps SYGRAPH from sorting the categories).

Figure 20

```
BOX   INCOME*REGION$/HEIGHT=3IN,WIDTH=4IN,SNORT
```

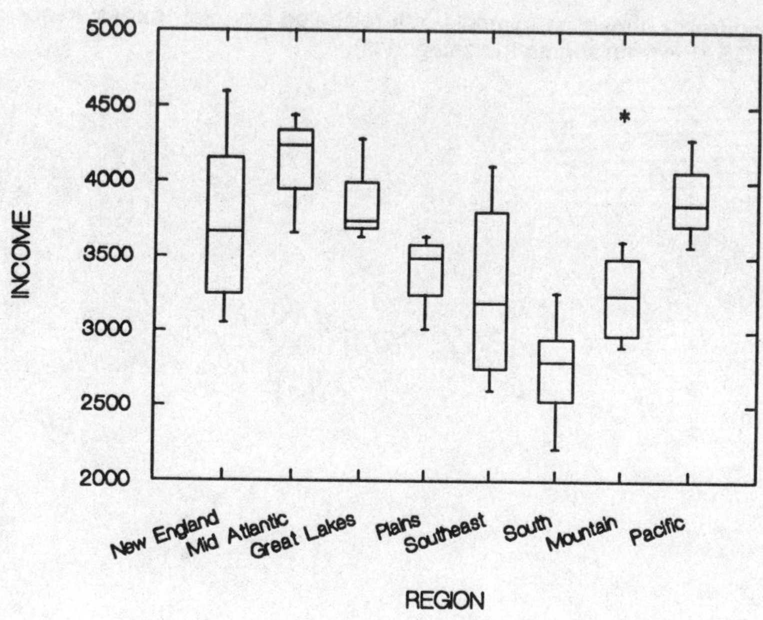

XLABEL,YLABEL *(Labeling a Box Plot)*

Box plots are usually labeled with the names of the variables you use in the **BOX** command. If you want different labels, use the **XLABEL** and/or **YLABEL** command, e.g.:

```
XLABEL='Group'
YLABEL='Per  Capita  Income'
XLABEL="Roger's  Groups"
XLABEL='Type  of  "Widgets"  Bid'
YLABEL='  '
```

The label text must be surrounded by quotes (") or apostrophes ('). If your text includes apostrophes, as in the third example, surround it with quotes. If it includes quotes, as in the fourth example, surround it with apostrophes. The last example shows how to remove labels from your graph. Just assign a blank (' ') to your label.

Grouped box plots have both X and Y labels. Single box plots, of course, have only an X label.

Figure 21 shows an example of a relabeled box plot (**SNORT** keeps SYGRAPH from sorting the categories).

Figure 21

```
BOX INCOME*REGION$/SNORT,
   YLABEL='1970 Per Capita Income',
   XLABEL='Region of U.S.'
```

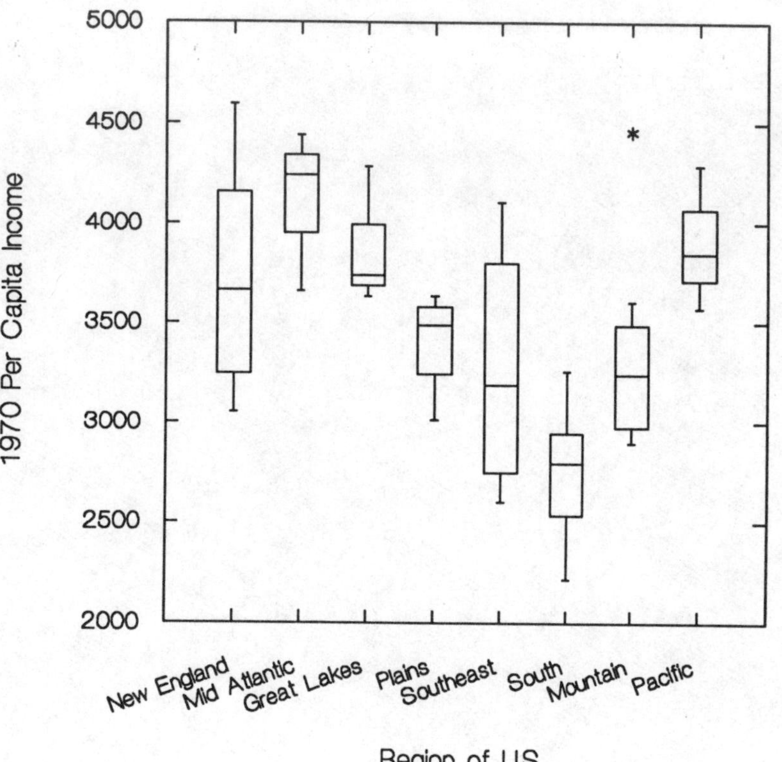

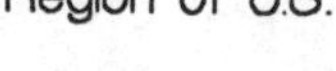

Chapter 4

CPLOT

The **CPLOT** (CATEGORICAL **PLOT**) command plots continuous against categorical variables. Many of the displays look like those produced by the **PLOT** command, which plots continuous against continuous variables. **CPLOT** is, in fact, more similar to the **BAR** command. A simple categorical plot will tally the counts of the different categories of a variable. A multi-way categorical plot computes and plots the averages of one or more continuous variables within the categories of a categorical variable.

Simple Categorical Plot

The **CPLOT** command will produce a two-way plot of counts in categories by a simple command. To tally counts of states in each Census region from the US file, for example, just type:

```
CPLOT  REGION$
```

SYGRAPH will read the file and tally duplicate values. The printed graph will show the counts of cases in the file.

If you have already tallied a variable, you can produce a category plot directly from the counts. Suppose your file looks like the following. Instead of 48 cases with duplicates, you have only 8 cases with a COUNT variable indicating duplicates.

REGION$	COUNT
New England	6
Mid Atlantic	3
Great Lakes	5
Plains	7
Southeast	8
South	8
Mountain	8
Pacific	3

To produce the same category plot, you can type:

```
WEIGHT=COUNT
CPLOT  REGION$
```

The categorical variable can be either character or numeric, with SYGRAPH displaying the corresponding categories as character strings or numbers, respectively. To produce a category plot of a continuous variable, use the BWIDTH option (see below).

Notice that SYGRAPH prints the labels for the categories at a slant. If there is not enough room to print the labels horizontally, SYGRAPH will automatically make this adjustment. Furthermore, if there are more than 10 categories on the horizontal axis, SYGRAPH will shrink the size of the lettering to fit the labels on the scale. You can do a category plot on up to 200 categories, but you will need an ultra high resolution device to display clearly the labels for that many categories.

You may notice that a bar graph of the data in Figure 1 might be preferable. The syntax and use of the **BAR** and **CPLOT** commands is identical because both are for plotting continuous against categorical data. In general, you should use the **BAR** command when the origin of the vertical scale is zero and **CPLOT** when the origin is arbitrary. In plain terms, bars are like houses. They should have a good foundation at ground zero (as in this example). Do not build your house on sand.

Figure 1

CPLOT REGION$

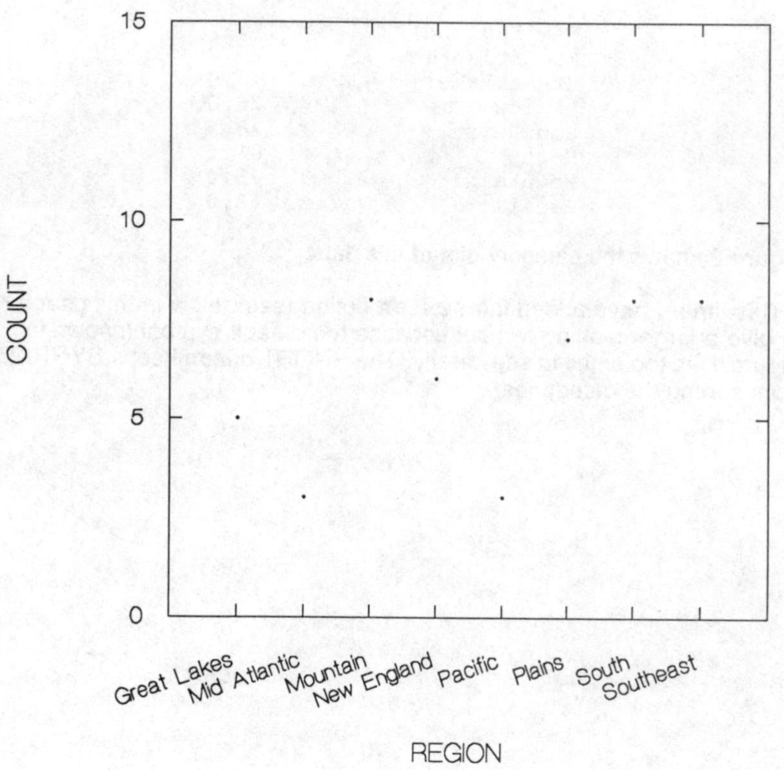

Two-way Category Plots

If you wish to produce a category plot of a continuous variable against categories, use the **CPLOT** command with two arguments, e.g.:

```
CPLOT   INCOME*REGION$
```

If you have more than one data value for a category, SYGRAPH calculates and plots the mean of that category.

From the above command, SYGRAPH computes and plots the following average summer temperatures in 1970 for each region in the US dataset.

REGION$	SUMMER
New England	70.7
Mid Atlantic	75.0
Great Lakes	73.8
Plains	76.0
Southeast	78.6
South	81.6
Mountain	75.4
Pacific	68.0

Figure 2 shows the category plot of this data.

This time, I have added the **SYMBOL** option (see below in this chapter) to give a larger plotting symbol because the default symbol (shown in Figure 1) is too small to see clearly. The SNORT option keeps SYGRAPH from sorting the categories.

Figure 2

```
CPLOT   SUMMER*REGION/SYMBOL=2,SNORT
```

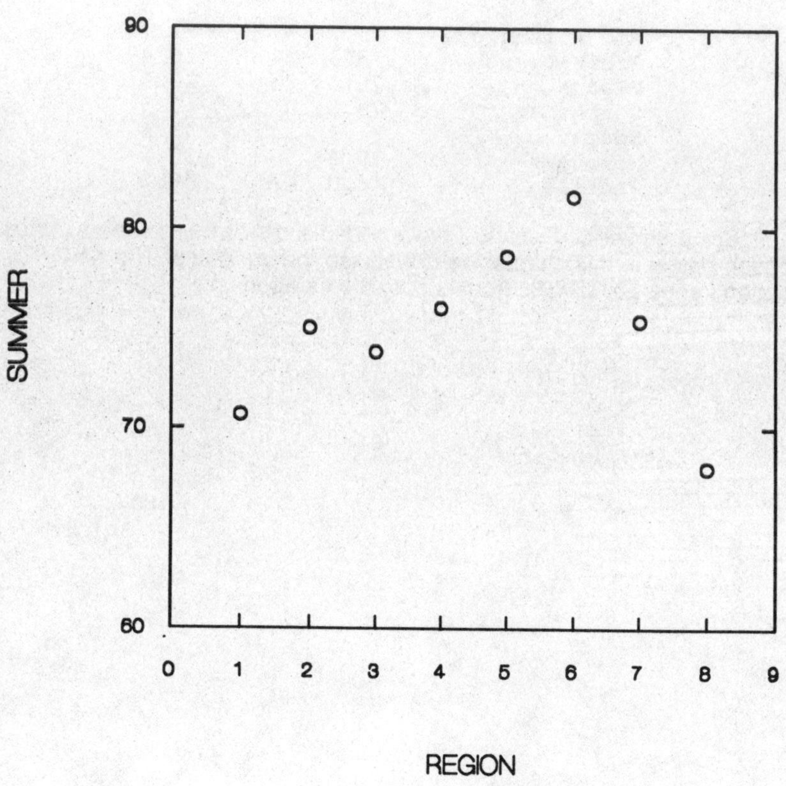

Multi-Valued Category Plots

You can plot up to 12 continuous variables against a categorical variable. We can produce a multi-valued chart with the following command:

```
CPLOT   SUMMER,WINTER*REGION$
```

Each variable on the left is placed on a common vertical scale against the categories on the horizontal scale. In this example, SYGRAPH computes and plots the following average summer and winter temperatures for each region in the US dataset in 1970.

REGION$	SUMMER	WINTER
New England	70.7	25.3
Mid Atlantic	75.0	31.7
Great Lakes	73.8	26.4
Plains	76.0	20.9
Southeast	78.6	43.5
South	81.6	45.3
Mountain	75.4	30.6
Pacific	68.0	40.0

Figure 3 shows the result. I have added **SYMBOL=2,3** (see **SYMBOL** option below in this chapter) to distinguish the variables. The SNORT option keeps SYGRAPH from sorting the categories.

Figure 3

```
CPLOT   SUMMER,WINTER*REGION$/SYMBOL=2,3,SNORT
```

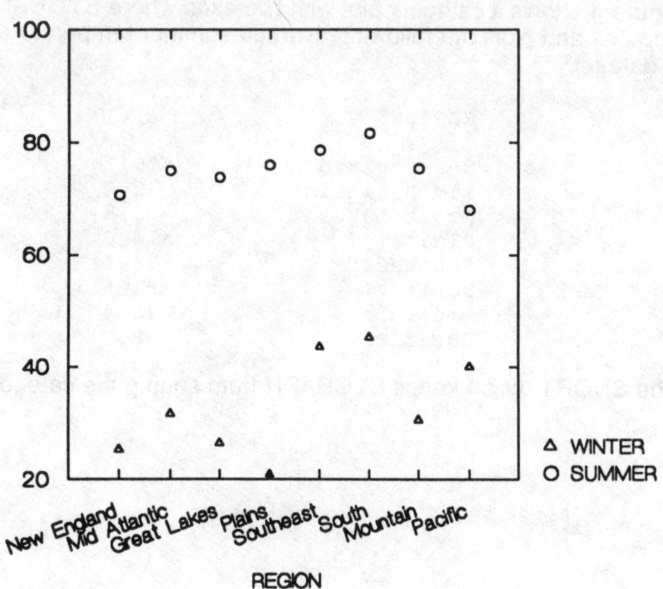

AXES *(Number of Axes)*

The **AXES** option controls the number of axes drawn in a category plot. Its syntax is:

```
AXES=n
```

where *n* is an integer from 0 to 4. If *n* is 0, no axes will be drawn. If *n* is an integer from 1 to 4, all axes from 1 to *n* will be drawn. Axes are numbered from 1 to 4 clockwise, beginning with the bottom axis:

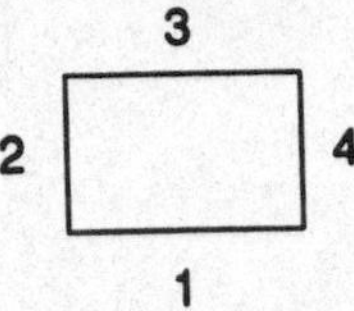

If *n* is negative, only the axis numbered with the absolute value of *n* will be drawn. The default (usual) value for **AXES** is 4.

Figure 4 shows a category plot with two axes where SYGRAPH computes and plots the following average summer temperatures from the US dataset.

REGION$	SUMMER
New England	70.7
Mid Atlantic	75.0
Great Lakes	73.8
Plains	76.0
Southeast	78.6
South	81.6
Mountain	75.4
Pacific	68.0

The SNORT option keeps SYGRAPH from sorting the categories.

Figure 4

```
CPLOT   SUMMER*REGION$/AXES=2,SYMBOL=2,FILL=1,SNORT
```

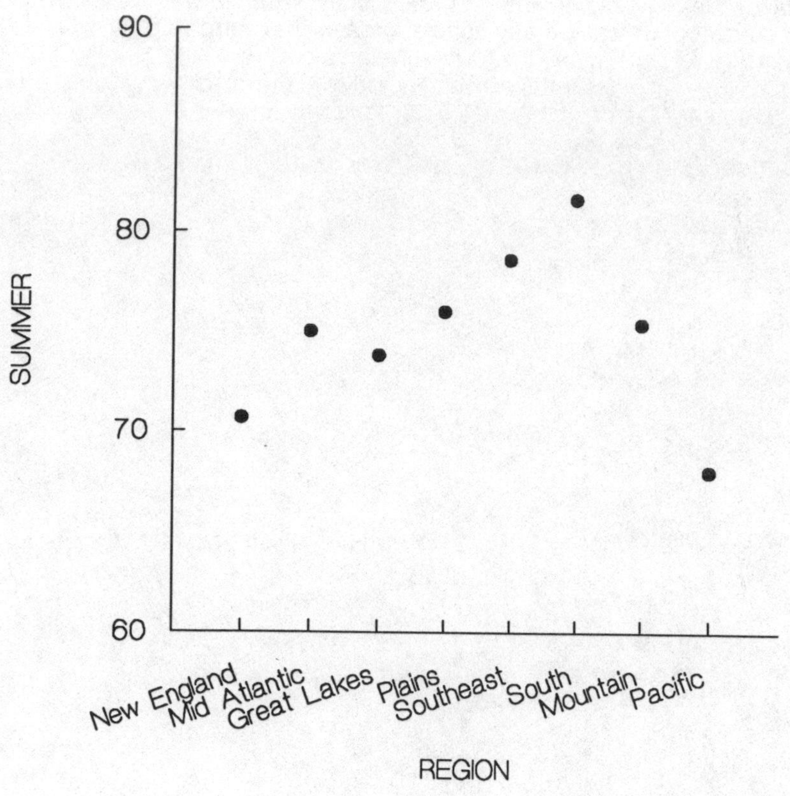

BWIDTH *(Cutpoints for Numerical Data)*

If you want to plot a category plot on a continuous variable (like INCOME), you can use the **BWIDTH** option to break the variable at evenly spaced cutpoints. In this case, the **CPLOT** command will not plot a single symbol for each separate data value. Instead, the data on the continuous variable will be binned into separate categories defined by cutpoints on the continuous variable. This works for simple and two-way category plots. For example, the following command collects the 48 states in the US dataset into temperature groups at each 10 degree increment:

```
CPLOT   SUMMER/XMIN=0,BWIDTH=10
```

You must specify the minimum value for the categories (**XMIN=0** in this case). See the **XMIN** option in this chapter for further information. The **BWIDTH** option can be any number greater than zero (e.g. **BWIDTH=3.5**). Figure 5 shows an example.

Figure 5

```
CPLOT   SUMMER/XMIN=0,BWIDTH=10,SYMBOL=2,FILL=1
```

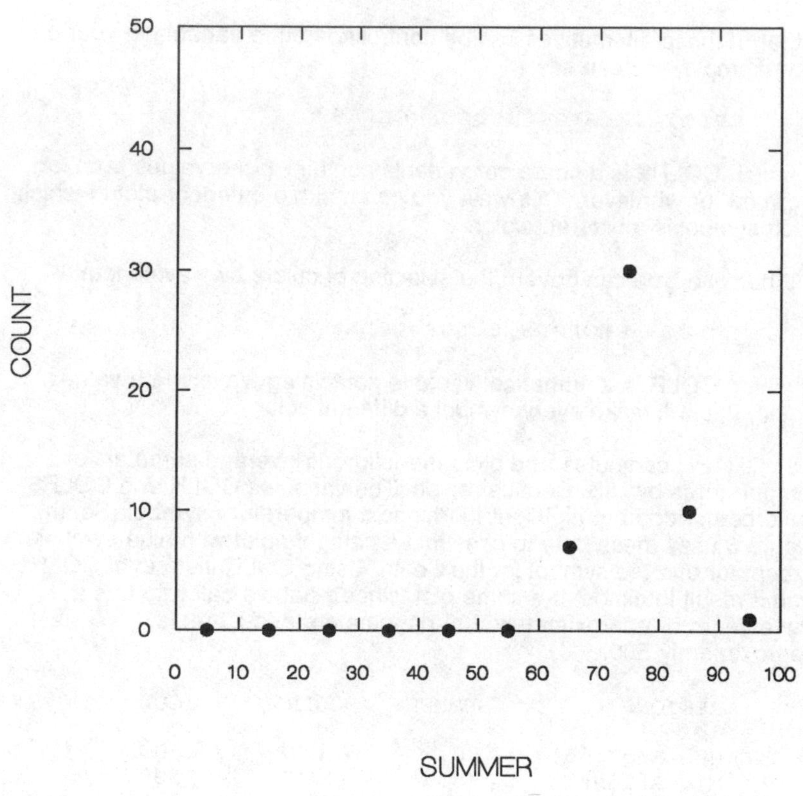

COLOR *(Setting Color of Symbols)*

You can choose a color for your symbols with the **COLOR** option. Choose either a name or a wavelength in nanometers. Possible colors and their approximate nanometer wavelengths are: **RED** (615), **ORANGE** (590), **YELLOW** (575), **GREEN** (505), **BLUE** (480), **VIOLET** (450). You may also name **BLACK**, **WHITE**, **GRAY**, and **BROWN**. The following command will make all symbols in the graph red:

```
CPLOT   REGION$/COLOR=RED
```

You can also specify color in nanometers wavelength. The following example will make all the symbols greenish:

```
CPLOT   REGION$/COLOR=540
```

Either of these alternatives can be controlled from a variable in your data. For example, you can say:

```
CPLOT   REGION$/COLOR=COLR$
```

in which COLR$ is a character variable containing the values '**RED**' or '**YELLOW**' or whatever. This way, you can make a category plot in which each symbol is a different color.

Otherwise, you can govern the selection of colors by wavelength:

```
CPLOT   REGION$/COLOR=COLR
```

in which COLR is a numerical variable containing wavelength values. Again, this will make every symbol a different color.

SYGRAPH computes and plots the following average summer temperatures by U.S. Census region. The variables COLR and COLR$ have been added to highlight the highest temperature symbol (South). Figure 6 uses these data to construct a category plot with blue symbols, except for one red symbol for the South. Using COLR instead of COLR$ would result in almost the same plot, since what we call **RED** has a wavelength of approximately 600 nanometers and **BLUE** is approximately 500.

REGION$	SUMMER	COLR$	COLR
New England	70.7	BLUE	500
Mid Atlantic	75.0	BLUE	500
Great Lakes	73.8	BLUE	500
Plains	76.0	BLUE	500
Southeast	78.6	BLUE	500
South	81.6	RED	600
Mountain	75.4	BLUE	500
Pacific	68.0	BLUE	500

Figure 6

```
CPLOT   SUMMER*REGION$,
  /COLOR=COLR$,SYMBOL=2,
   FILL=1,YLABEL='Average  Temperatures'
```

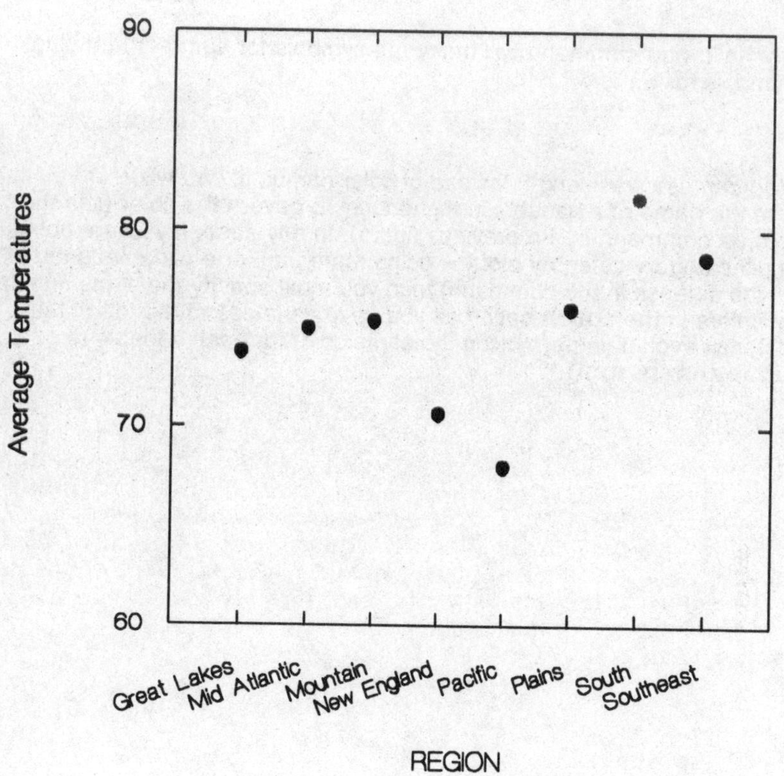

COLOR *(Multi-colored category plots)*

You can make category plots with a different color for each dependent variable. SYGRAPH computes and plots these average summer and winter temperatures for the given regions:

REGION$	SUMMER	WINTER
New England	70.7	25.3
Mid Atlantic	75.0	31.7
Great Lakes	73.8	26.4
Plains	76.0	20.9
Southeast	78.6	43.5
South	81.6	45.3
Mountain	75.4	30.6
Pacific	68.0	40.0

The following command will make red symbols for summer and blue symbols for winter:

```
CPLOT   SUMMER,WINTER*REGION$/COLOR=RED,BLUE
```

You can use wavelength instead of color names, if you wish, or you can use the name of a variable in the dataset to govern the color (see the **COLOR** command in the previous figure). In any case, if you are doing a multi-category category plot (by using more than one variable to the left of the asterisk in the command) then you must specify the same number of colors in the **COLOR** option as you have variables to the left of the asterisk even if you are using the same color for each variable (e.g. **COLOR=RED,RED**).

Figure 7

```
CPLOT   SUMMER,WINTER*REGION$,
      /COLOR=RED,BLUE,SYMBOL=2,2,FILL=1,1
```

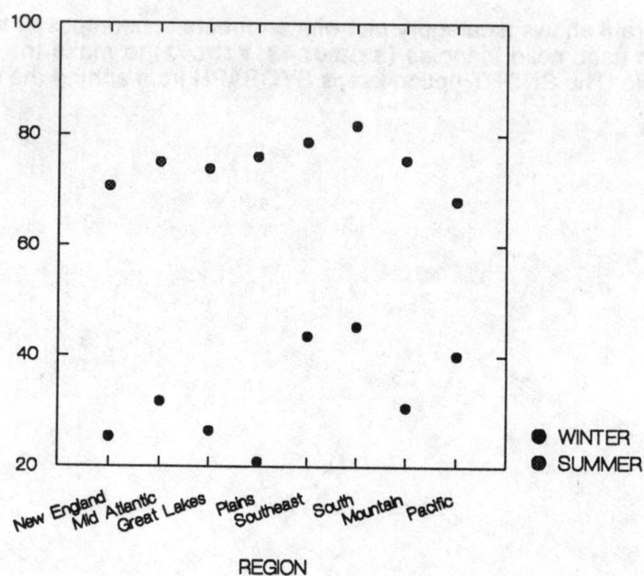

ERROR/ERROR1 *(Symmetric and One-Sided Error Bars)*

You can use an additional variable to represent errors in a category plot. The **ERROR** option works just as it does with the **BAR** and **PLOT** commands. It draws symmetric error bars above and below each symbol. The variable used for the error bars should have a value equal to one half the length of each error bar it specifies.

You can draw one-sided error bars with the ERROR1 option. If the variable you assign to ERROR1 is positive, the error bar will face upward. If it is negative, the bar will face downward.

Suppose we have the following data:

DENSITY	SE	ENERGY$
.09	.03	LOW
.40	.04	MEDIUM
.45	.02	HIGH

Figure 8 shows a category plot with error bars superimposed this way. I have used solid triangles (**SYMBOL=3,FILL=1**) to make the plot more visible. The SNORT option keeps SYGRAPH from sorting the categories.

Figure 8

```
TYPE=HERSHEY
CPLOT  DENSITY*ENERGY$,
   /ERROR=SE,SYMBOL=3,FILL=1,SNORT
```

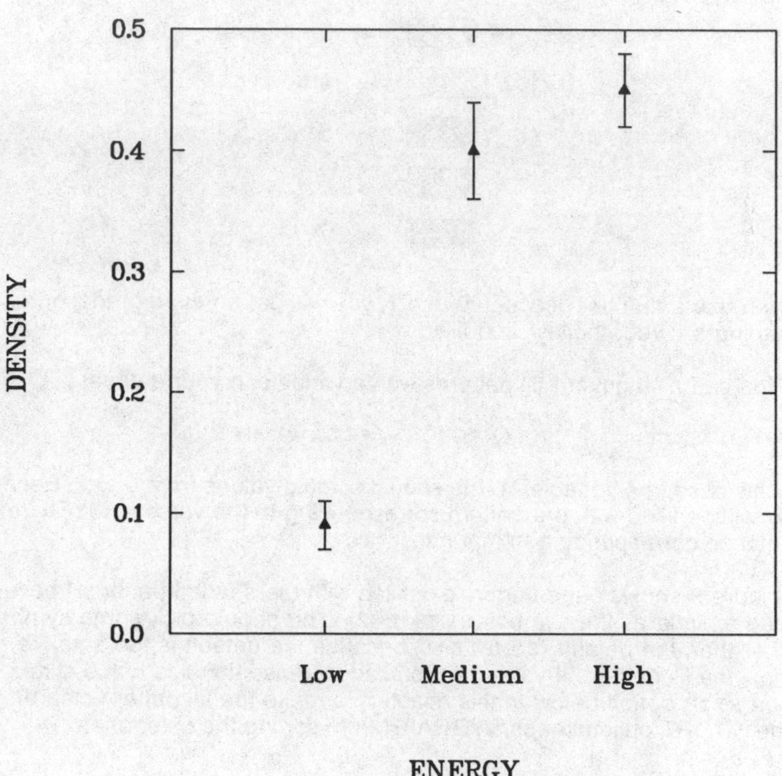

FILL *(Filling symbols)*

You can fill symbols with different patterns. The **FILL** option works this way:

```
CPLOT   INCOME*REGION$/FILL=2
```

The number you choose after "**FILL=**" determines the type of fill pattern. Here are the possibilities:

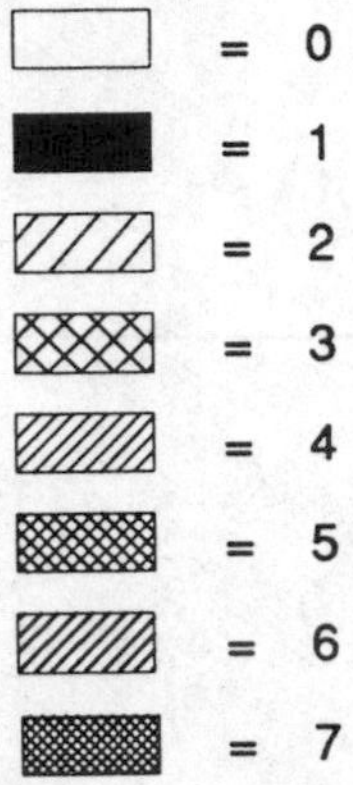

= 0

= 1

= 2

= 3

= 4

= 5

= 6

= 7

If you use a number between 0 and 1, you will get an even gradation of shading between hollow and filled.

You can also govern fill patterns with a variable in your dataset:

```
CPLOT   INCOME*REGION$/FILL=MYFIL
```

In this case, the variable MYFIL should contain values from 0 to 7. Each bar will be filled with the pattern corresponding to the value in MYFIL for the case corresponding to that bar.

Figure 9 shows our category plot filled with the shaded pattern. I have used a circle as the symbol (**SYMBOL=2**). You should pick some symbol other than the default (**SYMBOL=1**) because the default is too small to show the fill pattern. If you wish, you can increase the size of the symbols (see **SIZE** option below in this chapter) to make the fill pattern clearer. The SNORT option keeps SYGRAPH from sorting the categories.

Figure 9

```
CPLOT  INCOME*REGION$,
    /SYMBOL=2,FILL=4,SIZE=1.5,SNORT
```

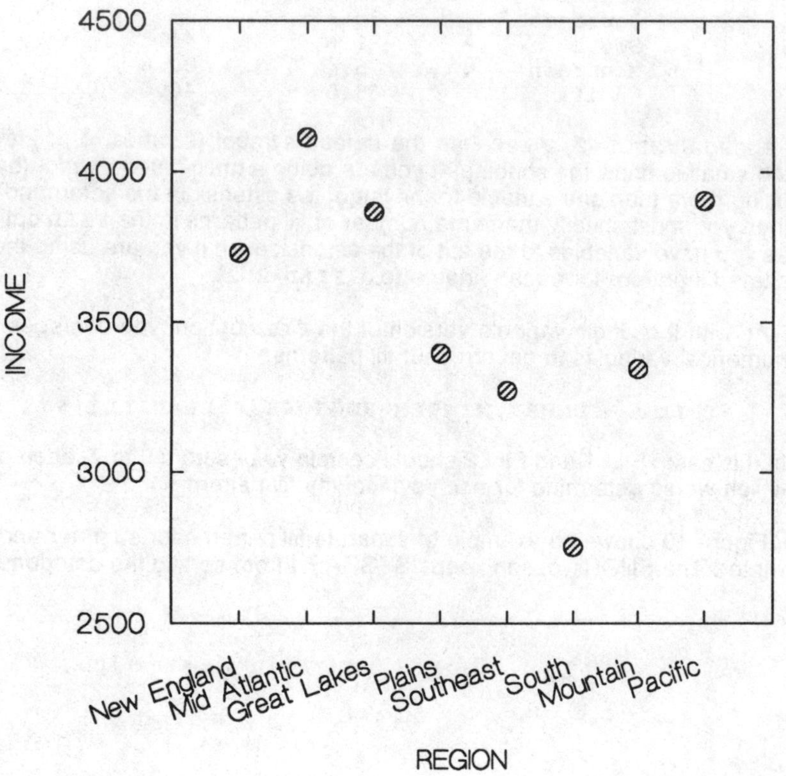

FILL *(Multi-filled category plots)*

You can do category plots with a different fill pattern for each dependent variable. The following **FILL** option will make solid symbols (1) for summer and shaded symbols (5) for winter:

```
CPLOT   SUMMER,WINTER*REGION$/FILL=1,5,SYMBOL=2,2
```

SYGRAPH computes and plots the following average temperatures:

REGION$	SUMMER	WINTER
New England	70.7	25.3
Mid Atlantic	75.0	31.7
Great Lakes	73.8	26.4
Plains	76.0	20.9
Southeast	78.6	43.5
South	81.6	45.3
Mountain	75.4	30.6
Pacific	68.0	40.0

I added **SYMBOL=2,2** because the default symbol (**SYMBOL=1,1**) is too small to show the shading. If you are doing a multi-category plot (by using more than one variable to the left of the asterisk in the command) then you must specify the same number of fill patterns in the **FILL** option as you have variables to the left of the asterisk even if you are using the same fill pattern for each variable (e.g. **FILL=2,2**).

As with the single variable version of the **FILL** option, you can specify numerical variables to govern your fill patterns:

```
CPLOT   SUMMER,WINTER*REGION$/FILL=FILL1,FILL2
```

In this case, FILL1 and FILL2 should contain values from 0 to 7, each of which would determine for each symbol the fill pattern.

Figure 10 shows an example of separate fill patterns for summer and winter. The SNORT option keeps SYGRAPH from sorting the categories.

Figure 10

```
CPLOT  SUMMER,WINTER*REGION$
  /FILL=0,1,SYMBOL=2,2,SNORT,
 YLABEL='Average  Temperature'
```

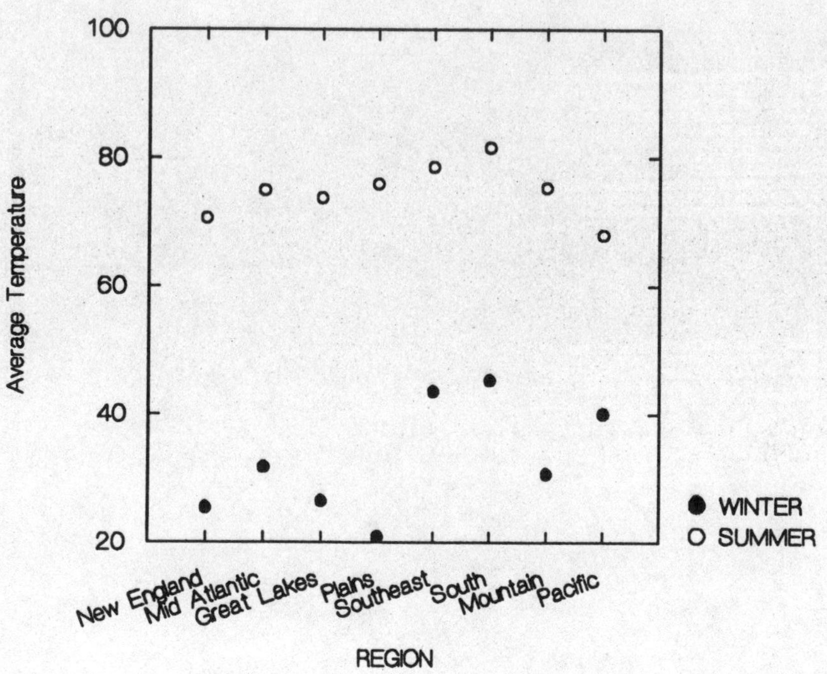

GRID *(Grid Marks)*

You can add grid marks to category plots with the **GRID** option. The possible values are:

`GRID=1`	*(vertical grid marks)*
`GRID=2`	*(horizontal grid marks)*
`GRID=3`	*(horizontal and vertical grid marks)*

Figure 11 shows an example with horizontal and vertical grid marks. The SNORT option keeps SYGRAPH from sorting the categories.

Figure 11

```
CPLOT  INCOME*REGION$,
/SYMBOL=2,FILL=1,GRID=3,SYMBOL=7,SNORT
```

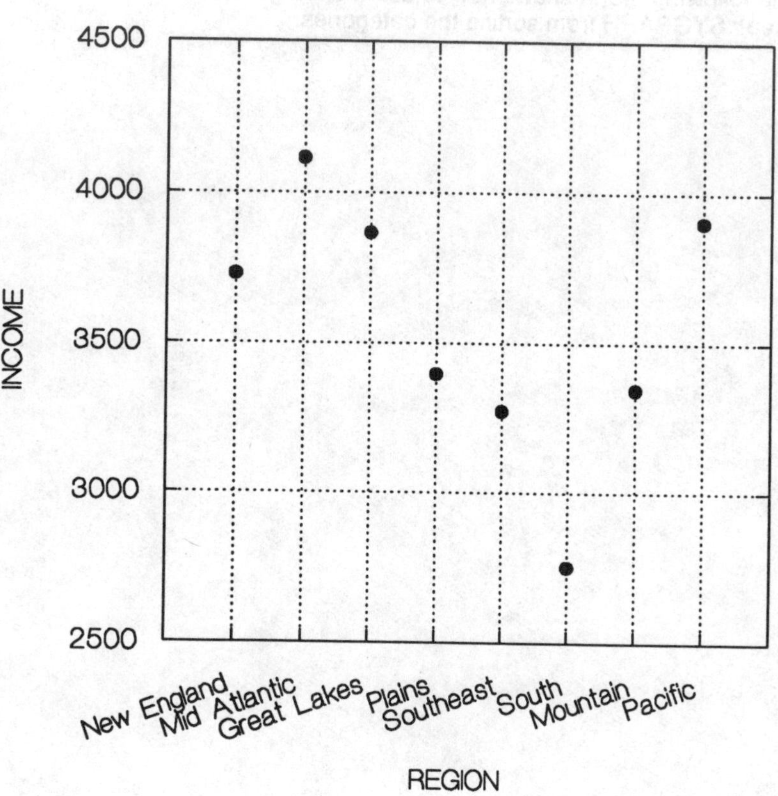

HEIGHT *(Physical Height of Plot)*

You can control the physical height of your category plot with the **HEIGHT** option. It works like this:

```
HEIGHT=50%      (or HEIGHT=50)
HEIGHT=4IN
HEIGHT=10CM
```

The first example specifies percent of display height. The second specifies inches, and the third centimeters.

When you use the **HEIGHT** option, you probably also want to use **WIDTH**, which works exactly the same way (see below in this chapter). The following graph shows how to use them together. The SNORT option keeps SYGRAPH from sorting the categories.

Figure 12

```
CPLOT   INCOME*REGION$,
     /HEIGHT=3IN,WIDTH=4IN,SYMBOL=7,SNORT
```

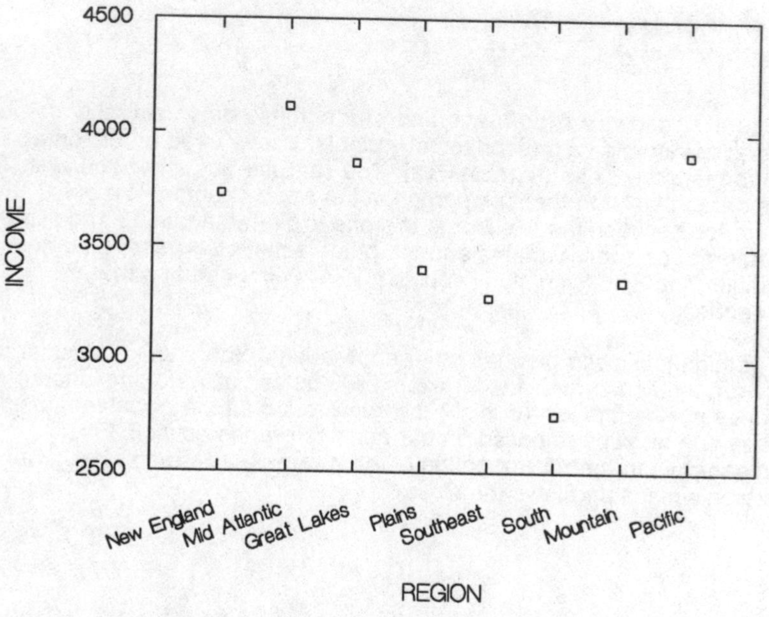

HILO *(HIGH-LOW-CLOSE Category Plots)*

Stock market daily, weekly, or monthly statistics are often most effectively plotted as a set of ranges between high and low prices with a marker for the closing price at each period. This is the way most newspapers plot the market. The HILO option allows you to produce this plot. Here are some typical data on a stock:

MONTH$	MONTH	HIGH	LOW	CLOSE
January	1	20.1	17.5	20.0
February	2	24.5	18.8	24.0
March	3	29.3	22.5	23.6
April	4	35.1	25.6	29.9
May	5	40.2	32.3	35.5
June	6	45.1	38.8	39.5
July	7	39.6	32.3	37.1
August	8	33.1	28.3	28.3
September	9	27.8	20.5	21.1
October	10	22.1	17.8	17.9
November	11	17.9	16.1	16.5
December	12	16.8	10.2	10.3

Figure 13 shows a **high-low-close plot** of these data using the month character variable as the horizontal variable. I have used a horizontal line to mark the close (**SYMBOL=12**). You can use any other you wish. Compare this plot to the same graph in the **PLOT** chapter. The only difference between the two is that this one is plotted against a (possibly unordered) category variable and the other is plotted against a numerical variable. The SNORT option keeps SYGRAPH from sorting the categories.

The high-low-close plot has other applications. You should consider it for asymmetrical error bars, for example. You can also do one-sided error bars by making the low (or high) the same value as the close variable. These can be superimposed on bar and line graphs as well. Finally, compare this to the **RANGE** option in the **BAR** plot. The range bar graph plots only highs and lows (no close).

Figure 13

```
CPLOT   HIGH,LOW,CLOSE*MONTH$,
/HILO,YLABEL='PRICE',SYMBOL=12,SNORT
```

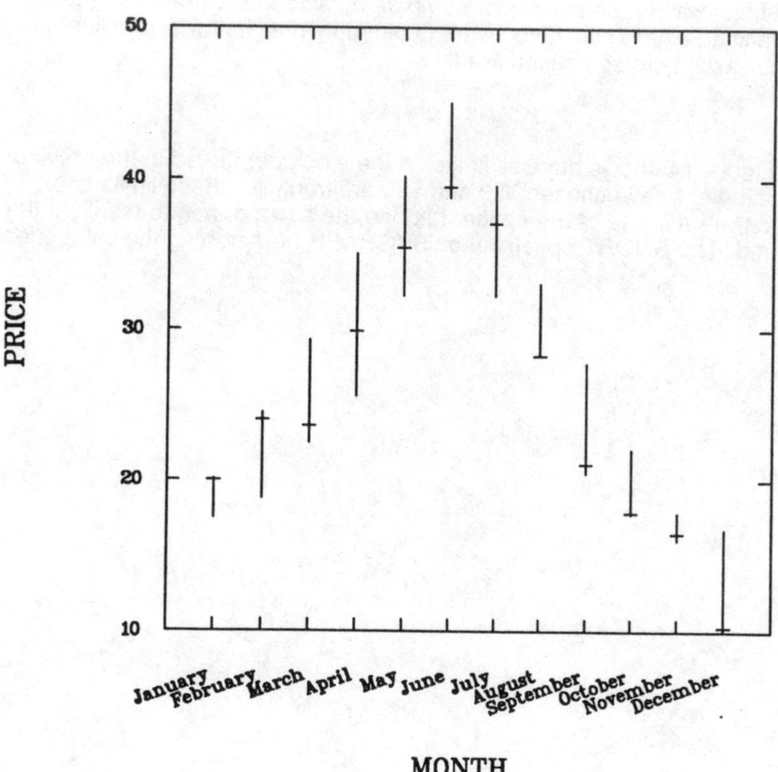

LIMIT *(Control Limits)*

You can add dashed lines to mark limits on the numerical axis of a category plot. **Quality control charts**, for example, mark upper and lower limits on an axis to indicate permissible bounds for a production process. Axis limits can be used in other applications to mark simultaneous standard errors. The **LIMIT** option works this way:

```
CPLOT  X$  /  LIMIT=3,8                              or,
CPLOT  Y*X$  /  LIMIT=.43,24.5
```

The first example places limits on counts, since there is only a grouping variable. The second example places limits on a two-way category plot. It is especially suited to quality control applications.

Limits will not be plotted for numbers outside the extremes of the specified axis. Thus, if you want to plot only one limit (dashed line) on your axis, type something like this:

```
BOX  X  /  LIMIT=2,-9999
```

Figure 14 shows buy-sell limits on the stock data used in the previous example. I have chosen $20 and $30 arbitrarily for these limits to illustrate the use of the option. I added the **LINE** option to highlight the trend. The SNORT option keeps SYGRAPH from sorting the categories.

Figure 14

```
CPLOT   CLOSE*MONTH$/LIMIT=20,30,LINE,SNORT
```

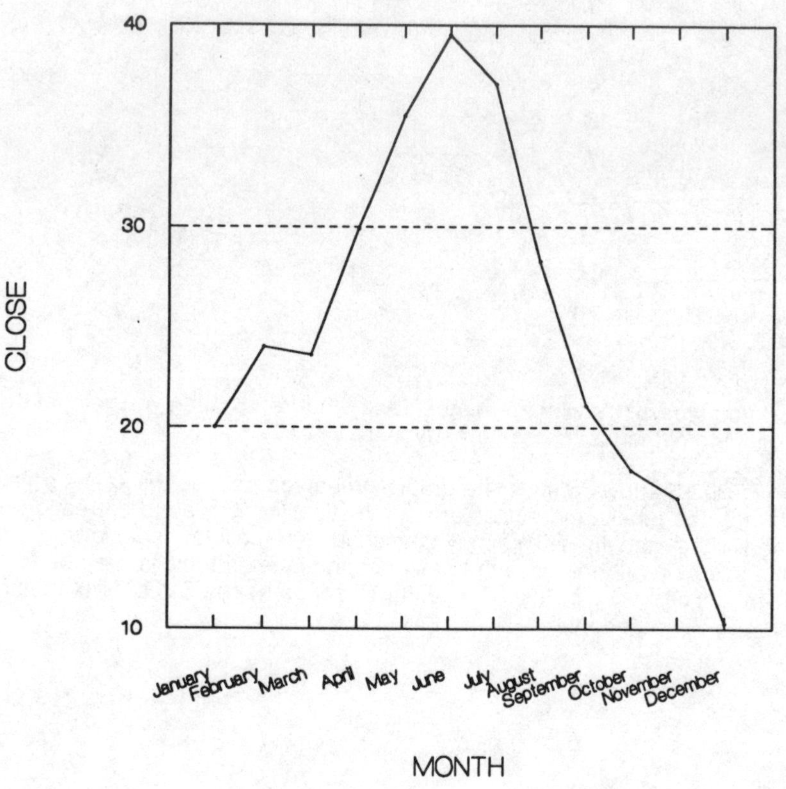

LINE *(Connecting Symbols with a Line)*

Connecting symbols with a line in a category plot can sometimes highlight trends or elevations. You can use the `LINE` option to do this. The resulting line will connect the centers of any symbols you draw. This is sometimes called a **profile plot**.

You may choose from 11 different types of lines by typing `LINE=`*n* , where *n* is one of the following numbers:

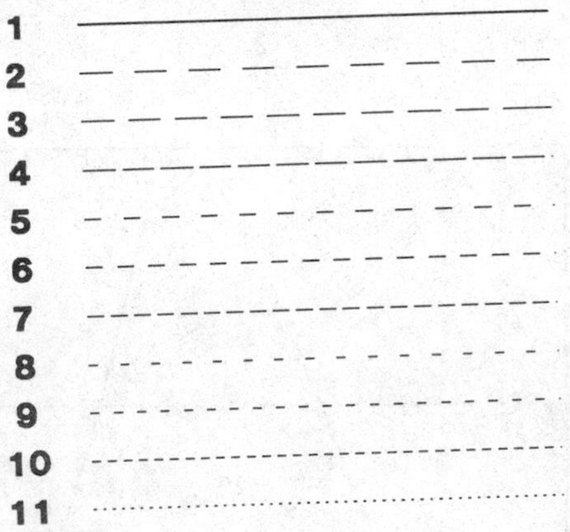

1
2
3
4
5
6
7
8
9
10
11

If you type `LINE` with no number, as in Figure 15, then you will get the solid line, which is the same as typing `LINE=1`.

Figure 15 shows a thick line graph. When you set line thickness greater than 5, the labels and scales are automatically enlarged to correspond to the width of the lines. This may cause labels to collide, especially in plots like this one with many categories and long labels. If this is a problem, then set `THICK=5` or less. The SNORT option keeps SYGRAPH from sorting the categories.

Figure 15

```
THICK=7
CPLOT  INCOME*REGION$/LINE,SNORT
```

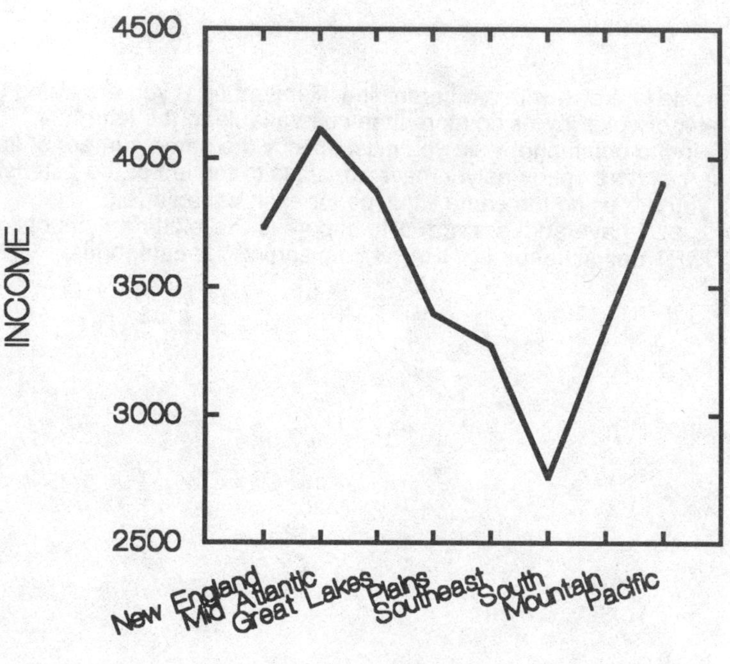

LINE *(Multi-line Category Plots)*

You can do category plots with a different type of line connecting the values of each dependent variable. Figure 16 shows a category (profile) plot of summer and winter temperatures against region. SYGRAPH computes and plots the following average temperatures for each region in the US dataset:

REGION$	SUMMER	WINTER
New England	70.7	25.3
Mid Atlantic	75.0	31.7
Great Lakes	73.8	26.4
Plains	76.0	20.9
Southeast	78.6	43.5
South	81.6	45.3
Mountain	75.4	30.6
Pacific	68.0	40.0

Each profile is drawn with a different line. Remember, if you are doing a multi-category plot (by using more than one variable to the left of the asterisk in the command) then you must specify the same number of line types in the **`LINE`** option as you have variables to the left of the asterisk, even if you are using the same line type for each variable (e.g. **`LINE=2,2`**). I have added **`SIZE=0`** to suppress the plotting symbols. The SNORT option keeps SYGRAPH from sorting the categories.

Figure 16

```
CPLOT  SUMMER,WINTER*REGION$,
/LINE=1,10,SIZE=0,SNORT
```

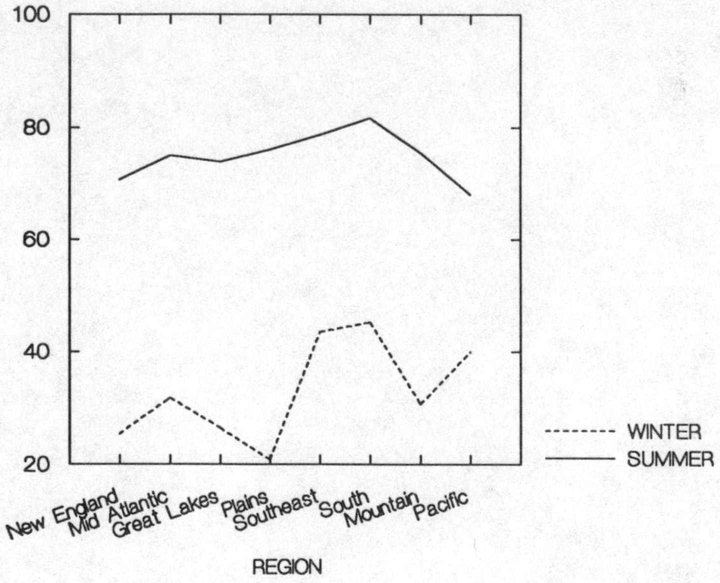

LOG *(Logging Data)*

You can log the vertical scale of your category plot with the `LOG` command. Logs may be computed to any base, e.g. `LOG=2`, `LOG=3`, `LOG=10`, `LOG=.5`. Natural logarithms will be computed if you use `LOG` with no argument, i.e. `LOG`. Only round number log bases (e.g. 0.5, 2, 3,10) will result in round number tick values, however.

`LOG` works with any form of the `CPLOT` command. The following command, for example, will log frequencies:

```
CPLOT  REGION$/LOG=10
```

The following logs INCOME.

```
CPLOT  INCOME*REGION$/LOG=10
```

Figure 17 shows this latter use of the option. The SNORT option keeps SYGRAPH from sorting the categories.

Figure 17

```
CPLOT  INCOME*REGION$,
/LOG=10,SYMBOL=5,FILL=1,PIP=9,TICK=1,SNORT
```

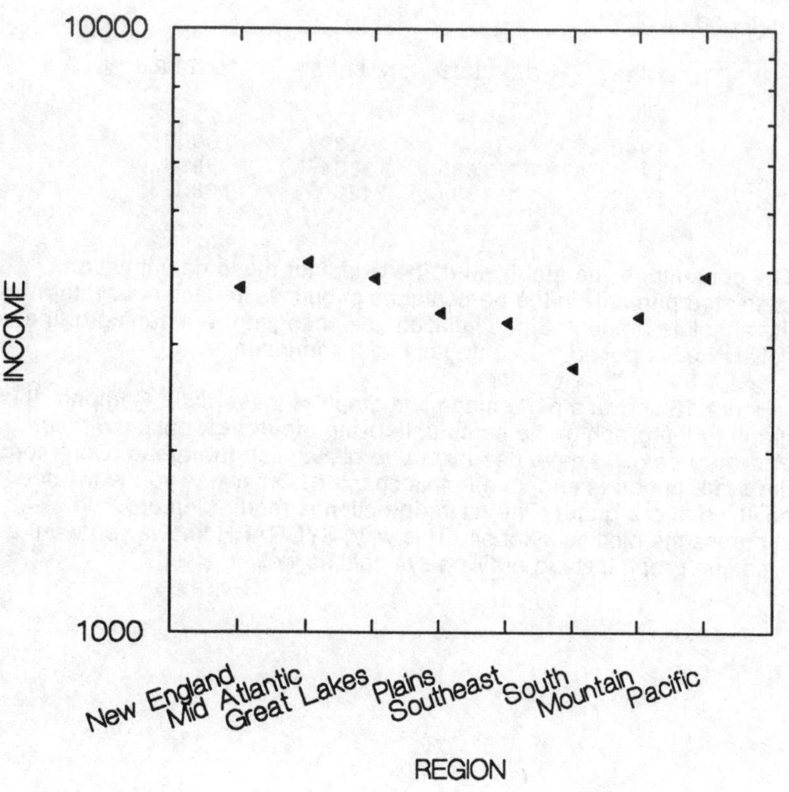

PERCENT *(Multi-variable Percentage, or Divided Line Graphs)*

If you wish to apportion several variables in a line graph, you can do it in a multi-variable percentage graph. This graph divides the vertical axis (denoting 100 percent) among several categories or variables. You need to use the **STACK** option (see below in this chapter) to divide the vertical axis this way. Otherwise, the percentages will not be summed on the vertical axis.

The multi-variable percentage line graph is exactly like connecting the tops of the bars in a multi-variable percentage bar graph. You should look at the **PERCENT** option in the **BAR** chapter to compare the two.

I used the following data in that chapter to illustrate the graph. They are U.S. expenditures in millions of dollars for defense, interest on public debt, and all other.

YEAR$	DEFENSE	INTEREST	OTHER
1950	9919	5750	23875
1960	43969	9180	39075
1970	78368	19304	98972
1980	136138	74860	368013

The percentage line graph would be useful for these data if we are interested primarily in the percentages of outlays in each year rather than the absolute amount. Since inflation has changed the meaning of these dollars in this period, percentages make some sense.

Figure 18 shows a percentage line graph of these data. Compare this graph to the graph of the same data using the **STACK** option without **PERCENT** below. I have used **FILL** to distinguish the areas. Don't forget the **LINE** option (see above in this chapter). Otherwise you won't see anything in the graph. The **SIZE=0** option is required in order to suppress the plotting symbols. This way, SYGRAPH knows you want a filled line graph instead of filling symbols as well.

Figure 18

```
CPLOT   DEFENSE,INTEREST,OTHER*YEAR$,
  /STACK,FILL=1,2,7,LINE,PERCENT,STICK,SIZE=0
```

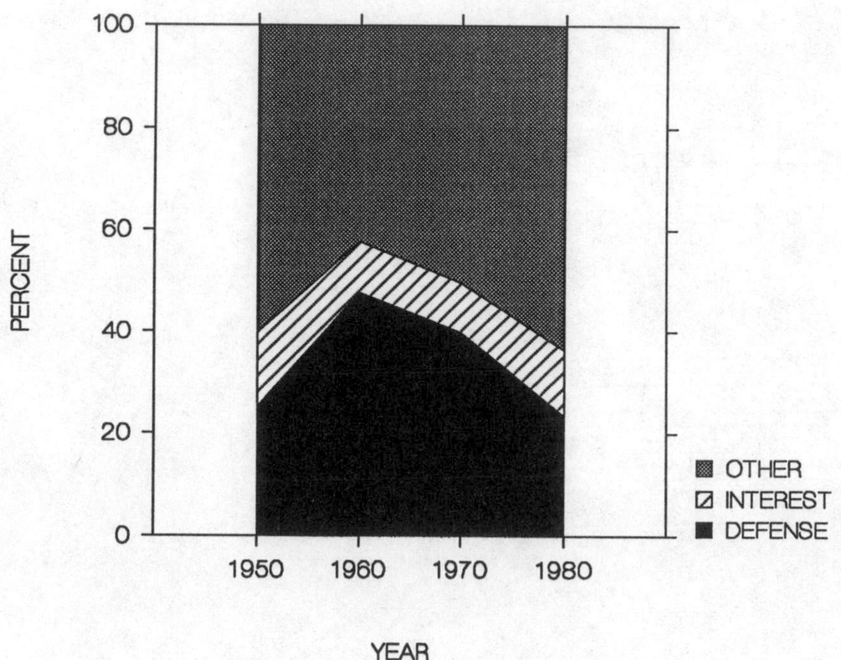

PIP *(Pip Marks)*

Pip marks are half sized tick marks. SYGRAPH normally omits pip marks from category plots. The `PIP` option adds them. Just specify the number you want. If you log a scale (see `LOG` option above in this chapter) the pip marks will be logarithmically spaced. Figure 19 shows an example with 10 pip marks. The SNORT option keeps SYGRAPH from sorting the categories.

Figure 19

```
CPLOT   INCOME*REGION$/PIP=10,SYMBOL=10,SNORT
```

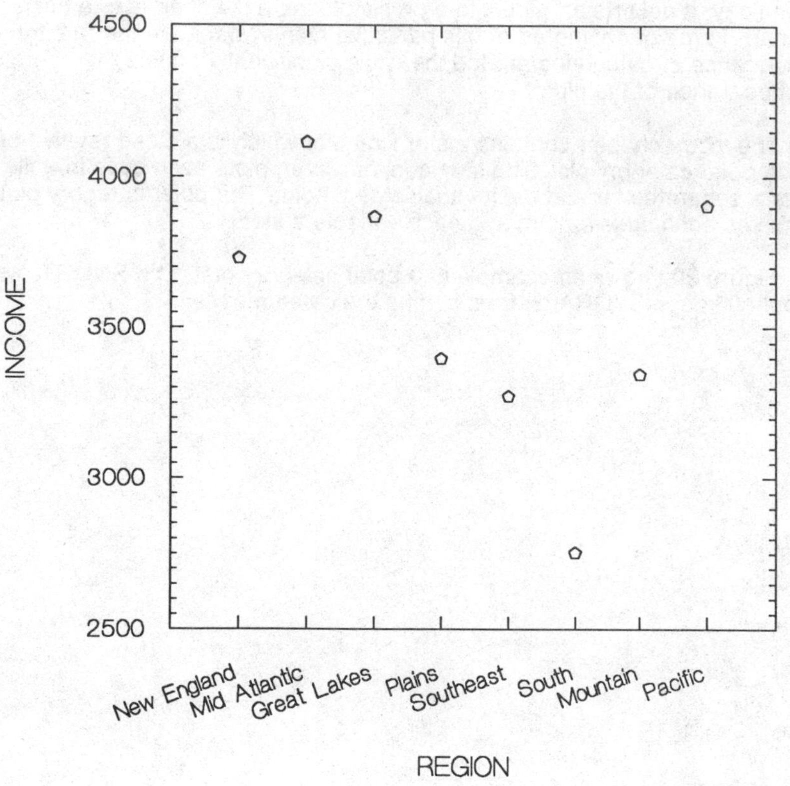

POLAR *(Polar Coordinate Category Plots)*

You can do category plots in polar coordinates. This may seem strange at first, but this is a way to produce what are sometimes called **star plots** or **snowflake plots**. To do these plots, it is best to use the **LINE** option (see above in this chapter) and to make the plotting symbols invisible by adding the option **SIZE=0** (see below in this chapter). For frills, you can add **GRID=3** to put grid marks inside the frame. You can fiddle with the other **CPLOT** options (e.g. **TICK**, **ERROR**, **AXES**, **YMIN/YMAX**, etc.) to produce variants.

Polar coordinates translate rectangular (Cartesian) coordinates into a circular arrangement. The X axis is transformed into an angle, or position around the circumference of a circle. The Y axis is transformed into a radius, or distance from the center of a circle. As an approximate analogy, a polar (star) plot is to a profile plot as a pie chart is to a bar chart. I am not enamored of this particular display because the (arbitrary) sequence of categories around the circle significantly affects the appearance of the plot.

The **ICON** chapter contains a star icon plot which is a close relative of the polar category plot. The star icon, however, plots each case in a file as a separate star and each variable as a point. The polar category plot makes each case a point and each variable a star.

Figure 20 shows an example of a polar category plot The SNORT option keeps SYGRAPH from sorting the categories.

Figure 20

```
CPLOT   INCOME*REGION$/SIZE=0,POLAR,LINE,SNORT
```

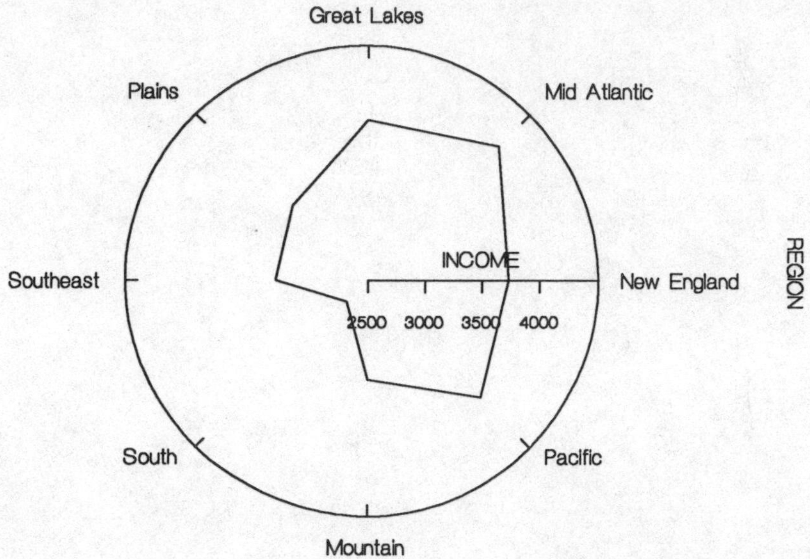

POW *(Powering Data)*

You can power the vertical scale of your category plot with the **POW** command. Powers may be computed to any exponent, e.g. **POW=.5** (square root), **POW=.33333** (cube root), **POW=-1** (inverse), **POW=2**. Square roots will be computed if you use **POW** with no argument, i.e. **POW**. Some exponents (e.g. 3) will produce non-integer tick marks. **POW** is implemented in SYGRAPH only for positive data. Negative values will be deleted.

POW works with any form of the **CPLOT** command. The following command, for example, will transform frequencies:

```
CPLOT   REGION$/POW=.5
```

The following command transforms INCOME.

```
CPLOT   INCOME*REGION$/POW=.5
```

Figure 21 shows the latter example.

Figure 21

```
CPLOT   INCOME*REGION$/POW=.5,SYMBOL=6,FILL=1
```

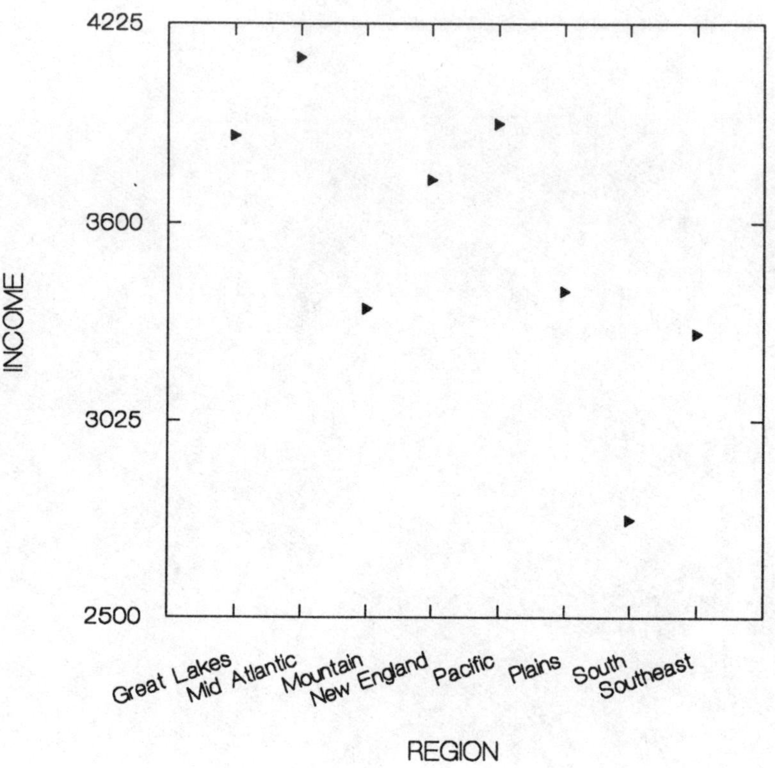

REV *(Reversing the Vertical Axis)*

You can reverse the vertical axis with the **REV** option.

Figure 22 shows an example of a reversed scale.

Figure 22

```
CPLOT   INCOME*REGION$/REV,SYMBOL=5,FILL=1
```

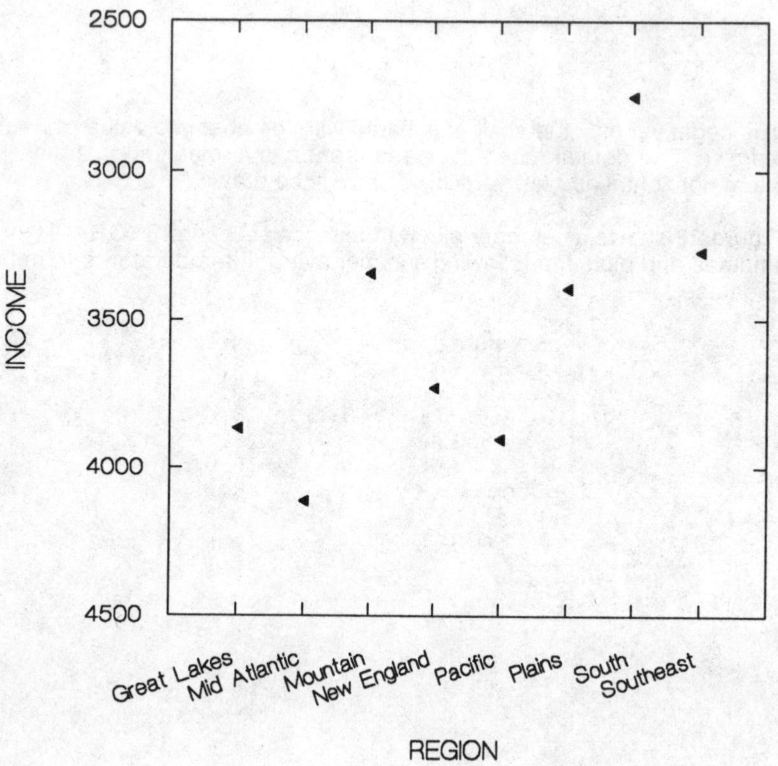

SCALE *(Number of Scales)*

Scales are the numbers which label the tick marks on an axis. The **SCALE** option controls the number of scales drawn in a category plot. Its syntax is:

```
SCALE=n
```

where *n* is an integer from 0 to 4. If *n* is 0, no scales will be drawn. If *n* is an integer from 1 to 4, all scales from 1 to *n* will be drawn. Scales are numbered from 1 to 4 clockwise, beginning with the bottom axis:

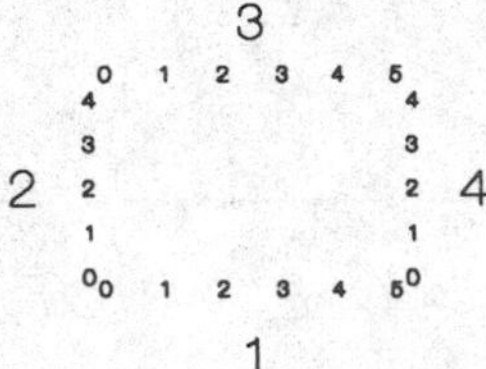

If *n* is negative, only the scale numbered with the absolute value of *n* will be drawn. The default (usual) value for **SCALE** is 2, meaning that the bottom horizontal and left vertical scales will be drawn.

Figure 23 shows a category plot with four scales where SYGRAPH computes and plots the following summer average temperatures from the US dataset.

REGION$	SUMMER
New England	70.7
Mid Atlantic	75.0
Great Lakes	73.8
Plains	76.0
Southeast	78.6
South	81.6
Mountain	75.4
Pacific	68.0

Figure 23

```
CPLOT   SUMMER*REGION$/SCALE=4,SYMBOL=17
```

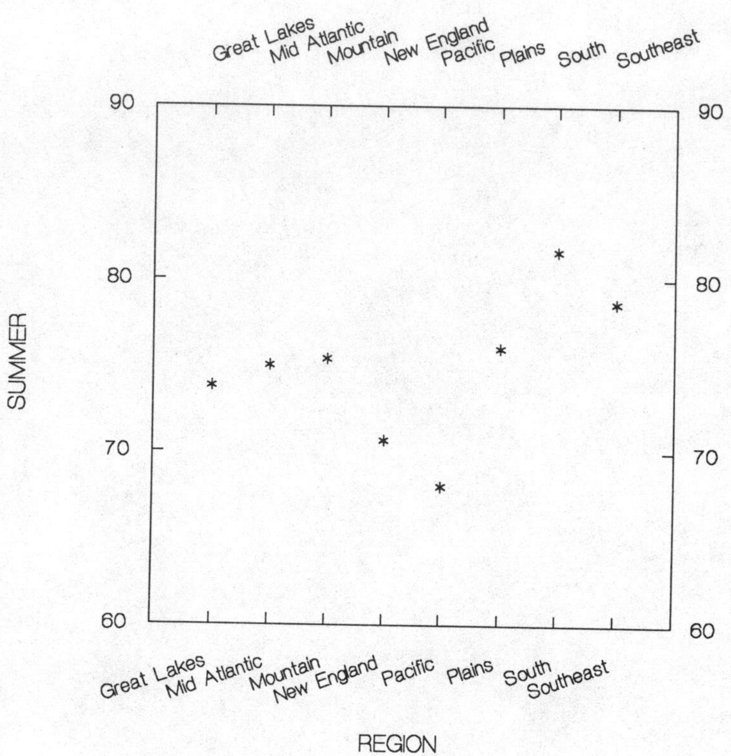

SIZE *(Changing Size of Plotting Symbols)*

You can alter the size of plotting symbols from invisible to as large as your entire graph. The standard value of all symbols is `SIZE=1`. `SIZE=2` produces symbols twice as large as the standard. `SIZE=.5` is half, and so on. `SIZE=0` makes the symbols invisible.

Figure 24 shows a category plot with symbols two and a half times larger than usual.

Figure 24

```
CPLOT  INCOME*REGION$/SYMBOL=8,SIZE=2.5
```

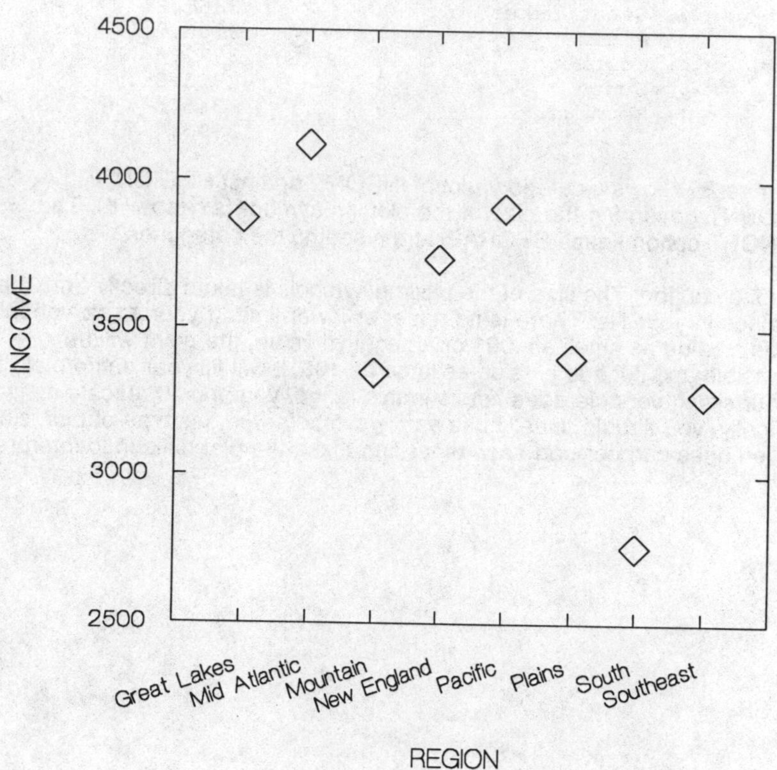

SIZE *(Representing a Variable by Size of Symbols)*

You can use the value of a variable in your file to control the size of a plotting symbol. This is especially useful when you are representing a third variable against two others in a two-way category plot.

Here are summary data from the US file on average INCOME (per-capita income) within REGION (Census region). The variable COUNT is the number of states in each region.

REGION$	COUNT	INCOME
New England	6	3730.2
Mid Atlantic	3	4114.0
Great Lakes	5	3867.2
Plains	7	3396.9
Southeast	8	3272.6
South	8	2753.8
Mountain	8	3345.5
Pacific	3	3903.7

Figure 25 shows a category plot of INCOME against REGION with COUNT governing the size of the plotting symbol (**SYMBOL=8**). The SNORT option keeps SYGRAPH from sorting the categories.

One caution. The size of the plotting symbols is taken directly from the values in your file. There is no upper or lower limit. If your **SIZE** variable has a value as small as .001 or a negative value, the point will be invisible and if it has a value as large as 100, it will fill your entire plot. If your sizing variable does not lie in this range, you should rescale it. Finally, you should usually use empty symbols with this type of plot, since filled ones can occlude each other and make the plot difficult to interpret.

Figure 25

```
CPLOT   INCOME*REGION$/SYMBOL=8,SIZE=COUNT,SNORT
```

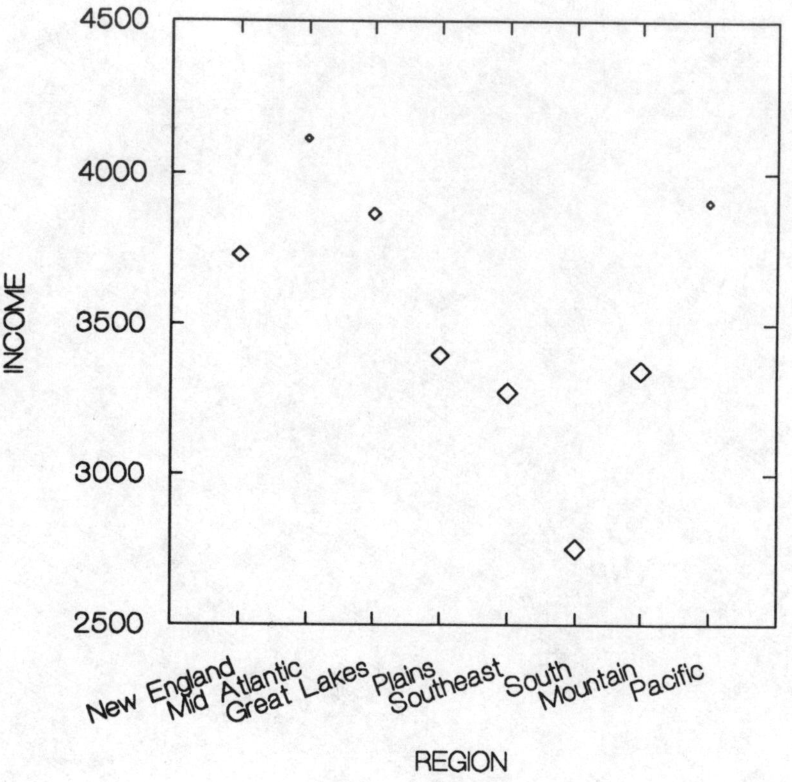

SORT/SNORT *(Sorting Categories)*

SYGRAPH automatically sorts the levels (categories) of categorical variables in ascending numeric or character order. If you want the categories arranged according to the order they appear in your data file, use the **SNORT** option. Figure 26 shows an example of the **SORT** option. Compare the bottom scale with that in other figures in this chapter to see how **SORT** and **SNORT** work.

Figure 26

```
CPLOT   SUMMER*REGION$/SORT,SYMBOL=19
```

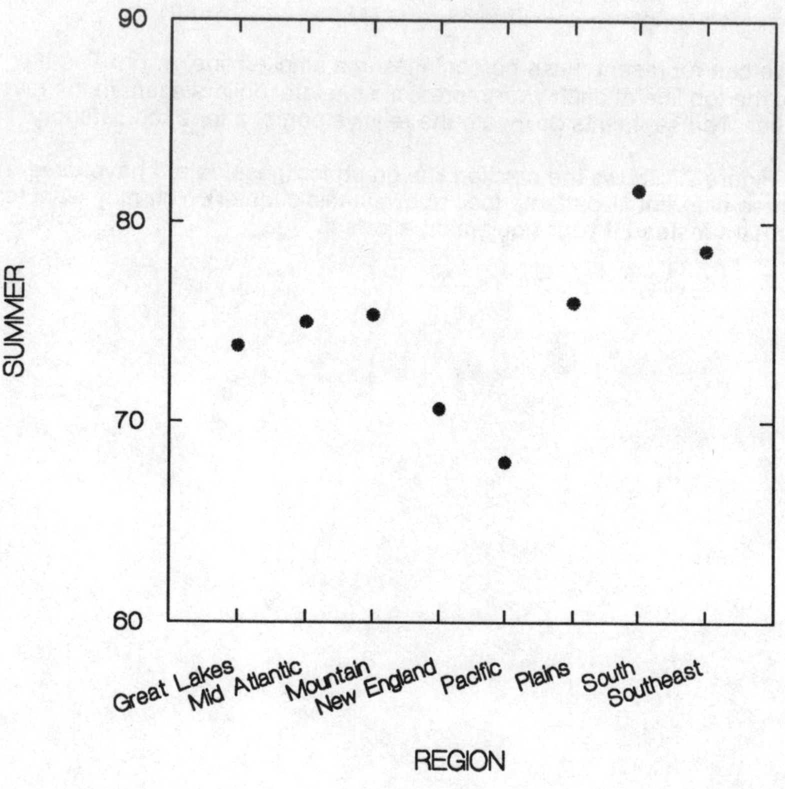

STACK *(Stacked or Cumulative Line Graphs)*

A stacked line graph works like a multi-valued line graph (see beginning of this chapter) except that the lines are cumulative at each value of the X or horizontal axis. As with the multi-valued line graphs, you can stack up to 12 different variables. These charts are most useful for comparing segments of a single variable over several categories, such as budget information. I used the following data to illustrate the **PERCENT** option above in this chapter. They are millions of dollars in U.S. budget outlays.

YEAR$	DEFENSE	INTEREST	OTHER
1950	9919	5750	23875
1960	43969	9180	39075
1970	78368	19304	98972
1980	136138	74860	368013

We can represent these percentages in a stacked line graph. The height of the top line at each year represents the total dollars spent in the given year. The segments delineate the relative portions for each category.

Figure 27 shows the stacked line graph for these data. I have used three different fill patterns (see above in this chapter). You may want to try **COLOR** instead if your equipment allows it.

Figure 27

```
CPLOT  DEFENSE,INTEREST,OTHER*YEAR$/STACK,
FILL=1,2,7,LINE,YMIN=0,YMAX=600000,SIZE=0
```

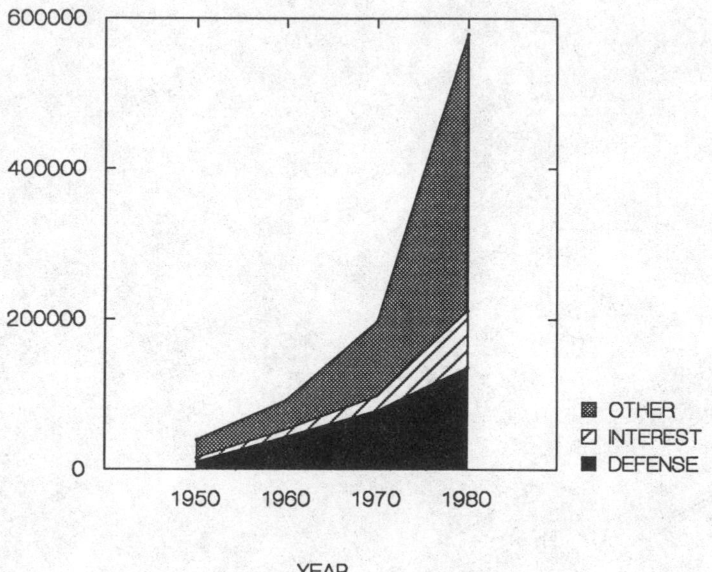

STICK *(Tick Marks Outside Frame)*
SYGRAPH normally places tick marks inside the frame. If you wish tick marks outside the frame, use the `STICK` option.

Figure 28 shows an example of a category plot with tick marks outside the frame.

Figure 28

```
CPLOT   SUMMER*REGION$/STICK,SYMBOL=3,FILL=1,SNORT
```

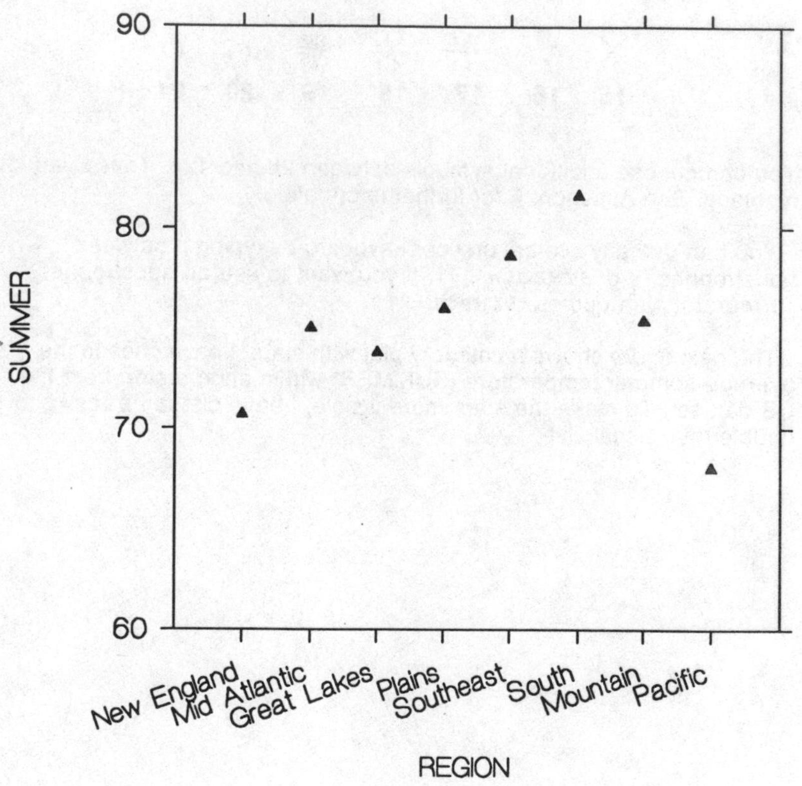

SYMBOL *(Plotting Symbols)*

You can choose a variety of symbols for your category plot. Just add the option: `SYMBOL=`*n* , where *n* is an integer denoting one of the following symbols:

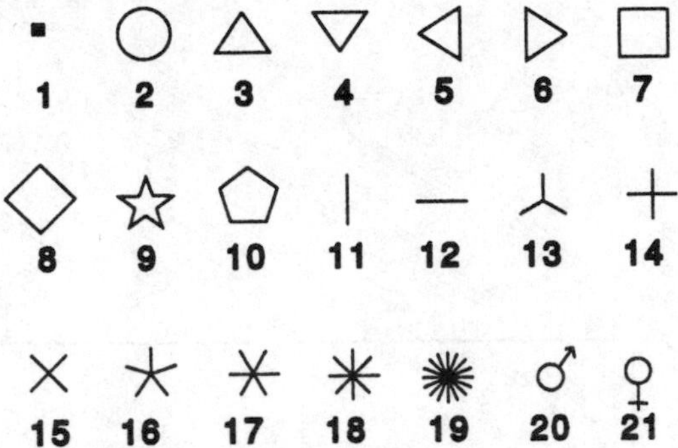

You can choose additional symbols between 28 and 128. These vary by typeface. See Appendix A for further information.

You can use any symbol on your keyboard by typing it between apostrophes, e.g. `SYMBOL='@'`. If you want to use an apostrophe, surround it with quotes: `SYMBOL="'"`.

The next figure shows a category plot with stars. I have chosen the average summer temperature (SUMMER) within each region from the US dataset. To make the stars more visible, I have chosen `SIZE=2` to double their usual size.

Figure 29

```
CPLOT   SUMMER*REGION$/SYMBOL=9,SIZE=2,FILL=7
```

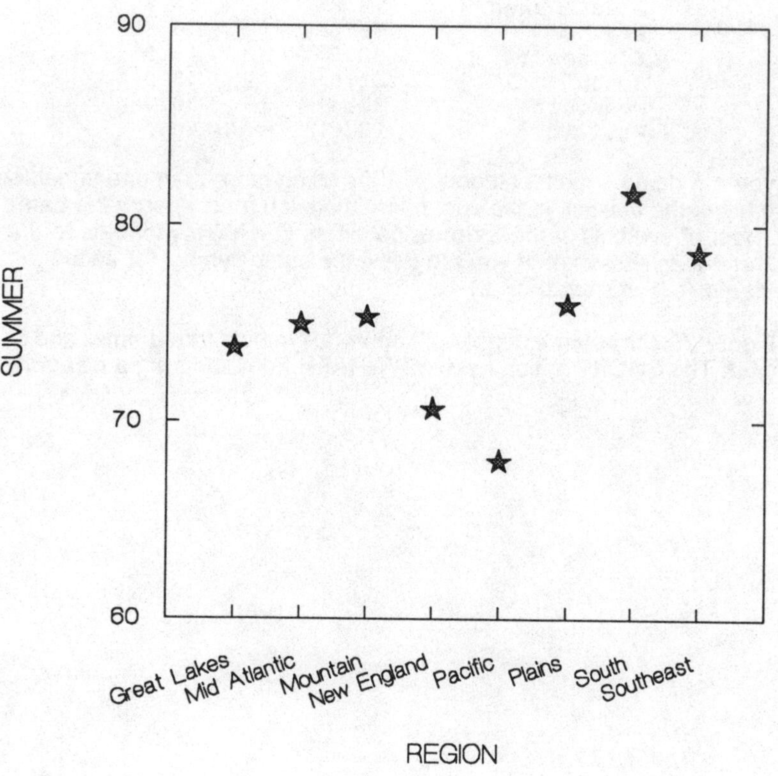

SYMBOL *(Multi-symbol category plots)*

You can do category plots with a different symbol for each dependent variable. The following command will make circles (2) for summer and triangles (5) for winter (see symbols above in this chapter):

```
CPLOT   SUMMER,WINTER*REGION$/SYMBOL=2,5
```

SYGRAPH computes and plots the following average temperatures for each region in the US dataset:

REGION$	SUMMER	WINTER
New England	70.7	25.3
Mid Atlantic	75.0	31.7
Great Lakes	73.8	26.4
Plains	76.0	20.9
Southeast	78.6	43.5
South	81.6	45.3
Mountain	75.4	30.6
Pacific	68.0	40.0

If you are doing a multi-category plot (by using more than one variable to the left of the asterisk in the command) then you must specify the same number of symbols in the **SYMBOL** option as you have variables to the left of the asterisk even if you are using the same symbol for each variable (e.g. **SYMBOL=2,2**).

Figure 30 shows an example of separate symbols for summer and winter. The SNORT option keeps SYGRAPH from sorting the categories.

Figure 30

```
TYPE=HERSHEY
CPLOT
SUMMER,WINTER*REGION$/SYMBOL=2,5,FILL=7,7,SNORT
```

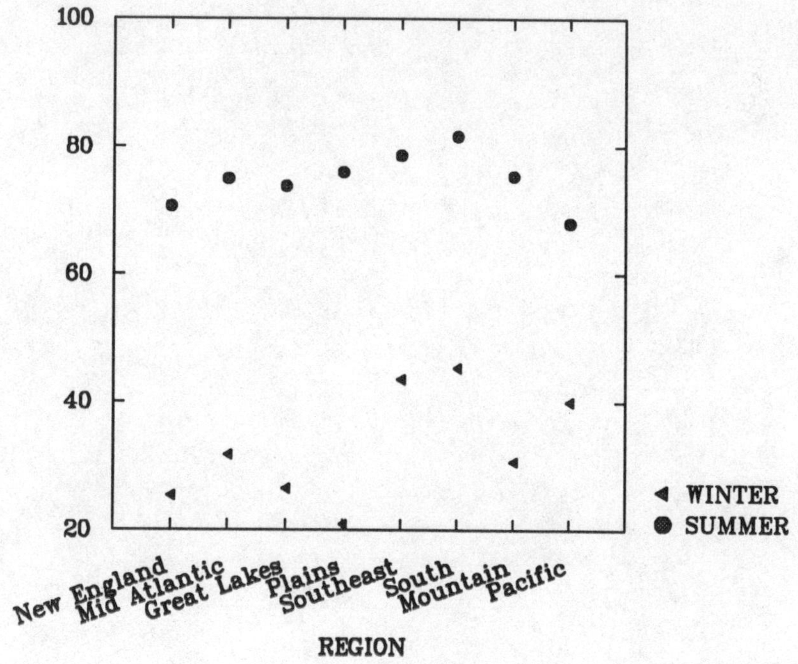

TICK *(Number of Tick Marks)*

SYGRAPH examines your data to determine how many tick marks to use on the vertical axis of a category plot. If you wish to modify this value, use the `TICK` option with a number. For example, `TICK=8` will force the vertical axis to have 8 tick marks. SYGRAPH will attempt to find minimum and maximum values for the scale such that the tick mark numbers are round. If it fails, you can control the values with the `YMIN` and `YMAX` options as well.

Figure 31 shows an example of a category plot with 10 tick marks. Notice that SYGRAPH automatically adjusts the size of the scale values when there are more tick marks. I have added `YMIN=0` (See below in this chapter) to force the minimum value of INCOME to 0.

Figure 31

```
CPLOT   INCOME*REGION$/TICK=10,SYMBOL=3,FILL=1
```

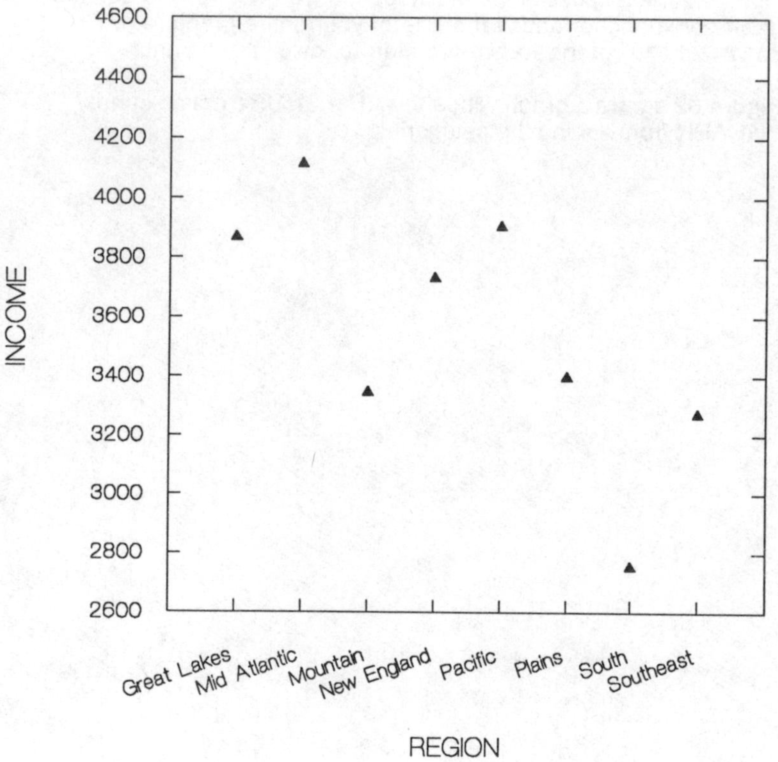

TITLE *(Graph Title)*
You can place a title at the top center of your graph with the **TITLE** option:

```
TITLE='Worldwide  Sales  in  U.S.  Dollars'
TITLE="Roger's  Fraudulent  Experiment"
TITLE='Perceived  variation  in  "Impact"'
```

The text must be surrounded by quotes (") or apostrophes ('). If your text includes apostrophes, as in the second example, surround it with quotes. If it includes quotes, as in the third example, surround it with apostrophes.

On some display devices the title will run off the top of the page because the standard display window is chosen to make the labels and graph as large as possible. If this happens, you will have to use the **SCALE** command to reduce the size of your entire graph (e.g. **SCALE=70,70**) or the **HEIGHT** option to lower the height.

Figure 32 shows a graph with a title. The SNORT option keeps SYGRAPH from sorting the categories.

Figure 32

```
TYPE=SWISS
CPLOT  INCOME*REGION$,
  /SYMBOL=2,FILL=1,SNORT,
   TITLE='Average Income within Region'
```

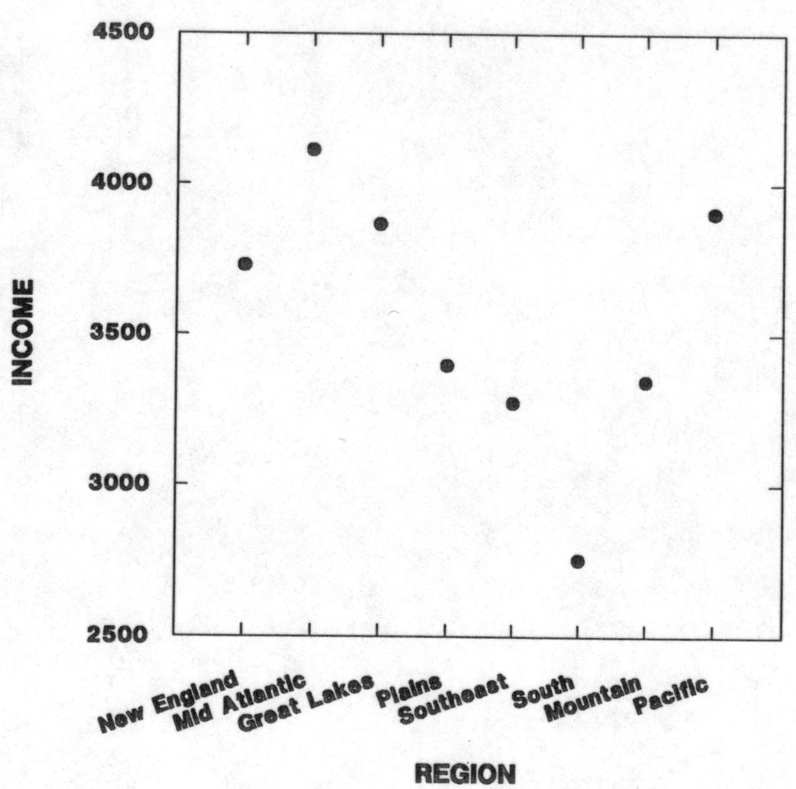

TRANS *(Transposing a Category Plot)*

You can transpose an entire category plot. To do this, just add the option **TRANS** to the **CPLOT** command.

TRANS affects everything in a graph. **XLABEL** becomes **YLABEL**, **XTICK** becomes **YTICK**, and so on. In other words, specify a graph as you would ordinarily and then add the **TRANS** option. Everything will be transposed appropriately, including the labels and scales.

Cleveland (1985) calls a transposed category plot with **SYMBOL=2** (dots) a **dot plot**. Figure 33 shows an example of this plot. To fit Cleveland's specifications, I have added horizontal grid lines (**GRID=2**) and dots for the plotting symbol (**SYMBOL=2**).

Figure 33

```
CPLOT   INCOME*REGION$/SYMBOL=2,FILL=1,GRID=2,TRANS
```

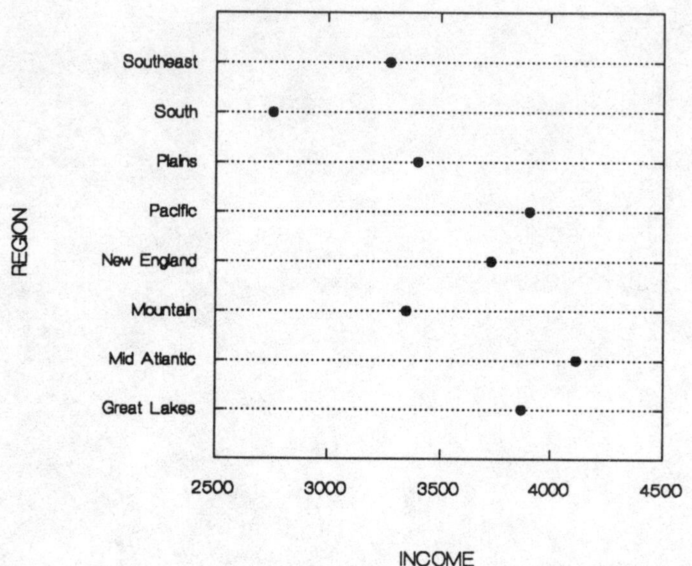

WIDTH *(Physical Width of Plot)*

You can control the physical width of your category plot with the **WIDTH** option. It works like this:

```
WIDTH=50%        (or WIDTH=50)
WIDTH=4IN
WIDTH=10CM
```

The first example specifies percent of display width. The second specifies inches, and the third centimeters.

When you use the **WIDTH** option, you probably also want to use **HEIGHT**, which works exactly the same way (see above in this chapter). The following graph shows how to use them together.

Figure 34

```
CPLOT   INCOME*REGION$,
   /HEIGHT=3IN,WIDTH=4IN,SYMBOL=6
```

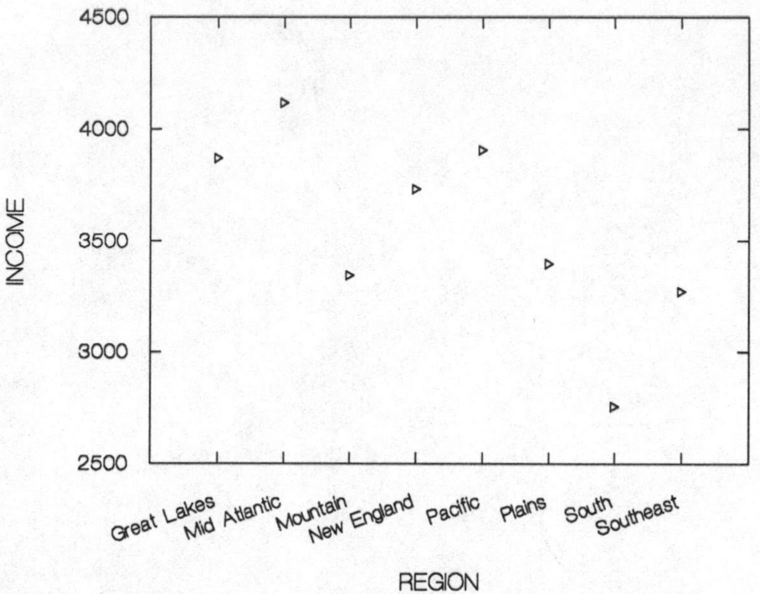

XLABEL,YLABEL *(Labeling a Bar Graph)*

Category plots are usually labeled with the names of the variables you use in the **CPLOT** command. If you want different labels, use the **XLABEL** and/or **YLABEL** command, e.g.

```
XLABEL='Proportion  of  Variance'
YLABEL='Per  Capita  Income'
XLABEL="Peter's  Portion"
XLABEL='Proportion  of  "Widgets"  Bid'
YLABEL='  '
```

The label text must be surrounded by quotes (") or apostrophes ('). If your text includes apostrophes, as in the third example, surround it with quotes. If it includes quotes, as in the fourth example, surround it with apostrophes. The last example shows how to remove labels from your graph. Just assign a blank (' ') to your label.

Figure 35 shows an example of a relabeled category plot.

Figure 35

```
CPLOT  INCOME*REGION$,
  /SYMBOL=2,FILL=1,
    YLABEL='1970 Per Capita Income',
    XLABEL='Region of U.S.'
```

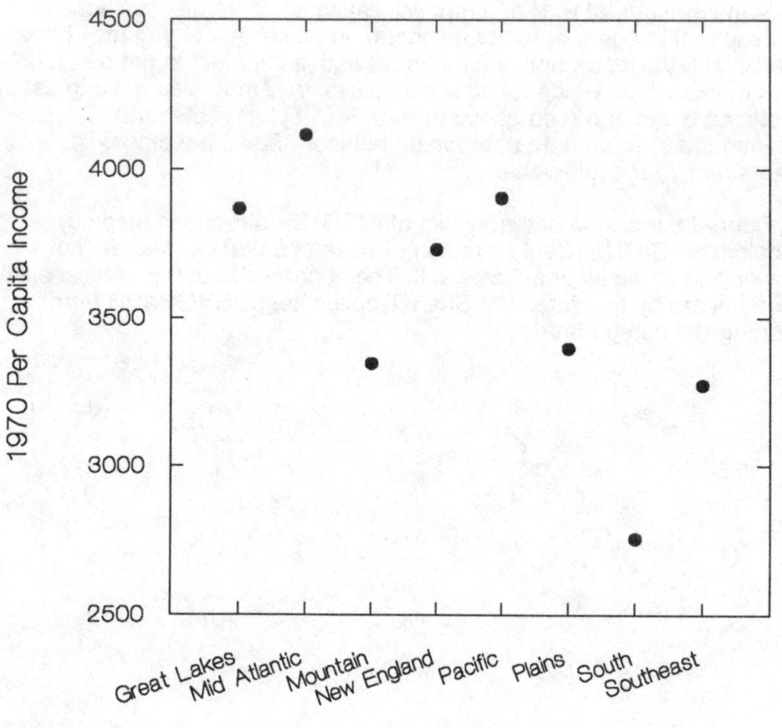

XMIN,YMIN,XMAX,YMAX *(Data Limits)*

SYGRAPH usually determines minimum and maximum scale values from the data in your file. If you wish to override this feature, use the **`MIN/MAX`** options. **`YMIN`** and **`YMAX`** control the lower and upper limits of the vertical scale. **`XMIN`** and **`XMAX`** do the same for the horizontal scale. Since the horizontal scale is categorical, however, you can use **`XMIN`** and/or **`XMAX`** only together with the **`BWIDTH`** option (see above in this chapter), which cuts a continuous variable into categories to make the horizontal scale.

If you set the **`MIN`** and **`MAX`** options inside the range of your data, you will zoom in to get a closer view, but you will eliminate certain data values from your plot. SYGRAPH will warn you when this happens.

Some settings of **`MIN`** and **`MAX`** will cause scale values to become messy (not integers or round numbers). In these cases, you may have to fiddle with the **`TICK`** option (see above in this chapter) to get a number of tick marks which yields round scale values. You may also have to use the **`FORMAT`** command (see above in Part 2, Chapter1, "General Commands") to print an appropriate number of decimal places to represent your scale values.

Figure 36 shows a category plot of INCOME (per-capita income) against REGION$ (Census region). I have used **`YMIN=0`** to anchor the lower end of the income scale to 0. The upper value of the vertical axis is determined by the data. The SNORT option keeps SYGRAPH from sorting the categories.

Figure 36

```
TYPE=STROKE/ITALIC
CPLOT  INCOME*REGION$,
  /YMIN=0,SYMBOL=2,FILL=1,SNORT,
   YLABEL='1970 Per Capita Income',
   XLABEL='Region of U.S.'
```

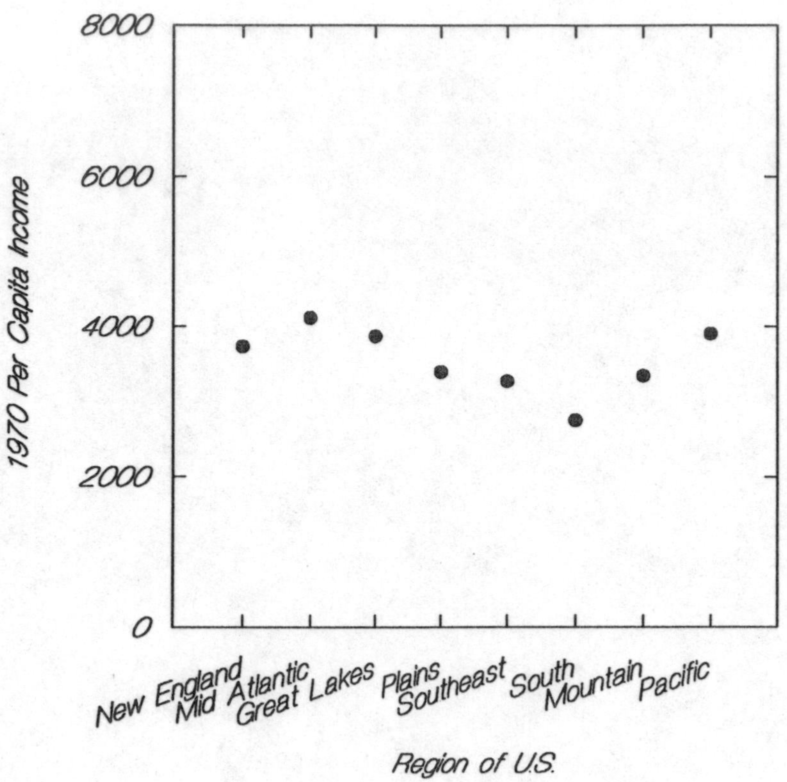

Chapter 5

DENSITY

The density of a sample is the relative concentration of data points at different sections of the scale on which the data are measured. Graphically representing the density of measurements on a variable is not a trivial problem. Most introductory statistics texts use a histogram, which is a crude density estimator. It is crude because the shape of a histogram depends on the choice of the number of bars. Most other graphical density estimation methods rest on more or less subjective choices of parameters or settings as well, which is one reason the general field of density estimation is rather controversial among statisticians (Wegman, 1982).

SYGRAPH offers several ways to represent a density. Both the **HISTOGRAM** and **DENSITY** commands produce garden variety histograms. The **POLY** option produces frequency polygons. **FUZZY** produces FUZZYGRAMS, which are probability enhanced histograms. **STRIPE** produces vertical stripes. **JITTER** produces jittered sample densities. The **SMOOTH** option offers several smooth probability distributions.

Figure 1 shows the standard display if you choose no options. This is a histogram of INCOME (per-capita income) from the US file. SYGRAPH chooses the number of bars based on a function of sample size and the shape of the distribution. The scale on the right measures the count in each bar. The scale on the left measures the proportion of cases falling in each bar divided by the sample standard deviation. Standardizing this axis this way makes it easier to compare histograms based on different scales.

Figure 1

```
DENSITY  INCOME
```

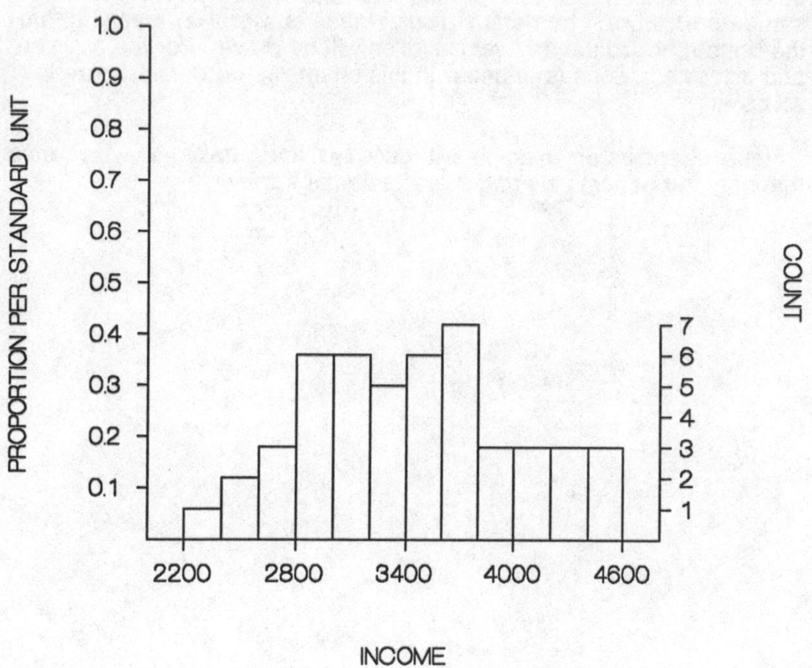

AXES *(Number of Axes)*

The **AXES** option controls the number of axes drawn in a histogram or density estimator. Its syntax is:

```
AXES=n
```

where *n* is an integer from 0 to 4. If *n* is 0, no axes will be drawn. If *n* is an integer from 1 to 4, all axes from 1 to *n* will be drawn. Axes are numbered from 1 to 4 clockwise, beginning with the bottom axis:

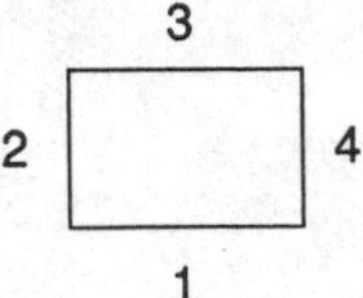

If *n* is negative, only the axis numbered with the absolute value of *n* will be drawn. Since SYGRAPH histograms have no top axis, **AXES=3** is the same as **AXES=2**. The default (usual) value is **AXES=4**, meaning that the bottom horizontal and vertical axes will be drawn. For the **STRIPE** and **JITTER** options (see below in this chapter), the default value is **AXES=1**.

Figure 2 shows an example with **AXES=1** and **SCALE=1**, which mean that only the bottom axis and scale values are drawn.

Figure 2

```
TYPE=SWISS
DENSITY  INCOME/AXES=1,SCALE=1
```

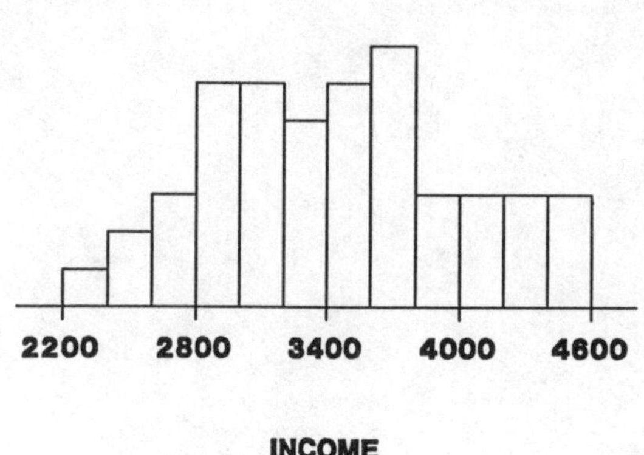

BARS *(Number of Bars)*

The BARS option controls the number of bars drawn in a histogram. SYGRAPH usually chooses an optimal number of bars via a statistical algorithm based on the binary log of the number of cases and other factors. You can force a different number of bars this way:

```
DENSITY   INCOME/BARS=20
```

This will leave SYGRAPH with the choice of scale values (cutpoints). If you with to manipulate the cutpoints as well, then use the **BWIDTH** option (see below in this chapter).

Figure 3 shows a histogram with 15 bars. Because SYGRAPH chose even cutpoints, the upper three bars were left empty and we were forced back to the same shape we had in Figure 1.

Figure 3

```
TYPE=HERSHEY
DENSITY INCOME/BARS=15
```

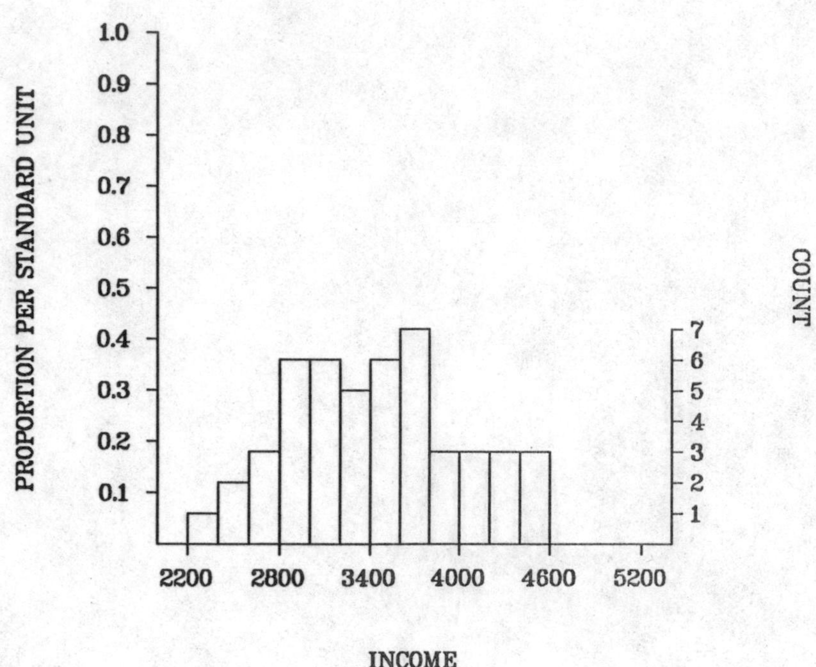

BWIDTH *(Width of Bars)*

The **BWIDTH** option controls the width of bars drawn in a histogram. Normally, SYGRAPH chooses the bar width (interval between cutpoints), number of bars, and scale values via an optimization algorithm. You can modify the chosen bar width with the **BWIDTH** option. Usually, you should set **MIN** (see below in this chapter) when you set **BWIDTH**. Otherwise, the SYGRAPH optimization algorithm may not give you the minimum values you wish. Figure 4 shows an example of this. By choosing **MIN** and **BWIDTH**, we have completely overridden the optimization algorithm.

Figure 4

```
DENSITY   INCOME/MIN=2000,BWIDTH=150
```

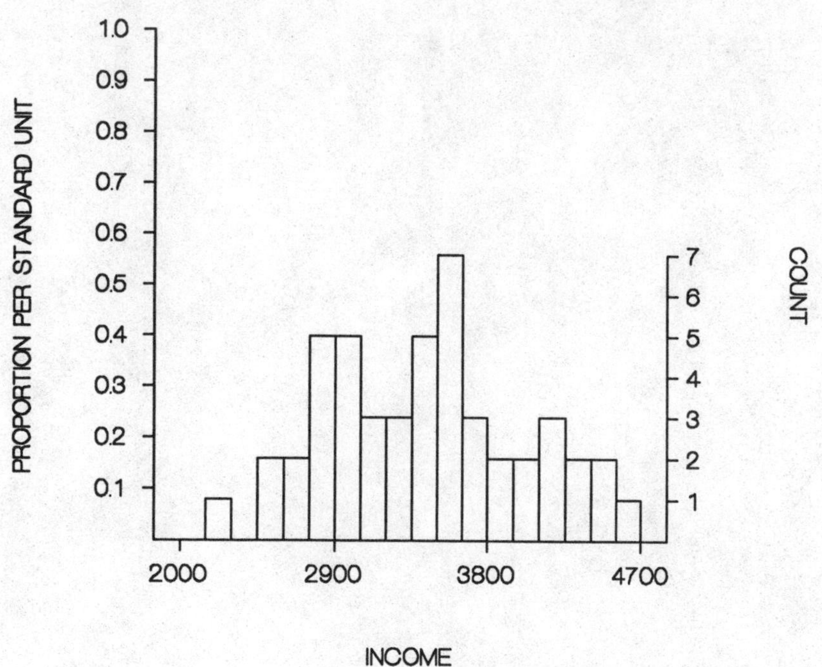

COLOR *(Setting Color of Bars)*

You can choose a color for your histogram with the **COLOR** option. Choose either a name or a wavelength in nanometers. Possible colors and their approximate nanometer wavelengths are: **RED** (615), **ORANGE** (590), **YELLOW** (575), **GREEN** (505), **BLUE** (480), **VIOLET** (450). You may also name **BLACK**, **WHITE**, **GRAY**, and **BROWN**. The following command will make all bars in the graph red:

```
DENSITY   REGION$/COLOR=RED
```

You can also specify color in nanometers wavelength. The following example will make all the bars greenish:

```
DENSITY   REGION$/COLOR=540
```

Figure 5 shows an example of a histogram with red bars. I used the SUMMER temperature from the US dataset.

Figure 5

```
DENSITY  SUMMER/COLOR=RED,FILL
```

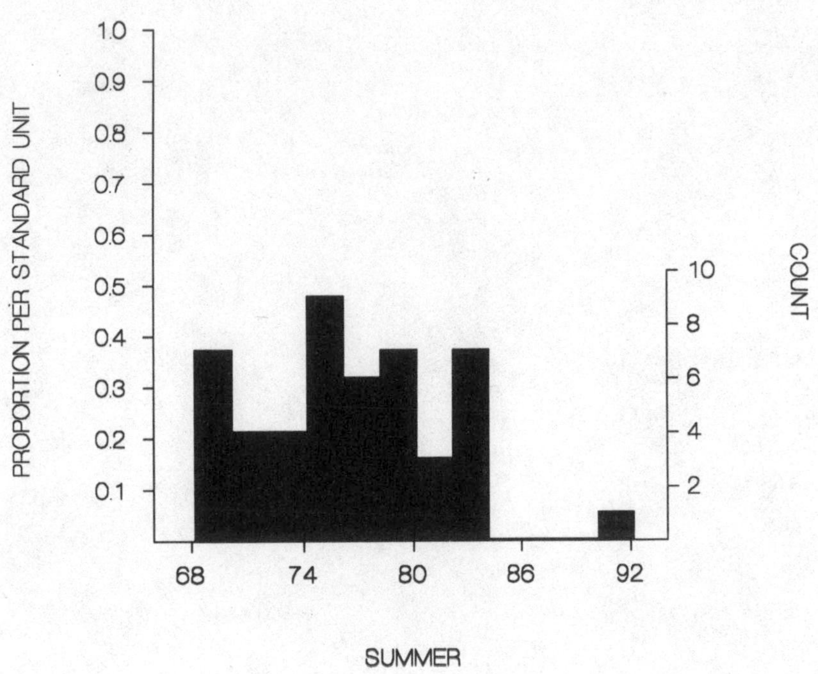

CUM *(Cumulative Histograms)*

The **CUM** option allows you to do a cumulative histogram. In a cumulative histogram, each bar's area is the sum of preceding bar's areas plus its own incremental area. This makes a cumulative histogram correspond to a cumulative frequency distribution or, for continuous data, a distribution function.

Figure 6 shows the result. Keep in mind that you can add the other **DENSITY** options to produce more complex histograms.

Figure 6

```
DENSITY  INCOME/CUM
```

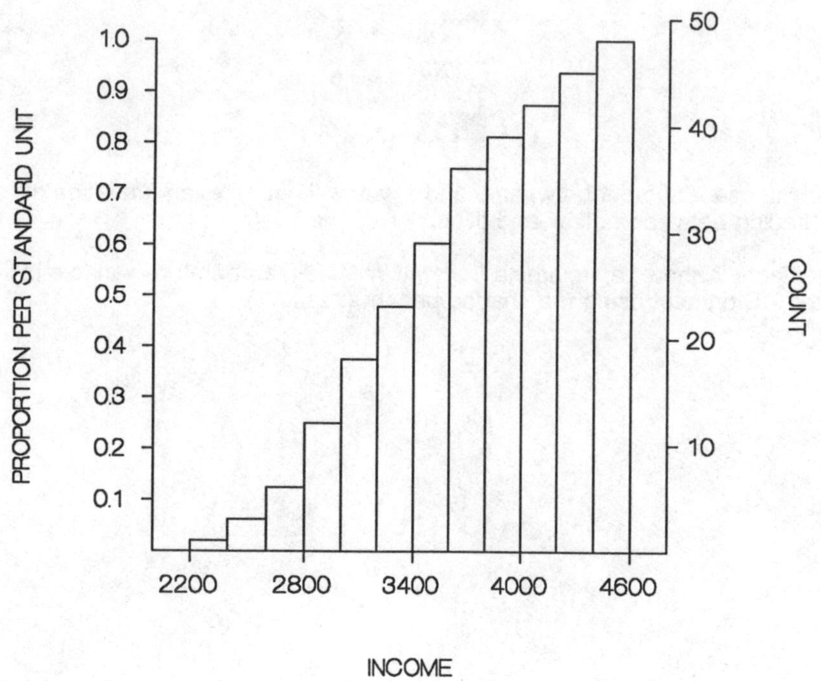

FILL *(Filling bars)*

You can fill bars with different patterns. The **FILL** option works this way:

```
DENSITY   WINTER/FILL=1
```

The number you choose after "**FILL=**" determines the type of fill pattern. Here are the possibilities:

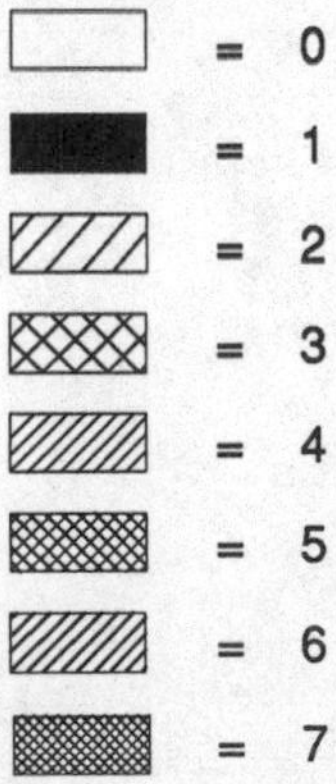

= 0

= 1

= 2

= 3

= 4

= 5

= 6

= 7

If you use a number between 0 and 1, you will get an even gradation of shading between hollow and filled.

Figure 7 shows an example from the WINTER temperature variable in the US dataset using the shaded pattern (**FILL=7**).

Figure 7

```
DENSITY  WINTER/FILL=7
```

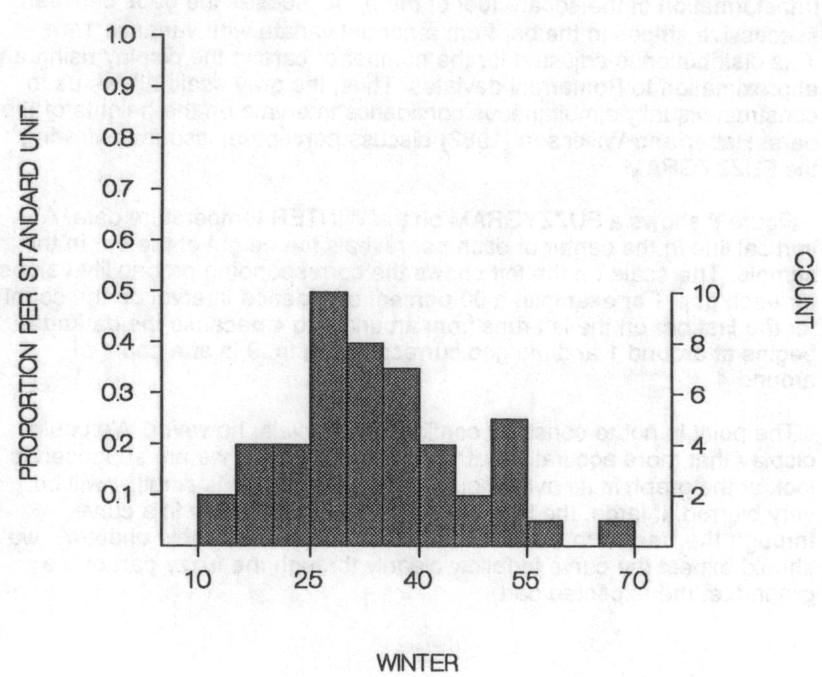

FUZZY *(Fuzzygrams)*

Wilkinson (1983) devised a variation of the histogram which superimposed a probability distribution on each bar. The purpose of this display is to make the bars for histograms based on small samples fuzzier than the bars for large sample histograms. This way, when we examine sample histograms to see if they plausibly represent a population distribution, we will not place too much faith in small sample variations or features.

Basically, it works like this. Let $p_i = n_i/n$ be the sample estimate of π_i the expected proportion of a sample of n values from a continuous distribution to fall in the i-th of k histogram bars (i=1,k). Assume k is selected such that $0 < \pi_i < 1$. A FUZZYGRAM is a histogram with bars represented by a gray scale distribution on $P_i = P(p_i > \pi_i)$. That is, the more likely p_i is greater than π_i, the lighter the bar.

The program computes the gray scale assuming that the joint distribution of the counts in the bars is multinomial. Using an arc sine transformation of the square root of the p_i, it chooses the gaps between successive stripes in the bar from a normal variate with variance $1/4n$. This distribution is adjusted for the number of bars in the display using an approximation to Bonferroni deviates. Thus, the gray scale allows us to construct visually simultaneous confidence intervals on the heights of the bars. Haber and Wilkinson (1982) discuss perceptual issues in viewing the FUZZYGRAM.

Figure 8 shows a FUZZYGRAM on the WINTER temperature data. A vertical line in the center of each bar reveals the height of the bar in the sample. The scale on the left shows the corresponding probability values for each gap. For example, a 90 percent confidence interval on the count for the first bar on the left runs from around 1 to 4 because the darkness begins at around 1 and the gap corresponding to .9 is at a count of around 4.

The point is not to construct confidence intervals, however. We could display that more accurately with tick marks. Rather, we are supposed to look at the graph in its overall blur. If the sample size is small, it will be very blurred. If large, the bars will be sharp. Finally, if we fit a curve through the bars with `SMOOTH=NORMAL` (see below in this chapter), we should expect the curve to follow cleanly through the fuzzy part of the graph (i.e. the expected part).

Figure 8

```
DENSITY  WINTER/FUZZY
```

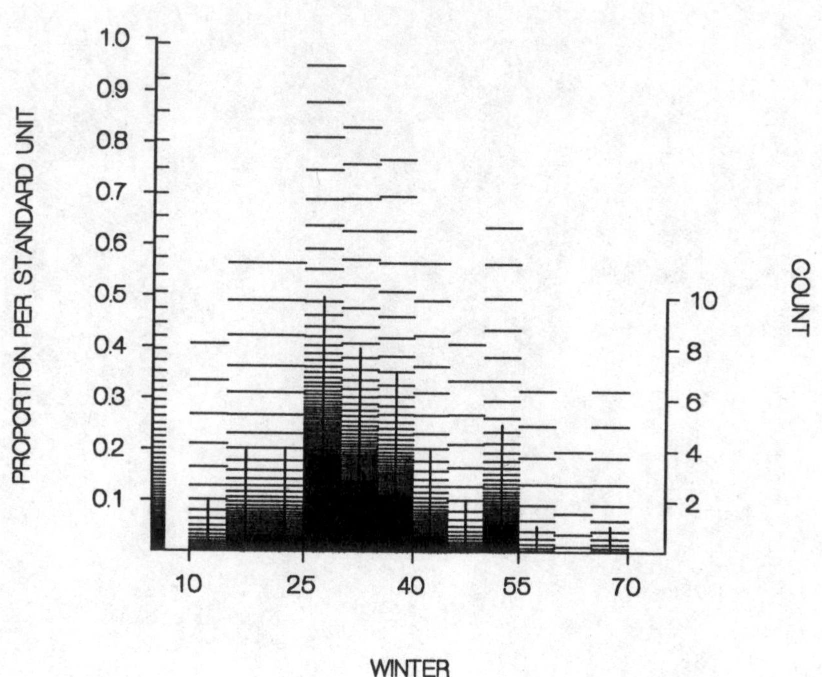

HEIGHT *(Physical Height of Plot)*

You can control the physical height of your display with the **HEIGHT** option. It works like this:

```
HEIGHT=50%      (or HEIGHT=50)
HEIGHT=4IN
HEIGHT=10CM
```

The first example specifies percent of display height. The second specifies inches, and the third centimeters.

When you use the **HEIGHT** option, you probably also want to use **WIDTH**, which works exactly the same way (see below in this chapter). The following graph shows how to use them together on the RAIN (annual rainfall) variable from the US dataset.

Figure 9

```
DENSITY   RAIN/HEIGHT=3IN,WIDTH=4IN
```

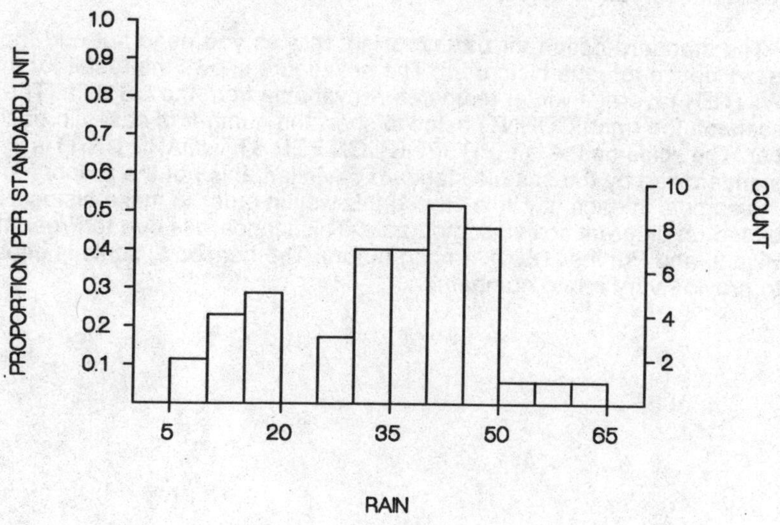

HIST *(Histograms)*

A histogram displays the sample density of a numerical variable. The word comes from a Greek word for a straight standing beam like a mast or loom frame (histos) and the word for picture (as in diagram) which derives from the word for writing. Thus, a histogram is a display of bars standing vertically.

Unlike bar charts, however, histograms in statistics are based on continuous variables. The bars are ordered along a continuum and the cutpoints between the bars are chosen to make the shape of the histogram particularly revealing of the distribution of a variable.

I mention this background to highlight the use of a histogram to display the shape of data. Many people use histograms to count data values. This is a misuse of the display. If you want to examine actual data values, you should use the `BAR` command or a stem and leaf diagram, offered with the `STEM` command in SYGRAPH.

SYGRAPH uses initial estimates and a heuristic strategy to pick the number of bars and scale values to produce an aesthetic histogram (Sturges, 1926; Doane, 1976; Scott, 1979). If there are too many empty bars (more than a half), the program reduces the number. If some bars are too tall, the program increases the number. Several options are available for you to adjust the values selected by the program.

The standard option for `DENSITY` is `HIST`, so you need not add the `HIST` option to get a histogram. The next figure shows the result for the WINTER (average winter temperature) variable from the US data. The scale on the right (COUNT) helps to show the number of cases in each bar. The scale on the left (PROPORTION PER STANDARD UNIT) is standardized by the sample standard deviation. It is not the proportion of the sample in each bar. It is printed this way in order to make histograms based on different scales comparable. This standard is due to Freedman, Pisani, and Purves (1980), among others. The horizontal scale is chosen to provide very round numbers.

Figure 10

```
DENSITY WINTER/HIST
```

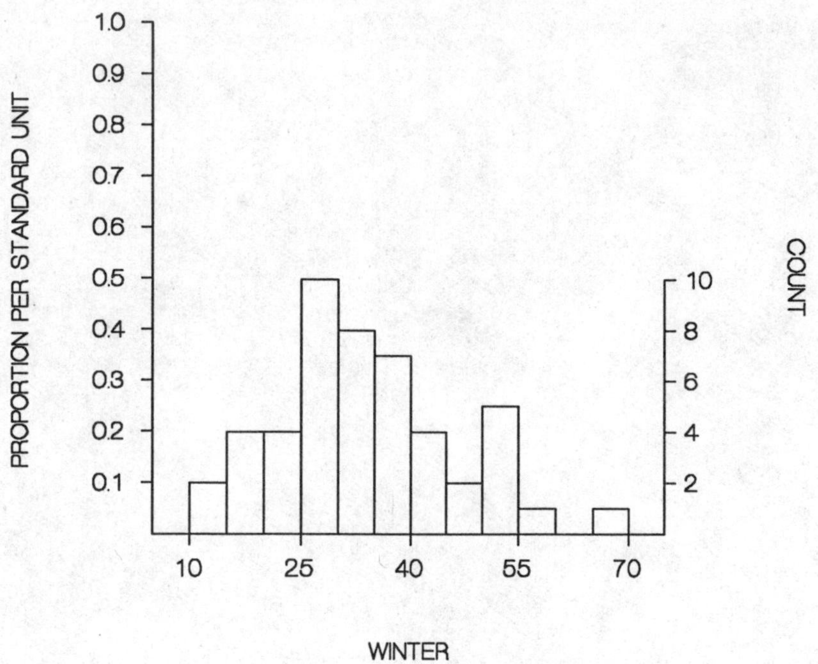

JITTER *(Jittered Density)*

A jittered density places points along a horizontal data scale at the locations of data values. In order to keep points from colliding, they are located randomly on a short vertical axis. Unlike histograms, no binning into bars is required. Unlike density stripes (see below in this chapter), jittered densities work well with large samples because points do not overlap. Jittering is less appropriate for small samples, however, because the quantity of points is usually not sufficient to indicate a density in a given region.

Figure 11 shows a jittered plot of POPDEN (population density). This sample is a bit too small for jittering. Compare it to Figure 19, which reveals the density better.

Figure 11

```
DENSITY POPDEN/JITTER
```

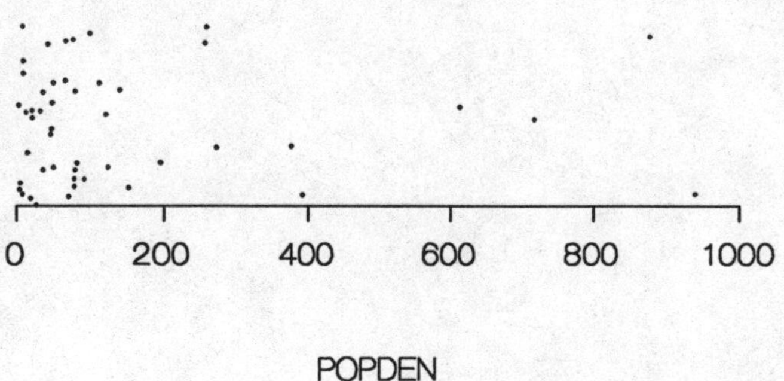

LOG *(Logging Data)*

You can log your data with the `LOG` command. Logs may be computed to any base, e.g. `LOG=2`, `LOG=3`, `LOG=10`, `LOG=.5`. Natural logarithms will be computed if you use `LOG` with no argument, i.e. `LOG`. Unlike elsewhere in SYGRAPH, the horizontal data scale is printed in the logged values rather than in the data values if you choose a histogram or FUZZYGRAM. This is because the bars are kept at a uniform width. If you choose the `STRIPE` or `JITTER` options (see below in this chapter), the raw data values will be printed with logarithmic spacing.

Figure 12 shows a striped density with a base 10 log. Compare this plot to Figure 19 below, which shows the density stripe for the raw data. The logging makes the density more symmetric.

Figure 12

`DENSITY POPDEN/STRIPE,LOG=10`

MAX *(Maximum Scale Value)*

You can limit the right end of your data scale with the **MAX** option. Usually, you should use this with the **MIN** option, which regulates the lower end of the data scale.

Figure 13 shows both options on the RAIN (annual rainfall) variable from the US dataset. I set **BARS=7** to keep the cutpoints even. Otherwise, SYGRAPH tries to choose the best number of bars based on sample size rather than the scale.

Figure 13

```
TYPE=BRITISH/ITALIC
DENSITY  RAIN/MIN=0,MAX=70,BARS=7
```

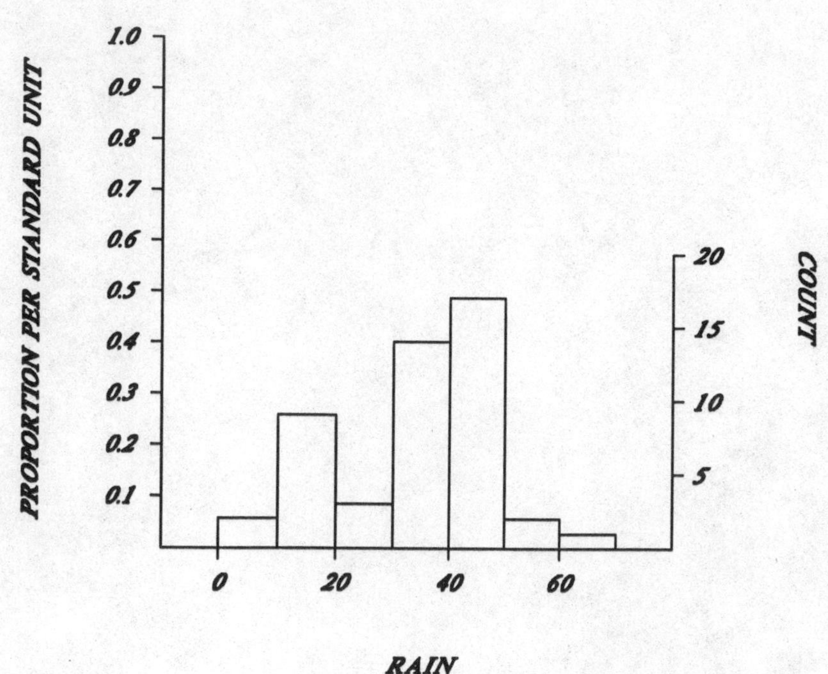

MIN *(Minimum Scale Value)*

You can limit the left end of your data scale with the `MIN` option.

Figure 14 shows how to begin INCOME (per-capita income) at zero.

Figure 14

```
TYPE=BRITISH/ITALIC
DENSITY  INCOME/MIN=0
```

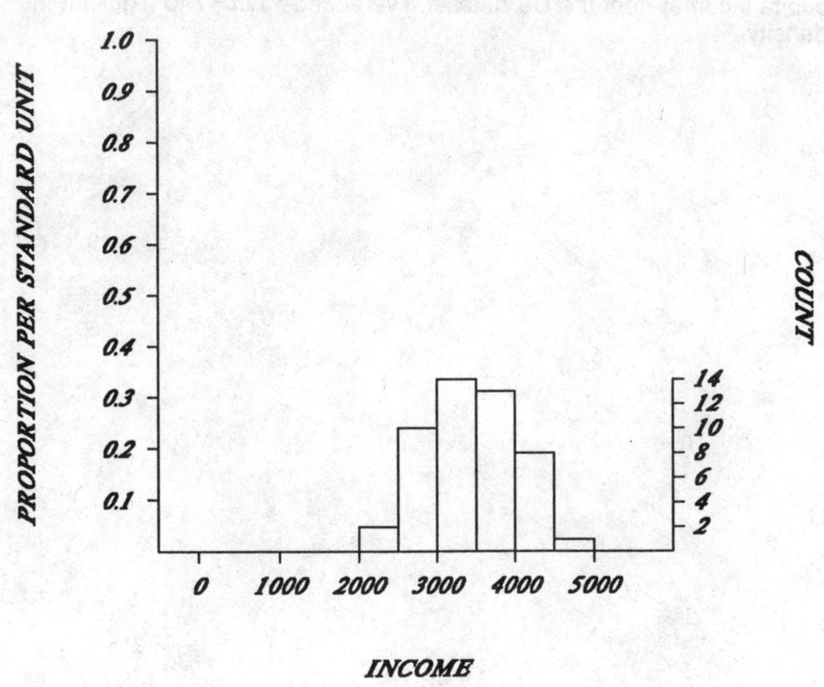

POLY *(Frequency Polygon)*

Frequency polygons can be produced by connecting the tops of the bars of a histogram with a line and then removing the bars. If we are thinking of a histogram as a sample density estimator, then a frequency polygon does a better job because it smooths the square edges of the bars.

It is simple to produce a frequency polygon instead of a histogram. Just type:

```
DENSITY  X/POLY
```

where X is the name of a variable. Remember, the shape of the polygon depends on the number of bars or cutpoints chosen. You may want to experiment with the **BARS** option (see above in this chapter) to see the differences.

Figure 15 shows a frequency polygon of the INCOME variable (per-capita income) from the US dataset. I've added **FILL=7** to highlight the density.

Figure 15

`DENSITY INCOME/POLY,FILL=7`

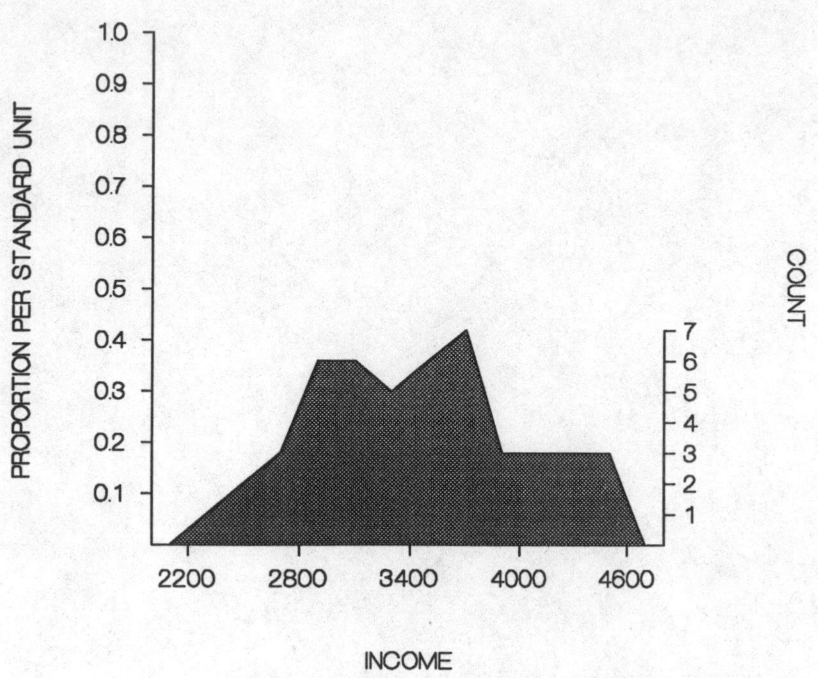

POW *(Powering Data)*

You can power your data with the **POW** command. Powers may be computed to any exponent, e.g. **POW=.5** (square root), **POW=.33333** (cube root), **POW=-1** (inverse), **POW=2**. Square roots will be computed if you use **POW** with no argument, i.e. **POW**. **POW** is implemented in SYGRAPH only for positive data. Negative values will be deleted.

Unlike elsewhere in SYGRAPH, the horizontal data scale is printed in the powered values rather than in the data values if you choose a histogram or FUZZYGRAM. This is because the bars are kept at a uniform width. If you choose the **STRIPE** or **JITTER** options (see below in this chapter), the raw data values will be printed with powered spacing.

Figure 16 shows the latter example on POPDEN (population density). I have used the default square root power (**POW=.5**), so I do not need to add a value. Compare this to Figure 12. Square rooting is not sufficient to symmetrize the distribution.

Figure 16

```
DENSITY  POPDEN/STRIPE,POW
```

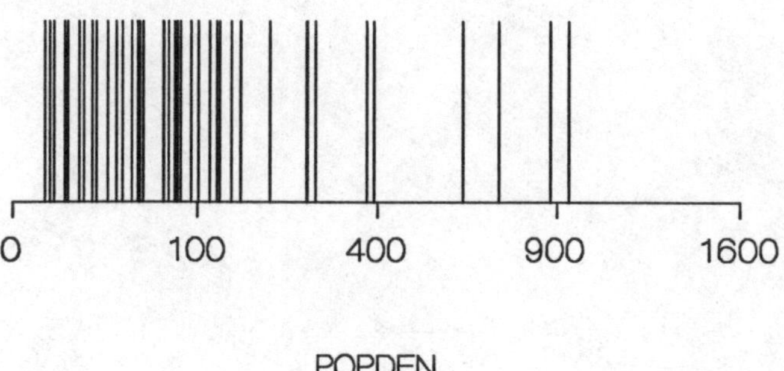

REV *(Reversing the Scale)*
You can reverse the scale of the horizontal axis with the REV option.

Figure 17 shows you an example of a reversed scale.

Figure 17

DENSITY POPDEN/STRIPE,POW,REV

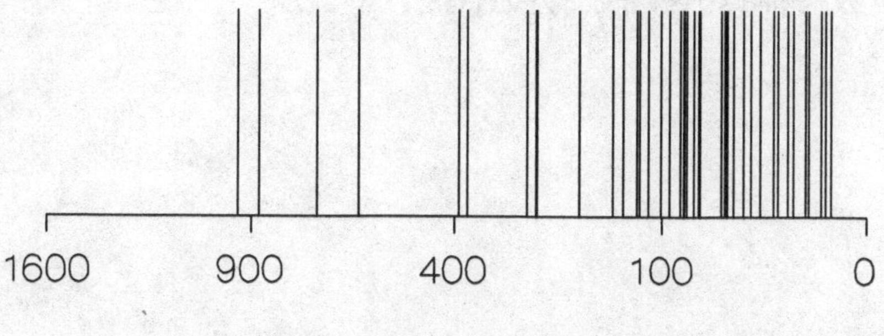

SCALE *(Number of Scales)*

Scales are the numbers which label the tick marks on an axis. The **SCALE** option controls the number of scales drawn in a histogram. Its syntax is:

```
SCALE=n
```

where *n* is an integer from 0 to 4. If *n* is 0, no scales will be drawn. If *n* is an integer from 1 to 4, all scales from 1 to *n* will be drawn. If *n* is negative, only the scale numbered with the absolute value of *n* will be drawn. Scales are numbered from 1 to 4 clockwise, beginning with the bottom axis:

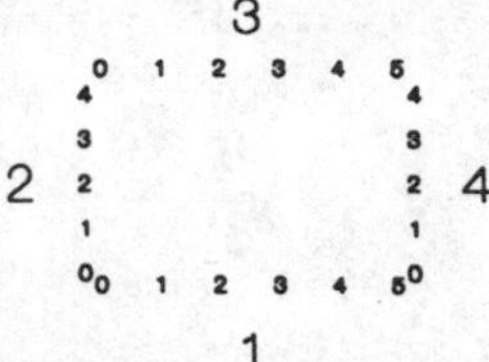

Because SYGRAPH histograms have no top axis, **SCALE=3** has no meaning. The default (usual) value for a histogram is **SCALE=4**, meaning that the bottom horizontal and both vertical scales will be drawn. For the **STRIPE** and **JITTER** options, the default value is **SCALE=1**.

Figure 18 shows a plot with two axes and scales. Usually, you will use the **AXES** and **SCALE** options together.

Figure 18

```
DENSITY  RAIN/AXES=2,SCALE=2
```

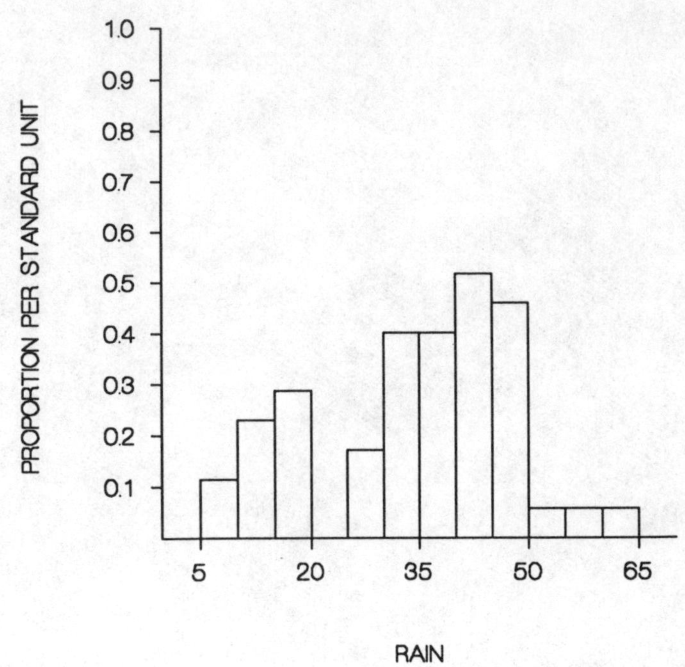

SMOOTH=NORMAL *(Smoothing with the Normal Density)*

If data are sampled from a normal distribution, then their histogram should tend to have a normal shape. We can examine this possibility by using the sample mean and standard deviation to superimpose a normal curve on a histogram. Just add the option **SMOOTH=NORMAL**. If you are doing a cumulative histogram (see **CUM** above in this chapter) then the cumulative normal curve will be used.

Figure 19 shows a normal smooth through the WINTER temperature data from the US file. The lower tail in the graph is a bit short, probably because we are not sampling temperatures as far north as we are south, given the geographic distribution of the continental U.S.

Figure 19

```
TYPE=BRITISH
DENSITY  WINTER/SMOOTH=NORMAL
```

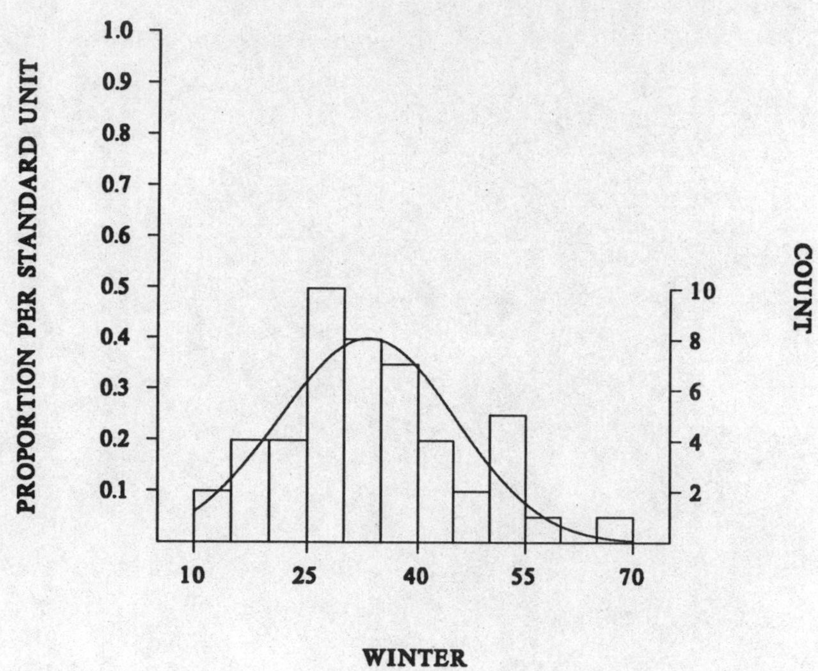

STRIPE *(Density Stripes)*

Density stripes are vertical lines placed at the location of data values on a horizontal data scale. Unlike histograms, no binning into bars is required, so density stripes are especially suited for small to moderate sized samples of continuous data. For larger datasets, stripes tend to overlap and produce black bars. In these cases, you should consider the `JITTER` option (see above in this chapter).

Figure 20 shows a density stripe plot of POPDEN (population density).

Figure 20

DENSITY POPDEN/STRIPE

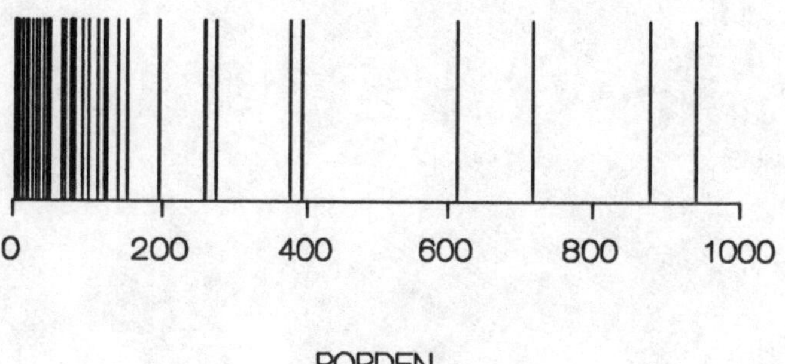

TITLE *(Graph Title)*

You can place a title at the top center of your graph with the `TITLE` option:

```
TITLE='Worldwide Sales in U.S. Dollars'
TITLE="Roger's Worthless Opinions"
TITLE='Perceived variation in "Impact"'
```

The text must be surrounded by quotes (") or apostrophes ('). If your text includes apostrophes, as in the second example, surround it with quotes. If it includes quotes, as in the third example, surround it with apostrophes.

On some display devices the title will run off the top of the page because the standard display window is chosen to make the labels and graph as large as possible. If this happens, you will have to use the **SCALE** command to reduce the size of your entire graph (e.g. **SCALE=70,70**) or the **HEIGHT** option to lower the height.

Figure 21 shows a graph with a title.

Figure 21

```
TYPE=SWISS/ITALIC
DENSITY  POPDEN/TITLE='Population  Density'
```

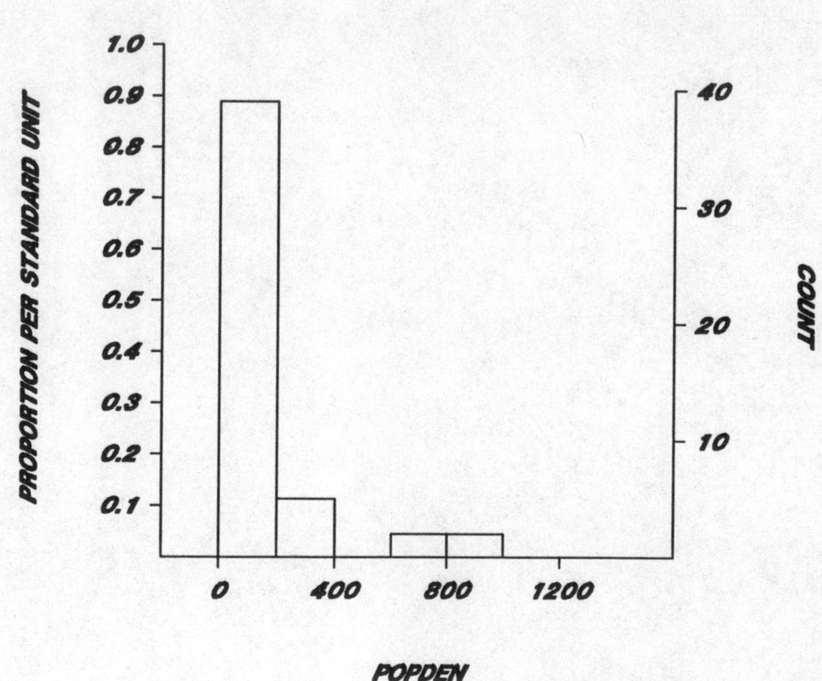

TRANS *(Transposed Density Stripes or Jitters)*

You can transpose density stripes or jitters with the `TRANS` option. It works the same as it does elsewhere in SYGRAPH. You cannot transpose histograms. Go back and read the introduction to this chapter. Histograms are straight standing masts. If you tip them sideways, they will sink.

Figure 22 shows a transposed density stripe plot of POPDEN, used in Figure 20.

Figure 22

```
DENSITY  POPDEN/STRIPE,TRANS
```

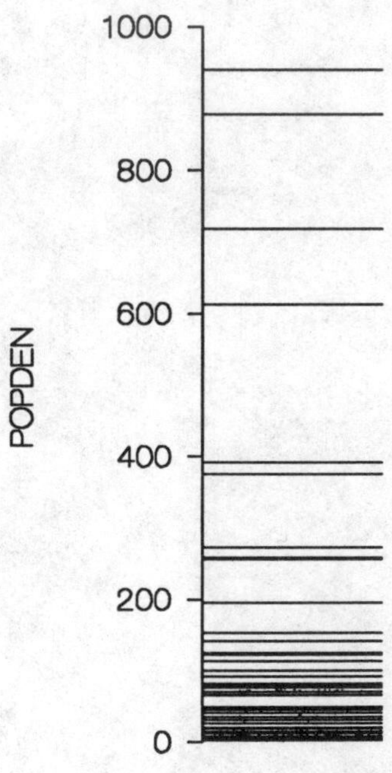

WIDTH *(Physical Width of Plot)*

You can control the physical width of your histogram with the **WIDTH** option. It works like this:

```
WIDTH=50%        (or WIDTH=50 )
WIDTH=4IN
WIDTH=10CM
```

The first example specifies percent of display width. The second specifies inches, and the third centimeters.

When you use the **WIDTH** option, you probably also want to use **HEIGHT**, which works exactly the same way (see above in this chapter). The following graph shows how to use them together on the PERSON variable (personal crimes per 100,000) from the US file.

Figure 23

```
DENSITY   PERSON/HEIGHT=4IN,WIDTH=3IN
```

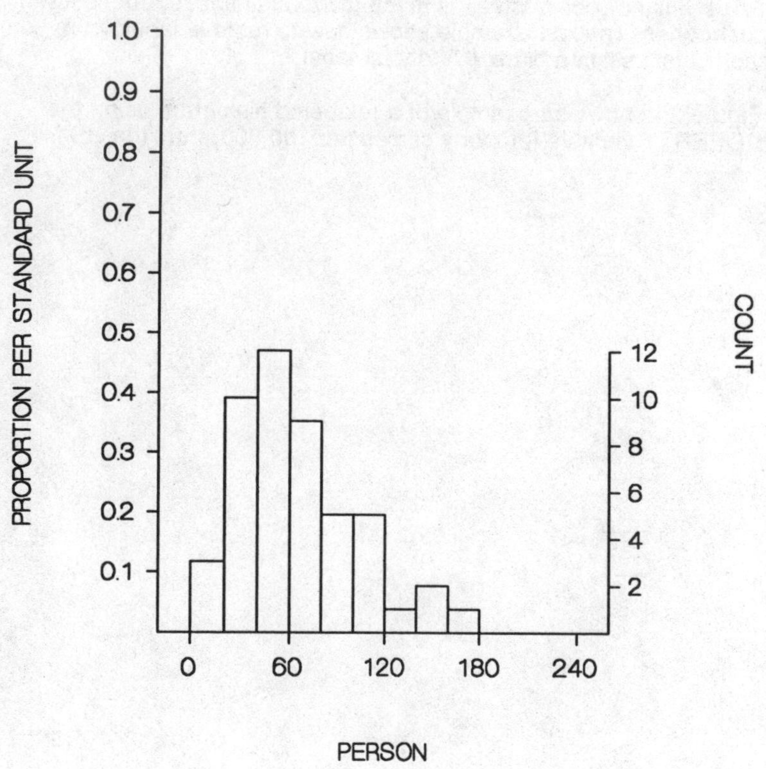

XLABEL,YLABEL *(Labeling a Histogram)*

Histograms are usually labeled at the bottom with the name of the variable you use in the **DENSITY** command and on the left side with 'PROPORTION PER STANDARD UNIT.' If you want different labels, use the **XLABEL** and/or **YLABEL** command, e.g.:

```
XLABEL='Proportion  of  Variance'
YLABEL='Proportion'
XLABEL="Peter's  Portion"
XLABEL='Proportion  of  "Widgets"  Bid'
YLABEL='  '
```

The label text must be surrounded by quotes (") or apostrophes ('). If your text includes apostrophes, as in the third example, surround it with quotes. If it includes quotes, as in the fourth example, surround it with apostrophes. The last example shows how to remove labels from your graph. Just assign a blank (' ') to your label.

Figure 24 shows an example of a relabeled histogram using the PROPERTY variable (property crimes per 100,000) from the US file.

Figure 24

```
DENSITY PROPERTY,
 /XLABEL='Property Crimes per 100,000'
```

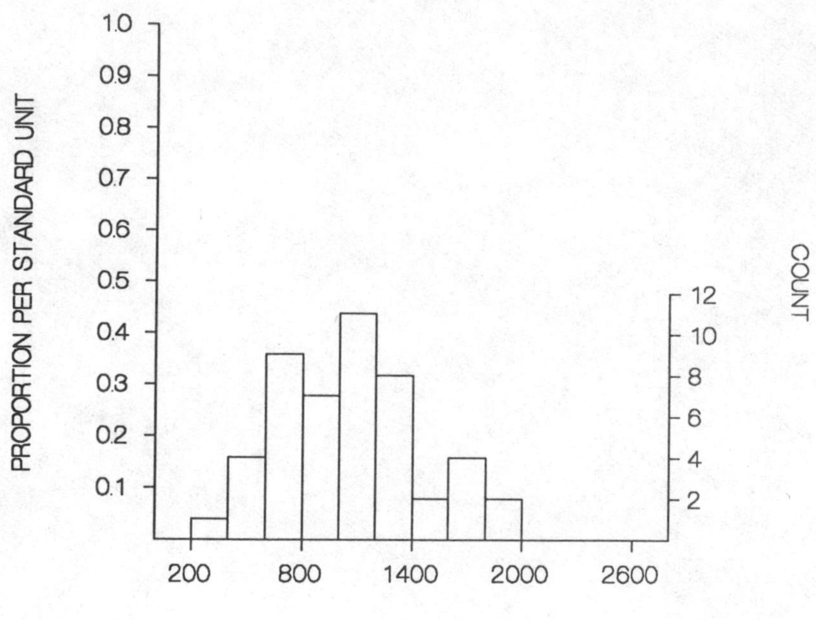

Chapter 6

DRAW

The **DRAW** command produces graphical primitives, namely boxes, ovals, lines, arrows, symbols, and triangles. You can use this command to annotate and revise the standard graphs in SYGRAPH. The standard syntax is:

```
DRAW  ARROW
DRAW  BOX
DRAW  LINE
DRAW  OVAL
DRAW  SYMBOL
DRAW  TRIANGLE
```

The options to these commands determine the type of primitive which is drawn. Here are the usual options which you would want to use with these commands:

```
ARROW:     COLOR,X1,Y1,X2,Y2,Z1,Z2
BOX:       CENTER,COLOR,FILL,HEIGHT,WIDTH,X,Y
LINE:      COLOR,X1,Y1,X2,Y2,Z1,Z2
OVAL:      COLOR,FILL,HEIGHT,WIDTH,X,Y
SYMBOL:    COLOR,FILL,HEIGHT,SYMBOL,WIDTH,X,Y
TRIANGLE:CENTER,COLOR,FILL,HEIGHT,WIDTH,X,Y
```

The default coordinates for all figures are **X=0** and **Y=0** (the lower left corner of the default graph axes). **BOX** and **TRIANGLE** positioned so that their lower left corner is at these location coordinates. **OVAL** and **SYMBOL** are centered on these coordinates. The default **HEIGHT** and **WIDTH** are the same as for the default graph axes. Thus, if you plot a **BOX** with no options, it will exactly overlap the typical graph frame for, say, the **PLOT** command. Since it is equilateral, the right-hand corner of **TRIANGLE** defaults to slightly wider than the graph frame. Its height, on the other hand, is exactly the height of a graph frame.

CENTER *(Center Figures)*

You can center boxes and triangles with the **CENTER** option. Normally, the **X** and **Y** options refer to the coordinates of the lower left corner of a box or triangle. Together with the **CENTER** option, they refer to the center of the box. The **CENTER** option applies only to boxes and triangles. Ovals and symbols are centered by default.

Figure 1 shows a centered box surrounding text.

Figure 1

```
WRITE  'Centered  Text',
  /CENTER,X=2IN,Y=2IN,HEIGHT=.2IN,WIDTH=.2IN
 DRAW  BOX/CENTER,X=2IN,Y=2IN,HEIGHT=1IN,WIDTH=3IN
```

Centered Text

COLOR *(Color Figures)*

You can choose a color for your primitive with the **COLOR** option. Choose either a name or a wavelength in nanometers. Possible colors and their approximate nanometer wavelengths are: **RED** (615), **ORANGE** (590), **YELLOW** (575), **GREEN** (505), **BLUE** (480), **VIOLET** (450). You may also name **BLACK**, **WHITE**, **GRAY**, and **BROWN**. The following command will make a red box:

```
DRAW  BOX/COLOR=RED
```

You can also specify color in nanometers wavelength. The following example will make a greenish circle:

```
DRAW  OVAL/COLOR=540
```

Figure 2 shows a filled red box.

Figure 2

```
DRAW  BOX/COLOR=RED,FILL=7
```

FILL *(Filling Figures)*

The `FILL` option specifies a fill pattern, e.g. FILL=1. The number you choose after "`FILL=`" determines the type of fill pattern for the whole primitive:

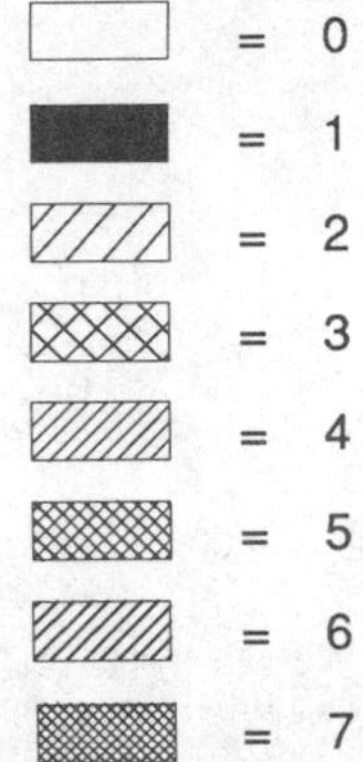

If you use a number between 0 and 1, you will get an even gradation of shading between hollow and filled.

Figure 3 shows an oval filled with the shaded pattern.

Figure 3

```
DRAW   OVAL/FILL=5,X=2IN,Y=2IN,HEIGHT=3IN,WIDTH=2IN
```

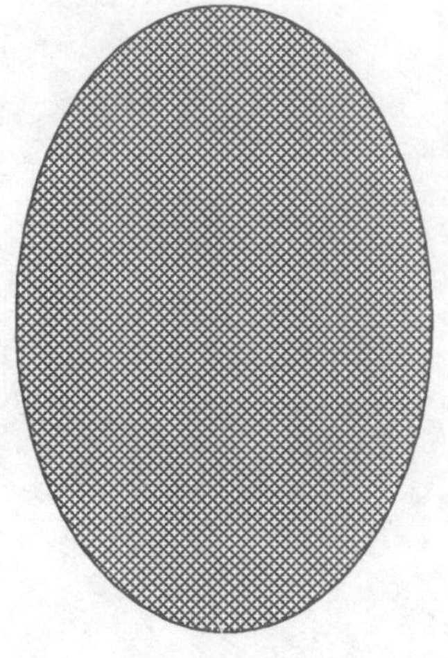

HEIGHT *(Physical Height of Figure)*

You can control the physical height of your primitive with the **HEIGHT** option. It works like this:

```
HEIGHT=50%      (or HEIGHT=50)
HEIGHT=4IN
HEIGHT=10CM
```

The first example specifies percent of display height. The second specifies inches, and the third centimeters.

The next figure shows how to make an oval (first ... squeeze a circle).

Figure 4

```
DRAW   OVAL/HEIGHT=3IN,WIDTH=4IN,X=2IN,Y=2IN
```

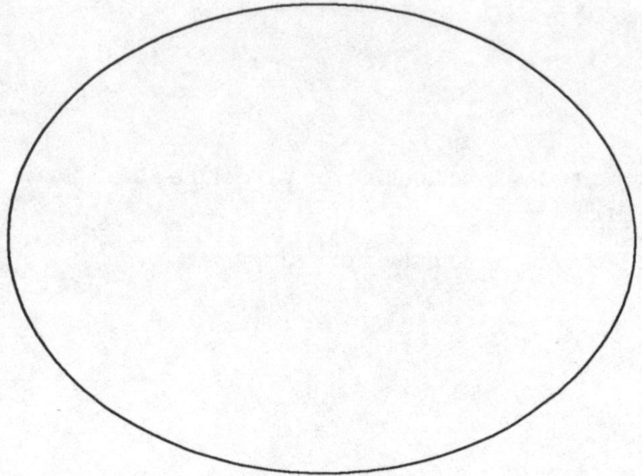

LINE *(Line Types)*
You may choose from 11 different types of lines by typing LINE=*n* , where *n* is one of the following numbers:

1
2
3
4
5
6
7
8
9
10
11

If you type `LINE` with no number you will get the solid line, which is the same as typing LINE=1.

Figure 5 shows how to draw a dotted line.

Figure 5

```
DRAW  LINE/LINE=2,X1=0,Y1=0,X2=3IN,Y2=4IN
```

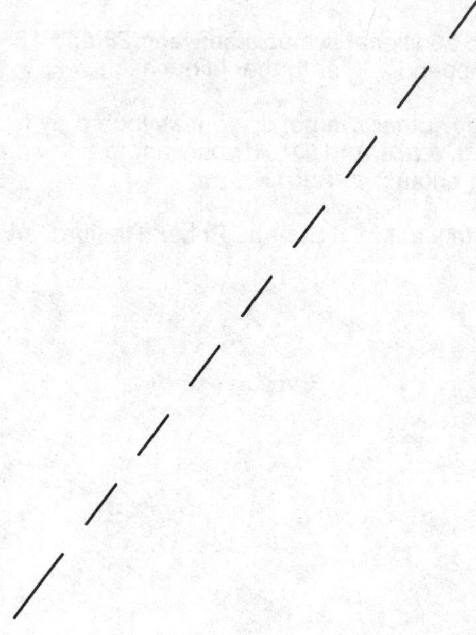

SYMBOL *(Plotting Symbols)*
You can draw a variety of symbols. Just add the option: **SYMBOL=***n* , where *n* is an integer denoting one of the following symbols:

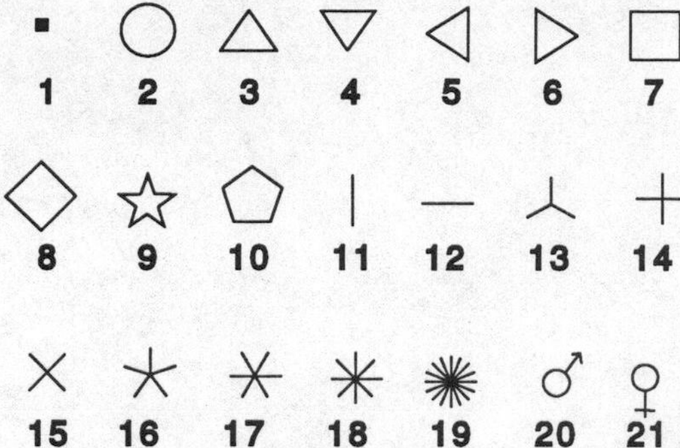

You can choose additional symbols between 28 and 128. These vary by typeface. See Appendix A for further information.

You can use any other symbol on your keyboard by typing it between apostrophes, e.g. **SYMBOL='@'**. If you want to use an apostrophe, surround it with quotes: **SYMBOL="'"**.

Here is a star (a.k.a. Meryl Streep, Robert Redford, and Rick Wessler).

Figure 6

```
DRAW  SYMBOL,
  /SYMBOL=9,X=2IN,Y=2IN,HEIGHT=3IN,WIDTH=3IN,FILL=5
```

WIDTH *(Physical Width of Text)*

You can control the physical width of your figure with the **WIDTH** option. It works like this:

```
WIDTH=50%        (or WIDTH=50)
WIDTH=4IN
WIDTH=10CM
```

The first example specifies percent of display width. The second specifies inches, and the third centimeters.

When you use the **WIDTH** option, you probably also want to use **HEIGHT**, which works exactly the same way (see above in this chapter). Here is how to draw a rectangle.

Figure 7

```
DRAW  BOX/HEIGHT=3IN,WIDTH=2IN
```

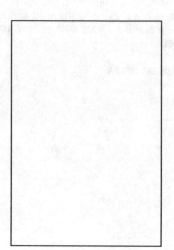

X,Y,Z *(Locating Text)*

SYGRAPH normally locates a figure at the default origin (0,0). You can place it anywhere else with the **X** and **Y** (and **Z**) options. They work like this:

```
X=50%        (or X=50)
X=4IN
Y=10CM
```

The first example specifies percent of display width. The second specifies inches, and the third centimeters.

For symbols and ovals, **X** and **Y** refer to their center. For boxes and triangles, they refer to their lower left corner, unless you add the **CENTER** option (see above in this chapter). For lines and arrows, you need two sets of coordinates, one for the beginning and one for the end. The beginning coordinates are **X1**,**Y1**, and the end are **X2**,**Y2**. To draw lines or arrows in three dimensions without using the **FACET** command, you need to add **Z1** and **Z2**.

Here is an example of an arrow.

Figure 8

```
DRAW   ARROW/X1=1IN,Y1=1IN,X2=3IN,Y2=4IN
```

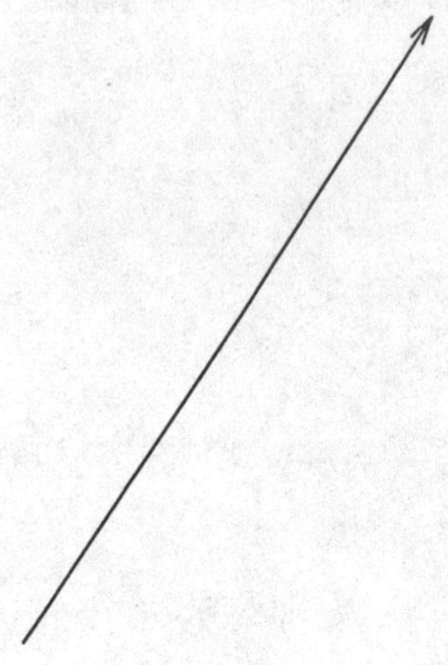

ZHEIGHT *(Three-Dimensional Boxes)*

If you add **ZHEIGHT** to the **HEIGHT** and **WIDTH** options when drawing a box, you will get a three-dimensional box in perspective. ZHEIGHT works just like **HEIGHT**, but it specifies the "altitude" of a box, or its height on the Z axis. It works like this:

```
ZHEIGHT=50%    (or ZHEIGHT=50)
ZHEIGHT=4IN
ZHEIGHT=10CM
```

The first example specifies percent of display height. The second specifies inches, and the third centimeters. Remember, **ZHEIGHT** is in real units, but the actual physical height of the object depends on the setting of the **EYE** command (see above in reference section). There is an example of a three-dimensional box in the 3-D chapter in the Advanced Applications section below, so there is no figure needed here.

Chapter 7
ICON

Icons are pictures for displaying multivariate data (Everitt, 1978; Cleveland, 1985). Given a dataset containing measurements of *n* cases on *p* variables, you plot *n* icons (one for each case) with *p* different features in each icon.

Unlike most graphs in SYGRAPH, icons are not designed to communicate absolute numerical information. They are intended, instead, for recognizing clusters of similar objects. Icons are useful for sorting or organizing objects which differ in many respects.

Some theorists find the use of icons subjective and ad hoc. They have ridiculed, for example, Chernoff's faces (see below in this chapter) as being facetious and cartoon-like. In such conclusions they have ignored the cognitive science research on multiattribute visual processing, which shows that people can accurately categorize multivariate data based on appropriate visual cues (Garner, 1974; Spohr and Lehmkuhle, 1982).

SYGRAPH offers a variety of icons for representing multivariate data: cartoon faces, Fourier blobs, stars, histograms, rectangles, and others. You should try several of these on the same data to see how they work. You should also compare them to automated techniques such as discriminant analysis and clustering. For some data you will be able to locate clusters that elude automated methods because your eye can perceive nonlinear, disjunctive relationships. ICONS cannot replace formal statistical models but they are indispensable exploratory tools.

For all icon methods, it is important to have all variables on common or comparable scales. Otherwise, individual features in each icon will dominate the whole picture, distorting comparisons. The US file variables SUMMER and WINTER, for example, are both measured in degrees Fahrenheit, so they would not need rescaling when used together. For other variables, however, you probably want to add the **STAND** option (see below in this chapter) which standardizes values on each variable to *z* scores before drawing icons.

The shape of icons depends on the mapping of variables to icon features. For all SYGRAPH icons, this mapping is done in the order you enter variables in the **ICON** command. With Chernoff's faces, for example, the first variable is assigned to mouth curvature, the second to angle of brow, and so on. Some have criticized icons for the arbitrariness of this assignment. There are ways to circumvent this problem, however. Research in cognitive processing (e.g. Garner and Felfoldy, 1970) has shown that integrated displays are more effective for communicating multidimensional information. Correlated information is best presented within integrated, rather than across disparate, features. One way to accomplish this is to order the variables by some seriation method before entering them into the **ICON** command. For example, use a cluster analysis program which orders tree branches (e.g. SYSTAT CLUSTER) and then use the ordering in the **ICON** command. Alternatively, order the variables according to the loadings on the first principal component of the correlation matrix of variables or, even better, the one dimensional multidimensional scaling (e.g. SYSTAT MDS) of this matrix. This way, similar features of **FACES**, **BLOBS**, **STARS**, etc. will be assigned to correlated variables. Freni-Titulaer and Louv (1984) have demonstrated that cluster-ordered icons result in fewer errors in judgment than randomly ordered icons. In the examples in this chapter, I have used the multidimensional scaling seriation of the correlation matrix of the variables to determine this order.

Sometimes you may wish to publish a matrix of icons clustered according to similarity. One way to do this is to cluster analyze a dataset and reorder the cases according to a seriation based on cluster membership. Then, when you use the ICON command, the icons will be arranged in clustered order. Another way to do this is to order the icons yourself and rearrange the cases in a file according to your visual ordering. Here is how to:

1) Make a hard copy plot and label each icon with a number.
2) Clip out each icon with scissors.
3) Sort them into piles of similar icons.
4) Enter the sorted numbers into the original data file.
5) Sort the file by your new sequence.
6) Plot the icons again in sorted order with their actual labels.

This procedure avoids the bias of knowing the categories in advance.

The `ICON` command has only one syntax: `ICON`. All the options determine the type of plot produced. If you add no options, you will get a `STAR` plot (see below in this chapter).

BLOB *(Fourier Blobs)*

Fourier blobs are polar coordinate Fourier waveforms. Fourier functions have the following form:

$$f(t) = y_1 / \sqrt{2} + y_2\sin(t) + y_3\cos(t) + y_4\sin(2t) + y_5\cos(2t) + \ldots$$

where *y* is a *p* dimensional variate and *t* varies from -3.14 to 3.14 (π radians on either side of zero). The result of this transformation is a set of waveforms made up of sine and cosine components. Each waveform corresponds to one case in the dataset. Cases which have similar values across all variables will have comparable waveforms. Cases with different patterns of variation will have contrasting waveforms. When these waveforms are transformed into polar coordinates, they look like blobs or amoebae. The information contained in Fourier blobs is therefore identical to the Andrews Fourier plot (see the **FOURIER** option below in the **PLOT** chapter. The advantage of blobs is that they do not overlap and they can be used as plotting symbols in a dimensional plot.

How do you interpret these blobs? What are the variable values? Keep in mind what I mentioned at the beginning of this chapter. The point of the icon is not to translate back to numerical values. The Fourier transformation is too complex for us to compute those values mentally. Instead, you should look for similar blobs and then go back to the raw data to examine actual values with other types of graphs.

The shape of the blobs depends on the order you input the variables in the **ICON** command. Earlier variables (those toward the left) are weighted with lower frequency components in the above equation and later ones with higher frequency. See the introduction to this chapter for the method I used to order the variables.

Figure 1 shows blobs of the variables in the US file. You can compare this result to the other icon representations in this chapter. I have added **LABEL=STATE$** to label the blobs with the state names and **STAND** to standardize the variables. You almost always want to do this with every icon type. To keep things clear on this small page, I have plotted only the New England states.

Figure 1

```
SELECT   REGION$='New  England'
ICON   INCOME,POPDEN,PROPERTY,PERSON,RAIN,WINTER,SUMMER,
   /LABEL=STATE$,STAND,BLOB
```

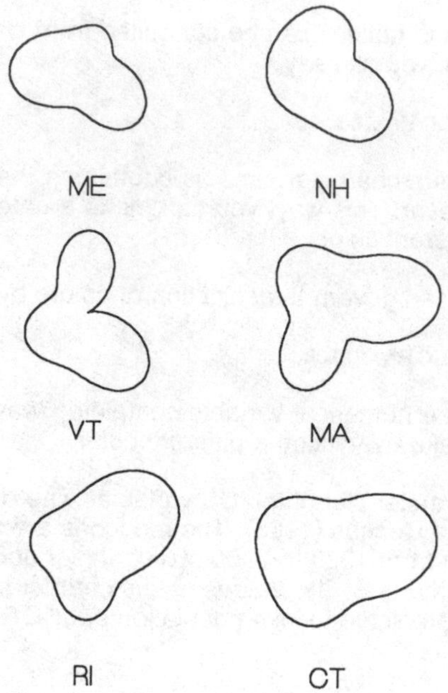

COLOR *(Setting Color of Symbols)*

You can choose a color for your symbols with the **COLOR** option. Choose either a name or a wavelength in nanometers. Possible colors and their approximate nanometer wavelengths are: **RED** (615), **ORANGE** (590), **YELLOW** (575), **GREEN** (505), **BLUE** (480), **VIOLET** (450). You may also name **BLACK**, **WHITE**, **GRAY**, and **BROWN**. The following command will make all icons in the graph red:

```
ICON/COLOR=RED
```

You can also specify color in nanometers wavelength. The following example will make all the icons greenish:

```
ICON/COLOR=540
```

Either of these alternatives can be controlled from a variable in your data. For example, you can say:

```
ICON/COLOR=COLR$
```

in which COLR$ is a character variable containing the values '**RED**' or '**YELLOW**' or whatever. This way, you can make a category plot in which each icon is a different color.

Otherwise, you can govern the selection of colors by wavelength:

```
ICON/COLOR=COLR
```

in which COLR is a numerical variable containing wavelength values. Again, this will make every icon a different color.

Figure 2 shows a star plot of the US variables The data are from the U.S. Bureau of the Census (1986). The red icons are for states predicted to lose population from 1990 to 2000. To do this, I added a variable called POPC$ to the U.S. file. Values of this character variable were "RED" for states predicted to lose population and "GREEN" otherwise.

Figure 2

```
ICON   INCOME,POPDEN,PROPERTY,PERSON,RAIN,WINTER,SUMMER,
  /STAND,COLOR=COLR$,FILL
```

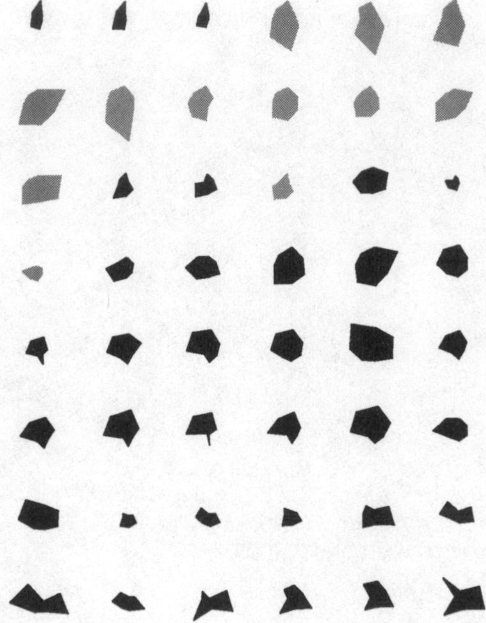

COLS *(Controlling the Number of Columns)*

As you have seen in the previous figure, SYGRAPH determines the number of rows and columns for displaying your icons. If you want a different shaped matrix, or rectangle of icons, use the `COLS` (and/or `ROWS`) option. If you set `COLS`, then SYGRAPH will draw as many rows as necessary to cover all your cases. If you set both `ROWS=`*r* and `COLS=`*c*, then SYGRAPH will draw only the first *rc* icons.

Figure 3 shows a star plot of the US variables with 4 columns. Notice that the symbols are reduced in size to fit in the window.

Figure 3

```
ICON   INCOME,POPDEN,PROPERTY,PERSON,RAIN,WINTER,SUMMER,
   /LABEL=STATE$,STAND,COLS=4
```

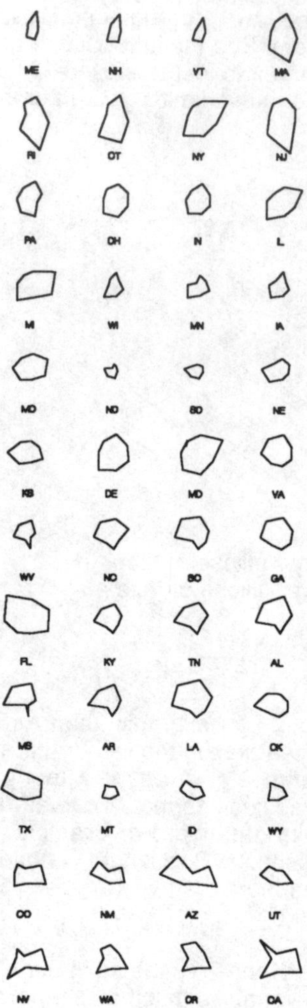

FACE *(Chernoff's Faces)*

Don't laugh. Faces are one of the most effective graphical icons for multivariate data, particularly for long term memory processing. Chernoff (1973) introduced the idea of using a cartoon face to represent many variables. Wang (1978) contains a number of articles on applications of faces to multivariate data. Wilkinson (1982) showed that faces can be more effective than many other icons for similarity comparisons.

Reviewers have criticized FACES for their arbitrary assignment of variables to features on the face. Chernoff and Rizvi (1975) and Jacob (1983) address this problem. See the introduction to this chapter for ways to make a rational assignment to features. Here is the order of features assigned by SYGRAPH to the variables you enter in the `ICON` command:

1 Curvature of mouth
2 Angle of brow
3 Width of nose
4 Length of nose
5 Length of mouth
6 Height of center of mouth
7 Separation of eyes
8 Height of center of eyes
9 Slant of eyes
10 Eccentricity of eyes
11 Half-length of eyes
12 Position of pupils
13 Height of eyebrow
14 Length of brow
15 Height of face
16 Eccentricity of upper ellipse of face
17 Eccentricity of lower ellipse of face
18 Ear level
19 Radius of ear
20 Hair length

If you type `ICON A,B,C,D` , for example, then A, B, C, and D will be assigned to the first four features in the list. You may repeat variables to make multiple assignments, e.g. `ICON A,A,B,C` , but I would do this only for correlated features such as mouth curvature and brow tilt. Finally, you can skip features with a period. For example, `ICON A,.,.,B,C` assigns A to curvature of mouth, B to length of nose, and C to length of mouth. Finally, if you type more than 20 variables, SYGRAPH will report an error instead of plotting.

Figure 4 shows `FACES` of the 7 variables in our US file. Notice the features not assigned to variables (such as shape of face) are constant.

Figure 4

```
SELECT  REGION$='New  England'
ICON   INCOME,POPDEN,PROPERTY,PERSON,RAIN,WINTER,SUMMER,
  /LABEL=STATE$,STAND,FACE
```

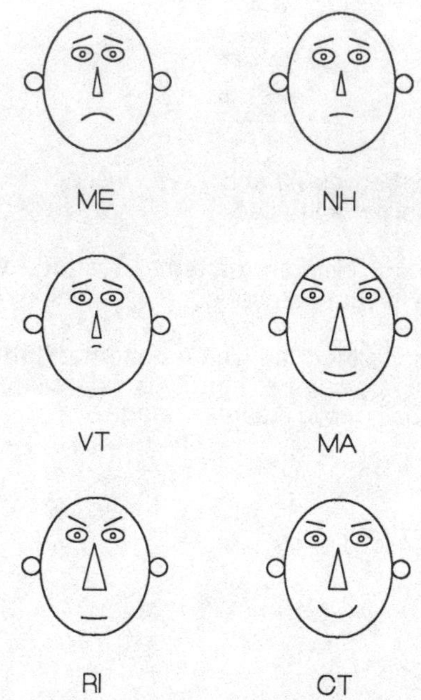

FILL *(Filling Icons)*

The **FILL** option specifies a fill pattern, e.g. **FILL=1**. The number you choose after "**FILL=**" determines the type of fill pattern for the whole pie:

(hollow)	=	0
(solid)	=	1
(wide diagonal hatch)	=	2
(crosshatch)	=	3
(diagonal hatch)	=	4
(fine crosshatch)	=	5
(fine diagonal hatch)	=	6
(dense crosshatch)	=	7

If you use a number between 0 and 1, you will get an even gradation of shading between hollow and filled.

You can fill icons with different patterns. Just add **FILL=MYFIL**, where MYFIL is a variable in your dataset containing values from 0 to 7.

Figure 5 shows star plots filled with a pattern determined by a variable called REGN, which is a number from 0 to 7 denoting the region of the US (0='New England',1='Mid Atlantic', etc.).

Figure 5

```
ICON   INCOME,POPDEN,PROPERTY,PERSON,RAIN,WINTER,SUMMER,
   /LABEL=STATE$,STAND,FILL=REGN
```

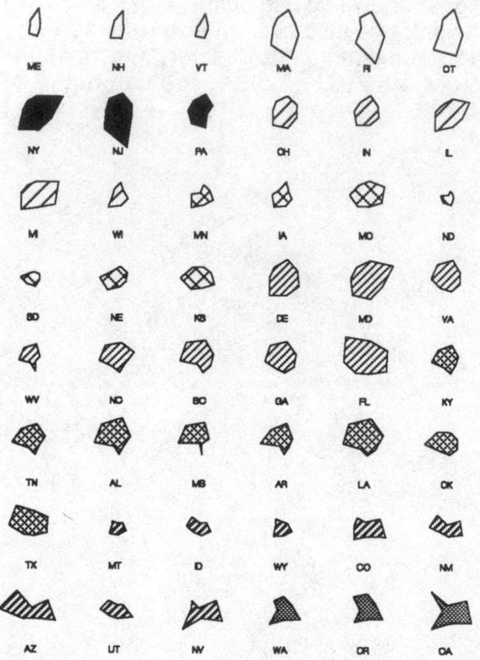

HEIGHT *(Physical Height of Plot)*

You can control the physical height of your plot with the **HEIGHT** option. It works like this:

```
HEIGHT=50%      (or HEIGHT=50)
HEIGHT=4IN
HEIGHT=10CM
```

The first example specifies percent of display height. The second specifies inches, and the third centimeters.

When you use the **HEIGHT** option, you probably also want to use **WIDTH**, which works exactly the same way (see below in this chapter). If you make the height and width different, you will distort the shape of the icons. The next figure shows how to flatten faces by choosing a width longer than the height. I've also chosen fewer cases with the **SELECT** command (see above in commands chapter). Once you have used **SELECT REGION$='New England'**, you can turn it off again by typing **SELECT** alone.

Figure 6

```
SELECT  REGION$='New  England'
ICON   INCOME,POPDEN,PROPERTY,PERSON,RAIN,WINTER,SUMMER,
   /FACE,LABEL=STATE$,STAND,HEIGHT=1.5IN,WIDTH=4IN
```

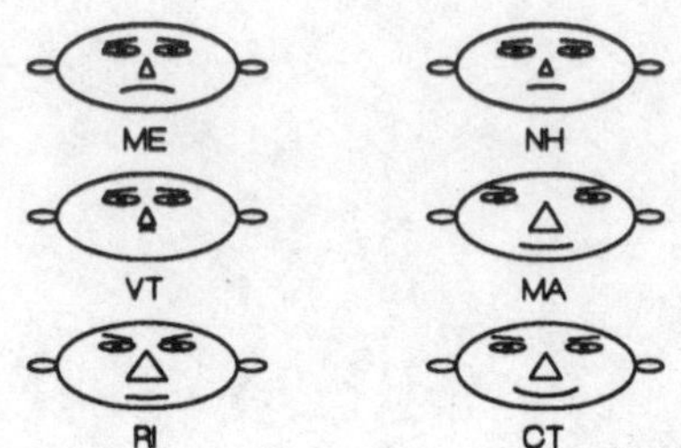

HIST *(Histogram Icons)*

The histogram icon assigns one histogram bar from left to right to each variable you choose from left to right in the **ICON** command. The bars are scaled so that the largest value in the data is the tallest bar and the smallest value is the shortest (i.e. zero height). Freni-Titulaer and Louv (1984) show examples of this icon.

It will help to order the variables according to a clustering or some other seriation. I have used the multidimensional scaling seriation of the variables to determine their order in the **ICON** command.

As with the other icons, you should make sure that the variables are on similar scales. Otherwise, one bar will be tall in all the icons and the rest will be barely visible. In the next figure, I have used **STAND** to standardize the variables on a common scale within the New England region before plotting. You can compare the results to blobs, faces, and the other icons in this chapter.

Figure 7

```
SELECT  REGION$='New England'
ICON   INCOME,POPDEN,PROPERTY,PERSON,RAIN,WINTER,SUMMER,
   /LABEL=STATE$,STAND,HIST
```

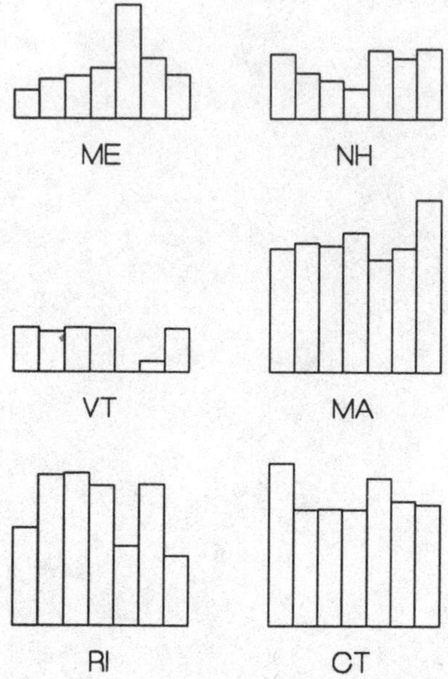

LABEL *(Labeling Icons)*

You can label each icon with a character string. These labels are specified with the `LABEL` option. With the value labels stored in the variable STATE$ in the US data, for example, we can label each icon by adding the option `LABEL=STATE$`. Whenever you plot icons in a rectangular array, you should use labels to identify them. All the examples in this chapter are labeled this way. Figure 8 shows a standardized star plot of the US file labeled with REGION$.

Figure 8

```
ICON   INCOME,POPDEN,PROPERTY,PERSON,RAIN,WINTER,SUMMER,
  /LABEL=REGION$,STAND
```

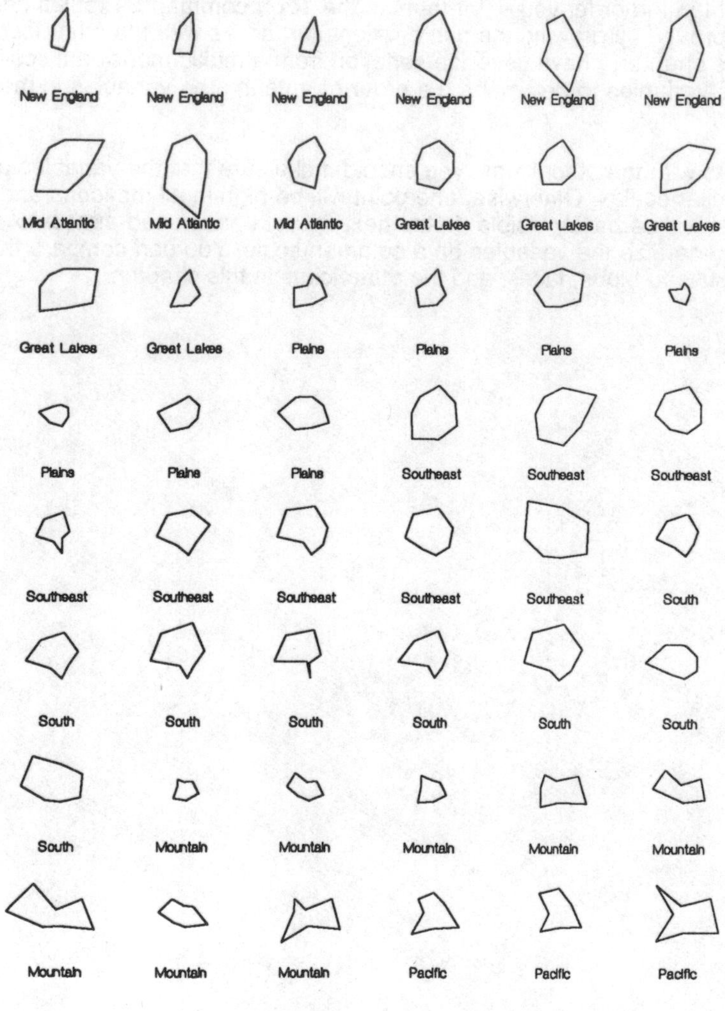

New England New England New England New England New England New England

Mid Atlantic Mid Atlantic Mid Atlantic Great Lakes Great Lakes Great Lakes

Great Lakes Great Lakes Plains Plains Plains Plains

Plains Plains Plains Southeast Southeast Southeast

Southeast Southeast Southeast Southeast Southeast South

South South South South South South

South Mountain Mountain Mountain Mountain Mountain

Mountain Mountain Mountain Pacific Pacific Pacific

PROF *(Profile Icons)*

Chambers, Cleveland, Kleiner, and Tukey (1983) discuss profile icons. They are identical to histogram icons (see **HIST** above in this chapter) except the tops of the bars are connected by lines and the bars are not drawn. **STARS** (see below in this chapter) are profile icons drawn in polar coordinates. To my knowledge, there is no research showing which of the three is better.

The **PROF** option assigns one profile point to each variable from left to right in the order you enter them in the **ICON** command. Profiles can be improved by drawing them in a rational order. As with the other icons in this chapter, I have used the seriation from a multidimensional scaling of the variables to determine the order of entering the variables in the **ICON** command.

As with the other icons, you should make sure that the variables are on similar scales. Otherwise, one point will be high in all the icons and the rest will be barely visible. In the next figure, I have used **STAND** to standardize the variables on a common scale. You can compare the results to blobs, faces, and the other icons in this chapter.

Figure 9

```
SELECT  REGION$='New  England'
ICON   INCOME,POPDEN,PROPERTY,PERSON,RAIN,WINTER,SUMMER,
   /LABEL=STATE$,STAND,PROF
```

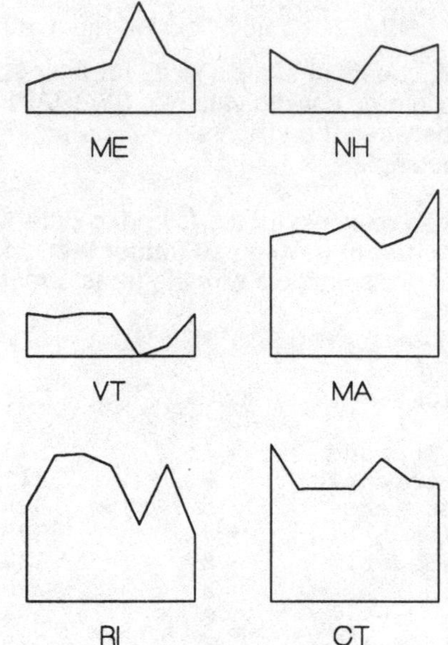

RECT *(Framed Rectangle Icons)*

Cleveland and McGill (1984) discussed an icon to represent a single variable. This framed rectangle graph contains a reference tick mark and uniform frame to ensure accurate comparisons. Unlike other icons in this chapter, only one variable can be represented. Thus, you use **RECT** this way:

```
ICON  INCOME/RECT
```

You name only one variable in the command. Thus, **RECT** is most useful for representing an extra variable on a map or scatterplot in combination with X and Y (see below in this chapter).

You can also represent two variables with **RECT**. Following Dunn (1987), I have made it possible to vary the width of each rectangle. In this case, you type the height and width variables in sequence:

```
ICON  INCOME,WIDTH/RECT
```

As Dunn points out, counts or sample sizes (or their square roots) are particularly appropriate as a width variable. SYGRAPH requires that the width variable be between 0 and 1. Values 1 or larger will produce a maximum width rectangle.

Figure 10 shows an example for the following data we used in the **CPLOT** chapter: In order to have areas (rather than width) represent COUNT, made the width variable with the transformation:

```
LET  WIDTH=SQR(COUNT/8)
```

REGION$	COUNT	INCOME
New England	6	3730.2
Mid Atlantic	3	4114.0
Great Lakes	5	3867.2
Plains	7	3396.9
Southeast	8	3272.6
South	8	2753.8
Mountain	8	3345.5
Pacific	3	3903.7

Figure 10

```
ICON   INCOME,WIDTH/LABEL=REGION$,RECT
```

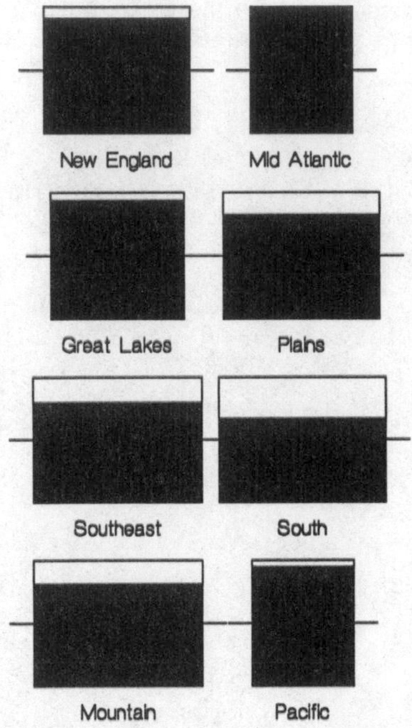

ROWS *(Controlling the Number of Rows)*

SYGRAPH automatically determines the number of rows and columns for displaying your icons. If you want a different shaped matrix, or rectangle of icons, use the **ROWS** (and/or **COLS**) option. If you set **ROWS**=*r*, then SYGRAPH will draw as many columns as necessary to cover all your cases. If you set both **ROWS**=*r* and **COLS**=*c*, then SYGRAPH will draw only the first *rc* icons.

Figure 11 shows a histogram plot of the US variables with 5 rows. Notice that the symbols are reduced in size to fit in the window.

Figure 11

```
ICON   INCOME,POPDEN,PROPERTY,PERSON,RAIN,WINTER,SUMMER,
   /LABEL=STATE$,STAND,HIST,ROWS=5
```

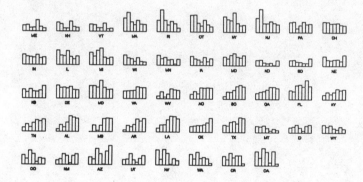

SIZE *(Changing Size of Icons)*

If you are using icons to enhance scatterplots with the **X** and **Y** options (see below in this chapter), you can alter the size of the icons from invisible to as large as your entire graph. The standard value of all icons is **SIZE=1**. **SIZE=2** produces icons twice as large as the standard. **SIZE=.5** is half, and so on. **SIZE=0** makes the icons invisible.

If you do not use the **X** and **Y** options, SYGRAPH will ignore the **SIZE** value.

Figure 12 shows a plot with half size rectangles. I have located the rectangles at the centroid latitudes and longitudes of the states.

Figure 12

```
ICON RAIN,
  /X=LABLON,Y=LABLAT,SIZE=.5,
    RECT,XMIN=-125,XMAX=-65,YMIN=25,YMAX=50,FILL
```

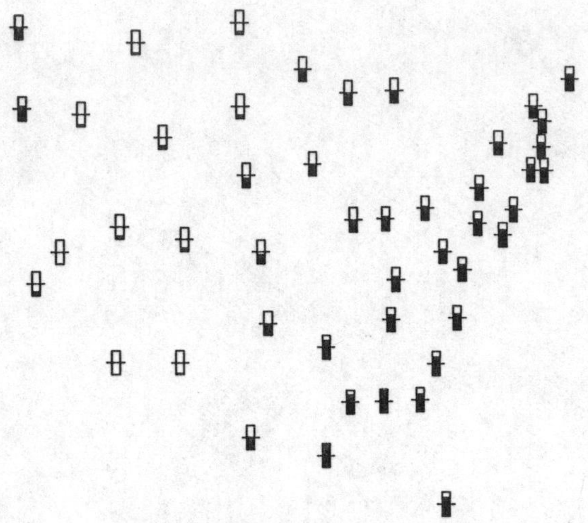

STAND *(Standardizing Scales)*

All the icons work best when the variables are on common scales. For example, all variables should be measured in inches, centimeters, minutes, degrees, etc.. If they are not, then some features of the icons will dominate others because some numbers are large relative to the others.

If variables are on different scales, then you can standardize them first to *z* scores by subtracting out the sample means and dividing by the sample standard deviations. You do this with the **STAND** option.

Because I have used **STAND** everywhere in this chapter, Figure 13 shows a plot without this option. Notice how INCOME dominates the histograms so that other variation is undetectable. Compare this result to the same plot standardized in Figure 7.

Figure 13

```
SELECT  REGION$='New  England'
ICON   INCOME,POPDEN,PROPERTY,PERSON,RAIN,WINTER,SUMMER,
  /LABEL=STATE$,HIST
```

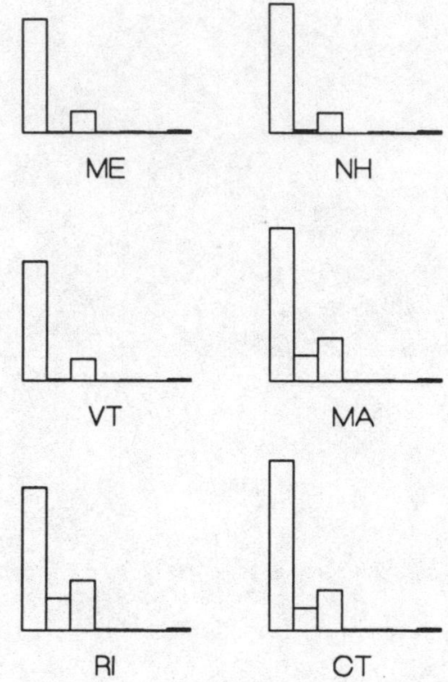

STAR *(Star Plots)*

Star plots are the default icon in this chapter. Stars are profiles in polar coordinates. Imagine that you have 12 variables, for example. Now imagine a clock. The hour hand is shorter than the minute hand. A star plot is like placing 12 hands on a clock at the position of each hour with the length of the hands determined by the value of the variables on a case. To make the plot more visible, the ends of the hands are connected instead of drawing the hands themselves. **STAR** can handle up to 200 variables (hands), but you usually don't want to do more than a few.

As with the other icons, it is helpful to order the variables around the circle (clock) so that correlated variables are near each other. I have done this by using the multidimensional scaling seriation of our US variables which I described in the introduction to this chapter.

Figure 14

```
SELECT  REGION$='New  England'
ICON   INCOME,POPDEN,PROPERTY,PERSON,RAIN,WINTER,SUMMER,
   /LABEL=STATE$,STAR,STAND
```

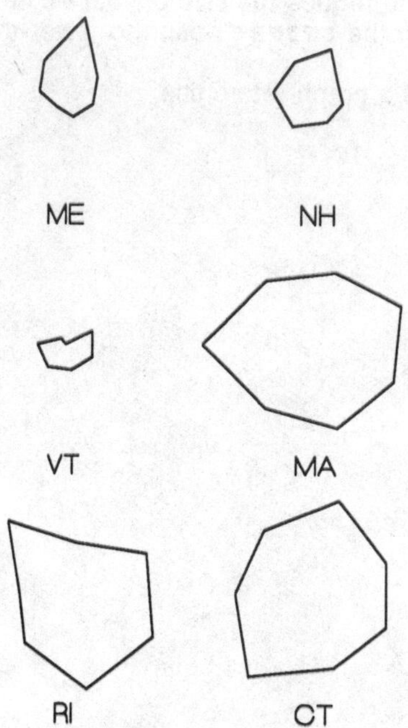

TITLE *(Graph Title)*

You can place a title at the top center of your graph with the **TITLE** option:

```
TITLE='Transistors from HF-103(a) Batch'
TITLE="Chernoff's Faces of Quality of Life"
TITLE='Market "Crash" Stimulates Investment'
```

The text must be surrounded by quotes (") or apostrophes ('). If your text includes apostrophes, as in the second example, surround it with quotes. If it includes quotes, as in the third example, surround it with apostrophes.

On some display devices the title will run off the top of the page because the standard display window is chosen to make the labels and graph as large as possible. If this happens, you will have to use the **SCALE** command to reduce the size of your entire graph (e.g. **SCALE=70,70**) or the **HEIGHT** option to lower the height.

Figure 15 shows a graph with a title.

Figure 15

```
SELECT  REGION$='New  England'
ICON  INCOME,POPDEN,PROPERTY,PERSON,RAIN,WINTER,SUMMER,
   /TITLE='Socio-Demo-Meteoro-Mumbo-Jumbo',STAND
```

Socio-Demo-Meteoro-Mumbo-Jumbo

WIDTH *(Physical Width of Plot)*

You can control the physical width of your plot with the **`WIDTH`** option. It works like this:

```
WIDTH=50%        (or WIDTH=50)
WIDTH=4IN
WIDTH=10CM
```

The first example specifies percent of display WIDTH. The second specifies inches, and the third centimeters.

When you use the **`WIDTH`** option, you probably also want to use **`HEIGHT`**, which works exactly the same way (see above in this chapter). If you make the WIDTH and height different, you will distort the shape of the icons. The next figure shows how to squeeze the faces by selecting a width narrower than the height. Compare this plot to Figure 6 below.

Figure 16

```
SELECT  REGION$='New  England'
ICON   INCOME,POPDEN,PROPERTY,PERSON,RAIN,WINTER,SUMMER,
     /FACE,LABEL=STATE$,STAND,HEIGHT=4IN,WIDTH=2IN
```

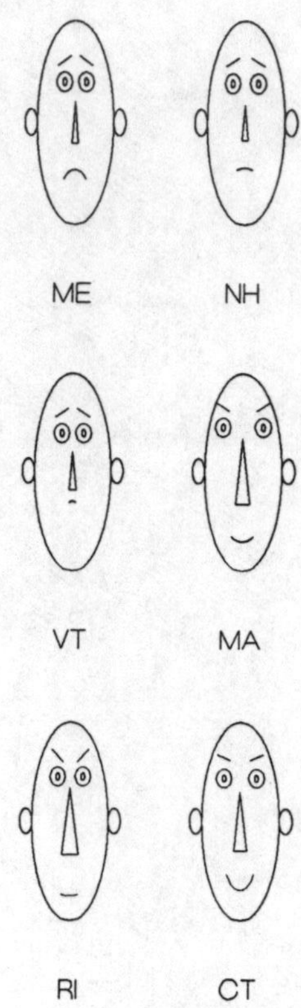

X,Y *(Locations—Icon Enhanced Scatterplots)*

Wainer and Thissen (1981), Chambers, Cleveland, Kleiner and Tukey (1983), and others discuss using icons to enhance scatterplots by placing them at the location of X and Y variables. Icons can be placed on maps, for example, or on scatterplots of two related variables.

To do this in SYGRAPH, use the **X** and **Y** options to specify the variables which determine the horizontal and vertical locations of the icons, respectively. You may have to fiddle with **SIZE** (see above in this chapter) and perhaps move the locations slightly to keep icons from colliding.

Figure 17 shows a plot of the Mountain states on the US variables. The two additional variables I have used, LABLAT and LABLON, are the latitudes and longitudes of the centers of the states respectively.

Figure 17

```
SELECT   REGION$='Mountain'
ICON   INCOME,POPDEN,PROPERTY.PERSON,RAIN,WINTER,SUMMER,
     /FACE,STAND,SIZE=2,X=LABLON,Y=LABLAT
MAP/XMIN=-120,XMAX=-105,YMIN=30,YMAX=50
```

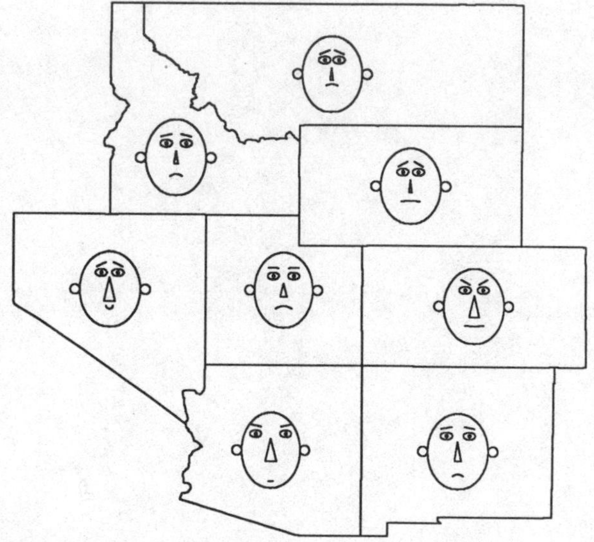

XMIN,YMIN,XMAX,YMAX *(Limits of Enhanced Scatterplots)*

These options control the axis limits if you are using the **X** and **Y** options (see directly above in this chapter). They work exactly the way they do for the **PLOT** command. Since axes are not drawn when you use icons this way, you may wonder why these limits are necessary, especially when SYGRAPH automatically can determine them from the data values. The reason they are here, however, is to allow you to combine maps, plots, and other graphs with icons in a single display and insure that the icons are correctly located.

Chapter 8

MAP

SYGRAPH produces maps with a single command: **MAP**. The standard package includes a boundary map of the continental United States with borders having a resolution of several miles. In this map file, which is used to plot the examples in this chapter, you can even see Wellfleet Harbor on the map of Cape Cod when it is enlarged. Because of this high resolution, the U.S. map takes a long time to draw. The **SKETCH** option (see below in this chapter) can produce rougher maps much more quickly.

City, county, state, and international maps are available from a variety of sources. SYGRAPH can process standard latitude and longitude text files from these sources. See Appendix B for further information on boundary files.

To use the **MAP** command, you must have two files accessible to SYGRAPH or in your local directory. Both must have the same name: one with the extension .MAP and the other with the extension .SYS. The boundaries of regions are taken from the .MAP file. Other labeling information is taken from the .SYS file. The two files used in these examples are US.MAP and US.SYS.

If you are going to do much work with maps, you really should read some of the research on map coloring, shading, and contouring. There is a large literature, of course, in geography on these topics. Gale (1982) discusses continuously shaded maps, which you can do in SYGRAPH with the **FILL** option. These run into problems with the perceptual biases I discussed in the perception chapter, however. Trumbo (1981) and Wainer and Francolini (1980) discuss problems in coloring statistical maps.

Figure 1 shows an example of an unlabeled map of the US. Since no projection is used, the actual latitudes and longitudes are plotted in rectangular coordinates. This map takes a while to draw because there are tens of thousands of boundary points in the US.MAP file. If you use maps with lower resolution, they will draw much faster. On some computers, you may not have enough memory to draw this map. Try the **SKETCH** option (see below in this chapter) if this happens or choose a map file with fewer coordinates.

Figure 1

MAP

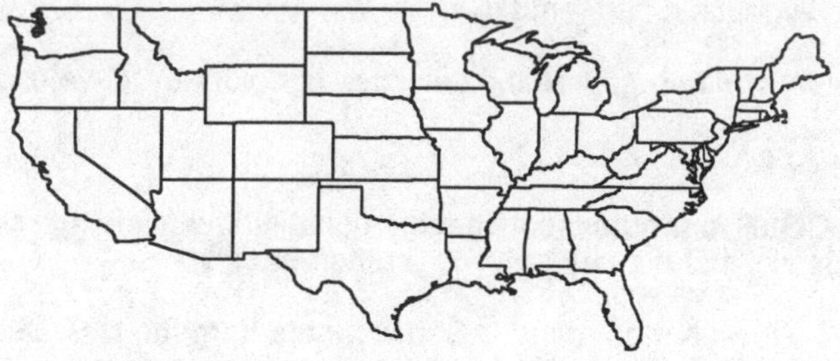

COLOR *(Setting Color of Map)*

You can choose a color for your map with the **COLOR** option. Choose either a name or a wavelength in nanometers. Possible colors and their approximate nanometer wavelengths are: **RED** (615), **ORANGE** (590), **YELLOW** (575), **GREEN** (505), **BLUE** (480), **VIOLET** (450). You may also name **BLACK**, **WHITE**, **GRAY**, and **BROWN**. The following command will make the map red:

```
MAP/COLOR=RED
```

You can also specify color in nanometers wavelength. The following example will make the map greenish:

```
MAP/COLOR=540
```

Either of these alternatives can be controlled from a variable in your data. For example, you can say:

```
MAP/COLOR=COLR$
```

in which COLR$ is a character variable containing the values '**RED**' or '**YELLOW**' or whatever. This way, you can make a map in which each state or polygon is a different color.

Otherwise, you can govern the selection of colors by wavelength:

```
MAP/COLOR=COLR
```

in which COLR is a numerical variable containing wavelength values. Again, this will make every polygon a different color.

Figure 2 shows a map of the U.S. using data from the U.S. Bureau of the Census (1986). The red states in the map are predicted to lose population from 1990 to 2000. I created this map by adding a variable called POPC$ to the U.S. file. Values of this character variable were "RED" for states predicted to lose population and "GREEN" otherwise. I have added the **FILL** option (see below in this chapter) to make the whole states (not just their outlines) colored.

Figure 2

```
MAP/COLOR=POPC$,FILL,PROJECT=STEREO
```

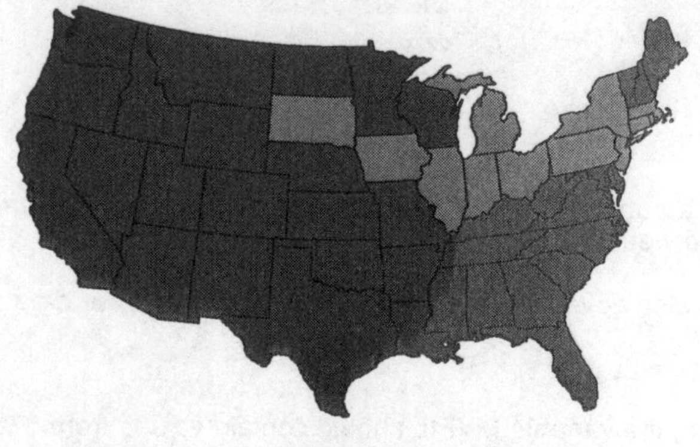

FILL *(Filling Map Polygons)*
You can fill polygons with different patterns. The **FILL** option works this way:

```
MAP/FILL=2
```

The number you choose after "**FILL=**" determines the type of fill pattern. Here are the possibilities:

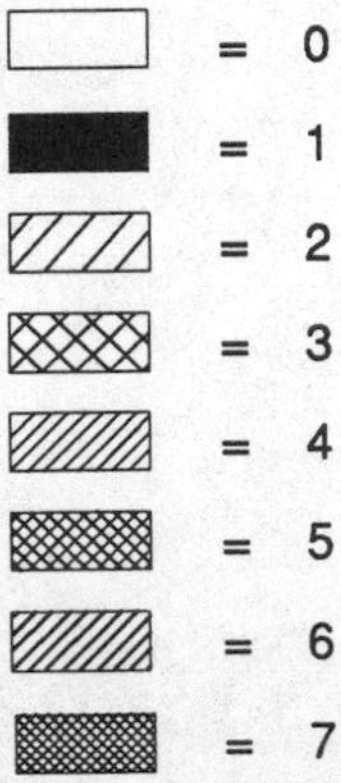

= 0

= 1

= 2

= 3

= 4

= 5

= 6

= 7

If you use a number between 0 and 1, you will get an even gradation of shading between hollow and filled.

You can also govern fill patterns with a variable in your dataset:

```
MAP/FILL=MYFIL
```

In this case, the variable MYFIL should contain values from 0 to 7. Each plotting symbol will be filled with the pattern corresponding to the value in MYFIL for the case corresponding to that symbol.

Figure 3 shows a map of the U.S. with different shades of darkness to reveal rainfall. The variable RAI was created with the following transformation:

```
LET  RAI=RAIN/65
```

This caused the values to range from about .1 to .9, which are within the region of light to dark values. I have also used a stereographic projection (see below in this chapter) to provide a different view.

Figure 3

```
MAP/PROJECT=STEREO,FILL=RAI
```

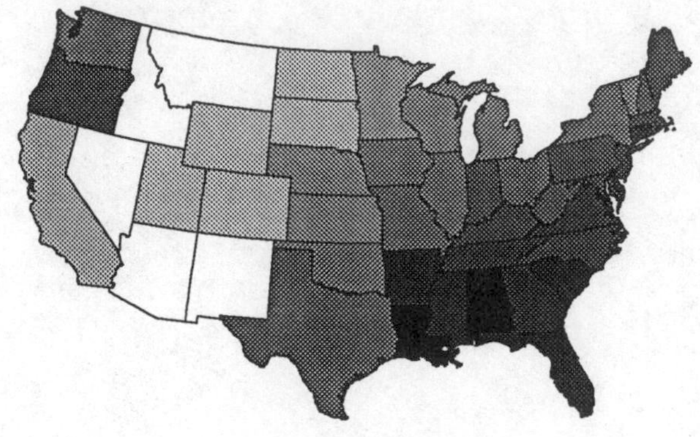

HEIGHT *(Physical Height of Map)*

You can control the physical height of your map with the **HEIGHT** option. It works like this:

```
HEIGHT=50%      (or HEIGHT=50)
HEIGHT=4IN
HEIGHT=10CM
```

The first example specifies percent of display height. The second specifies inches, and the third centimeters.

When you use the **HEIGHT** option, you probably also want to use **WIDTH**, which works exactly the same way (see below in this chapter). The following map shows how to use them together. I have also used the **SELECT** command (see general commands chapter above) to choose only the New England region.

Figure 4

```
SELECT  REGION$='New  England'
MAP/HEIGHT=4IN,WIDTH=4IN
```

LABEL *(Labeling Points)*

You can label points in a map with character strings. These are specified with the **LABEL** option. With the value labels stored in the variable STATE$ in the US data, for example, we can draw labels in the center of each state by adding the option **LABEL=STATE$**. Your data file must contain two variables called LABLAT and LABLON, respectively, showing the latitude and longitude of the points where labels are to be inserted. See Appendix B for further details.

Here is a map of the Pacific states with labels.

Figure 5

```
SELECT REGION$='Pacific'
MAP/LABEL=STATE$
```

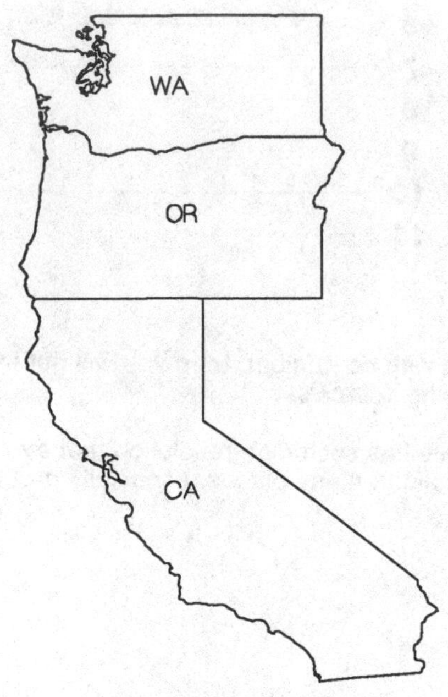

LINE *(Choosing Map lines)*

Sometimes you want to draw a map in faint outlines or add features in a different type of line. The **LINE** option allows you to choose the type of line used to draw a map.You may choose from 11 different types of lines by typing **LINE=***n* , where *n* is one of the following numbers:

1
2
3
4
5
6
7
8
9
10
11

If you type **LINE** with no number, then you will get the solid line, which is the same as typing **LINE=1**.

The US.MAP file has such high resolution that even the finest dotted line (11) looks solid in many places, especially around detailed coastlines.

Figure 6

```
SELECT REGION$='New England'
MAP/LINE=11
```

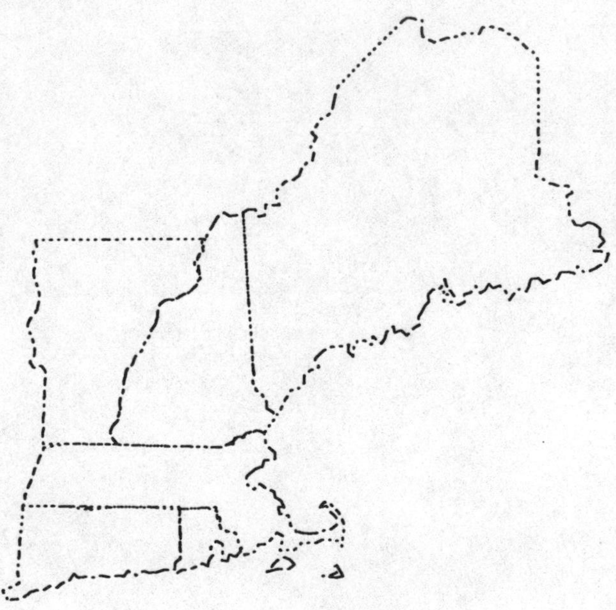

PROJECT *(Geographic Projections)*

Projections are transformations of spherical to rectangular coordinates. You can think of them as mathematical methods for taking an orange peel and stretching it to lie flat on a table. The **MAP** option offers the following projections:

PROJECT=GNOMON	*(oblique gnomonic)*
PROJECT=STEREO	*(oblique stereographic)*
PROJECT=MERCATOR	*(Mercator conformal)*
PROJECT=ORTHO	*(oblique orthographic)*

These projections are documented in Appendix B of Richardus and Adler (1972).

Figure 7 shows a map of the U.S. using a Mercator conformal projection.

Figure 7

MAP/PROJECT=MERCATOR

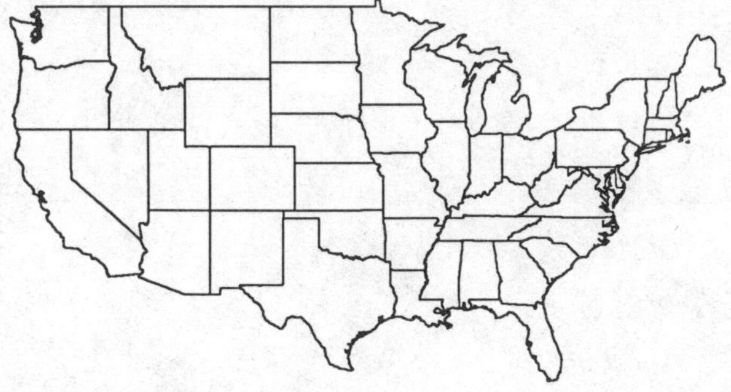

SKETCH *(Sketching Maps)*

Sometimes you want a quicker look at a complex map before drawing it in high resolution. The **SKETCH** option produces maps with lower resolution and saves time and storage. You can expect to save a half to a tenth of the normal computing time depending on the size of a map. The lower resolution slightly compromises boundaries between states or regions, however.

Figure 8 shows a map of New England using this option.

Figure 8

```
SELECT  REGION$='New  England'
MAP/SKETCH
```

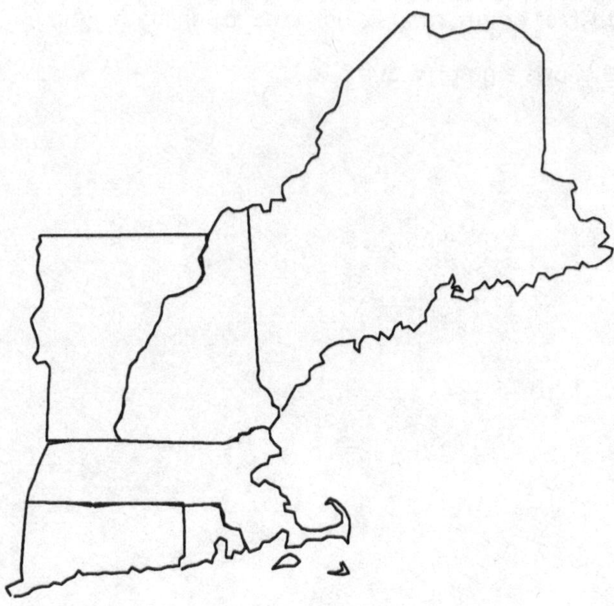

TITLE *(Graph Title)*

You can place a title at the top center of your map with the **TITLE** option:

```
TITLE='Worldwide Sales in U.S. Dollars'
TITLE="Roger's View of Kansas"
TITLE='Flow of "Ixolotl" River'
```

The text must be surrounded by quotes (") or apostrophes ('). If your text includes apostrophes, as in the second example, surround it with quotes. If it includes quotes, as in the third example, surround it with apostrophes.

On some display devices the title will run off the top of the page because the standard display window is chosen to make the labels and graph as large as possible. If this happens, you will have to use the **SCALE** command to reduce the size of your entire graph (e.g. **SCALE=70,70**) or the **HEIGHT** option to lower the height.

Figure 9 shows a graph with a title.

Figure 9

```
SELECT REGION$='Great Lakes'
TYPE=SWISS
MAP/TITLE='Great Lakes Region'
```

Great Lakes Region

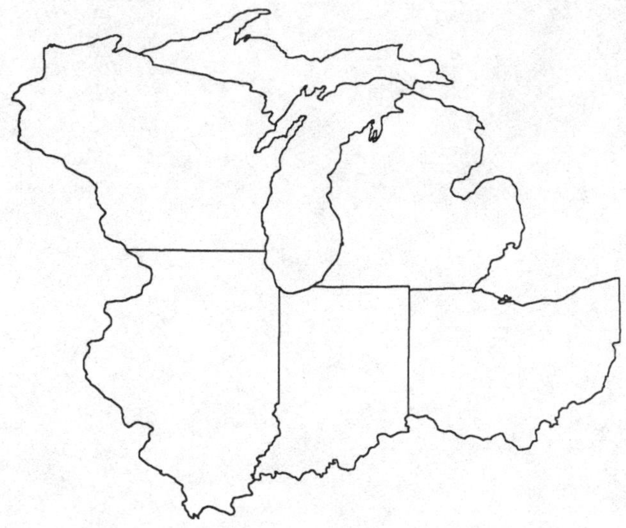

WIDTH *(Physical Width of Map)*

You can control the physical width of your map with the **WIDTH** option. It works like this:

```
WIDTH=50%        (or WIDTH=50)
WIDTH=4IN
WIDTH=10CM
```

The first example specifies percent of display width. The second specifies inches, and the third centimeters.

When you use the **WIDTH** option, you probably also want to use **HEIGHT**, which works exactly the same way (see above in this chapter). The following map shows how to use them together. Here is a tiny map of the U.S. suitable for a postage stamp. If you want to go into business, you can use SYGRAPH to put maps on sweatshirts, ball point pens, and designer jeans.

Figure 10

```
MAP/HEIGHT=1IN,WIDTH=1IN
```

XMIN,YMIN,XMAX,YMAX *(Limits of Maps)*

These options control the axis limits of latitude and longitude in case you need to superimpose plots on a map. They work exactly the way they do for the PLOT command. Since axes are not drawn when you do maps, you may wonder why these limits are necessary, especially when SYGRAPH automatically can determine them from the data values. The reason they are here, however, is to allow you to combine maps, plots, and other graphs in a single display and insure that the points are correctly located. You can see some examples of this in the Advance Applications chapters.

Here is how to squish the U.S. sideways. In Figure 11 I've set the axis limits to two different ranges. Keep in mind that the scales you use affect the horizontal and vertical orientation. If you wish to proportion the map more familiarly, make the ranges the same. This will make the projections sensible as well. The limits you select are identical to the ones you would get if you plot latitude and longitude with the PLOT command. This way, any numerical information you have in a data file can be coordinated with the map.

Figure 11

```
MAP/XMIN=-140,XMAX=-60,YMIN=20,YMAX=50
```

Chapter 9

PIE

A pie chart displays continuous against categorical variables. It is particularly suited for displaying portions of wholes. Although many statisticians and graphic designers have attacked the pie chart, recent studies (e.g., Simkin & Hastie, 1987) have shown it to be more effective than bar charts for displaying proportional data. SYGRAPH produces a variety of pie charts.

Simple Pie Chart

The **PIE** command will produce a pie chart of counts in categories by a simple command. To tally counts of states in each Census region from the US file, for example, just type:

```
PIE  REGION$
```

SYGRAPH will read the file and tally duplicate values. The printed pie chart will show the counts of cases in the file as a proportion of total count.

If you have already tallied a variable, you can produce a pie chart directly from the counts. Suppose your file looks like the following. Instead of 48 cases with duplicates, you have only 8 cases with a COUNT variable indicating duplicates.

REGION$	COUNT
New England	6
Mid Atlantic	3
Great Lakes	5
Plains	7
Southeast	8
South	8
Mountain	8
Pacific	3

To produce the same pie chart, you can type:

```
WEIGHT=COUNT
PIE  REGION$
```

You can use either a numeric or character categorical variable. SYGRAPH displays the categories as either character character strings or numbers, respectively, and sorts them in ascending alphabetic or numeric order counter-clockwise around the pie. To arrange the values in the order they appear in the file, use the **SNORT** option (see below).

Figure 1

```
PIE  REGION$/SNORT
```

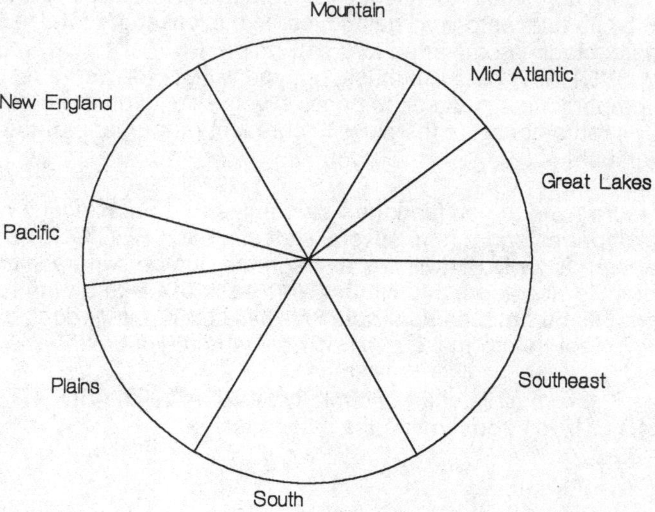

Two-way Pie Charts

If you wish to produce a pie chart of a continuous variable against categories, use the **PIE** command with two arguments. Assume, for example, that we have the following sales data by region. SALES contains percentages which total to 100.

REGION$	SALES
New England	10
Mid Atlantic	10
Great Lakes	20
Plains	5
Southeast	5
South	30
Mountain	10
Pacific	10

We can do a pie chart of these data with the following command:

```
PIE  SALES*REGION$
```

To compute portions of the pie for each category, SYGRAPH divides SALES by its total across all categories. In this case, the total is 100, so each percentage is converted to a proportion. Normally, you would be feeding SYGRAPH data like these, but you will get the same result if you feed it proportions instead of percents. If you feed it some other kind of numbers, remember that the pie will represent proportions of the total of your numbers.

One more thing. If you feed the **PIE** command a dataset with more than one value per category (e.g. several states in each REGION$ as in the US dataset), SYGRAPH will first average the numbers in each category, then total the averages, and finally divide each average by the total of the averages. If you have an application for this sort of thing, don't call SYSTAT. Feel free to make a million dollars on it yourself.

Figure 2 shows a pie chart of our nifty sales data. The SNORT option keeps SYGRAPH from sorting the categories.

Figure 2

```
TYPE=BRITISH
PIE  SALES*REGION$/SNORT
```

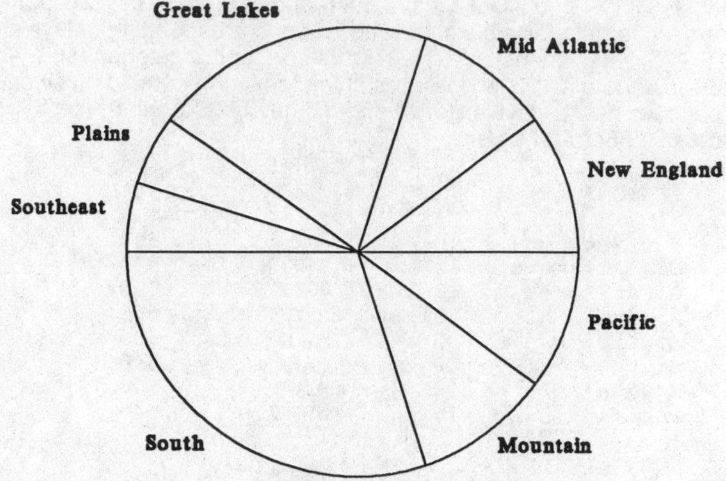

COLOR *(Setting Color of Pie)*

You can choose a color for your pie with the **COLOR** option. Choose either a name or a wavelength in nanometers. Possible colors and their approximate nanometer wavelengths are: **RED** (615), **ORANGE** (590), **YELLOW** (575), **GREEN** (505), **BLUE** (480), **VIOLET** (450). You may also name **BLACK**, **WHITE**, **GRAY**, and **BROWN**. You can make all slices in the pie red (strawberry-rhubarb) by adding **COLOR=RED**, for example. You can also specify color in nanometers wavelength, **COLOR=540**, which is a greenish (key lime) color.

To make each slice a different color, you need to use a variable in your data. For example, you can add **COLOR=COLR$**, in which COLR$ is a character variable containing the values '**RED**' or '**YELLOW**' or whatever. Otherwise, you can govern the selection of colors by wavelength: **COLOR=COLR**, in which COLR is a numerical variable containing wavelength values. Again, this will make every slice a different color.

Suppose we have the following data on average sales by region. The variables COLR and COLR$ have been added to color the slices. Figure 3 uses these data for a pie chart with colors corresponding to levels of SALES (SNORT keeps SYGRAPH from sorting the categories). Using COLR instead of COLR$ would result in almost the same plot, since what we call **RED** has a wavelength of approximately 600 nanometers, **ORANGE** is 580, and so on.

```
REGION$          SALES     COLR$       COLR

New England        10      RED          600
Mid Atlantic       10      GREEN        540
Great Lakes        20      BLUE         500
Plains              5      RED          600
Southeast           5      BLUE         500
South              30      GREEN        540
Mountain           10      BLUE         500
Pacific            10      GREEN        540
```

Figure 3

```
TYPE=BRITISH
PIE   SALES*REGION$/COLOR=COLR$,FILL,SNORT
```

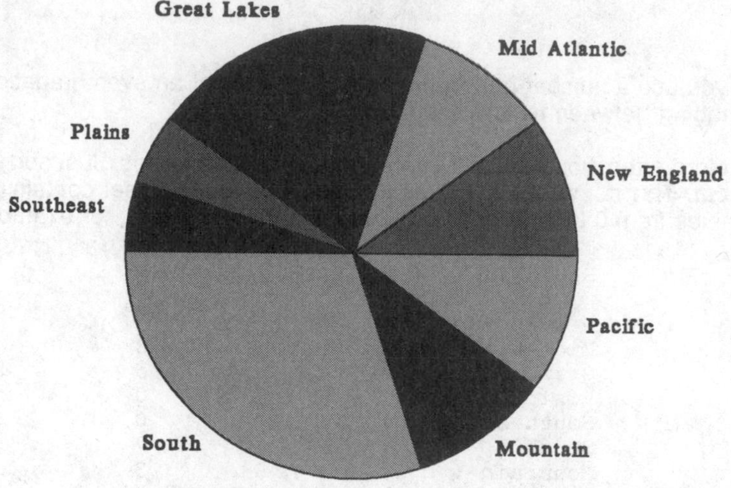

FILL *(Filling Pie Slices)*

The **FILL** option specifies a fill pattern, e.g. **FILL=1**. The number you choose after "**FILL=**" determines the type of fill pattern for the whole pie:

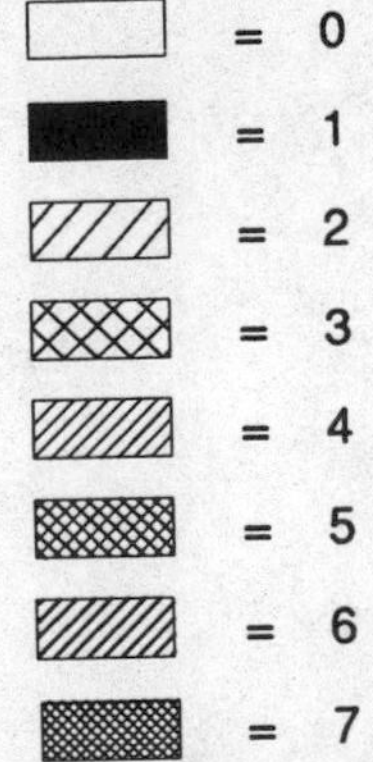

If you use a number between 0 and 1, you will get an even gradation of shading between hollow and filled.

More often, you want to fill slices with different patterns. Just add **FILL=MYFIL**, where MYFIL is a variable in your dataset containing values from 0 to 7. Suppose we have the following data, for example:

REGION$	SALES	MYFIL
New England	10	3
Mid Atlantic	10	3
Great Lakes	20	5
Plains	5	0
Southeast	5	0
South	30	7
Mountain	10	3
Pacific	10	3

The command to fill slices with the patterns in MYFIL would be:

```
PIE   SALES*REGION$/FILL=MYFIL
```

Figure 4 shows our pie chart filled with the shaded pattern determined by the variable MYFIL. The SNORT option keeps SYGRAPH from sorting the categories.

Figure 4

```
TYPE=SWISS
PIE   SALES*REGION$/FILL=MYFIL,SNORT
```

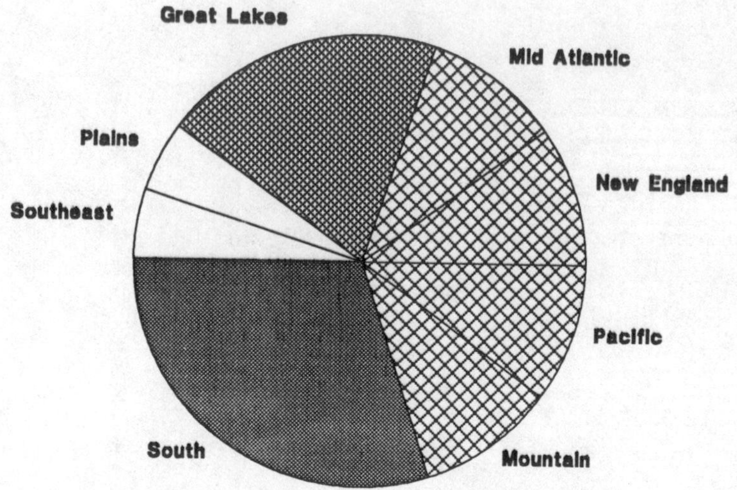

HEIGHT *(Physical Height of Plot)*

You can control the physical height of your pie chart with the **HEIGHT** option. It works like this:

```
HEIGHT=50%      (or HEIGHT=50)
HEIGHT=4IN
HEIGHT=10CM
```

The first example specifies percent of display height. The second specifies inches, and the third centimeters.

When you use the **HEIGHT** option, you probably also want to use **WIDTH**, which works exactly the same way (see below in this chapter). If you don't, you will get elliptical pie charts. Maybe you like them, but you'll lose your job when management finds out you see crooked.

Figure 5

```
TYPE=HERSHEY/ITALIC
PIE
SALES*REGION$/HEIGHT=4IN,WIDTH=3IN,SNORT
```

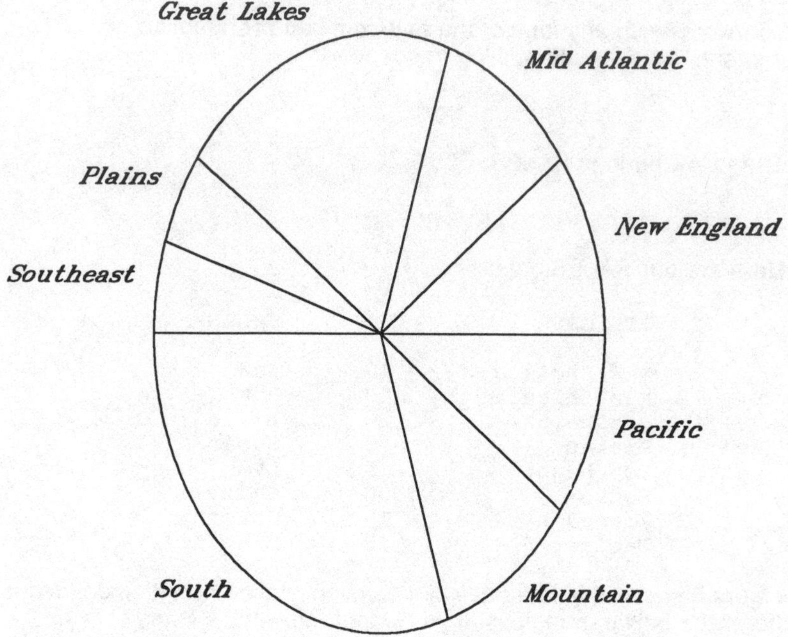

LOG *(Logging Data)*

Why would you log data for a pie chart? Don't ask me. The commands in SYGRAPH are orthogonal, however. This means that the **PIE** command is designed for plotting continuous against categorical data and there is no good reason why the commands which work in this context shouldn't work for **PIE**. Besides, some biochemist in Arizona is going to call up SYSTAT with the perfect application for logged pie charts and we're going to send her a free T-shirt when she does.

Logs may be computed to any base, e.g. **LOG=2**, **LOG=3**, **LOG=10**, **LOG=.5**. Natural logarithms will be computed if you use **LOG** with no argument, i.e. **LOG**. Only round number log bases (e.g. 0.5, 2, 3,10) will result in round number tick values, however.

LOG works with any form of the **PIE** command. The following command, for example, will log frequencies:

```
PIE  REGION$/LOG=10
```

The following logs SALES:

```
PIE  SALES*REGION$/LOG=10
```

Here are our SALES data:

REGION$	SALES	SALESMAN
New England	10	Leah
Mid Atlantic	10	Ruth
Great Lakes	20	Lydia
Plains	5	Susan
Southeast	5	Eve
South	30	Harry
Mountain	10	Dorothy
Pacific	10	Michelle

Figure 6 shows this latter use of the option. Notice how it smooths out differences between regions. If you want to downplay Harry's performance in the South, use log pie charts. Just a matter of emphasis, isn't it? Hey, whose job is on the line?

Figure 6

```
TYPE=STROKE/ITALIC
PIE   SALES*REGION$/LOG=10,SNORT
```

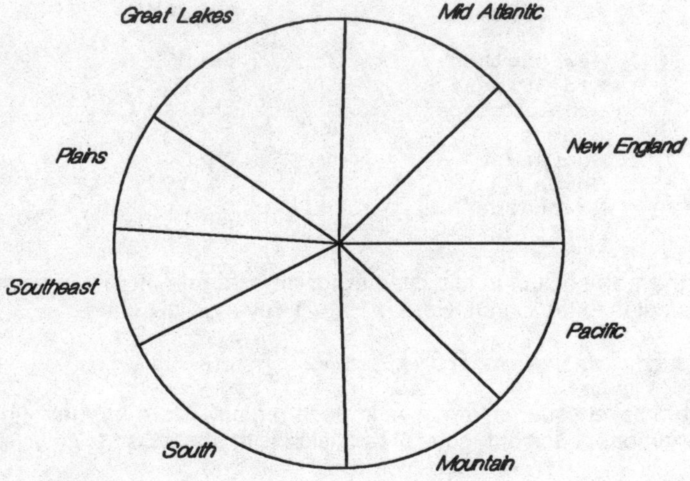

POW *(Powering Data)*

If we can do log pie charts, why not power pie charts. These are for power users. Powers may be computed to any exponent, e.g. **POW=.5** (square root), **POW=.33333** (cube root), **POW=-1** (inverse), **POW=2**. Square roots will be computed if you use **POW** with no argument, i.e. **POW**. **POW** is implemented in SYGRAPH only for positive data. Negative values will be deleted.

POW works with any form of the **PIE** command. The following command, for example, will transform frequencies:

```
PIE  REGION$/POW=.5
```

The following transforms SALES:

```
PIE  SALES*REGION$/POW=.5
```

Let's examine our SALES data with a power pie chart.

REGION$	SALES	SALESMAN
New England	10	Leah
Mid Atlantic	10	Ruth
Great Lakes	20	Lydia
Plains	5	Susan
Southeast	5	Eve
South	30	Harry
Mountain	10	Dorothy
Pacific	10	Michelle

See the **LOG** section in this chapter for an example of how to downplay Harry's sales in the South. Here is Harry's revenge pie chart :

```
PIE  SALES*REGION$/POW=2
```

This command squares the sales in each region before normalizing them as proportions. Look at Figure 7. Isn't lying with statistics fun?

Figure 7

```
TYPE=HERSHEY
PIE  SALES*REGION$/POW=2,SNORT
```

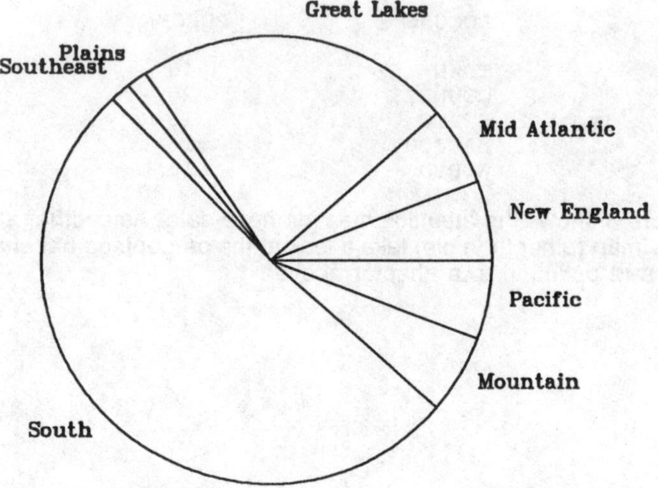

RING *(Ring Plots or Attention Maps)*

Let's make donuts instead of pies. Imagine the categories of a pie ordered from inside to outside. The ring plot draws a set of concentric rings beginning with a smallest ring for the first category. The radius of each ring is the sum of the previous radii plus the amount due to the corresponding category. This plot is sometimes used by newspapers as an attention map showing a paper's relative rates of reporting from local to international news.

The option to produce this chart is **`RING`**. I decided to make it an option to the **`PIE`** command because they are both basically baked goods and it's important with human-computer interfaces to be consistent.

It's best to have an ordered scale of categories for this type of chart. So here are some typical attention data for *The Cape Codder*, a salty local paper. I have expressed the attention values as percents. If you don't, SYGRAPH will add them together and compute percents before drawing the map, just as it does with pies.

```
LOCUS$              PERCENT

TOWN                   40
COUNTY                 20
STATE                  10
NATION                 16
WORLD                  14
```

Figure 8 shows the attention map for these data. As another alternative to this map (other than pie) take a look at the percentage bar chart (see **`PERCENT`** option in **`BAR`** chapter above).

Figure 8

```
TYPE=BRITISH/ITALIC
PIE   PERCENT*LOCUS$/RING,SNORT
```

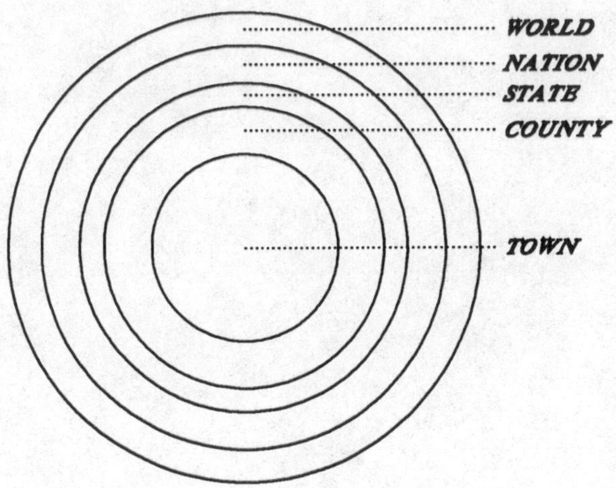

SCALE *(Altering the Pie Scales)*

Scales are the numbers or characters which label the slices of the pie chart. If you add **SCALE=0**, you can remove the printing around the pie. This might be useful for custom lettering with the **WRITE** command (see the **WRITE** chapter) or for embedding pies in other graphs.

Figure 9 shows our pie chart of SALES without the scale.

REGION$	SALES
New England	10
Mid Atlantic	10
Great Lakes	20
Plains	5
Southeast	5
South	30
Mountain	10
Pacific	10

Figure 9

```
PIE   SALES*REGION$/SCALE=0,SNORT
```

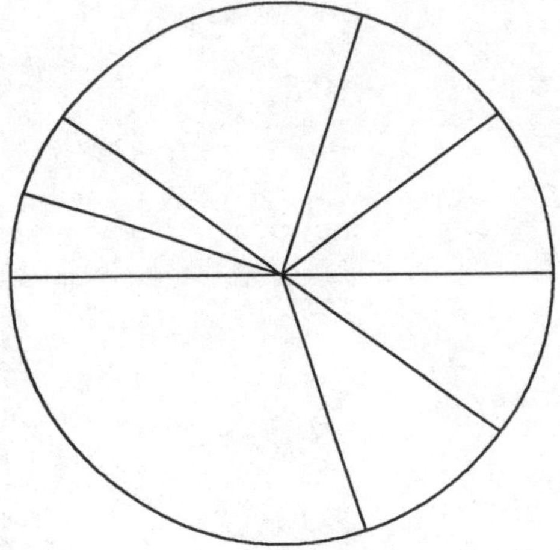

SORT/SNORT *(Sorting Categories)*

SYGRAPH automatically sorts the levels (categories) of categorical variables in ascending numeric or character order. If you want the categories arranged according to the order they appear in your data file, use the **SNORT** option. Figure 10 shows an example of the **SORT** option. Compare the bottom scale with those in other figures in this chapter to see how **SORT** and **SNORT** work.

```
REGION$              SALES

New England            10
Mid Atlantic           10
Great Lakes            20
Plains                  5
Southeast               5
South                  30
Mountain               10
Pacific                10
```

Figure 10

```
TYPE=SWISS
PIE  SALES*REGION$/SORT
```

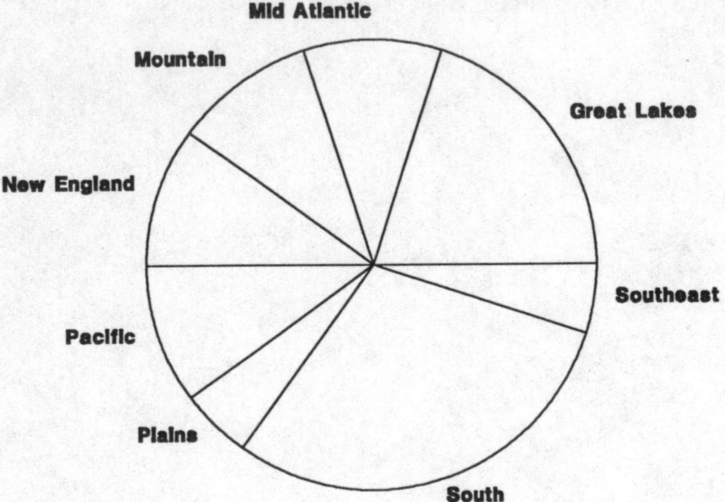

TITLE *(Graph Title)*

You can place a title at the top center of your pie graph with the **TITLE** option:

```
TITLE='Worldwide Sales in U.S. Dollars'
TITLE="Roger's Preferences"
TITLE='CPM for "Soft" Media'
```

The text must be surrounded by quotes (") or apostrophes ('). If your text includes apostrophes, as in the second example, surround it with quotes. If it includes quotes, as in the third example, surround it with apostrophes.

On some display devices the title will run off the top of the page because the standard display window is chosen to make the labels and graph as large as possible. If this happens, you will have to use the **SCALE** command to reduce the size of your entire graph (e.g. **SCALE=70,70**) or the **HEIGHT** option to lower the height.

Figure 11 shows the pie chart in Figure 10 with a title.

Figure 11

```
TYPE=SWISS/ITALIC
PIE  SALES*REGION$,
   /TITLE='Regional  Sales',SNORT
```

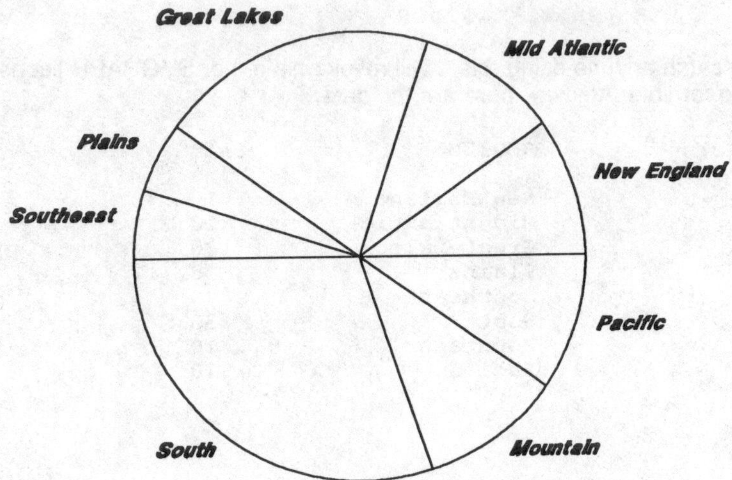

WIDTH *(Physical Width of Plot)*

You can control the physical width of your pie chart with the **WIDTH** option. It works like this:

```
WIDTH=50%        (or WIDTH=50)
WIDTH=4IN
WIDTH=10CM
```

The first example specifies percent of display width. The second specifies inches, and the third centimeters.

When you use the **WIDTH** option, you probably also want to use **HEIGHT**, which works exactly the same way (see above in this chapter). The following graph shows how to use them together. I've done an elliptical pie chart. This will make your viewers sick and keep them off-guard. If you really want some glitz, use the **FACET** command (see beginning of reference section) and do a 3-D pie chart:

```
FACET=Z
PIE  SALES*REGION$
```

If I catch anyone doing this, I will revoke his or her SYGRAPH license and sue for libel. Anyway, here are the data:

REGION$	SALES
New England	10
Mid Atlantic	10
Great Lakes	20
Plains	5
Southeast	5
South	30
Mountain	10
Pacific	10

Figure 12

```
PIE   SALES*REGION$/HEIGHT=1IN,WIDTH=3IN,SNORT
```

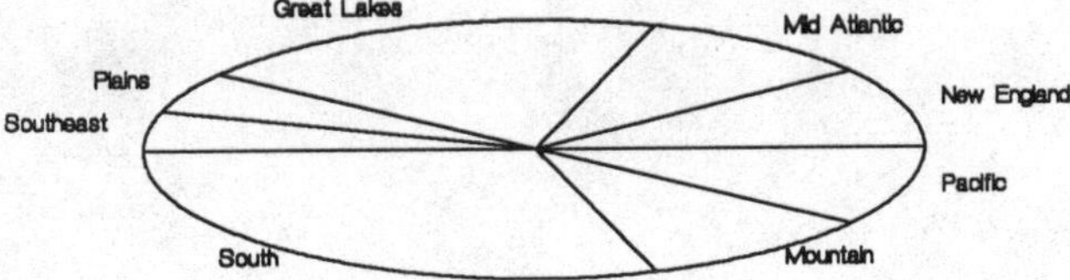

Chapter 10

PLOT

The **PLOT** command produces two- and three-way plots of continuous variables against each other. **PLOT** can use data you provide or it can generate its own data by plotting mathematical functions. It incorporates as options a large number of graphs which are treated as separate displays in other graphics packages. This is because **PLOT** is the general SYGRAPH command for plotting continuous against continuous data.

Scatterplots

To make a scatterplot, you **USE** a file and **PLOT Y*X**, where Y is the vertical axis variable and X is the horizontal. Figure 1 shows a plot of SUMMER (summer temperatures) against LABLAT (latitude) using the US file.

Figure 1

```
TYPE=BRITISH
PLOT  SUMMER*LABLAT
```

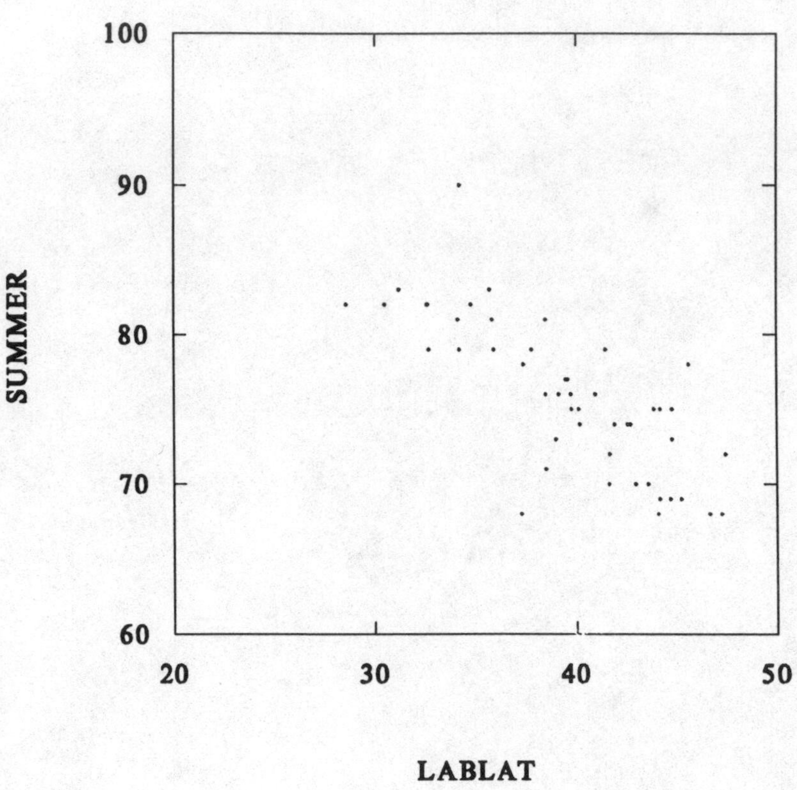

Multi-Valued Scatterplots

To plot several variables against another variable on the same graph, just add them to the first variable in the **PLOT** command, e.g.:

```
PLOT  A,B,C*D
```

When you do this, it is usually a good idea to use a different symbol (see **SYMBOL** option below in this chapter) for each vertical axis variable. Although SYGRAPH can plot up to 12 variables on the vertical axis against one on the horizontal, it is not a good idea to do more than two or three. Figure 2, for example, shows SUMMER and WINTER values plotted against LABLAT using circles and triangles (**SYMBOL=2,3**) for the points.

Figure 2

```
PLOT   SUMMER,WINTER*LABLAT/SYMBOL=2,3
```

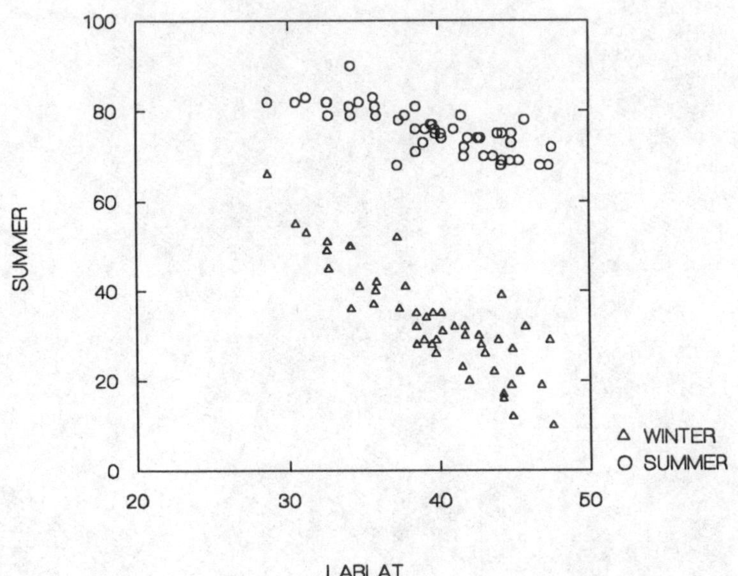

Three-dimensional scatterplots

You can plot three variables against each other in a three-dimensional graph. The syntax for this plot is:

```
PLOT  Z*Y*X
```

All the usual options work with 3-D plots (see elsewhere in this chapter).

As I discussed in the graphical perception chapter, three-dimensional plots can be confusing unless they are constructed carefully. Although the SYGRAPH plots are in true perspective, a long focal length has been chosen to avoid distortions.

Figure 3 shows a three-dimensional plot of INCOME (per-capita income) against LABLAT (latitude) and LABLON (longitude) from the US file. I have added the **SYMBOL** and **SPIKE** options (see below in this chapter) to make the values more visible.

Figure 3

```
PLOT   INCOME*LABLAT*LABLON/SYMBOL=2,FILL=1,SPIKE
```

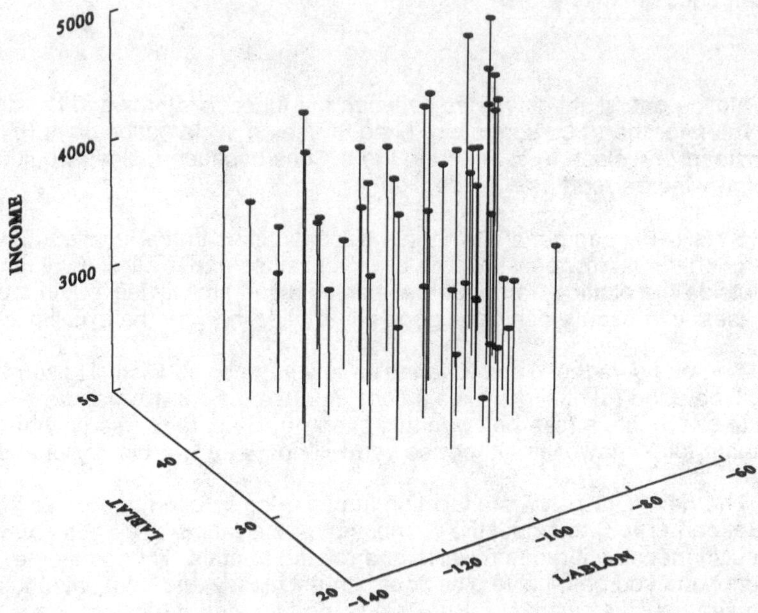

Function Plots

You can plot mathematical functions as well as data with the **PLOT** command. Just type the equation of the function you wish to plot. SYGRAPH will analyze your function, determine axis values, and plot it in smooth lines. You need not generate sample values to produce the plot. The notation and syntax for equations follow standard BASIC. For example, you could type the following to produce the equation for a parabola:

```
PLOT  Y=X^2
```

SYGRAPH determines the plotting domain (horizontal axis limits) and range (vertical axis limits) of the function by numerically computing the second derivatives (rate of change in Y versus change in X) and examining their behavior. For most non-periodic functions, it can do a good job at finding the interesting part of your function to plot. It has more trouble with periodic (e.g. trigonometric) functions. If it fails, however, you can choose limits yourself, e.g.:

```
PLOT  Y=X^2!XMIN=-3,XMAX=3,YMIN=0,YMAX=9
```

Notice one slight difference between the function syntax and the data syntax for the **PLOT** command. I had to use an exclamation point (!) instead of a slash (/) to separate the options because a slash would otherwise be read as a divide sign.

SYGRAPH can generally handle discontinuities in the function as well. It should not blow up with large or small values and it will clip values outside the plotting frame. Sometimes its algorithm will fail, but in these cases, you usually can get a good plot by fiddling with the axis limits.

You can give the Y and X variables any names you wish. These names will be used to label the axes unless you use the **XLABEL** and/or **YLABEL** options (see below in this chapter). Be sure to use only one name for X, however. Otherwise you will not get a two-dimensional plot.

The next figure shows a function from the family used by Rudnic and Gaspari (1987) to model the distribution of the radius of gyration of multidimensional random walks and related fractals. Try some other functions yourself. I love plotting arbitrarily messy and unusual functions to see how they work out. Here are some fun ones. Some require a lot of time to compute.

```
PLOT  Y=SIN(COS(TAN(X)))
PLOT  Y=1/SIN(X)
PLOT  Y=SIN(EXP(X))
PLOT  Y=SIN(1/X)
PLOT  Y=ATH(COS(X))
PLOT  Y=1/X^2-SIN(X)
PLOT  Y=1/LOG(ABS(TAN(X)))
```

Figure 4

```
TYPE=HERSHEY
PLOT  P=SQR(R)*EXP(-R),
  !XMIN=0,XMAX=10,YMIN=0,YMAX=.5
```

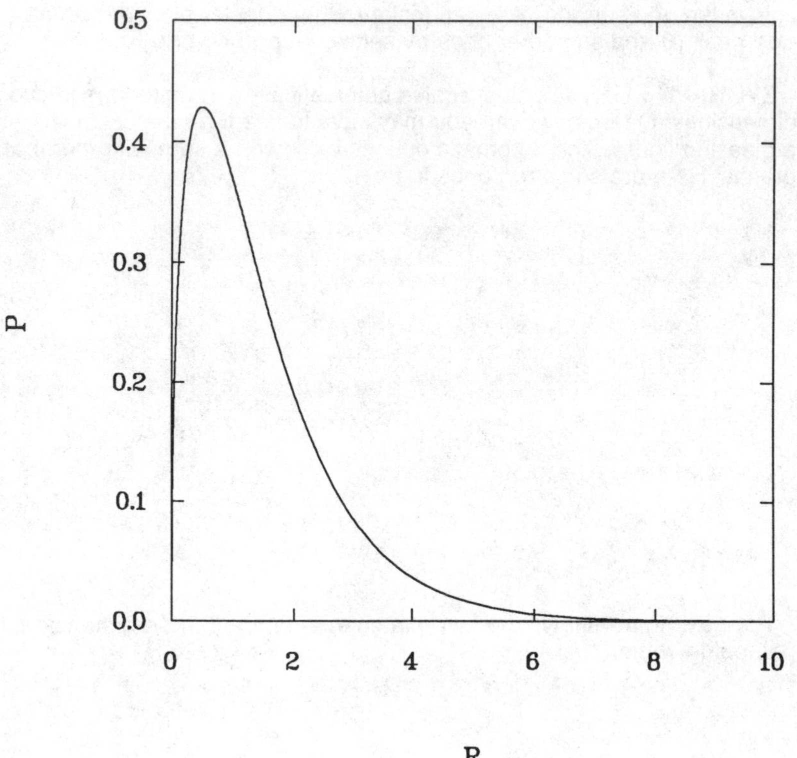

Three-Dimensional Function Plots

SYGRAPH produces three-dimensional function plots when you have two predictors in the **PLOT** equation. For example, if you type:

```
PLOT  Z=X^2-Y^2
```

the program will recognize the two predictors X and Y automatically and place the plot in three-dimensional perspective.

Almost always, you should use the **HIDE** option (see below in this chapter) because most mathematical functions produce overlapping surfaces when viewed in perspective. You can try some preliminary plots without **HIDE** to save time, however. Another way to save time is to use the **CUT** option (see below in this chapter), which modifies the number of cuts in the grid surface. You can make rougher, faster plots by setting **CUT** near 10 and smoother ones by setting it up to 40 or 50.

SYGRAPH will try to adjust scales automatically just as it does in two dimensions. Often, however, you may have to fine tune the scales to get a pleasing figure. The automatic options work with a surprising number of graphs. Here are some fun ones to try:

```
PLOT  Z=X*Y*(X^2-Y^2)/(X^2+Y^2)!,
XMIN=-10,XMAX=10,YMIN=-10,YMAX=10,
ZMIN=-100,ZMAX=100,HIDE

PLOT  Z=SIN(SQR(X*X+Y*Y))!,
XMIN=-5,XMAX=5,YMIN=-5,YMAX=5,
ZMIN=-1,ZMAX=1,HIDE

PLOT  Z=X*X/8-Y*Y/12!XMIN=-10,XMAX=10,
YMIN=-10,YMAX=10,
ZMIN=-10,ZMAX=10,HIDE

PLOT  Z=2*SIN(2*SQR(X^2+Y^2))/SQR(X^2+Y^2)!,
XMIN=-5,XMAX=5,YMIN=-5,YMAX=5,
ZMIN=-5,ZMAX=5,HIDE
```

The next figure shows the last example, a damped three-dimensional polar sine wave.

Figure 5

```
PLOT   Z=2*SIN(2*SQR(X^2+Y^2))/SQR(X^2+Y^2),
   !XMIN=-5,XMAX=5,
    YMIN=-5,YMAX=5,
     ZMIN=-5,ZMAX=5,HIDE
```

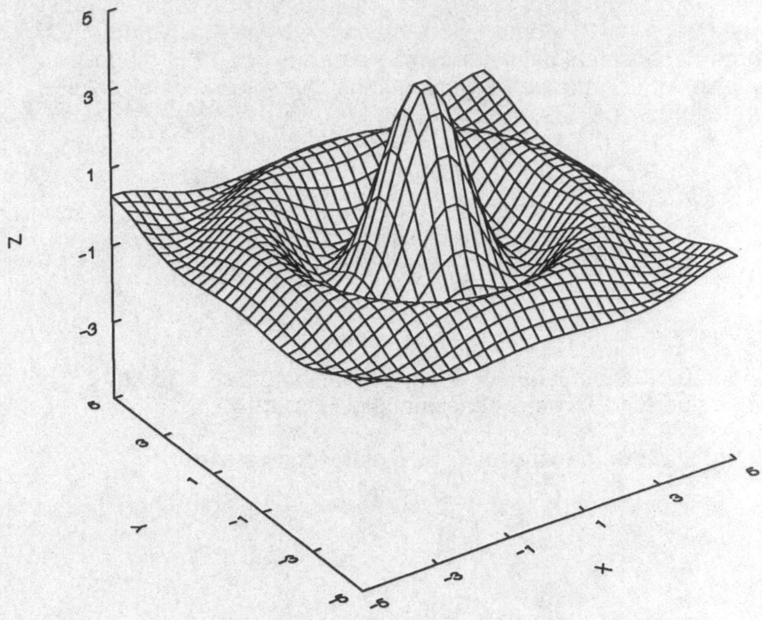

AXES *(Number of Axes)*

The **AXES** option controls the number of axes drawn in a plot. Its syntax is:

```
AXES=n
```

where *n* is an integer from 0 to 12. If *n* is 0, no axes will be drawn. If *n* is an integer from 1 to 12, all axes from 1 to *n* will be drawn. If *n* is negative, only the axis numbered with the absolute value of *n* will be drawn.

Two-dimensional axes are numbered from 1 to 4 clockwise, beginning with the bottom axis:

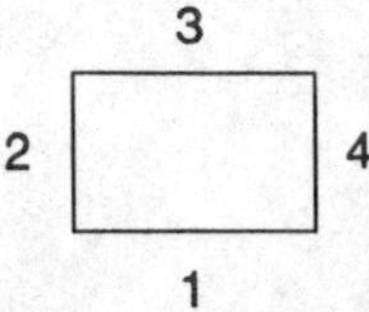

Three-dimensional axes are numbered from 1 to 12 in the following way (see AXIS in the general commands chapter above for more information):

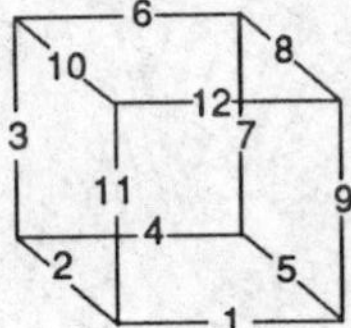

The default (usual) value for a two-dimensional plot is **AXES=4**. The usual value for a three-dimensional plot is **AXES=3**.

Figure 6 shows a two-dimensional plot with two axes.

Figure 6

```
PLOT  SUMMER*WINTER/AXES=2
```

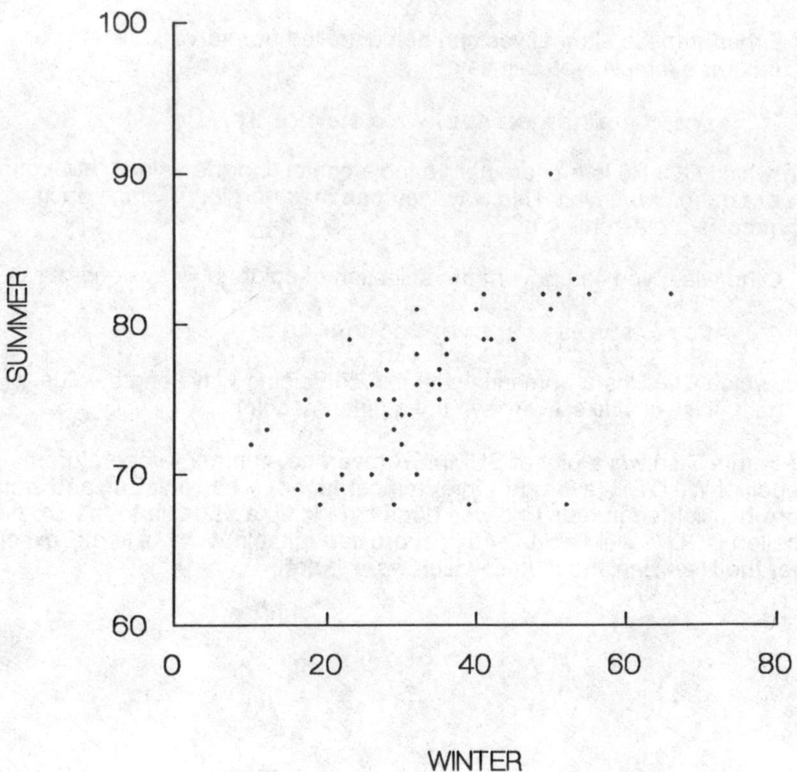

COLOR *(Setting Color of Symbols)*

You can choose a color for your symbols with the **COLOR** option. Choose either a name or a wavelength in nanometers. Possible colors and their approximate nanometer wavelengths are: **RED** (615), **ORANGE** (590), **YELLOW** (575), **GREEN** (505), **BLUE** (480), **VIOLET** (450). You may also name **BLACK**, **WHITE**, **GRAY**, and **BROWN**. The following command will make all symbols in the graph red:

```
PLOT   SUMMER*WINTER/COLOR=RED
```

You can also specify color in nanometers wavelength. The following example will make all the symbols greenish:

```
PLOT   SUMMER*WINTER/COLOR=540
```

Either of these alternatives can be controlled from a variable in your data. For example, you can say:

```
PLOT   SUMMER*WINTER/COLOR=COLR$,
```

in which COLR$ is a character variable containing the values '**RED**' or '**YELLOW**' or whatever. This way, you can make a plot in which each symbol is a different color.

Otherwise, you can govern the selection of colors by wavelength:

```
PLOT   SUMMER*WINTER/COLOR=COLR,
```

in which COLR is a numerical variable containing wavelength values. Again, this will make every symbol a different color.

Figure 7 shows a plot of SUMMER (average summer temperatures) against WINTER (average winter temperatures). The New England states are highlighted in red. This was done by adding a variable to the US file called COLR$. All values of this character variable were "**BLACK**" except for the New England states, which were "**RED**".

Figure 7

```
PLOT   SUMMER*WINTER/COLOR=COLR$,SYMBOL=2,FILL=1
```

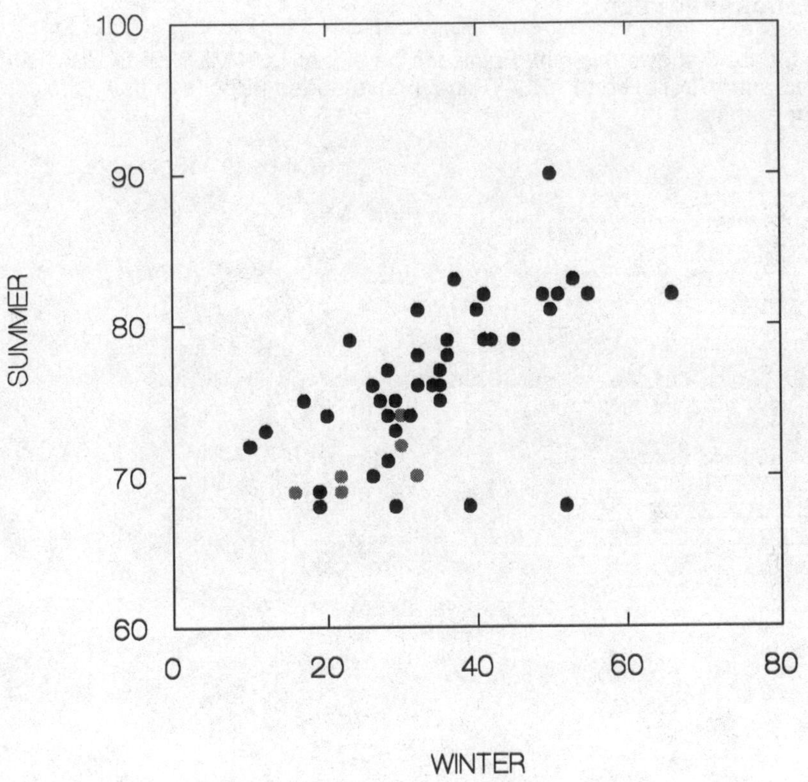

COLOR *(Multi-colored multiple variable plots)*

You can make plots with a different color for each dependent variable. The following command will make red symbols for summer and blue symbols for winter, for example:

```
PLOT   SUMMER,WINTER*LABLAT/COLOR=RED,BLUE
```

You can use wavelength instead of color names, if you wish, or you can use the name of a variable in the dataset to govern the color (see the **COLOR** command in the previous figure). In any case, if you are doing a multi-category category plot (by using more than one variable to the left of the asterisk in the command) then you must specify the same number of colors in the **COLOR** option as you have variables to the left of the asterisk even if you are using the same color for each variable (e.g. **COLOR=RED,RED**).

Figure 8 shows this plot. Points for the plot of SUMMER on LABLAT are red and WINTER on LABLAT blue. I have added larger symbols (circles) for emphasis.

Figure 8

```
PLOT  SUMMER,WINTER*LABLAT,
   /COLOR=RED,BLUE,SYMBOL=2,2,FILL=1,1,
    YLABEL='Average  Temperatures'
```

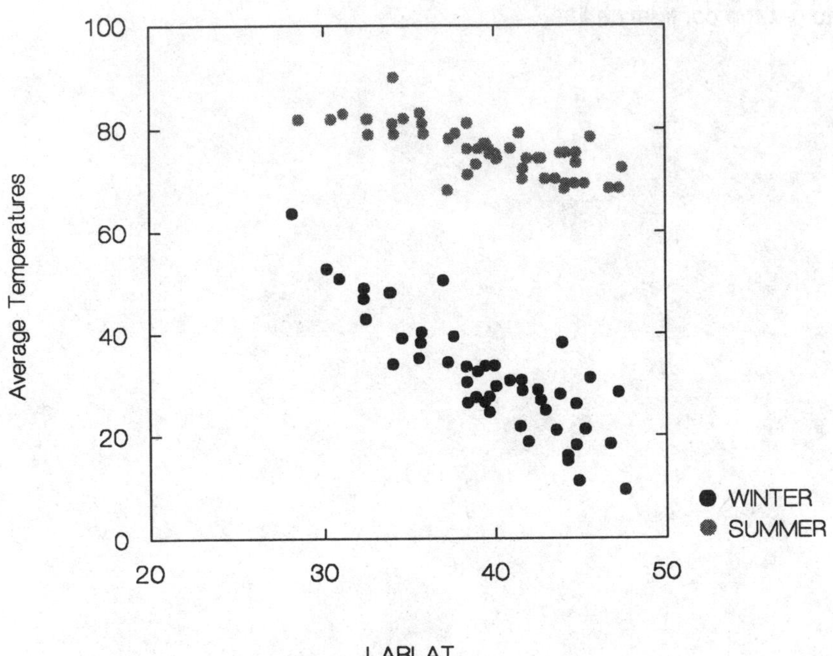

CONFI *(Confidence Interval on Regression Line)*

Often, we want a confidence interval on a regression line we have fitted. You can choose any level you wish for the confidence interval (e.g. `CONFI=.87`). If you do not choose a value (just typing `CONFI`), then it defaults to .95. Say we choose `CONFI=.90`. This will cause SYGRAPH to draw upper and lower hyperbolic bands around the actual fitted line. These bands mean the following: if the discrepancies (residuals) between the fitted and observed values for Y at each X are normally distributed and independent of each other and have the same spread (variance), then 90 times out of a hundred, confidence intervals constructed by SYGRAPH from data sampled in the same way you found these data will cover the true regression line relating Y to X.

The next figure shows the 95 percent confidence intervals on the regression line of WINTER (average winter temperature) on LABLAT (latitude). You must include `SMOOTH=LINEAR`, as I have done, in order to get the confidence line.

Figure 9

```
TYPE=HERSHEY
PLOT   WINTER*LABLAT/SMOOTH=LINEAR,CONFI=.95
```

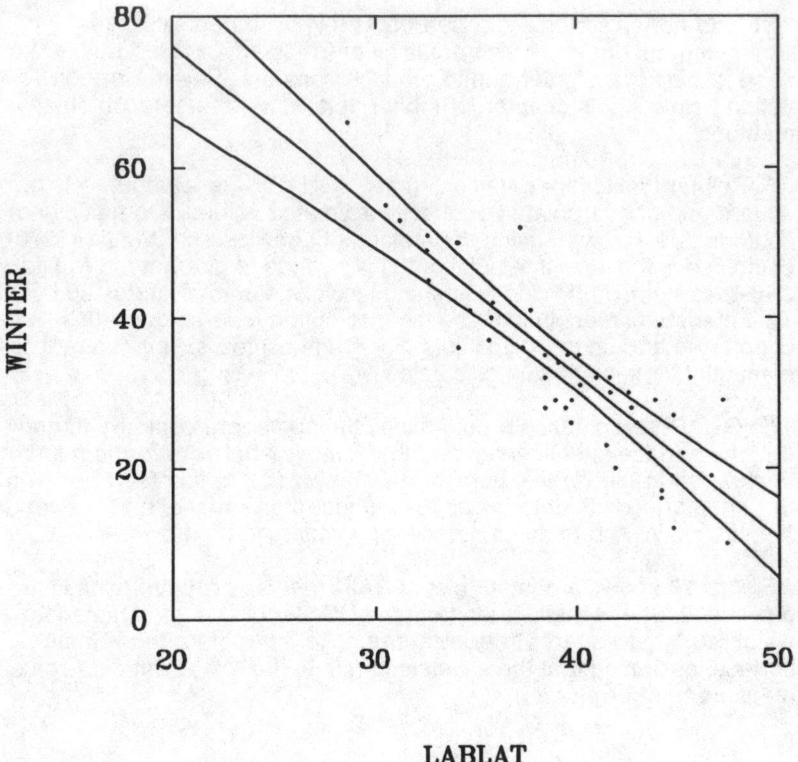

CONTOUR *(Contour Plotting with Lines)*

You can produce contour plots of functions and smoothed surfaces with the **CONTOUR** option. For mathematical functions, simply add the **CONTOUR** option:

```
PLOT   Z=X^2-Y^2!CONTOUR
```

For contouring data from a file, you may also include one of the following **SMOOTH** options to interpolate points, e.g.:

```
PLOT   Z*Y*X/SMOOTH=LINEAR,CONTOUR
PLOT   Z*Y*X/SMOOTH=QUAD,CONTOUR
PLOT   Z*Y*X/SMOOTH=DWLS,CONTOUR
PLOT   Z*Y*X/SMOOTH=NEXPO,CONTOUR
```

If you do not select one, **SMOOTH=NEXPO** is assumed. All of the smoothing options work with regularly or irregularly spaced points. You need not input a regular grid to produce contours. See the **SMOOTH** option below in this chapter for further details on the interpolation methods used.

For either function or data contours, SYGRAPH first computes its own square grid of interpolated or directly estimated values. From this grid, contours are followed using the method of Lodwick and Whittle (1970) combined with linear interpolation. This method is guaranteed to find proper contours if the grid is fine enough. The standard grid is 30 by 30. To increase this resolution, use the **CUT** option (see below in this chapter) to add up to 60 grid cuts. For rough contours, you can reduce computing time by setting cuts below 30.

SYGRAPH automatically determines the number of contours to draw so that the surface is delineated and the contour labels are round numbers. If you wish to modify this number, use the **ZTICK** option (see below in this chapter), which determines the number of tick marks on the third (vertical) axis, and thus the number of contours to be drawn.

Figure 10 shows a contour plot of RAIN (average annual rainfall) against latitude and longitude from the US file. I have used distance weighted least squares (**SMOOTH=DWLS**) to interpolate the rainfall surface, assuming that the estimate of rain at the state centroids contains measurement error.

Figure 10

```
PLOT  RAIN*LABLAT*LABLON,
  /ZTICK=10,SMOOTH=DWLS,CONTOUR
```

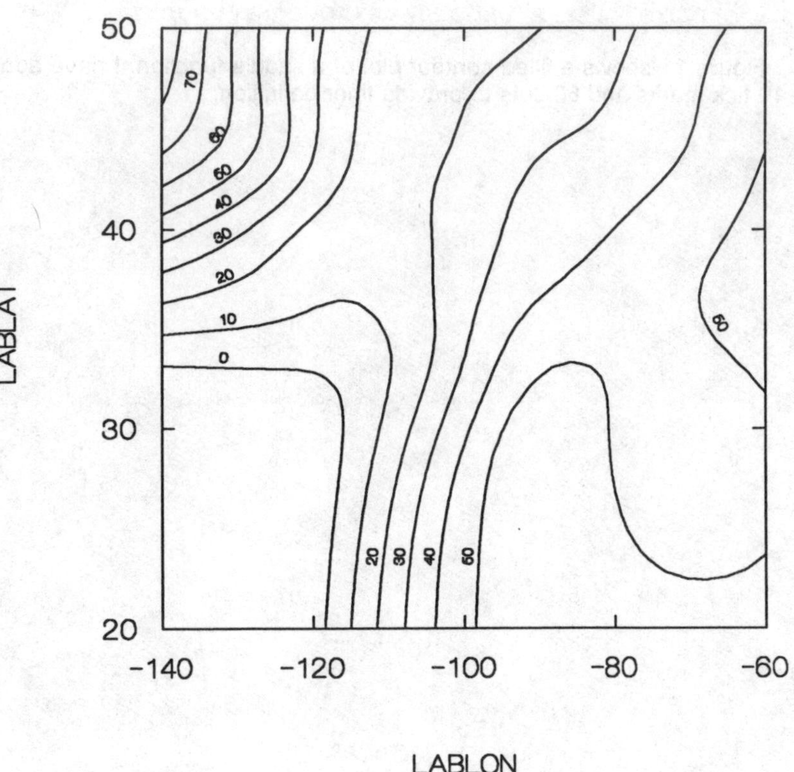

CONTOUR *(Contour Plotting with Shading)*

You can produce shaded contour plots of functions and smoothed surfaces with the **CONTOUR** and **FILL** options used together. Instead of lines, this method uses fill patterns from empty (white) to full (black) in even gradations which are determined by the height of the function at a given pixel (grid square). The syntax of the option for functions is:

```
PLOT   Z=X^2-Y^2!CONTOUR,FILL
```

And for smoothed data it is:

```
PLOT   Z*Y*X/SMOOTH=LINEAR,CONTOUR,FILL
PLOT   Z*Y*X/SMOOTH=QUAD,CONTOUR,FILL
PLOT   Z*Y*X/SMOOTH=DWLS,CONTOUR,FILL
PLOT   Z*Y*X/SMOOTH=NEXPO,CONTOUR,FILL
```

Figure 11 shows a filled contour plot of a saddle function. I have added 10 tick marks and 60 cuts to provide finer definition.

Figure 11

```
PLOT  Z=X^2-Y^2,
   !CONTOUR,FILL,ZTICK=10,ZMIN=-2,ZMAX=2,CUT=60
```

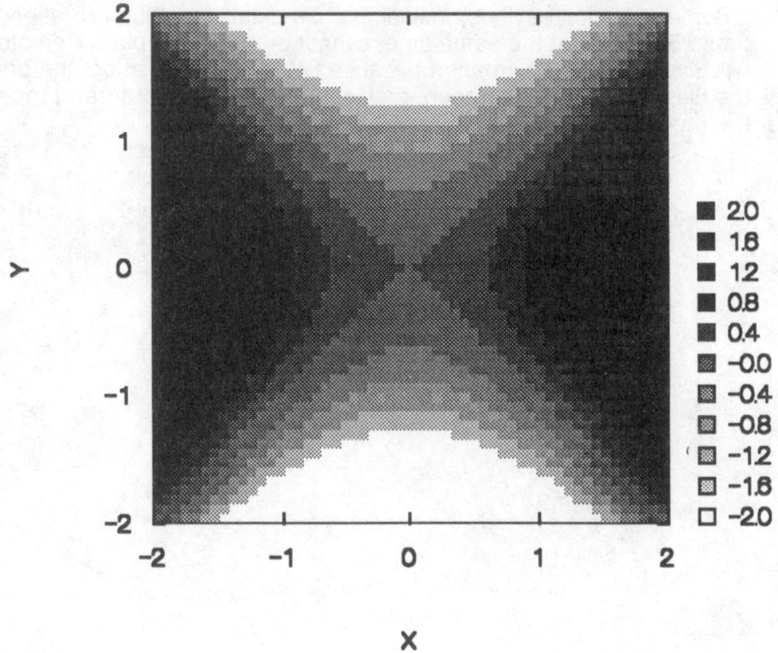

CONTOUR *(Contour Plotting with Color)*

You can produce color contour plots of functions and smoothed surfaces with the **CONTOUR** and **COLOR** options used together. Instead of lines, this method uses fill patterns from blue to red in even perceptual gradations which are determined by the height of the function at a given pixel (grid square). The syntax of the option for functions is:

```
PLOT   Z=X^2-Y^2!CONTOUR,COLOR
```

And for smoothed data it is:

```
PLOT   Z*Y*X/SMOOTH=LINEAR,CONTOUR,COLOR
PLOT   Z*Y*X/SMOOTH=QUAD,CONTOUR,COLOR
PLOT   Z*Y*X/SMOOTH=DWLS,CONTOUR,COLOR
PLOT   Z*Y*X/SMOOTH=NEXPO,CONTOUR,COLOR
```

Figure 12 shows a color contour plot of the saddle function used in Figure 11. Because this manual is printed in only three colors, I have had to keep ZTICK=3.

Some graphics devices, including color displays which represent fewer than 256 colors at the same time, cannot produce this plot. Pen plotters will give a fair approximation because SYGRAPH will select the pen with the closest color appearance, provided the pens are ordered properly in the carousel.

Figure 12

```
PLOT  Z=X^2-Y^2,
  !CONTOUR,COLOR,ZTICK=3,ZMIN=-2,ZMAX=2,CUT=60
```

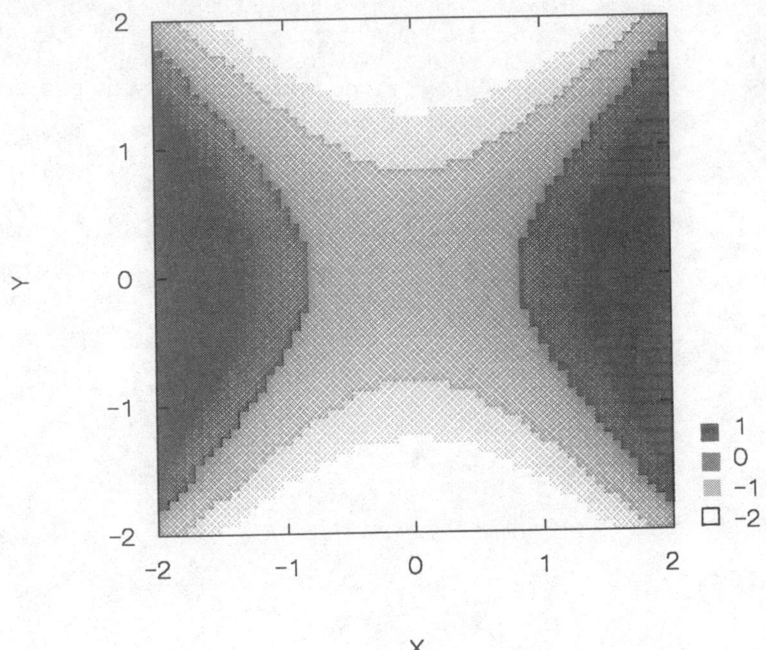

CUT *(Picking Number of Cuts in a Grid)*

For contouring and surface plotting in three dimensions, SYGRAPH computes a 30 by 30 square grid. This is usually sufficient to give good resolution while conserving computer time. You can change this value with the **CUT** option, e.g. **CUT=40** or **CUT=10**. You may choose up to 60 cuts and as few as 2 on most machines, but you should rarely need fewer than 10 or more than 40.

Setting **CUT=10** and omitting **HIDE** (see above in this chapter) is the best way to save computer time when you are trying to get a rough sketch of a surface. If you want a more detailed view, use the **HIDE** option and, perhaps, set **CUT=35**. You may need an even larger value for some complex mathematical functions with steep cliffs.

Figure 13 shows an example of an error function plot with 60 cuts. I have used **ZMIN** and **ZMAX** (see below in this chapter) to scale the vertical axis. The **HIDE** option (see above in this chapter) keeps the rear of the surface hidden.

Figure 13

```
TYPE=HERSHEY
PLOT   Z=EXP(-X^2-Y^2)!ZMIN=0,ZMAX=1,HIDE,CUT=60
```

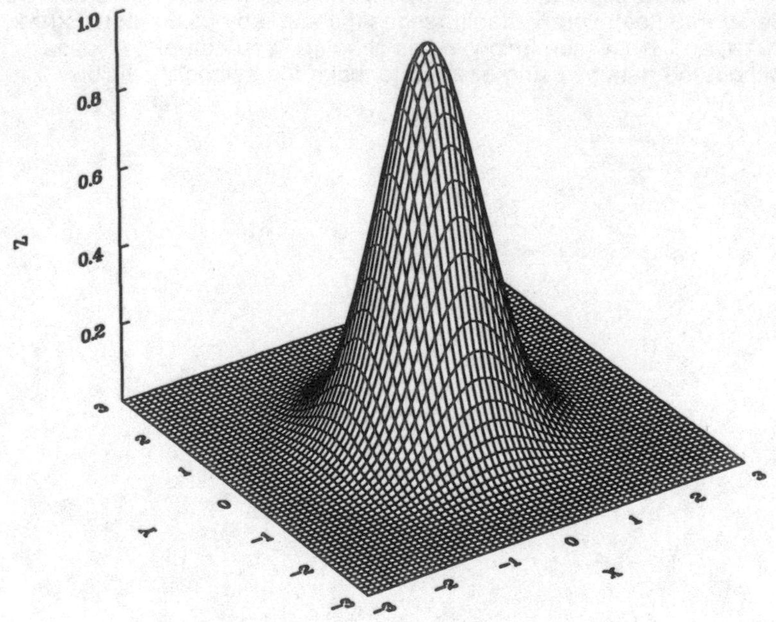

ELL *(Gaussian Bivariate Ellipsoids)*
You can draw bivariate ellipses on scatterplots assuming a Gaussian (Normal) bivariate distribution for your data. The ellipse produced is centered on the sample means of the X and Y variables. Its major axes are determined by the unbiased sample standard deviations of X and Y and its orientation is determined by the sample covariance between X and Y. You choose the size of the ellipse by specifying a probability value between 0 and 1, e.g. **`ELL=.95`**. If you make an extremely large ellipse (e.g. **`ELL=.999`**), it may extend beyond the axes of your plot. If you do not choose a value, (by typing only **`ELL`**), then .5 is assumed.

Figure 14 shows an ellipse superimposed on the plot of PERSON (person crimes) against PROPERTY (property crimes). I have used a 50 percent confidence region on the data values (**`ELL=.5`**). If the data were bivariate normal, then we would expect to find half the data points inside the ellipse. This is approximately the case.

If you have two or more samples, such as in a discriminant analysis, you can draw separate ellipses by superimposing them on the same plot. Be sure to keep your variable ranges the same by using **`XMIN`**, **`XMAX`**, **`YMIN`**, and **`YMAX`** (see below in this chapter). You can plot ellipses without the data by using **`SIZE=0`** to make the symbols invisible.

Figure 14

```
TYPE=HERSHEY
PLOT   PERSON*PROPERTY/SYMBOL=2,ELL=.5
```

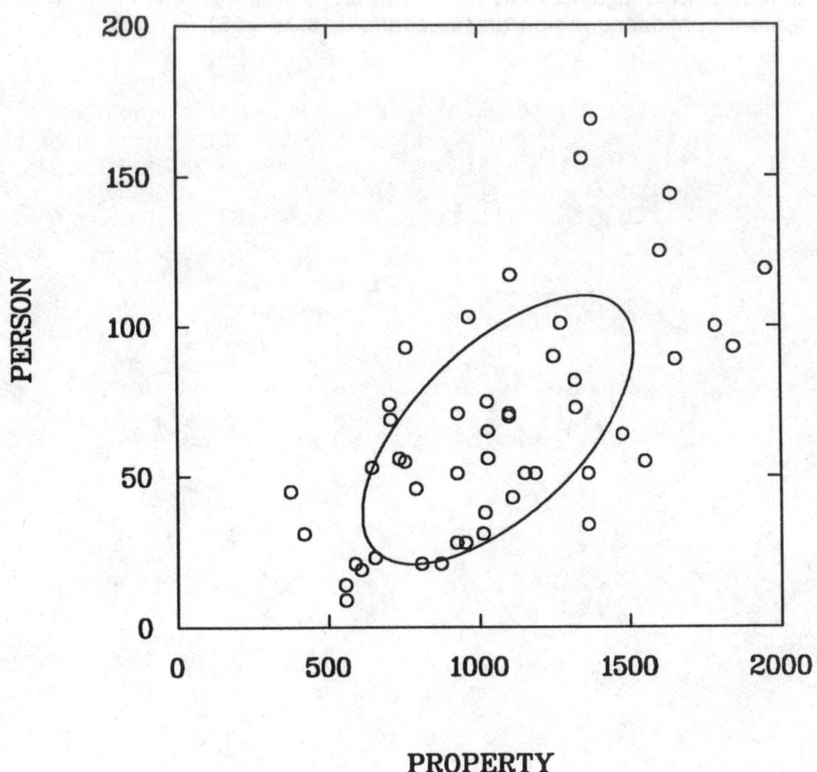

ELM *(Gaussian Confidence Intervals on Bivariate Centroids)*

You can draw bivariate confidence intervals on centroids with the **ELM** option. As with the **ELL** option (see directly above), the ellipse produced is centered on the sample means of the X and Y variables. Its major axes are determined by the unbiased sample standard deviations of X and Y and its orientation is determined by the sample covariance between X and Y. You choose the size of the ellipse by specifying a probability value between 0 and 1, e.g. **ELM=.95**. This size is adjusted by the sample size so that the ellipse will always be smaller than that produced by the **ELL** option. If you do not choose a value, (by typing only **ELM**), then .95 is assumed.

Figure 15 shows an ellipse superimposed on the plot of PERSON (person crimes) against PROPERTY (property crimes). I have used a 95 percent confidence region on the centroid (**ELM=.95**).

Figure 15

```
TYPE=HERSHEY
PLOT   PERSON*PROPERTY/SYMBOL=2,ELM=.95
```

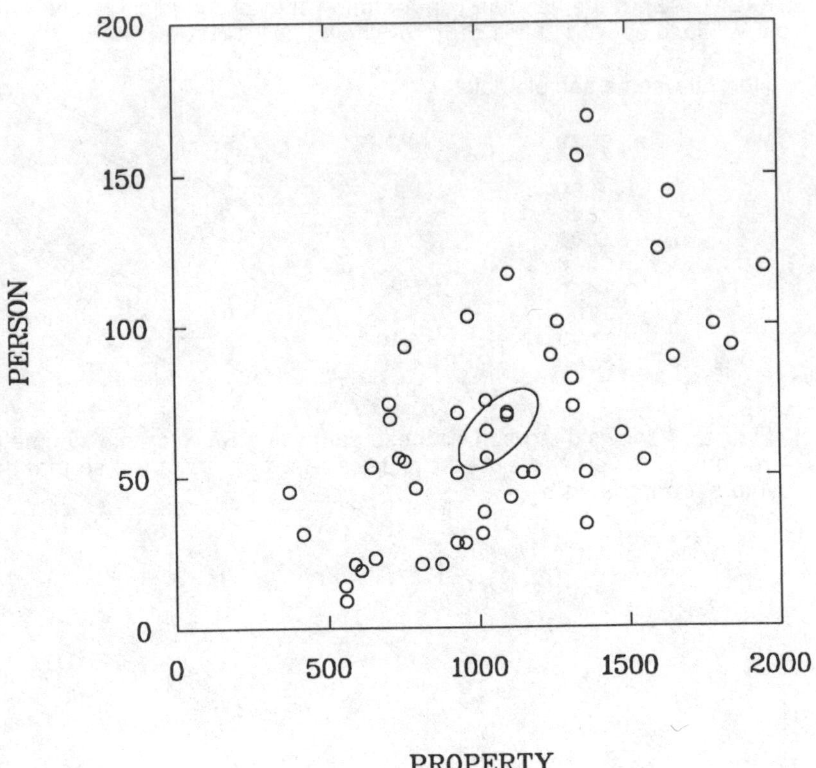

ERROR/ERROR1 *(Symmetric and One-Sided Error Bars)*

Sometimes we want plots which show standard errors around plotted points. For example, each point might represent a group of plants receiving the same dose of a growth hormone. In this case, you can plot the standard error of the mean around the mean for the group using the **ERROR** option. It is up to you whether you choose standard deviations, standard errors of the mean, two times the standard deviation, or some other measure of spread. SYGRAPH simply takes the value from the file and plots tick marks on each side of the point by the same amount. As with the **SIZE** option, you are responsible for insuring that your tick marks fit the graph. If they go outside the axes, you can use the **MIN** and **MAX** options for Y or X to keep them inside.

You can draw one-sided error bars with the **ERROR1** option (e.g., **ERROR1=SE**). If the variable you assign to **ERROR1** is positive, the error bar will face upward. If it is negative, the bar will face downward.

Here are some sample data:

DOSE	GROWTH	SE
500	110	5
800	112	6
1000	116	7
1200	118	9
1400	120	13
1700	135	20
1900	140	22
2200	150	24
2900	210	26

Figure 16 shows the graph for these data using SE to create symmetric error bars. I have used closed circles (**SYMBOL=2,FILL=1**) so that the centers are more visible.

Figure 16

```
PLOT   GROWTH*DOSE/SYMBOL=2,FILL=1,ERROR=SE
```

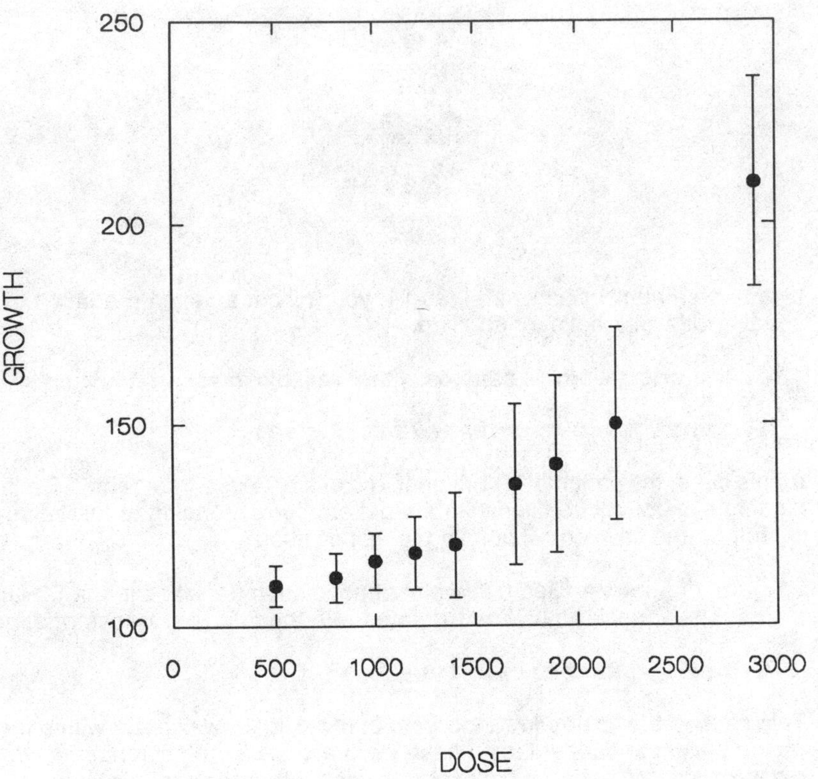

FILL *(Filling symbols)*

You can fill symbols with different patterns. The **FILL** option works this way:

```
PLOT   INCOME*POPDEN/FILL=2
```

The number you choose after "**FILL=**" determines the type of fill pattern. Here are the possibilities:

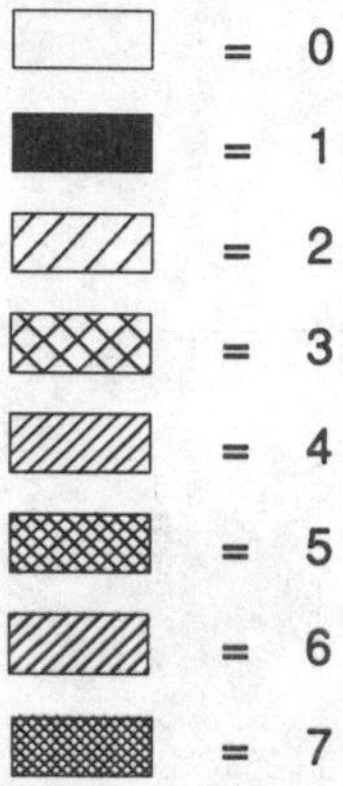

= 0

= 1

= 2

= 3

= 4

= 5

= 6

= 7

If you use a number between 0 and 1, you will get an even gradation of shading between hollow and filled.

You can also govern fill patterns with a variable in your dataset:

```
PLOT   INCOME*POPDEN/FILL=MYFIL
```

In this case, the variable MYFIL should contain values from 0 to 7. Each plotting symbol will be filled with the pattern corresponding to the value in MYFIL for the case corresponding to that symbol.

Figure 17 shows a filled circle plot of population densities in the 50 U.S. states. The variable PDEN was created with the following transformation:

```
LET   PDEN=POPDEN/1000
```

This caused the values to range from about .1 to .9, which are within the region of light to dark values. I have used a circle as the symbol (**SYMBOL=2**). You should pick some symbol other than the default (**SYMBOL=1**) because the default is too small to show the fill pattern. I have also increased the symbol size (**SIZE=2**) so that the shading is more visible.

Figure 17

```
PLOT    LABLAT*LABLON/SYMBOL=2,SIZE=2,FILL=PDEN
```

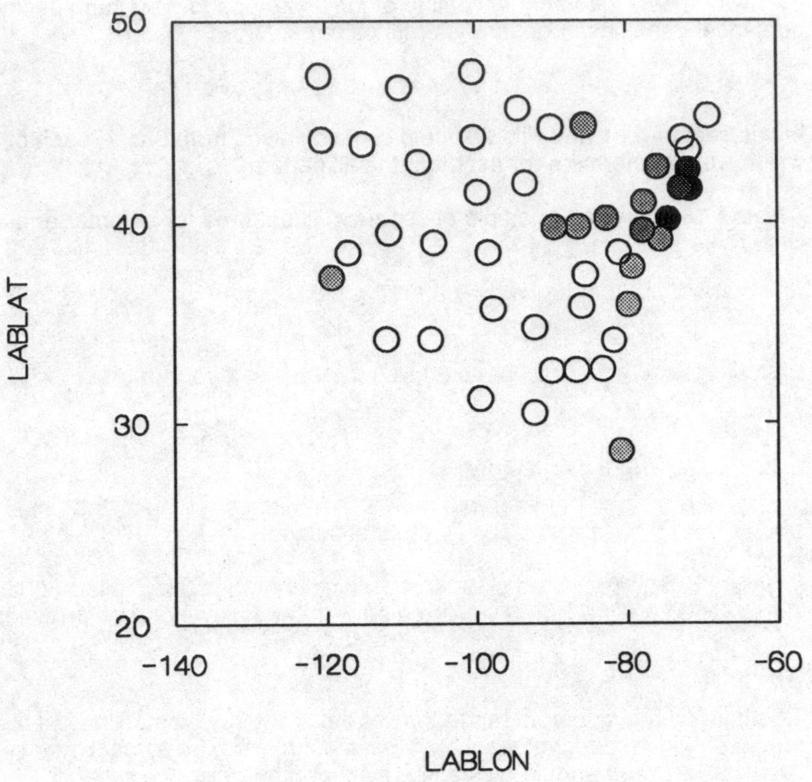

FILL *(Multi-filled plots)*

You can do plots with a different fill pattern for each dependent variable. For example, the SUMMER and WINTER temperatures from the US file can be plotted as empty and filled with the following command:

```
PLOT   SUMMER,WINTER*LABLAT/FILL=0,1,SYMBOL=2,2
```

I added **SYMBOL=2,2** because the default symbol (**SYMBOL=1,1**) is too small to show the shading. If you are doing a multi-variable plot (by using more than one variable to the left of the asterisk in the command) then you must specify the same number of fill patterns in the **FILL** option as you have variables to the left of the asterisk even if you are using the same fill pattern for each variable (e.g. **FILL=2,2**).

As with the single variable version of the **FILL** option, you can specify numerical variables to govern your fill patterns:

```
PLOT   SUMMER,WINTER*LABLAT/FILL=FILL1,FILL2
```

In this case, FILL1 and FILL2 should contain values from 0 to 7, each of which would determine for each bar the fill pattern.

Figure 18 shows an example of separate fill patterns for summer and winter.

Figure 18

```
PLOT  SUMMER,WINTER*LABLAT,
    /FILL=0,1,SYMBOL=2,2,YLABEL='Temperature'
```

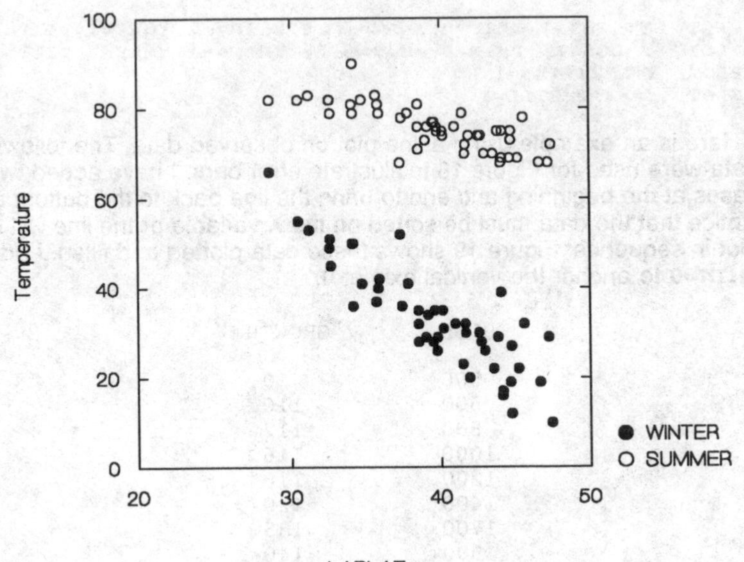

FILL *(Filled Line and Function Plots)*

You can fill a line plot or curve with one of the available fill patterns to highlight its shape. For example, you may want to plot a theoretical probability density with the area under the curve shaded. Or you may wish to reveal the trend across observed data by shading under a line graph. To do this, just add the **FILL** option exactly as it is used to fill plotting symbols (see directly above in this chapter). If you are using the **LINE** option to connect data points (see below in this chapter) and if you set **SIZE=0**, then the area bounded by the line and a straight line connecting the two endpoints of the line will be filled. If you are plotting a function, then adding the **FILL** option will fill the area bounded by the curve and a straight line connecting the two endpoints of the curve.

The exact area filled is easier to show in a graph than to explain further. Try the following functions to see what I mean. You will see that if you want to fill areas under a curve and down to the bottom of the Y axis, you will have to include points at the end of the curve which touch the X axis.

```
PLOT  Y=SIN(X)!XMIN=0,XMAX=6.28,YMIN=-1,YMAX=1,FILL=1
PLOT  Y=COS(X)!XMIN=0,XMAX=6.28,YMIN=-1,YMAX=1,FILL=1
PLOT  Y=X^2!FILL=1
PLOT  Y=-X^2!FILL=1
```

Here is an example using a line plot on observed data. The following data were used for Figure 16 to illustrate error bars. I have added two cases at the beginning and end to bring the line back to the bottom axis. Notice that the data must be sorted on the X variable or the line will not plot in sequence. Figure 19 shows these data plotted and filled. I added **YMIN=0** to anchor the vertical axis at 0.

DOSE	GROWTH
500	0
500	110
800	112
1000	116
1200	118
1400	120
1700	135
1900	140
2200	150
2900	210
2900	0

Figure 19

```
PLOT  GROWTH*DOSE/FILL=5,SIZE=0,LINE,YMIN=0
```

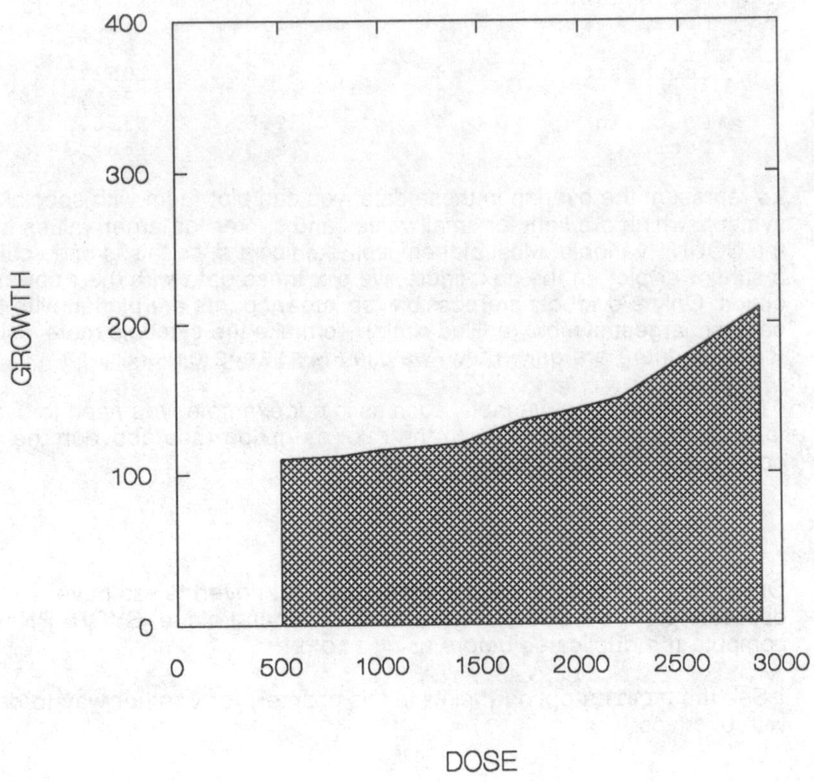

FLOWER *(Sunflower Plots)*

Sometimes we have data which overlap at exactly the same values. For example, we may have a questionnaire with a 7 point scale and we wish to plot two items against each other. There are only 49 possible points where we may plot the data. Or, we may have aggregate data and wish to plot them in a scatterplot. Here are the means of PERSON (personal crimes) and PROPERTY (property crimes) within regions of the variables in the US file. COUNT shows the number of states over which the means were computed.

REGION$	COUNT	PERSON	PROPERTY
New England	6	33.2	899.0
Mid Atlantic	3	97.3	1038.3
Great Lakes	5	81.8	1148.8
Plains	7	41.3	891.3
Southeast	8	87.3	1052.3
South	8	67.9	801.5
Mountain	8	59.5	1356.0
Pacific	3	79.3	1661.3

To represent the overlap in these data, you can plot them with special symbols which are light for small values and darker for larger values of the COUNT variable. Most of them look like flowers, so this is often called a sunflower plot. In the next figure, we plot these data with the **FLOWER** option. Only 9 symbols are possible, so larger counts are plotted with the darkest, largest symbol (a filled circle). To make the symbols more visible (because there are only a few) we use the **SIZE=2** option.

If you have a count variable, such as in our example, you need to use it to **WEIGHT** cases before using the **FLOWER** option (see above in the general commands chapter):

```
WEIGHT=COUNT
PLOT  Y*X/FLOWER
```

Otherwise, if your data are not aggregated but nevertheless have duplicate pairs of values, use the **PLOT** command alone. SYGRAPH will compute the duplicates before using **FLOWER**.

See the **JITTER** option (below in this chapter) for another way to deal with overlaps.

Figure 20

```
WEIGHT=COUNT
 PLOT  PERSON*PROPERTY/FLOWER,SIZE=2
```

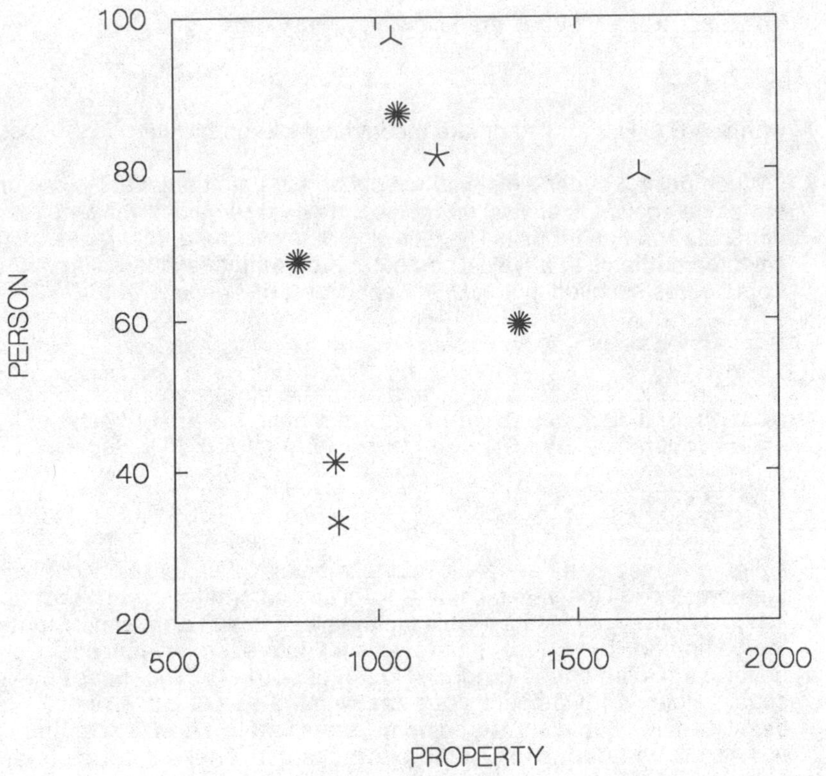

FOURIER *(Andrews' Fourier Plots)*

A particularly powerful method for identifying clusters of cases in a multivariate dataset is to plot their Fourier components. Andrews (1972) developed these plots. Fourier functions have the following form:

$$f(t) = y_1 / \sqrt{2} + y_2\sin(t) + y_3\cos(t) + y_4\sin(2t) + y_5\cos(2t) + ...$$

where y is a p dimensional variate and t varies from -3.14 to 3.14 (π radians on either side of zero). The result of this transformation is a set of waveforms made up of sine and cosine components. Each waveform corresponds to one case in the dataset. Cases which have similar values across all variables will have overlapping waveforms in the plot. Cases with different patterns of variation will have contrasting waveforms.

The **FOURIER** plot has the following syntax:

```
PLOT  A,B,C,D,E,   .../FOURIER
```

where A,B,C,D,E and so on are the variables to be included in the plot.

When using Fourier plots, you should be sure all the variables are on the same scale. Otherwise, variables having large values will tend to dominate the Fourier plot. The following data are the percentages of selected nutrients in a typical computer programmer's diet, estimated from figures supplied by the U.S. Department of Agriculture.

FOOD$	WATER	PROTEIN	FAT	CARBO
Twinkie	22.0	5.4	13.6	57.0
Eggroll	55.0	6.2	8.2	20.0
Cola	90.0	0.0	0.0	8.0
Pizza	45.0	9.3	8.0	35.8
Fudge	8.0	3.5	13.8	72.7
Peanuts	2.0	26.1	50.8	19.1

Figure 21 shows a Fourier plot of these data. Notice that I did not type the names of all the variables after the **PLOT** command. If you want to include all the numerical variables in the file, it is sufficient simply to type the command. The Fourier plot reveals the four essential nutrition groups: beverage (Cola), entree (Eggroll, Pizza), dessert (Twinkie, Fudge), and snack (Peanuts). Compare **FOURIER** with the **PARALLEL** axes plot (see below in this chapter). Also compare **FOURIER** to **ICON/BLOB** and **PARALLEL** to **ICON/STAR** in the **ICON** chapter. These latter plots are polar coordinate versions of Fourier and parallel coordinate plots, respectively.

Figure 21

```
TYPE=HERSHEY
PLOT/FOURIER,LABEL=FOOD$
```

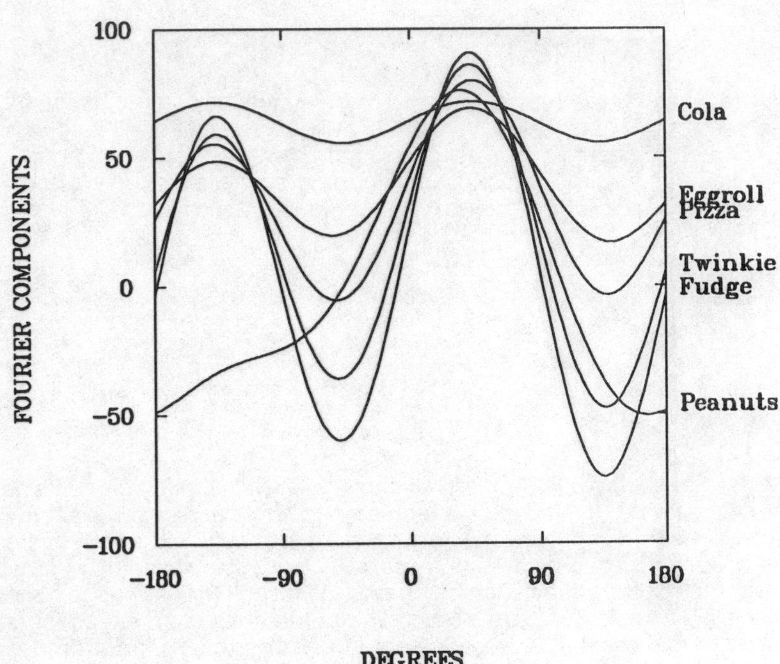

GRID *(Grid Marks)*

You can add grid marks to plots with the **GRID** option. The possible values are:

```
GRID=1      (vertical grid marks)
GRID=2      (horizontal grid marks)
GRID=3      (horizontal and vertical grid marks)
```

Grids can be added to the back and side panels of three-dimensional plots by using the **FACET** command (see above in general commands chapter) and one of the three settings for **GRID**. See the advanced applications chapter for an example.

Figure 22 shows an example with vertical and horizontal grid marks.

Figure 22

```
PLOT   INCOME*LABLAT/GRID=3,SYMBOL=2,FILL=1
```

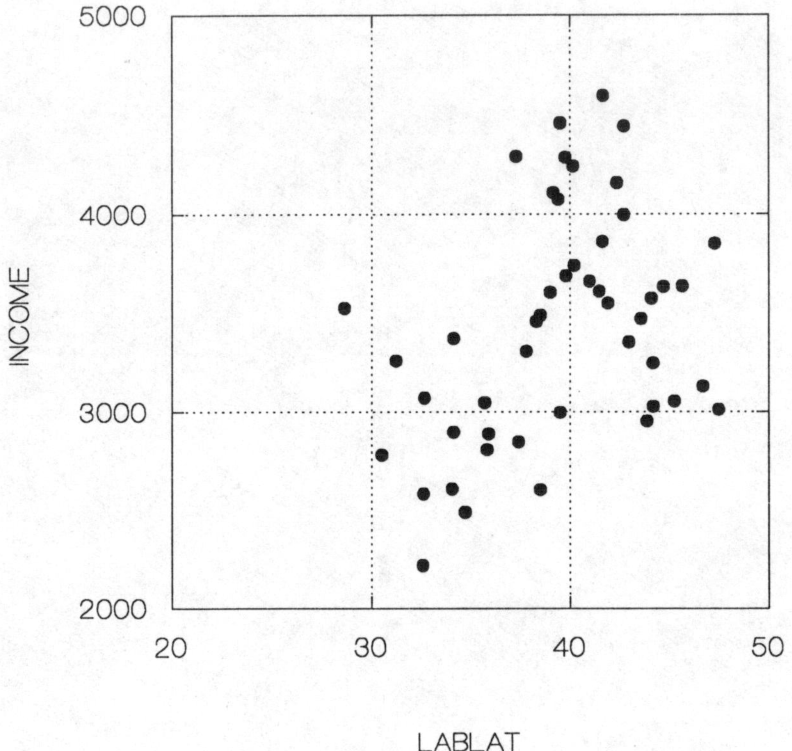

HEIGHT *(Physical Height of Plot)*

You can control the physical height of your plot with the **HEIGHT** option. It works like this:

```
HEIGHT=50%      (or HEIGHT=50)
HEIGHT=4IN
HEIGHT=10CM
```

The first example specifies percent of display height. The second specifies inches, and the third centimeters.

When you use the **HEIGHT** option, you probably also want to use **WIDTH**, which works exactly the same way (see below in this chapter). The following graph shows how to use them together.

Figure 23

```
PLOT   INCOME*LABLAT/HEIGHT=3IN,WIDTH=4IN
```

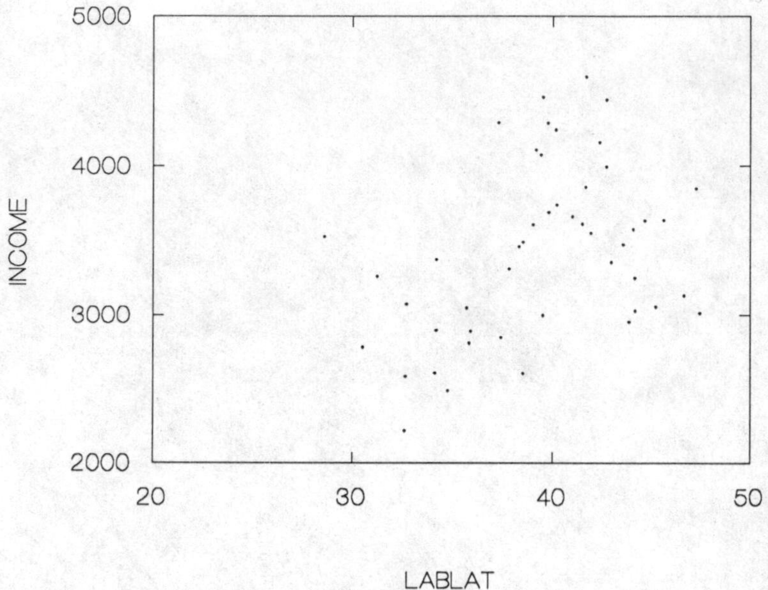

HIDE *(Hidden Surface 3-D Plotting)*

When you plot surfaces in three dimensions, you can occasionally encounter "see through" portions, where parts of the surface overlap. This will happen either when you are plotting a function (see 3-D function plotting at the beginning of this chapter) or when you are using a 3-D `SMOOTH` option (see below in this chapter). To prevent this overlap, add the `HIDE` option to your `PLOT` command.

`HIDE` takes longer to compute, so you may not want to use it until you have a final production graph. On faster machines, you may be able to use it all the time.

The next figure shows `HIDE` for a substantially overlapping figure which looks like a cowboy hat. I have set the axis limits to keep the figure in scale.

Figure 24

```
PLOT  Z=SIN(SQR(X*X+Y*Y)),
   !XMIN=-5,XMAX=5,YMIN=-5,YMAX=5,
    ZMIN=-1,ZMAX=1,HIDE
```

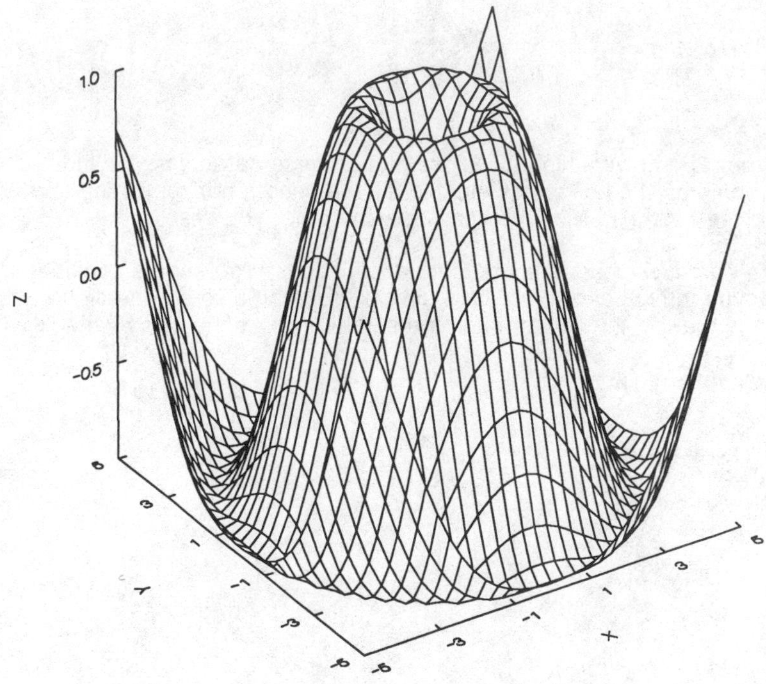

HILO *(HIGH-LOW-CLOSE Plots)*

Stock market daily, weekly, or monthly statistics are often most effectively plotted as a set of ranges between high and low prices with a marker for the closing price at each period. This is the way most newspapers plot the market. The **HILO** option allows you to produce this plot. Here are some typical data on a stock which we used in the **CPLOT** chapter:

MONTH	MONTH	HIGH	LOW	CLOSE
January	1	20.1	17.5	20.0
February	2	24.5	18.8	24.0
March	3	29.3	22.5	23.6
April	4	35.1	25.6	29.9
May	5	40.2	32.3	35.5
June	6	45.1	38.8	39.5
July	7	39.6	32.3	37.1
August	8	33.1	28.3	28.3
September	9	27.8	20.5	21.1
October	10	22.1	17.8	17.9
November	11	17.9	16.1	16.5
December	12	16.8	10.2	10.3

Figure 25 shows a high-low-close plot of these data using the index of the month as the horizontal variable. I have used a horizontal line to mark the close (**SYMBOL=12**). You can use any other you wish.

The high-low-close plot has other applications. You should consider it for asymmetrical error bars, for example. You can also do one-sided error bars by making the low (or high) the same value as the close variable.

Figure 25

```
PLOT   HIGH,LOW,CLOSE*MONTH/HILO,SYMBOL=12
```

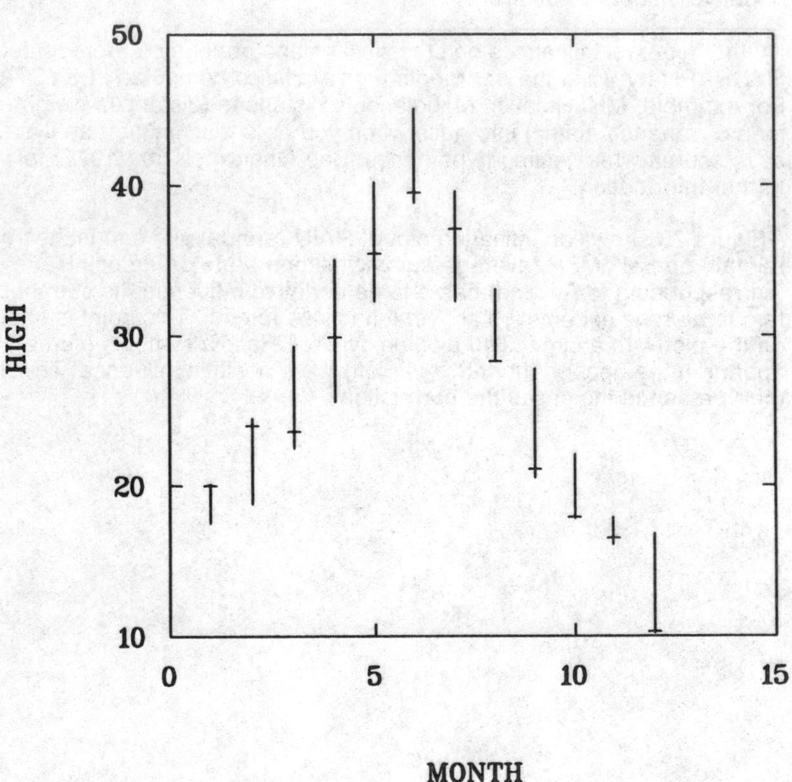

INFLUENCE *(Influence Plots)*

The influence of a point in a scatterplot on the correlation coefficient is the amount the correlation would change if that point were deleted. Plotting influences can help us determine whether a linear fit to the scatterplot is relatively robust or is dependent on just a few points. The **PLOT** command has an **INFLUENCE** option which makes the size of the plotting symbol represent the extent of influence from each point. A scale to the right of the plot helps us judge the extent of the influence. If any large points appear in the plot, we should scrutinize them before we draw any conclusions concerning the correlation.

You can use any symbol for influence plots, although circles are standard. Positive influences are represented by hollow symbols and negative influences by filled.

Other types of influences on statistical estimators can be represented in SYGRAPH by using the **SIZE** option on statistics computed in SYSTAT. For example, MGLH saves Mahalanobis distances (distances weighted by a covariance matrix) into a file when you do a discriminant analysis or save scores when testing hypotheses. See Gnanadesikan (1977) for further information.

Figure 26 shows an influence plot of RAIN (annual average inches of rainfall) on SUMMER (average summer temperature). One point (corresponding to Arizona) has a large negative influence. Its summer temperature is extremely high, yet it has little rainfall. This point is shown on the plot with a large filled plotting symbol. Hollow symbols (some appear in the upper right and lower left) have positive influence. That is, their presence increases the correlation.

Figure 26

```
TYPE=HERSHEY
PLOT  RAIN*SUMMER/INFLUENCE
```

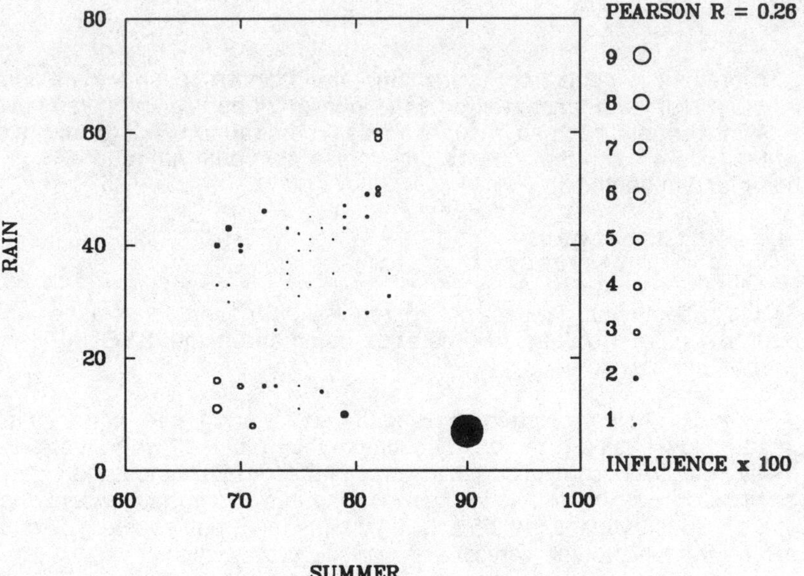

JITTER *(Jittered Plots)*

Sometimes we have data which overlap at exactly the same values. For example, we may have a questionnaire with a 7 point scale and we wish to plot two items against each other. There are only 49 possible points where we may plot the data. Or, we may have aggregate data and wish to plot them in a scatterplot. Here are the means of PERSON (personal crimes) and PROPERTY (property crimes) within regions of the variables in the US file. COUNT shows the number of states over which the means were computed.

REGION$	COUNT	PERSON	PROPERTY
New England	6	33.2	899.0
Mid Atlantic	3	97.3	1038.3
Great Lakes	5	81.8	1148.8
Plains	7	41.3	891.3
Southeast	8	87.3	1052.3
South	8	67.9	801.5
Mountain	8	59.5	1356.0
Pacific	3	79.3	1661.3

To prevent symbols from overlapping, the **JITTER** option adds a small amount of uniform random error to the location of each point. If you have a count variable, such as in our example, you need to use it to **WEIGHT** cases before using the **JITTER** option (see above in the general commands chapter):

```
WEIGHT=COUNT
PLOT  Y*X/JITTER
```

Otherwise, if your data are not aggregated but nevertheless have duplicate pairs of values, use the **PLOT** command alone. SYGRAPH will jitter all the duplicates.

Figure 27 shows a scatterplot using the above aggregate data. I have used hollow circles (**SYMBOL=2**) because they plot well when there are many near overlaps. Notice that if you plot these data without the **JITTER** option, the correlation between the items is not as evident. One of the values overlaps the top axis. If you find this troublesome, you can extend the limits of the vertical axis with the **YMAX** option.

Figure 27

```
WEIGHT=COUNT
 PLOT  PERSON*PROPERTY/SYMBOL=2,JITTER
```

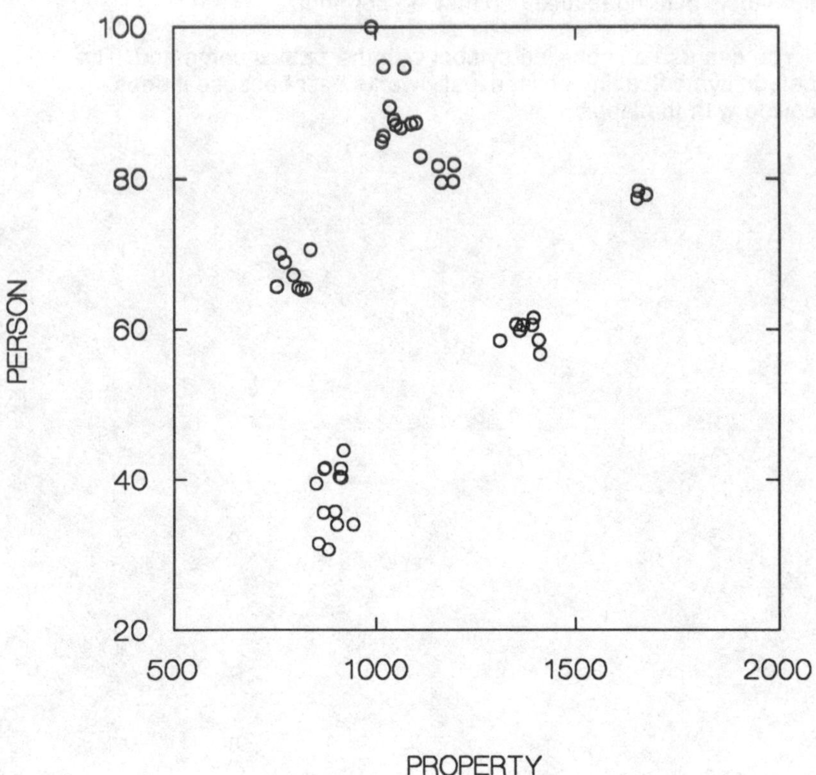

LABEL *(Labeling Points)*

You can label points in a plot with character strings. These are specified with the **LABEL** option. With the value labels stored in the variable STATE$ in the US data, for example, we can plot points with tiny labels by adding the option **LABEL=STATE$**. Here is an example identifying the influential state (Arizona) in Figure 26. Note that a few of the labels collided. SYGRAPH will avoid this if possible. First, it adjusts the size of the labels according to the number of points. Then it plots the labels to the left or right of the points in order to avoid overwriting other points or axes. When the points become too dense, as in the lower left of the plot, there is nothing left to do but to print the labels. You can move the points slightly in the original file to avoid collisions or make some of the labels missing (blanks) so they do not print.

You can use any plotting symbol with the **LABEL** command. The default symbol, a tiny point, usually works best because it does not collide with the labels.

Figure 28

```
PLOT   RAIN*SUMMER/LABEL=STATE$
```

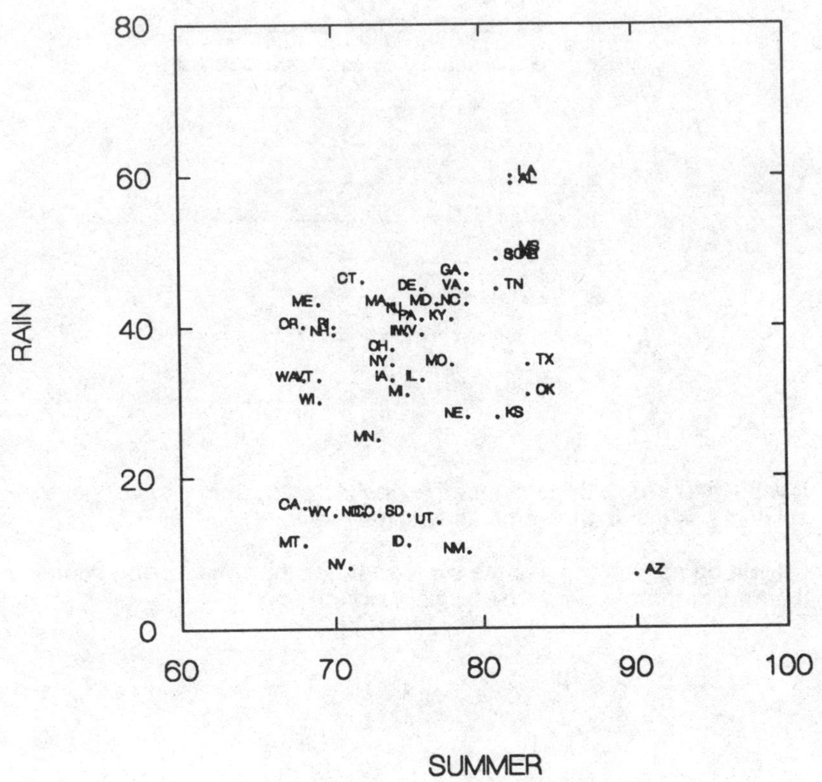

LINE *(Line Graphs)*

Time series and other data plot best when the points are connected with a line. This is easy to do in SYGRAPH. Just use the `LINE` option. The next figure shows the U.S. adjusted Gross National Product in millions of dollars plotted against year for 100 years. The data are in time order in the file. If the data were in some other order, the `LINE` option would connect successive points and produce a messy spider web.

You may choose from 11 different types of lines by typing `LINE=`*n* , where *n* is one of the following numbers:

1
2
3
4
5
6
7
8
9
10
11

If you type `LINE` with no number, as in Figure 29, then you will get the solid line, which is the same as typing `LINE=1`.

If you do not want to see the symbols which the `LINE` option connects, then make them invisible by typing `SIZE=0`.

Figure 29

```
TYPE=BRITISH
PLOT   GNP*YEAR/LINE,SIZE=0
```

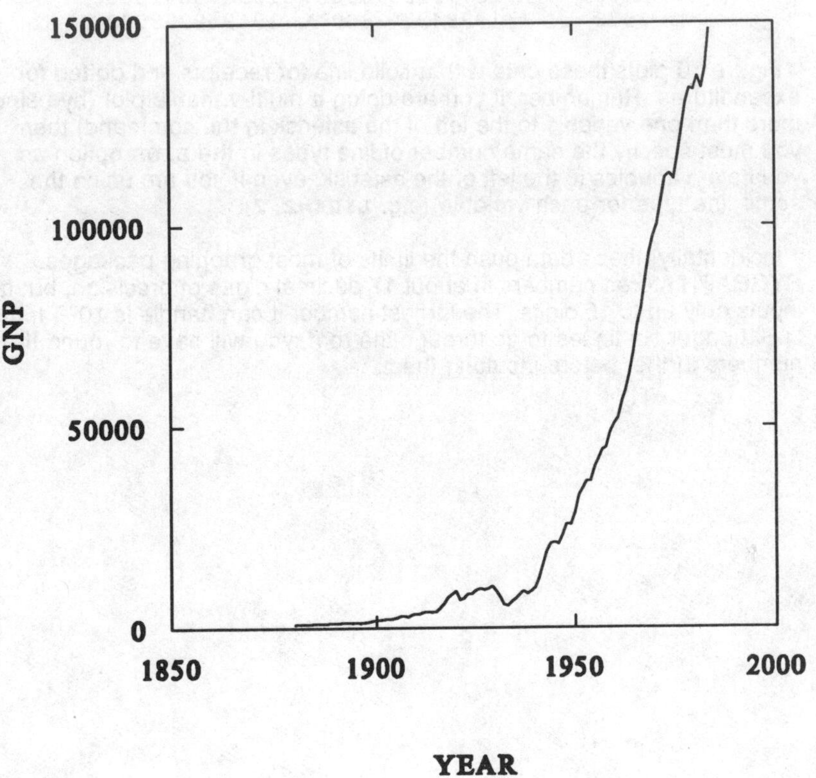

LINE *(Multi-valued Line Graphs)*

You can use a different line for each dependent variable in a multi-variable plot. Here are data on U.S. receipts and expenditures in dollars since 1960, taken from U.S. Treasury annual reports.

YEAR	RECEIPT	EXPENSE
1961	77659424905	81515167453
1962	81409092072	87786766580
1963	86357020251	92589764029
1964	89458664071	97684374794
1965	93071796891	96506904210
1966	106978344155	104727263667
1967	149554815000	153183886000
1968	187792337000	183079841000
1970	193843791000	194968258000

Figure 30 plots these data with a solid line for receipts and dotted for expenditures. Remember, if you are doing a multi-variable plot (by using more than one variable to the left of the asterisk in the command) then you must specify the same number of line types in the **LINE** option as you have variables to the left of the asterisk, even if you are using the same line type for each variable (e.g. **LINE=2,2**).

Incidentally, these data push the limits of most graphing packages. SYGRAPH stores numbers in about 17 decimal digits of precision, but it inputs only up to 15 digits. The largest number it can handle is 10^{35}. If the U.S. budget continues to go through the roof, you will have to round the numbers further before inputting them.

Figure 30

```
TYPE=HERSHEY
  PLOT  RECEIPT,EXPENSE*YEAR/LINE=1,3
```

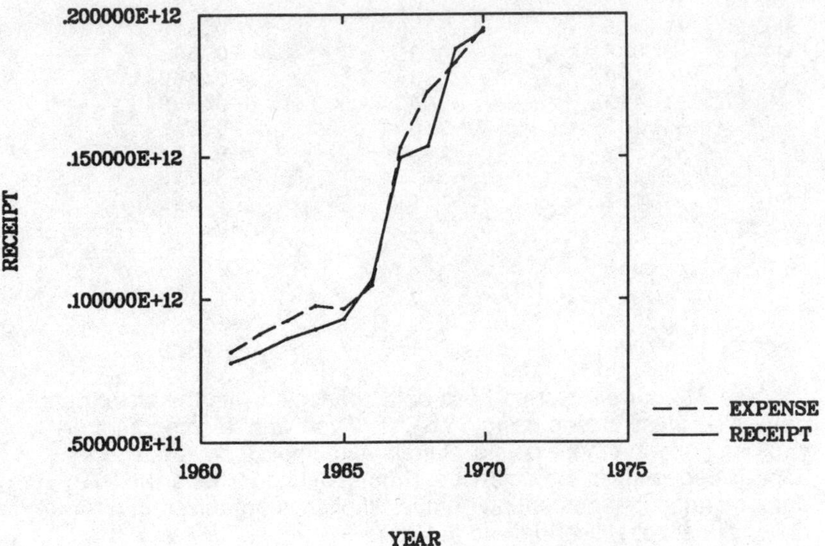

LINE *(Three-dimensional Line Graphs)*

You can plot line graphs in three dimensions. The following data comprise a spiral in three dimensions.

X	Y	Z
0.068	0.036	0.923
0.087	0.127	0.846
0.028	0.229	0.769
-0.109	0.288	0.692
-0.288	0.255	0.615
-0.448	0.110	0.538
-0.523	-0.129	0.461
-0.460	-0.408	0.385
-0.245	-0.648	0.308
0.093	-0.764	0.231
0.481	-0.696	0.154
0.818	-0.428	0.077
1.000	0.001	0.000
0.953	0.502	-0.077
0.654	0.951	-0.154
0.147	1.222	-0.231
-0.466	1.222	-0.308
-1.038	0.917	-0.385
-1.420	0.347	-0.462
-1.493	-0.371	-0.539
-1.207	-1.074	-0.616
-0.597	-1.584	-0.693
0.217	-1.756	-0.770
1.052	-1.517	-0.846
1.705	-0.890	-0.923
2.000	0.005	-1.000
1.837	0.970	-1.077
1.219	1.776	-1.154
0.263	2.216	-1.231
-0.824	2.156	-1.308

Figure 31 shows a plot of these data connected with the **LINE** option. I generated these values using SYSTAT. If you want a smoother curve, you can generate more points. Spirals and other geometric figures appear frequently in the sciences. Krumhansl and Shepard (1979) demonstrated that perception of musical pitch is organized in a three dimensional spiral like the one in Figure 31.

Figure 31

`PLOT  Z*Y*X/LINE`

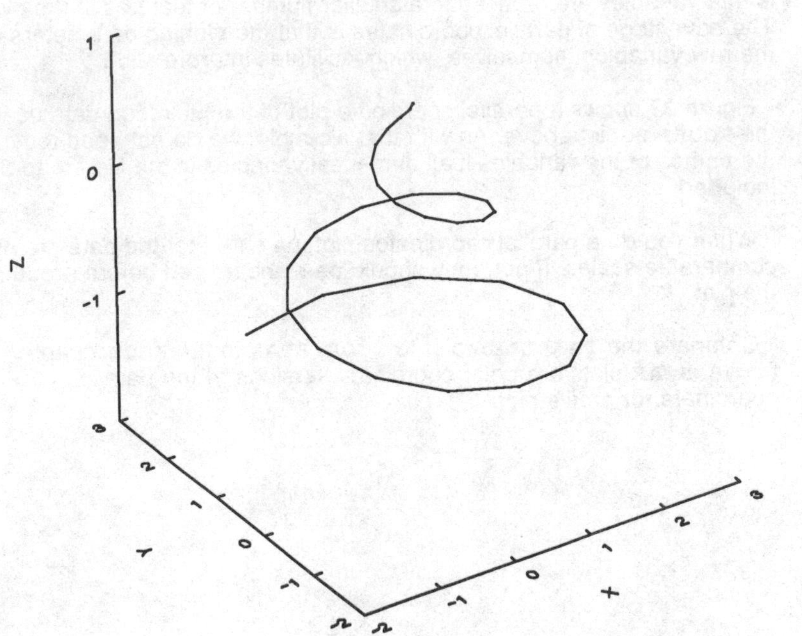

PARALLEL *(Parallel Coordinate Plots)*

Cartesian coordinates are computed on perpendicular axes. This works fine for two and three dimensional plots. Higher dimensions, however, would be difficult to visualize. Inselberg (1985) proposed making coordinate axes parallel for these higher dimensional plots. See Wegman (1986) and Curtis, Burton & Campbell (1987) for further information.

The **PARALLEL** option to the **PLOT** command implements parallel coordinates this way:

```
PLOT  A,B,C,D,E,  .../PARALLEL
```

The syntax is similar to that for the **FOURIER** option (see above in this chapter). Indeed, parallel and Fourier coordinates are alternative representations of the same data. The advantage of Fourier coordinates is that variables are reduced to a smaller number of features in the plot. The advantage of parallel coordinates is that the plotting parameters are the raw variables themselves, which facilitates interpretation.

Figure 32 shows a parallel coordinate plot of the junk food data used in the **FOURIER** plot above. As with that example, we do not need to type the names of the variables if all numerical variables in the file are to be included.

When you do a parallel coordinates plot, be sure that the data are on comparable scales. If not, they should be standardized before producing the plot.

Compare the **PARALLEL** plot to **ICON/STAR** in the **ICON** chapter above. **STAR** plots are polar coordinate versions of the parallel coordinate, or profile plot.

Figure 32

PLOT/PARALLEL

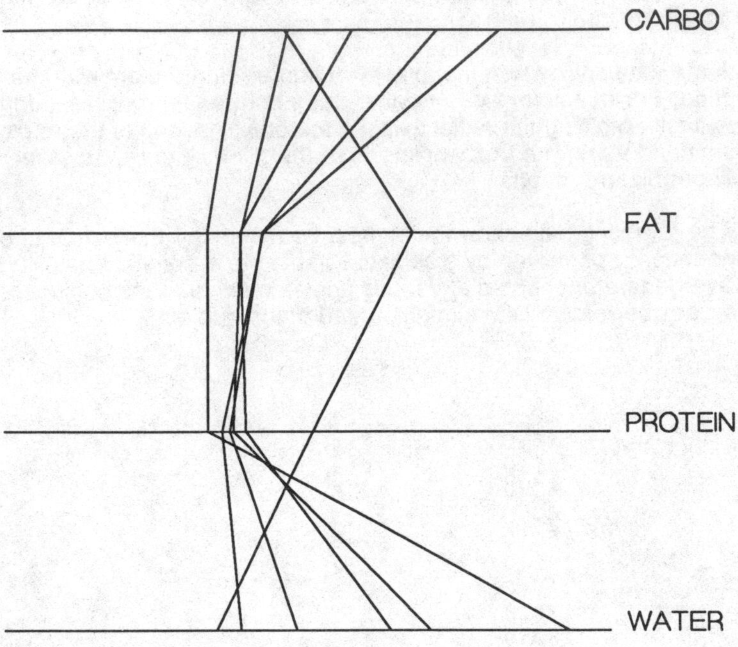

POLAR *(Polar Data Plots)*

You can plot data in polar coordinates with the **POLAR** option of the **PLOT** command. Either functions or data can be plotted in this way. With polar coordinates, the "Y" axis is the distance of a point from the origin of a circle and the "X" axis is the angle between the horizontal axis and a line from the origin to the point. Polar coordinates may seem confusing in some contexts but they are handy for representing many mathematical equations and data profiles.

SYGRAPH automatically scales polar graphs as well as rectangular graphs. The units printed on the scales are those of the data. You may alter these scales with the **YMIN** and **YMAX** option for Y and the **XMIN** and **XMAX** option for X. **YMIN** is always at the center of the circle and **YMAX** at its periphery. **XMIN** and **XMAX** always coincide at the right edge (0 radians).

If the data collide with the axes, you can eliminate them with the **AXES** option. For example, **AXES=0** eliminates both axes. **AXES=1** prints only the circle, omitting the radial axis. All the other options of the **PLOT** command work with **POLAR** plots. Use them intelligently, however, or you will get bizarre graphs.

The following data show the highest frequency (in thousands of cycles per second) perceived by a subject listening to a constant amplitude sine wave generator oriented at various angles relative to the subject. Zero degrees corresponds to straight ahead of the subject.

ANGLE	FREQ
0.0	12.1
20.0	12.4
40.0	12.4
60.0	12.6
80.0	12.9
100.0	12.8
120.0	12.7
140.0	12.4
160.0	12.1
180.0	11.9
200.0	12.0
220.0	12.3
240.0	12.8
260.0	14.1
280.0	14.3
300.0	13.8
320.0	13.4
340.0	12.6
360.0	12.1

Figure 33 shows the polar plot of these data with the points connected by a spline smooth. Notice that the profile shows hearing impairment in the left ear relative to the right.

Figure 33

```
PLOT FREQ*ANGLE,
   /POLAR,SMOOTH=SPLINE,SYMBOL=2,XMIN=0,XMAX=360
```

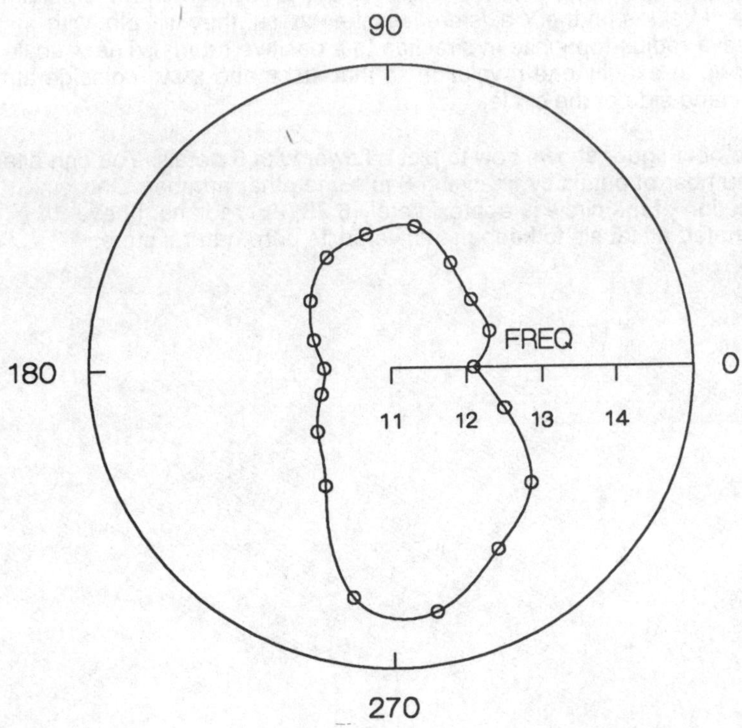

POLAR *(Polar Function Plots)*

Functions plot in polar coordinates the way you would expect. Just type the function and add the polar options, e.g.:

```
PLOT Y = X^2!POLAR
```

Remember to use the exclamation point instead of the slash to delimit the options.

You can add scaling options to size the function plot. You may alter these scales with the **YMIN** and **YMAX** options for Y and the **XMIN** and **XMAX** options for X. If you do not set it, **YMIN** is automatically set to zero, making the origin for the Y axis always at the center of the polar circle. If values on the Y axis are less than **YMIN**, they will plot with negative radius (opposite in direction to a positive radius). The X scale is mapped to exactly one revolution so that **XMIN** and **XMAX** coincide at the right hand side of the circle.

The next figure shows how to plot a flower with 8 petals. You can alter the number of petals by changing 8 to some other number. One revolution of the circle is approximately 6.28 (2π) radians. I have eliminated all labels to keep the flower in its pure natural state.

Figure 34

```
PLOT  Y=SIN(8*X),
  !POLAR,YMAX=1,XMIN=0,XMAX=6.28,AXES=0,SCALE=0,
  XLABEL='  ',YLABEL='  '
```

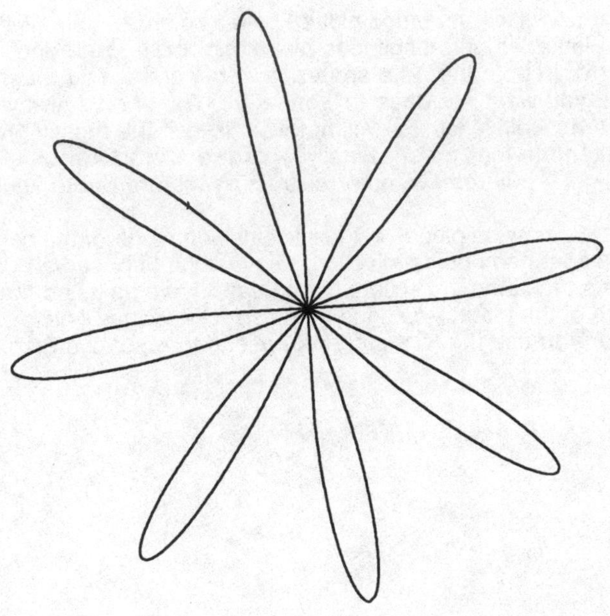

PROJECT *(Geographic Projections)*

Sometimes you want to plot on top of a map which you have drawn with the **MAP** command. If you used a projection with **MAP**, then you will have to use one with **PLOT**. The same projections are available with both commands:

PROJECT=GNOMON	*(oblique gnomonic)*
PROJECT=STEREO	*(oblique stereographic)*
PROJECT=MERCATOR	*(Mercator conformal)*
PROJECT=ORTHO	*(oblique orthographic)*

These projections are documented in Appendix B of Richardus and Adler (1972)

In order to make a map and plotted points coincide, you must use common latitudes and longitudes by setting **XMIN**,**XMAX** and **YMIN**,**YMAX** in both the **MAP** and **PLOT** commands. You *must* use these options if you want **PROJECT** to work at all. You should always add **SCALE=0** as well, since you will not want to see the messy projection coordinates on your graph. Finally, **AXES=0** and **XLABEL=' '** and **YLABEL=' '** will remove other distracting features from your graph.

Figure 35 shows a plot of latitude against longitude of the centers of the states using a gnomonic projection. I have superimposed a map of the U.S. using the same projection. Notice that I have adjusted the height and width of the plot to scale the map correctly. You will have to do this whenever you use the **MIN** and **MAX** options to rescale a map.

Figure 35

```
PLOT  LABLAT*LABLON,
   /XMIN=-125,XMAX=-65,YMIN=25,YMAX=50,
    PROJECT=GNOMON,SYMBOL=2,SIZE=.5,
    HEIGHT=3IN,WIDTH=5IN,AXES=0,SCALE=0,
   XLABEL=' ',YLABEL=' '
MAP,
   /XMIN=-125,XMAX=-65,YMIN=25,YMAX=50,
    PROJECT=GNOMON,HEIGHT=3IN,WIDTH=5IN
```

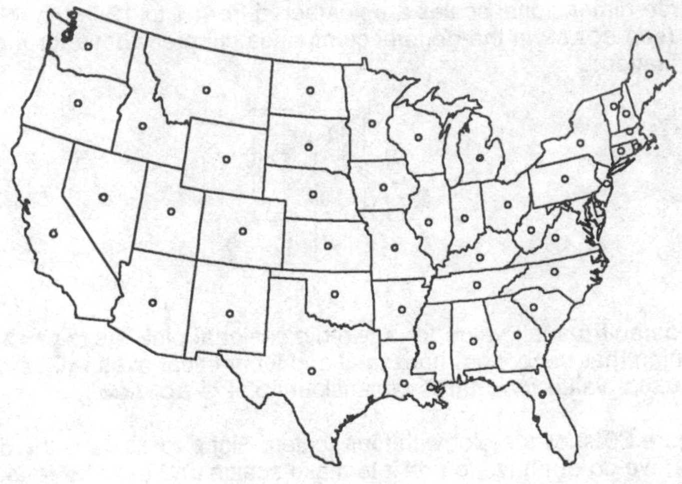

SCALE *(Number of Scales)*

Scales are the numbers which label the tick marks on an axis. The **SCALE** option controls the number of scales drawn in a plot. Its syntax is:

```
SCALE=n
```

where *n* is an integer from 0 to 12. If *n* is 0, no scales will be drawn. If *n* is an integer from 1 to 12, all scales from 1 to *n* will be drawn. If *n* is negative, only the scale numbered with the absolute value of *n* will be drawn.

Two-dimensional scales are numbered from 1 to 4 clockwise, beginning with the bottom axis:

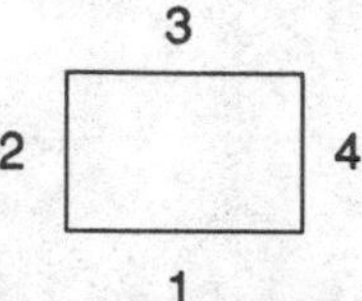

Three-dimensional scales are numbered from 1 to 12 in the following way (see **SCALE** in the general commands chapter above for more information):

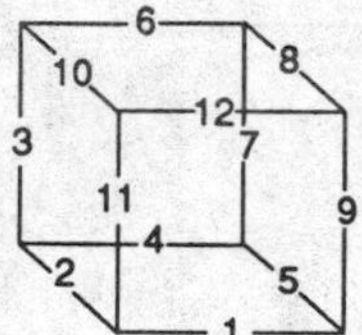

The default (usual) value for a two-dimensional plot is **SCALE=2**, meaning that the bottom horizontal and left vertical axes will be drawn. The usual value for a three-dimensional plot is **SCALE=3**.

Figure 36 shows a plot with four scales. Since **AXES=4** is the default value, we do not have to add it to make scales and axes correspond.

Figure 36

```
PLOT   INCOME*LABLAT/SCALE=4
```

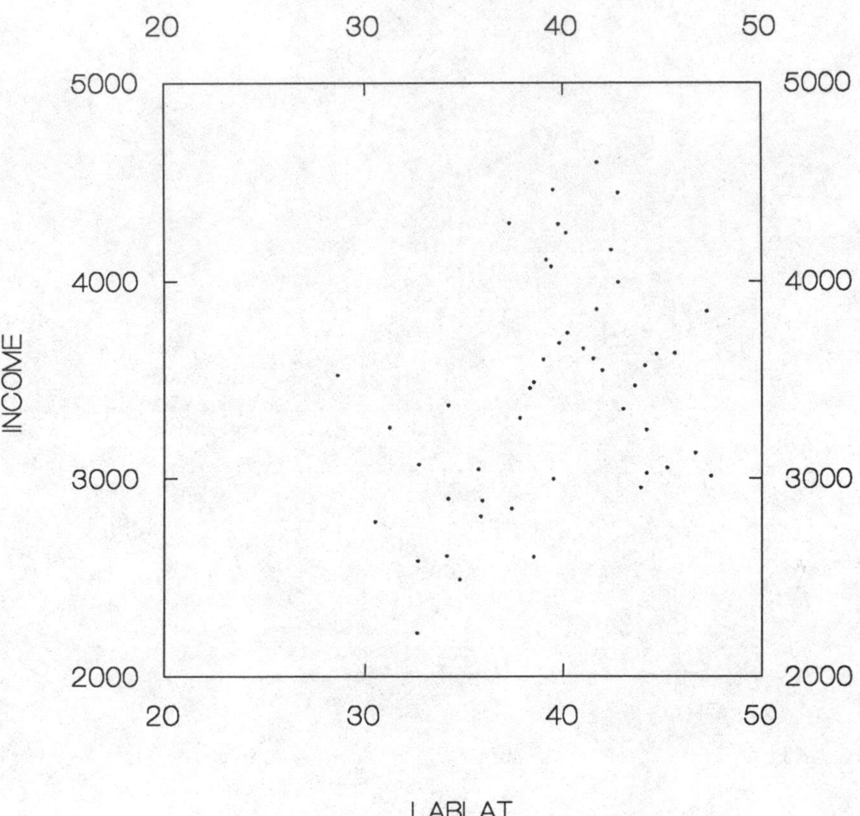

SHORT *(Shortening the Domain of Smoothing)*

Sometimes you can get into trouble by extrapolating beyond the range of your data when making a prediction. Many of the smoothing methods in SYGRAPH (see **SMOOTH** option below in this chapter) yield curves which extend from the left to the right edges of the plotting frame. If you wish to limit the domain of the smooth to the extreme values of the data on the horizontal axis, add the **SHORT** option.

Figure 37 shows a plot with a linear function and confidence interval limited to the range of the X data with the **SHORT** option. Compare this to the extrapolated version in Figure 9 above.

Figure 37

```
PLOT   WINTER*LABLAT/SMOOTH=LINEAR,CONFI=.95,SHORT
```

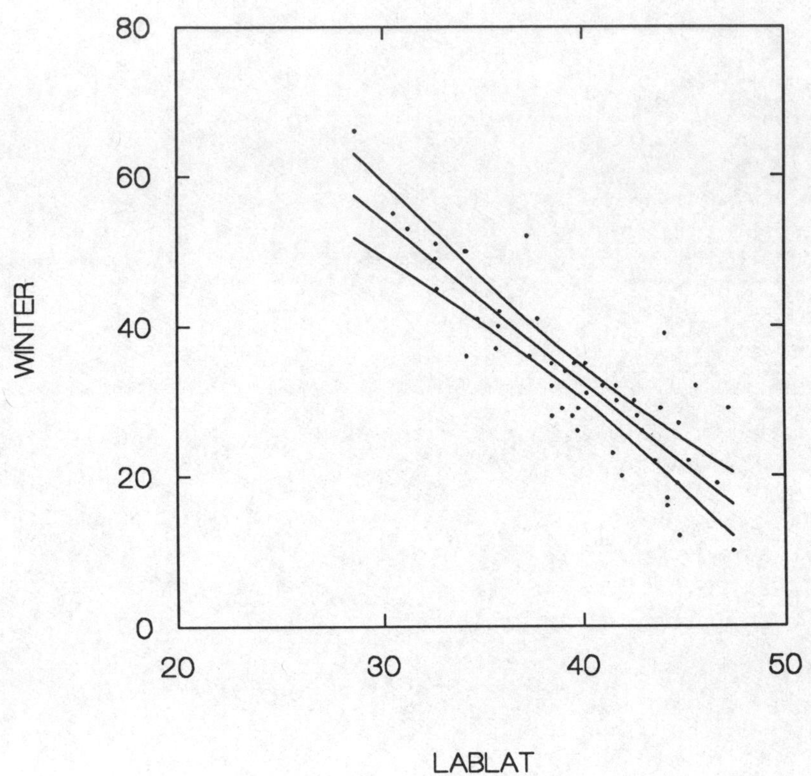

SIZE *(Changing Size of Plotting Symbols)*

You can alter the size of plotting symbols from invisible to as large as your entire graph. The standard value of all symbols is `SIZE=1`. `SIZE=2` produces symbols twice as large as the standard. `SIZE=.5` is half, and so on. `SIZE=0` makes the symbols invisible.

Figure 38 shows a plot with symbols one and a half times larger than usual. Just for fun, I've used hollow stars (`SYMBOL=9`).

Figure 38

```
PLOT   INCOME*LABLAT/SYMBOL=9,SIZE=1.5
```

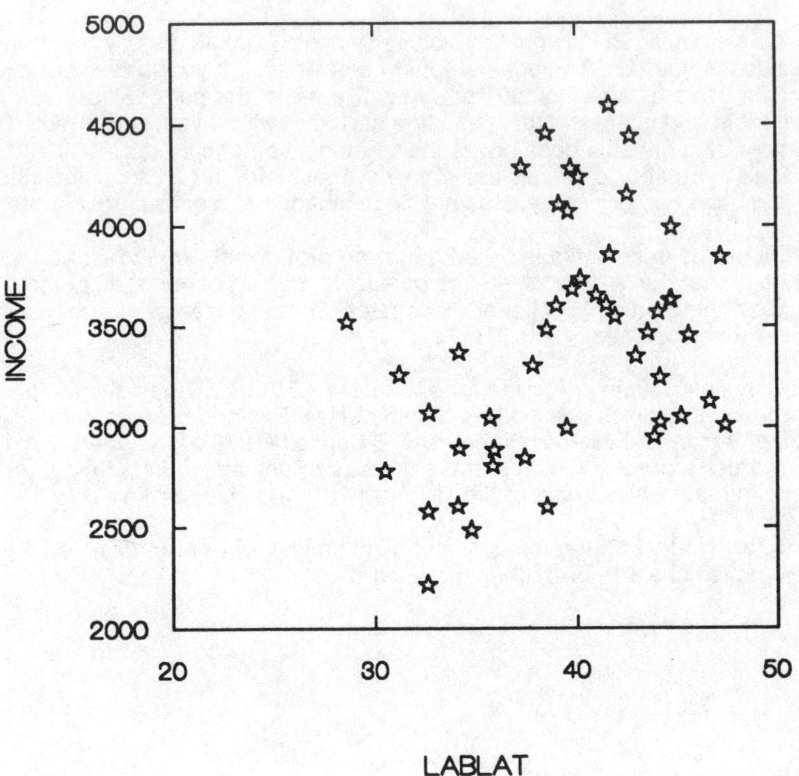

SIZE *(Representing a Variable by Size of Symbols in a 2-D Plot)*

You can use the value of a variable in your file to control the size of a plotting symbol. This is especially useful when you are representing a third variable against two others in a two-way plot.

Here is an example. I made a new variable using POPDEN from the US file:

```
LET DEN = 4*SQR(POPDEN/1000)
```

By this transformation, I have placed the new variable DEN in the range of 0 to 4. I selected a square root because I want the area of the symbols (not their diameter) to be proportional to the value of POPDEN. Now we can use this variable to determine the size of a plotting symbol.

One caution. The size of the plotting symbols is taken directly from the values in your file. There is no upper or lower limit. If your `SIZE` variable has a value as small as .001 or a negative value, the point will be invisible and if it has a value as large as 100, it will fill your entire plot. If your sizing variable does not lie in this range, you should rescale it. Finally, you should usually use empty symbols with this type of plot, since filled ones can occlude each other and make the plot difficult to interpret.

Figure 39 is sometimes called a **bubble plot**, for obvious reasons. Notice that the large circles (high population density) are not all at the upper right of the plot. Higher crime rates do not necessarily correspond to higher population densities.

Cleveland, Kleiner, McRae, and Warner (1976) used open circles to represent levels of pollution on a map of New England. You can use other symbols. Bickel, Hammel, and O'Connell (1975) used open squares (`SYMBOL=7`) to represent the size of university departments in plotting admissions data at the University of California, Berkeley.

`SIZE` works in three-dimensional plots as well. See the advanced examples chapter for more information.

Figure 39

```
PLOT   PERSON*PROPERTY/SYMBOL=2,SIZE=DEN
```

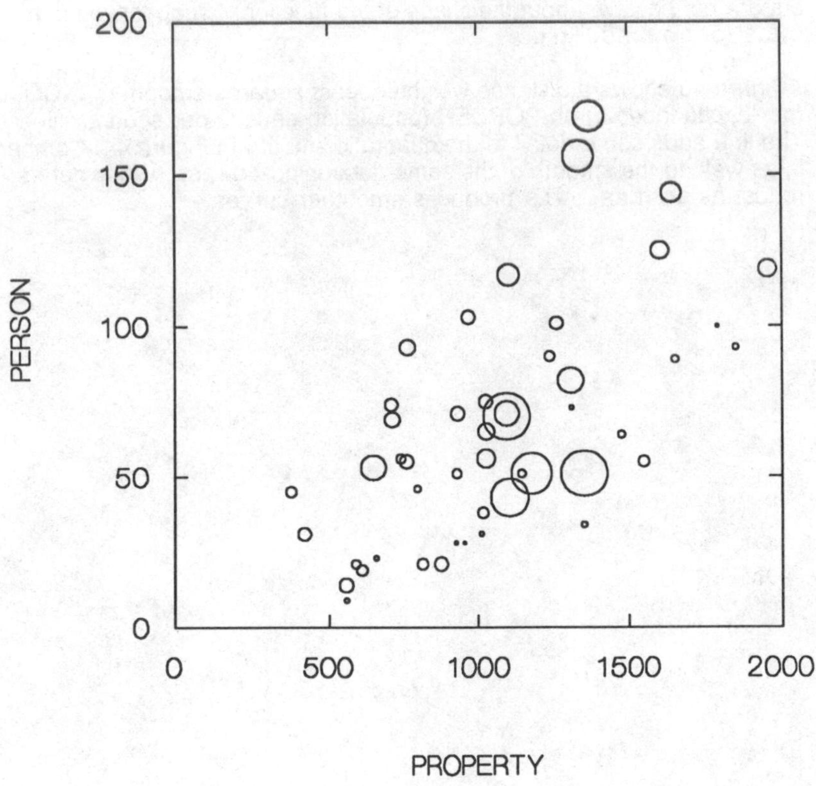

SMOOTH=DWLS *(Distance Weighted Least Squares Smoothing)*

Distance weighted least squares fits a line through a set of points by least squares. Unlike linear or low order polynomial smoothing, however, the surface is allowed to flex locally to fit the data better. The amount of flex is controlled by a tension parameter (see **TENSION** below in this chapter).

If you use **SMOOTH=DWLS** on a two-dimensional plot, be prepared to wait a while, particularly on slow machines. Every point on the smoothed line requires a weighted quadratic multiple regression on all the points. The wait is worth it, however. This method produces a true, locally weighted curve running through the points using an algorithm due to McLain (1974). If you want to do a regression of one variable on another, but are not positive about the shape of the function, I suggest you use **DWLS** (or **LOWESS**) first.

Figure 40 shows a distance weighted least squares smooth of INCOME (per-capita income) on POPDEN (population density per square mile). The line adds some detail to the quadratic smooth in Figure 44. Compare it, as well, to the smooth of the same data using **LOWESS**. While not as robust as **LOWESS**, **DWLS** produces smoother curves.

Figure 40

```
PLOT   INCOME*POPDEN/SMOOTH=DWLS,SYMBOL=2,SIZE=.5
```

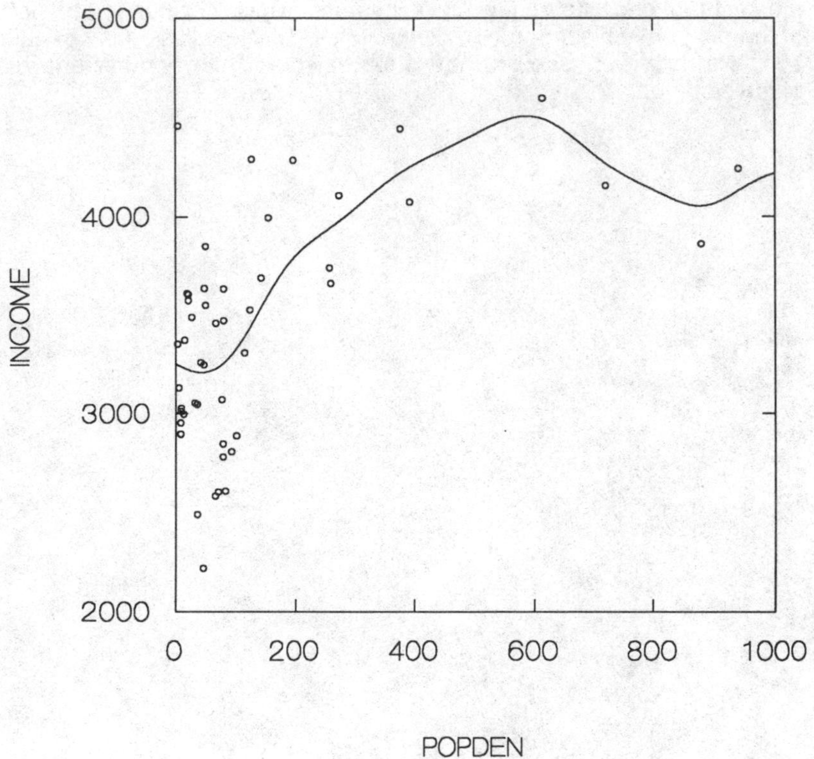

SMOOTH=LINEAR *(Linear Regression Smoothing)*

Regression fits a function to data such that the value predicted by the function at each observed value of X is as close as possible to the observed value of Y at the same value of X. Ordinary linear regression uses a straight line for the function and makes the squared discrepancies between predicted and observed Y values as small as possible. The equation for this function looks like this:

$$Y = a + bX,$$

where *a* is a constant term and *b* is a slope coefficient.

You fit this function with the option **SMOOTH=LINEAR** (or just **SMOOTH**, because the default smoothing is linear). Figure 41 shows the linear regression of PROPERTY (property crimes) onto LABLON (longitude of the center of each state). It would appear that western states (on the left of the plot) have higher property crime rates. This conclusion is not quite accurate, however. See **SMOOTH=LOWESS** (below) for another analysis of the same data.

Figure 41

```
PLOT PROPERTY*LABLON/SMOOTH=LINEAR,SYMBOL=2
```

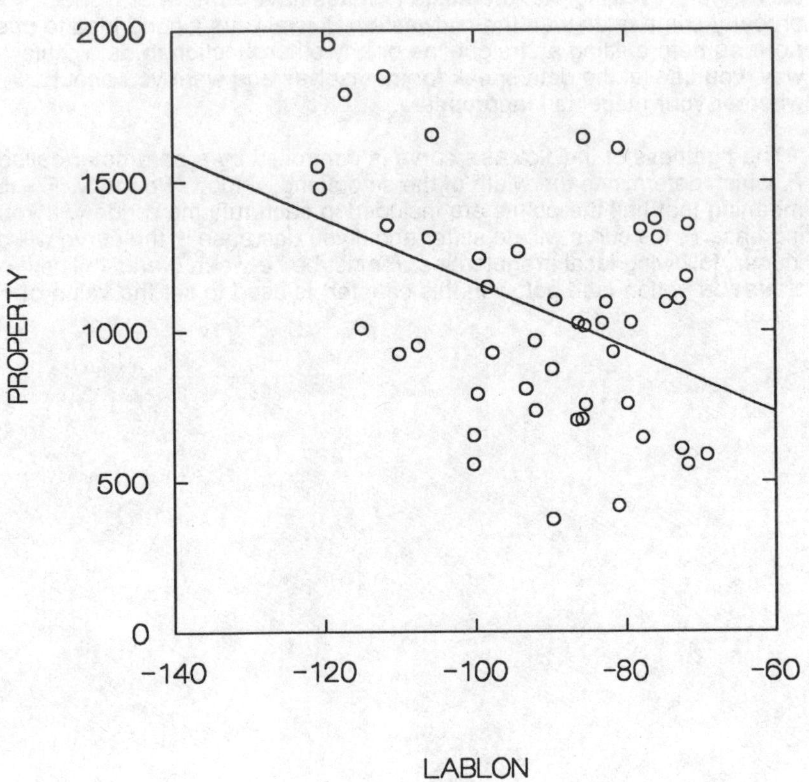

SMOOTH=LOWESS *(Locally Weighted Scatterplot Smoothing)*
Linear, quadratic and other parametric smoothers presuppose the shape of the function. SYGRAPH offers a smoothing method (**SMOOTH=LOWESS**) which requires only that the smooth be a function (i.e. unique Y value for every X). This method is called LOWESS (Cleveland, 1979,1981). It produces a smooth by running along the X values and finding predicted values from a weighted average of nearby Y values. Because a lot of computations are involved, the **LOWESS** option can be time consuming for large scatterplots.

The next figure shows the result for the regression of PROPERTY (property crime) on LABLON (longitude of center of state) which we used above to illustrate **SMOOTH=LINEAR**. Notice that the fit is distinctly curvilinear, revealing that the eastern states have somewhat higher property crime rates than the midwestern. It is always a good idea to use **LOWESS** before fitting a straight line or any other function to data. This way, you can let the data speak for themselves and warn you about whether your model is inappropriate.

The tightness of the **LOWESS** curve is controlled by a parameter called *F*, which determines the width of the smoothing window. Normally, $F = .5$, meaning that half the points are included in each running window. If you increase *F*, the curve will be stiffer and if you decrease it, the curve will be looser, following local irregularities. *F* must be between 0 and 1. The **TENSION** option (see below in this chapter) is used to set the value of *F*.

Figure 42

PLOT PROPERTY*LABLON/SMOOTH=LOWESS,SYMBOL=2

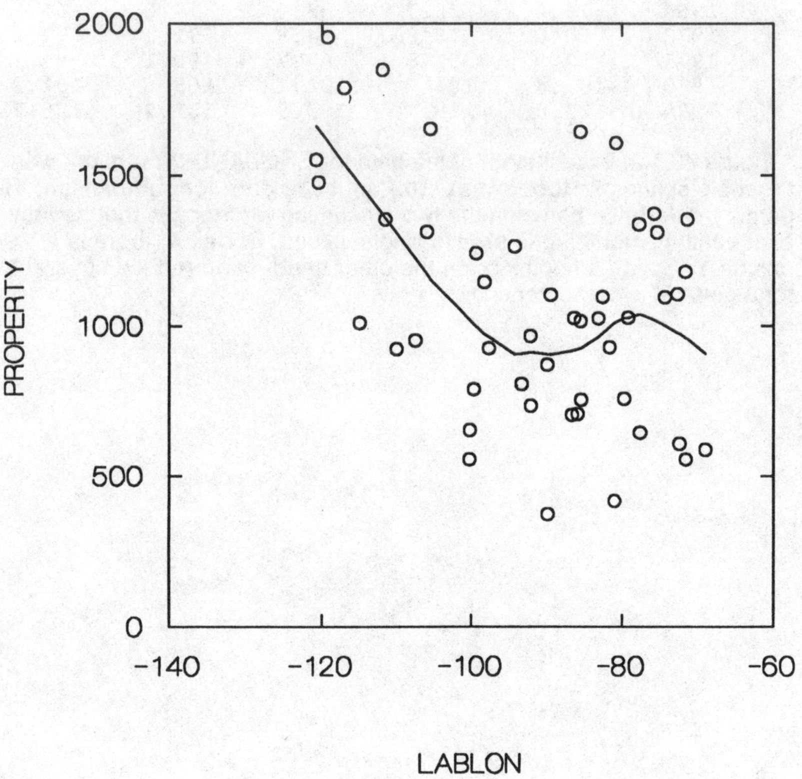

SMOOTH=NEXPO *(Negative Exponentially Weighted Smoothing)*

Negative exponentially weighted smoothing fits a curve through a set of points such that the influence of neighboring points decreases exponentially with distance. It is an alternative to **SPLINE** smoothing (see below in this chapter) for interpolation. The smoothing algorithm is due to McLain (1974). It is closely related to distance weighted least squares regression smoothing (see **DWLS** above in this chapter).

The following data show output productivity per labor hour in 1977 U.S. dollars for a 15 year period from the U.S. Bureau of Labor Statistics.

YEAR	US	CANADA	JAPAN	GERMANY	ENGLAND
1960	62.2	50.3	23.2	40.3	53.8
1965	76.6	62.7	35.0	54.0	63.9
1970	80.0	76.8	64.8	71.2	77.6
1975	92.9	91.8	87.7	90.1	94.3
1980	101.4	101.9	122.7	108.6	101.2
1985	121.8	115.1	159.9	131.9	129.7

Figure 43 shows a smooth of the data for ENGLAND. You might want to try cubic splines (**SMOOTH=SPLINE**) on these data for comparison. The primary difference between the two smoothing methods is that negative exponential smoothing is always single valued. For all X, there is a unique Y. Spline smoothing, on the other hand, can produce several Y for a given X in some contexts.

Figure 43

```
PLOT   ENGLAND*YEAR/SMOOTH=NEXPO,SYMBOL=2,FILL
```

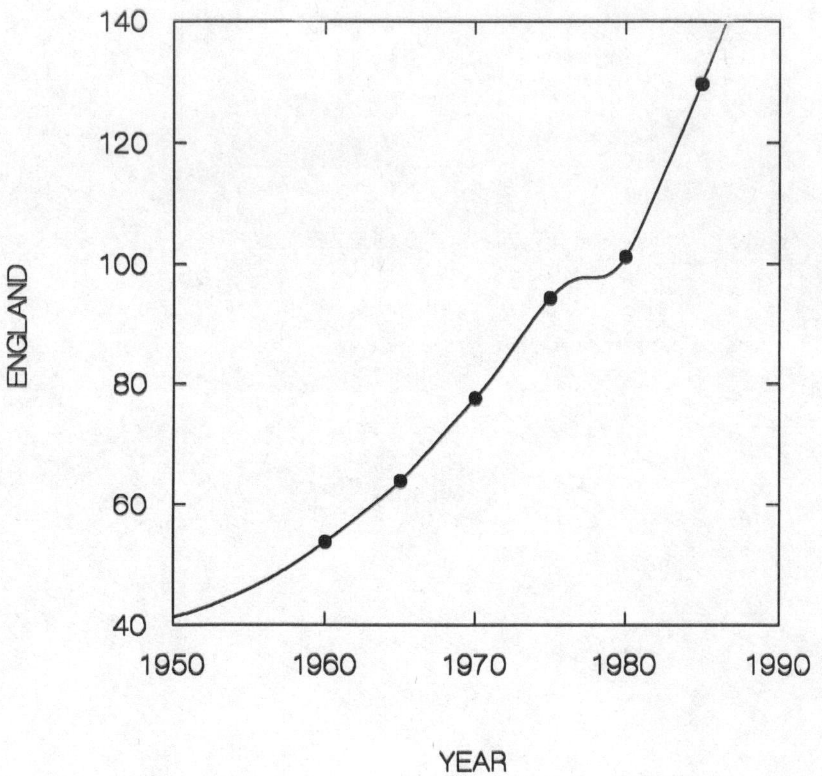

SMOOTH=QUAD *(Quadratic Smoothing)*

You can fit a quadratic regression curve to your data with the `SMOOTH=QUAD` option. This fits the following type of equation to the data:

$$Y = a + bX + cX^2,$$

where a is a constant and b and c are slope coefficients.

Figure 44 shows the quadratic regression of INCOME (per-capita income) onto POPDEN (people per square mile).

Figure 44

```
PLOT   INCOME*POPDEN/SMOOTH=QUAD,SYMBOL=2,SIZE=.5
```

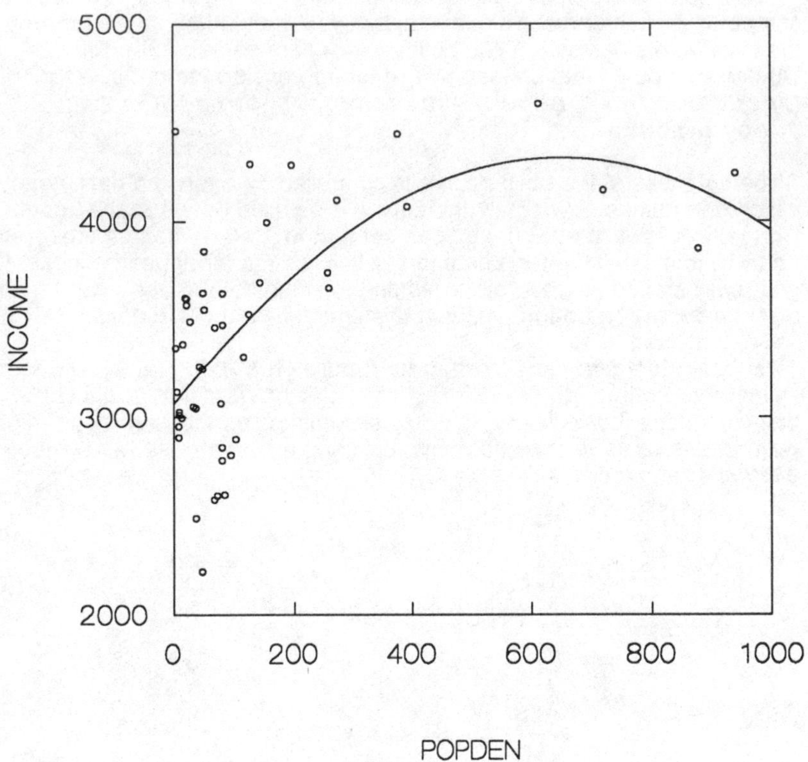

SMOOTH=SPLINE *(Spline Smoothing)*

You can fit a spline curve to your data with the **SMOOTH=SPLINE** option. Spline smoothing fits a curved line through every point in the plot such that the curve is smooth everywhere. SYGRAPH employs cubic splines (Brodlie, 1980) for smoothing. Cubic splines involve fitting several sections of the curve with cubic equations:

$$Y = a + bX + cX^2 + dX^3$$

where a is a constant, and b, c, and d are coefficients. These curves are joined smoothly at "knots," which usually coincide with the data points themselves.

Cubic splines are especially useful for interpolation, when you need a computer French curve. This means that you should use splines through the data points only when you believe your data contain no error. Otherwise, you should choose one of the regression methods (**SMOOTH=LINEAR**, **SMOOTH=QUAD**, **SMOOTH=DWLS**, or **SMOOTH=LOWESS**).

The tightness of the spline curve is controlled by a tension parameter, which determines how tightly the curves are pulled between the knots. Normally, **TENSION=2**, but you can set it down to 0 to make it looser and up to 10 to make it tighter. I hate to say this is a matter of aesthetics, but you really should try several values on the same data to see what I mean. See the **TENSION** option below in this chapter for more details.

The following data were taken from Brodlie (1980). Figure 45 shows a spline smooth through the points. I have used **SYMBOL=2** to show the point locations more clearly. In many circumstances, however, you might want to use **SIZE=0** (see above in this chapter) to remove the symbols altogether and leave only a curve.

X	Y
2.5	6.90
5.0	2.20
10.0	0.80
15.0	0.50
20.0	0.35
25.0	0.25
30.0	0.20
40.0	0.15

Figure 45

```
PLOT   Y*X/SMOOTH=SPLINE,SYMBOL=2,FILL=1
```

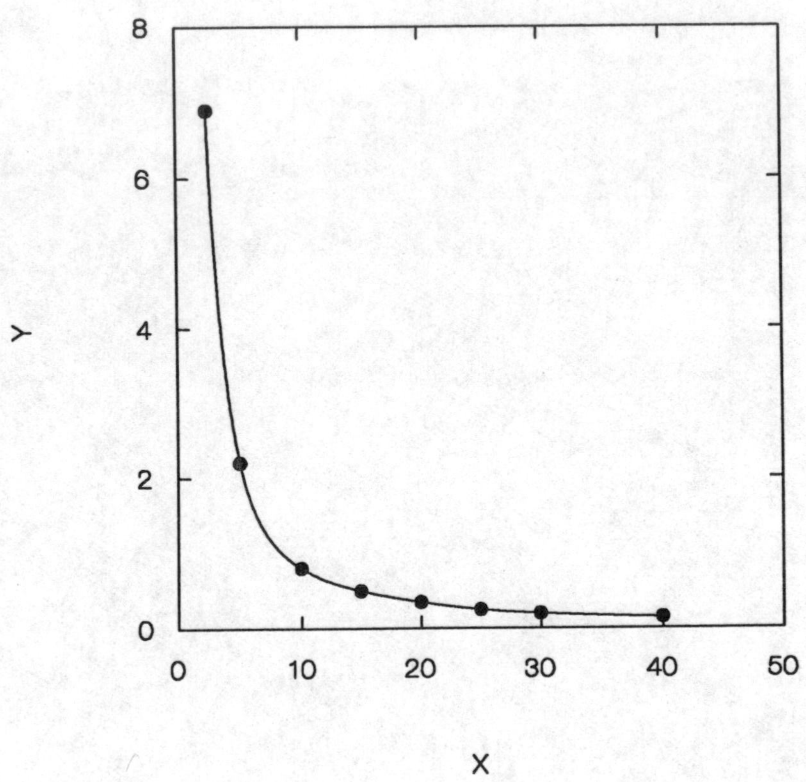

SMOOTH=STEP *(Step Smoothing)*

You can fit a step function to your data with the `SMOOTH=STEP` option. The function begins at the point with the smallest X value and drops (or rises) to the point with the next larger X value. If you wish to drop (or rise) immediately from the first point to the second, you need to shift the Y data values one lag down the list for each X in your data.

Figure 46 shows the step smooth for the data used in the spline example in Figure 45.

Figure 46

```
PLOT  Y*X/SMOOTH=STEP,SYMBOL=2,FILL=1
```

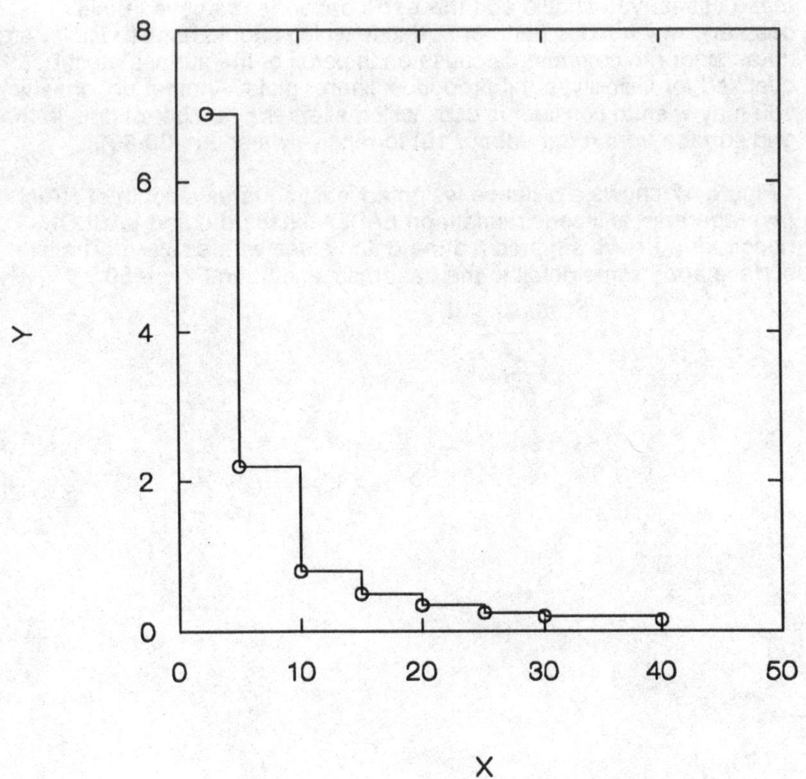

SMOOTH=DWLS *(Distance Weighted Least Squares 3-D Smoothing)*

Distance weighted least squares fits a surface through a set of points by least squares. Unlike linear or low order polynomial smoothing, however, the surface is allowed to flex locally to fit the data better. The amount of flex is controlled by a tension parameter (see `TENSION` below in this chapter).

If you use `SMOOTH=DWLS` on a three-dimensional plot, be prepared to wait a while, particularly on slow machines. Every patch on the surface requires four weighted multiple regressions on all the points. This method produces a true, locally weighted three-dimensional surface using an algorithm due to McLain (1974).

This method may occasionally produce surfaces which overlap. In these cases, you should add the `HIDE` option (see above in this chapter), which hides parts of surfaces which should not be visible. `HIDE` takes longer to compute, because each patch of the surface must be checked for visibility, but it produces clearer plots. Another option which you may wish to consider is `CUT`, which alters the number of cuts in the grid surface from rough (about 10) to relatively smooth (30-60).

Figure 47 shows a distance weighted least squares smooth of RAIN (average annual inches rainfall) on LABLAT (latitude) and LABLON (longitude). I have suppressed the data values with `SIZE=0`. The surface adds some detail to the quadratic smooth in Figure 50.

Figure 47

```
PLOT   RAIN*LABLAT*LABLON/SMOOTH=DWLS,SIZE=0,HIDE
```

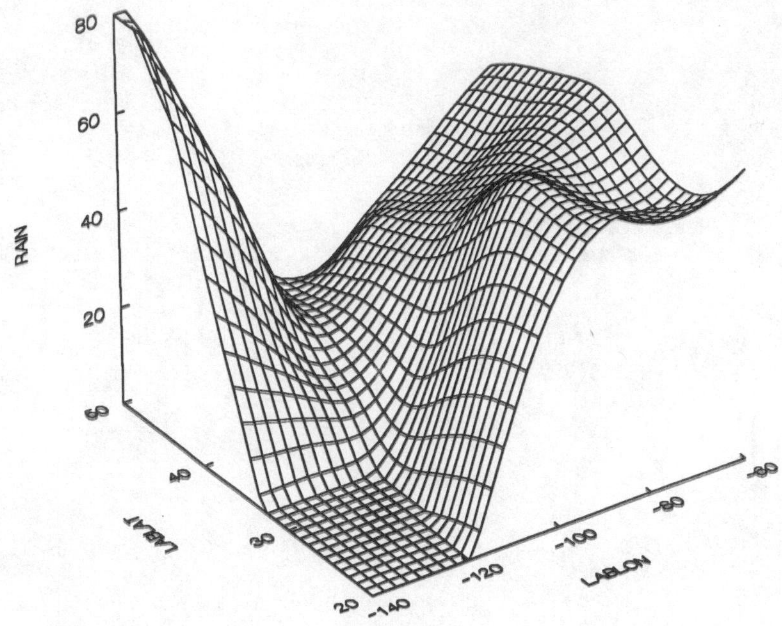

SMOOTH=LINEAR *(Linear Smoothing Three-Dimensional Data Plots)*
When you are plotting three-dimensional data (see the beginning of this chapter), the `SMOOTH=LINEAR` option produces a surface based on an equation of the following form:

$$Z = a + bX + cY$$

The data will be plotted with the default symbol (a tiny point). If you wish to see them better, use one of the larger symbols (e.g. `SYMBOL=2`). If you want them not to show, use `SIZE=0`. Another option you may wish to consider is `CUT`, which sets the number of cuts in the grid surface.

Figure 48 shows a linear smooth of RAIN (average annual inches rainfall) on LABLAT (latitude) and LABLON (longitude). The surface shows higher rainfall in the northeast.

Figure 48

```
PLOT   RAIN*LABLAT*LABLON/SMOOTH=LINEAR,SIZE=0
```

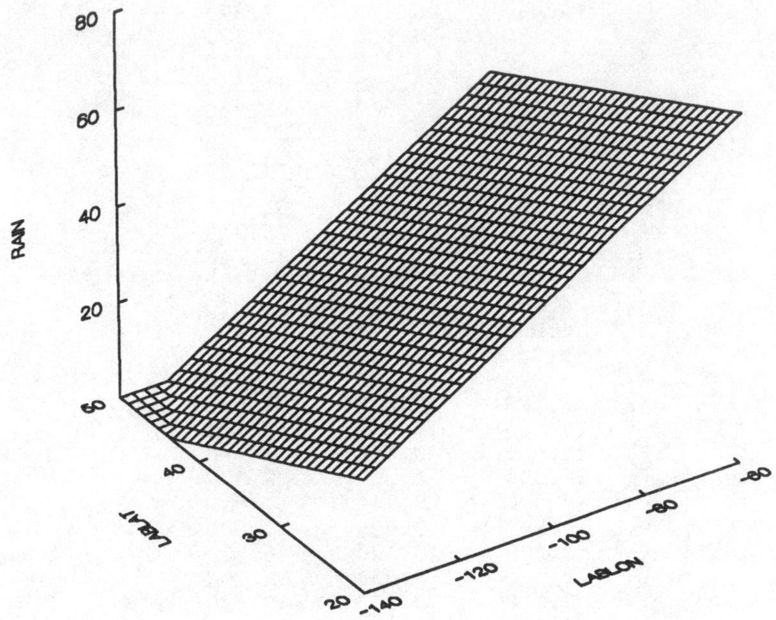

SMOOTH=NEXPO *(3-D Negative Exponential Interpolation)*
You can interpolate a smooth surface through points in 3-D. The method is derived from McLain (1974), in which negative exponential weights are computed from distances between points in a regular grid and the irregularly spaced data points in the XY plane. These weights are used in a quadratic function to compute the height of the surface at each grid point.

Akima, 1978, derived a similar method for 3-D interpolation, which is implemented in SAS (1986). Negative exponential smoothing outperforms Akima's method on Akima's own data, however. Akima sampled the following values from a more detailed surface to see how well his spline interpolation method would do in recovering the original surface.

X	Y	Z
11.160	1.240	22.150
24.200	16.230	2.830
19.850	10.720	7.970
10.350	4.110	22.330
19.720	1.390	16.830
0.000	20.000	34.600
20.870	20.000	5.740
19.990	4.620	14.720
10.280	15.160	21.590
4.510	20.000	15.610
0.000	4.480	61.770
16.700	19.650	6.310
6.080	4.580	35.740
25.000	11.870	4.400
14.900	3.120	21.700
0.000	0.000	58.200
9.660	20.000	4.730
5.220	14.660	40.360
11.770	10.470	13.620
15.100	17.190	12.570
25.000	3.870	8.740
25.000	0.000	12.000
14.590	8.710	14.810
15.200	0.000	21.600
5.230	10.720	26.500
2.140	15.030	53.100
0.510	8.370	49.430
25.000	20.000	0.600
21.670	14.360	5.520
3.310	0.130	44.080

I used **XREV** and **YREV** (see below in this chapter) to display the surface more clearly. You can try **CONTOUR** (see above in this chapter) to compare the results with Akima's original figures.

Figure 49

```
PLOT  Z*Y*X,
   /SMOOTH=NEXPO,XREV,YREV,SIZE=0,
     XMIN=0,XMAX=25,YMIN=0,YMAX=20
```

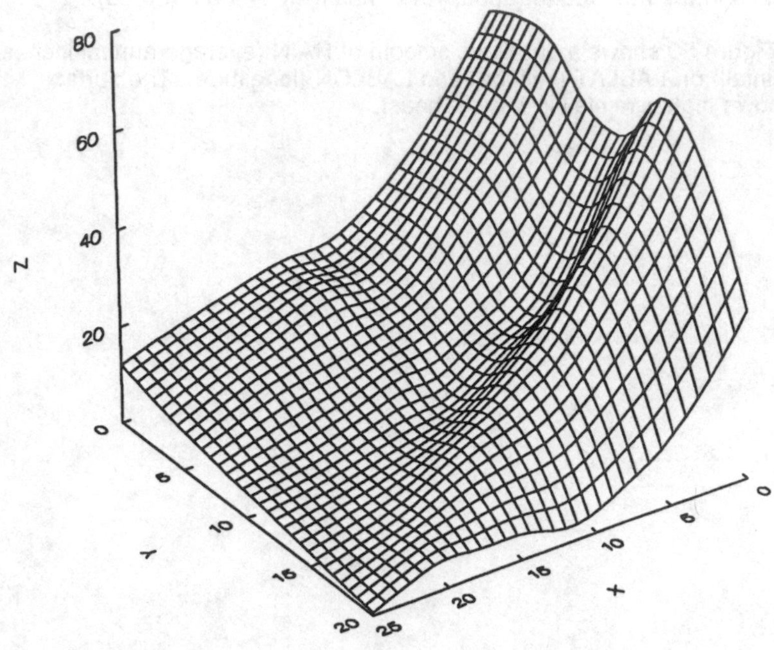

SMOOTH=QUAD *(Quadratic Smoothing Three-Dimensional Data Plots)*
When you are plotting three-dimensional data (see the beginning of this chapter), the **SMOOTH=QUAD** option produces a surface based on an equation of the following form:

$$Z = a + bX + cY + dX^2 + eY^2 + fXY$$

This way, the fitted surface can have curvature and tilt.

This method may occasionally produce surfaces which overlap. In these cases, you should add the **HIDE** option (see above in this chapter), which hides parts of surfaces which should not be visible. **HIDE** takes longer to compute, because each patch of the surface must be checked for visibility, but it produces clearer plots. Another option which you may wish to consider is **CUT**, which alters the number of cuts in the grid surface from rough (about 10) to relatively smooth (30-60).

Figure 50 shows a quadratic smooth of RAIN (average annual inches rainfall) on LABLAT (latitude) and LABLON (longitude). The surface shows higher rainfall in the northeast.

Figure 50

```
PLOT   RAIN*LABLAT*LABLON/SMOOTH=QUAD,SIZE=0
```

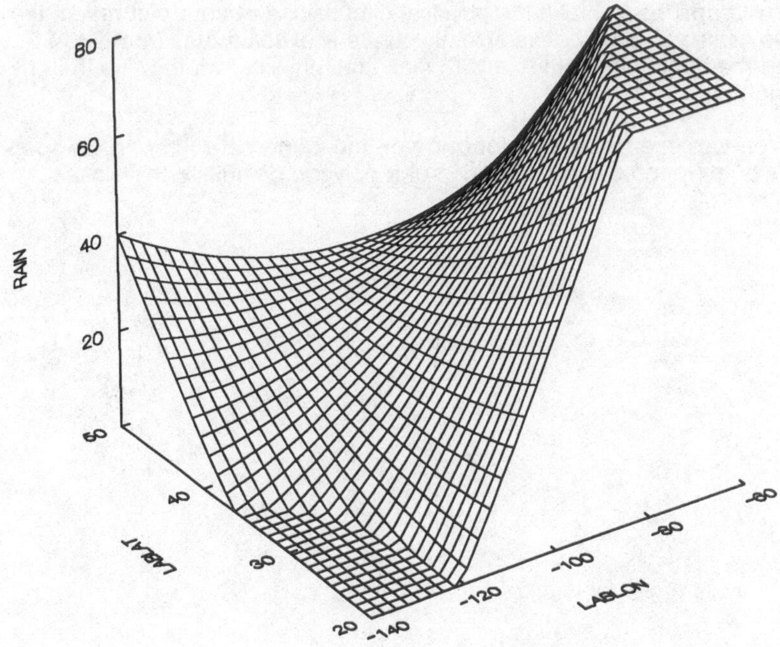

SPAN *(Minimum Spanning Tree)*
A minimal spanning tree connects a set of points in a space such that the sum of the lengths of the connecting line segments is as small as possible (Hartigan, 1975). Imagine, for example, that you have a map of the U.S. and you must connect one city in each state with a computer network. The network may have any shape, provided there is only one path along the network from one city to any other. You wish to spend as little as possible on optical cable for the network. The solution to your problem is a minimum spanning tree with the **SPAN** option.

Figure 51 shows a minimum spanning tree connecting the centroids of each state. You can use **SPAN** in a three-dimensional plot, but it can become cluttered with a lot of points.

As with the **VORONOI** option, which draws Voronoi polygons (see below in this chapter), the **SPAN** option presumes you have equivalent distances on the X and Y axis. If your scales differ, use the **HEIGHT** and **WIDTH** options to make the physical dimensions of your plot reflect the true scale values. For example, if your vertical scale runs from 0 to 50 and the horizontal from 0 to 100, make the physical width twice the height.

You can use **SPAN** and **VORONOI** on the same data. If so, each span will be perpendicular to the edge of a polygon delimiting the closest points.

Figure 51

```
PLOT   LABLAT*LABLON/SPAN,HEIGHT=2IN,WIDTH=4IN
```

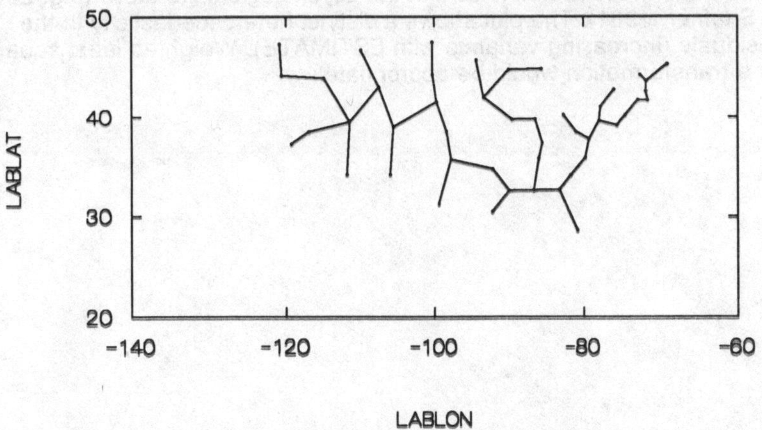

SPIKE *(Spikes to Data Points in Two Dimensions)*

To represent deviations from a constant value, you can plot data with the **SPIKE** option. This is handy, for example, in plotting residuals from a regression. If you use **SPIKE** with no value, e.g.:

```
PLOT  Y*X/SPIKE
```

then lines will be drawn from each plotting symbol down to the horizontal axis. If you add a value, e.g.

```
PLOT  Y*X/SPIKE=10
```

then lines will be drawn from each symbol to the level on the vertical axis corresponding to the value you have picked.

Figure 52 shows an example plotting residuals from the linear regression of SUMMER (average summer temperatures) on WINTER (average winter temperatures for the 48 continental states). These residuals were computed by SYSTAT, but you could get them from any statistical package. Notice that there is no need to draw a horizontal line at the 0 level of RESIDUAL because we impose our own "subjective contour" at this point anyway. This perception of a horizontal line along spikes like these is well known in the psychological literature (e.g. Levine & Shefner, 1981). The plot shows a distinct heteroscedasticity in the residuals (increasing variance with ESTIMATE). Weighted least squares or a transformation would be appropriate.

Figure 52

```
PLOT   RESIDUAL*ESTIMATE/SPIKE=0,YMIN=-20,YMAX=20
```

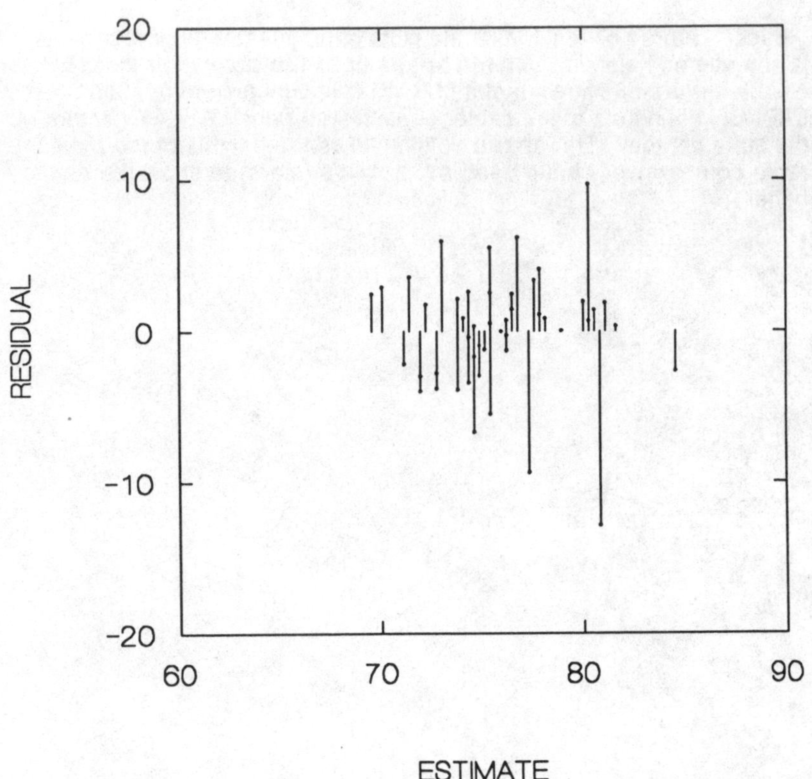

SPIKE *(Spikes to Data Points in Three Dimensions)*

To represent deviations from a constant value, you can plot data with the **SPIKE** option in three dimensions. This is handy, for example, in plotting residuals from a regression. If you use **SPIKE** with no value, e.g.:

```
PLOT  Z*Y*X/SPIKE
```

then lines will be drawn from each plotting symbol down to the horizontal plane. If you add a value, e.g.:

```
PLOT  Z*Y*X/SPIKE=10
```

then lines will be drawn from each symbol to the horizontal plane at level on the vertical axis corresponding to the value you have picked.

Because three dimensional data plots often seem to float nebulously, it is sometimes helpful to use the **SPIKE** option to show their location more clearly. Figure 53 shows a plot of RAIN (average annual rainfall) against LABLON (longitude of the center of each state) and LABLAT (latitude of the state centers). The **SPIKE** option makes the heights of the points more comparable. I have used **SYMBOL=18** (stars) to show the points better.

Figure 53

```
PLOT   RAIN*LABLAT*LABLON/SYMBOL=18,SPIKE
```

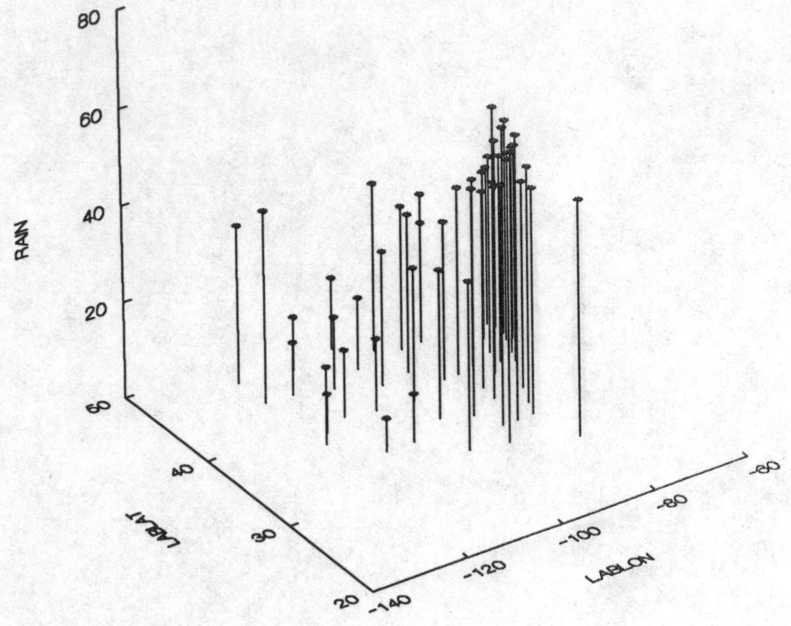

STICK *(Tick Marks Outside Frame)*

SYGRAPH normally places tick marks inside the frame. If you wish tick marks outside the frame, use the **STICK** option.

Figure 54 shows an example of a plot with tick marks outside the frame.

Figure 54

```
PLOT   SUMMER*WINTER/STICK
```

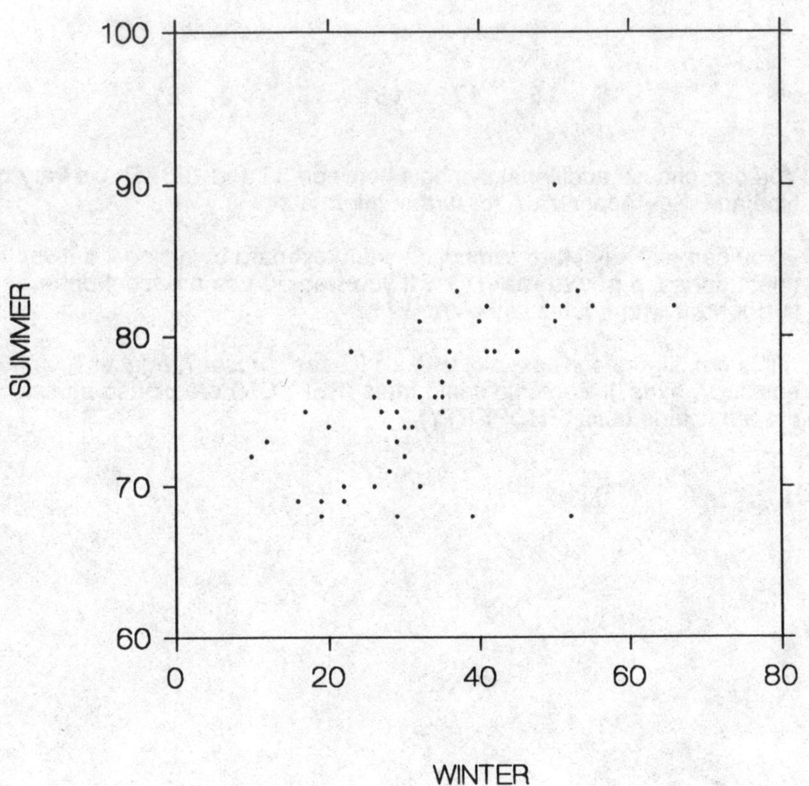

SYMBOL *(Plotting Symbols)*

You can choose a variety of symbols for your plot. Just add the option: `SYMBOL=`*n* , where *n* is an integer denoting one of the following symbols:

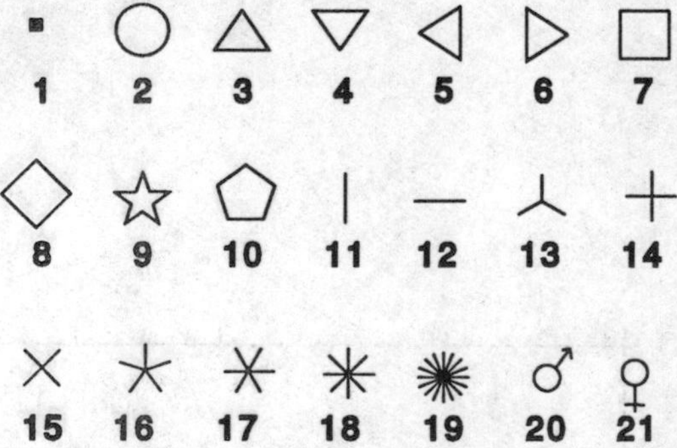

You can choose additional symbols between 32 and 128. These vary by typeface. See Appendix A for further information.

You can use any other symbol on your keyboard by typing it between apostrophes, e.g. `SYMBOL='@'`. If you want to use an apostrophe, surround it with quotes: `SYMBOL="'"`.

The next figure shows a plot with x's (ekses?, ecses?, eggses?, equises?, exes?). Personal crime rates (PERSON) are plotted against property crime rates (PROPERTY).

Figure 55

`PLOT PERSON*PROPERTY/SYMBOL=15`

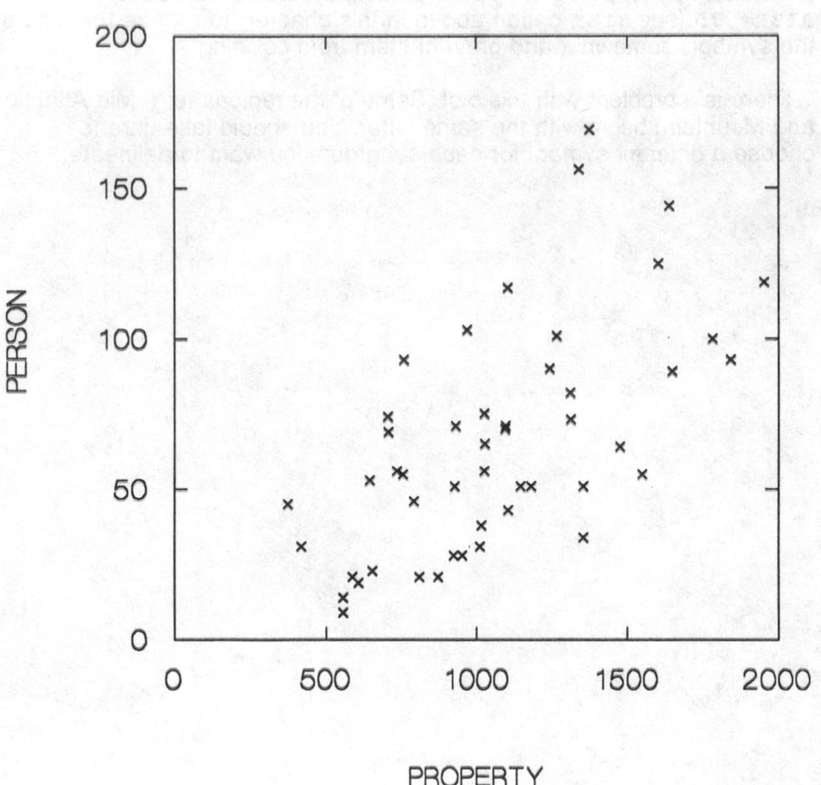

SYMBOL *(Data Based Plotting Symbols)*

You can use a character or numeric variable in your data file to determine the plotting symbol for each point. This can be handy when you are trying to denote experimental and control groups, or males and females in a plot without using labels (see **`LABEL`** option above in this chapter).

SYGRAPH uses the first character in a character variable when you use this option. The symbols are centered at their proper locations in the graph.

Figure 56 shows a plot of SUMMER (average summer temperature) against WINTER (average winter temperature), using the first character in REGION$ (Census Region) as the plotting symbol. I have used **`SIZE=.75`** (see **`SIZE`** option above in this chapter) to reduce the size of the symbols somewhat and prevent them from colliding.

There is a problem with this plot. Some of the regions (e.g. Mid Atlantic and Mountain) begin with the same letter. You should take care to choose a different symbol for each subgroup you want to delineate.

Figure 56

```
PLOT   SUMMER*WINTER/SYMBOL=REGION$,SIZE=.75
```

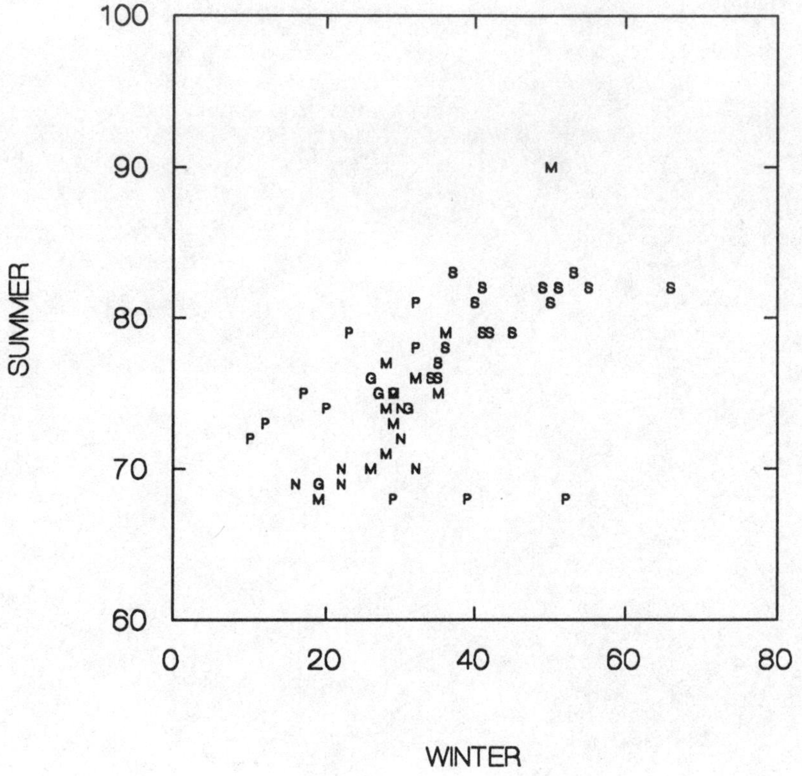

SYMBOL *(Multi-symbol plots)*

You can do plots with a different symbol for each dependent variable. The following command, for example, will make circles (2) for summer and triangles (5) for winter (see symbols above in this chapter):

```
PLOT   SUMMER,WINTER*LABLAT/SYMBOL=2,5
```

If you are doing a multi-symbol plot (by using more than one variable to the left of the asterisk in the command) then you must specify the same number of symbols in the **SYMBOL** option as you have variables to the left of the asterisk even if you are using the same symbol for each variable (e.g. **SYMBOL=2,2**).

Figure 57 shows an example of separate symbols for summer and winter.

Figure 57

```
PLOT   SUMMER,WINTER*LABLAT/SYMBOL=2,5,FILL=1,1
```

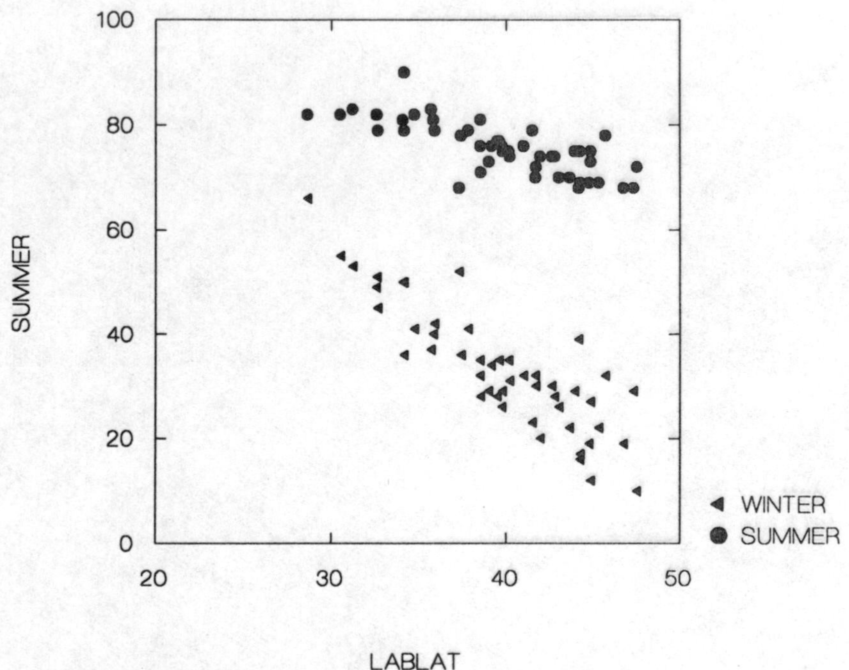

TENSION *(Tension Parameter for LOWESS or Splines or DWLS)*

The **TENSION** option controls a stiffness parameter for **LOWESS** or **SPLINE** or **DWLS** smoothing. The default value for **LOWESS** is **TENSION=.5** and for **SPLINE**, **TENSION=2**. For **DWLS**, tension is set at the inverse of the number of cases (1/*n*). The limits for **LOWESS** are between 0 and 1 and for **SPLINE** and **DWLS**, between 0 and 10. Increasing these values makes the smooths stiffer and decreasing them makes them looser, more curvy, more susceptible to individual data points, or however you wish to think about it.

Figure 58 shows the same plot used to illustrate **LOWESS** in Figure 42 (see **SMOOTH** above in this chapter) with the tension set higher (**TENSION=.9**). In this case, 90 percent of the data points are used to smooth each value on the curve.

Figure 58

```
PLOT   PROPERTY*LABLON/SMOOTH=LOWESS,TENSION=.9
```

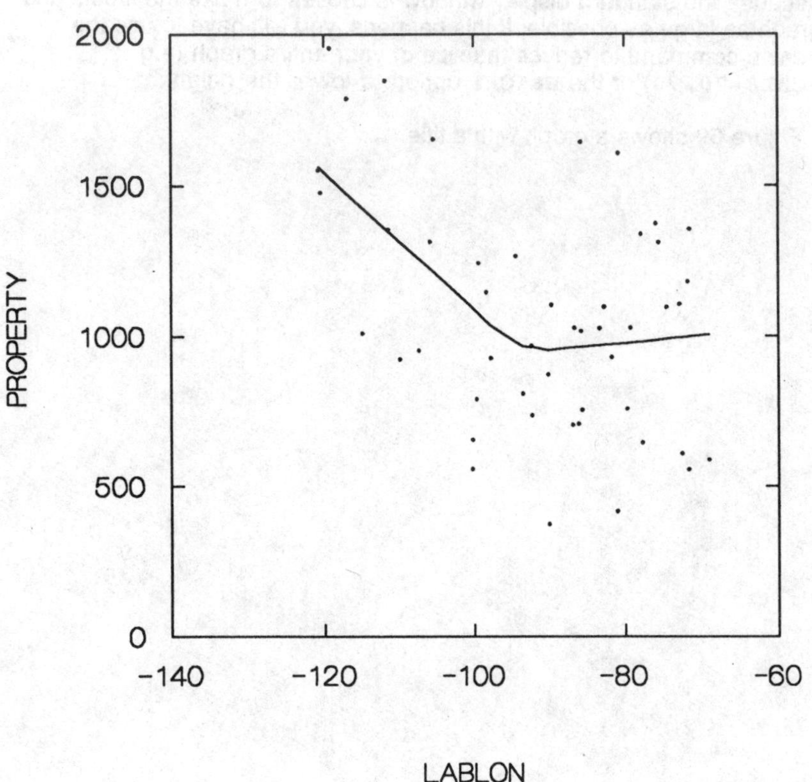

TITLE *(Graph Title)*

You can place a title at the top center of your plot with the **TITLE** option:

```
TITLE='Comparison of Four Pheromones'
TITLE="Roger's Z8-12:OAc+6%"
TITLE='Response "Flooding" from Stimulation'
```

The text must be surrounded by quotes (") or apostrophes ('). If your text includes apostrophes, as in the second example, surround it with quotes. If it includes quotes, as in the third example, surround it with apostrophes.

On some display devices the title will run off the top of the page because the standard display window is chosen to make the labels and graph as large as possible. If this happens, you will have to use the **SCALE** command to reduce the size of your entire graph (e.g. **SCALE=70,70**) or the **HEIGHT** option to lower the height.

Figure 59 shows a graph with a title.

Figure 59

```
TYPE=HERSHEY
PLOT   Z=X*Y*(X^2-Y^2)/(X^2+Y^2),
   !XMIN=-10,XMAX=10,YMIN=-10,YMAX=10,
     ZMIN=-100,ZMAX=100,HIDE,AXES=0,SCALE=0,
    XLABEL='  ',YLABEL='  ',ZLABEL='  ',
     TITLE='PROPELLOR  FUNCTION'
```

PROPELLOR FUNCTION

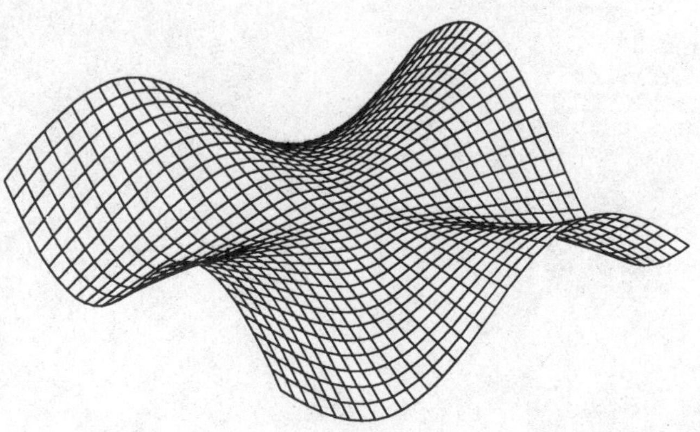

TRANS*(Transposing a Plot)*

You can transpose a plot with the **TRANS** option. **TRANS** affects everything in a graph. **XLABEL** becomes **YLABEL**, **XTICK** becomes **YTICK**, and so on. In other words, specify a graph as you would ordinarily and then add the **TRANS** option. Everything will be transposed appropriately, including the labels and scales.

In figure 60, TRANS is used to make horizontal error bars. Compare this graph with figure 16.

Figure 60

```
PLOT   GROWTH*DOSE/SYMBOL=2,FILL=1,
   ERROR=SE,TRANSPOSE
```

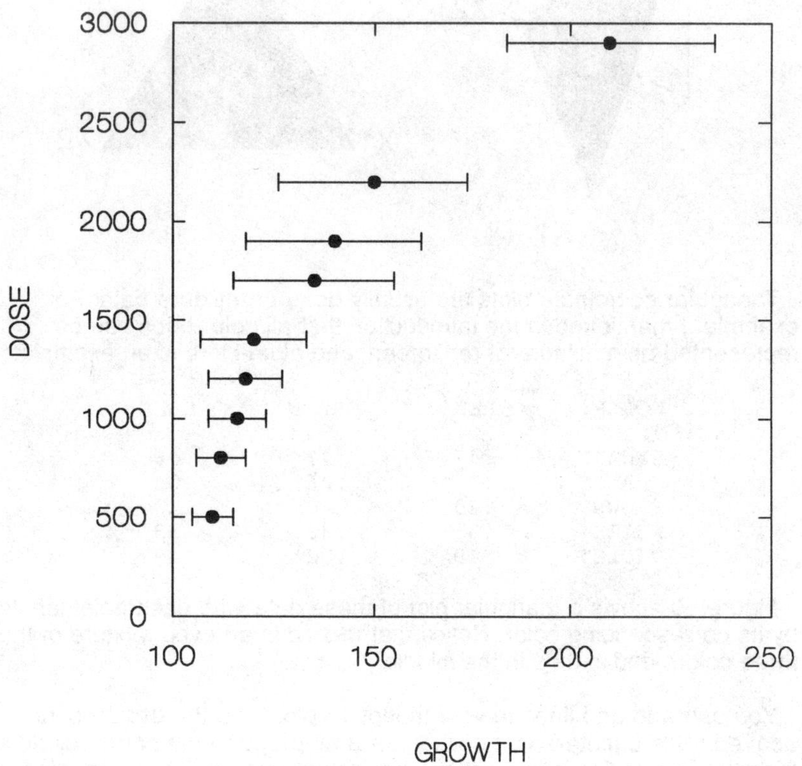

TRI *(Triangular Coordinates)*

You can plot three variables in two dimensions with triangular coordinates. Consider the figure below. The graph on the left shows a perspective plot of three variables. If we assume that all points in this plot (X1,X2,X3) sum to a constant (SYGRAPH makes them sum to 1), then they fall on a plane, which is represented by the dark triangle in the plot. If we place this plane on the plotting surface, then the original axes correspond to the three vertices of a triangle.

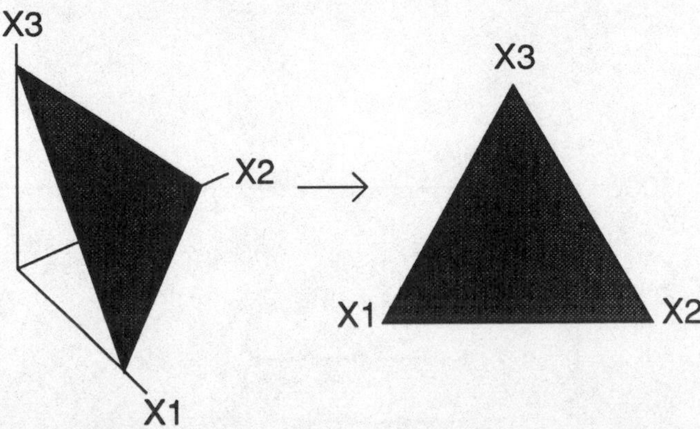

Triangular coordinate plots are usually done on mixture data. For example, I mentioned in the introduction that all color hues can be represented as a mixture of red, green, and blue. Here is an example:

COLOR$	RED	GREEN	BLUE
CANARY	.47	.47	.06
ORANGE	.70	.26	.04
BROWN	.40	.40	.20
WHITE	.33	.33	.33
VIOLET	.49	.02	.49

Figure 60 shows a triangular plot of these data with each point labeled by its corresponding color. Notice that **WHITE** is an even mixture of the three colors and is thus in the middle.

You can add grid lines to your triangular plot (see the **GRID** option above in this chapter). **GRID=1,2,** or **3** all produce the same result: a triangular grid. The other options like **LINE**, **COLOR**, **FILL**, **SYMBOL**, **SIZE**, and **JITTER** work as well. The **SMOOTH** options do not work with triangular plots, however. For surface analyses, see the **CONTOUR** option with **TRI** directly below.

Figure 61

```
TYPE=SWISS
PLOT   RED*GREEN*BLUE/TRI,SYMBOL=COLOR$
```

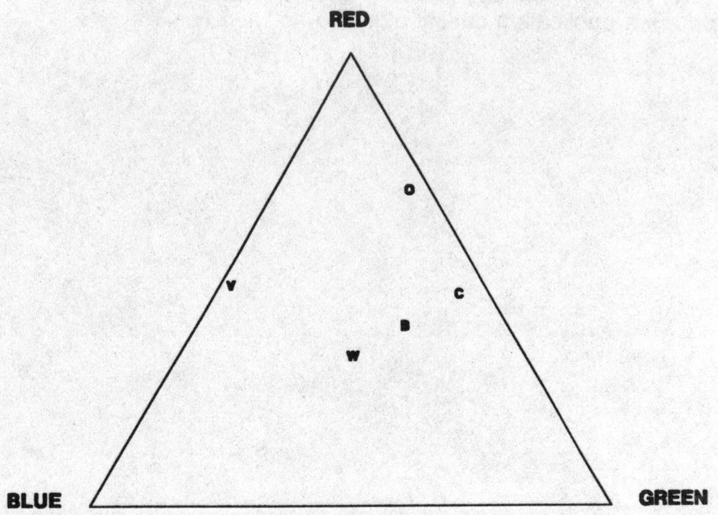

TRI *(Contouring with Triangular Coordinates)*

You can contour with triangular coordinates. This feature allows you to analyze mixture experiments and examine four dimensional data in two dimensions. See the previous figure for an explanation of triangular coordinates. Diamond (1981) summarizes their use and references more advanced material.

Figure 62 shows a triangular plot of a cubic response surface. This is the only place in SYGRAPH where you can enter three predictors in an equation. Notice that I set the parameters of the contouring axis with **ZMIN**, **ZMAX**, and **ZTICK**.

You can add grid lines to your triangular plot (see the **GRID** option above in this chapter). **GRID=1, 2,** or **3** all produce the same result: a triangular grid. If you have a linear or nonlinear statistical package like SYSTAT, you can estimate trend surfaces and use the coefficients here to produce a publication quality plot.

Figure 62

```
PLOT   U=V+W^2+X^3-2.5*V*W*X,
   !CONTOUR,ZTICK=10,ZMIN=0,ZMAX=1,TRI
```

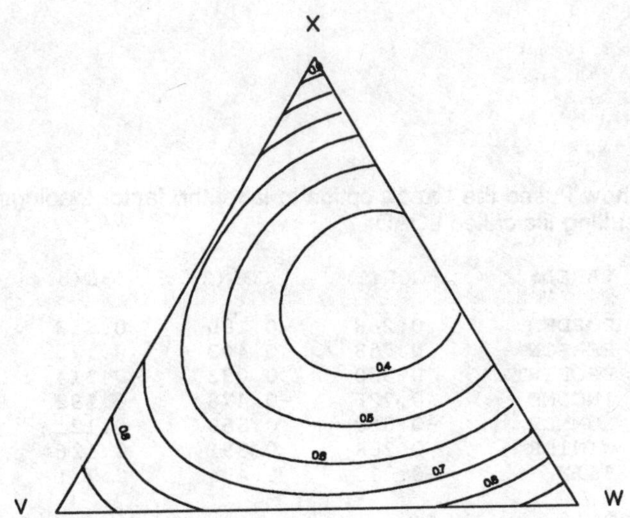

VECTOR *(Two-dimensional Vector Plots)*

The **VECTOR** option works like **SPIKE**, except that each point is connected to one point rather than to an axis or plane. This type of plot is especially useful for representing factor loadings and other vector models.

Let's get some factor loadings to plot. I took the US data and computed principal components in the SYSTAT FACTOR module and saved the loadings:

```
FACTOR
USE US
NUMBER=3
ROTATE=VARIMAX
SAVE  TEMP/LOADINGS
FACTOR
QUIT

DATA
USE  TEMP
SAVE  LOAD
TRANS
RUN
QUIT
```

Notice how I used the **LABEL** option to label the factor loadings. Here is the resulting file called LOAD:

LABEL$	COL(1)	COL(2)	COL(3)
POPDEN	0.248	-0.180	0.858
PERSON	0.758	0.462	0.170
PROPERTY	0.950	0.033	-0.114
INCOME	0.726	-0.478	0.392
SUMMER	-0.060	0.859	-0.121
WINTER	0.208	0.891	0.126
RAIN	-0.313	0.494	0.731

Figure 63 shows a plot of the first two components, labeled with the variable name. If you type **VECTOR** with no number following, then the vectors will be drawn to the lower left corner of the plotting window. With these data, because the vectors must emanate from 0 on each axis, I have typed **VECTOR=0**.

Notice that the plot shows the weather variables grouping together, the crime variables together, and POPDEN and INCOME straggling off somewhere else.

Figure 63

```
PLOT   COL(2)*COL(1)/VECTOR=0,LABEL=LABEL$
```

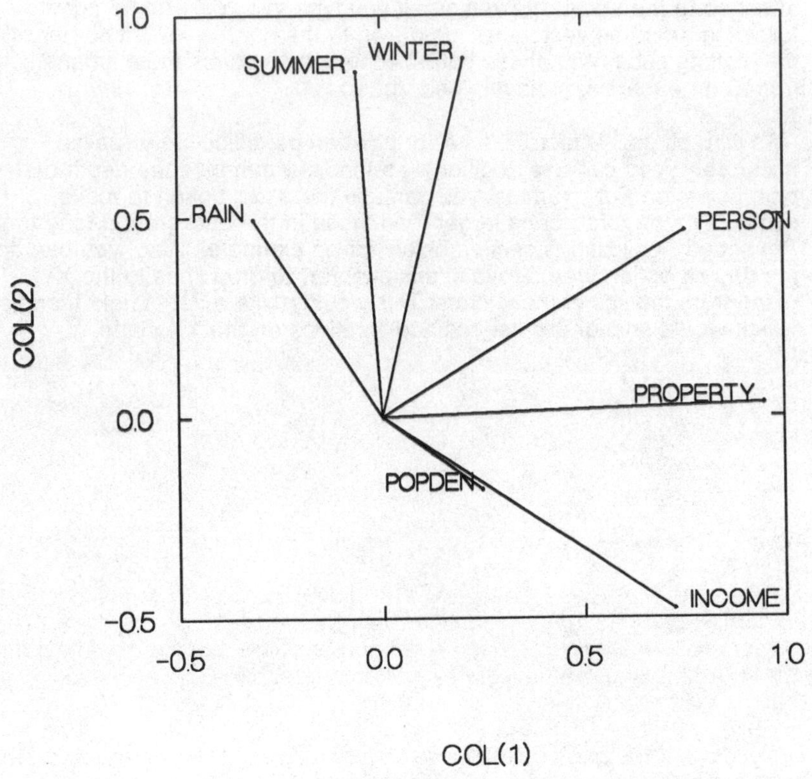

VECTOR *(Three Dimensional Vector Plots)*

You can plot factor loadings and other types of vectors in three dimensions. Let's do the same factor loadings I used for the last figure:

LABEL$	COL(1)	COL(2)	COL(3)
POPDEN	0.248	-0.180	0.858
PERSON	0.758	0.462	0.170
PROPERTY	0.950	0.033	-0.114
INCOME	0.726	-0.478	0.392
SUMMER	-0.060	0.859	-0.121
WINTER	0.208	0.891	0.126
RAIN	-0.313	0.494	0.731

Figure 64 plots the three components in perspective with the labels attached to the end of the vectors. If you type **VECTOR** with no number following, then the vectors will be drawn to the near lower left corner of the plotting cube. With these data, because the vectors must emanate from 0 on each axis, I have typed **VECTOR=0.**

As with other 3-D plots, the vector plot can be difficult to visualize accurately. You can use additional methods to enhance the depth of the plot, however. For example, you can use the **SIZE** option to make symbols in the foreground larger than those in the background (see the Advanced Applications section below for an example). Also, you can add the **SPIKE** option (see above in this chapter) to drop lines to the XY plane from the tips of the vectors. This would make a set of right triangles, which would anchor the heights and locations on the XY plane.

Figure 64

```
PLOT   COL(3)*COL(2)*COL(1)/LABEL=LABEL$,VECTOR=0
```

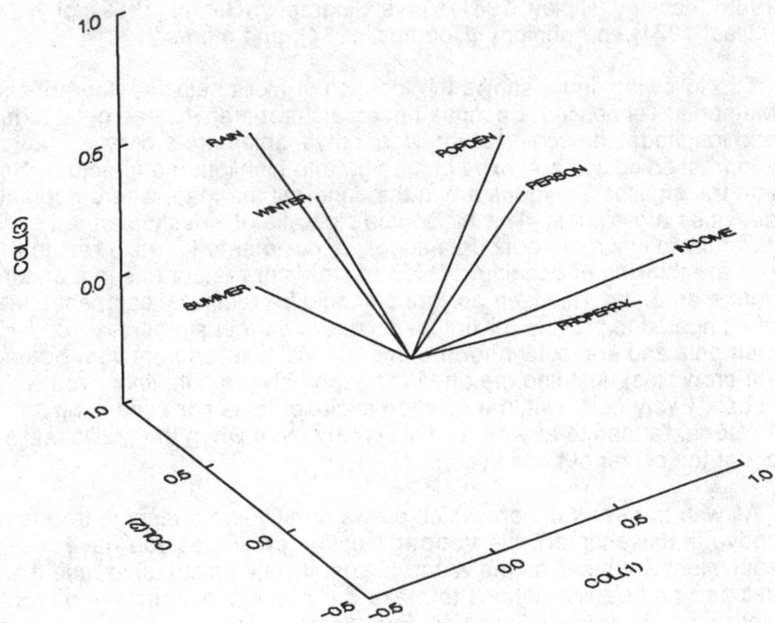

VORONOI *(Voronoi Tesselation)*

This is my favorite plot in the whole package. I've become attached to it because it has so many applications, it's so pretty, and because I managed to program it in only a few lines of code. This plot takes a long time to compute, on the order of the square of the number of points. There are faster algorithms than mine for large datasets (e.g. Green and Sibson, 1978; Preparata and Shamos, 1985), but they require much more storage and code.

The **Voronoi tesselation** is also known as the **Dirichlet tesselation** or the **Thiessen diagram**. Imagine placing little balls of hot roll dough at irregular spacings in a baking pan. After letting them rise, you notice that the boundaries between rolls are straight and approximately half way between the points where you placed the balls. The same thing happens with colonies of yeast irregularly spaced on a Petri dish or grass fires started at different points on a plain or cats establishing their turf in the city. These boundaries appear in diverse physical phenomena: geography (Rhynsburger, 1973), hydrology (Croley and Hartmann, 1985), ecology (Ripley, 1981), crystallography (Gilbert, 1962), physics (Miles, 1974), psychology (Coombs, 1964), and others.

The following figure shows the location of McDonald's restaurants in Memphis, Tennessee. Because I used a street map instead of latitude and longitude, the scales of the location variables are arbitrary. I have suppressed scales and axes in the figure to highlight the structure. Notice that the smallest polygons are in the center of the map, where population densities are highest. The McDonald's people obviously planned carefully to insure an adequate supply of customers for each restaurant. If you are thinking of opening a chain of stores or restaurants in a uniformly dense area, the Thiessen polygons should be relatively compact instead of elongated to provide maximum access to your customers. If you live in Memphis and are looking for the nearest McDonald's from your home (as the crow flies), just find the one inside the polygon containing your house. Every point within a polygon is closer to its corresponding McDonald's than to any other. This is true even when the McDonald's is not at the center of the polygon.

As with the **SPAN** option, which draws a minimum spanning tree (see above in this chapter), the **VORONOI** option presumes you have equivalent distances on the X and Y axis. If your scales differ, use the **HEIGHT** and **WIDTH** options to make the physical dimensions of your plot reflect the true scale values. For example, if your vertical scale runs from 0 to 50 and the horizontal from 0 to 100, make the physical width twice the height.

Figure 65

```
PLOT  Y*X,
  /SYMBOL='M',AXES=0,SCALE=0,
   XLABEL='  ',YLABEL='  ',VORONOI
```

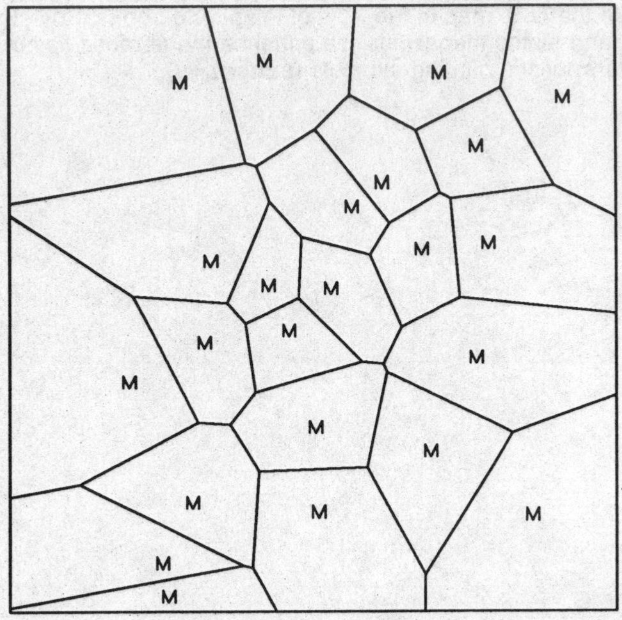

WIDTH *(Physical Width of Plot)*

You can control the physical width of your plot with the **WIDTH** option. It works like this:

```
WIDTH=50%       (or WIDTH=50)
WIDTH=4IN
WIDTH=10CM
```

The first example specifies percent of display width. The second specifies inches, and the third centimeters.

When you use the **WIDTH** option, you probably also want to use **HEIGHT**, which works exactly the same way (see above in this chapter). The following graph shows how to use them together. I've adjusted the height and width of the LABLAT by LABLON plot to make the plot look more like the U.S. map in the front of telephone books, Soviet satellite photos, and airline magazines. To enhance the patriotic flavor, I've used open stars for the plotting symbols (**SYMBOL=9**).

Figure 66

```
PLOT   LABLAT*LABLON/HEIGHT=3IN,WIDTH=5IN,SYMBOL=9
```

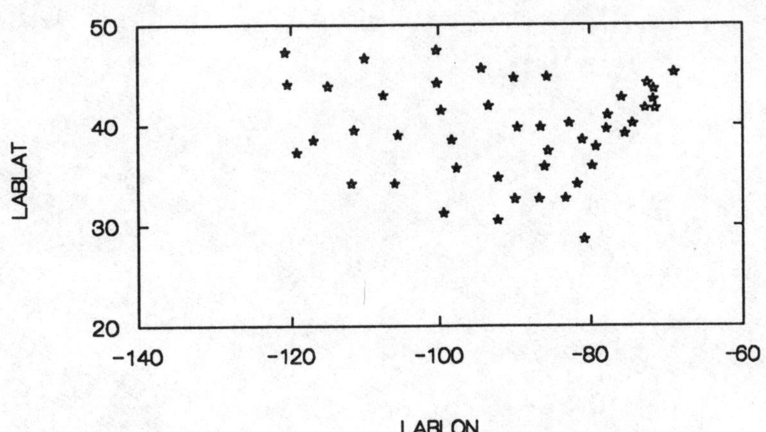

XLABEL,YLABEL,ZLABEL *(Labeling a Plot)*

Plots are usually labeled with the names of the variables you use in the **PLOT** command. If you want different labels, use the **XLABEL** and/or **YLABEL** and/or **ZLABEL** option(s), e.g.:

```
XLABEL='Concentration  Na'
YLABEL='Per  Capita  Income'
XLABEL="Roger's  Bogus  Data"
ZLABEL='Weight  of  "Widgets"  Bid'
YLABEL='  '
```

The label text must be surrounded by quotes (") or apostrophes ('). If your text includes apostrophes, as in the third example, surround it with quotes. If it includes quotes, as in the fourth example, surround it with apostrophes. The last example shows how to remove labels from your graph. Just assign a blank (' ') to your label.

Figure 67 shows an example of a relabeled 3-D graph. Because of the labels, the command takes several lines. Notice that I connected them with a comma at the end of each, until the last. I added **SYMBOL=10** because it is cute.

Figure 67

```
PLOT SUMMER*LABLAT*LABLON,
  /XLABEL='Longitude',
  YLABEL='Latitude',
  ZLABEL='Average  Summer  Temperature',
   SYMBOL=10,FILL=1,HEIGHT=3IN,WIDTH=4IN
```

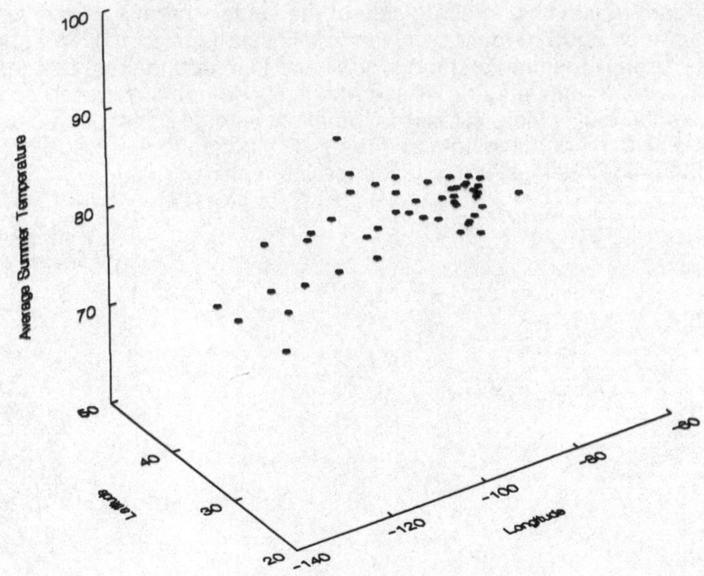

XLIMIT, YLIMIT *(Control Limits)*

You can add dashed lines to mark limits on each axis of a two-way plot. **Control (Shewhart) charts**, for example, mark upper and lower limits on one axis to indicate permissible bounds for a production process. Axis limits can be used in other applications to mark standard errors. The **LIMIT** option works this way:

```
PLOT  Y*X  /  XLIMIT=2,6,YLIMIT=3.1,5.2
```

Notice that you must specify two numbers for each limit (upper and lower). They need not be in order. Limits will not be plotted for numbers outside the extremes of the specified axes. Thus, if you want to plot only one limit (dashed line) on an axis, type something like this:

```
PLOT  Y*X  /  XLIMIT=2,-9999
```

Figure 68 shows a plot of SUMMER (summer temperature) against WINTER (winter temperature) with limits set at approximately two standard deviations on either side of the sample means. I have added a simultaneous 95 percent confidence ellipsoid (see **ELL** option above in this chapter) to contrast the marginal and joint boundaries. Because I rounded the numbers, the ellipse and limits do not correspond exactly. If you teach multivariate statistics, you might want to construct a chart like this one with your own data and the *F* distribution to illustrate simultaneous versus joint confidence intervals.

Figure 68

```
PLOT SUMMER*WINTER,
    /XLIMIT=9,57,YLIMIT=65,85,ELL=.95
```

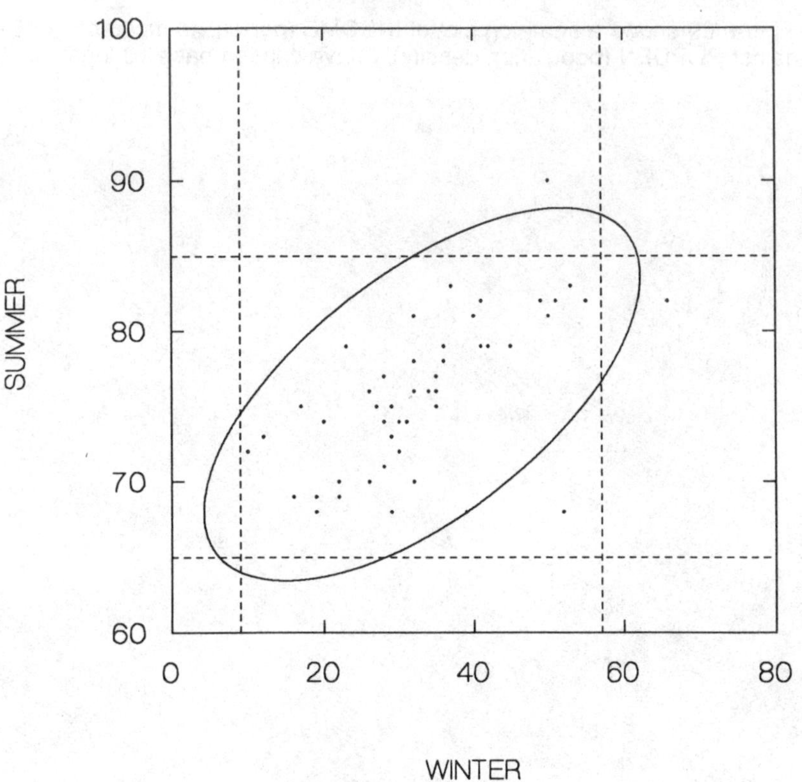

XLOG, YLOG, ZLOG *(Logging Data)*

You can log any scale(s) of your plot with the `LOG` option. The X axis is transformed with the `XLOG` option, Y with `YLOG` and Z (if you are doing 3-D) with `ZLOG`. Logs may be computed to any base, e.g. `XLOG=2`, `XLOG=3`, `YLOG=10`, `ZLOG=.5`. Natural logarithms will be computed if you use `XLOG`, `YLOG`, or `ZLOG` with no argument, i.e. `ZLOG`. Only round number log bases (e.g. 0.5, 2, 3,10) will result in round number tick values, however.

Plots with one axis logged are often called semi-log plots. Those with two axes logged are called log-log plots. Those with three axes logged are called log-log-log. Those with four, log-log-log-log. But I digress.

Figure 69 shows a semi-log plot of INCOME (per-capita income) against POPDEN (population density). I have chosen base 10 logs.

Figure 69

```
PLOT   INCOME*POPDEN/XLOG=10
```

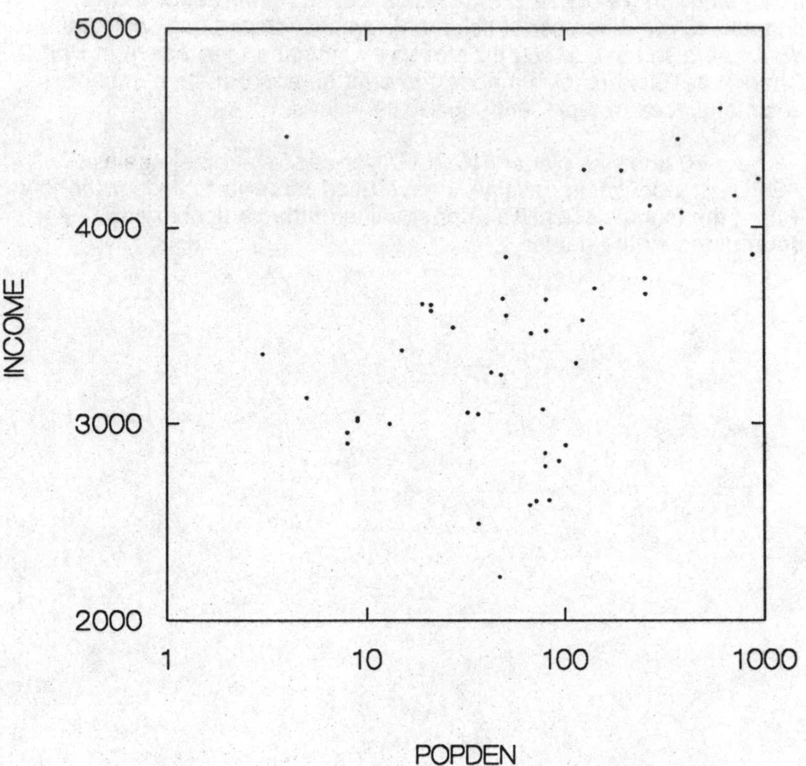

XMIN,YMIN,XMAX,YMAX,ZMIN,ZMAX *(Data Limits)*

SYGRAPH usually determines minimum and maximum scale values from the data in your file. If you wish to override this feature, use the **MIN/MAX** options. **YMIN** and **YMAX** control the lower and upper limits of the vertical scale. **XMIN** and **XMAX** do the same for the horizontal scale. **ZMIN** and **ZMAX** do so for the third dimension.

If you set the **MIN** and **MAX** options inside the range of your data, you will zoom in to get a closer view, but you will eliminate certain data values from your plot. SYGRAPH will warn you when this happens.

Some settings of **MIN** and **MAX** will cause scale values to become messy (not integers or round numbers). In these cases, you may have to fiddle with the **XTICK**, **YTICK**, **ZTICK** options (see below in this chapter) to get a number of tick marks which yields round scale values. You may also have to use the **FORMAT** command (see above in Part 2, Chapter 1, "General Commands") to print an appropriate number of decimal places to represent your scale values.

Figure 70 shows a plot of INCOME (per-capita income) against POPDEN (population density). I have used **YMIN=0** to anchor the lower end of the income scale. The upper value of the vertical axis is determined by the data.

Figure 70

```
PLOT   INCOME*POPDEN/YMIN=0,SYMBOL=2,SIZE=.5
```

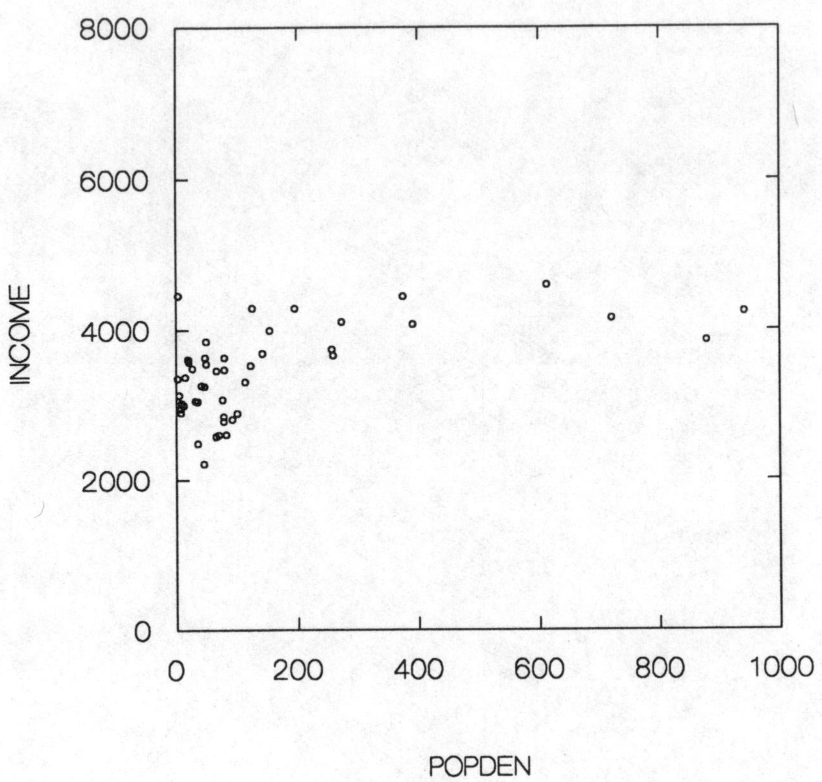

XPIP,YPIP,ZPIP *(Pip Marks)*

Pip marks are half sized tick marks. SYGRAPH normally omits pip marks from plots. The `PIP` option adds them. Just specify the number you want. `XPIP` controls the X axis, `YPIP` the Y axis, and (if you are doing 3-D) `ZPIP` controls the Z axis. If you log a scale (see `LOG` option above in this chapter) the pip marks will be logarithmically spaced.

Figure 71 shows an example with 10 pip marks on each axis.

Figure 71

```
PLOT   RAIN*LABLAT/XPIP=10,YPIP=10
```

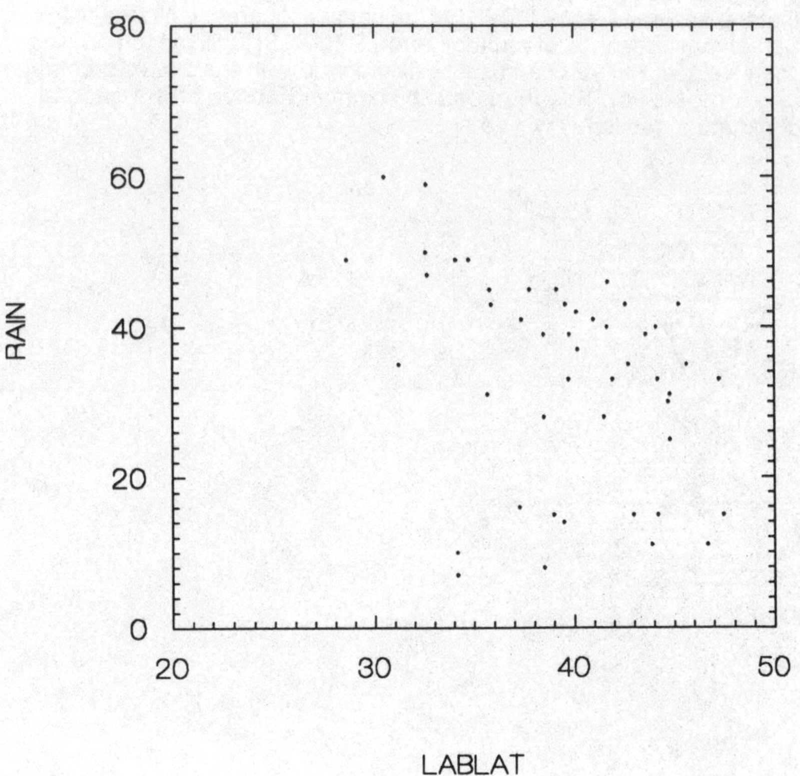

XPOW,YPOW,ZPOW *(Powering Data)*

You can power the scales of your plot with the **POW** command. **XPOW** governs the X axis, **YPOW** the Y, and **ZPOW** the Z (if you are doing 3-D). Powers may be computed to any exponent, e.g. **XPOW=.5** (square root), **YPOW=.33333** (cube root), **ZPOW=-1** (inverse), **XPOW=2**. Square roots will be computed if you use **POW** with no argument, i.e. **YPOW**. Some exponents (e.g. 3) will produce non-integer tick marks. **POW** is implemented in SYGRAPH only for positive data. Negative values will be deleted.

Figure 72 shows a plot of INCOME (per-capita income) against the square root (**XPOW=.5**) of POPDEN (population density). Compare this plot to the log plot in Figure 69. Notice that the square root is not strong enough to remove the curvature in the plot. A log is needed. Notice, also, that the scale values of POPDEN are perfect squares. Isn't that nifty? Sometimes, because of roundoff error, SYGRAPH will fail to find nice scale values, but you can usually fix them up with the **FORMAT** command (e.g. **FORMAT=0**). See the **FORMAT** command above in the general commands section. Try **XPOW=.2**.

Figure 72

```
PLOT  INCOME*POPDEN/XPOW=.5
```

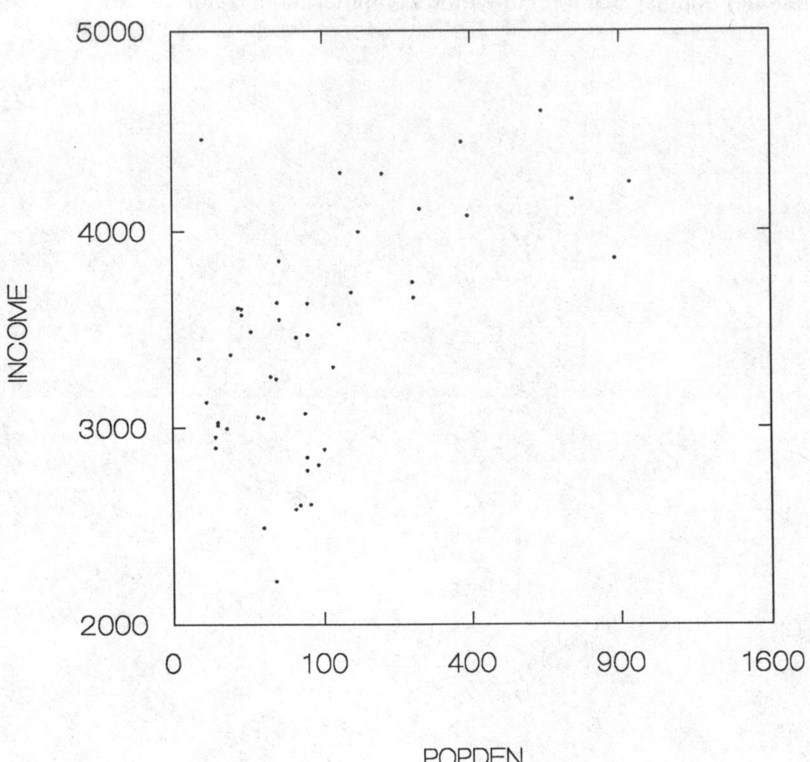

XREV,YREV, ZREV *(Reversing Axes)*

You can reverse axes with the **REV** option. **XREV** reverses the X axis, **YREV** the Y, and **ZREV** the Z (if you have 3-D). There are two principal applications of these options. First, you can orient 3-D surfaces so that they slope upwards toward the rear, as in Figure 49 in this chapter. This is often handier than trying to rotate the figure with the **EYE** command.

The second application is to do back-to-back plots. Two plots can share a common vertical scale, for example, and be anti-symmetrical to reveal dissimilarities. See the Advanced Applications in two dimensions chapter for examples.

Figure 73 shows an example of a reversed scale plotting RAIN (annual rainfall) against SUMMER (average summer temperature).

Figure 73

```
PLOT   RAIN*SUMMER/XREV
```

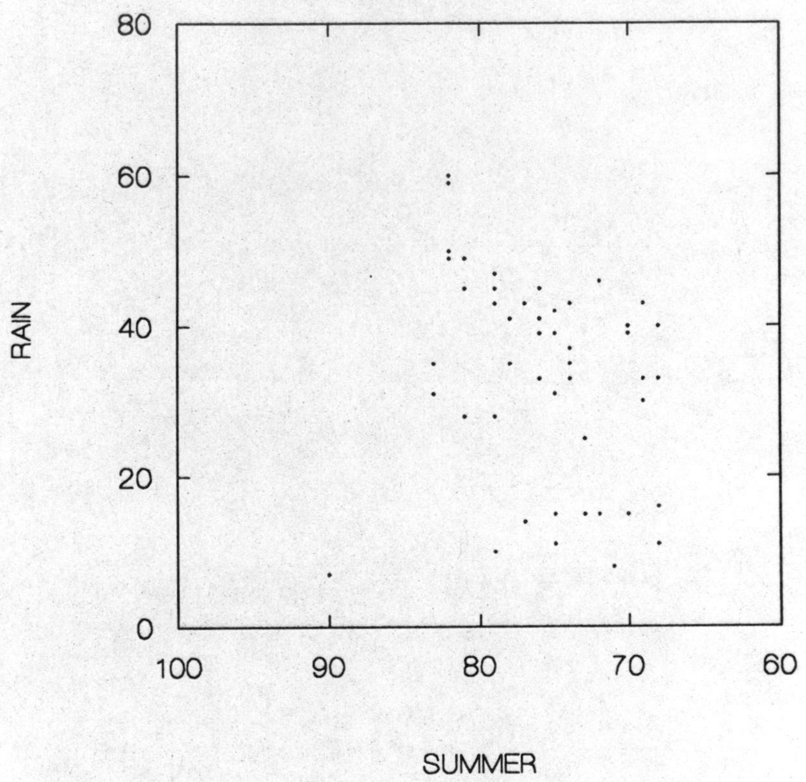

XTICK, YTICK, ZTICK *(Number of Tick Marks)*

SYGRAPH examines your data to determine how many tick marks to use on the axes of a plot. If you wish to modify this value, use the **TICK** option with a number. **XTICK** refers to the X axis, **YTICK** to the Y, and **ZTICK** to the Z (if you are doing 3-D). For example, **YTICK=8** will force the vertical axis to have 8 tick marks. SYGRAPH will attempt to find minimum and maximum values for the scale such that the tick mark numbers are round. If it fails, you can control the values with the **YMIN** and **YMAX** options as well.

Figure 74 shows an example of a plot with 10 tick marks. Notice that SYGRAPH automatically adjusts the size of the scale values when there are more tick marks. For you compulsives, I have added 10 pip marks to give the impression of precision.

Figure 74

```
PLOT  PERSON*PROPERTY,
   /XTICK=10,YTICK=10,XPIP=10,YPIP=10
```

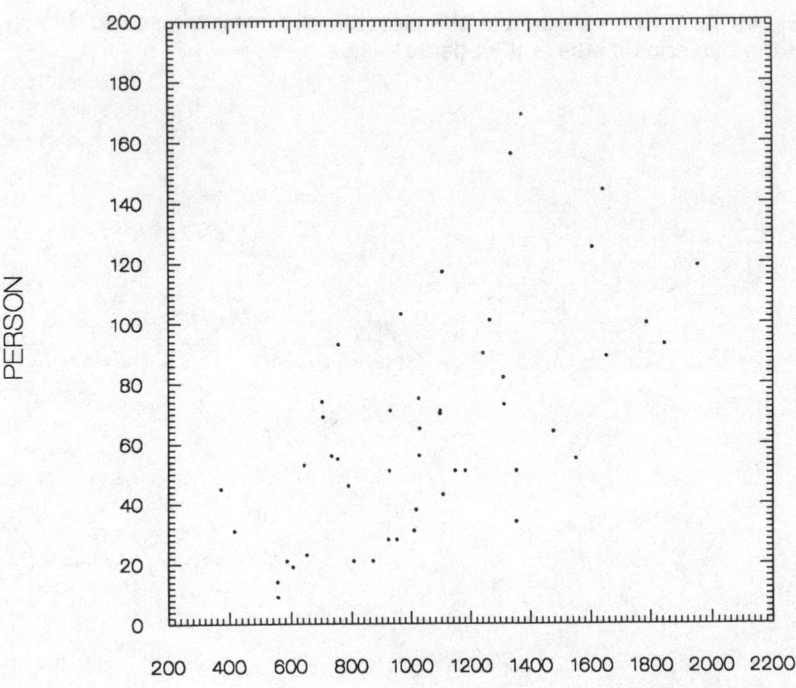

ZHEIGHT *(Height of 3-D Axis)*

You can control the height of the third axis in a 3-D plot with the **ZHEIGHT** option. **HEIGHT** and **WIDTH** refer to the first two axes for a three-dimensional plot. If you do not use the **ZHEIGHT** option, then the third axis will have the same relative dimension as the second.

Keep in mind that the actual size of the axes in 3-D plots is adjusted for the point of view you choose with the **EYE** command (see above in the Reference section). If you place your viewing eye far from the graph (e.g. **EYE=-1,-10,2**), then the axes will look small. If you place your eye close (e.g. **EYE=-1,-1,.5**), then the axes will be large. **XHEIGHT**, **YHEIGHT**, and **ZHEIGHT** thus control the actual size of the object in 3-D space. How it appears in two dimensions depends on your viewing position.

Figure 75 shows an example of a plot with all three axes scaled. I have left the eye coordinates at their default value.

Figure 75

```
PLOT  RAIN*LABLAT*LABLON,
  /WIDTH=4IN,HEIGHT=3IN,ZHEIGHT=5IN,
   SYMBOL=2,SPIKE
```

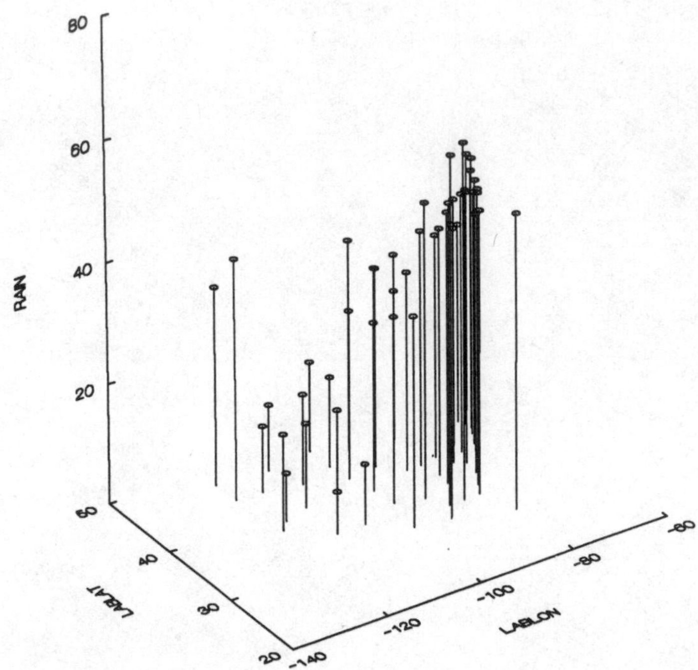

Chapter 11

PPLOT

A histogram is a rather poor method for determining the distribution of your data. A much more powerful visual display is to plot the values of a variable against corresponding percentage points of a theoretical distribution (Gnanadesikan, 1977). Graphs like this are called **probability plots** or **P plots**. Specifically, let *r* be the rank order of an observation in a batch of *n* observations sorted from smallest to largest. Assume for the moment that we are looking at the normal Gaussian distribution. We estimate an expected normal value corresponding to that observation as the standard normal value corresponding to the probability $(r\text{-}.5)/n$. We plot this value on the vertical axis against the value of the observation on the horizontal axis. If the data are from a normal distribution, the plotted values will lie on a straight line. For further information, consult Chambers, Cleveland, Kleiner, and Tukey (1983).

Normal Probability Plot

You can choose from a variety of distributions: normal, half-normal, uniform, exponential, Weibull, gamma, and chi-square. If you do not choose a reference distribution as an option, you will get the standard normal. Figure 1 shows a plot of PERSON (person crimes per 100,000) against a standard normal variable.

Figure 1

```
PPLOT  PERSON
```

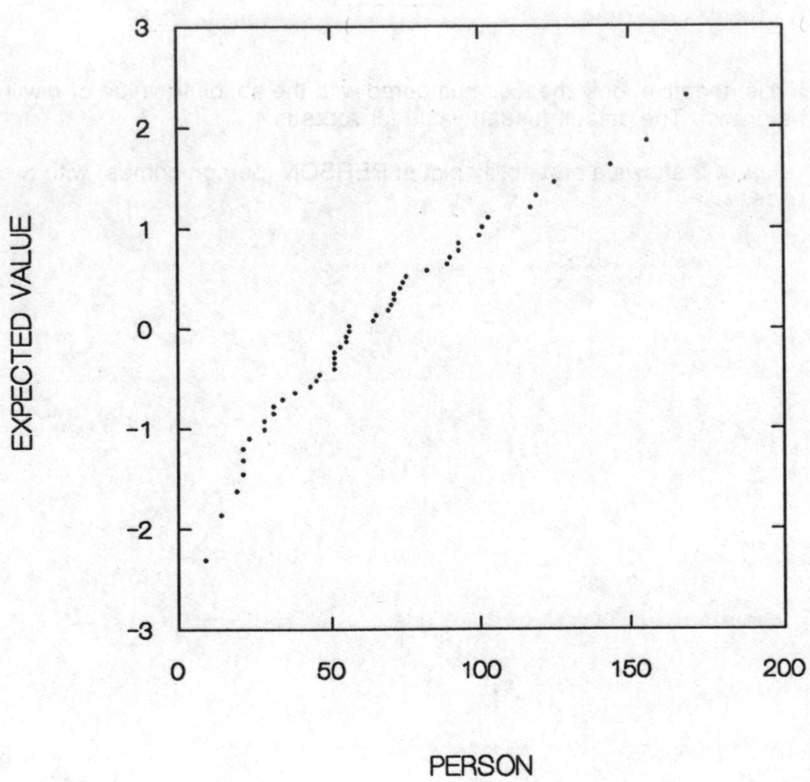

AXES *(Number of Axes)*

The **AXES** option controls the number of axes drawn in a probability plot. Its syntax is:

```
AXES=n
```

where *n* is an integer from 0 to 4. If *n* is 0, no axes will be drawn. If *n* is an integer from 1 to 4, all axes from 1 to *n* will be drawn. Axes are numbered from 1 to 4 clockwise, beginning with the bottom axis:

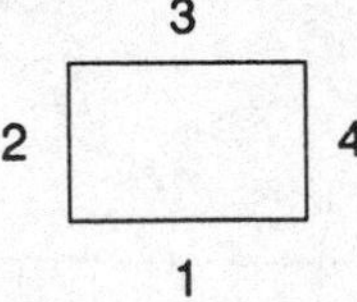

If *n* is negative, only the axis numbered with the absolute value of *n* will be drawn. The default (usual) value for **AXES** is 4.

Figure 2 shows a probability plot of PERSON (person crimes) with two axes.

Figure 2

```
TYPE=SWISS
PPLOT  PERSON/AXES=2
```

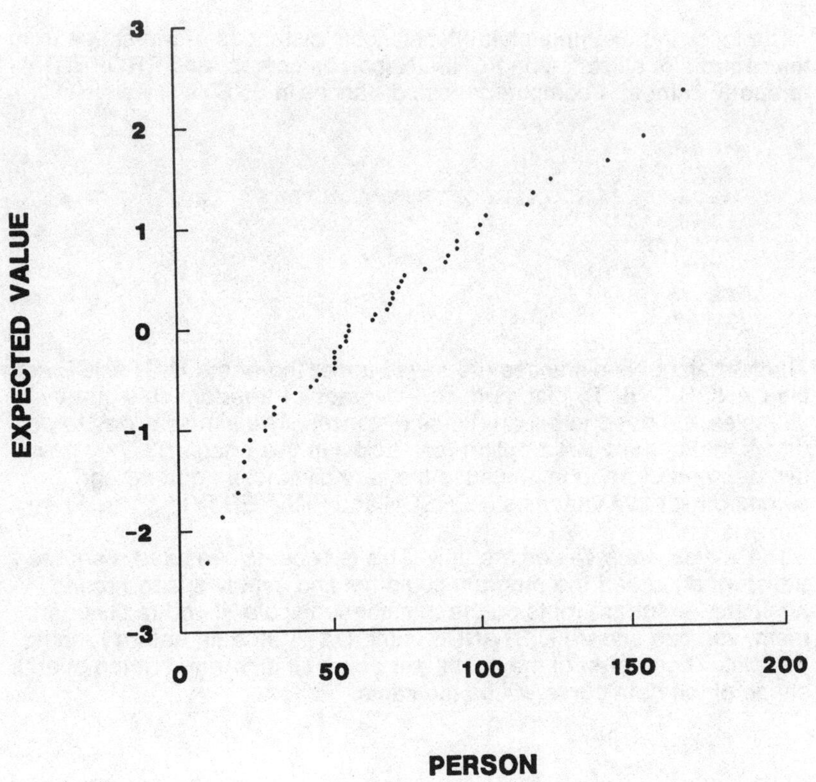

CHISQ *(Chi-Square Probability Plot)*

A chi-square variable is the sum of the squares of one or more normal variables. You can plot your data against the quantiles of a chi-square distribution with the `CHISQ` option. You must choose the degrees of freedom in the option, e.g. `CHISQ=5`.

Where can we get chi-square data to fool around with? Typically, sums of squares in analysis of variance and Mahalanobis squared distances in multivariate analysis are chi-square distributed when the normality assumptions are appropriate (see, for example, Gnanadesikan, 1977 or Winer, 1971). If you have a 2 by 2 by 2 by 2 ... analysis of variance, for example, the sums of squares for all effects are single degree of freedom chi-square variables. Probability plots will show you which effects stand out.

The following example plots Mahalanobis distances of the states from the centroid of all states on PERSON (person crimes) and PROPERTY (property crimes). I computed these distances in SYSTAT:

```
MGLH
USE US
MODEL   PERSON,PROPERTY=CONSTANT
ESTIMATE
HYPOTHESIS
SAVE  CANON
TEST
QUIT
```

The Mahalanobis distances are saved under the name DISTANCE in the file CANON.SYS. To plot them as 2 degrees-of-freedom chi-square variables, we need to square these distances. The simplest way to do that is to use the `POW=2` option (see below in this chapter). They have two degrees of freedom because they are distances squared and summed over two variables (PERSON and PROPERTY).

The X axis scale values are ugly. This is because we used a square transformation and the program could not find evenly spaced round numbers for square roots on the transformed scale. If you really need them, you can square DISTANCE in the DATA module before running this plot. The spread of the points will look a bit different, but the overall shape of the data curve will be the same.

Figure 3

```
PPLOT  DISTANCE/POW=2,SMOOTH=LINE,CHISQ=2
```

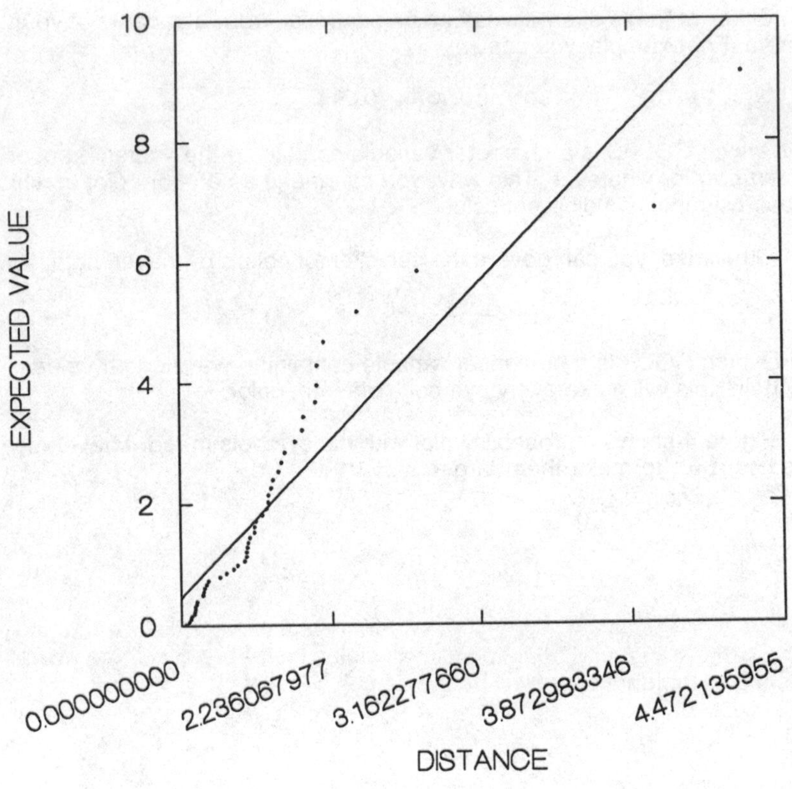

COLOR *(Setting Color of Symbols)*

You can choose a color for your symbols with the **COLOR** option. Choose either a name or a wavelength in nanometers. Possible colors and their approximate nanometer wavelengths are: **RED** (615), **ORANGE** (590), **YELLOW** (575), **GREEN** (505), **BLUE** (480), **VIOLET** (450). You may also name **BLACK**, **WHITE**, **GRAY**, and **BROWN**. The following command will make all symbols in the graph red:

```
PPLOT   PERSON/COLOR=RED
```

You can also specify color in nanometers wavelength. The following example will make all the symbols greenish:

```
PPLOT   PERSON/COLOR=540
```

Either of these alternatives can be controlled from a variable in your data. For example, you can say:

```
PPLOT   PERSON/COLOR=COLR$
```

in which COLR$ is a character variable containing the values '**RED**' or '**YELLOW**' or whatever. This way, you can make a category plot in which each symbol is a different color.

Otherwise, you can govern the selection of colors by wavelength:

```
PPLOT   PERSON/COLOR=COLR
```

in which COLR is a numerical variable containing wavelength values. Again, this will make every symbol a different color.

Figure 4 shows a probability plot with the symbols in red. I have used **SYMBOL=2** to make them larger.

Figure 4

```
PPLOT  INCOME/COLOR=RED,SYMBOL=2,FILL=1
```

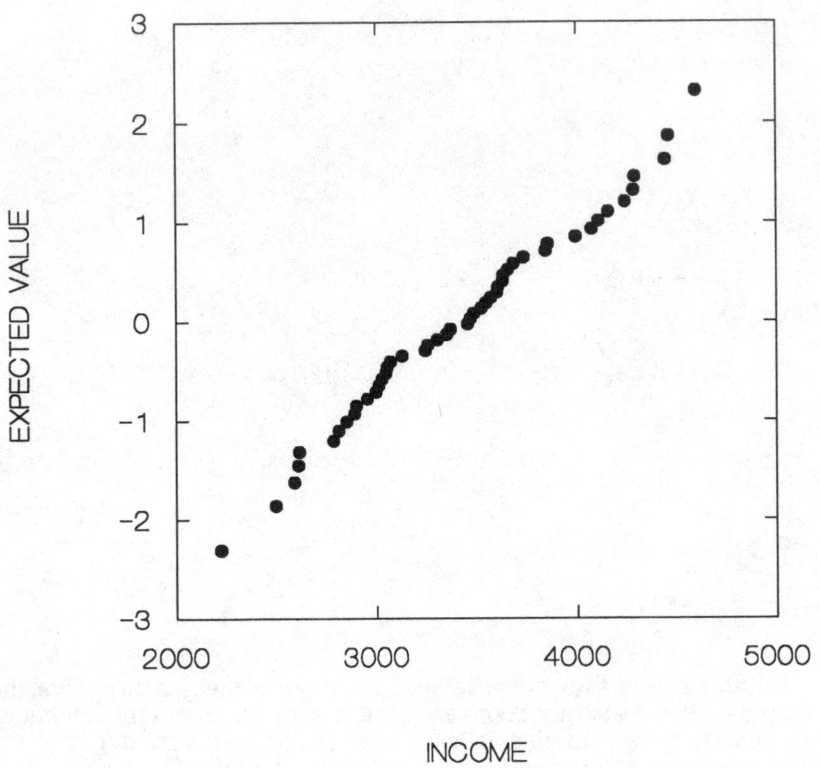

EXPO *(Exponential Distribution)*

You can plot your data against an exponential distribution with the EXPO option. The exponential distribution function is:

$$f(y) = 1 - \exp(-y/s)$$

where *s* is a spread parameter. In the transposed probability plot, the slope of the line through the plotted points is an estimate of *s.*

Here are some data from an unpublished memo by Taylor cited in Maltz (1984) and elsewhere. The data record the number of Illinois parolees observed to have failed conditions of their parole each month after release. An additional 149 parolees were observed to have failed after 22 months, but we will not graph the data beyond this point.

MONTH	COUNT
.5	29
1	15
2	9
3	8
4	9
5	6
6	5
7	5
8	3
9	2
10	2
11	3
12	3
13	0
14	0
15	2
16	2
17	2
18	0
19	0
20	0
21	0
22	3

Figure 5 shows an exponential probability plot of these data. Notice that I have used the **`WEIGHT`** command (see above in the general commands chapter) to cover duplicate values. I have also used the **`TRANS`** and **`SMOOTH=LINEAR`** options (see below in this chapter). The model appears to fit poorly in the tails, especially the lower.

Figure 5

```
WEIGHT=COUNT
 PPLOT  MONTH/TRANS,SMOOTH=LINEAR,EXPO
```

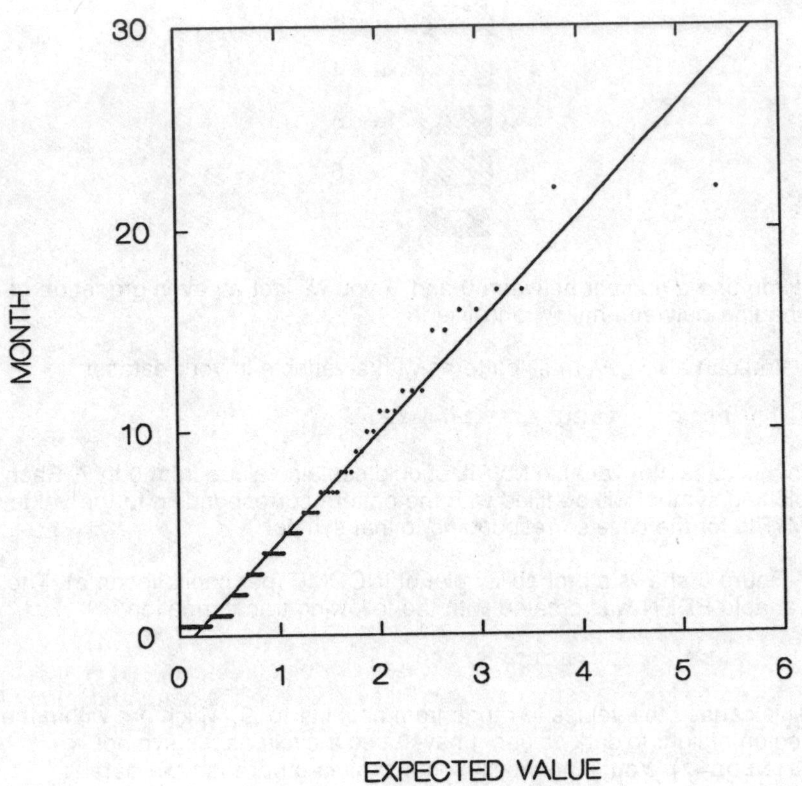

FILL *(Filling symbols)*

You can fill symbols with different patterns. The **FILL** option works this way:

```
PPLOT   INCOME/FILL=2
```

The number you choose after "**FILL=**" determines the type of fill pattern. Here are the possibilities:

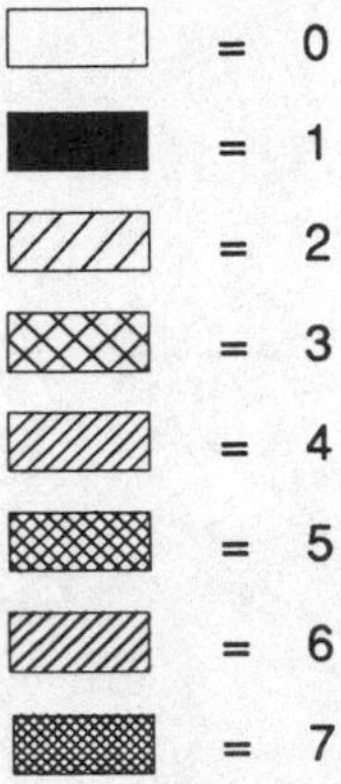

= 0

= 1

= 2

= 3

= 4

= 5

= 6

= 7

If you use a number between 0 and 1, you will get an even gradation of shading between hollow and filled.

You can also govern fill patterns with a variable in your dataset:

```
PPLOT   INCOME/FILL=MYFIL
```

In this case, the variable MYFIL should contain values from 0 to 7. Each plotting symbol will be filled with the pattern corresponding to the value in MYFIL for the case corresponding to that symbol.

Figure 6 shows a probability plot of INCOME (per capita income). The variable PDEN was created with the following transformation:

```
LET   PDEN=POPDEN/1000
```

This caused the values to range from about .1 to .9, which are within the region of light to dark values. I have used a circle as the symbol (**SYMBOL=2**). You should pick some symbol other than the default (**SYMBOL=1**) because the default is too small to show the fill pattern. Notice that higher population densities are at the upper end of the income distribution.

Figure 6

```
PPLOT   INCOME/SYMBOL=2,FILL=PDEN,XTICK=6
```

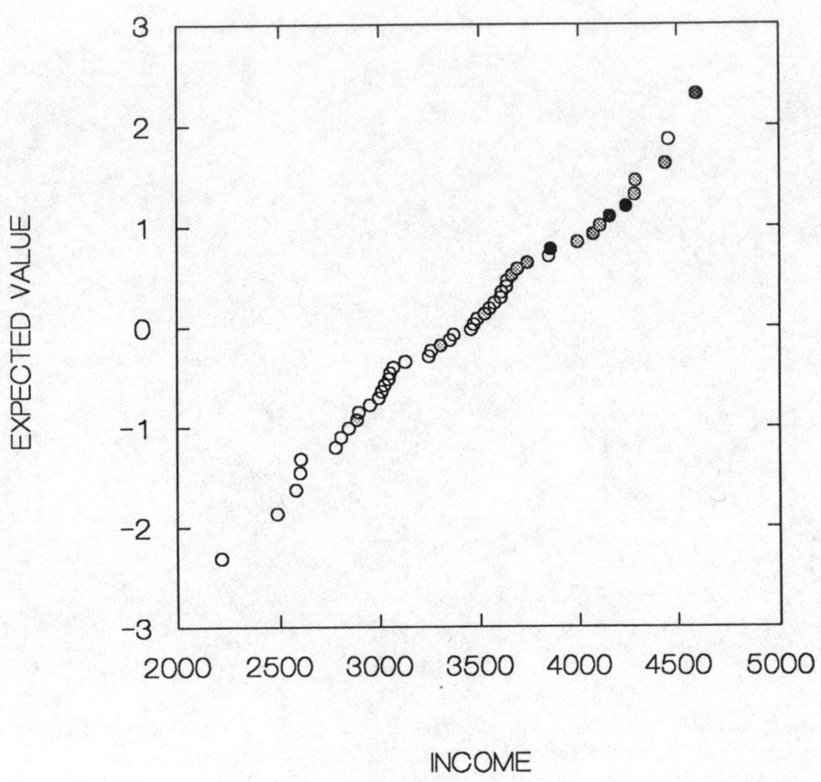

GAMMA *(Gamma Probability Plot)*

A gamma distribution is a transformed chi-square with real degrees of freedom. You can plot your data against the quantiles of a gamma distribution with the **GAMMA** option. Like the chi-square, you must specify a shape parameter, e.g. **GAMMA=.8**. Chambers, Cleveland, Kleiner, and Tukey (1983) discuss applications of gamma probability plots in univariate models and Gnanadesikan (1977) shows how to use them for analyzing multivariate data.

Figure 7 shows an example. I have plotted the recidivism data used to illustrate **EXPO** against a gamma distribution with shape parameter equal to .5. The fit to these data is better than those for the other distributions in this chapter.

Figure 7

```
WEIGHT=COUNT
PPLOT   MONTH/TRANS,SMOOTH=LINEAR,GAMMA=.5
```

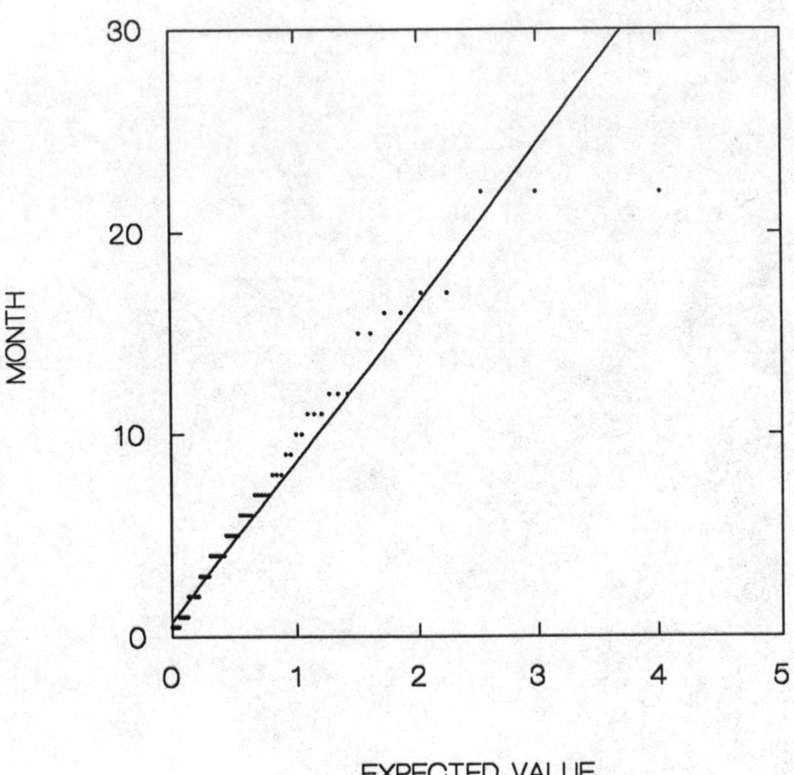

GRID *(Grid Marks)*

You can add grid marks to plots with the **GRID** option. The possible values are:

`GRID=1`	*(vertical grid marks)*
`GRID=2`	*(horizontal grid marks)*
`GRID=3`	*(horizontal and vertical grid marks)*

Figure 8 shows an example with vertical and horizontal grid marks.

Figure 8

```
PPLOT  SUMMER/GRID=3
```

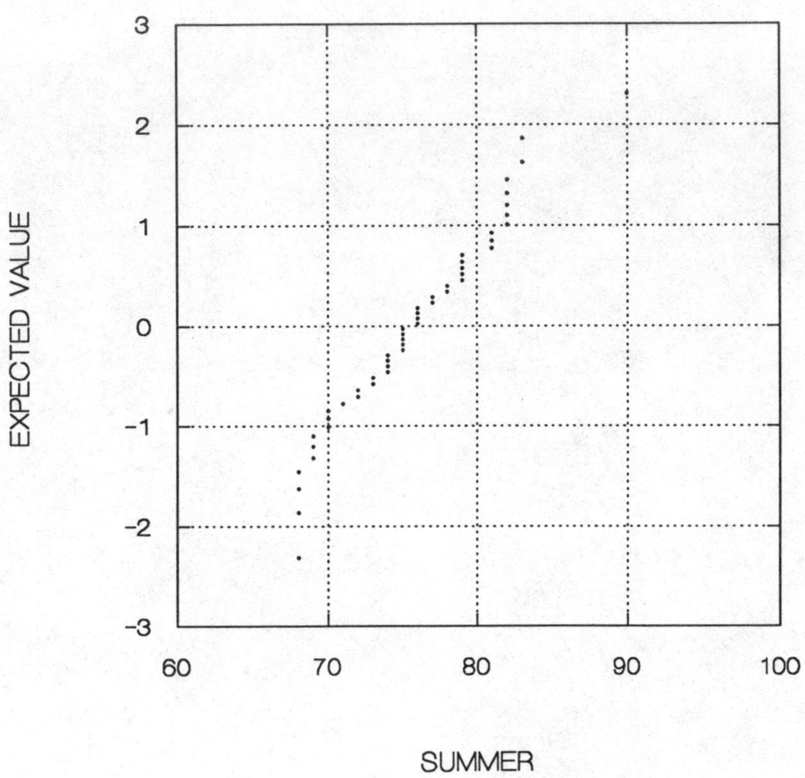

HALF *(Half-normal Probability Plot)*

A half-normal distribution is the absolute value of a normal (or the square root of a chi-square with one degree of freedom). You can plot your data against the quantiles of a half-normal distribution with the **HALF** option.

Figure 9 shows an example. POPDEN looks like half a normal distribution if you do a stem-and-leaf diagram (see **STEM** chapter). The half-normal probability plot shows it to be otherwise, however, since the points do not plot in a straight line.

Figure 9

```
PPLOT   POPDEN/HALF
```

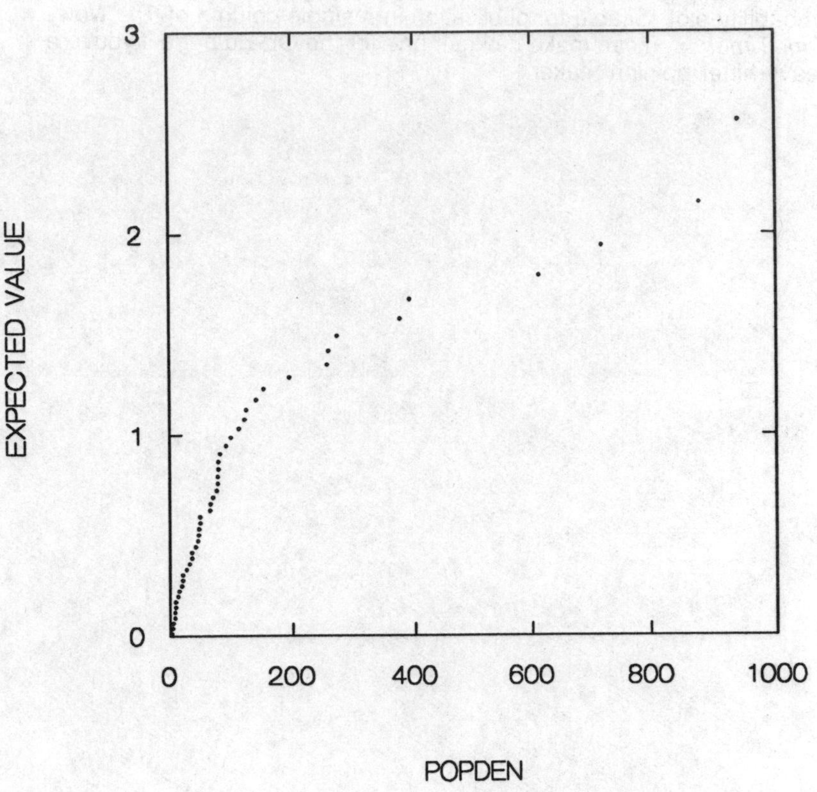

HEIGHT *(Physical Height of Plot)*

You can control the physical height of your plot with the **HEIGHT** option. It works like this:

```
HEIGHT=50%      (or HEIGHT=50)
HEIGHT=4IN
HEIGHT=10CM
```

The first example specifies percent of display height. The second specifies inches, and the third centimeters.

When you use the **HEIGHT** option, you probably also want to use **WIDTH**, which works exactly the same way (see below in this chapter). The following graph shows how to use them together. This is a probability plot suitable for publication in a single column of *The New York Times*. You can make a bigger one for the Op-Ed page if you're a heavy-hitter opinion maker.

Figure 10

```
PPLOT   SUMMER/HEIGHT=5IN,WIDTH=2IN
```

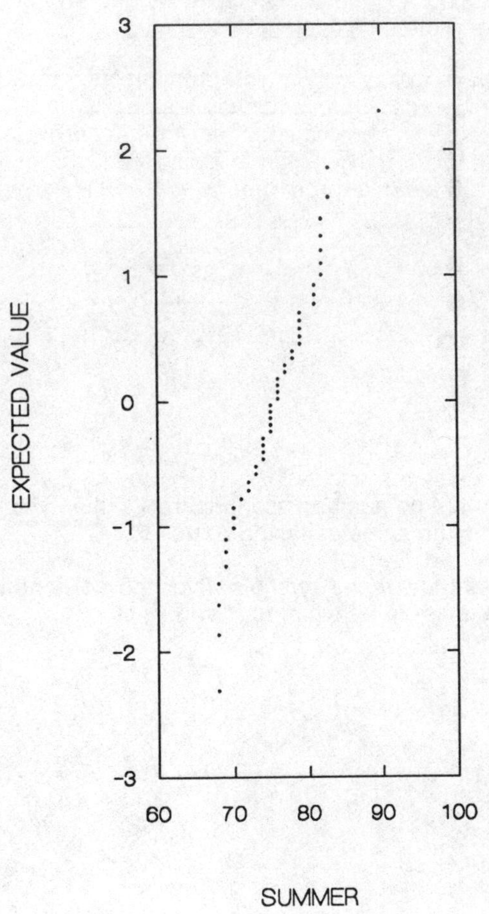

LINE *(Line Graphs)*

When you have only a few data points in a probability plot, it sometimes helps to connect them with a line. This is easy to do in SYGRAPH. Just use the **LINE** option. You may choose from 11 different types of lines by typing **LINE=***n* , where *n* is one of the following numbers:

1

2

3

4

5

6

7

8

9

10

11

If you type **LINE** with no number, as in Figure 11, then you will get the solid line, which is the same as typing **LINE=1**.

If you do not want to see the symbols which the **LINE** option connects, then make them invisible by typing **SIZE=0**.

Figure 11

```
PPLOT  RAIN/LINE,SIZE=0
```

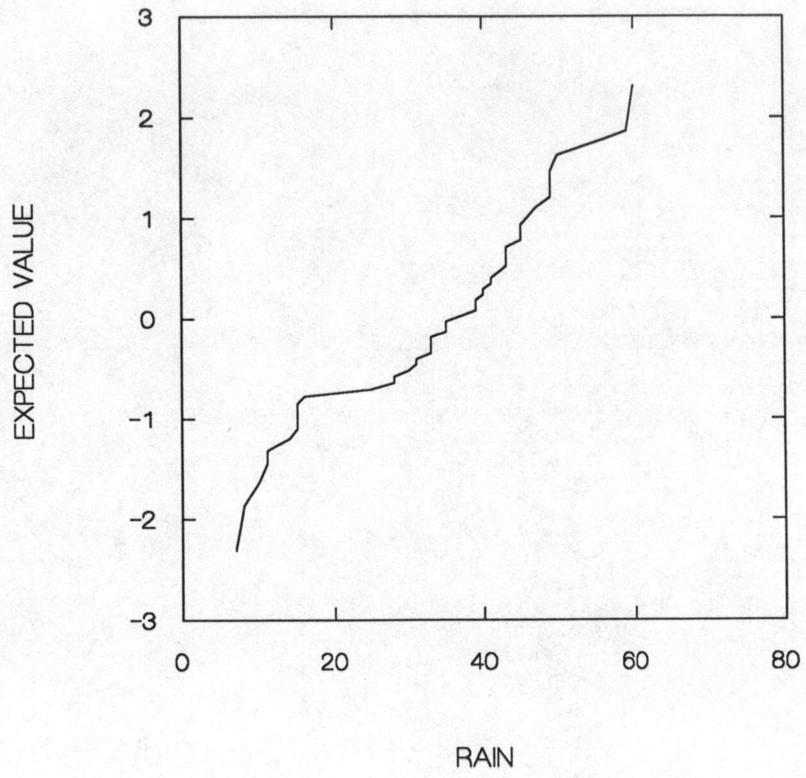

LOG *(Logging Data)*

You can log the data scale of your probability plot with the `LOG` command. This can be handy for testing log normal distributions, for example. Logs may be computed to any base, e.g. `LOG=2`, `LOG=3`, `LOG=10`, `LOG=.5`. Natural logarithms will be computed if you use `LOG` with no argument, i.e. `LOG`. Only round number log bases (e.g. 0.5, 2, 3,10) will result in round number tick values, however.

Figure 12 shows a log normal probability plot of POPDEN (population density). Compare this plot to Figure 8. We have managed to straighten out the distribution considerably.

Figure 12

```
PPLOT   POPDEN/LOG=10,SMOOTH=LINEAR
```

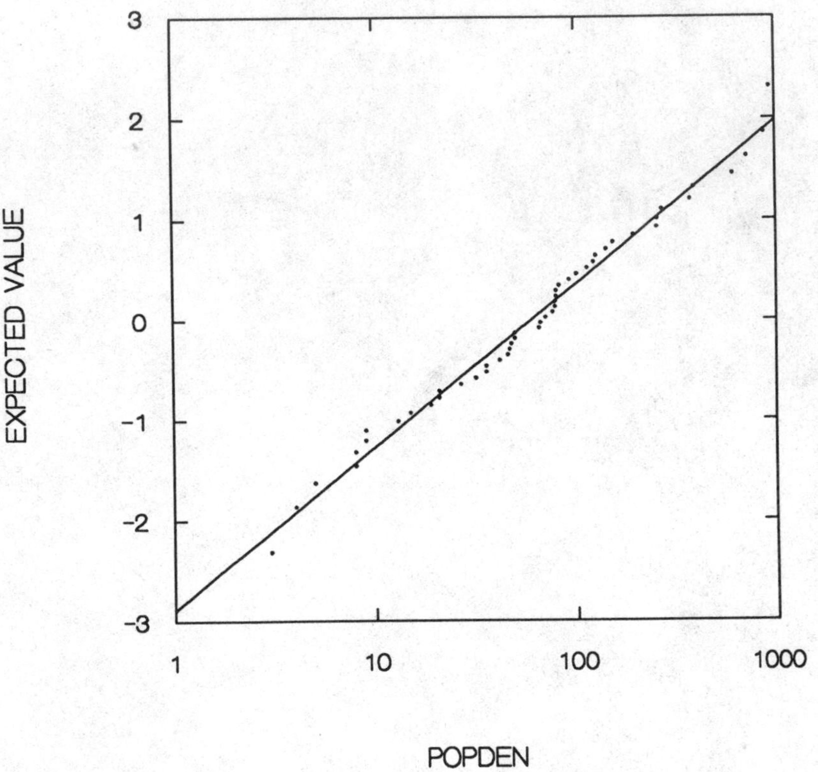

NORM *(Normal Probability Plot)*

The **NORM** option produces a normal probability plot. If you don't use any option, **NORM** is assumed anyway, so I've included the **NORM** option for those of you who don't trust computers and insist on telling them exactly what to do.

Figure 13 shows an example. I used the SYSTAT random number generator to produce 500 normal random numbers. You can try some other random number seeds or use another statistical package.

```
SAVE  RAND
RSEED=1339
LET  Z  =  ZRN
REPEAT  500
RUN
```

Figure 13

`PPLOT  Z/NORM`

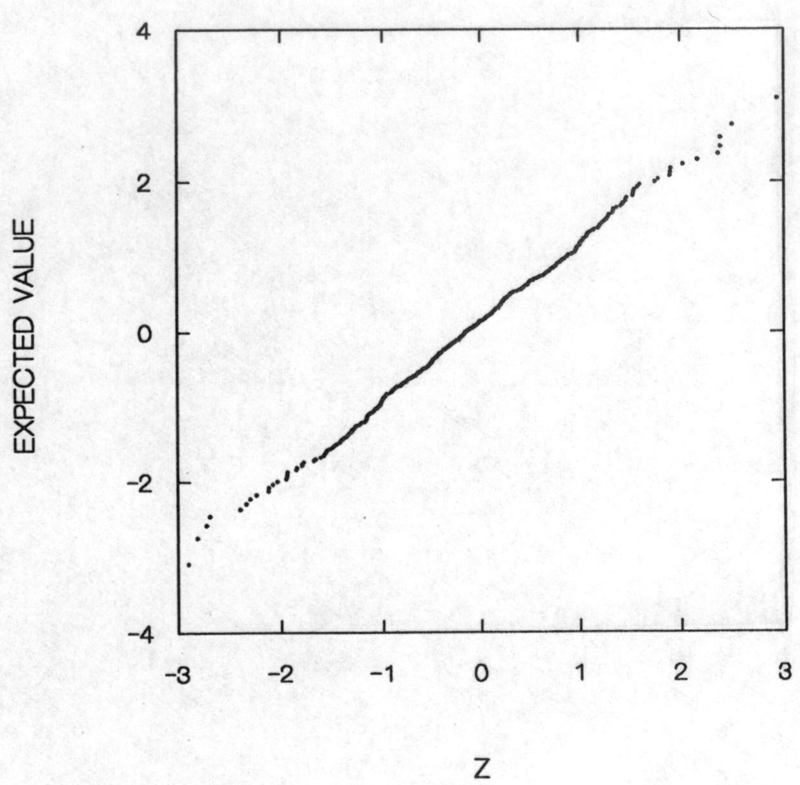

POW *(Powering Data)*

You can power the horizontal scale of your probability plot with the `POW` command. Powers may be computed to any exponent, e.g. `POW=.5` (square root), `POW=.33333` (cube root), `POW=-1` (inverse), `POW=2`. Square roots will be computed if you use `POW` with no argument, i.e. `POW`. Some exponents (e.g. 3) will produce non-integer tick marks. `POW` is implemented in SYGRAPH only for positive data. Negative values will be deleted.

Figure 14 shows a square root transformation of the POPDEN (population density) variable. Notice that the square root does not pull the upper tail in sufficiently to make it look normal. Compare the result to the logging of Figure 12.

Figure 14

```
PPLOT   POPDEN/POW=.5,SMOOTH=LINEAR
```

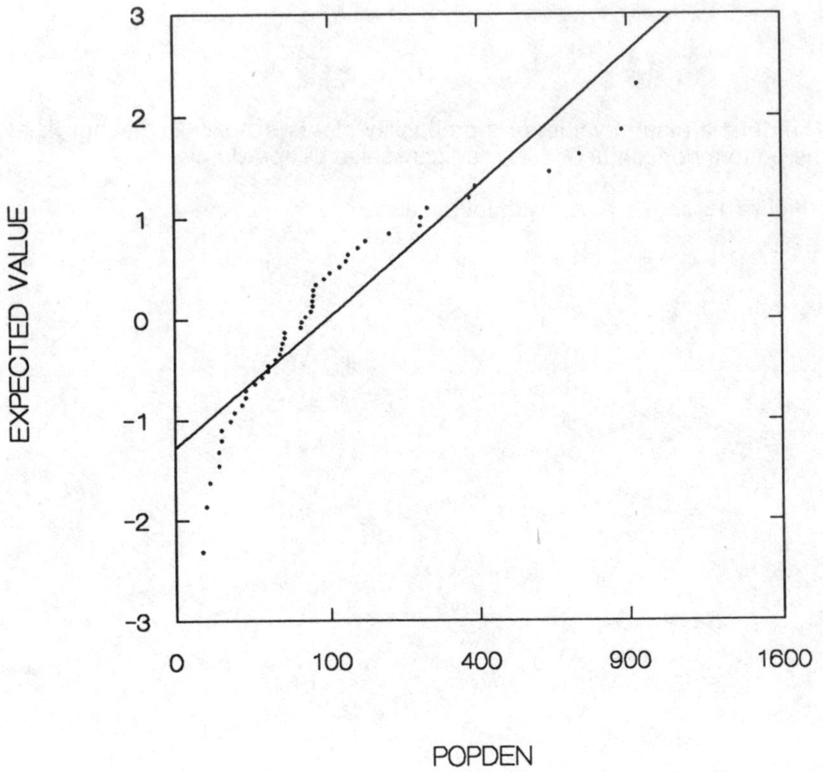

SCALE *(Number of Scales)*

Scales are the numbers which label the tick marks on an axis. The **SCALE** option controls the number of scales drawn in a plot. Its syntax is:

```
SCALE=n
```

where n is an integer from 0 to 4. If n is 0, no scales will be drawn. If n is an integer from 1 to 4, all scales from 1 to n will be drawn. If n is negative, only the scale numbered with the absolute value of n will be drawn. Scales are numbered from 1 to 4 clockwise, beginning with the bottom axis:

```
              3
     0  1  2  3  4  5
     4              4
     3              3
 2   2              2   4
     1              1
     0              0
     0  1  2  3  4  5
              1
```

The default (usual) value for a probability plot is **SCALE=2**, meaning that the bottom horizontal and left vertical scales will be drawn.

Figure 15 shows a plot with four scales.

Figure 15

```
PPLOT  WINTER/SCALE=4
```

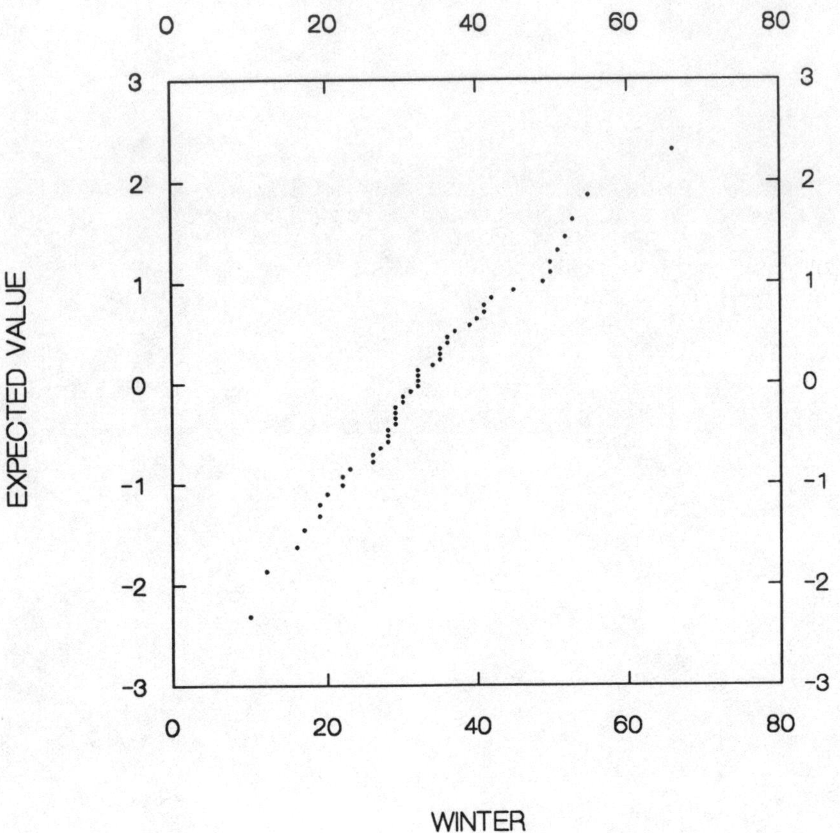

SHORT *(Shortening the Domain of Smoothing)*

Sometimes you can get into trouble by extrapolating beyond the range of your data when smoothing. The linear and quadratic smoothing for probability plots yield curves which extend from the left to the right edges of the plotting frame. If you wish to limit the domain of the smooth to the extreme values of the data, add the **SHORT** option.

Figure 16 shows a plot with a quadratic smooth limited to the range of the data with the **SHORT** option. Compare this to the extrapolated version in Figure 20 below.

Figure 16

```
PPLOT  WINTER/TRANS,SMOOTH=QUAD,SHORT
```

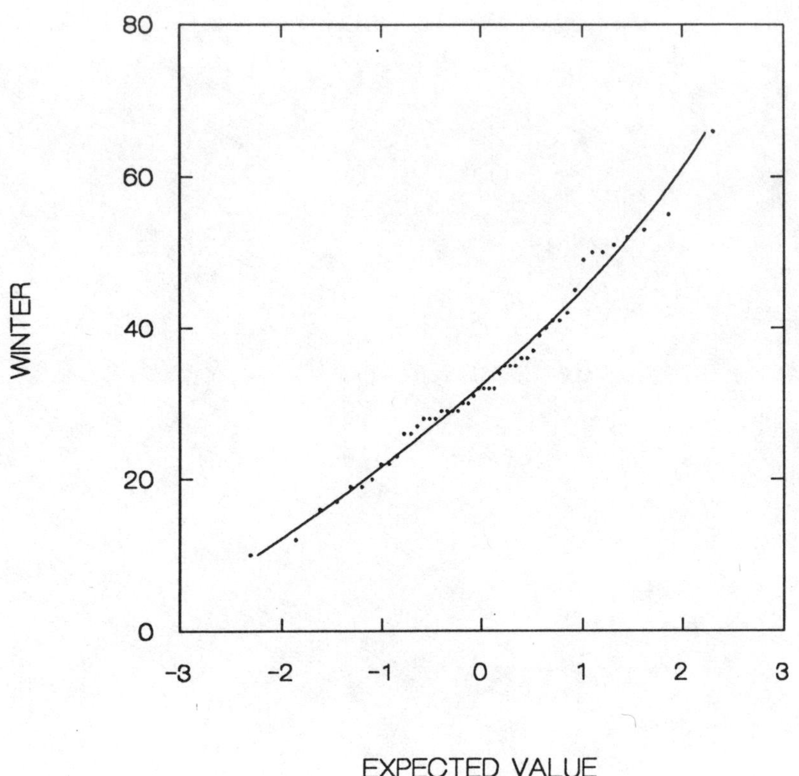

SIZE *(Changing Size of Plotting Symbols)*

You can alter the size of plotting symbols from invisible to as large as your entire graph. The standard value of all symbols is `SIZE=1`. `SIZE=2` produces symbols twice as large as the standard. `SIZE=.5` is half, and so on. Anything equal to or smaller than `SIZE=.001` makes the symbols invisible.

Figure 17 shows a probability plot with symbols half their usual size. I've used hollow circles for the symbols (`SYMBOL=2`).

Figure 17

```
PPLOT  PERSON/SYMBOL=2,SIZE=.5
```

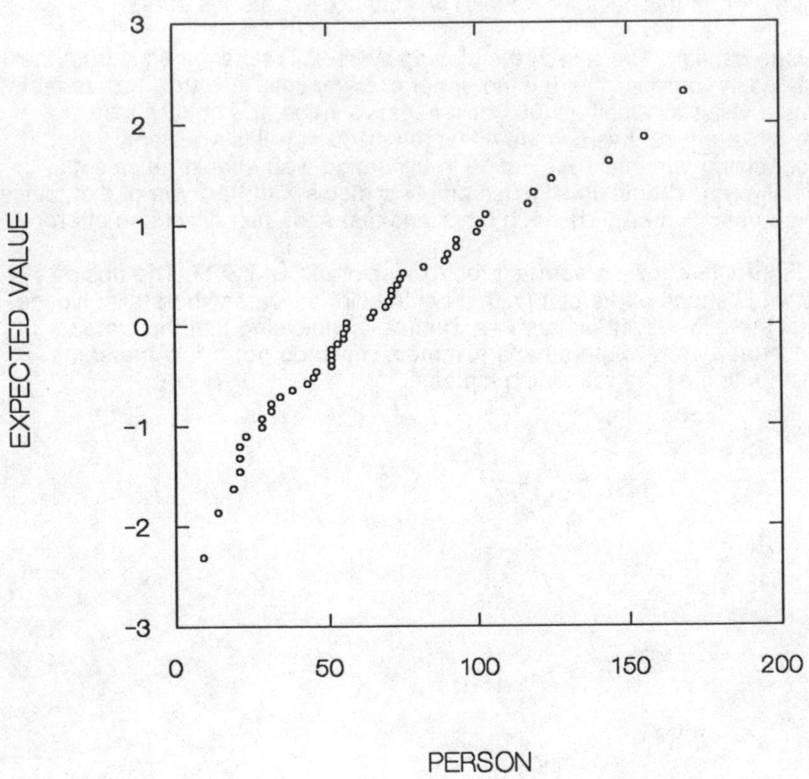

SIZE *(Representing a Variable by Size of Symbols in a Probability Plot)*
You can use the value of a variable in your file to control the size of a plotting symbol. I'm not sure why you'd want to do this, but I saw no reason to prevent you from doing it. Actually, I do have an idea. Suppose you have two variables and you wish to see whether the marginal distribution of one of them is related in some way to the marginal distribution of the other. Here is an example. I took the US file and made a new variable WIN:

```
LET WIN = WINTER/25
```

This brought the values of WIN within 0 and 3. Now it can serve as a **SIZE** variable. Normally, I would square root this variable when using it to determine symbol sizes because we pay more attention to area than diameter. In this case, however, I want to accentuate the effect.

One caution. The size of the plotting symbols is taken directly from the values in your file. There is no upper or lower limit. If your **SIZE** variable has a value as small as .001 or a negative value, the point will be invisible and if it has a value as large as 100, it will fill your entire plot. If your sizing variable does not lie in this range, you should rescale it. Finally, you should usually use empty symbols with this type of plot, since filled ones can occlude each other and make the plot difficult to interpret.

Figure 18 shows a normal probability plot of SUMMER. The upside down U shape of the plot (with a central dip) indicates short tails. Notice that the larger symbols are near both tails, indicating that the states with unusually warm winters have summers which do not follow the same distribution as the remaining states.

Figure 18

`PPLOT   SUMMER/SYMBOL=2,SIZE=WIN`

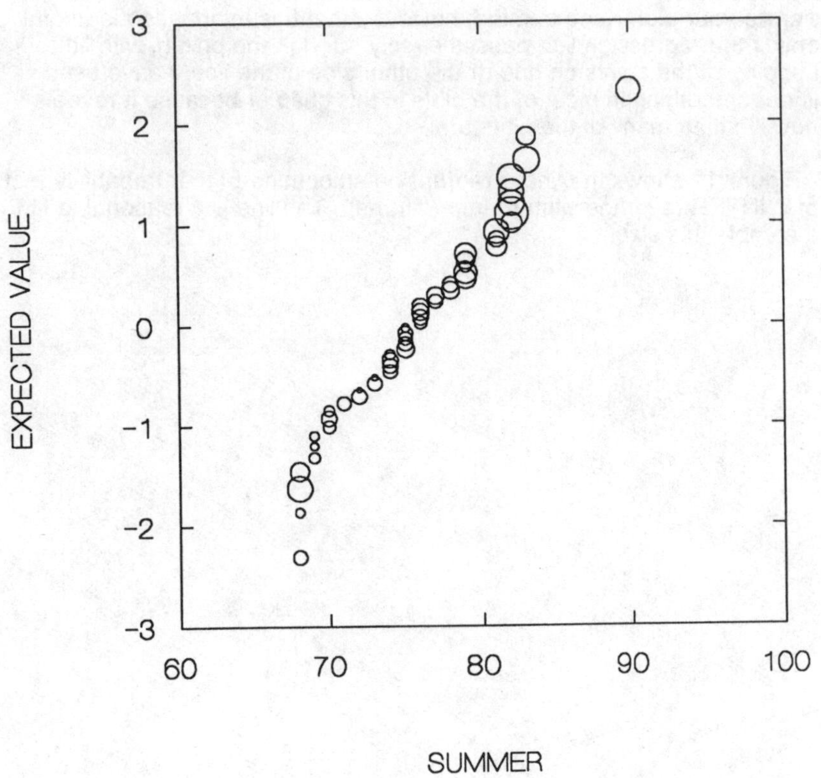

SMOOTH=LINEAR *(Linear Regression Smoothing)*

You can fit a linear regression to your probability plot with the option **SMOOTH=LINEAR**. Regression fits a function to data such that the value predicted by the function at each observed value of X is as close as possible to the observed value of Y at the same value of X. Ordinary linear regression uses a straight line for the function and makes the squared discrepancies between predicted and observed Y values as small as possible. The equation for this function looks like this:

$$Y = a + bX$$

where *a* is a constant term and *b* is a slope coefficient.

The slope and intercept provide rough estimates of the spread and location parameters in most of the distributions in **PPLOT**, provided you **TRANS** your plot. Keep in mind, however, that this information is useful only if the regression line passes evenly through the points, with little bending of the points on one or the other side of the line. I have used linear smoothing in most of the plots in this chapter because it reveals how ill-fitting many of the plots are.

Figure 19 shows the linear regression smoothing of the probability plot of WINTER (average winter temperatures) . The line is a reasonable fit for a sample this size.

Figure 19

`PPLOT   WINTER/TRANS,SMOOTH=LINEAR`

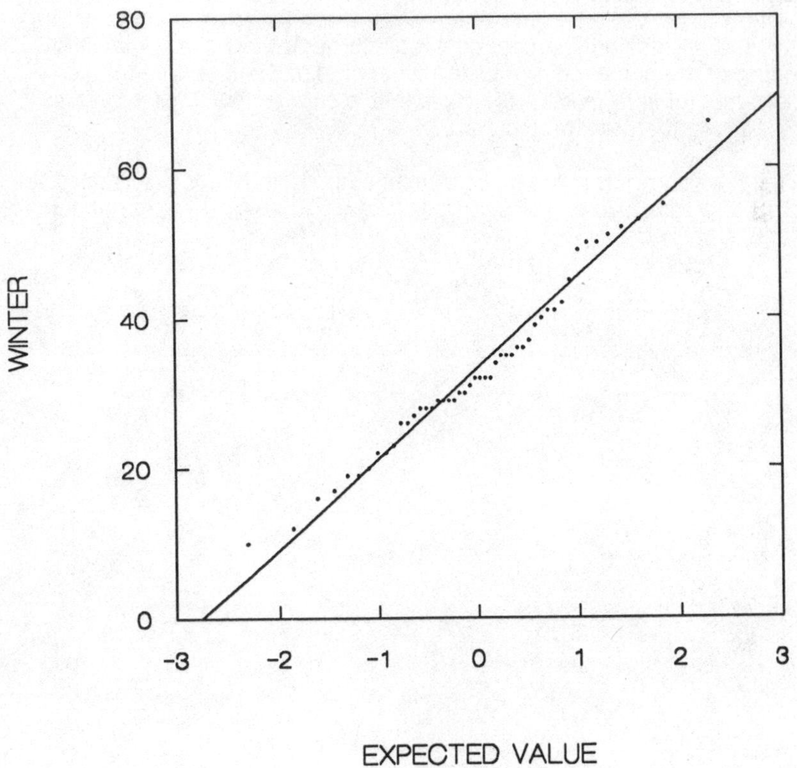

SMOOTH=QUAD *(Quadratic Smoothing)*

You can fit a quadratic regression curve to your data with the SMOOTH=QUAD option. This fits the following type of equation to the data:

$$Y = a + bX + cX^2$$

where *a* is a constant and *b* and *c* are slope coefficients.

You might want to use this option to enhance visually any bendings in your probability plot. The more curved the fit, the poorer fit is the distribution.

Figure 20 shows the quadratic regression of the same data (WINTER) used in Figure 19 for linear smoothing.

Figure 20

```
PPLOT  WINTER/TRANS,SMOOTH=QUAD
```

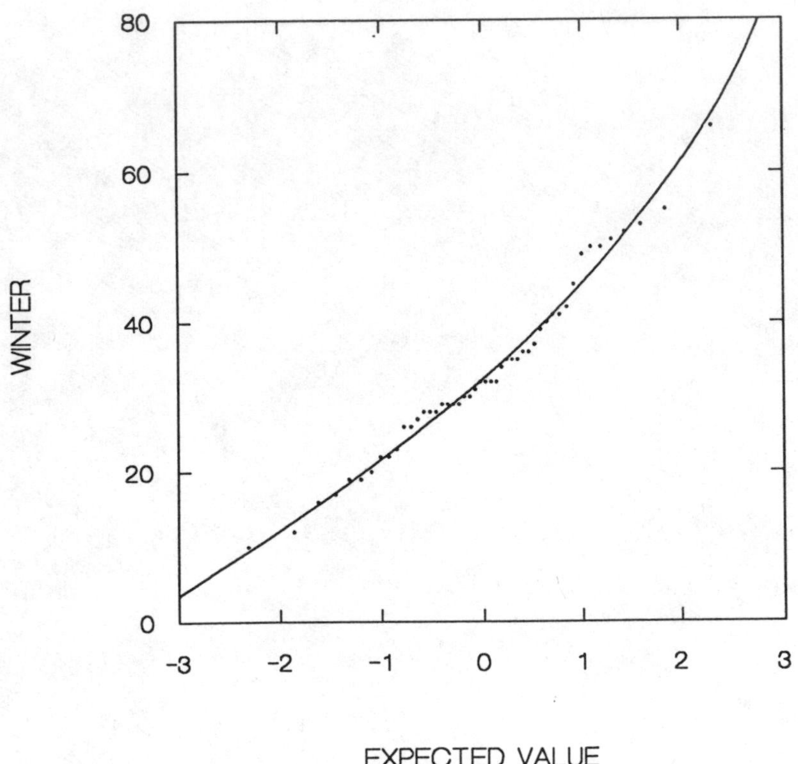

STICK *(Tick Marks Outside Frame)*

SYGRAPH normally places tick marks inside the frame. If you wish tick marks outside the frame, use the **STICK** option.

Figure 21 shows an example of a probability plot with tick marks outside the frame.

Figure 21

```
PPLOT  SUMMER/STICK
```

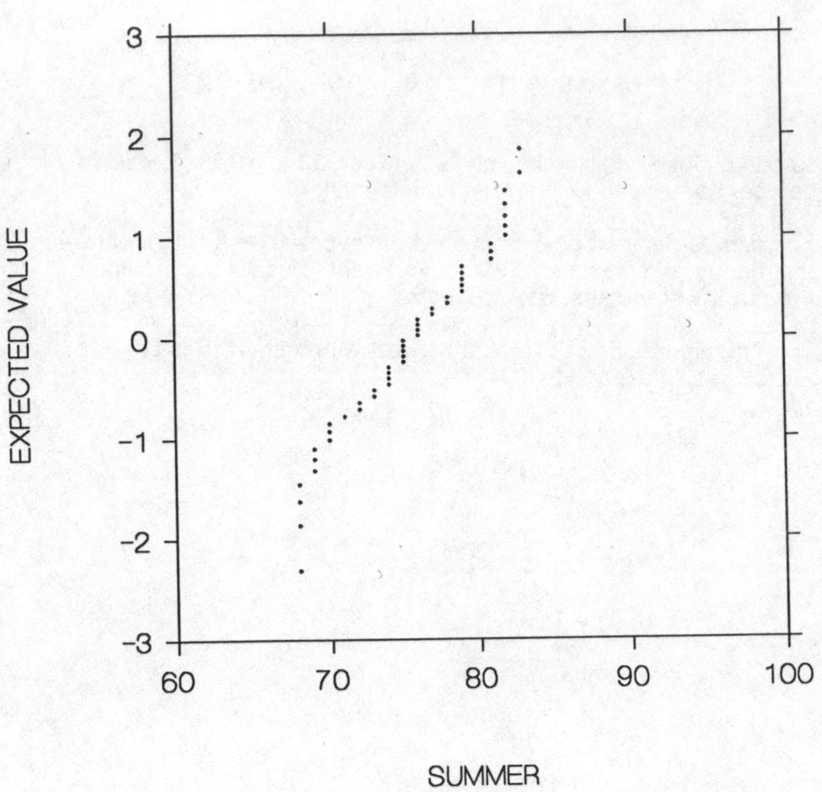

SYMBOL *(Plotting Symbols)*
You can choose a variety of symbols for your probability plot. Just add the option: `SYMBOL=`*n* , where *n* is an integer denoting one of the following symbols:

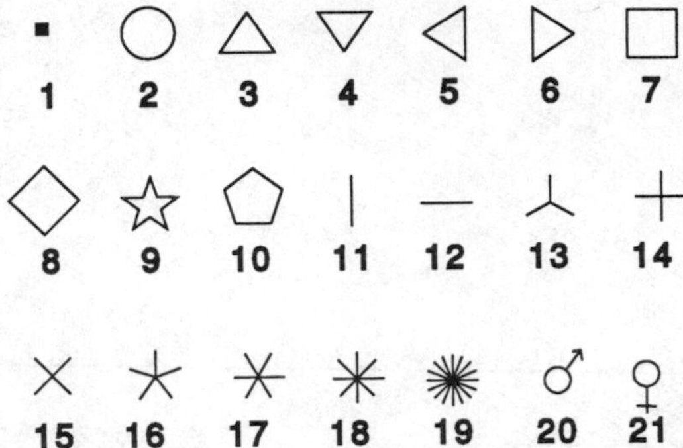

You can choose additional symbols between 32 and 128. These vary by typeface. See Appendix A for further information.

You can use any other symbol on your keyboard by typing it between apostrophes, e.g. `SYMBOL='@'`. If you want to use an apostrophe, surround it with quotes: `SYMBOL="'"`.

The next figure shows a probability plot with half sized (`SIZE=.5`) open circles (`SYMBOL=2`).

Figure 22

```
PPLOT  RAIN/SYMBOL=2,SIZE=.5
```

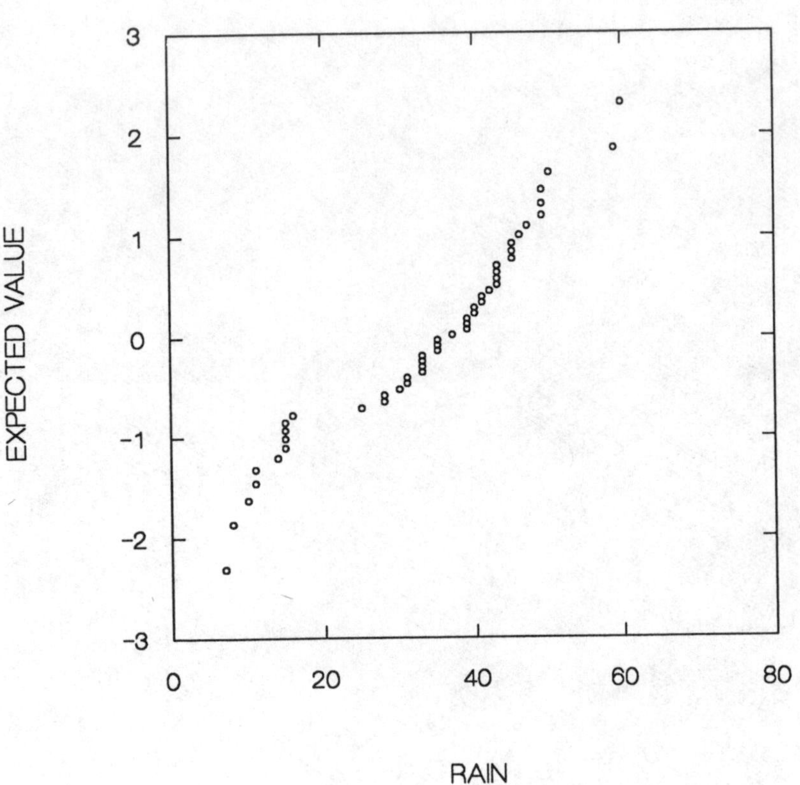

SYMBOL *(Data Based Plotting Symbols)*

You can use a character variable in your data file to determine the plotting symbol for each point. This can be handy when you are trying to identify subgroups or individual cases which are influencing your probability plot.

SYGRAPH uses the first character in a character variable when you use this option. The symbols are centered at their proper locations in the graph.

Figure 23 shows a probability plot of SUMMER (summer temperatures) using the first letter of each state to identify the points. I have used `SIZE=.75` (see `SIZE` option above in this chapter) to reduce the size of the symbols somewhat and prevent them from colliding.

Figure 23

```
PPLOT  SUMMER/SYMBOL=STATE$,SIZE=.5
```

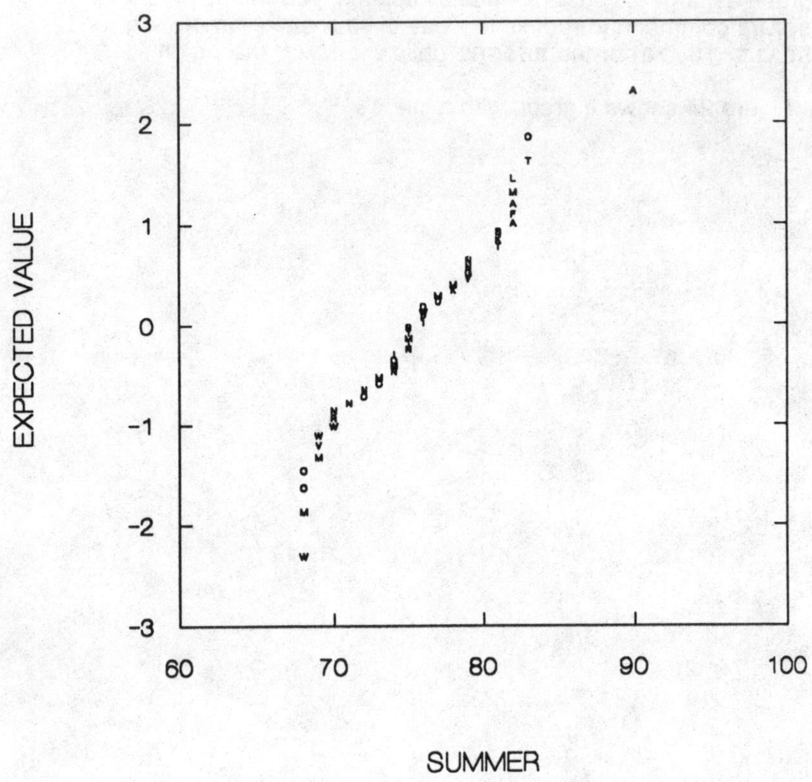

TITLE *(Graph Title)*

You can place a title at the top center of your probability plot with the **TITLE** option:

```
TITLE='Gamma Probability Plot of Recidivism'
TITLE="(ABC'-D)'(X'X)(ABC'-D)"
TITLE='Distribution of "Excellent" Responses'
```

The text must be surrounded by quotes (") or apostrophes ('). If your text includes apostrophes, as in the second example, surround it with quotes. If it includes quotes, as in the third example, surround it with apostrophes.

On some display devices the title will run off the top of the page because the standard display window is chosen to make the labels and graph as large as possible. If this happens, you will have to use the **SCALE** command to reduce the size of your entire graph (e.g. **SCALE=70,70**) or the **HEIGHT** option to lower the height.

Figure 24 shows a graph with a title.

Figure 24

```
TYPE=HERSHEY
PPLOT  WINTER/TITLE='Winter  Temperatures'
```

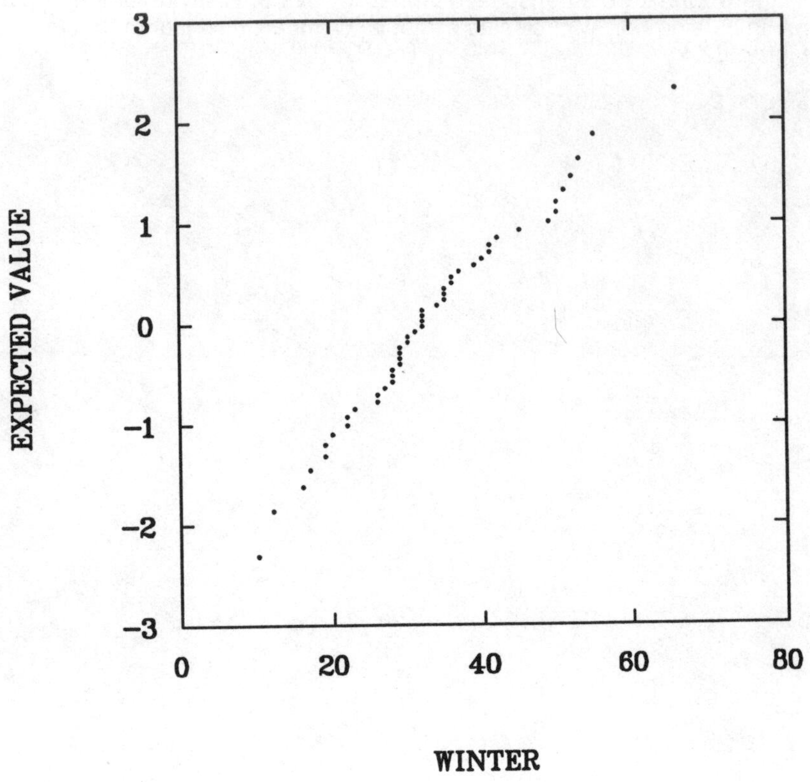

TRANS *(Transposing a Probability Plot)*

You can transpose a probability plot with the **TRANS** option. **TRANS** affects everything in a graph. **XLABEL** becomes **YLABEL**, **XTICK** becomes **YTICK**, and so on. In other words, specify a graph as you would ordinarily and then add the **TRANS** option. Everything will be transposed appropriately, including the labels and scales.

As you can see from many of the examples in this chapter, you may want to use the **TRANS** option frequently to be able to estimate the spread and location of distributions by examining the slope and intercept of the line through the points. Since there is not universal agreement on which way the probability plot should be, you can have it either way in SYGRAPH with the **TRANS** option.

Figure 25 shows a transposed probability plot of RAIN (average annual rainfall) using hollow circles as symbols. Compare this plot to that in Figure 22.

Figure 25

```
PPLOT   RAIN/SYMBOL=2,SIZE=.5,TRANS
```

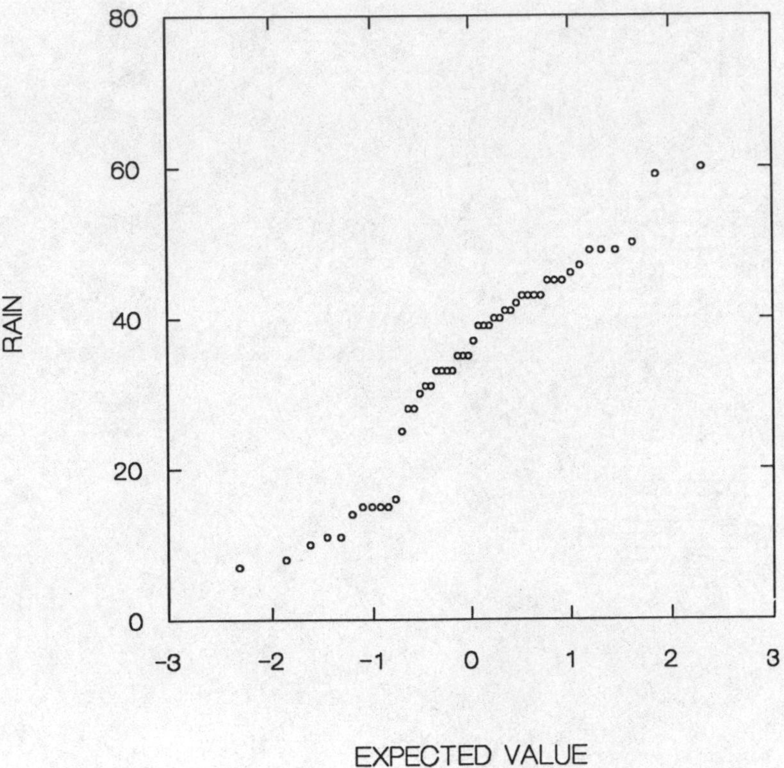

UNIFORM *(Uniform Distribution Probability Plot)*

The UNIFORM option produces a uniform probability plot. The uniform distribution has two parameters:

$$f(y) = (y - m)/s$$

where m is a location and s is a spread parameter. If you use the **TRANS** option, then the slope of the line fitting the points estimates spread and the intercept estimates location.

Figure 26 shows an example. I used the uniform random number generator in SYSTAT to produce 500 uniform random numbers:

```
SAVE  URAND
RSEED=1339
LET  X  =  URN
REPEAT  500
RUN
```

Figure 26

`PPLOT X/UNIFORM`

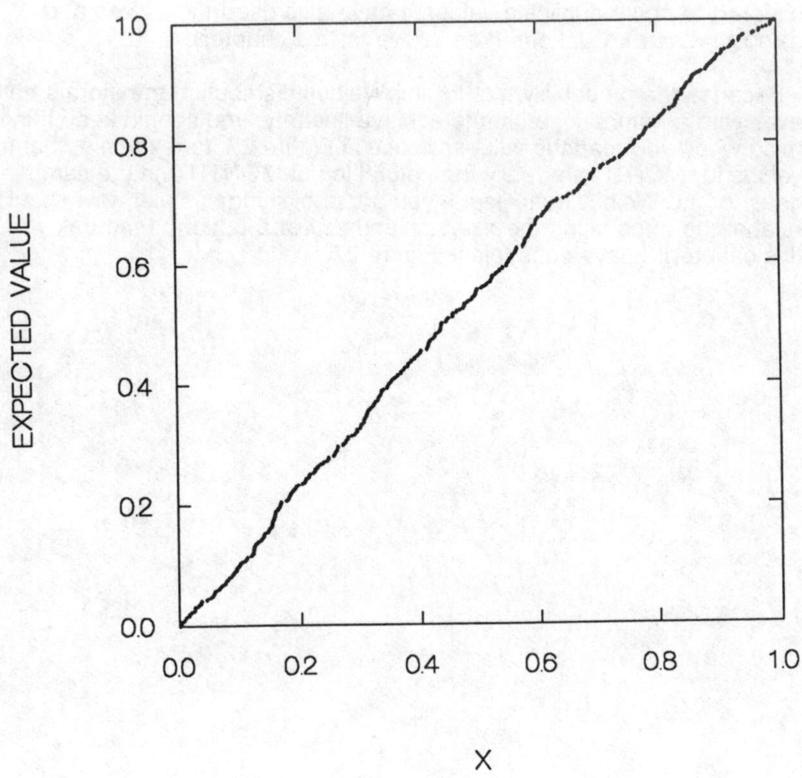

WEIBULL *(Weibull Distribution)*

You can plot your data against a Weibull distribution with the **WEIBULL** option. The Weibull is a powered exponential distribution:

$$f(y) = 1 - \exp\{-(y/s)^t\}$$

where *s* is a spread and *t* is a power (or shape) parameter. In the probability plot, the slope of the line through the plotted points is an estimate of the inverse of *t* and the intercept is an estimate of the log of *s*. Both axes in the plot are on a natural log scale.

Figure 27 shows a Weibull distribution probability plot of the recidivism data used in the **EXPO** option above in this chapter. Notice that I have used the **WEIGHT** command (see above in the general commands chapter) to cover duplicate values. I have also used the **TRANS** and **SMOOTH=LINEAR** options (see above in this chapter).

Because the probability plot for the Weibull distribution transforms both axes with a natural logarithm to achieve linearity, you should keep this in mind when you read the values. Notice in Figure 27, for example, that the values for MONTH are really the natural log of MONTH and the same goes for the Weibull quantiles. If you are publishing this plot, you should relabel the axes using the **XLABEL** and **YLABEL** options (see below in this chapter). I have done this in Figure 27.

Figure 27

```
WEIGHT=COUNT
PPLOT  MONTH,
  /TRANS,SMOOTH=LINEAR,WEIBULL,
    XLABEL='Log  of  Recidivism  Month',
    YLABEL='Log  Weibull  Quantiles'
```

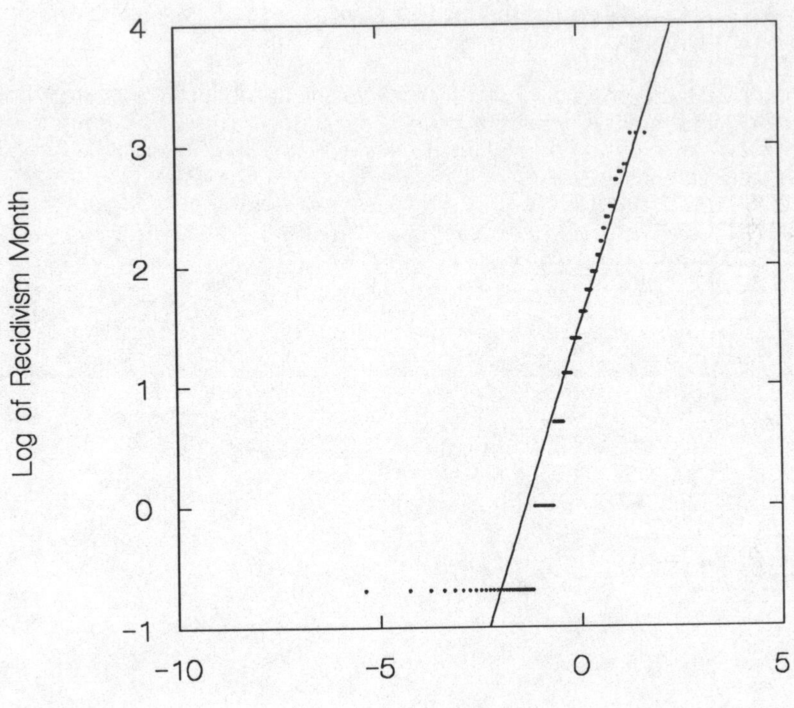

WIDTH *(Physical Width of Plot)*

You can control the physical width of your plot with the **WIDTH** option. It works like this:

```
WIDTH=50%        (or WIDTH=50)
WIDTH=4IN
WIDTH=10CM
```

The first example specifies percent of display width. The second specifies inches, and the third centimeters.

When you use the **WIDTH** option, you probably also want to use **HEIGHT**, which works exactly the same way (see above in this chapter). The following graph shows how to use them together.

Figure 28

```
PPLOT  SUMMER/HEIGHT=2IN,WIDTH=4IN
```

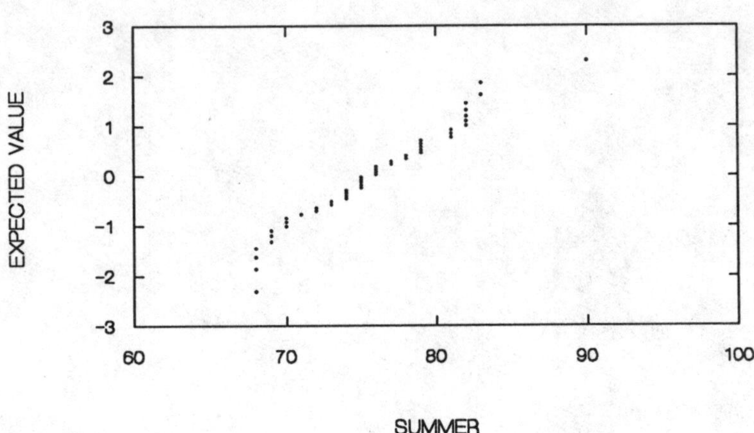

XLABEL,YLABEL *(Labeling a Plot)*

Probability plots are usually labeled with the names of the variables you use in the **PPLOT** command. If you want different labels, use the **XLABEL** and/or **YLABEL** option(s), e.g.:

```
XLABEL='Rainfall'
YLABEL='Exponential  Quantiles'
XLABEL="Roger's  Wacky  Data"
XLABEL='Cost  of  "Widgets"  Bid'
YLABEL='  '
```

The label text must be surrounded by quotes (") or apostrophes ('). If your text includes apostrophes, as in the third example, surround it with quotes. If it includes quotes, as in the fourth example, surround it with apostrophes. The last example shows how to remove labels from your graph. Just assign a blank (' ') to your label.

Figure 29 shows an example of a relabeled probability plot. Notice that the labels describe the axes before transposition.

Figure 29

```
WEIGHT=COUNT
PPLOT  MONTH,
  /TRANS,SMOOTH=LINEAR,GAMMA=.25,
   XLABEL='Failure  Month',
   YLABEL='Gamma  Quantiles'
```

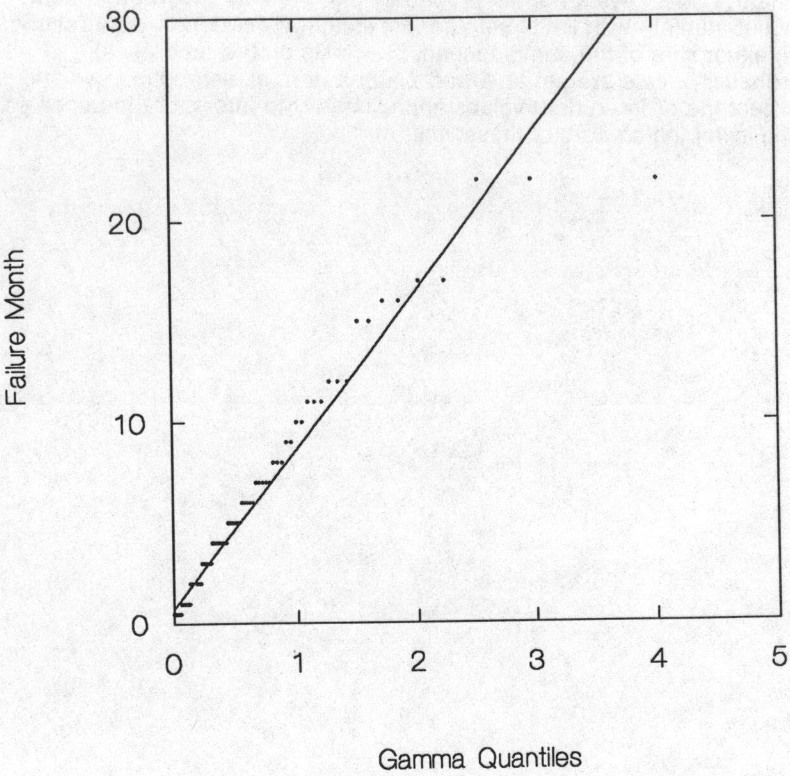

XLIMIT, YLIMIT *(Control Limits)*

You can add dashed lines to mark limits on each axis of a probability plot. The **LIMIT** option works this way:

```
PPLOT  X  /  XLIMIT=2,6,YLIMIT=-2,2
```

Notice that you must specify two numbers for each limit (upper and lower). They need not be in order. Limits will not be plotted for numbers outside the extremes of the specified axes. Thus, if you want to plot only one limit (dashed line) on an axis, type something like this:

```
PPLOT  X  /  XLIMIT=2,-9999
```

Figure 30 shows a normal probability plot of RAIN (average annual inches rainfall) with limits set at approximately two standard deviations on either side of the sample mean. The limits on the theoretical probability scale are set at -2 and 2. For a normal distribution, we should expect the ordered data values approximately to intersect the upper right and lower left corners of these limits.

Figure 30

```
PPLOT  RAIN/XLIMIT=6.2,61.4,YLIMIT=-2,2
```

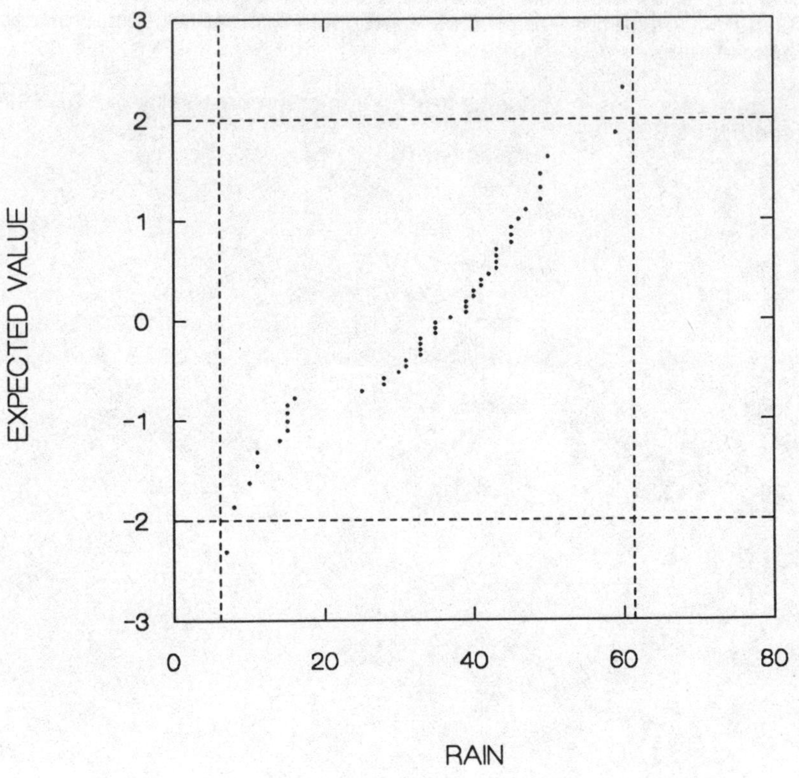

XMIN,YMIN,XMAX,YMAX *(Scale Limits)*

SYGRAPH usually determines minimum and maximum scale values from the data in your file. If you wish to override this feature, use the **MIN/MAX** options. **YMIN** and **YMAX** control the lower and upper limits of the vertical scale. **XMIN** and **XMAX** do the same for the horizontal scale.

If you set the **MIN** and **MAX** options inside the range of your data, you will zoom in to get a closer view, but you will eliminate certain data values from your plot.

Some settings of **MIN** and **MAX** will cause scale values to become messy (not integers or round numbers). In these cases, you may have to fiddle with the **XTICK**, **YTICK**, **ZTICK** options (see below in this chapter) to get a number of tick marks which yields round scale values. You may also have to use the **FORMAT** command (see Part 2, Chapter 1, "General Commands") to print an appropriate number of decimal places to represent your scale values.

Figure 31 zooms in on the central portion of the probability plot of RAIN (see Figure 30).

Figure 31

```
PPLOT   RAIN/XMIN=20,XMAX=50,YMIN=-1,YMAX=1
```

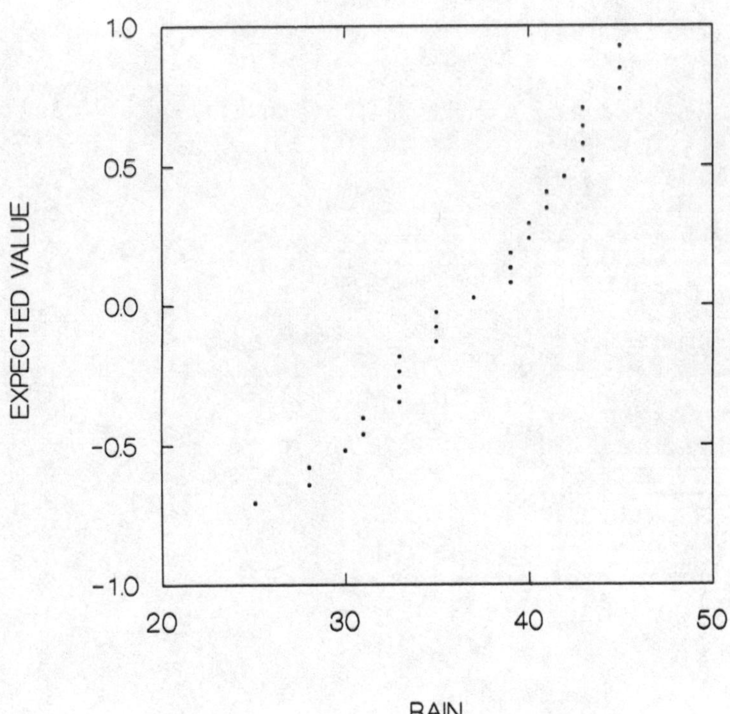

XPIP,YPIP *(Pip Marks)*

Pip marks are half sized tick marks. SYGRAPH normally omits pip marks from probability plots. The `PIP` option adds them. Just specify the number you want. `XPIP` controls the X axis, `YPIP` the Y axis. If you log a scale (see `LOG` option above in this chapter) the pip marks will be logarithmically spaced.

Figure 32 shows an example with 10 pip marks on the horizontal axis and 5 on the vertical.

Figure 32

```
PPLOT  WINTER/XPIP=10,YPIP=5
```

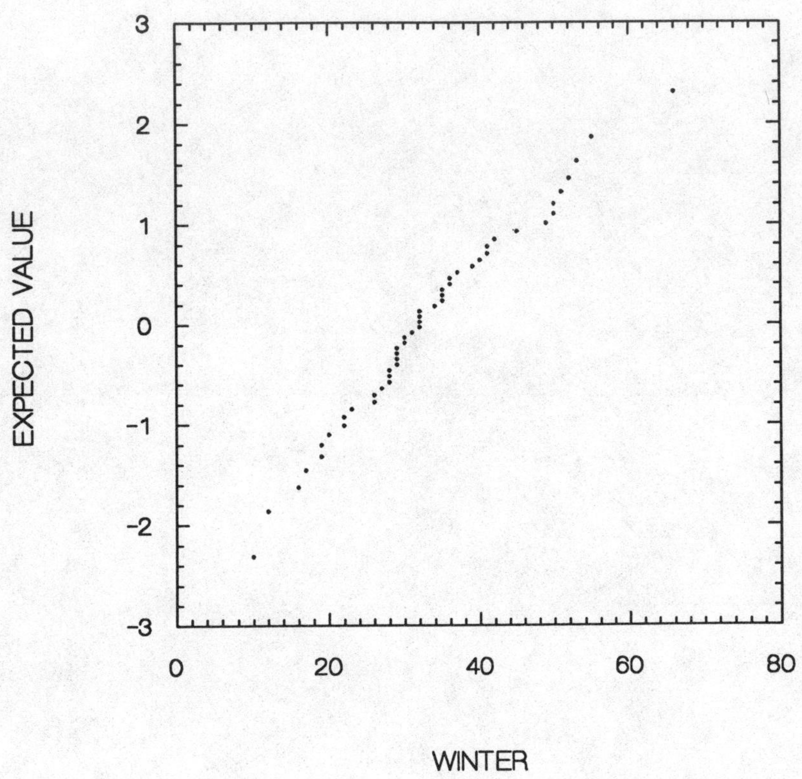

XTICK,YTICK *(Number of Tick Marks)*

SYGRAPH examines your data to determine how many tick marks to use on the axes of a probability plot. If you wish to modify this value, use the `TICK` option with a number. `XTICK` refers to the X axis and `YTICK` to the Y. For example, `YTICK=8` will force the vertical axis to have 8 tick marks.

Figure 33 shows an example of a probability plot with 6 tick marks on the horizontal axis.

Figure 33

```
PPLOT  INCOME/XTICK=6
```

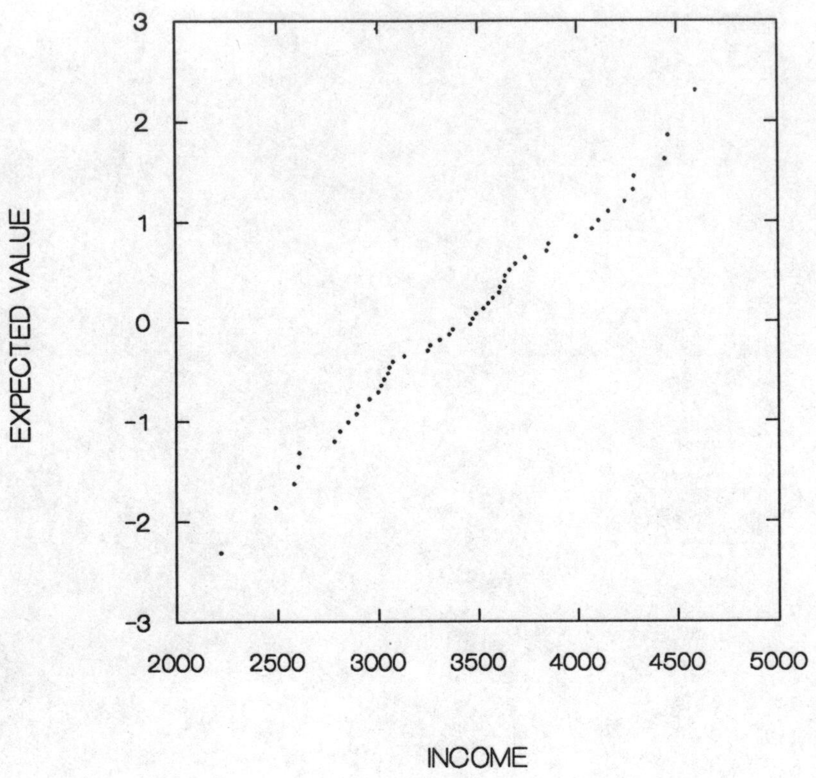

Chapter 12

QPLOT

The QPLOT command produces **quantile plots**, or **Q plots** (Gnanadesikan, 1977). We have seen how probability plots compare a sample to a theoretical probability distribution. Sometimes we want to compare a sample to its own quantiles or two samples to each other. The quantile of a sample is the data point corresponding to a given fraction of the data.

Quantile Plots

A single sample quantile plot looks like a cumulative sample distribution function. A sample from a normal distribution, for example, should plot in an S, or ogive shape. A sample from a uniform distribution should plot roughly as a straight line. Samples from skewed distributions should plot as asymmetric functions.

The next figure shows a Q plot for INCOME (per-capita income) from the US dataset. The plot is slightly S shaped, indicating lumpiness in the middle and two tails.

Figure 1

```
QPLOT INCOME
```

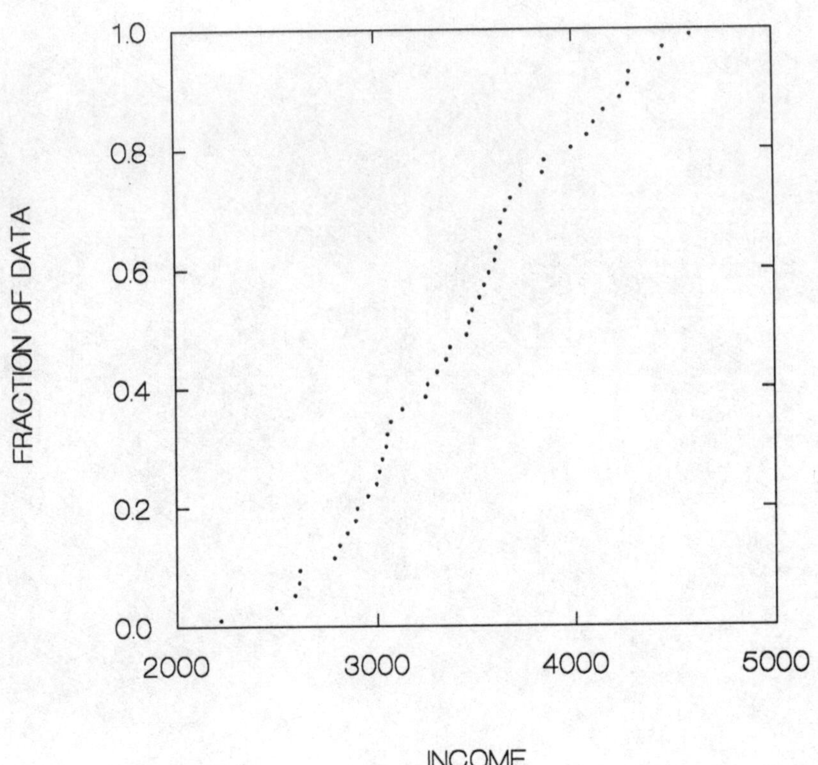

Quantile-Quantile Plots

A two-sample quantile plot relates two sample distributions. It should look approximately like a straight line if the two samples are from the same distribution. Otherwise, the quantile plot can reveal the area of the distribution where they differ the most. These are sometimes called Q-Q plots.

Here is a Q-Q plot of PERSON (person crimes) against PROPERTY (property crimes) from the US dataset.

Figure 2

QPLOT PERSON*PROPERTY

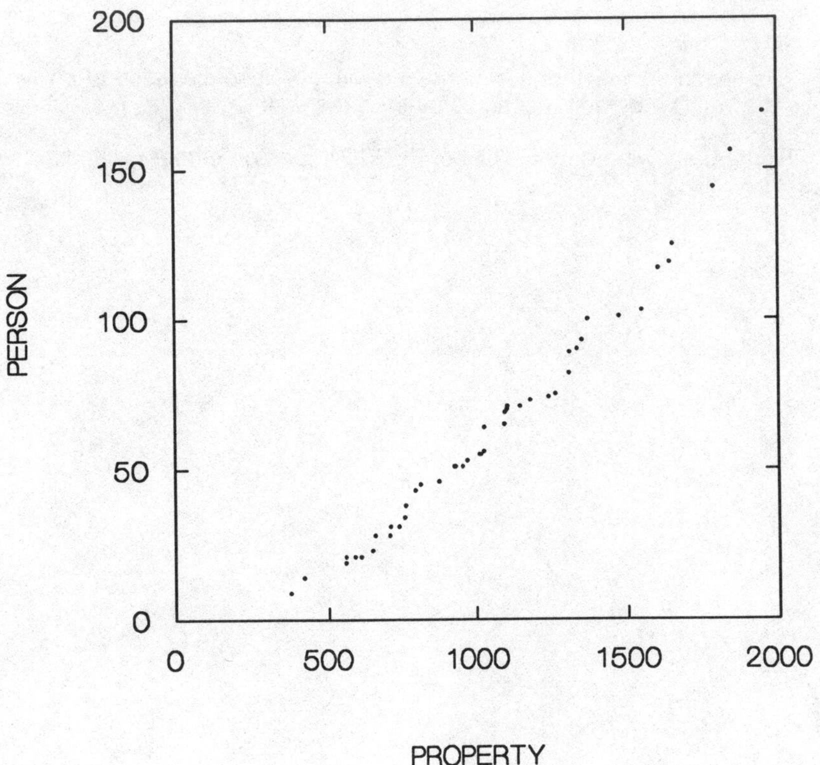

AXES *(Number of Axes)*

The **AXES** option controls the number of axes drawn in a quantile plot. Its syntax is:

```
AXES=n
```

where *n* is an integer from 0 to 4. If *n* is 0, no axes will be drawn. If *n* is an integer from 1 to 4, all axes from 1 to *n* will be drawn. Axes are numbered from 1 to 4 clockwise, beginning with the bottom axis:

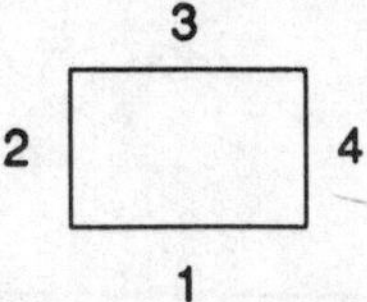

If *n* is negative, only the axis numbered with the absolute value of *n* will be drawn. The default (usual) value for **AXES** is 4.

Figure 3 shows a quantile plot of PERSON (person crimes) with two axes.

Figure 3

```
QPLOT  PERSON/AXES=2
```

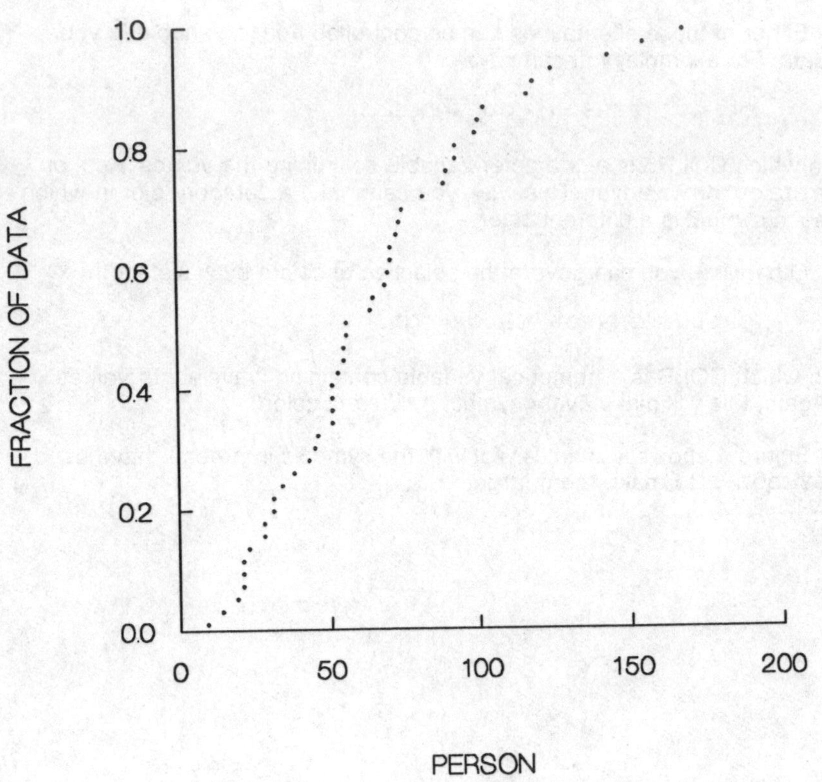

COLOR *(Setting Color of Symbols)*

You can choose a color for your symbols with the **COLOR** option. Choose either a name or a wavelength in nanometers. Possible colors and their approximate nanometer wavelengths are: **RED** (615), **ORANGE** (590), **YELLOW** (575), **GREEN** (505), **BLUE** (480), **VIOLET** (450). You may also name **BLACK**, **WHITE**, **GRAY**, and **BROWN**. The following command will make all symbols in the graph red:

```
QPLOT   PERSON/COLOR=RED
```

You can also specify color in nanometers wavelength. The following example will make all the symbols greenish:

```
QPLOT   PERSON/COLOR=540
```

Either of these alternatives can be controlled from a variable in your data. For example, you can say:

```
QPLOT   PERSON/COLOR=COLR$
```

in which COLR$ is a character variable containing the values '**RED**' or '**YELLOW**' or whatever. This way, you can make a category plot in which each symbol is a different color.

Otherwise, you can govern the selection of colors by wavelength:

```
QPLOT   PERSON/COLOR=COLR
```

in which COLR is a numerical variable containing wavelength values. Again, this will make every symbol a different color.

Figure 4 shows a quantile plot with the symbols in green. I have used **SYMBOL=2** to make them larger.

Figure 4

```
QPLOT   INCOME/COLOR=GREEN,SYMBOL=2,FILL=1
```

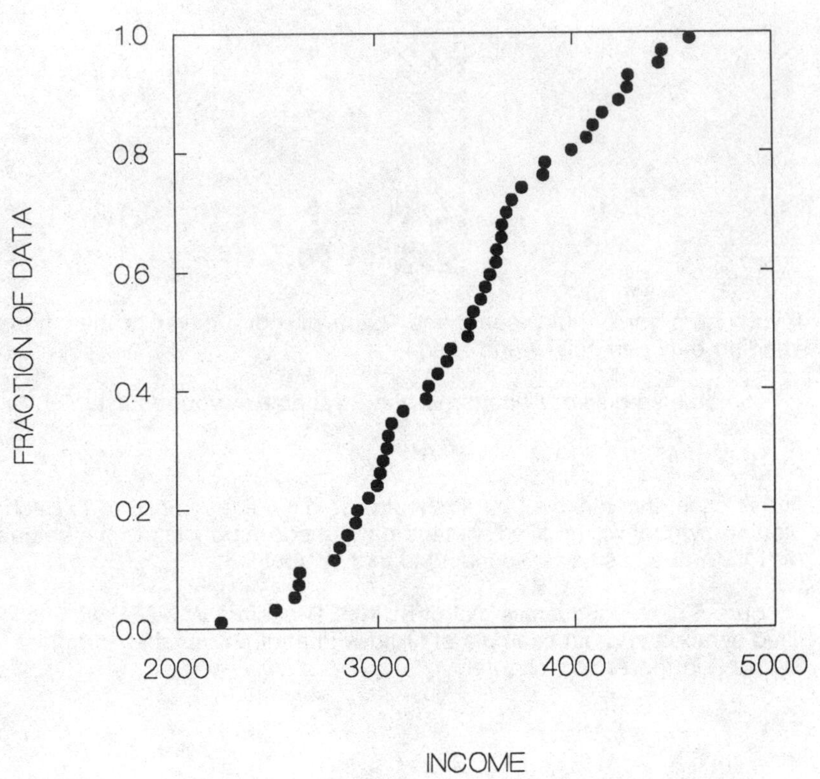

FILL *(Filling symbols)*

You can fill symbols with different patterns. The **FILL** option works this way:

```
QPLOT   INCOME/FILL=2
```

The number you choose after "**FILL=**" determines the type of fill pattern. Here are the possibilities:

= 0

= 1

= 2

= 3

= 4

= 5

= 6

= 7

If you use a number between 0 and 1, you will get an even gradation of shading between hollow and filled.

You can also govern fill patterns with a variable in your dataset:

```
QPLOT   INCOME/FILL=MYFIL
```

In this case, the variable MYFIL should contain values from 0 to 7. Each plotting symbol will be filled with the pattern corresponding to the value in MYFIL for the case corresponding to that symbol.

Figure 5 shows a quantile plot of SUMMER against WINTER with solid filled symbols. For an example of filling with another variable, compare Figure 6 in the **PPLOT** chapter.

Figure 5

```
QPLOT   SUMMER*WINTER/SYMBOL=2,SIZE=.5,FILL
```

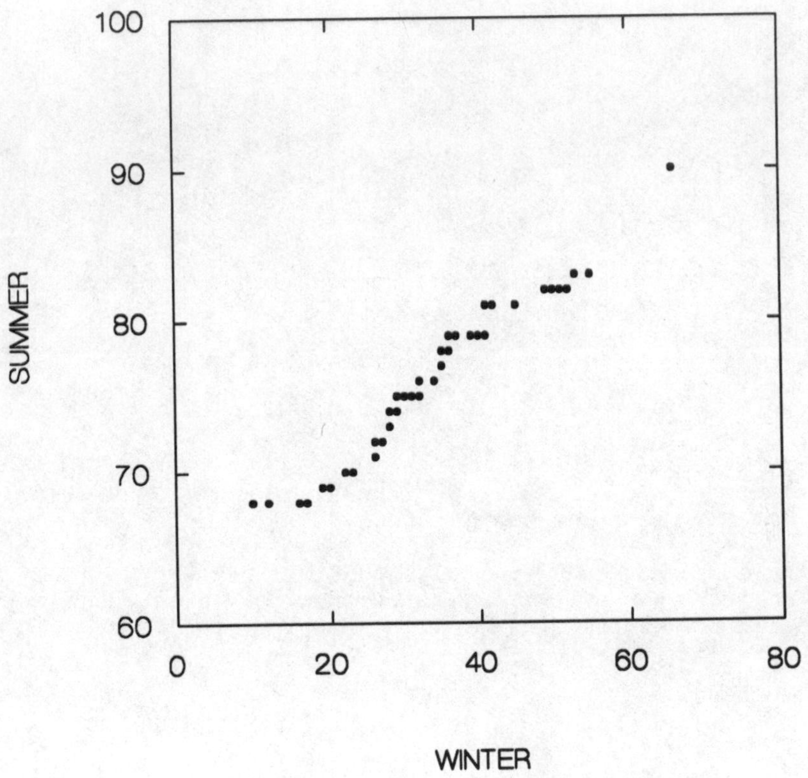

GRID *(Grid Marks)*

You can add grid marks to plots with the **GRID** option. The possible values are:

```
GRID=1      (vertical grid marks)
GRID=2      (horizontal grid marks)
GRID=3      (horizontal and vertical grid marks)
```

Figure 6 shows an example with vertical and horizontal grid marks. I have added **SYMBOL=2** to highlight the data.

Figure 6

```
QPLOT   SUMMER*WINTER/GRID=3,SYMBOL=2,FILL
```

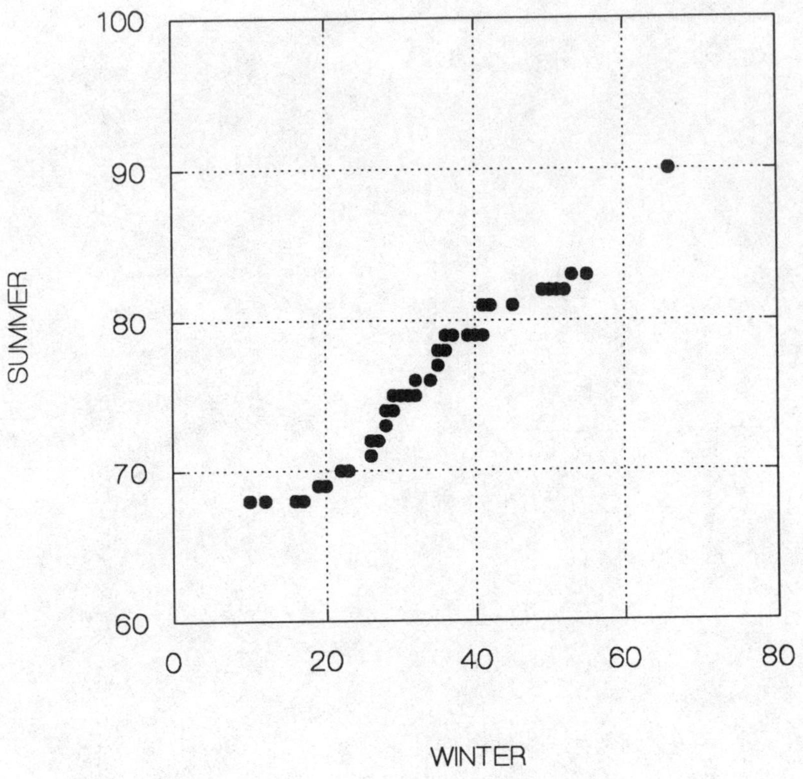

HEIGHT *(Physical Height of Plot)*

You can control the physical height of your plot with the **HEIGHT** option. It works like this:

```
HEIGHT=50%        (or HEIGHT=50)
HEIGHT=4IN
HEIGHT=10CM
```

The first example specifies percent of display height. The second specifies inches, and the third centimeters.

When you use the **HEIGHT** option, you probably also want to use **WIDTH**, which works exactly the same way (see below in this chapter). The following graph shows how to use them together.

Figure 7

`QPLOT   SUMMER/HEIGHT=4IN,WIDTH=3IN`

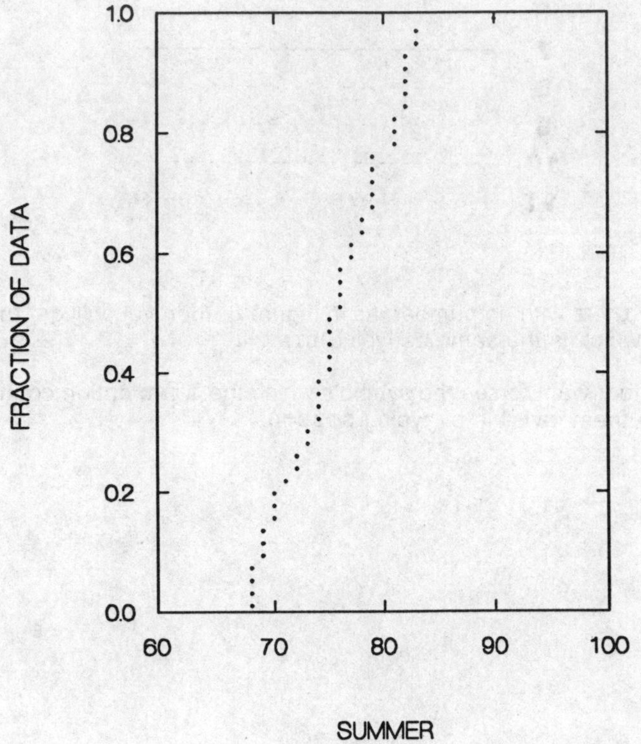

LINE *(Line Graphs)*

When you have only a few data points in a quantile plot, it sometimes helps to connect them with a line. This is easy to do in SYGRAPH. Just use the `LINE` option. You may choose from 11 different types of lines by typing `LINE=`*n* , where *n* is one of the following numbers:

1
2
3
4
5
6
7
8
9
10
11

If you type `LINE` with no number, as in Figure 8, then you will get the solid line, which is the same as typing `LINE=1`.

If you do not want to see the symbols which the `LINE` option connects, then make them invisible by typing `SIZE=0`.

Figure 8

```
QPLOT  RAIN/LINE,SIZE=0
```

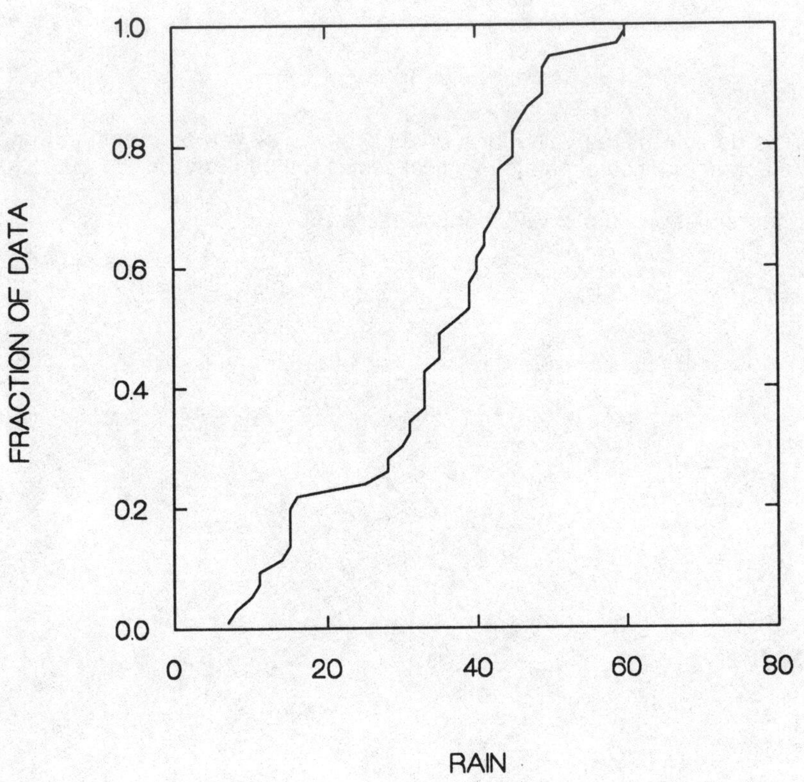

SCALE *(Number of Scales)*

Scales are the numbers which label the tick marks on an axis. The **SCALE** option controls the number of scales drawn in a plot. Its syntax is:

```
SCALE=n
```

where *n* is an integer from 0 to 4. If *n* is 0, no scales will be drawn. If *n* is an integer from 1 to 4, all scales from 1 to *n* will be drawn. If *n* is negative, only the scale numbered with the absolute value of *n* will be drawn. Scales are numbered from 1 to 4 clockwise, beginning with the bottom axis:

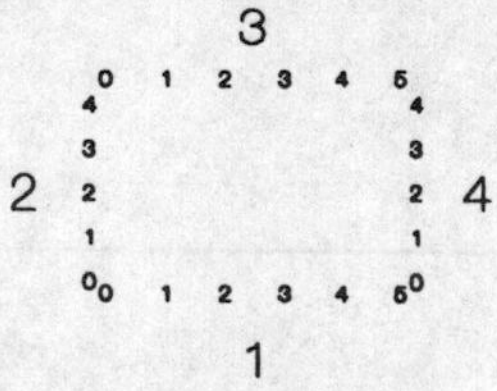

```
                3
      0   1   2   3   4   5
      4                   4
      3                   3
   2  2                   2  4
      1                   1
      0 0  1   2   3   4  5 0
                1
```

The default (usual) value for a quantile plot is **SCALE=2**, meaning that the bottom horizontal and left vertical scales will be drawn.

Figure 9 shows a plot with four scales.

Figure 9

```
QPLOT SUMMER*WINTER/SCALE=4
```

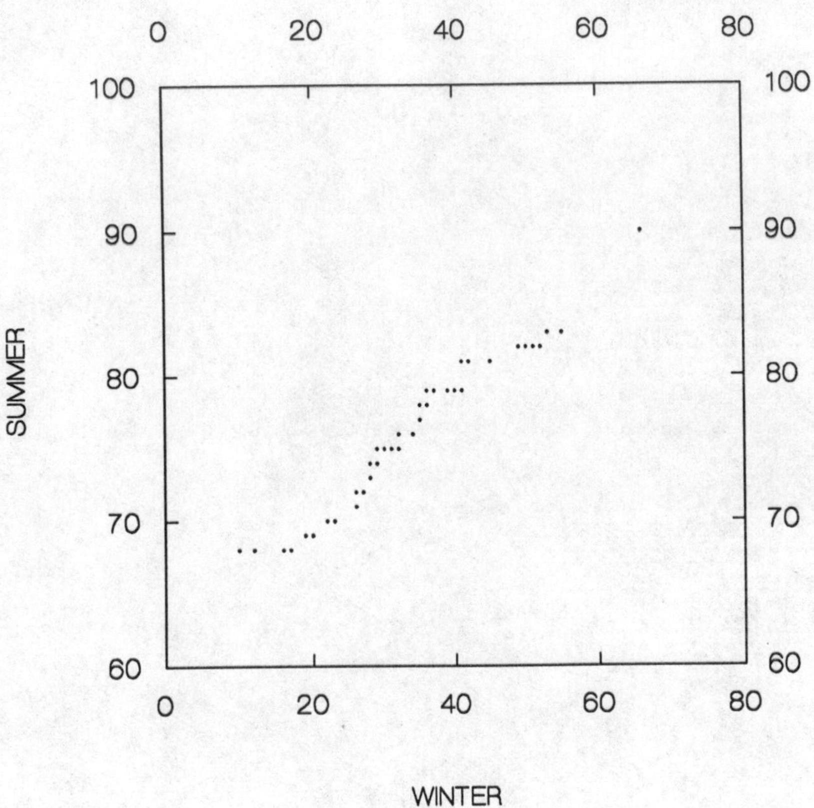

SHORT *(Shortening the Domain of Smoothing)*

Sometimes you can get into trouble by extrapolating beyond the range of your data when smoothing. The linear and quadratic smoothing for quantile plots yield curves which extend from the left to the right edges of the plotting frame. If you wish to limit the domain of the smooth to the extreme values of the data, add the **SHORT** option.

Figure 10 shows a plot with a quadratic smooth limited to the range of the data with the **SHORT** option. Compare this to the extrapolated version in Figure 14 below.

Figure 10

```
QPLOT  PERSON/SMOOTH=QUAD,SHORT
```

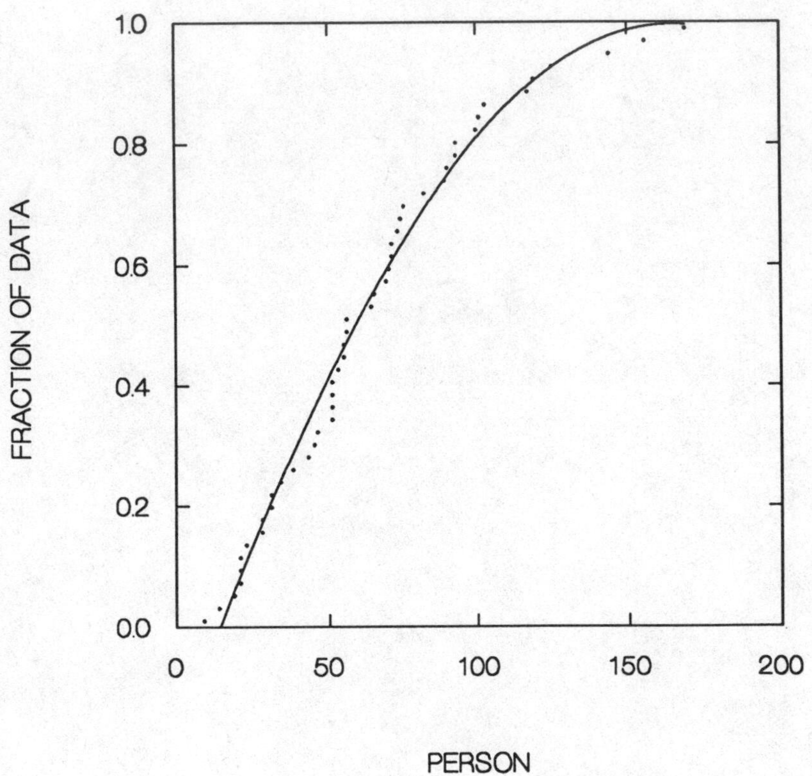

SIZE *(Changing Size of Plotting Symbols)*

You can alter the size of plotting symbols from invisible to as large as your entire graph. The standard value of all symbols is **SIZE=1**. **SIZE=2** produces symbols twice as large as the standard. **SIZE=.5** is half, and so on. **SIZE=0** makes the symbols invisible.

Figure 11 shows a quantile plot with symbols half their usual size. I've used hollow circles for the symbols (**SYMBOL=2**).

Figure 11

```
QPLOT POPDEN/SYMBOL=2,SIZE=.5
```

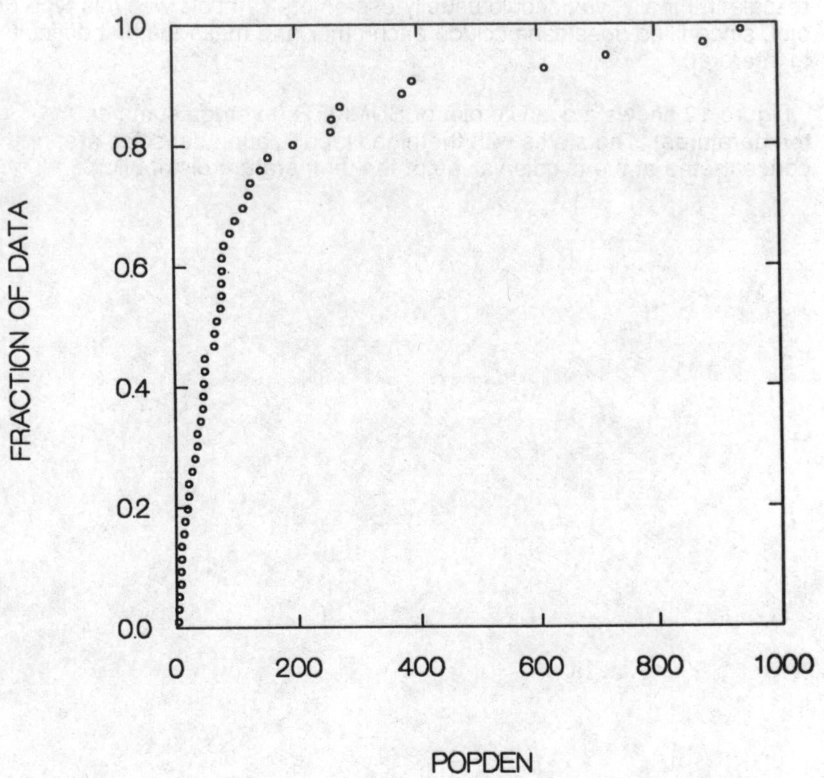

SIZE *(Representing a Variable by Size of Symbols in a Probability Plot)*

You can use the value of a variable in your file to control the size of a plotting symbol. See the **PPLOT** chapter for an example of this feature in probability plots. Here is an example for quantile plots. I took the US file and made a new variable DEN:

```
LET DEN = 4*SQR(POPDEN/1000)
```

This brought the values of DEN within 0 and 4. Now it can serve as a **SIZE** variable. Remember, the size of the plotting symbols is taken directly from the values in your file. There is no upper or lower limit. If your **SIZE** variable has a value as small as .001 or a negative value, the point will be invisible and if it has a value as large as 100, it will fill your entire plot. If your sizing variable does not lie in this range, you should rescale it. Finally, you should usually use empty symbols with this type of plot, since filled ones can occlude each other and make the plot difficult to interpret.

Figure 12 shows a quantile plot of SUMMER (average summer temperatures). The states with the highest population densities are concentrated at the middle values of the temperature distribution.

Figure 12

```
QPLOT  SUMMER/SYMBOL=2,SIZE=DEN
```

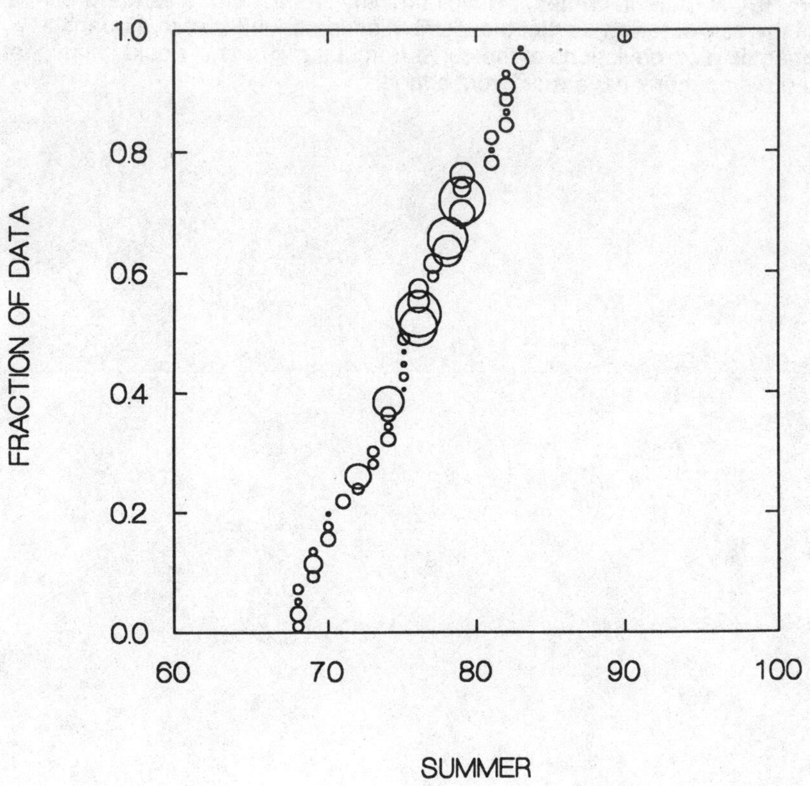

SMOOTH=LINEAR *(Linear Regression Smoothing)*

You can fit a linear regression to your quantile plot with the option `SMOOTH=LINEAR`. Regression fits a function to data such that the value predicted by the function at each observed value of X is as close as possible to the observed value of Y at the same value of X. Ordinary linear regression uses a straight line for the function and makes the squared discrepancies between predicted and observed Y values as small as possible. The equation for this function looks like this:

$$Y = a + bX$$

where *a* is a constant term and *b* is a slope coefficient.

Figure 13 shows the linear regression smoothing of the quantile plot of PERSON (person crimes) . Notice how the line accentuates the S shape of the curve, telling us that the distribution is not uniform. In a quantile-quantile plot, deviations of the curve from a straight line would tell us that the distributions have a different shape.

Figure 13

`QPLOT PERSON/SMOOTH=LINEAR`

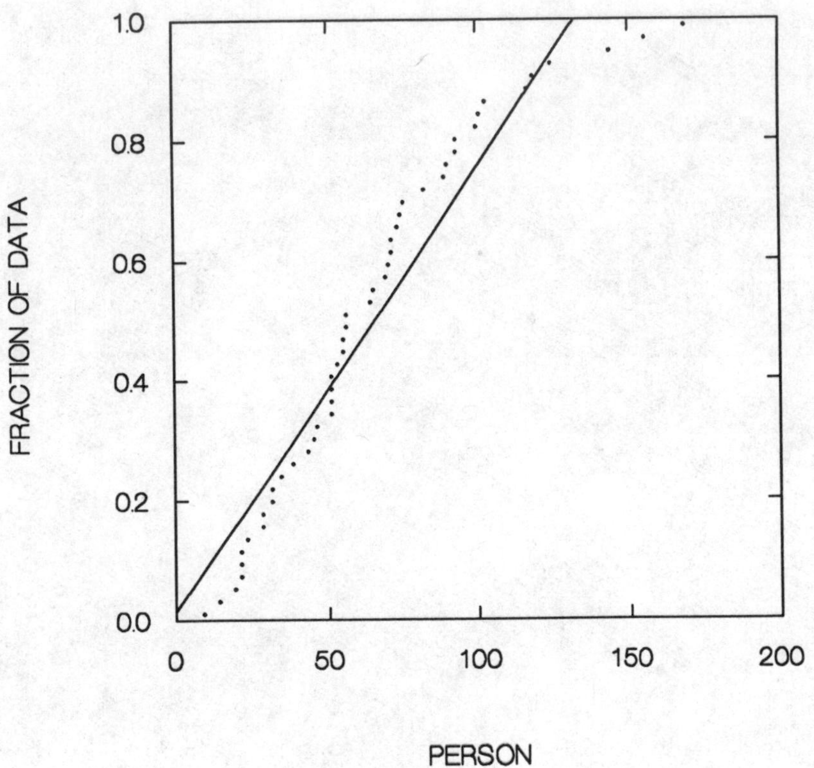

SMOOTH=QUAD *(Quadratic Smoothing)*

You can fit a quadratic regression curve to your data with the `SMOOTH=QUAD` option. This fits the following type of equation to the data:

$$Y = a + bX + cX^2$$

where *a* is a constant and *b* and *c* are slope coefficients.

You might want to use this option to enhance visually any bendings in your quantile plot.

Figure 14 shows the quadratic regression of the same data (PERSON) used in Figure 13 for linear smoothing.

Figure 14

```
QPLOT  PERSON/SMOOTH=QUAD
```

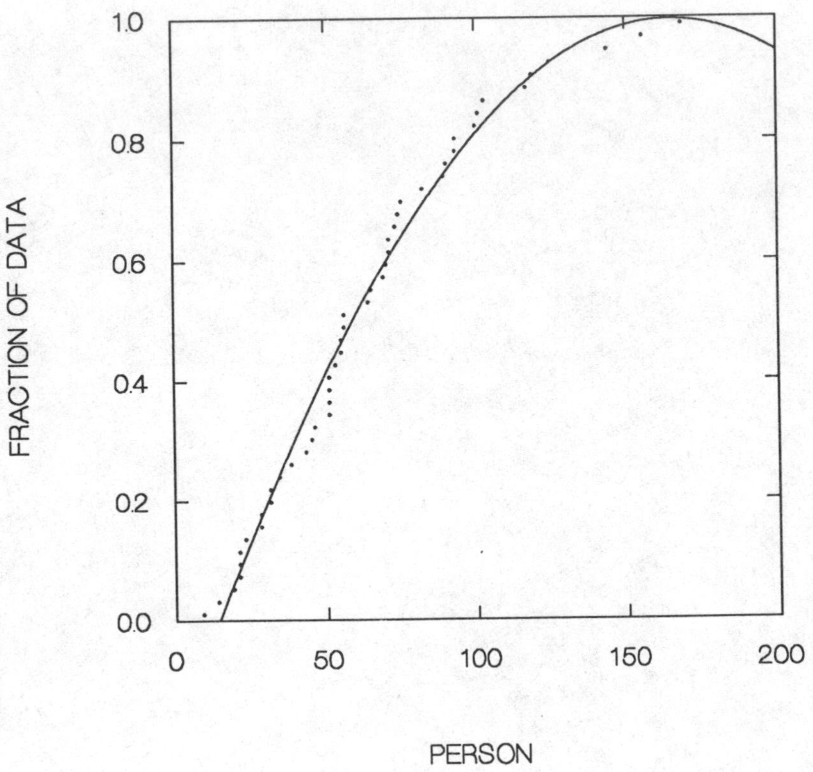

STICK *(Tick Marks Outside Frame)*
SYGRAPH normally places tick marks inside the frame. If you wish tick marks outside the frame, use the **STICK** option.

Figure 15 shows an example of a quantile plot with tick marks outside the frame.

Figure 15

```
QPLOT   SUMMER*WINTER/STICK
```

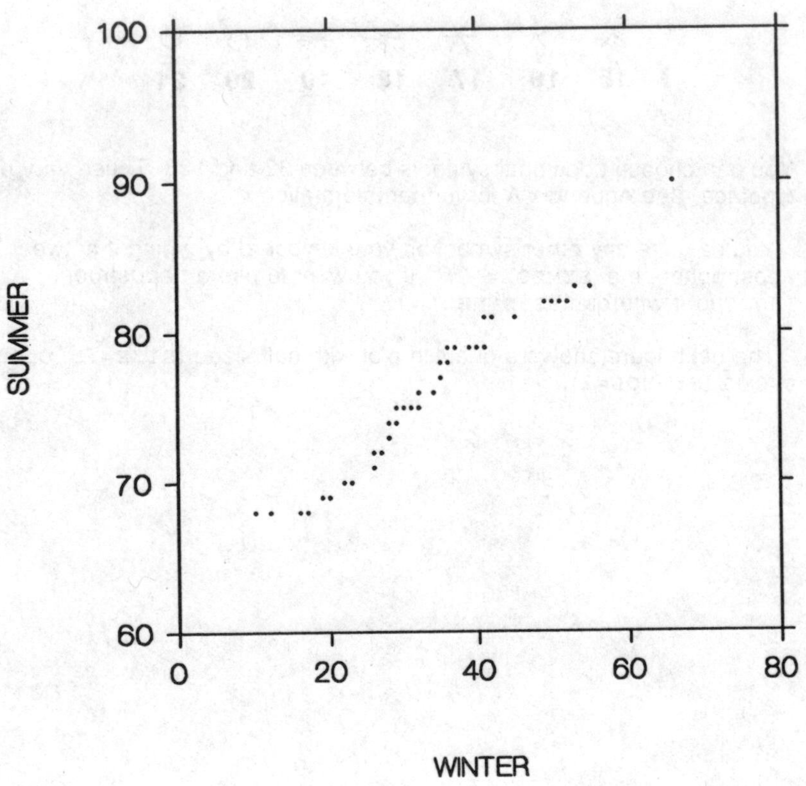

SYMBOL *(Plotting Symbols)*
You can choose a variety of symbols for your quantile plot. Just add the option: **SYMBOL=***n* , where *n* is an integer denoting one of the following symbols:

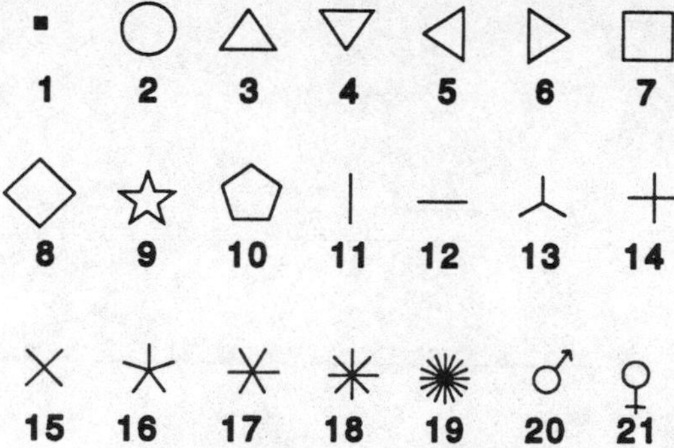

You can choose additional symbols between 32 and 128. These vary by typeface. See Appendix A for further information.

You can use any other symbol on your keyboard by typing it between apostrophes, e.g. **SYMBOL='@'**. If you want to use an apostrophe, surround it with quotes: **SYMBOL="'"**.

The next figure shows a quantile plot with half sized (**SIZE=.5**) open circles (**SYMBOL=2**).

Figure 16

```
QPLOT  RAIN/SYMBOL=2,SIZE=.5
```

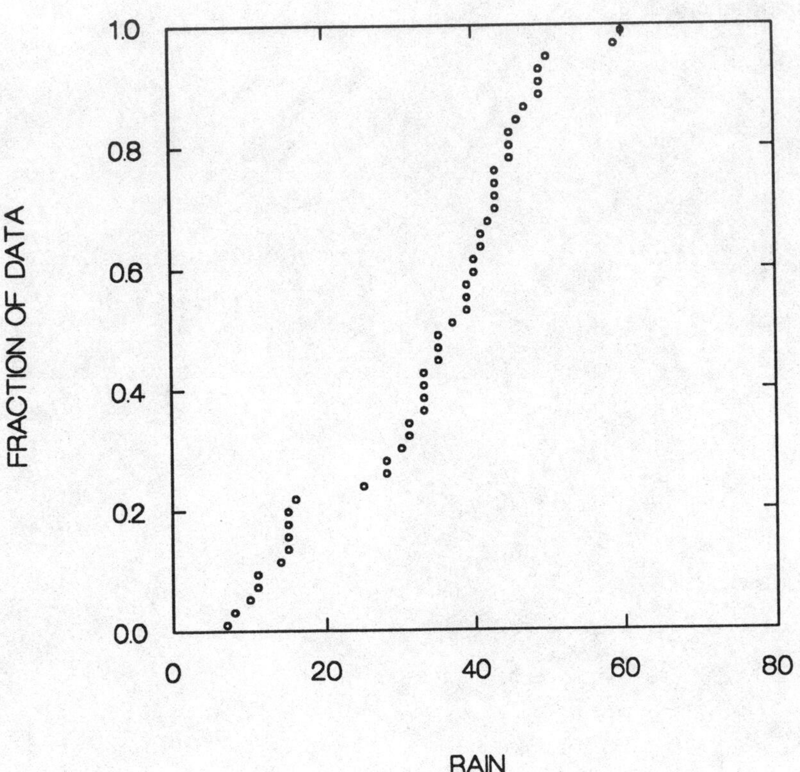

SYMBOL *(Data Based Plotting Symbols)*

You can use a character variable in your data file to determine the plotting symbol for each point. This can be handy when you are trying to identify subgroups or individual cases which are influencing your quantile plot.

SYGRAPH uses the first character in a character variable when you use this option. The symbols are centered at their proper locations in the graph.

Figure 17 shows a quantile plot of SUMMER (summer temperatures) against WINTER (winter temperatures) using the first letter of each state to identify the points. I have used `SIZE=.5` (see `SIZE` option above in this chapter) to reduce the size of the symbols somewhat and prevent them from colliding.

Figure 17

```
QPLOT   SUMMER*WINTER/SYMBOL=STATE$,SIZE=.5
```

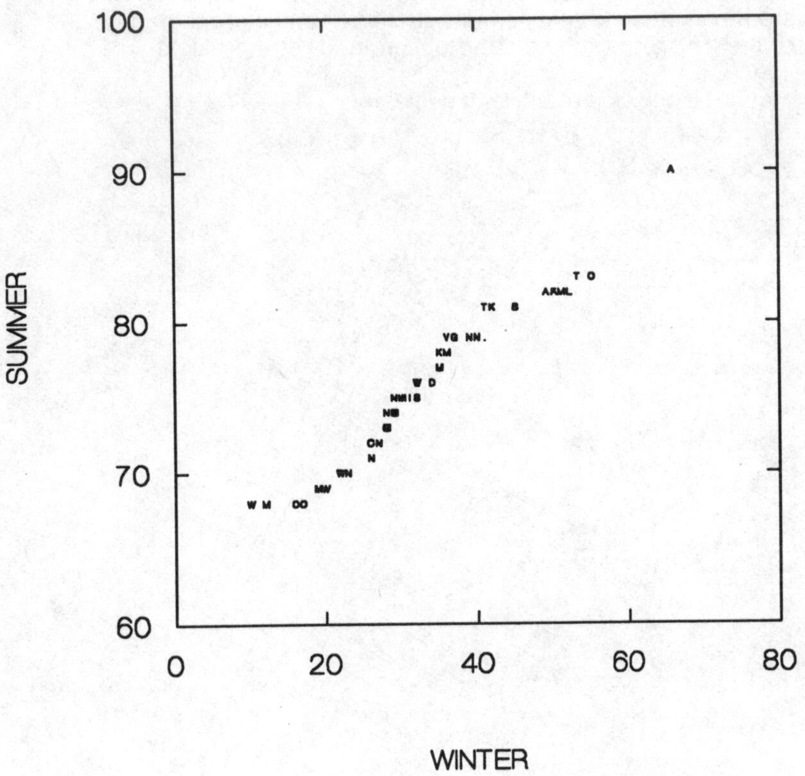

TITLE *(Graph Title)*

You can place a title at the top center of your quantile plot with the **TITLE** option:

```
TITLE='IgG  Antihuman  Urokinase  Sample'
TITLE="Segmented  T'  Cells"
TITLE='Proto  "Sequencing"  Quantiles'
```

The text must be surrounded by quotes (") or apostrophes ('). If your text includes apostrophes, as in the second example, surround it with quotes. If it includes quotes, as in the third example, surround it with apostrophes.

On some display devices the title will run off the top of the page because the standard display window is chosen to make the labels and graph as large as possible. If this happens, you will have to use the **SCALE** command to reduce the size of your entire graph (e.g. **SCALE=70,70**) or the **HEIGHT** option to lower the height.

Figure 18 shows a graph with a title.

Figure 18

```
TYPE=BRITISH
QPLOT  PERSON*PROPERTY,
  /TITLE='Person  vs.  Property  Crimes'
```

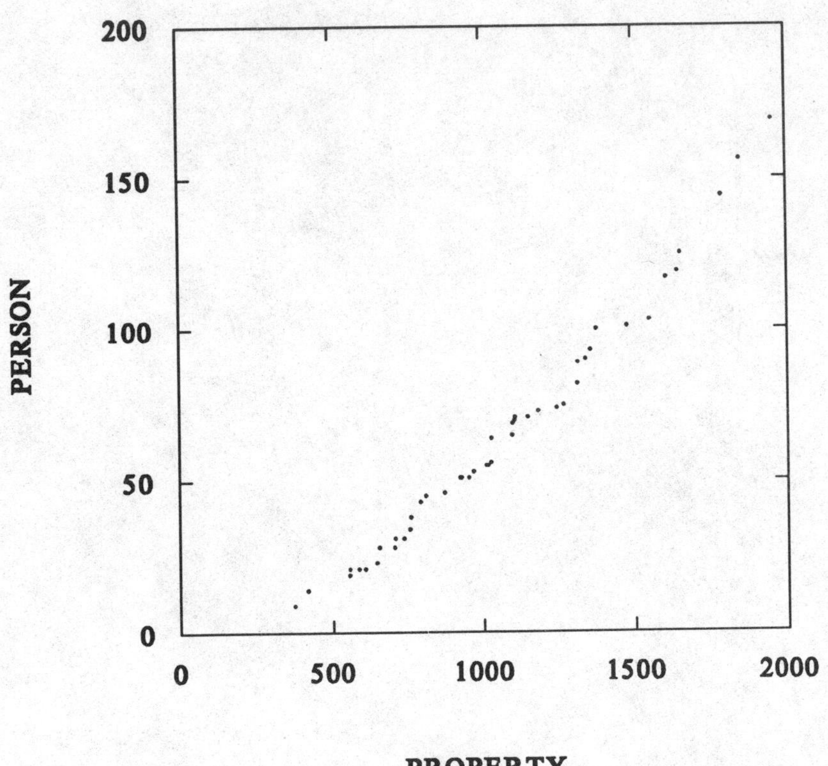

TRANS *(Transposing a Quantile Plot)*

You can transpose a quantile plot with the **TRANS** option. **TRANS** affects everything in a graph. **XLABEL** becomes **YLABEL**, **XTICK** becomes **YTICK**, and so on. In other words, specify a graph as you would ordinarily and then add the **TRANS** option. Everything will be transposed appropriately, including the labels and scales.

Figure 19 shows a transposed quantile plot of RAIN (average annual rainfall) using hollow circles as symbols. Compare this plot to that in Figure 16.

Figure 19

```
QPLOT  RAIN/SYMBOL=2,SIZE=.5,TRANS
```

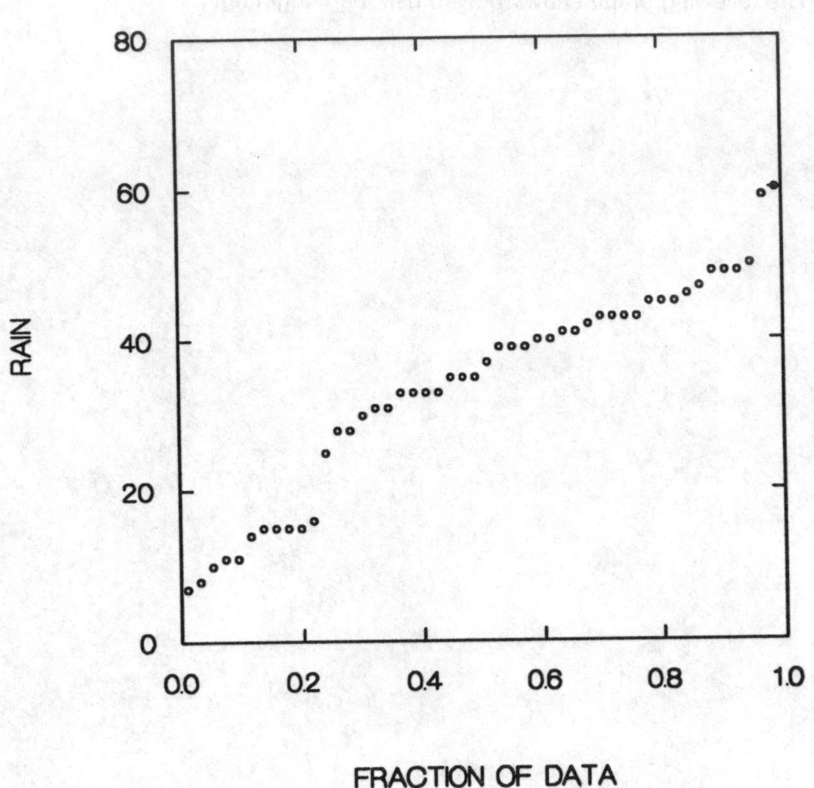

WIDTH *(Physical Width of Plot)*

You can control the physical width of your plot with the **WIDTH** option. It works like this:

```
WIDTH=50%        (or WIDTH=50)
WIDTH=4IN
WIDTH=10CM
```

The first example specifies percent of display width. The second specifies inches, and the third centimeters.

When you use the **WIDTH** option, you probably also want to use **HEIGHT**, which works exactly the same way (see above in this chapter). The following graph shows how to use them together.

Figure 20

```
QPLOT   SUMMER/HEIGHT=2IN,WIDTH=4IN
```

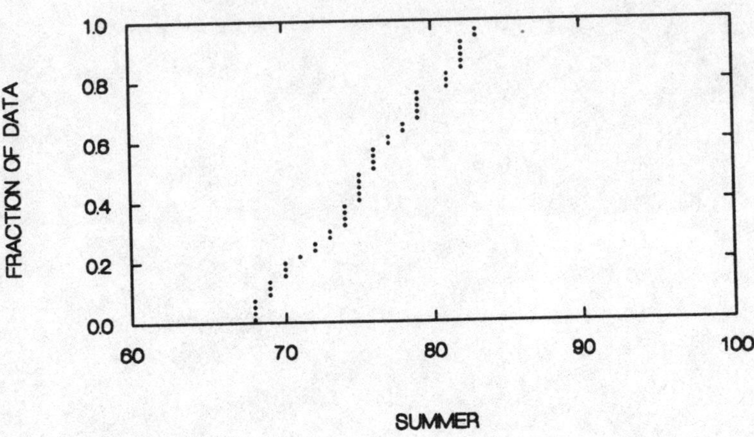

XLABEL,YLABEL *(Labeling a Plot)*

Quantile plots are usually labeled with the names of the variables you use in the **QPLOT** command. If you want different labels, use the **XLABEL** and/or **YLABEL** option(s), e.g.:

```
XLABEL='Rainfall'
YLABEL='U.S. Personal Crime in 1970'
XLABEL="Roger's Tacky Data"
XLABEL='Cost of "MAES" Bid'
YLABEL=' '
```

The label text must be surrounded by quotes (") or apostrophes ('). If your text includes apostrophes, as in the third example, surround it with quotes. If it includes quotes, as in the fourth example, surround it with apostrophes. The last example shows how to remove labels from your graph. Just assign a blank (' ') to your label.

Figure 21 shows an example of a relabeled quantile plot. It shows how a creative person can get ahead in business. Who will ever know where you got the data?

Figure 21

```
TYPE=BRITISH/ITALIC
QPLOT  PERSON,
  /SYMBOL=2,SIZE=0,
    LINE,XLABEL='MONTH',
    YLABEL="Roger's  Sales"
```

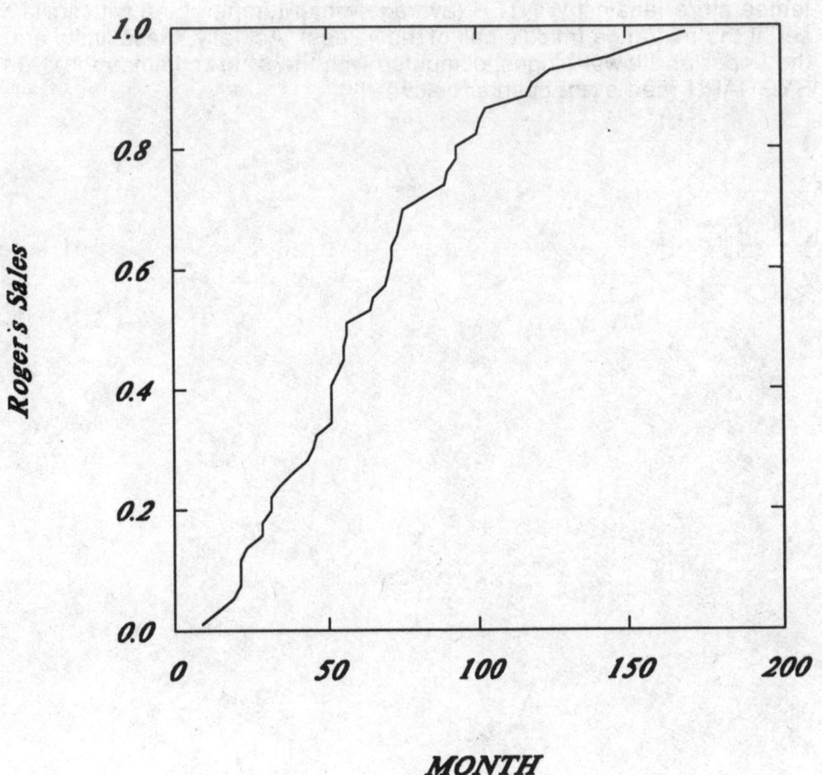

XLIMIT, YLIMIT *(Control Limits)*

You can add dashed lines to mark limits on each axis of a quantile plot. The **LIMIT** option works this way:

```
QPLOT  X  /  XLIMIT=2,6,YLIMIT=.2,.8          or,
QPLOT  A*B  /  XLIMIT=1,3,YLIMIT=15,45
```

Notice that you must specify two numbers for each limit (upper and lower). They need not be in order. Limits will not be plotted for numbers outside the extremes of the specified axes. Thus, if you want to plot only one limit (dashed line) on an axis, type something like this:

```
QPLOT  X  /  XLIMIT=2,-9999
```

Figure 22 shows a quantile plot of SUMMER (average summer temperature) against WINTER (average winter temperature) with limits set at the midrange (middle half of the values). Actually, these limits are the upper and lower hinges, computed with the **STEM** command in SYGRAPH (see **STEM** chapter below).

Figure 22

```
TYPE=STROKE/ITALIC
QPLOT   SUMMER*WINTER/XLIMIT=26.5,40.5,YLIMIT=72,79
```

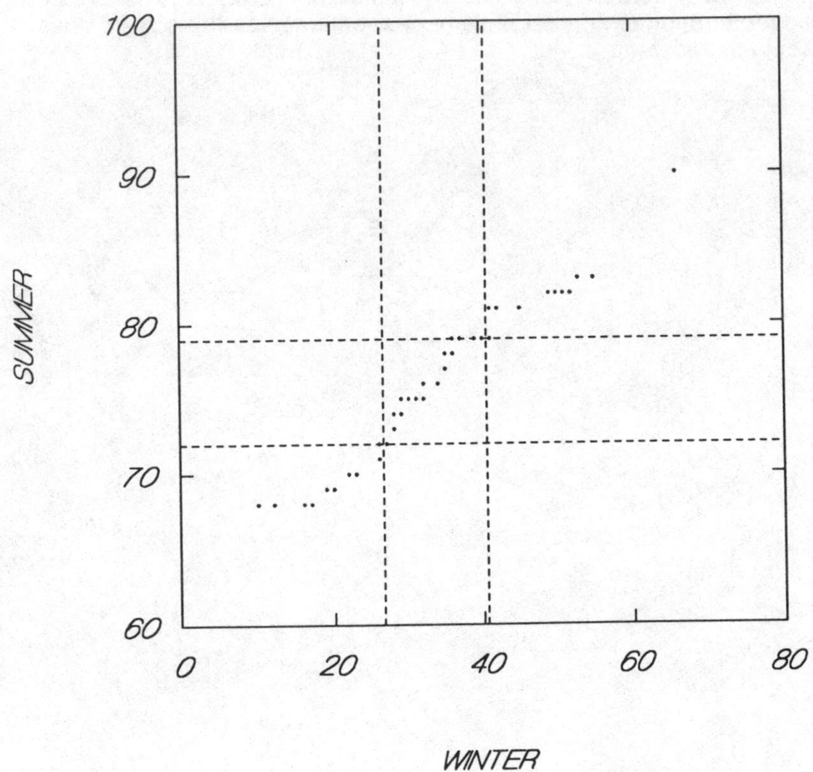

XLOG,YLOG *(Logging Data)*

You can log the data scale of one or both variables in your quantile plot with the **XLOG** or **YLOG** command. Logs may be computed to any base, e.g. **XLOG=2, YLOG=3, XLOG=10, XLOG=.5**. Natural logarithms will be computed if you use **LOG** with no argument, i.e. **YLOG**. Only round number log bases (e.g. 0.5, 2, 3,10) will result in round number tick values, however. If you are doing a quantile plot, then use only **XLOG** to transform your one variable, as in the figure below. If you are doing a quantile-quantile plot, use **XLOG** and **YLOG** to log both variables if you wish.

Figure 23 shows a logged quantile plot of POPDEN (population density). Compare this plot to Figure 10. We have managed to straighten out the distribution considerably. I used logs to the base 2 to show you what the values would look like. The plot would not change shape if you logged to another number base (e.g. **XLOG=10**), but the scale values would be different.

Figure 23

```
QPLOT   POPDEN/XLOG=2
```

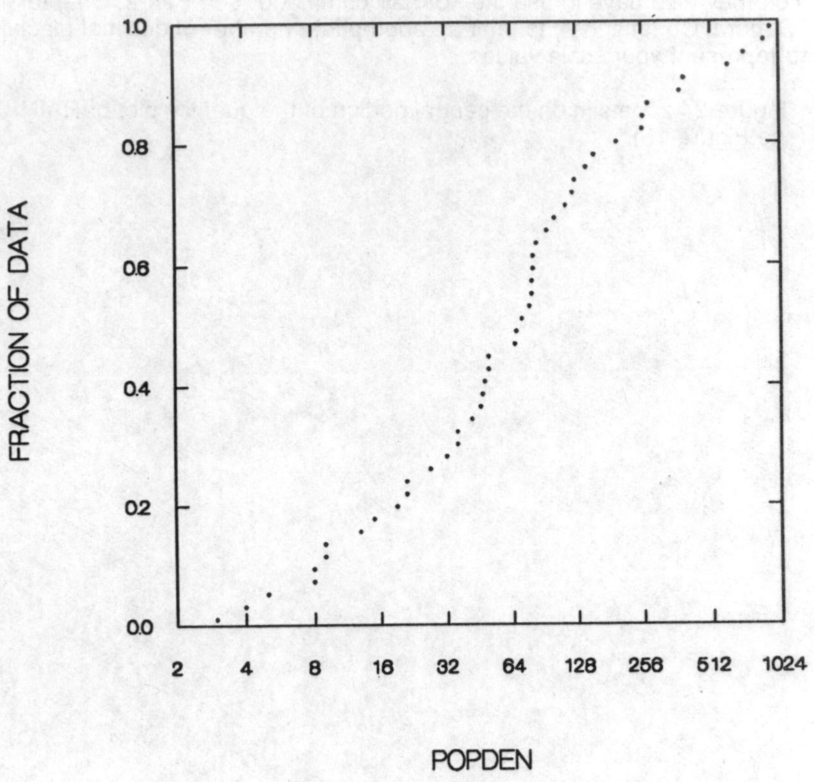

XMIN,YMIN,XMAX,YMAX *(Scale Limits)*

SYGRAPH usually determines minimum and maximum scale values from the data in your file. If you wish to override this feature, use the **MIN/MAX** options. **YMIN** and **YMAX** control the lower and upper limits of the vertical scale. **XMIN** and **XMAX** do the same for the horizontal scale.

If you set the **MIN** and **MAX** options inside the range of your data, you will zoom in to get a closer view, but you will eliminate certain data values from your plot.

Some settings of **MIN** and **MAX** will cause scale values to become messy (not integers or round numbers). In these cases, you may have to fiddle with the **XTICK**, **YTICK**, **ZTICK** options (see below in this chapter) to get a number of tick marks which yields round scale values. You may also have to use the **FORMAT** command (see Part 2, Chapter 1, "General Commands") to print an appropriate number of decimal places to represent your scale values.

Figure 24 zooms in on the central portion of the quantile plot of RAIN (see Figure 16).

Figure 24

```
QPLOT   RAIN/XMIN=20,XMAX=55,YMIN=.2
```

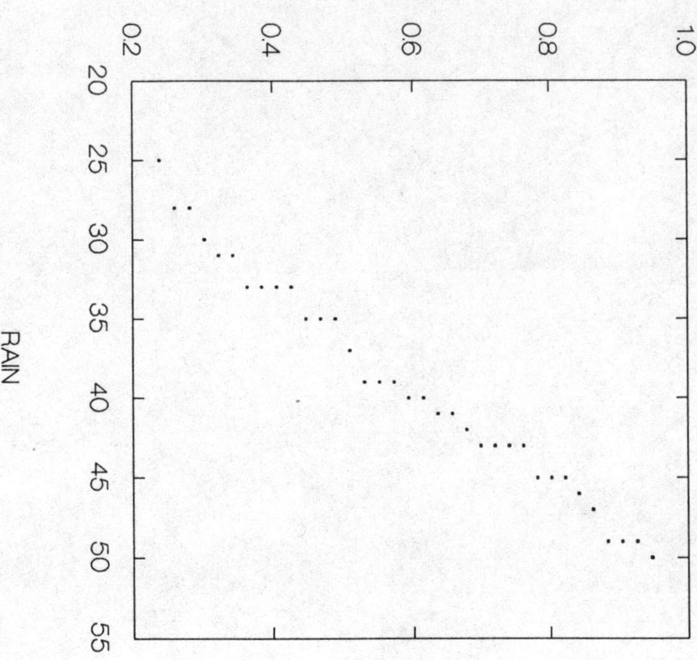

XPIP,YPIP *(Pip Marks)*

Pip marks are half sized tick marks. SYGRAPH normally omits pip marks from quantile plots. The **PIP** option adds them. Just specify the number you want. **XPIP** controls the X axis, **YPIP** the Y axis. If you log a scale (see **XLOG** option above in this chapter) the pip marks will be logarithmically spaced.

Figure 25 shows the same plot I used to illustrate **XLOG** in Figure 22. This time, however, I used logs to the base 10. With logs to this base, you want to specify **XPIP=9** to make the tick marks work properly. Notice how they are spaced on the horizontal axis like the markings on a slide rule.

Figure 25

```
QPLOT   POPDEN/XLOG=10,XPIP=9,YPIP=10
```

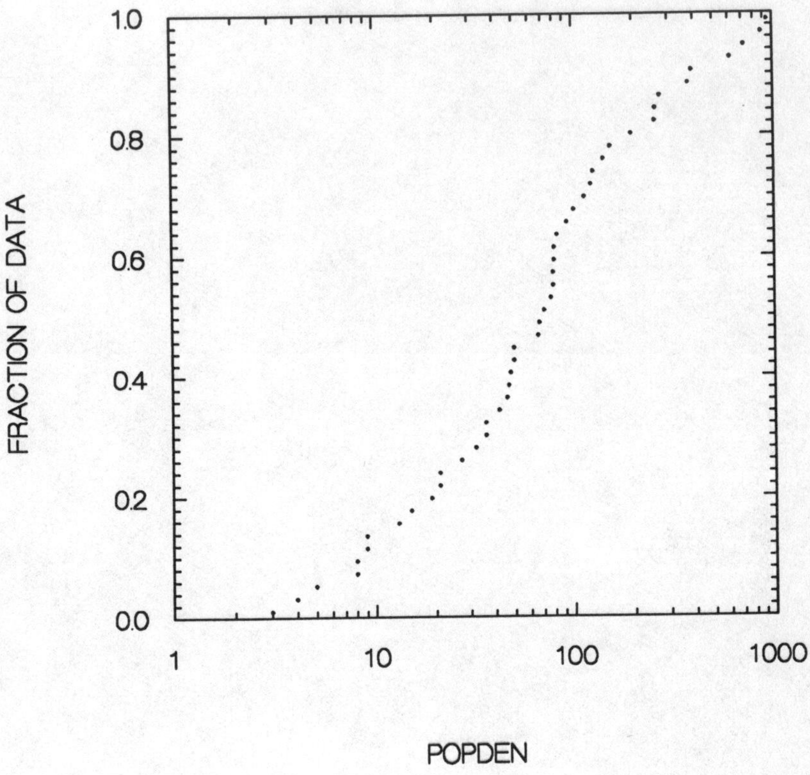

XPOW,YPOW *(Powering Data)*

You can power the horizontal and/or vertical scales of your quantile plot with the `POW` command. Powers may be computed to any exponent, e.g. `POW=.5` (square root), `POW=.33333` (cube root), `POW=-1` (inverse), `POW=2`. Square roots will be computed if you use `POW` with no argument, i.e. `POW`. Some exponents (e.g. 3) will produce non-integer tick marks. `POW` is implemented in SYGRAPH only for positive data. Negative values will be deleted.

Figure 26 shows a square root transformation of the POPDEN (population density) variable. Notice that the square root does not pull the upper tail in sufficiently to make it look normal. Compare the result to the logging of Figure 23.

Figure 26

QPLOT POPDEN/XPOW=.5

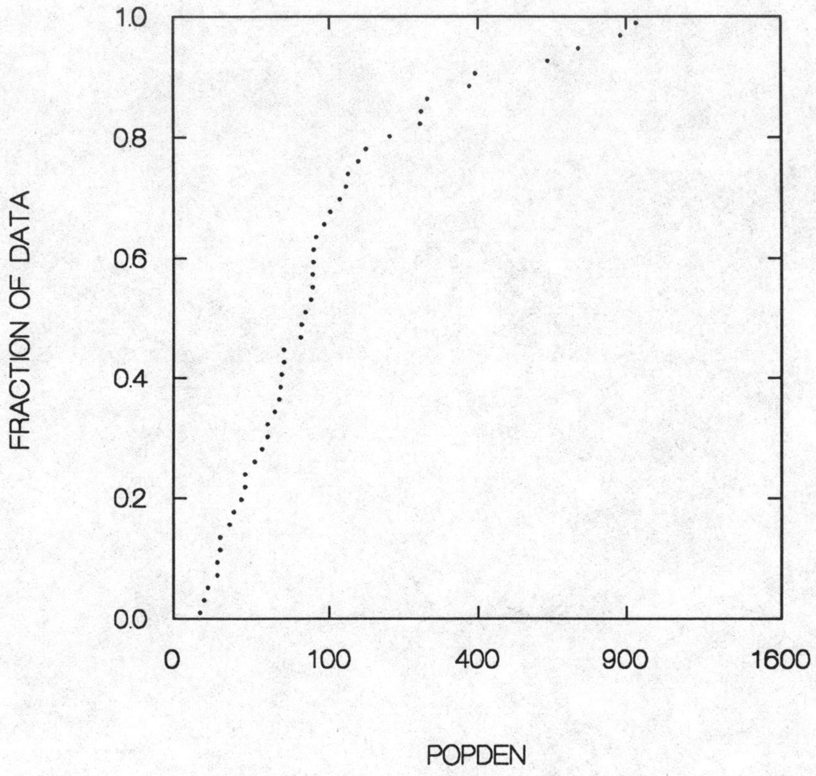

XTICK,YTICK *(Number of Tick Marks)*

SYGRAPH examines your data to determine how many tick marks to use on the axes of a probability plot. If you wish to modify this value, use the **TICK** option with a number. **XTICK** refers to the X axis and **YTICK** to the Y. For example, **YTICK=8** will force the vertical axis to have 8 tick marks.

Figure 27 shows an example of a quantile plot with 6 tick marks on the horizontal axis.

Figure 27

```
QPLOT INCOME/XTICK=6
```

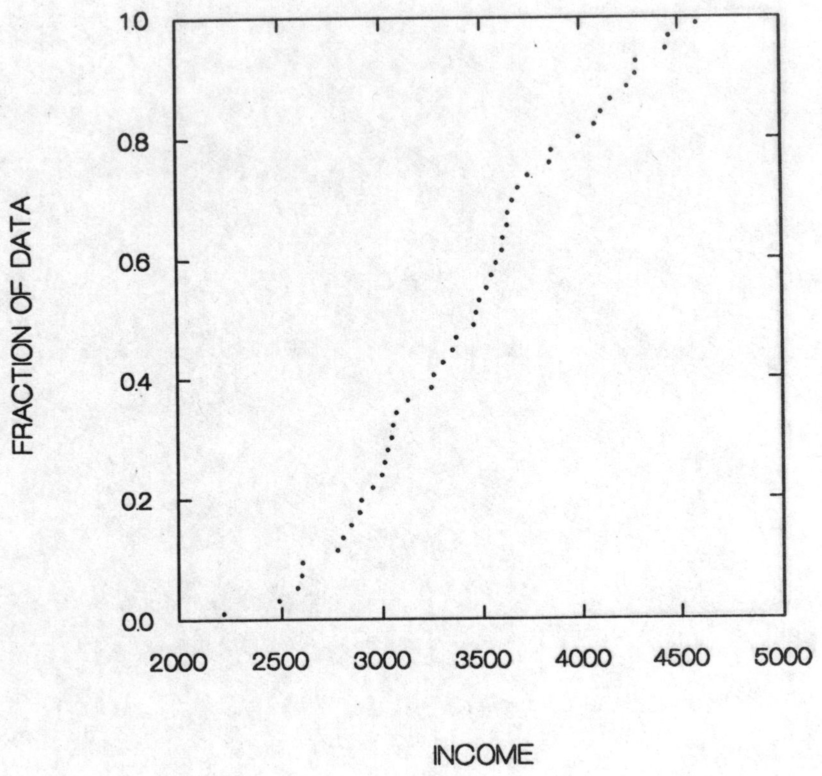

Chapter 13

SPLOM

SPLOM stands for "**S**catter**PLO**t **M**atrix." It is also called "casement plot." (Cleveland, 1985; Chambers, Cleveland, Kleiner, and Tukey, 1983). Although this graph has been rediscovered several times, the first published reference I can find is in Hartigan (1975a), where it is described as a **pairwise plot**. The point of the plot is simple. When you have many variables to plot against each other in scatterplots, why not arrange them in row and column order? GRAPH offers several types of symmetrical and asymmetrical SPLOMs.

Full Symmetric SPLOMs

Figure 1 shows a **SPLOM** of the US data. To read the **SPLOM**, locate the row variable (e.g. POPDEN on the first row) and the column variable (e.g. PERSON in the second column). The intersection is the scatterplot of the row variable on the vertical axis against the column variable on the horizontal. Each column and row is scaled exactly as it is in the **PLOT** command so that the points fill each frame. Tick marks and other labels are omitted because they would distract from the clarity of the plot. If you need scale information on any variable, you can use the **PLOT** command to produce a separate plot.

Because SPLOMs are real scatterplots, you can use almost every option available in the **PLOT** command, including **SMOOTH**, **SIZE**, and **SYMBOL**. The following figure uses the defaults. Notice that the scatterplots above the diagonal are reflections of those below because the row and column variables are complementary. The overall plot is skew symmetric (the upper half is the mirror image of the lower).

Notice, also, that I didn't need to type the names of the variables. If you leave out the names, the **SPLOM** command uses every numeric variable in the file. Watch out if you have a large file of, say, more than a 100 variables. You'll get a scatterplot matrix looking like a patchwork quilt!

Figure 1

SPLOM

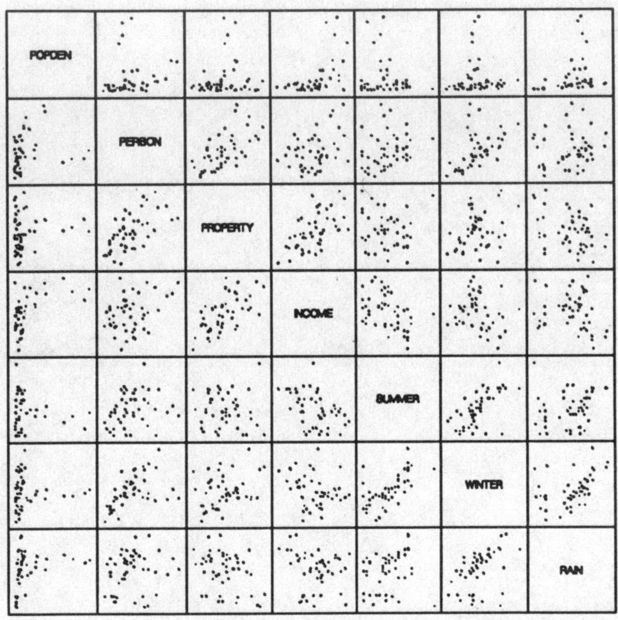

Asymmetric SPLOMs

You can plot one set of variables against another set by using an asterisk to divide sets in the **SPLOM** command. The next example shows SUMMER, WINTER, RAIN against PERSON, PROPERTY. These particular pairs show up in the earlier SPLOMs, but this orientation allows you to look at cross-relations more easily.

Figure 2

```
SPLOM   SUMMER,WINTER,RAIN*PERSON,PROPERTY
```

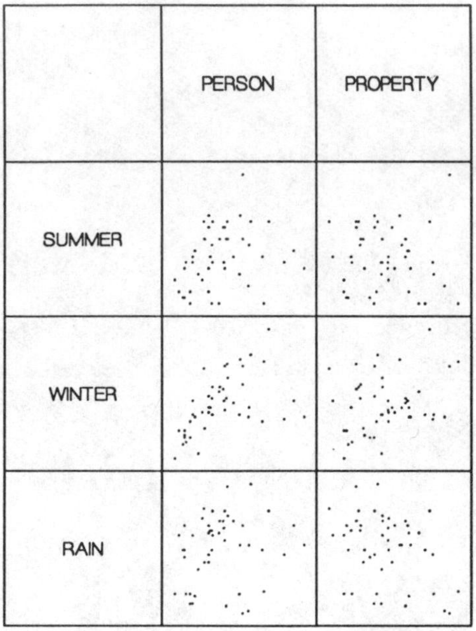

AXES *(Number of Axes)*

You can remove axes from your **SPLOM** by adding the option **AXES=0**. Other values of **AXES** are not allowed as in the other plot routines because they would not make sense in this context.

Figure 3 shows a **SPLOM** of PERSON (person crimes) against PROPERTY (property crimes) with axes removed.

Figure 3

```
SPLOM PERSON,PROPERTY/AXES=0
```

COLOR *(Setting Color of Symbols)*

You can choose a color for your symbols with the **COLOR** option. Choose either a name or a wavelength in nanometers. Possible colors and their approximate nanometer wavelengths are: **RED** (615), **ORANGE** (590), **YELLOW** (575), **GREEN** (505), **BLUE** (480), **VIOLET** (450). You may also name **BLACK**, **WHITE**, **GRAY**, and **BROWN**. The following command will make all symbols in the graph red:

```
SPLOM/COLOR=RED
```

You can also specify color in nanometers wavelength. The following example will make all the symbols greenish:

```
SPLOM/COLOR=540
```

Either of these alternatives can be controlled from a variable in your data. For example, you can say:

```
SPLOM/COLOR=COLR$
```

in which COLR$ is a character variable containing the values '**RED**' or '**YELLOW**' or whatever. This way, you can make a **SPLOM** in which each symbol is a different color.

Otherwise, you can govern the selection of colors by wavelength:

```
SPLOM/COLOR=COLR
```

in which COLR is a numerical variable containing wavelength values. Again, this will make every symbol a different color.

Figure 4 shows a **SPLOM** with the symbols in blue. I have used **SYMBOL=2** to make them larger.

Figure 4

```
SPLOM   SUMMER,WINTER,RAIN/COLOR=BLUE,SYMBOL=2
```

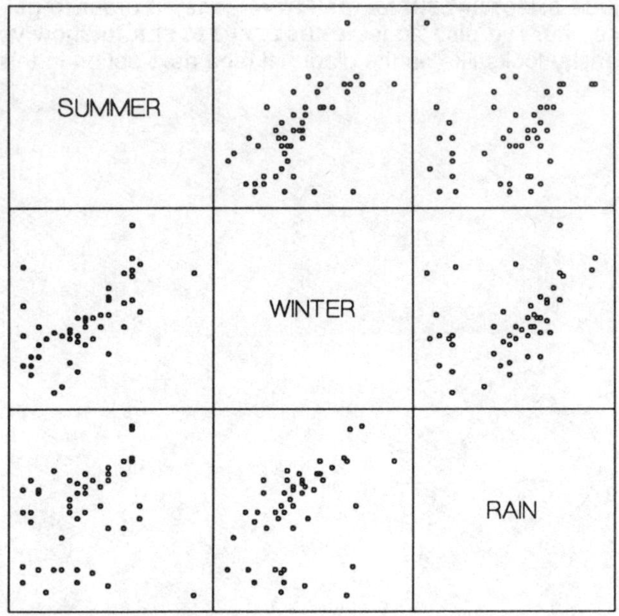

CONFI *(Confidence Bands)*

Often, we want a confidence interval on a regression line we have fitted in each cell of a **`SPLOM`** (see **`SMOOTH=LINEAR`** below). You can choose any level you wish for the confidence interval (e.g. **`CONFI=.87`**). If you do not choose a value (just typing **`CONFI`**), then it defaults to .95. Say we choose **`CONFI=.90`**. This will cause SYGRAPH to draw upper and lower hyperbolic bands around the actual fitted line. These bands mean the following: if the discrepancies (residuals) between the fitted and observed values for Y at each X are normally distributed and independent of each other and have the same spread (variance), then 90 times out of a hundred, confidence intervals constructed by SYGRAPH from data sampled in the same way you found these data will cover the true regression line relating Y to X.

The next figure shows the 95 percent confidence intervals on the regression lines of SUMMER, WINTER, and RAIN on each other. You must include **`SMOOTH=LINEAR`**, as I have done, in order to get the confidence line. I've also added **`DENSITY=JITTER`** to show you what a jittered density looks like on the diagonal (see next option in this chapter).

Figure 5

```
SPLOM   SUMMER,WINTER,RAIN,
   /SMOOTH=LINEAR,CONFI=.95,DENSITY=JITTER
```

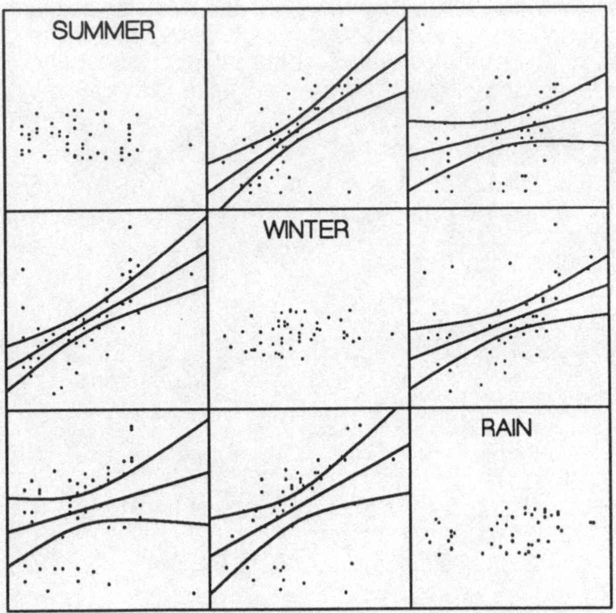

DENSITY *(Filling Densities in the Diagonal or Marginal Cells)*

Following Hartigan (1975a), you can insert cute little histograms into the empty cells or diagonal or margins of the scatterplot matrix. The option to do this is `DENSITY=HIST`. You can see an example of this in Figure 8. If you want to add density stripes (see `STRIPE` option in the `DENSITY` chapter or the figure below) add `DENSITY=STRIPE`. To add jittered densities, add `DENSITY=JITTER`.

The next figure shows density stripes instead of histograms in the diagonal elements. These stripes are drawn for each observation on the variable.

Figure 6

```
SPLOM   SUMMER,WINTER,RAIN/DENSITY=STRIPE
```

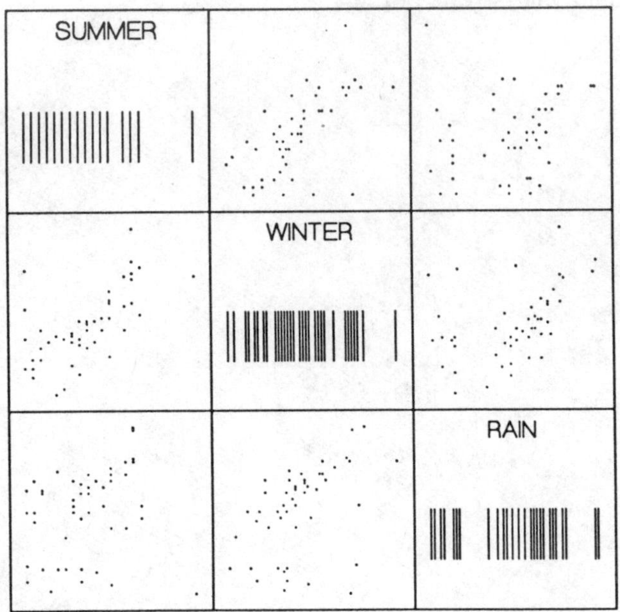

ELL *(Gaussian Bivariate Ellipsoids)*

You can draw bivariate ellipses on scatterplot matrices assuming a Gaussian (Normal) bivariate distribution for your data. The ellipse produced is centered on the sample means of the X and Y variables. Its major axes are determined by the unbiased sample standard deviations of X and Y and its orientation is determined by the sample covariance between X and Y. You choose the size of the ellipse by specifying a probability value between 0 and 1, e.g. `ELL=.95`. If you make an extremely large ellipse (e.g. `ELL=.999`), it may extend beyond the axes of your plot. If you do not choose a value, (by typing only `ELL`), then .5 is assumed.

Figure 7 shows ellipses superimposed on the splom of SUMMER, WINTER, and RAIN. I have used the default 50 percent confidence region on the data values (`ELL` or `ELL=.5`).

Figure 7

```
SPLOM   SUMMER,WINTER,RAIN/ELL
```

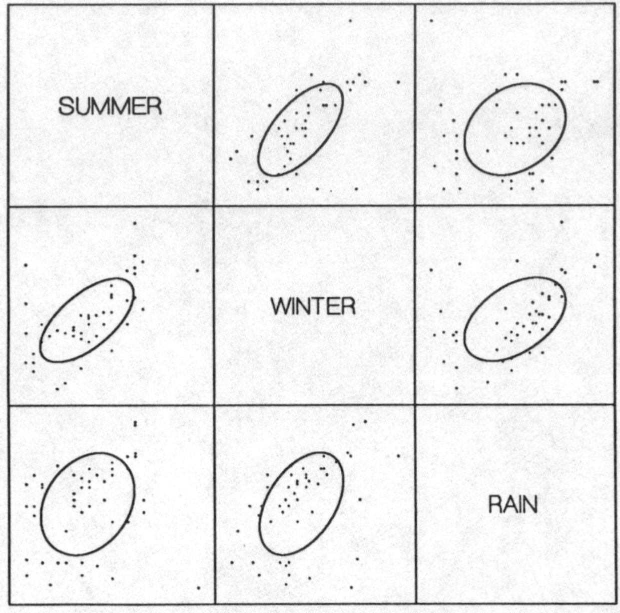

ELM *(Gaussian Confidence Intervals on Bivariate Centroids)*

You can draw bivariate confidence intervals on centroids in sploms with the **ELM** option. As with the **ELL** option (see directly above), the ellipse produced is centered on the sample means of the X and Y variables. Its major axes are determined by the unbiased sample standard deviations of X and Y and its orientation is determined by the sample Pearson correlation between X and Y. You choose the size of the ellipse by specifying a probability value between 0 and 1, e.g. **ELM=.95**. This size is adjusted by the sample size so that the ellipse will always be smaller than that produced by the **ELL** option. If you do not choose a value, (by typing only **ELM**), then .95 is assumed.

Figure 8 shows an ellipse superimposed on the splom of SUMMER, WINTER, and RAIN. I have used a 99 percent confidence region on the centroids (**ELM=.99**).

Figure 8

```
TYPE=SWISS
SPLOM   SUMMER,WINTER,RAIN/ELM=.99,DENSITY=HIST
```

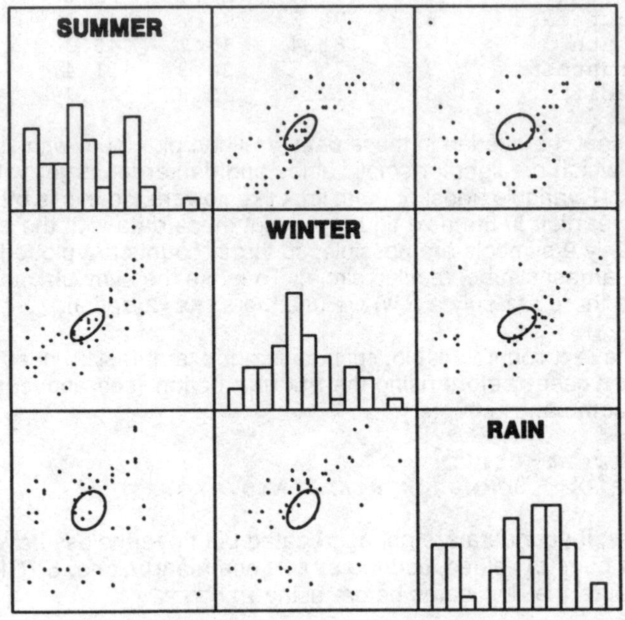

FLOWER (*Sunflower Plots)*

Sometimes we have data which overlap at exactly the same values. For example, we may have a questionnaire with a 7 point scale and we wish to plot two items against each other. There are only 49 possible points where we may plot the data. Or, we may have aggregate data and wish to plot them in a scatterplot. Here are the means of SUMMER, WINTER, and RAIN within regions of the variables in the US file. COUNT shows the number of states over which the means were computed.

REGION$	COUNT	SUMMER	WINTER	RAIN
New England	6	70.3	25.2	40.7
Mid Atlantic	3	74.8	31.3	39.3
Great Lakes	5	73.6	26.3	34.0
Plains	7	75.7	20.7	25.6
Southeast	8	78.3	43.2	45.0
South	8	81.4	45.1	46.3
Mountain	8	75.3	30.3	11.4
Pacific	3	67.7	39.8	29.7

To represent the overlap in these data, you can plot them with special symbols which are light for small values and darker for larger values of the COUNT variable. Most of them look like flowers, so this is often called a sunflower plot. In the next figure, we plot these data with the **FLOWER** option. Only 9 symbols are possible, so larger counts are plotted with the darkest, largest symbol (a filled circle). To make the symbols more visible (because there are only a few) we use the **SIZE=2** option.

If you have a count variable, such as in our example, you need to use it to **WEIGHT** cases before using the **FLOWER** option (see above in the general commands chapter):

```
WEIGHT=COUNT
SPLOM   SUMMER,WINTER,RAIN/FLOWER
```

Otherwise, if your data are not aggregated but nevertheless have duplicate pairs of values, use the **SPLOM** command alone. SYGRAPH will compute the duplicates before using **FLOWER**.

See the **JITTER** option (below in this chapter) for another way to deal with overlaps.

Figure 9

```
WEIGHT=COUNT
SPLOM   SUMMER,WINTER,RAIN/FLOWER,SIZE=2
```

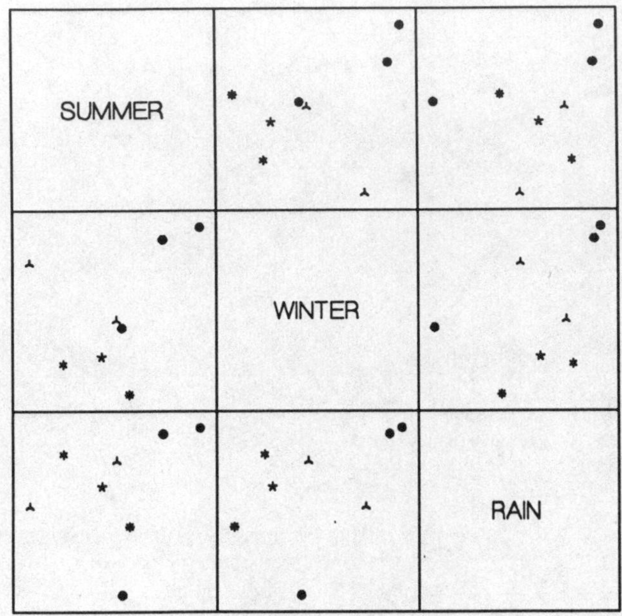

HALF *(Half Symmetric Sploms)*

You can plot only the lower half of a symmetric **SPLOM** by using the **HALF** option. Remember, the full symmetric **SPLOM** has the same plots above the diagonal but they are transposed. If you can flip things around in your mind's eye, you may want to use the **HALF** option all the time. It makes a cleaner graph. The next example shows all the variables in a half **SPLOM**.

Figure 10

TYPE=SWISS
SPLOM/HALF

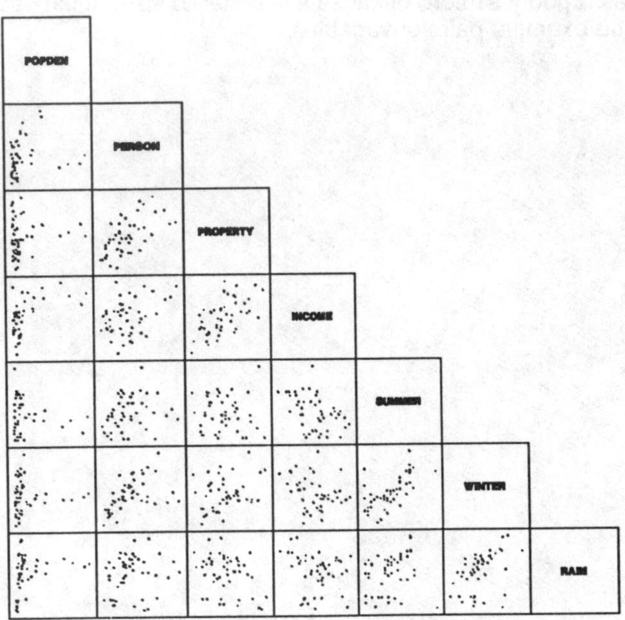

HEIGHT *(Physical Height of SPLOM)*

You can control the physical height of your **SPLOM** with the **HEIGHT** option. It works like this:

```
HEIGHT=50%      (or HEIGHT=50)
HEIGHT=4IN
HEIGHT=10CM
```

The first example specifies percent of display height. The second specifies inches, and the third centimeters.

When you use the **HEIGHT** option, you probably also want to use **WIDTH**, which works exactly the same way (see below in this chapter). The following graph shows how to use them together. I think this produces a goofy **SPLOM**, because it is better to keep things square when you examine pairs of variables.

Figure 11

```
SPLOM   SUMMER,WINTER,RAIN/HEIGHT=3IN,WIDTH=4IN
```

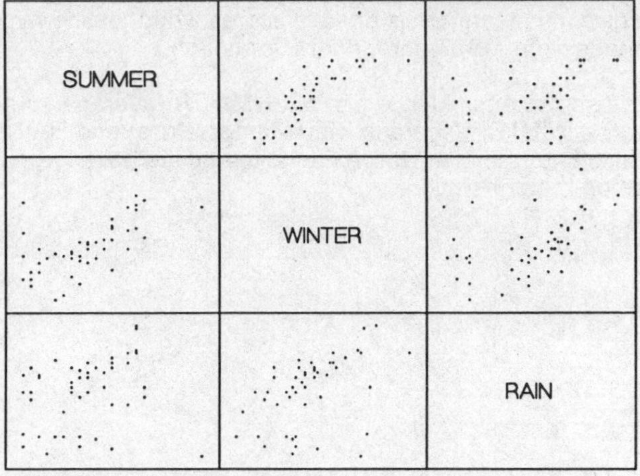

INFLUENCE *(Influence Plots)*

The influence of a point in a scatterplot on the correlation coefficient is the amount the correlation would change if that point were deleted. Plotting influences can help us determine whether a linear fit to the scatterplot is relatively robust or is dependent on just a few points. The `SPLOM` command has the same `INFLUENCE` option found in `PLOT`, which makes the size of the plotting symbol represent the extent of influence from each point. If any large points appear in the plot, we should scrutinize them further with the `PLOT` command before we draw any conclusions concerning the correlation.

You can use any symbol for influence plots, although circles are standard. Positive influences are represented by hollow symbols and negative influences by filled.

Other types of influences on statistical estimators can be represented in SYGRAPH by using the `SIZE` option on statistics computed in SYSTAT or another statistical package. For example, MGLH saves Mahalanobis distances (distances weighted by a covariance matrix) into a file when you do a discriminant analysis or save scores when testing hypotheses. See Gnanadesikan (1977) for further information.

Figure 12 shows an influence plot of SUMMER (average summer temperature), WINTER (average winter temperature) and RAIN (annual average inches of rainfall). Notice that some points have large negative influences on the correlation.

Figure 12

```
SPLOM   SUMMER,WINTER,RAIN/INFLUENCE
```

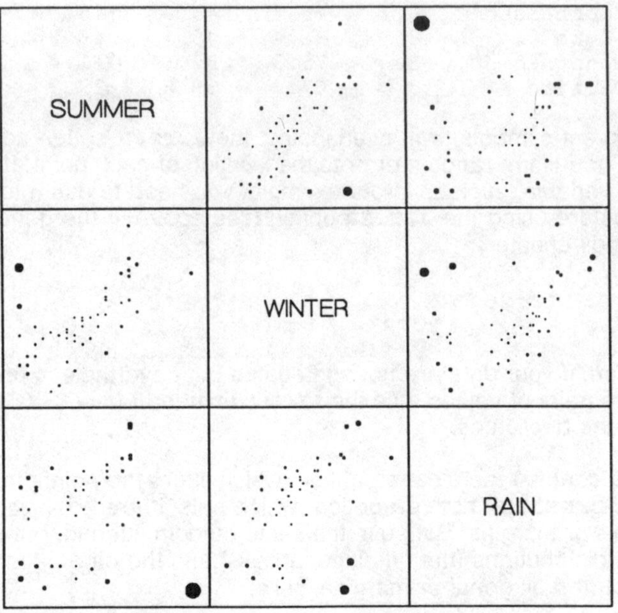

JITTER *(Jittered SPLOMS)*

Sometimes we have data which overlap at exactly the same values. For example, we may have a questionnaire with a 7 point scale and we wish to plot two items against each other. There are only 49 possible points where we may plot the data. Or, may have aggregate data and wish to plot them in a scatterplot. Here are the means of SUMMER, WINTER, and RAIN within regions of the variables in the US file. COUNT shows the number of states over which the means were computed.

REGION$	COUNT	SUMMER	WINTER	RAIN
New England	6	70.3	25.2	40.7
Mid Atlantic	3	74.8	31.3	39.3
Great Lakes	5	73.6	26.3	34.0
Plains	7	75.7	20.7	25.6
Southeast	8	78.3	43.2	45.0
South	8	81.4	45.1	46.3
Mountain	8	75.3	30.3	11.4
Pacific	3	67.7	39.8	29.7

To prevent symbols from overlapping, the **JITTER** option adds a small amount of uniform random error to the location of each point. If you have a count variable, such as in our example, you need to use it to **WEIGHT** cases before using the **JITTER** option (see above in the general commands chapter):

```
WEIGHT=COUNT
PLOT  Y*X/JITTER
```

Otherwise, if your data are not aggregated but nevertheless have duplicate pairs of values, use the **PLOT** command alone. SYGRAPH will jitter all the duplicates.

Do not confuse the **JITTER** option, which jitters the points in the cells, with the **DENSITY=JITTER** option, which puts jittered densities into the diagonals or margins. Both use the same random jittering, but one is for the joint distributions (the off-diagonal cells) and the other is for the marginal (the diagonal or marginal cells).

Figure 13 shows a scatterplot using the above aggregate data. I have used hollow circles (**SYMBOL=2**) because they plot well when there are many near overlaps.

Figure 13

```
WEIGHT=COUNT
SPLOM   SUMMER,WINTER,RAIN/SYMBOL=2,JITTER
```

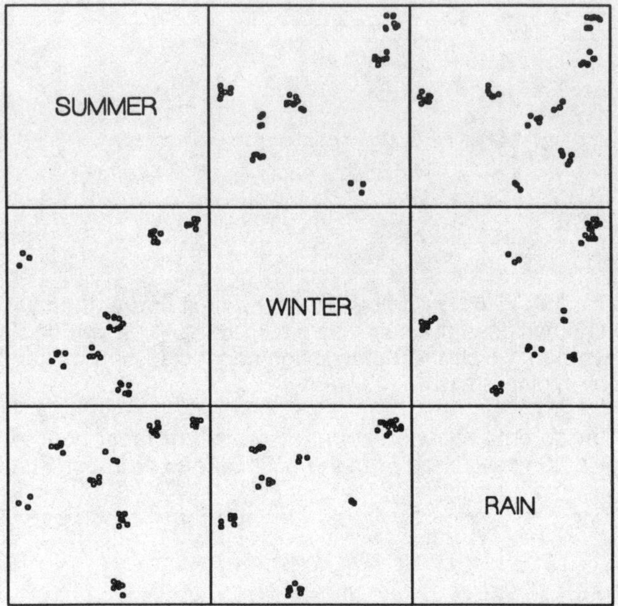

LINE *(Line Graphs)*

Time series and other data plot best when the points are connected with a line. This is easy to do in SYGRAPH. Just use the **LINE** option. You may choose from 11 different types of lines by typing **LINE=***n*, where *n* is one of the following numbers:

1
2
3
4
5
6
7
8
9
10
11

If you type **LINE** with no number, as in the next figure, then you will get the solid line, which is the same as typing **LINE=1**. If you do not want to see the symbols which the **LINE** option connects, then make them invisible by typing **SIZE=0**.

The following data show output productivity per labor hour in 1977 U.S. dollars for a 25 year period from the U.S. Bureau of Labor Statistics.

YEAR	US	CANADA	JAPAN	GERMANY	ENGLAND
1960	62.2	50.3	23.2	40.3	53.8
1965	76.6	62.7	35.0	54.0	63.9
1970	80.0	76.8	64.8	71.2	77.6
1975	92.9	91.8	87.7	90.1	94.3
1980	101.4	101.9	122.7	108.6	101.2
1985	121.8	115.1	159.9	131.9	129.7

The data are in time order in the file. If the data were in some other order, the **LINE** option would connect successive points and produce a messy spider web in each cell of the **SPLOM**. Figure 14 shows a **SPLOM** of each country's productivity against the YEAR variable. I have used the **HEIGHT** and **WIDTH** options to scale the series better. Finally, I have used the **YMIN** and **YMAX** options to keep the vertical scale of each cell the same.

Figure 14

```
SPLOM  US,CANADA,JAPAN,GERMANY,ENGLAND*YEAR,
  /LINE,SIZE=0,HEIGHT=3IN,WIDTH=4IN,
   YMIN=0,YMAX=200
```

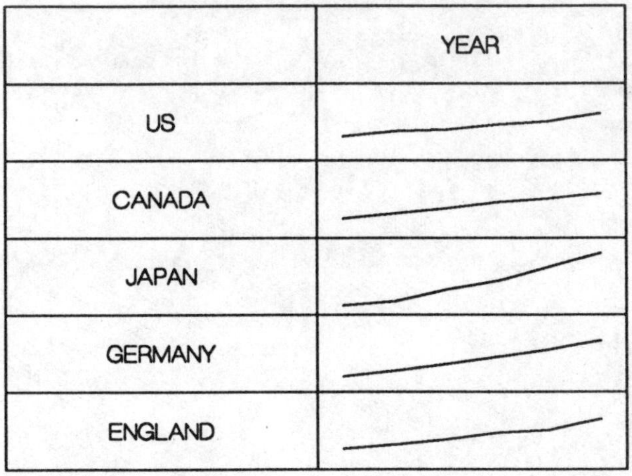

	YEAR
US	
CANADA	
JAPAN	
GERMANY	
ENGLAND	

SHORT *(Shortening the Domain of Smoothing)*

Sometimes you can get into trouble by extrapolating beyond the range of your data when making a prediction. Many of the smoothing methods in SYGRAPH (see `SMOOTH` option below in this chapter) yield curves which extend from the left to the right edges of the plotting frame. If you wish to limit the domain of the smooth to the extreme values of the data on the horizontal axis, add the `SHORT` option.

Figure 15 shows a `SPLOM` with a linear function and confidence interval limited to the range of the X data with the `SHORT` option. Compare this to the extrapolated version in Figure 5 above.

Figure 15

```
SPLOM   SUMMER,WINTER,RAIN,
   /SMOOTH=LINEAR,CONFI,SHORT
```

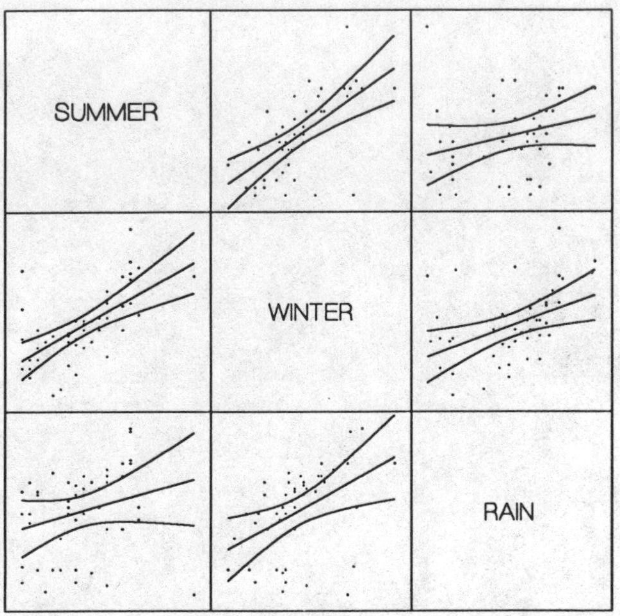

SIZE *(Changing Size of Plotting Symbols)*

You can alter the size of plotting symbols from invisible to as large as your entire graph. The standard value of all symbols is **SIZE=1**. **SIZE=2** produces symbols twice as large as the standard. **SIZE=.5** is half, and so on. **SIZE=0** makes the symbols invisible.

Figure 16 shows a **SPLOM** with stars (**SYMBOL=9**) one and three quarters larger than usual. I've added histograms to the margins to pretty it up.

Figure 16

```
SPLOM   SUMMER,WINTER,RAIN*PERSON,PROPERTY,
   /SYMBOL=9,SIZE=1.75,DENSITY=HIST
```

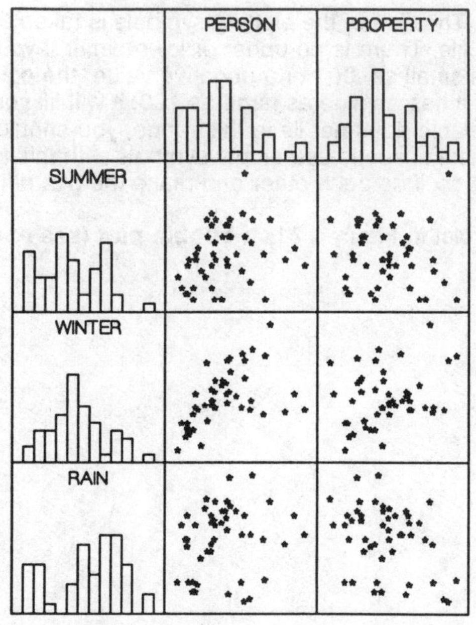

SIZE *(Representing a Variable by Size of Symbols in a SPLOM)*
You can use the value of a variable in your file to control the size of a plotting symbol. This is especially useful when you are representing a third variable against the other variables in a **SPLOM**.

Here is an example. I made a new variable using POPDEN from the US file:

```
LET DEN = POPDEN/300
```

By dividing POPDEN by 300, I have placed the new variable DEN in the range of 0 to 4. Now we can use this variable to determine the size of a plotting symbol. Figure 16 shows scatterplots of climate conditions enhanced by population density.

One caution. The size of the plotting symbols is taken directly from the values in your file. There is no upper or lower limit. If your **SIZE** variable has a value as small as .001 or a negative value, the point will be invisible and if it has a value as large as 100, it will fill your entire plot. If your sizing variable does not lie in this range, you should rescale it. Finally, you should usually use empty symbols with this type of plot, since filled ones can occlude each other and make the plot difficult to interpret.

Each scatterplot in Figure 17 is a **bubble plot** (see **PLOT** chapter above).

Figure 17

```
SPLOM    SUMMER,WINTER,RAIN/SYMBOL=2,SIZE=DEN
```

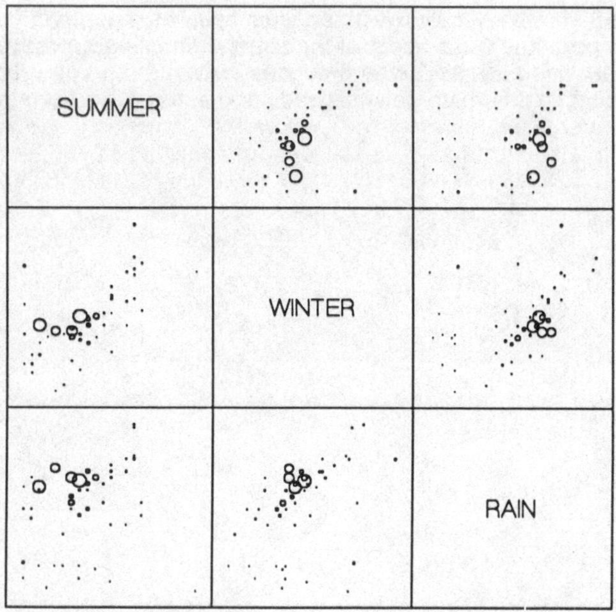

SMOOTH=DWLS *(Distance Weighted Least Squares Smoothing)*

Distance weighted least squares fits a line through a set of points by least squares. Unlike linear or low order polynomial smoothing, however, the surface is allowed to flex locally to fit the data better. The amount of flex is controlled by a tension parameter (see **TENSION** below in this chapter).

If you use **SMOOTH=DWLS**, be prepared to wait a while, particularly on slow machines. Every point on the smoothed line requires a weighted quadratic multiple regression on all the points. This method produces a true, locally weighted curve running through the points using an algorithm due to McLain (1974). If you want to do a regression of one variable on another, but are not positive about the shape of the function, I suggest you use **DWLS** (or **LOWESS**) first.

Figure 18 shows a locally weighted least squares smooth of the climate data. Compare it to the smooth of the same data using **LOWESS**. While not as robust as **LOWESS**, **DWLS** produces smoother curves. I added **SHORT** because it is extremely misleading to extrapolate from the data using **DWLS**.

Figure 18

```
SPLOM   SUMMER,WINTER,RAIN/SMOOTH=DWLS,SHORT
```

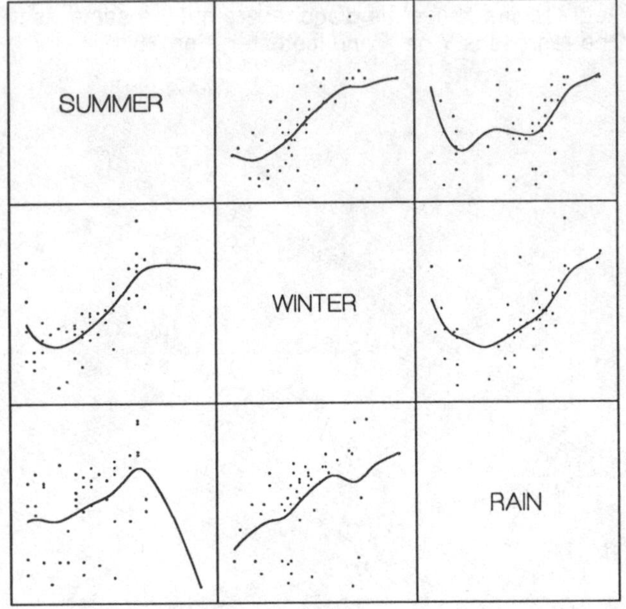

SMOOTH=LINEAR *(Linear Regression Smoothing)*

SYGRAPH offers several ways to smooth plots of data. The most popular is linear regression. Regression fits a function to data such that the value predicted by the function at each observed value of X is as close as possible to the observed value of Y at the same value of X. Ordinary linear regression uses a straight line for the function and makes the squared discrepancies between predicted and observed Y values as small as possible. The equation for this function looks like this:

$$Y = a + bX$$

where *a* is a constant term and *b* is a slope coefficient.

You fit this function with the option **SMOOTH=LINEAR**. Figure 19 shows the linear regression smoothing of the climate variables **SPLOM**. Notice that the regressions above the diagonal are not the same as those below. One regresses Y on X and the other X on Y.

Figure 19

```
SPLOM   SUMMER,WINTER,RAIN/SMOOTH=LINEAR
```

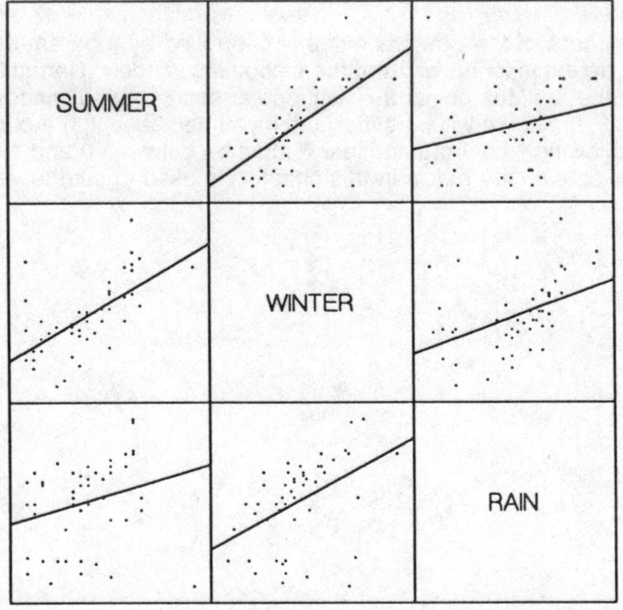

SMOOTH=LOWESS *(LOWESS, or Locally Weighted Smoothing)*

Quadratic smoothing, like linear smoothing, presupposes the shape of the function. SYGRAPH offers a smoothing method which requires only that the smooth be a function (i.e. unique Y value for every X). This method is called **LOWESS** (Cleveland, 1979,1981). It produces a smooth by running along the X values and finding predicted values from a weighted robust average of nearby Y values. Because a lot of computations are involved, the **LOWESS** option can be time consuming for large scatterplots.

The next figure shows the result for the climate data **SPLOM**. Notice that the fit is distinctly curvilinear in most of the cells. It is always a good idea to use **LOWESS** before fitting a straight line or any other function to data. This way, you can let the data speak for themselves and warn you about whether your model is inappropriate.

The tightness of the **LOWESS** curve is controlled by a parameter called *F*, which determines the width of the smoothing window. Normally, $F = .5$, meaning that half the points are included in each running window. If you increase *F*, the curve will be stiffer and if you decrease it, the curve will be looser, following local irregularities. *F* must be between 0 and 1. The **TENSION** option (see below in this chapter) is used to set the value of F.

Figure 20

```
SPLOM   SUMMER,WINTER,RAIN/SMOOTH=LOWESS
```

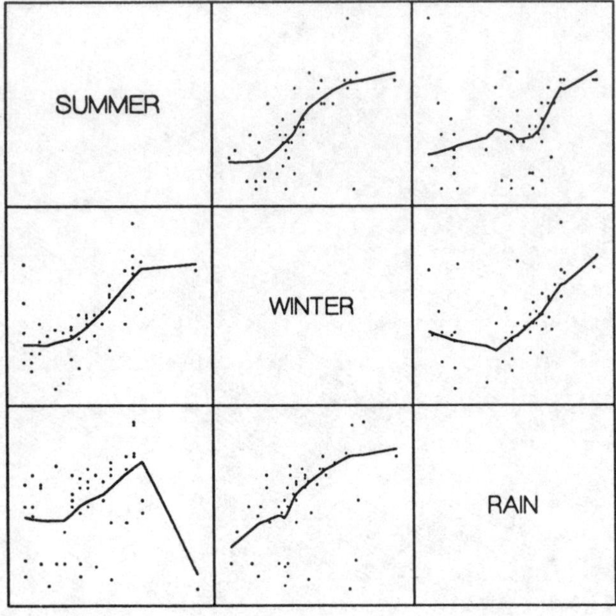

SMOOTH=NEXPO *(Negative Exponentially Weighted Smoothing)*

Negative exponentially weighted smoothing fits a curve through a set of points such that the influence of neighboring points decreases exponentially with distance. It is an alternative to **SPLINE** smoothing (see below in this chapter) for interpolation. The smoothing algorithm is due to McLain (1974). It is closely related to distance weighted least squares regression smoothing (see **DWLS** above in this chapter).

Figure 21 shows a smooth of the data used to illustrate spline smoothing below in this chapter. The primary difference between the two smoothing methods is that negative exponential smoothing is always single valued. For all X, there is a unique Y. Spline smoothing, on the other hand, can produce several Y for a given X in some contexts.

Figure 21

```
SPLOM  US,CANADA,JAPAN,GERMANY,ENGLAND*YEAR,
  /SMOOTH=NEXPO,SIZE=0,HEIGHT=3IN,WIDTH=4IN,
   YMIN=0,YMAX=200
```

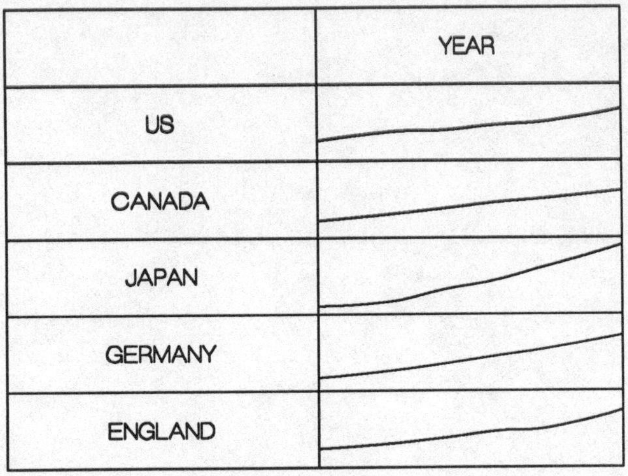

SMOOTH=QUAD *(Quadratic Smoothing)*

You can fit a quadratic regression curve to your data with the **QUAD** option. This fits the following type of equation to the data:

$$Y = a + bX + cX^2$$

where *a* is a constant and *b* and *c* are slope coefficients.

Figure 22 shows the quadratic regression of the climate data. Compare it to the results in Figure 20.

Figure 22

```
SPLOM  SUMMER,WINTER,RAIN/SMOOTH=QUAD
```

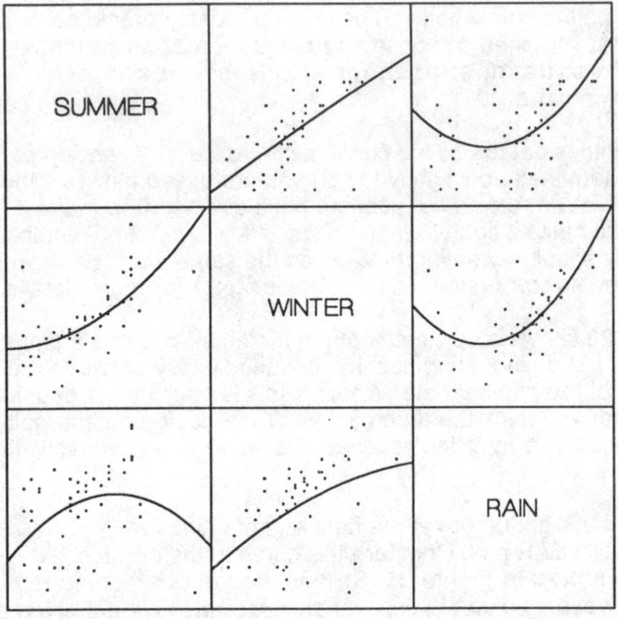

SMOOTH=SPLINE *(Spline Smoothing)*

You can fit a spline curve to your data with the **SMOOTH=SPLINE** option. Spline smoothing fits a curved line through every point in the plot such that the curve is smooth everywhere. SYGRAPH employs cubic splines (Brodlie, 1980) for smoothing. Cubic splines involve fitting several sections of the curve with cubic equations:

$$Y = a + bX + cX^2 + dX^3$$

where *a* is a constant, and *b*, *c*, and *d* are coefficients. These curves are joined smoothly at "knots," which usually coincide with the data points themselves.

Cubic splines are especially useful for interpolation, when you need a computer French curve. This means that you should use splines through the data points only when you believe your data contain no error. Otherwise, you should choose one of the regression methods (**SMOOTH=LINEAR**, **SMOOTH=QUAD**, **SMOOTH=DWLS** or **SMOOTH=LOWESS**).

The tightness of the spline curve is controlled by a tension parameter, which determines how tightly the curves are pulled between the knots. Normally, **TENSION=2**, but you can set it down to 0 to make it looser and up to 10 to make it tighter. I hate to say this is a matter of aesthetics, but you really should try several values on the same data to see what I mean. See the **TENSION** option below in this chapter for more details.

Figure 23 shows a spline smooth of the time series data plotted in Figure 14. The smoothing has interpolated flexibly between the 5 year intervals of the original data. Whether this is appropriate depends on how much error you think the data contain. You should use interpolating splines like this only when you want the curve to pass exactly through the points.

Notice the slight upturn at the right end of the curve in the ENGLAND*YEAR plot. Compare this curve to the one for **SMOOTH=NEXPO** in Figure 21. Splines are not guaranteed to be single valued for every value of the X variable. Because we are fitting a function in this case, the negative exponential smoothing is preferable to the splines.

Figure 23

```
SPLOM   US,CANADA,JAPAN,GERMANY,ENGLAND*YEAR,
  /SMOOTH=SPLINE,SIZE=0,HEIGHT=3IN,WIDTH=4IN,
   YMIN=0,YMAX=200
```

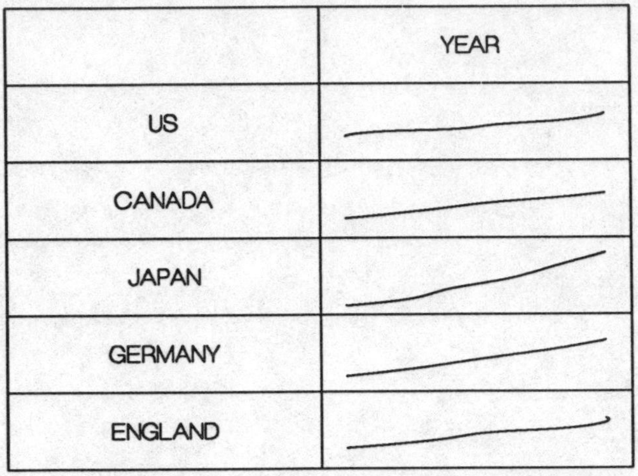

	YEAR
US	
CANADA	
JAPAN	
GERMANY	
ENGLAND	

SMOOTH=STEP *(Step Smoothing)*

You can fit a step function to your data with the `SMOOTH=STEP` option. The function begins at the point with the smallest X value and drops (or rises) to the point with the next larger X value. If you wish to drop (or rise) immediately from the first point to the second, you need to shift the Y data values one lag down the list for each X in your data.

Figure 24 shows the step smooth for the time series data used in the spline example in Figure 23. Of all the smoothing methods for these data, this one is the least appropriate, since it suggests that productivity changes were discontinuous at five year intervals.

Figure 24

```
SPLOM  US,CANADA,JAPAN,GERMANY,ENGLAND*YEAR,
   /SMOOTH=STEP,SIZE=0,HEIGHT=3IN,WIDTH=4IN,
   YMIN=0,YMAX=200
```

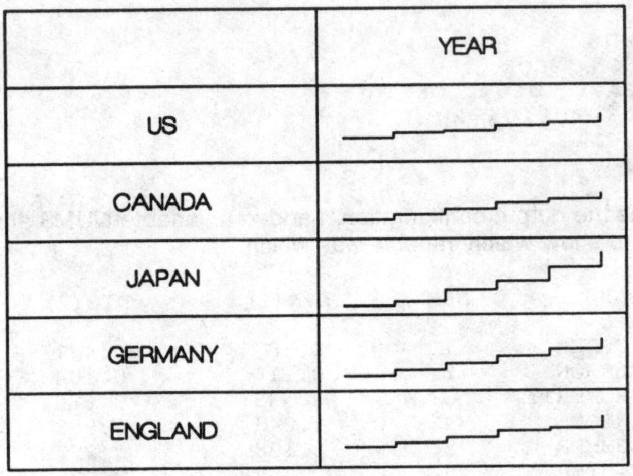

YEAR

US

CANADA

JAPAN

GERMANY

ENGLAND

SPAN *(Minimum Spanning Tree)*

OK, folks, what's a minimal spanning tree doing in a **SPLOM** routine? Well, here's one application. Suppose you've done factor analyses or smallest space analyses or multidimensional scalings in more than two dimensions. Analyzing graphic results from these analyses can be difficult, as many of you know who have pored over printouts trying to look at pairs of dimensions on different pages.

Well, here's the super-duper SPAN-SPLOM! As an example, I did a multidimensional scaling on the US data. First, I computed a Pearson correlation matrix on the data using SYSTAT:

```
CORR
USE US
SAVE UCOR
PEARSON
QUIT
```

Then I did an MDS:

```
MDS
USE UCOR
SAVE UCON/CONFIG
DIMENSION=3
SCALE
QUIT
```

Here is the output configuration. I added a variable NUM$ and a label (LAB$) to show which variable was which.

LAB$	NUM$	DIM(1)	DIM(2)	DIM(3)
POPDEN	1	0.587	-0.471	-0.643
PERSON	2	0.114	0.104	0.520
PROPERTY	3	0.533	0.680	0.350
INCOME	4	1.243	-0.052	0.066
SUMMER	5	-1.138	0.227	0.221
WINTER	6	-0.759	0.320	-0.022
RAIN	7	-0.579	-0.808	-0.492

Figure 25 shows a minimum spanning tree connecting the points in the climate data MDS configuration **SPLOM**. I've used the numbers in NUM$ to label the points, although you might prefer other symbols. The axis limits have been set with the **MIN/MAX** options in order to keep every cell on the same scale.

Figure 25

```
SPLOM  DIM(1-3),
  /SPAN,SYMBOL=NUM$,SIZE=3,
    XMIN=-1.5,XMAX=1.5,YMIN=-1.5,YMAX=1.5
```

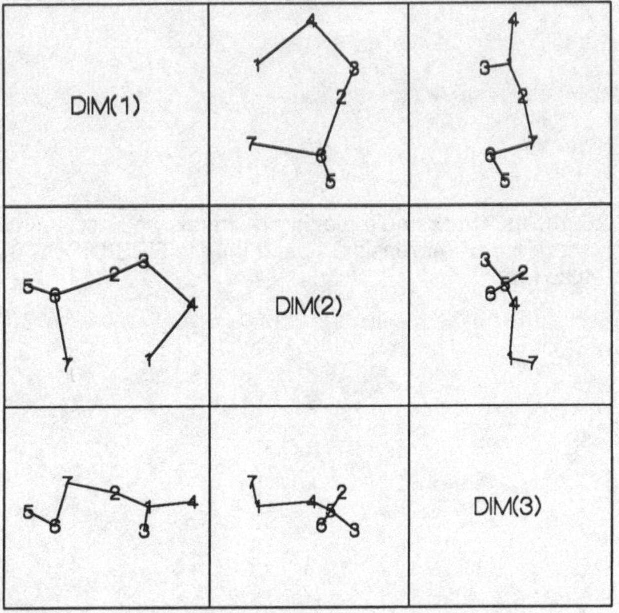

SPIKE (Vertical Spikes to Data Points)

To represent deviations from a constant value, you can plot data with the **SPIKE** option. This is handy, for example, in plotting residuals from a regression. If you use **SPIKE** with no value, e.g.:

```
SPLOM/SPIKE
```

then lines will be drawn from each plotting symbol down to the horizontal axis in each cell. If you add a value, e.g.:

```
SPLOM/SPIKE=10
```

then lines will be drawn from each symbol to the level on the vertical axis corresponding to the value you have picked.

I computed residuals from the following regression in SYSTAT:

```
MGLH
USE US
MODEL  SUMMER,WINTER,RAIN=CONSTANT+LABLAT+LABLON
SAVE  RESID
ESTIMATE
QUIT
```

Figure 26 shows an example plotting residuals against estimates from this multivariate linear regression. I used the file RESID.SYS from the file saved in MGLH.

Figure 26

```
SPLOM  RESIDUAL(1-3)*ESTIMATE(1-3)/SPIKE=0
```

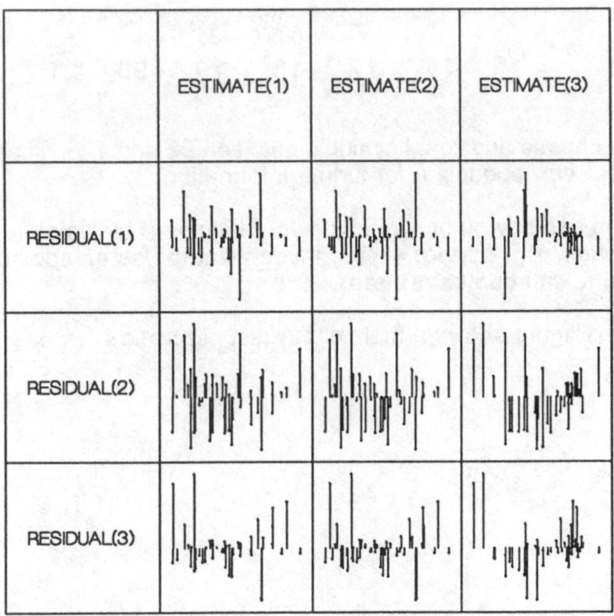

SYMBOL *(Plotting Symbols)*

You can choose a variety of symbols for your **SPLOM**. Just add the option: **SYMBOL=***n* , where *n* is an integer denoting one of the following symbols:

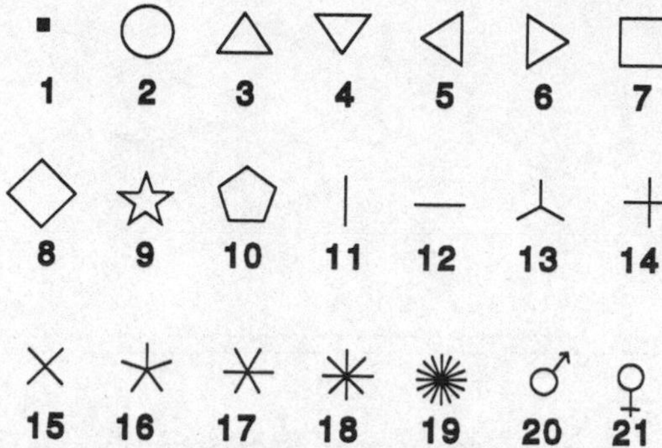

You can choose additional symbols between 32 and 128. These vary by typeface. See Appendix A for further information.

You can use any other symbol on your keyboard by typing it between apostrophes, e.g. **SYMBOL='@'**. If you want to use an apostrophe, surround it with quotes: **SYMBOL="'"**.

The next figure shows a male chauvinist pig **SPLOM**.

Figure 27

```
SPLOM   SUMMER,WINTER,RAIN/SYMBOL=20,SIZE=2
```

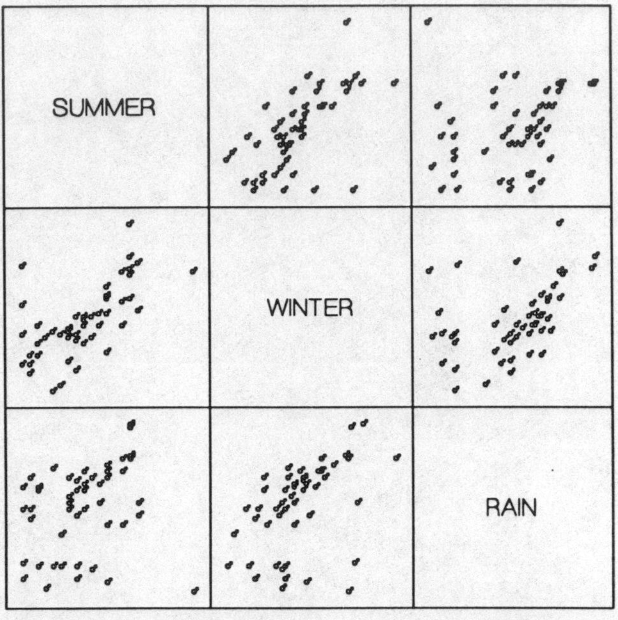

SYMBOL *(Data Based Plotting Symbols)*
You can use a character variable in your data file to determine the plotting symbol for each point. This can be handy when you are trying to denote experimental and control groups, or males and females in a plot without using labels (see **LABEL** option above in this chapter).

SYGRAPH uses the first character in a character variable when you use this option. The symbols are centered at their proper locations in the graph.

Figure 28 shows a **SPLOM** with the first letter of each state as the plotting symbol.

Figure 28

```
SPLOM   SUMMER,WINTER,RAIN/SYMBOL=STATE$,SIZE=2
```

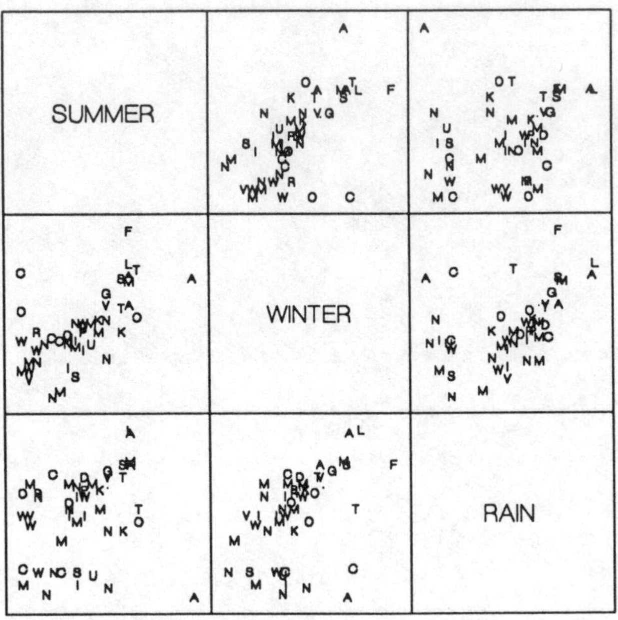

TENSION *(Tension Parameter for LOWESS or Splines or DWLS)*
The **TENSION** option controls a stiffness parameter for **LOWESS** or **SPLINE** or **DWLS** smoothing. The default value for **LOWESS** is **TENSION=.5** and for **SPLINE**, **TENSION=2**. For **DWLS**, tension is set at the inverse of the number of cases (1/*n*). The limits for **LOWESS** are between 0 and 1 and for **SPLINE** and **DWLS**, between 0 and 10. Increasing these values makes the smooths stiffer and decreasing them makes them looser, more curvy, more susceptible to individual data points, or however you wish to think about it.

Figure 29 shows the same plot used to illustrate **LOWESS** in Figure 20 (see **SMOOTH** above in this chapter) with the tension set higher (**TENSION=.9**). In this case, 90 percent of the data points are used to smooth each value on the curve.

Figure 29

```
SPLOM   SUMMER,WINTER,RAIN/SMOOTH=LOWESS,TENSION=.9
```

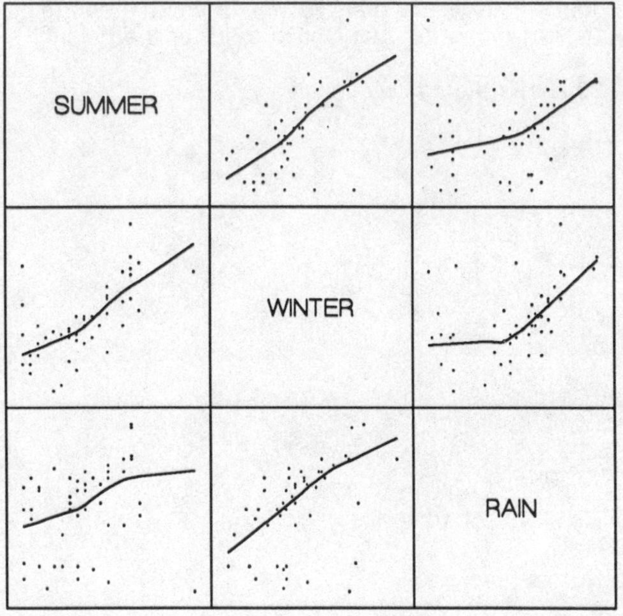

TITLE *(Graph Title)*

You can place a title at the top center of your **SPLOM** with the **TITLE** option:

```
TITLE='Quality of Life Variables'
TITLE="Stick's Segments"
TITLE='"Poor" Judgments'
```

The text must be surrounded by quotes (") or apostrophes ('). If your text includes apostrophes, as in the second example, surround it with quotes. If it includes quotes, as in the third example, surround it with apostrophes.

On some display devices the title will run off the top of the page because the standard display window is chosen to make the labels and graph as large as possible. If this happens, you will have to use the **SCALE** command to reduce the size of your entire graph (e.g. **SCALE=70,70**) or the **HEIGHT** option to lower the height.

Figure 30 shows a graph with a title.

Figure 30

```
TYPE=SWISS/ITALIC
SPLOM   PERSON,PROPERTY,POPDEN,
  /TITLE='Crime  and  Population  Density'
```

Crime and Population Density

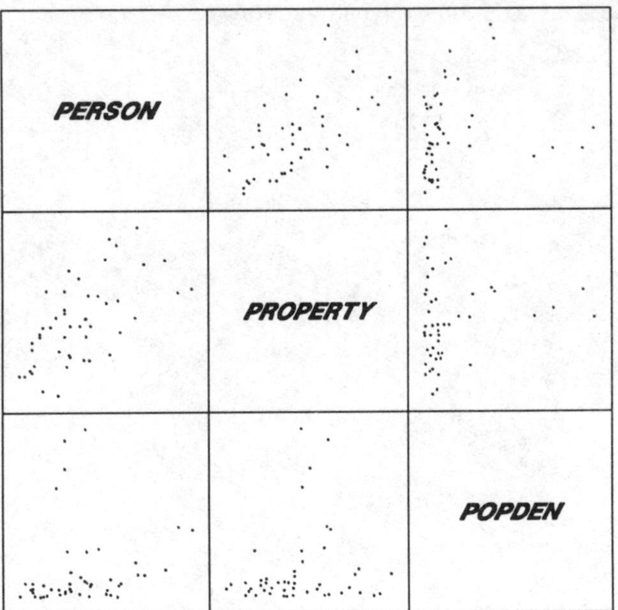

VECTOR *(Vector SPLOMS)*

You can plot factor loadings and other types of vectors in each cell of a **SPLOM**. The **VECTOR** option connects points to a single point, usually the origin (0,0). Let's use the same factor loadings I used for illustrating the **VECTOR** option in the **PLOT** chapter:

LABEL$	NUM$	COL(1)	COL(2)	COL(3)
POPDEN	1	0.248	-0.180	0.858
PERSON	2	0.758	0.462	0.170
PROPERTY	3	0.950	0.033	-0.114
INCOME	4	0.726	-0.478	0.392
SUMMER	5	-0.060	0.859	-0.121
WINTER	6	0.208	0.891	0.126
RAIN	7	-0.313	0.494	0.731

I've added the variable NUM$ to label each vector in the next figure. Let's plot all three possible pairs of loadings in a single **SPLOM** with a symbol used at the end of each vector. If you type **VECTOR** with no number following, then the vectors will be drawn to the near lower left corner of each cell. With these data, because the vectors must emanate from 0 on each axis, I have typed **VECTOR=0**.

Figure 31

```
SPLOM  COL(1-3),
    /XMIN=-1,XMAX=1,YMIN=-1,YMAX=1,
     SYMBOL=NUM$,SIZE=2,VECTOR=0
```

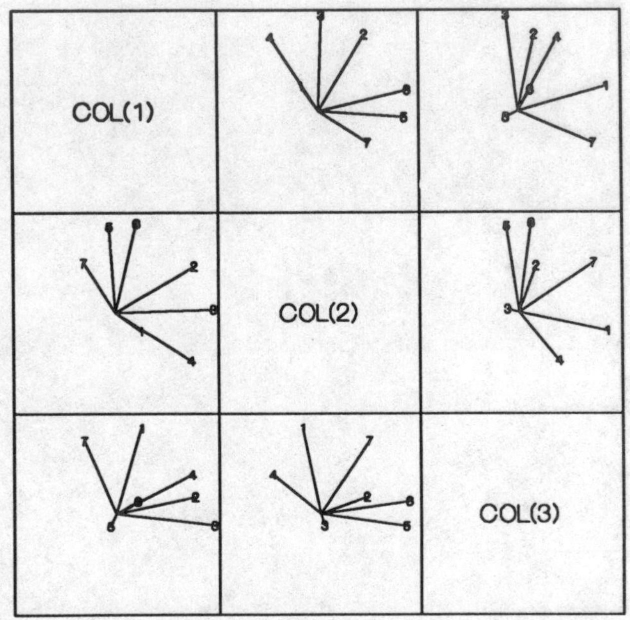

WIDTH (*Physical Width of SPLOM)*

You can control the physical width of your **SPLOM** with the **WIDTH** option. It works like this:

```
WIDTH=50%        (or WIDTH=50)
WIDTH=4IN
WIDTH=10CM
```

The first example specifies percent of display width. The second specifies inches, and the third centimeters.

When you use the **WIDTH** option, you probably also want to use **HEIGHT**, which works exactly the same way (see above in this chapter). The following graph is a thinner version of the one in Figure 14.

Figure 32

```
SPLOM  US,CANADA,JAPAN,GERMANY,ENGLAND*YEAR,
  /LINE,SIZE=0,YMIN=0,YMAX=200,
   HEIGHT=3IN,WIDTH=3IN
```

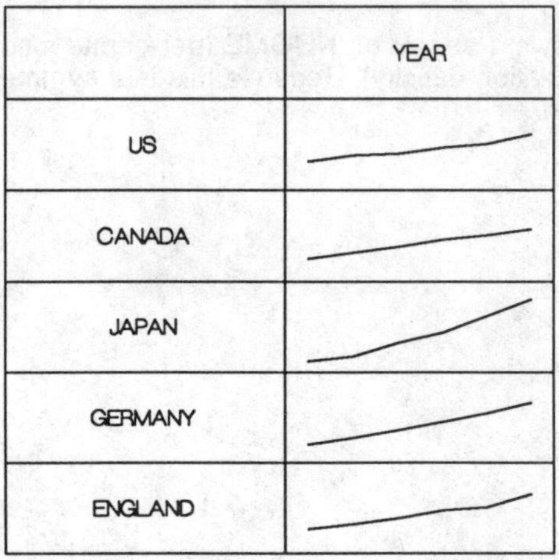

YEAR

US

CANADA

JAPAN

GERMANY

ENGLAND

XLOG, YLOG *(Logging Data in a SPLOM)*

You can log the vertical and/or horizontal scales of your **SPLOM** with the **LOG** option. The horizontal axis is transformed with the **XLOG** option and the vertical with **YLOG**. If you use either **XLOG** or **YLOG** with a symmetric **SPLOM**, both axes will receive the same transformation.

Logs may be computed to any base, e.g. **XLOG=2, XLOG=3, YLOG=10**. Natural logarithms will be computed if you use **XLOG** or **YLOG** with no argument, i.e. **YLOG**. Since **SPLOMS** have no scales, it won't matter what base you choose. You might as well use natural logs. Did you ever wonder why you get the same significance values in statistical tests when you log the same data to different bases? The reason is the same as for **SPLOMS**.

Asymmetric **SPLOMS** with one axis logged are often called semi-log **SPLOMS** (actually, I just made that up, but it's accurate). Those with two axes logged are called log-log **SPLOMS**. Be careful when interpreting semi-log **SPLOMS**. If you use **YLOG**, the row variables will be logged, but not the column variables.

Figure 33 shows a **SPLOM** of INCOME (per-capita income) against POPDEN (population density). Because this is a symmetric **SPLOM**, both axes are logged.

Figure 33

```
TYPE=HERSHEY
SPLOM  INCOME,POPDEN/XLOG
```

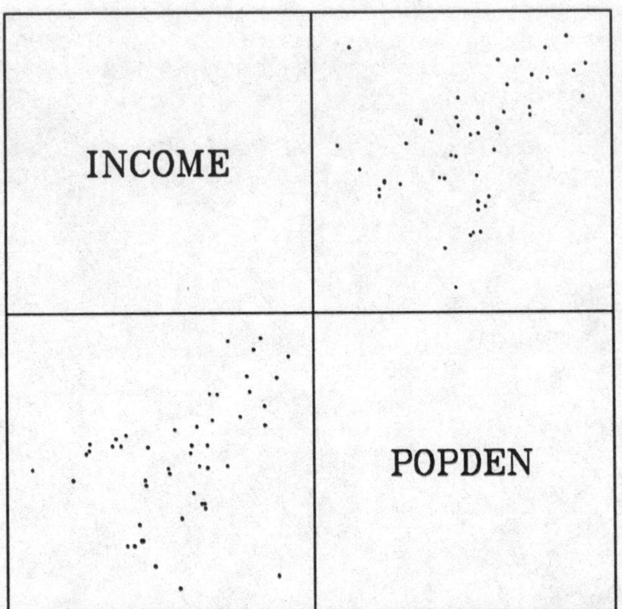

XMIN,YMIN,XMAX,YMAX *(Data Limits)*

SYGRAPH usually determines minimum and maximum scale values from the data in your file. If you wish to override this feature, use the **`MIN/MAX`** options. **`YMIN`** and **`YMAX`** control the lower and upper limits of the vertical scale. **`XMIN`** and **`XMAX`** do the same for the horizontal scale.

If you set the **`MIN`** and **`MAX`** options inside the range of your data, you will zoom in to get a closer view, but you will eliminate certain data values from your plot. SYGRAPH will warn you when this happens.

Figure 34 shows a plot of SUMMER (summer temperature), WINTER (winter temperature) and RAIN (annual rainfall) with fixed limits between 0 and 100. You can compare it to Figure 29 to see how the data ranges affect the plots.

Figure 34

```
SPLOM   SUMMER,WINTER,RAIN,
   /XMIN=0,XMAX=100,YMIN=0,YMAX=100
```

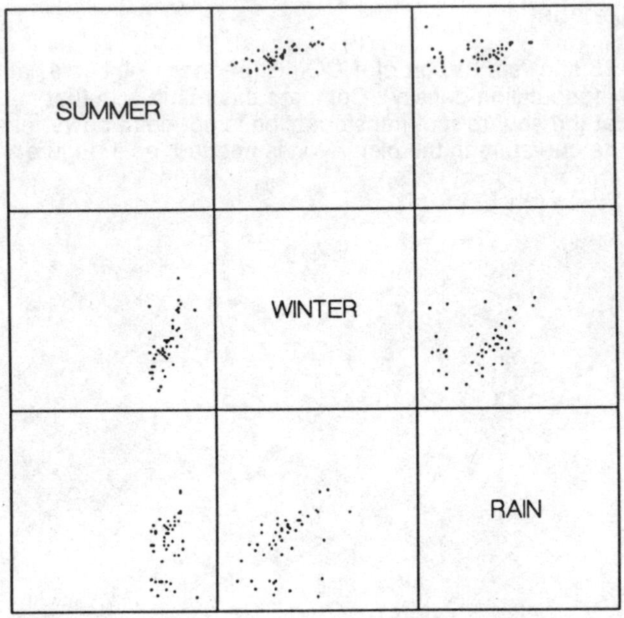

SUMMER

WINTER

RAIN

XPOW,YPOW *(Powering Data)*

You can power the vertical and/or horizontal scales of your **SPLOM** with the **POW** command. **XPOW** governs the horizontal axis and **YPOW** the vertical. If you use either **XPOW** or **YPOW** with a symmetric **SPLOM**, both axes will receive the same transformation.

Powers may be computed to any exponent, e.g. **POW=.5** (square root), **POW=.33333** (cube root), **POW=-1** (inverse), **POW=2**. Square roots will be computed if you use **POW** with no argument, i.e. **POW**. **POW** is implemented in SYGRAPH only for positive data. Negative values will be deleted.

Unlike logs, where different bases do not matter for SPLOMs, different powers do make a difference. You should read Velleman and Hoaglin (1981) or Chambers, Cleveland, Kleiner, and Tukey (1983) to see why **LOG** is like **POW=0**.

Figure 35 shows a **SPLOM** of INCOME (per-capita income) against POPDEN (population density). Compare this result with that in Figure 33. Notice that the square root transformation is not quite powerful enough to remove the curvature in the plot. A log is needed, as in Figure 33.

Figure 35

```
TYPE=HERSHEY/ITALIC
SPLOM  INCOME,POPDEN/XPOW=.5
```

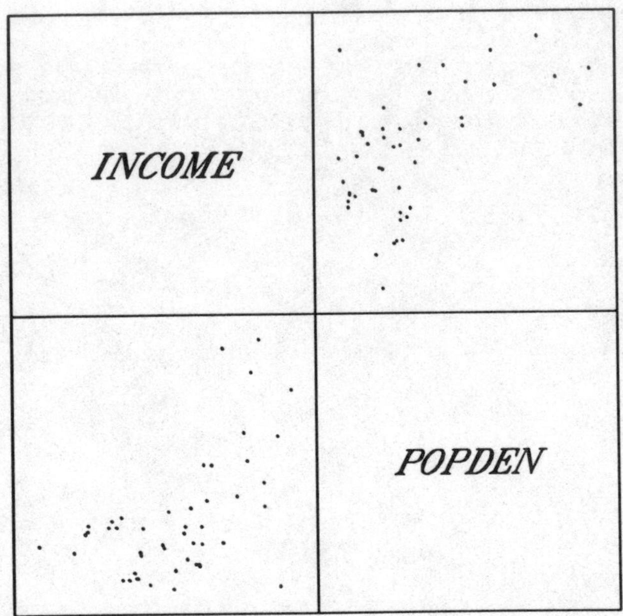

Chapter 14

STEM

The stem-and-leaf display looks like a sideways histogram or tally. Unlike the histogram, however, the stem-and-leaf display shows the numerical values of the variable. The stems are printed on the left side. These are the most significant digits in which variation occurs. The leaves are printed to the right. These are taken from the next decimal digit after each stem for each case. The leaves are not rounded, so that the original data can be recovered to the precision of the leaves. For more information, consult Tukey (1977) or Velleman and Hoaglin (1981).

SYGRAPH constructs the display in an heuristic manner similar to the way it does histograms. It first chooses the number of lines to use based on the number of observations in the batch of data. Then it picks a stem (the number on the left) which will allow roughly the number of lines chosen for the display. The difference between adjacent stems is a very round number $\{1,2,5\}*10^n$, where n is an integer. Next, the leaves (the numbers on the right) are taken from the next digit after the stem value for each case. The leaf for each case is written on the line corresponding to the stem for the observation and leaves for other cases with the same stem are written next to each other on the same line. If there are more leaves than can fit on one line, an asterisk is printed at the end of the line to indicate the overflow. This should rarely happen, since more lines are used when there are more data values.

SYGRAPH prints the median (M) and the hinges or quartiles (H) in the vertical area between stems and leaves. See the discussion of `BOX` plots for more information on these statistics. Any values outside the inner fences are printed on additional lines separated from the inner values by a line of text: ***OUTSIDE VALUES*** .

This is the world's slowest stem-and-leaf program. It is intended for presentation quality graphics only. Consequently, all the typography, color, and other options slow down the printing. If you need a quick, exploratory stem-and-leaf program which uses the ordinary character output of your computer, consider the same command in SYSTAT.

If you use the `FACET` command together with `STEM`, you will have the world's only three-dimensional stem-and-leaf diagram. I will send a SYSTAT sweatshirt to anyone who manages to get such a monstrosity past the editors of a reputable scientific journal and into print.

Figure 1 shows an example from the US data. This one is black on white. If you want a color stem-and-leaf diagram (blasphemy!), add **COLOR GRAPH=RED** (or some other color) before the **STEM** command.

You will notice that STEM adjusts the height and width of numerals to make the entire plot fit the usual plotting frame. The left edge of the "leaves" is set at the left edge of the usual frame. This can sometimes cause squished looking diagrams. You can cure this with the **HEIGHT** and **WIDTH** options (see below). In addition, the height is adjusted only for the values inside the inner fences. If you have a lot of outliers, you will need to make additional adjustments.

Figure 1

STEM INCOME

```
2   2
2   45
2   667
2   888899
3H  000001
3   22333
3M  444555
3H  6666667
3   889
4   011
4   222
4   445
```

HEIGHT *(Physical Height of Plot)*

You can control the physical height of your stem-and-leaf diagram with the **HEIGHT** option. It works like this:

```
HEIGHT=50%        (or HEIGHT=50)
HEIGHT=4IN
HEIGHT=10CM
```

The first example specifies percent of display height. The second specifies inches, and the third centimeters.

When you use the **HEIGHT** option, you probably also want to use **WIDTH**, which works exactly the same way (see below in this chapter). The height and width of each number in the stem-and-leaf diagram are adjusted to fit the overall height and width you request. This way, you can get thin or fat numbers, depending on the dimensions. The following graph shows how to use them together.

Figure 2

```
TYPE=SWISS
STEM   SUMMER/HEIGHT=4IN,WIDTH=2IN
```

```
68   0000
69   000
70   000
71   0
72H  00
73   00
74   0000
75M  00000
76   0000
77   00
78   00
79H  00000
80
81   000
82   00000
83   00
     ***OUTSIDE VALUES***
90   0
```

LINES *(Setting the Number of Lines)*

If your diagram is too coarse, you can increase the number of lines with the **LINES** option, e.g.:

```
STEM  ROBBERY/LINES=15
```

It may take you several tries to set the number of lines correctly. If you set too many, your stem-and-leaf diagram will look long and stringy. If too few, it will be too coarse.

Figure 3 shows the same stem-and-leaf diagram as in Figure 1 with more lines. Notice that you will not necessarily get the exact number you specify. SYGRAPH has to back and fill to cover all the values and come as close as it can to the number you request.

Figure 3

```
STEM   INCOME/LINES=30,HEIGHT=3.5IN,WIDTH=2IN
```

```
22    1
23
24    8
25    8
26    00
27    8
28    0489
29    59
30H   12457
31    3
32    45
33    057
34M   578
35    247
36    003358
37H   3
38    45
39    9
40    7
41    05
42    489
43
44    45
45    9
```

LOG *(Logging Data)*

You can log your data with the `LOG` option before doing a stem-and-leaf diagram. Logs may be computed to any base, e.g. `LOG=2, LOG=3, LOG=10`. Natural logarithms will be computed if you use `LOG` with no argument, i.e. `LOG`.

Figure 4 shows a stem-and-leaf diagram of INCOME (per-capita income). Compare its shape to that of Figure 1, which shows the raw data.

Figure 4

```
STEM INCOME/LOG=10
```

```
33    4
33
33    9
34    111
34
34    445
34H   66777
34    88889
35    111
35M   223
35    4445555
35H   66667
35    88
36    0011
36    233
36    44
36    6
```

POW *(Powering Data)*

You can power your data with the `POW` command before doing a stem-and-leaf diagram. Powers may be computed to any exponent, e.g. `POW=.5` (square root), `POW=.33333` (cube root), `POW=-1` (inverse), `POW=2`. Square roots will be computed if you use `POW` with no argument, i.e. `POW`. `POW` is implemented in SYGRAPH only for positive data. Negative values will be deleted.

Unlike logs, where different bases do not affect the overall shape of the stem-and-leaf diagram, different powers do make a difference. You should read Velleman and Hoaglin (1981) or Chambers, Cleveland, Kleiner, and Tukey (1983) to see why `LOG` is like `POW=0`.

Figure 5 shows a stem-and-leaf diagram of INCOME (per-capita income). Compare this result with that in Figure 4. Notice that the square root transformation is not quite powerful enough to normalize the data. A log is needed, as in Figure 4.

Figure 5

```
STEM  INCOME/POW=.5
```

4	7
4	9
5	011
5	22333
5H	44455555
5	6777
5M	8889999
6H	0000001
6	2233
6	44555
6	667

TITLE *(Graph Title)*

You can place a title at the top center of your stem-and-leaf diagram with the **TITLE** option:

```
TITLE='Distribution of Offices'
TITLE="Avco's Share of Market"
TITLE='Sections "Lighted"'
```

The text must be surrounded by quotes (") or apostrophes ('). If your text includes apostrophes, as in the second example, surround it with quotes. If it includes quotes, as in the third example, surround it with apostrophes.

On some display devices the title will run off the top of the page because the standard display window is chosen to make the labels and graph as large as possible. If this happens, you will have to use the **SCALE** command to reduce the size of your entire graph (e.g. **SCALE=70,70**) or the **HEIGHT** option to lower the height.

Figure 6 shows a stem-and-leaf diagram with a title. I had to adjust the height because it overflows the page.

Figure 6

```
STEM  POPDEN,
  /TITLE='Population  Density',HEIGHT=2IN,WIDTH=3IN
```

Population Density

```
0    0000000111
0H   222333
0    444455
0M   667777
0    8889
1    01
1H   22
1    45
1
1    9
2
2
2    55
2    7
     ***OUTSIDE VALUES***
3    79
6    1
7    1
8    7
9    4
```

WIDTH (*Physical Width of Stem-and-leaf Diagram)*

You can control the physical width of your graph with the **WIDTH** option. It works like this:

```
WIDTH=50%        (or WIDTH=50)
WIDTH=4IN
WIDTH=10CM
```

The first example specifies percent of display width. The second specifies inches, and the third centimeters.

When you use the **WIDTH** option, you probably also want to use **HEIGHT**, which works exactly the same way (see above in this chapter). The following graph is a wider version of the one in Figure 2.

Figure 7

```
STEM   SUMMER/HEIGHT=3IN,WIDTH=2IN
```

```
68    0000
69    000
70    000
71    0
72H   00
73    00
74    0000
75M   00000
76    0000
77    00
78    00
79H   00000
80
81    000
82    00000
83    00
      ***OUTSIDE VALUES***
90    0
```

Chapter 15

WRITE

The **WRITE** command plots text in a graph. You can use it to make signs for office parties and to annotate scientific graphs. Together with **TYPE**, which chooses type faces, you can produce publication quality text. The standard syntax for **WRITE** is:

```
WRITE  'Text'          e.g.
WRITE  'Group'
WRITE  'Per  Capita  Income'
WRITE  "Roger's  Party"
WRITE  'Type  of  "Widgets"  Bid'
WRITE  '  '
```

The text must be surrounded by quotes (") or apostrophes ('). If your text includes apostrophes, as in the third example, surround it with quotes. If it includes quotes, as in the fourth example, surround it with apostrophes. The last example shows how to write nothing. This can be thrilling, like the sound of one hand clapping.

The following examples in this chapter are taken from a single author. Can you guess who?

Writing a Line of Text

Whatever you write will begin in the lower left corner of the standard graph frame and it will be approximately a tenth of the height of the frame. Here is an example, using the **BRITISH** typeface.

Figure 1

```
TYPE=BRITISH/ITALIC
WRITE "TRICHINOSIS, the pig's reply to pork chops"
```

TRICHINOSIS, the pig's reply to pork chops

ANGLE *(Angle of Text)*

You can write text at any angle from 0 (the default) to 360 degrees. Just add the option **ANGLE=***n* , where *n* is a number from 0 to 360. Figure 2 shows some text written at a 50 degree angle in the **SWISS** typeface.

Figure 2

```
TYPE=SWISS
WRITE "POSITIVE, mistaken at the top of one's voice",
  /ANGLE=50
```

POSITIVE, mistaken at the top of one's voice

CENTER *(Centering Text)*

Normally, SYGRAPH positions text beginning at the location specified by **X** and **Y** (see below in this chapter) or at the default location 0,0. If you wish to center text at **X** and **Y**, use the **CENTER** option. Here is an example of centering text at the middle of a standard size box. I have used the **DRAW** command to produce the box (see the **DRAW** chapter above).

Figure 3

```
DRAW  BOX/HEIGHT=2IN,WIDTH=4IN
TYPE=HERSHEY
WRITE  'VIRTUES,  certain  abstentions',
   /CENTER,X=2IN,Y=1IN,HEIGHT=.1IN,WIDTH=.1IN
```

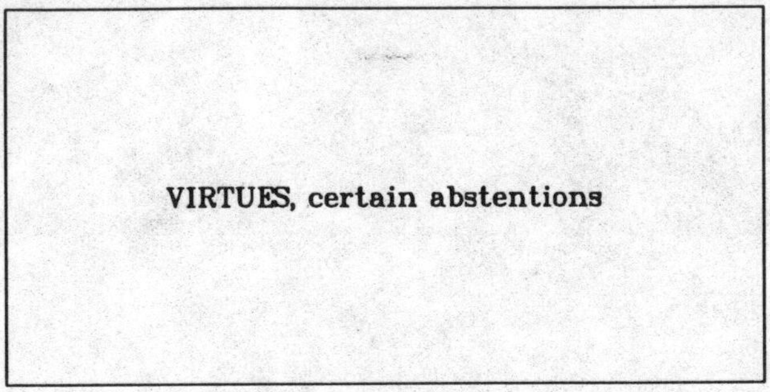

VIRTUES, certain abstentions

COLOR *(Color Writing)*

You can choose a color for your text with the **COLOR** option. Choose either a name or a wavelength in nanometers. Possible colors and their approximate nanometer wavelengths are: **RED** (615), **ORANGE** (590), **YELLOW** (575), **GREEN** (505), **BLUE** (480), **VIOLET** (450). You may also name **BLACK**, **WHITE**, **GRAY**, and **BROWN**. The following command will make all text red:

```
WRITE  'RED'/COLOR=RED
```

You can also specify color in nanometers wavelength. The following example will make the text greenish:

```
WRITE  'GREENISH'/COLOR=540
```

Figure 4 shows blue text.

Figure 4

```
TYPE=BRITISH
WRITE 'PLATITUDE, a moral without a fable',
  /COLOR=BLUE
```

PLATITUDE, a moral without a fable

HEIGHT (*Physical Height of Text*)

You can control the physical height of your text with the **HEIGHT** option. It works like this:

```
HEIGHT=50%      (or HEIGHT=50)
HEIGHT=4IN
HEIGHT=10CM
HEIGHT=12PT
```

The first example specifies percent of display height. The second specifies inches, and the third centimeters. The last is in point sizes.

The next figure shows height and width specified for a text using point sizes. SYGRAPH points are actually 72 per inch of full height. No allowance is made for leading.

Figure 5

```
TYPE=BRITISH
WRITE 'LOVE, a temporary insanity cured by marriage',
  /HEIGHT=30PT,WIDTH=7PT
```

LOVE, a temporary insanity cured by marriage

WIDTH *(Physical Width of Text)*

You can control the physical width of your text with the **WIDTH** option. It works like this:

```
WIDTH=50%        (or WIDTH=50
WIDTH=4IN
WIDTH=10CM
WIDTH=10PT
```

The first example specifies percent of display width. The second specifies inches, and the third centimeters. The last is type size in points.

When you use the **WIDTH** option, you probably also want to use **HEIGHT**, which works exactly the same way (see above in this chapter). The following figure shows them together.

Figure 6

```
TYPE=BRITISH
WRITE 'ALONE, in bad company',
  /HEIGHT=2IN,WIDTH=3IN
```

ALONE, in bad company

X,Y *(Locating Text)*

SYGRAPH normally locates text at the lower left corner of the graph window. You can place text anywhere else with the **X** and **Y** options. They work like this:

```
X=50%        (or X=50)
X=4IN
Y=10CM
```

The first example specifies percent of display width. The second specifies inches, and the third centimeters. If you use the **CENTER** option (see above in this chapter), then **X** and **Y** refer to the location of the center of the string rather than the lower left hand corner.

Here is an example of a title placed at the upper center of a figure area.

Figure 8

```
TYPE=GREEK/ITALIC
WRITE  'a'/X=1IN,Y=1IN,HEIGHT=2IN,WIDTH=2IN
```

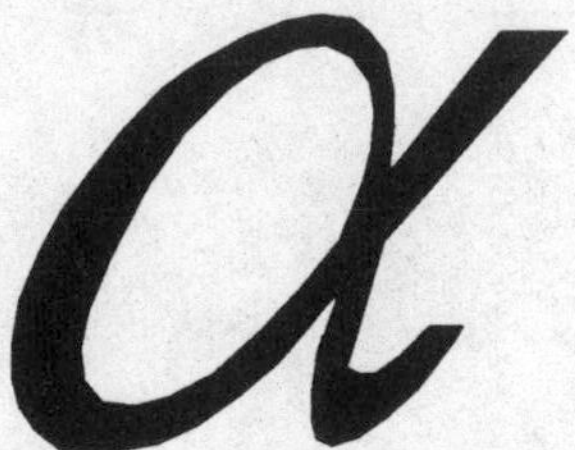

Part 3
Chapter 1

Two-Dimensional Plots

This chapter concerns special applications of two-dimensional graphics. Since SYGRAPH is like a computer language in many respects, you can use it to construct complex graphs. If you have a language which generates files of commands, such as BASIC or the SYSTAT MACRO processor, you can automatically produce graphs for different datasets. This is what distinguishes SYGRAPH from paint programs and menu oriented graphics packages which require you to set features by hand for every new graph.

To do these graphs, you must be able to draw repeatedly on a single page or screen. The `BEGIN` and `END` commands (see above in the General Commands section on page 105) allow you to overlay several SYGRAPH commands. All the examples in this and the next chapter were surrounded with `BEGIN` and `END` markers and submitted from a command file or the `FEDIT` full screen editor.

Plotting a Curve on Points from a Spreadsheet

Spreadsheets can perform sophisticated numerical analyses and can produce simple XY plots and line plots. When you use a spreadsheet for forecasting or creating theoretical mathematical curves, however, there is no way to plot a smooth curve unless you compute many points and connect them with a line. The interpolation methods in SYGRAPH offered in the **SMOOTH** option allow you to do this.

The following data are adapted from Nelson (1987). They constitute the results of a Lotus 1-2-3 analysis using the @IRR (internal rate of return) and @NPV (net present value) Lotus functions on figures from an undeveloped land holding. Nelson standardized both measures to allow a common vertical scale on his graph. Although Lotus calculated the values of these functions for only 8 points (years), we can plot them as continuous functions with the **SMOOTH=SPLINE** option in SYGRAPH. Figure 1 shows the result.

YEAR	IRR	NPV
1	-24.9	-12.07
2	12.8	-3.54
3	19.6	2.98
4	20.9	7.80
5	20.9	11.19
6	20.6	13.37
7	20.1	14.54
8	19.7	14.87

You should compare Figure 1 with the graph in the original article to see the improvement with smoothing. Spline smoothing will work well provided you have enough points to define the curve which underlies the points. I increased the standard tension (**TENSION=5**) in order to make the IRR curve straighter on the left.

Figure 1

```
TYPE=BRITISH
PLOT  IRR,NPV*YEAR,
    /SMOOTH=SPLINE,SYMBOL=2,3,FILL=1,1,
     TENSION=5,YLABEL='YIELD'
```

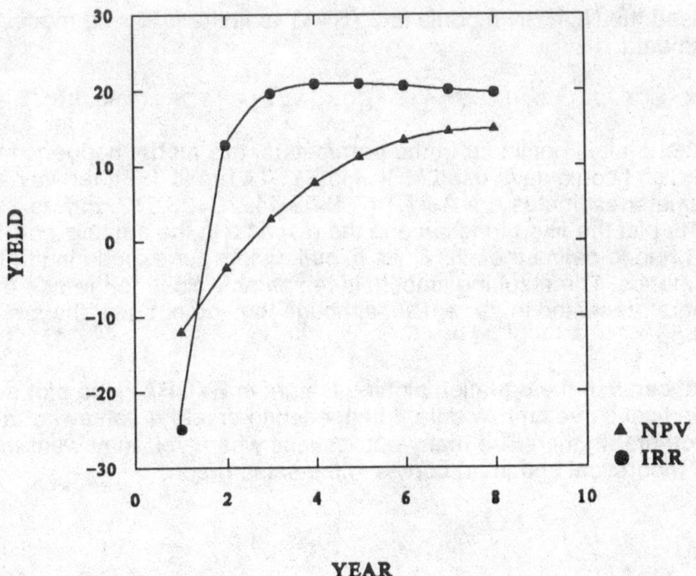

Plotting a Theoretical Curve on Data.

You can plot a theoretical curve on top of data in two steps. The following data are adapted from Giloh and Sedat (1982), who showed that the chemical *n*-propyl gallate reduces the rate of fading of fluorescence of cell structures labeled with tetramethylrhodamine for microscopy. The variable T_HALF represents time in minutes for 50 percent loss of initial fluorescence and CONCENT represents concentration of propyl gallate (percentage, weight to volume).

CONCENT	T_HALF
.2	1.8
.3	5.0
.6	10.0
1.0	15.0
2.0	18.0
4.0	27.0
10.0	34.0

I used the NONLIN module in SYSTAT to fit the following model to these data:

```
MODEL   T_HALF=A+B*CONCENT+C*SQR(CONCENT)
```

Although it is nonlinear in the parameters, this model happens to be linear, so I could have used MGLH in SYSTAT to fit it. Either way, the parameter estimates are A=-7.147, B=-3.446, C=23.882. Figure 2 shows how to plot the fitted function and the raw data in the same graph. Notice that I had to define the axis limits to make them correspond in the two plot commands. The resulting smooth is remarkably close to the one the authors presented in the article, although they do not give the smoothing method.

You can use the equation plotting feature in SYGRAPH to plot any theoretical curve on raw data. I happened to create a somewhat ad-hoc smoother, but there are many applications where you may want to plot both theoretical and fitted curves in the same graph.

Figure 2

```
PLOT  T_HALF*CONCENT,
  /AXES=2,SYMBOL=2,FILL=1,
   XMIN=0,XMAX=10,YMIN=0,YMAX=40,
   XLABEL='Concentration  of  propyl  gallate',
   YLABEL='t1/2  (minutes)'
PLOT  Y=-7.147-3.446*X+23.882*SQR(X),
  !AXES=0,SCALE=0,
   XMIN=0,XMAX=10,YMIN=0,YMAX=40,
   XLABEL='  ',YLABEL='  '
```

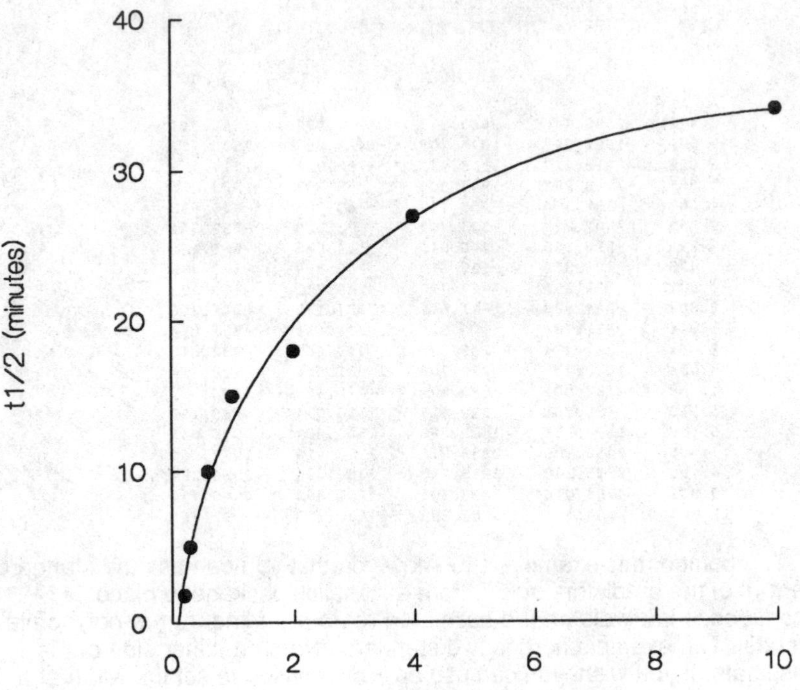

Plotting Confidence Limits for Polynomial Regression Models

The following variables X and Y were created in SYSTAT using the equation:

$x = u + i - 10$
$y = 2 + 3x + 4x^2 + 5x^3 + 500z$, where

u is a uniform random variable
i is an index running from 1 to 20
z is a standard normal random variable.

The variable ESTIMATE was estimated from a cubic regression model computed with the MGLH regression program in SYSTAT. Finally, the variables UPPER and LOWER were computed in the DATA module of SYSTAT from the variable SEPRED (standard error of the predicted values) created by MGLH. UPPER is two standard errors above ESTIMATE and LOWER is two standard errors below.

```
LET   UPPER=ESTIMATE+2*SEPRED
LET   LOWER=ESTIMATE-2*SEPRED
```

X	Y	ESTIMATE	UPPER	LOWER
-8.472	-2598.746	-2680.917	-1915.487	-3446.347
-7.570	-1981.547	-1975.207	-1419.687	-2530.727
-6.058	-916.427	-1113.931	-713.743	-1514.119
-5.666	-1543.242	-947.304	-555.893	-1338.715
-4.005	392.356	-450.719	-50.705	-850.733
-3.353	-501.377	-330.748	71.349	-732.844
-2.898	-516.368	-266.045	134.056	-666.145
-1.425	-406.352	-133.613	242.519	-509.745
-0.081	321.691	-62.792	283.751	-409.335
0.807	-844.989	-11.042	324.172	-346.256
1,006	-211.789	3.306	337.631	-331.018
2.064	311.474	108.577	449.465	-232.310
3.054	1070.435	270.706	631.626	-90.214
4.238	1188.001	580.501	970.489	190.513
5.510	459.061	1099.617	1510.074	689.160
6.150	1594.951	1449.868	1862.904	1036.831
7.398	2438.986	2335.840	2743.716	1927.964
8.108	2535.208	2975.190	3386.096	2564.284
9.902	4708.076	5096.305	5651.865	4540.744
11.000	7250.791	6802.599	7607.337	5997.861

The point of this example is to show you that you can use the standard errors of the predictors output from a statistics package to place confidence intervals on the estimated regression line from a polynomial model. The example here is two standard errors on either side of the estimate. If you wish, you can use an F distribution to set the width at a given probability value (see, for example, Daniel and Wood, 1971). Figure 3 shows the values plotted and smoothed. Notice that I have suppressed the axes and labels the second time around.

Figure 3

```
PLOT  Y*X/SYMBOL=2
PLOT  UPPER,ESTIMATE,LOWER*X,
   /SMOOTH=SPLINE,SIZE=0,AXES=0,SCALE=0,
    XLABEL='  ',YLABEL='  ',  SHORT
```

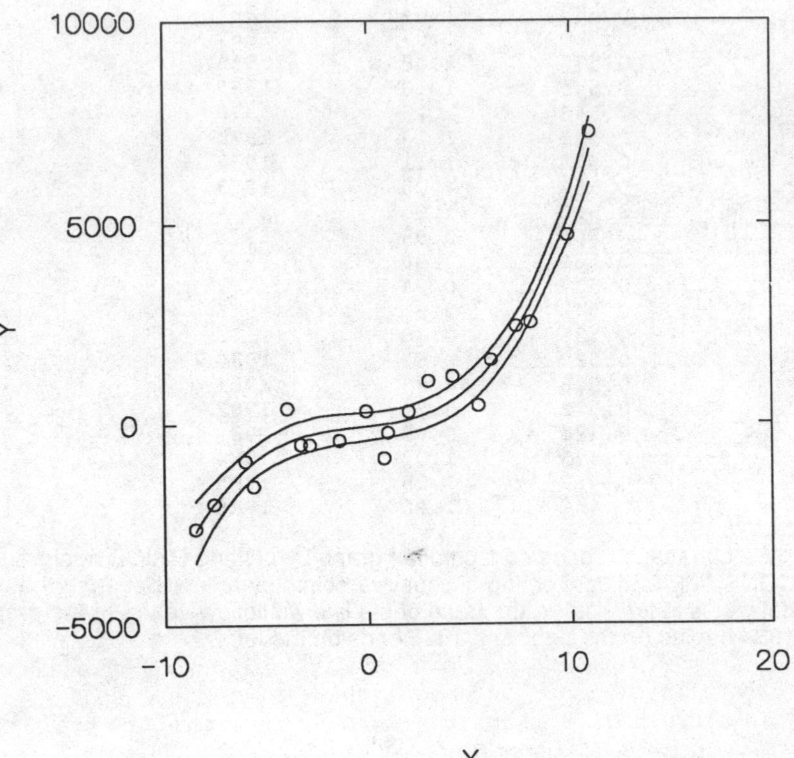

Flow Graphs for Price/Consumption and Other Data

Line graphs can be used to trace dynamic flow and price/consumption indices in economics. In these graphs, successive points are connected in a trace that is not a function of the horizontal axis variable. A price/consumption chart shows price plotted against consumption with points connected in time order.

The following data are adapted from a graph in Harris (1987) on tobacco prices and consumption. PRICE is in 1986 dollars a pack and CONSUMP is in packs per person per day.

CONSUMP	PRICE	YEAR
0.575	1.00	1964
0.584	1.02	1965
0.588	1.04	1966
0.580	1.07	1967
0.575	1.08	1968
0.545	1.10	1969
0.543	1.13	1970
0.552	1.10	1971
0.553	1.11	1972
0.567	1.05	1973
0.566	1.00	1974
0.565	0.98	1975
0.561	0.96	1976
0.557	0.94	1977
0.543	0.91	1978
0.530	0.88	1979
0.529	0.83	1980
0.526	0.80	1981
0.512	0.85	1982
0.480	0.99	1983
0.475	1.02	1984
0.462	1.05	1985
0.450	1.10	1986

We can make a price/consumption graph by plotting PRICE against CONSUMP and connecting successive points by a line. Because the dataset is in time order, the trace of the line will follow years. In the graph, 1964 begins on the right and 1986 ends on the left.

Figure 4

```
TYPE=SWISS
PLOT  PRICE*CONSUMP,
   /LINE,SYMBOL=2,HEIGHT=3IN,WIDTH=4IN,FILL=1,
    YLAB='Price  per  Pack',
    XLAB='Packs  Consumed  per  Day'
WRITE  '1964',
  /X=3.5IN,Y=1.6IN,
    HEIGHT=6PT,WIDTH=6PT,CENTER
WRITE  '1986',
  /X=1IN,Y=2.6IN,
    HEIGHT=6PT,WIDTH=6PT,CENTER
```

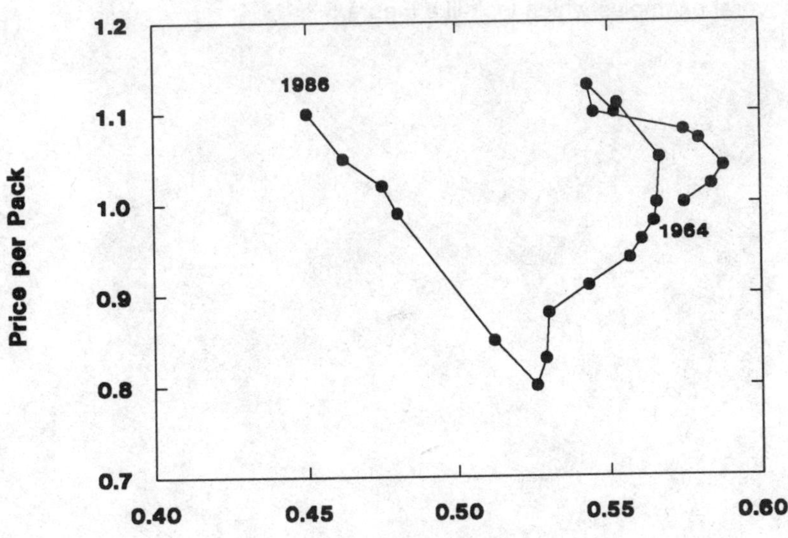

Random Walks

A random walk is a two-dimensional trace of a path in which the direction taken at each step is a random variable. Here is a program in SYSTAT for generating a random walk in two dimensions.

```
SAVE WALK
REPEAT 1000
HOLD
LET R=URN
IF R<.25 THEN LET X=X+1
ELSE IF R<.5 THEN LET Y=Y+1
ELSE IF R<.75 THEN LET X=X-1
ELSE LET Y=Y-1
RUN
```

Figure 5 shows a plot of the output of this program. I have left out the axes to emphasize the shape itself. This elongated (non-globular) shape is typical of random walks and is somewhat counter-intuitive. Rudnick and Gaspari (1987) discuss the shapes of random walks and show several examples which look like Figure 5.

Figure 5

```
PLOT  Y*X,
   /LINE,AXES=0,SCALE=0,HEIGHT=4IN,WIDTH=4IN,
    SIZE=0,XLABEL='  ',YLABEL='  '
```

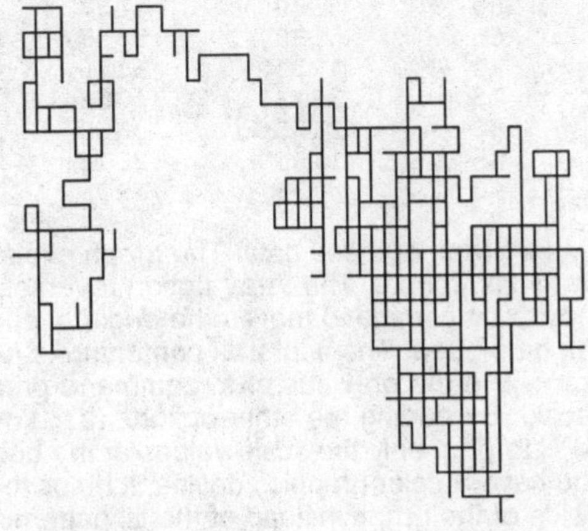

Dual Histograms and Pyramid Graphs

Dual histograms and pyramid graphs reveal differences between distributions in groups because they place them side by side. The most popular form of these graphs is the **age-sex pyramid**. The following data from the 1980 U.S. Census show the distributions of males and females within age groups. Each age group is the upper age limit of its members. The last group (90) is open ended.

AGE	MALES	FEMALES
5	9230	8806
10	8608	8213
15	8762	8340
20	9445	9107
25	10515	10479
30	10886	10865
35	10096	10171
40	8741	8967
45	6889	7166
50	5679	5969
55	5281	5660
60	5380	5957
65	5120	5877
70	4254	5176
75	3213	4352
80	2135	3360
85	1153	2176
90	773	1938

Figure 6 shows a graph of these data. The graph explains itself, but there are a few things to note. The **YREV** option reverses the left graph segment. The **ORIGIN** command moves the origin over so that the second half can be plotted. The final **BAR** command is necessary because **SCALE=-4** in the previous **BAR** command prints only the right-hand vertical scale. By adding the other options (**SIZE=0**, etc.), we cause SYGRAPH to print only the scale values at the bottom right side of the graph. If you have a color graphics device, it helps to use a different color for each side of the graph instead of the fill patterns.

Figure 6

```
TYPE=HERSHEY
BAR  MALES*AGE,
  /TRANS,XMIN=0,YMIN=0,YMAX=12000,BWID=5,
    FILL=5,HEIGHT=4IN,WIDTH=2IN,TICK=4,YREV
ORIGIN=2IN,0
BAR  FEMALES*AGE,
  /TRANS,XMIN=0,YMIN=0,YMAX=12000,BWID=5,
    FILL=7,HEIGHT=4IN,WIDTH=2IN,TICK=4,
   XLABEL='  ',SCALE=-4
BAR  FEMALES*AGE,
  /TRANS,XMIN=0,YMIN=0,YMAX=12000,AXES=0,
    SCALE=1,HEIGHT=4IN,WIDTH=2IN,TICK=4,
   XLABEL='  ',YLABEL='  '
```

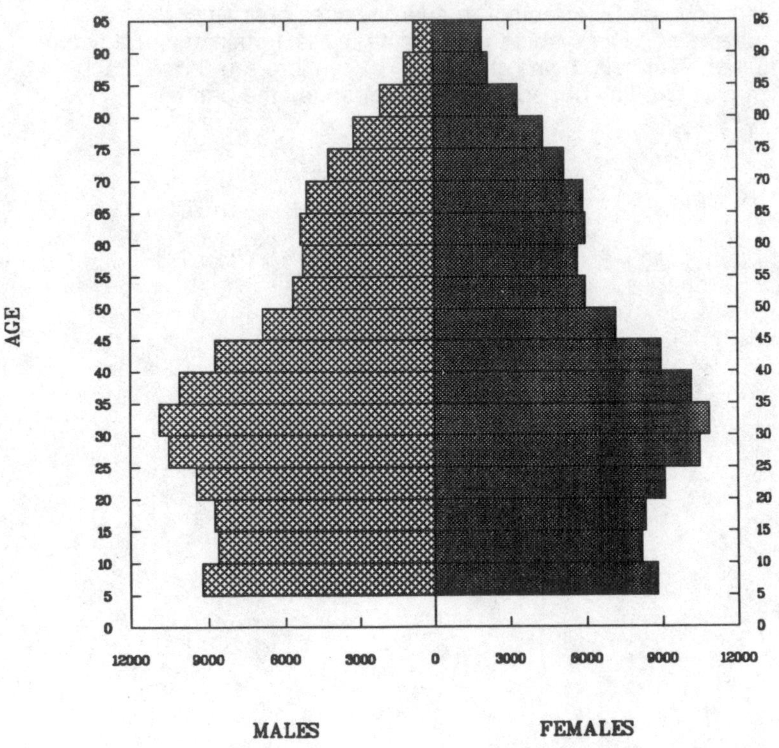

A Pretty Bar Graph

The following data are adapted from an editorial in *The New York Times* (December 3, 1987). They represent the duration of various plays, films, and operas. Figure 7 shows a bar graph of these data.

TITLE$	HOURS
SHOA	9.0
ELECTRA	6.5
NICKLEBY	8.6
MAHABHAR	9.0
EINSTEIN	4.0
PARSIFAL	5.0
STALIN	12.0

I plotted this graph in italic Hershey font to suit the nature of the titles. While there are many commands, most of them are devoted to annotating the graph. The positioning of the text is determined by the height and width I chose. By keeping an even number (**HEIGHT=4.5IN, WIDTH=6IN**), I was able to determine the text positions in advance. The 4.5 inches of height was chosen because there are 8 bars each a half an inch plus two half bar spaces on either end of the bars.

Figure 7

```
TYPE=HERSHEY
ORIGIN=-1IN,0
BAR  HOURS*TITLE$,
   /FAT,TRANS,AXES=1,SCALE=1,XLABEL=' ',
     YMIN=0,YMAX=12,TICK=12,STICK,HEIGHT=4.5IN,WIDTH=6IN
WRITE   'OPERA'/X=-.3IN,Y=3.5IN,ANGLE=90
WRITE   'THEATER'/X=-.3IN,Y=2IN,ANGLE=90
WRITE   'FILM'/X=-.3IN,Y=.75IN,ANGLE=90
WRITE 'THE LIFE AND TIMES OF JOSEPH STALIN',
   /X=.1IN,Y=3.9IN,HEIGHT=.2IN,WIDTH=.1IN,STYLE=ITALIC
WRITE  'PARSIFAL',
   /X=.1IN,Y=3.4IN,HEIGHT=.2IN,WIDTH=.1IN,STYLE=ITALIC
WRITE 'EINSTEIN ON THE BEACH',
   /X=.1IN,Y=2.9IN,HEIGHT=.2IN,WIDTH=.1IN,STYLE=ITALIC
WRITE  'THE  MAHABHARATA',
   /X=.1IN,Y=2.4IN,HEIGHT=.2IN,WIDTH=.1IN,STYLE=ITALIC
WRITE  'NICHOLAS  NICKLEBY',
   /X=.1IN,Y=1.9IN,HEIGHT=.2IN,WIDTH=.1IN,STYLE=ITALIC
WRITE  'MOURNING  BECOMES  ELECTRA',
   /X=.1IN,Y=1.4IN,HEIGHT=.2IN,WIDTH=.1IN,STYLE=ITALIC
WRITE  'SHOA',
   /X=.1IN,Y=.9IN,HEIGHT=.2IN,WIDTH=.1IN,STYLE=ITALIC
WRITE  'OUR  HITLER',
   /X=.1IN,Y=.4IN,HEIGHT=.2IN,WIDTH=.1IN,STYLE=ITALIC
```

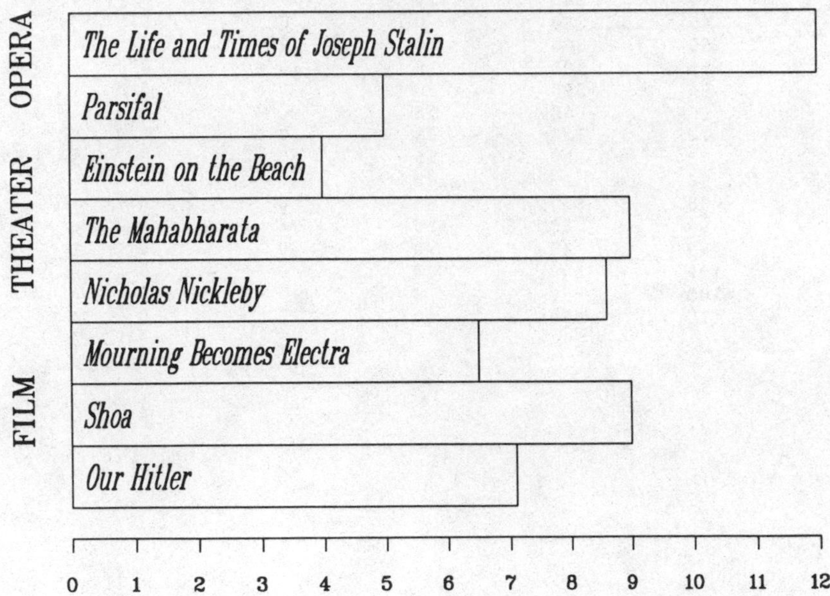

A Really Complicated Bar Graph

The following example is adapted from Warner, Mathewes and Clague (1982). The data give the incidence of fossil specimens of various flora found at various elevations of a site in British Columbia. The numbers have been interpolated from the graph, and may not accurately reflect the original data. Nevertheless, I have attempted to reproduce the graph literally, except for selecting four flora out of ten to save room in the dataset below. I have also omitted an illustration of the geological strata next to the vertical scale. This graph takes a lot of work to produce. Notice that two of the bottom scales are logarithmic and the widths have been adjusted to fit on a page. I have included this example to show you how much custom work you can do with SYGRAPH. Despite the lengthy setup, it should take less time than consulting with an illustrator.

HEIGHT	CHARA	NITELLA	JUNCUS	RUMEX
5	1	0	52	0
10	2	0	65	4
15	1	0	18	20
20	0	0	9	10
25	0	0	4	8
30	3	0	4	4
35	180	0	0	9
40	260	18	0	0
45	280	0	0	0
50	500	0	10	0
55	190	18	0	0
60	390	20	0	0
65	690	38	0	4
70	720	95	0	0
75	600	85	0	0
80	425	148	10	0
85	550	85	0	0
90	30	50	6	0
95	40	90	0	0
100	550	12	0	0
105	550	0	0	0
110	550	0	0	0

Figure 8

```
PLOT  CHARA*HEIGHT,
   /SIZE=0,AX=-2,SCALE=-2,YTICK=12,YMIN=0,YMAX=120,YPIP=2,
     HEIGHT=2IN,WIDTH=3.25IN,STICK
    YLABEL='Height  of  sampled  exposure  (cm)',
    XLABEL='Macrofossils  per  100  cubic  centimeters'
WRITE  '(logarithmic  scale)  <-|'/HEIGHT=6PT,WIDTH=6PT,
  X=1.12IN,Y=-.4IN
ORIGIN=.125IN,0
BAR  CHARA*HEIGHT,
   /LOG=10,XMIN=0,YMIN=0,BWID=5,FILL=1,TRANS,AXES=-1,SCALE=-1,
     XLABEL='  ',YLABEL='  ',HEIGHT=2IN,WIDTH=1IN,PIP=9,STICK
WRITE  'Chara  oospores'/X=.1IN,Y=2.1IN,HEIGHT=6PT,WIDTH=6PT,
  ANGLE=40
ORIGIN=1.25IN,0
BAR  NITELLA*HEIGHT,
   /LOG=10,XMIN=0,YMIN=0,BWID=5,FILL=1,TRANS,AXES=-1,SCALE=-1,
     XLABEL='  ',YLABEL='  ',HEIGHT=2IN,WIDTH=1IN,PIP=9,STICK
WRITE  'Nitella  oospores'/X=.1IN,Y=2.1IN,HEIGHT=6PT,WIDTH=6PT,
  ANGLE=40
ORIGIN=2.375IN,0
BAR  JUNCUS*HEIGHT,
   /XMIN=0,YMIN=0,BWID=5,FILL=1,TRANS,AXES=-1,SCALE=-1,
     XLABEL='  ',YLABEL='  ',HEIGHT=2IN,WIDTH=1IN,PIP=5,STICK
WRITE  'Juncus'/X=.1IN,Y=2.1IN,HEIGHT=6PT,WIDTH=6PT,ANGLE=40
ORIGIN=3.5IN,0
BAR  RUMEX*HEIGHT,
   /XMIN=0,YMIN=0,BWID=5,FILL=1,TRANS,AXES=-1,SCALE=-1,
     XLABEL='  ',YLABEL='  ',HEIGHT=2IN,WIDTH=1IN,PIP=5,STICK
WRITE  'Rumex'/X=.1IN,Y=2.1IN,HEIGHT=6PT,WIDTH=6PT,ANGLE=40
```

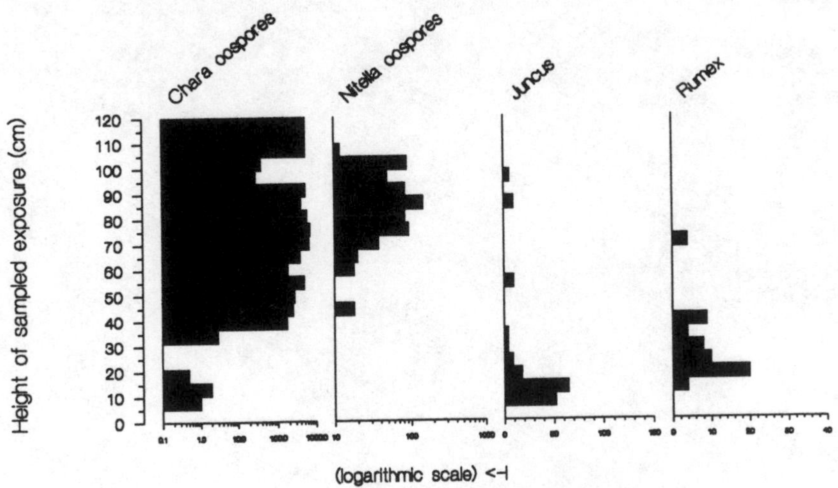

Bordering Scatterplots

You can do several panels of scatterplots on a common scale bordered by box plots or other types of graphs. Here is an example using our U.S. data. You might want to substitute **DENSITY/STRIPE** or **DENSITY/JITTER** for the box plots.

Figure 9

```
TYPE=HERSHEY
PLOT  RAIN*SUMMER,
  /HEIGHT=3IN,WIDTH=1.5IN,SYMBOL=2
ORIGIN=2.5IN,0
PLOT  RAIN*WINTER,
  /AXES=4,HEIGHT=3IN,WIDTH=1.5IN,SYMBOL=2
ORIGIN=4IN,0
BOX  RAIN,
  /TRANS,AXES=0,SCALE=0,HEIGHT=3IN,WIDTH=1.5IN,
   XLABEL=' '
ORIGIN=2.5IN,3IN
BOX  WINTER,
  /AXES=0,SCALE=0,HEIGHT=1.5IN,WIDTH=1.5IN,
   XLABEL=' '
ORIGIN=0,3IN
BOX  SUMMER,
  /AXES=0,SCALE=0,HEIGHT=1.5IN,WIDTH=1.5IN,
   XLABEL=' '
```

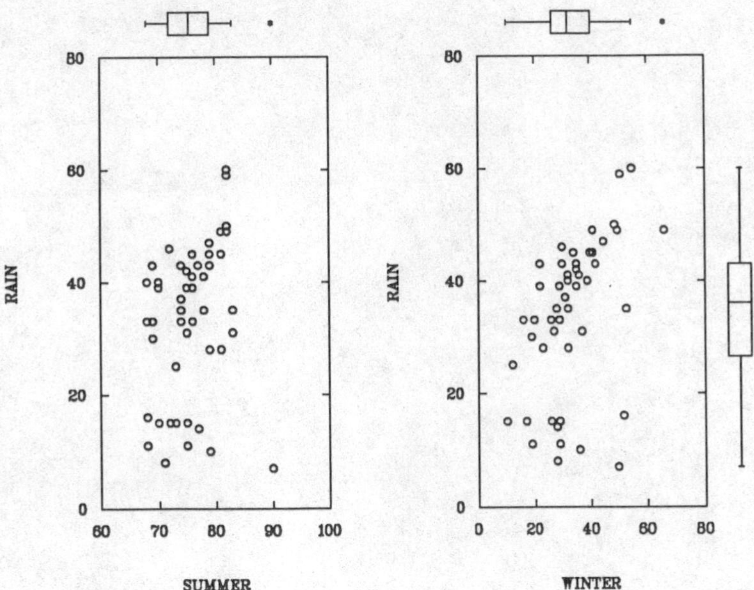

Plotting Long Time Series

Long time series often require long, thin graphs. This is easy to do with SYGRAPH. Just use the **HEIGHT** and **WIDTH** options to rescale the size of the graph. Cleveland, McGill, and McGill (1986) discuss the implications of this scaling for plotting time series and other data. The next figure shows a series of 256 points scaled in this way. I have removed the points themselves by including **SIZE=0**. In the upper section of the figure, I have used the **FILL** option to highlight the periodicity in the same data.

Figure 10

```
TYPE=HERSHEY
ORIGIN=-.5IN,0
PLOT  RATE*TIME,
  /HEIGHT=.75IN,WIDTH=5IN,LINE,SIZE=0,
   XMIN=0,XMAX=7
ORIGIN=-.5IN,3IN
PLOT  RATE*TIME,
  /HEIGHT=.75IN,WIDTH=5IN,LINE,SIZE=0,
   XMIN=0,XMAX=7,FILL=1
```

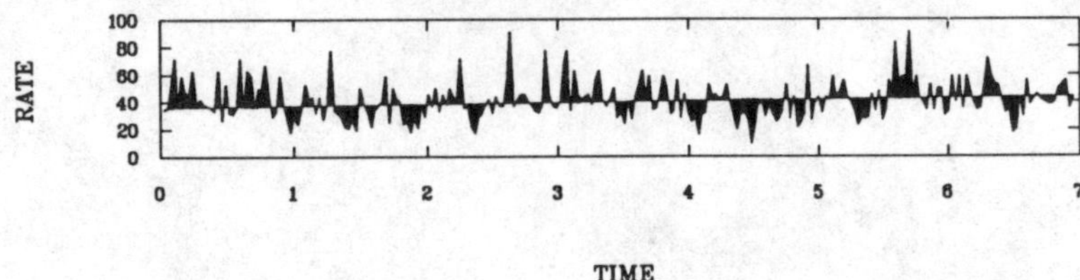

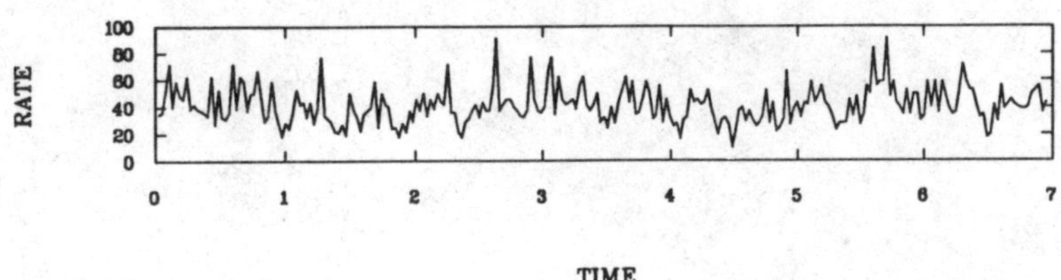

Multi-Valued Category Plots with Lines (ANOVA Plots)

In the analysis of variance, we often plot the results of a factorial design using lines connecting levels of a factor. This highlights interaction effects and trends. Here are the cell means from a repeated measures example in Winer (1971, page 525).

```
  A1          A2          B$

2.33        5.33        B1
1.33        3.67        B2
5.33        7.00        B3
3.00        7.67        B4
```

Figure 11 shows how to plot these data. Notice that you should use the **CPLOT** command because the factors are categorical. Choose the factor you want on the horizontal axis for your character variable in the file (B$ in this case) and make a separate variable for each level of the other factor (A in this case). You can plot up to 12 levels on the second factor this way in a single **CPLOT** command. If there are more groups, you can use separate **CPLOT** commands (with **AXES=0** and **MIN** and **MAX** options) to superimpose results.

Figure 11

```
TYPE=SWISS
CPLOT  A1,A2*B$/LINE,SYMBOL=2,3,FILL=1,1,SIZE=2
```

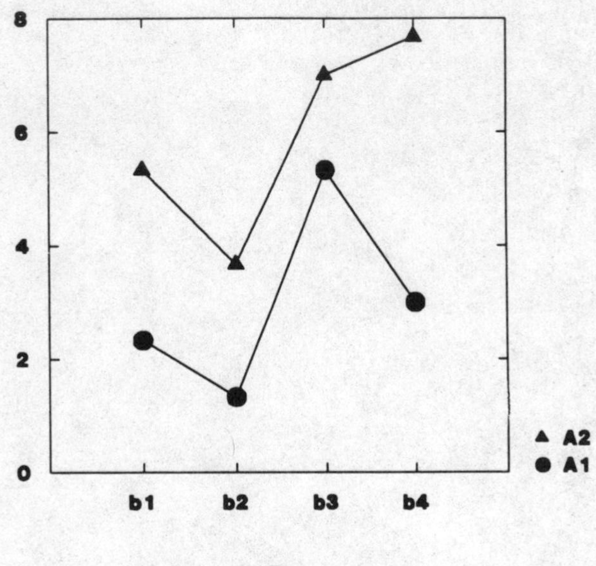

Contouring over Filled Contours

You can enhance filled contours by adding contour lines for reference. Figure 12 shows an example of this. These are contours of INCOME (per-capita income) against LABLAT and LABLON (latitude and longitude of the centers of the states). The contours help to delineate the darker and lighter areas without destroying the continuity of the gray scale.

Figure 12

```
PLOT  INCOME*LABLAT*LABLON,
  /CONTOUR,FILL,
    XMIN=-125,XMAX=-65,YMIN=25,YMAX=50
PLOT  INCOME*LABLAT*LABLON,
  /CONTOUR,ZTICK=10,
    XMIN=-125,XMAX=-65,YMIN=25,YMAX=50
```

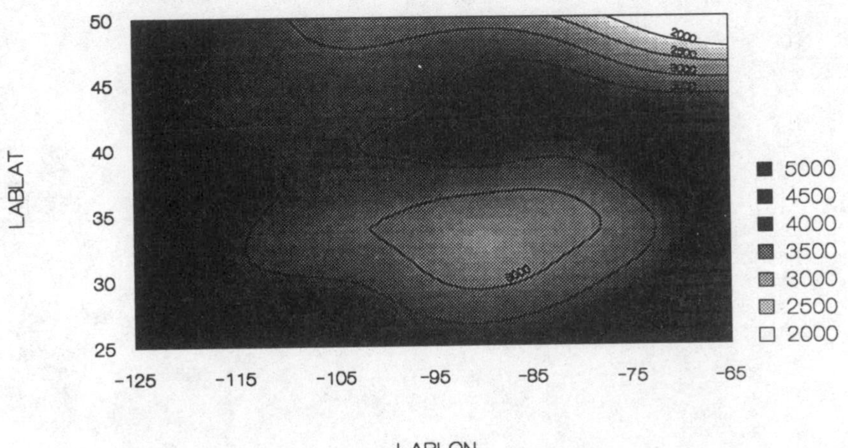

Part 3
Chapter 2

Three-Dimensional Plots

Working in three dimensions requires thinking about facets of the graph you are creating. You can apply any two-dimensional plot like wallpaper on the surface of a three-dimensional box in perspective with the **FACET** command. The examples in this chapter show some applications.

The commands you will need for more complex 3-D graphics are **EYE**, **FACET**, and **DEPTH**. You can read about these commands at the beginning of the Reference section above. These commands regulate the *perspective*, *orientation*, and *position* of planes in a 3-D space. What you draw on those planes depends on the subsequent graphics commands you choose. Once you have set these three control commands, you may proceed with other graphics commands as if you were working in two dimensions.

The **EYE** command regulates perspective. You need to specify three coordinates of the viewing eye to change the standard perspective. These coordinates are multiples of a standard unit cube whose lower near left corner (from the standard viewing perspective) is the (0,0,0) origin. The default setting is **EYE=-8,-12,8**. You may put your viewing eye anywhere, including inside the cube, but some viewpoints will produce weird perspectives. Figure 1 shows some examples. The first example uses the default perspective. By typing **EYE** with no numbers following, the perspective is reset to the default perspective. If you have not set it to some other value during your session, this is optional. The last example in Figure 1 shows a viewpoint underneath the cube.

As with the two-dimensional plots in the previous chapter, you will need to use the **BEGIN** and **END** commands to superimpose several graphics commands on the same screen or page. The examples in this chapter were created this way and submitted from a command file or the **FEDIT** full screed editor.

The **FACET** command defines the facet of 3-D space on which you wish to plot 2-D graphs. **FACET=XY** defines the XY plane. **FACET=YZ** defines the YZ. **FACET=XZ** defines the XZ.

The position of a plane along a facet is defined by the **DEPTH** command. The normal setting is **DEPTH=50**, which is 50 percent of the viewing area before perspective transformation. For the XY facet, **DEPTH=50** defines the top of the default viewing cube. For the YZ facet, it defines the right rear plane. For the XZ facet, it defines the left rear plane. It is usually easier to define a depth in inches or centimeters, however, so you can think of the actual measurements of the physical object you are constructing. The examples in this chapter are done this way. In Figure 1, I have chosen **DEPTH=0** with **FACET=XY** to mark the floor of the standard cube.

Figure 1

```
EYE
FACET=XY
DEPTH=0
DRAW   BOX/HEIGHT=2IN,WIDTH=2IN,FILL=5
DRAW   BOX/HEIGHT=2IN,WIDTH=2IN,ZHEIGHT=2IN

ORIGIN=3IN,0
EYE=.3,-.5,.5
FACET=XY
DEPTH=0
DRAW   BOX/HEIGHT=2IN,WIDTH=2IN,FILL=5
DRAW   BOX/HEIGHT=2IN,WIDTH=2IN,ZHEIGHT=2IN

ORIGIN=0,2IN
EYE=-.5,-.5,.5
FACET=XY
DEPTH=0
DRAW   BOX/HEIGHT=2IN,WIDTH=2IN,FILL=5
DRAW   BOX/HEIGHT=2IN,WIDTH=2IN,ZHEIGHT=2IN

ORIGIN=-2IN,0
EYE=.2,-1,-.8
FACET=XY
DEPTH=0
DRAW   BOX/HEIGHT=2IN,WIDTH=2IN,FILL=5
DRAW   BOX/HEIGHT=2IN,WIDTH=2IN,ZHEIGHT=2IN
```

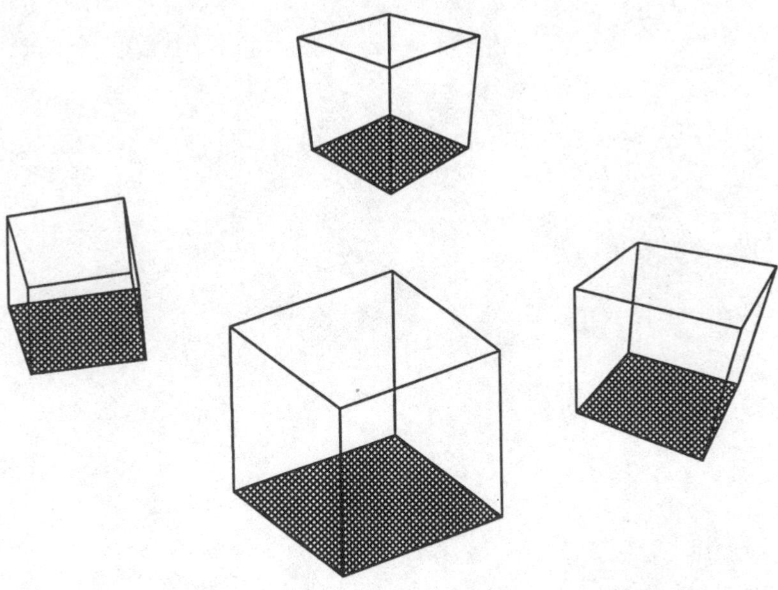

Drawing on the Facets

Let's try plotting on the faces of a rectangular box to see how these options work. Figure 2 is an outlandish graph which has no real application. Its purpose, however, is to show you how the **EYE**, **FACET**, and **DEPTH** commands interact with the graphics commands to produce a complex 3-D plot. Notice that you have to keep track of which facet of the box you are laying a graph on. **HEIGHT** and **WIDTH** always refer to the height and width of the selected facet.

This example plots all the graphs on the surface of a box. I drew the box simply to make the orientations clear. You can adjust **DEPTH** to any setting you wish, but you have to take care to keep things from colliding or going off the page. When you are working in 3-D, it may take several tries to get things right.

Two other commands should be of use. **ORIGIN** will set the 2-D origin to wherever you wish. If you precede the 3-D plotting commands with an **ORIGIN** command (see above in Reference chapter), then the entire graph will be shifted to the area you wish. Furthermore, if your final graph proves too large or small, you can use the **SCALE** command to reduce or enlarge the entire image.

Figure 2

```
TYPE=SWISS
DRAW   BOX/ZHEIGHT=3IN,HEIGHT=4IN,WIDTH=5IN
FACET=ZX
DEPTH=4IN
WRITE  'A  Whatsit  Plot'/HEIGHT=.4IN,WIDTH=.25IN,
   X=2.5IN,Y=3.75IN,CENTER
SPLOM  SUMMER,WINTER,RAIN/HEIGHT=3IN,WIDTH=5IN,ELL=.5
SELECT  REGION=1
FACET=XY
DEPTH=0
MAP/HEIGHT=4IN,WIDTH=5IN
FACET=ZY
DEPTH=5IN
PLOT   Y=SIN(COS(TAN(X))),
   !HEIGHT=3IN,WIDTH=4IN,AXES=0,SCALE=0,XLAB='  ',YLAB='  '
```

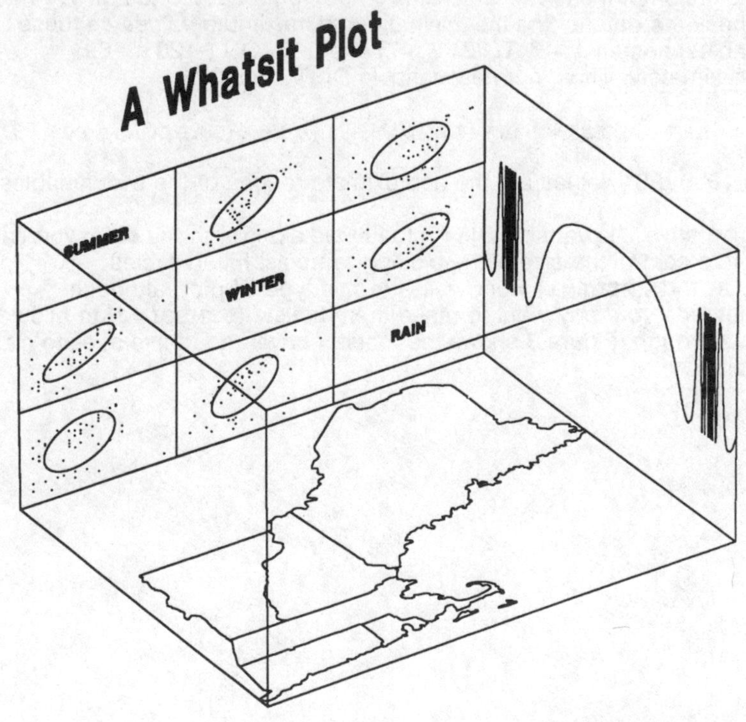

Representing a Variable by Size of Symbols in a 3-D Plot

The perspective transformation in SYGRAPH is mild. That is, the graphs have a long focal length so as to avoid perspective distortions. Close points in a 3-D plot are in fact larger than distant points, but the effect is barely noticeable. Sometimes you might want to enhance the perspective effect, however, when you are trying to distinguish among plotting symbols.

One way to do this is to create a variable which you can use with the **SIZE** option to make close points larger and distant points smaller. This variable (say, DIST) should be a weighted sum of the two variables used on the bottom XY plane for the normal viewing position. This way, if a point has large values on X and Y, the DIST variable will have a large value and if the X and Y values are small, the DIST variable will be small.

I have found that the DIST variable should range from about .5 to 2.5 when used to size plotting symbols. If you let it range more broadly, the depth effect will be too exaggerated. Let's consider plotting RAIN (annual rainfall) against LABLAT (latitude) and LABLON (longitude) from the US file. Since LABLAT and LABLON will be on the XY plane, we want a combination of these two which will range from about .5 to 2.5. We need to check the data to find the minimum and maximum values on these variables, namely LABLAT (31 ... 47) and LABLON (-120 ... -69) approximately. Thus, our new variable DIST should be:

```
LET   DIST=2.5-(LABLAT-31)/16-(LABLON+120)/51
```

The 16 and 51 values are the approximate ranges of the two variables.

If you save this variable DIST into the file along with the data, you can use it to control the size of the plotting symbols. Filled circles (**SYMBOL=2,FILL=1**) work well with this type of plot, although sometimes you may want to make them hollow (**SYMBOL=2**) to allow show-through. Figure 3 shows the result. I have added five axes to clarify it a bit.

Figure 3

```
PLOT   RAIN*LABLAT*LABLON/SIZE=DIST,SYMBOL=2,AXES=5
```

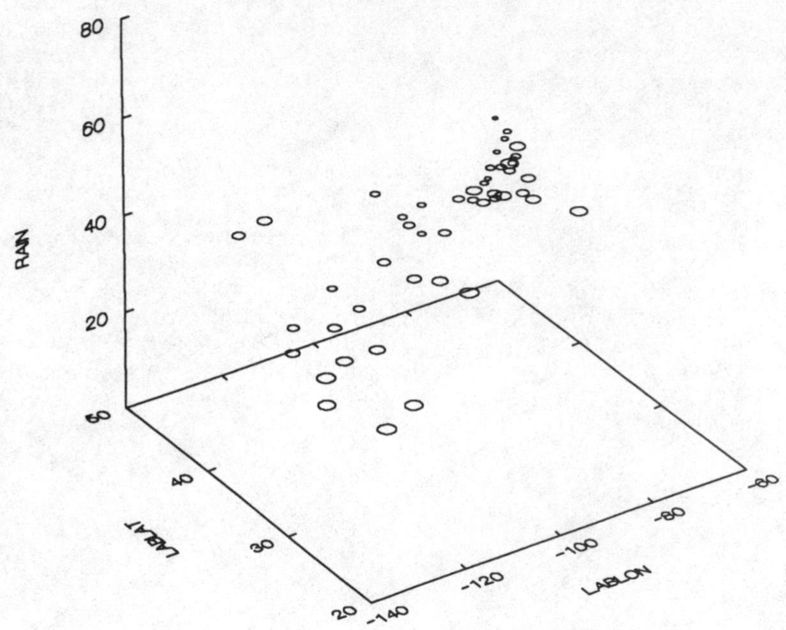

Overlaying Facets in Three Dimensions

The next example shows how you can overlay three-dimensional plots. For this example, I plotted RAIN against SUMMER and WINTER temperatures in a 3-D scatterplot. I chose the symbols to be filled circles (`SYMBOL=2,FILL=1`) in double size (`SIZE=2`).

Next, I plotted two scatterplots at the margins of SUMMER and WINTER. The first I placed on the XZ facet, perpendicular to the Y axis on the left rear. This panel reveals the joint distribution of RAIN and WINTER temperatures. Then I changed the facet to YZ, perpendicular to the X axis on the right rear in order to plot RAIN against SUMMER temperatures. Notice that I had to use XREV to reverse the bottom axis because of the location of the origin. Finally, I reverted to the bottom of the graph on the Z facet (`FACET=Z` and `DEPTH=0`) to plot contours.

Figure 4

```
PLOT  RAIN*SUMMER*WINTER,
  /SYMBOL=2,SIZE=2,FILL=1,AXES=0
FACET=XZ
PLOT  RAIN*WINTER,
  /SCALE=0,XLABEL=' ',YLABEL=' ',ZLABEL=' '
FACET=YZ
PLOT  RAIN*SUMMER,
  /XREV,SCALE=0,XLABEL=' ',YLABEL=' ',ZLABEL=' '
FACET=XY
DEPTH=0
PLOT  RAIN*SUMMER*WINTER,
  /SCALE=0,CONTOUR,SMOOTH=DWLS,ZTICK=10,
   XLABEL=' ',YLABEL=' '
```

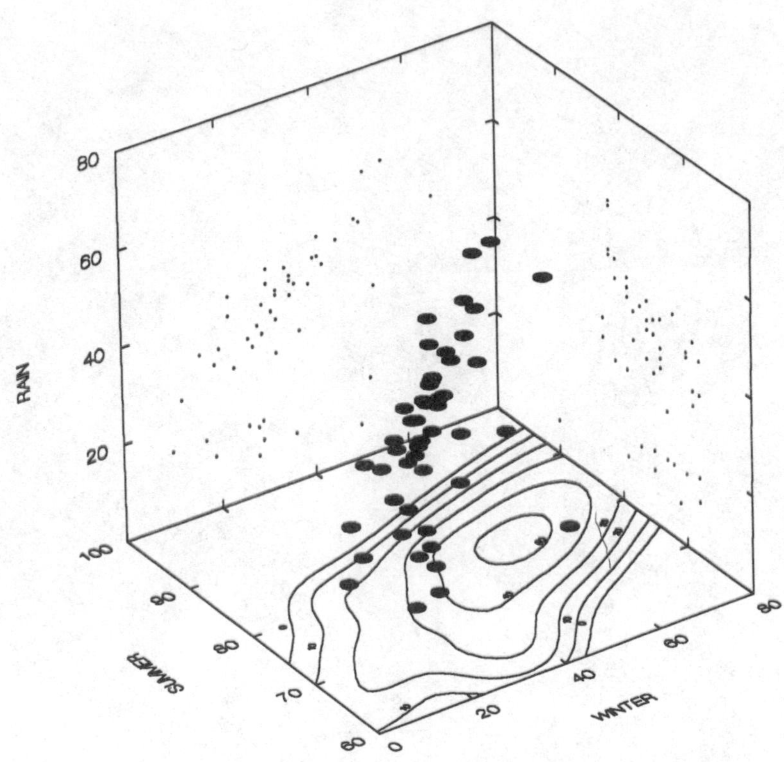

Three-Dimensional Grid Lines

The next example shows how to place grid lines on any facet of a three-dimensional plot. The default grid lines for 3-D plots are on the bottom facet of the axis frame. To put grid lines or other material on the other facets, use the **FACET** command. The **XREV** option in the second **PLOT** command is not necessary because we are not plotting data or scale values. Nevertheless, you should keep in mind that plots on the XZ facet need to be reversed on the X axis if you are blending them with 3-D plots.

Figure 5 shows the result.

Figure 5

```
PLOT  RAIN*LABLAT*LABLON,
   /SYMBOL=2,SIZE=2,AXES=9,GRID=3
FACET=YZ
PLOT  RAIN*LABLAT,
   /XREV,SCALE=0,GRID=3,SIZE=0,
    XLABEL='  ',YLABEL='  ',
FACET=XZ
PLOT  RAIN*LABLON,
   /SCALE=0,GRID=3,SIZE=0,
    XLABEL='  ',YLABEL='  '
```

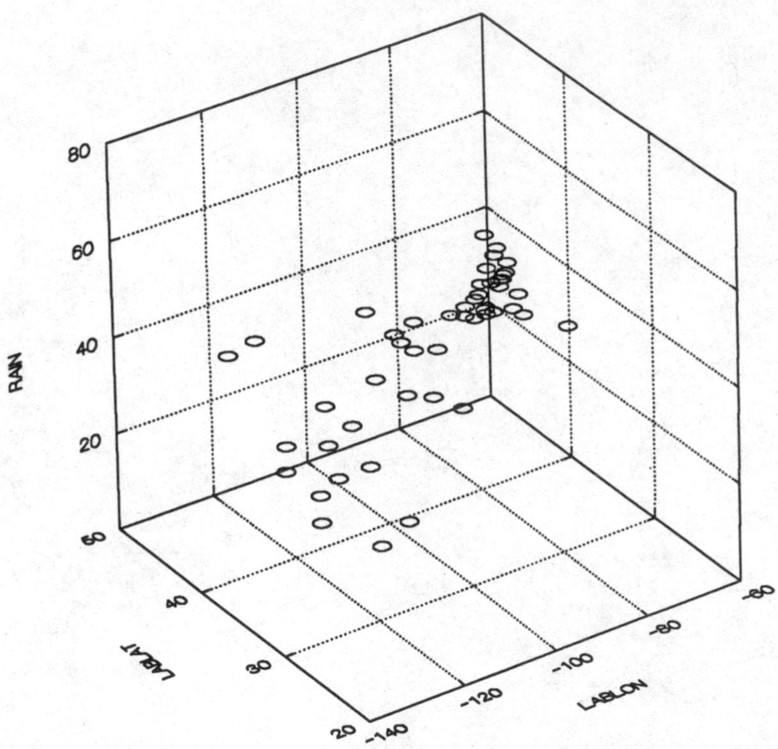

Perspective Contours

The next example shows a perspective surface with contouring below. You may need to fiddle with the **EYE** command or the **XREV** and **YREV** options to get an unobstructed view of contours and surface. Notice that I made the map rectangular with the **HEIGHT** and **WIDTH** commands.

Figure 6

```
TYPE=HERSHEY
PLOT  WINTER*LABLAT*LABLON,
  /HEIGHT=3IN,WIDTH=5IN,SIZE=0,
   SMOOTH=DWLS,AXES=5,HIDE
FACET=XY
DEPTH=0
PLOT  WINTER*LABLAT*LABLON,
  /HEIGHT=3IN,WIDTH=5IN,SMOOTH=DWLS,CONTOUR,
   ZTICK=10,AXES=0,SCALE=0,XLABEL='  ',YLABEL='  '
```

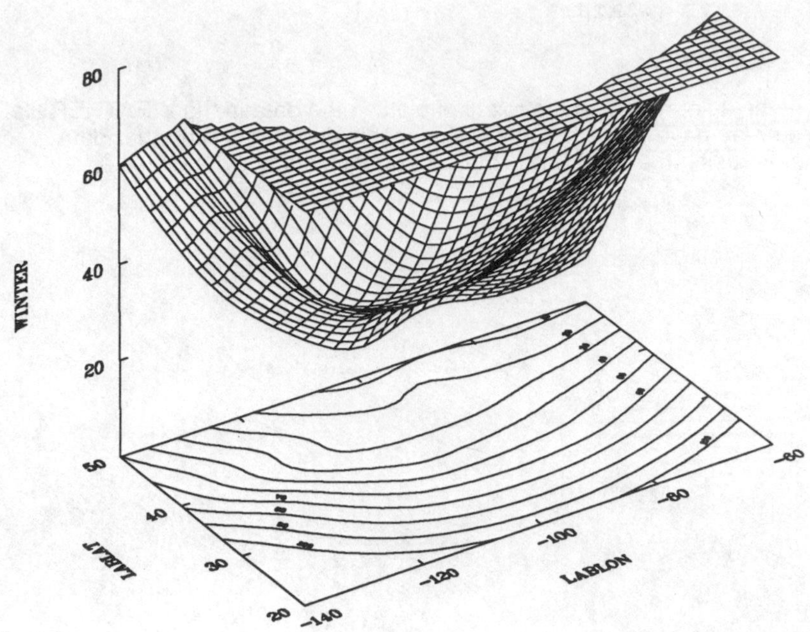

Three-Dimensional Mahalanobis Distance Plots

As I mentioned above, you can plot Mahalanobis distances to detect multivariate outliers in a distribution. Here is an example of how to do it in three dimensions. I used MGLH in SYSTAT to compute the distances and then used them with the **SIZE** option to represent outliers. Then I used DATA to merge the distances with the variables in the US file and saved them into a new file called WEATHER

```
MGLH
USE US
MODEL  SUMMER,WINTER,RAIN  =  CONSTANT
ESTIMATE
HYPOTHESIS
SAVE  CANON
TEST
QUIT

DATA
USE US  CANON
SAVE  WEATHER
RUN
QUIT
```

The next figure shows the result of plotting the data in the WEATHER file. You may have to rescale the Mahalanobis distances with other data before using them to control the size of the plotting symbols.

Figure 7

```
TYPE=HERSHEY
PLOT   RAIN*SUMMER*WINTER/SYMBOL=2,SIZE=DISTANCE
```

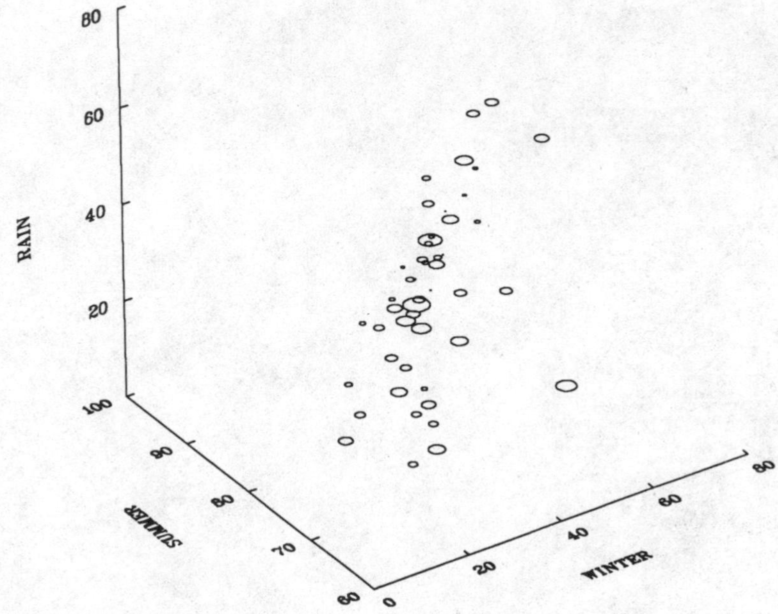

Perspective Maps

Although they can distort, perspective maps have their uses. The trick in producing them in SYGRAPH is to line up the scales for whatever you are plotting over the map and the scales for the map itself. Figure 8 shows how to do this with the US map. Setting `FACET=XY` and `DEPTH=0` places the map on the floor of the subsequent plot.

I have chosen a stereographic projection for the map and plots. Notice that we must specify axis limits in order to use the `PROJ` option in the `PLOT` command. How do you know what limits to choose? Check the MINLAT, MINLON, MAXLAT, and MAXLON variables in the SYS file accompanying your map. Round the largest and smallest of these values up and down, respectively, to make the map fit as much of the plotting window as possible. See Appendix B for further details.

Figure 8

```
TYPE=HERSHEY
FACET=XY
DEPTH=0
MAP,
   /XMIN=-125,XMAX=-65,YMIN=25,YMAX=50,
    HEIGHT=3IN,WIDTH=5IN,PROJ=STEREO
ORIGIN=0,1.5IN
PLOT   RAIN*LABLAT*LABLON,
   /XMIN=-125,XMAX=-65,YMIN=25,YMAX=50,
    SMOOTH=NEXPO,HIDE,HEIGHT=3IN,WIDTH=5IN,
    AXES=0,SCALE=0,PROJ=STEREO,SIZE=0,
   XLABEL=' ',YLABEL=' ',ZLABEL=' '
WRITE 'Average Annual U.S. Rainfall',
   /X=2.5IN,Y=4.5IN,CENTER
```

Average Annual U.S. Rainfall

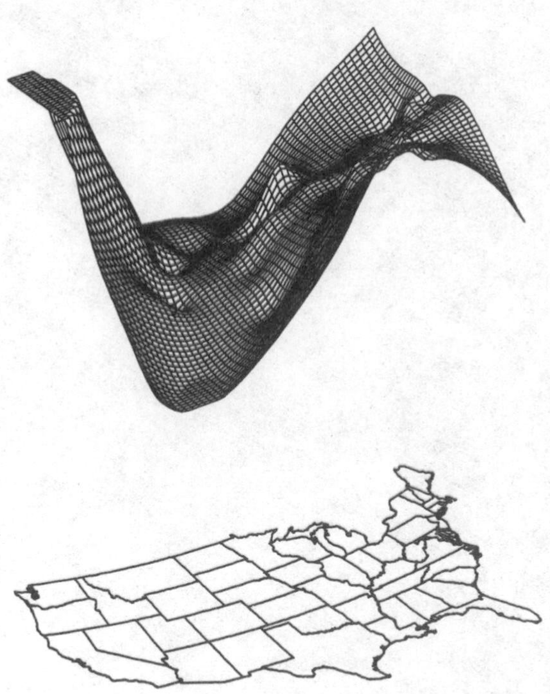

Three-Dimensional Functions and Contours

You can place contours below 3-D function plots in the same graph. Figure 9 shows an error function with contours below. I chose the default perspective and lengthened the Z axis (**ZHEIGHT=75** instead of the default **ZHEIGHT=50**) to keep the upper plot from hiding the contours. You may wish to try two other methods to keep the plots visible. First, you can adjust the perspective with the **EYE** command (e.g. **EYE=-9,-8,3**). Second, you can use the **ORIGIN** command to move the surface higher (e.g. **ORIGIN=0,1IN**).

In the figure, I plotted the contours first. I set **FORMAT=1** to keep the labels on the contours to one decimal. I set **CUT=50** to make the contours smoother and **ZTICK=20** to draw more than a few contours. Next, I did the upper plot. This time, I set **CUT=60** to make the mesh finer. Finally, I made **ZHEIGHT=75** to enlarge the vertical axis. The normal size of 3-D figure axes is 50 percent of the display area.

The final set of commands draws the axes. This is a rather sleazy method just to produce axes, but it works and saves having an extra command. Any old data will do. We just make **SIZE=0** so that the plotting symbols don't appear.

Figure 9

```
TYPE=HERSHEY
FORMAT 1
FACET=XY
DEPTH=0
COLOR  GRAPH=RED
PLOT   Z=EXP(-X^2)*EXP(-Y^2)*X,
  !CONTOUR,ZMIN=-.5,ZMAX=.5,CUT=50,ZTICK=20,
   AXES=0,SCALE=0,XLABEL='  ',YLABEL='  '
COLOR  GRAPH=BLUE
PLOT   Z=EXP(-X^2)*EXP(-Y^2)*X,
  !ZMIN=-.5,ZMAX=.5,HIDE,AXES=0,SCALE=0,
   CUT=60,XLABEL='  ',YLABEL='  ',ZLABEL='  ',ZHEIGHT=75
COLOR  GRAPH=BLACK
PLOT  X*X*X,
  /XMIN=-3,XMAX=3,YMIN=-3,YMAX=3,ZMIN=-.5,ZMAX=.5,SIZE=0,
    XLABEL='X',YLABEL='Y',ZLABEL='Z',AXES=5,ZHEIGHT=75
```

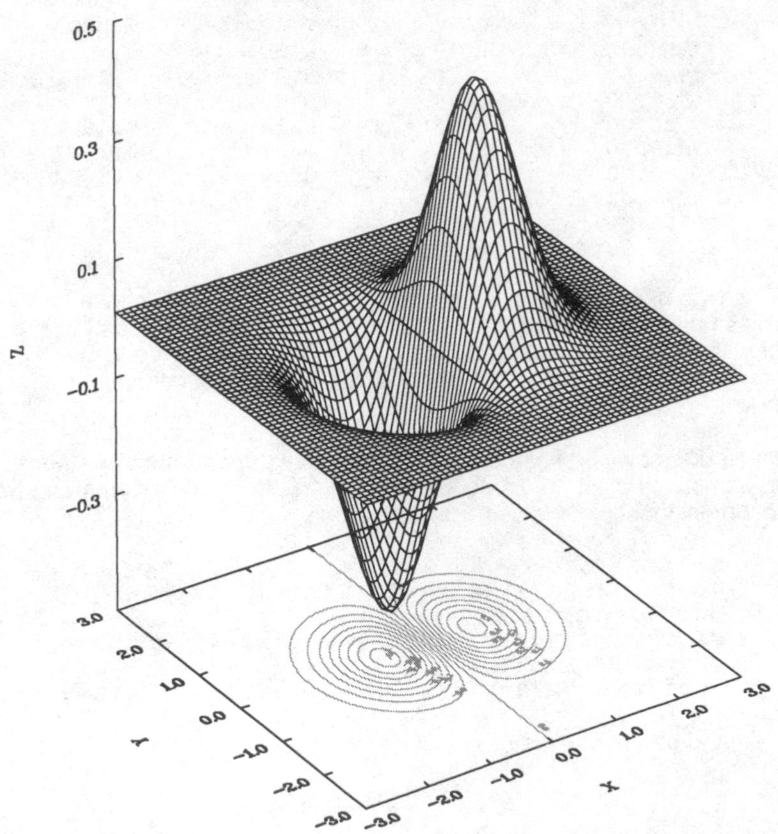

Time Ordered Spectra and 3-D Function Plots

Time ordered spectral plots are used frequently in chemistry, acoustics, image processing, medicine, and other fields. Two forms are popular. The first uses darkness to represent magnitude across time. This plot is produced by some laboratory spectral decomposition equipment. Speech samples and bird calls, for example, have been displayed this way. The graph looks like a smear of light and dark patches. The second form is a three-dimensional plot in which magnitude is assigned to the third dimension. This latter graph looks like a range of mountains in perspective.

Figure 10 shows this second type of spectral plot. The data are from Michalske and Bunker (1987). They are the Fourier transformed infrared spectroscopy data for a chemical reaction involving methanol. This graph shows spectra at only three time points. I have estimated the data by interpolating their graph at several points. The vertical scale was not given in the article, so I standardized it to 1.0 maximum.

FREQ	TIME1	TIME2	TIME3
950.00	0.40	0.30	0.15
940.00	0.50	0.31	0.16
930.00	0.44	0.29	0.14
920.00	0.55	0.32	0.19
910.00	0.79	0.51	0.23
900.00	0.81	0.58	0.26
890.00	0.98	0.76	0.31
880.00	0.50	0.49	0.13
870.00	0.02	0.02	0.01

This type of plot is useful for other purposes. You can display a family of curves (such as chi-square with increasing degrees of freedom) in one plot with each curve plotted behind the last. By choosing your perspective carefully, you can show all the curves in a continuous surface.

If you do not wish to use the mild perspective transformation as here, you can accomplish the same effect by using the **ORIGIN** command with two-dimensional plots to shift the curves, e.g.

```
ORIGIN=0,0
PLOT   Y=SQR(X)*EXP(-X)!AXES=0,SCALE=0
ORIGIN=1CM,1CM
PLOT   Y=SQR(2*X)*EXP(-2*X)!AXES=0,SCALE=0
ORIGIN=2CM,2CM
PLOT   Y=SQR(3*X)*EXP(-3*X)!AXES=0,SCALE=0
```

and so on.

Figure 10

```
FACET=ZX
DEPTH=0
PLOT  TIME1*FREQ,
   /SMOOTH=SPLINE,XMIN=870,XMAX=950,XTICK=8,XREV,YMIN=0,YMAX=1,
     HEIGHT=3IN,WIDTH=4IN,AXES=1,SCALE=1,
    XLABEL='WAVENUMBERS',YLABEL='  '
DRAW  BOX/HEIGHT=3IN,WIDTH=4IN
DEPTH=1IN
PLOT  TIME2*FREQ,
   /SMOOTH=SPLINE,XMIN=870,XMAX=950,XTICK=8,XREV,YMIN=0,YMAX=1,
     HEIGHT=3IN,WIDTH=4IN,AXES=1,SCALE=0,
    XLABEL='  ',YLABEL='  '
DRAW  BOX/HEIGHT=3IN,WIDTH=4IN
DEPTH=3IN
PLOT  TIME3*FREQ,
   /SMOOTH=SPLINE,XMIN=870,XMAX=950,XTICK=8,XREV,YMIN=0,YMAX=1,
     HEIGHT=3IN,WIDTH=4IN,AXES=1,SCALE=0,
    XLABEL='  ',YLABEL='MAGNITUDE'
DRAW  BOX/HEIGHT=3IN,WIDTH=4IN
FACET=XY
DEPTH=0
DRAW  BOX/HEIGHT=3IN,WIDTH=4IN
WRITE  'TIME  (MINUTES)',
   /X=-.8IN,Y=1.5IN,CENTER,ANGLE=270,HEIGHT=.1IN,WIDTH=.1IN
```

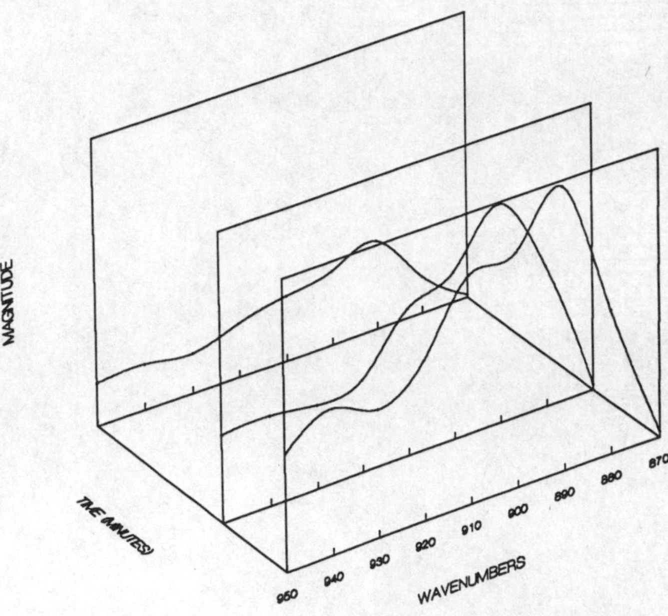

Figure 11

```
TYPE=SWISS
FACET=XY
DEPTH=0
SELECT  STATE$='IL'
MAP/HEIGHT=6IN,WIDTH=6IN
COLOR  GRAPH=GREEN
ORIGIN=-.2IN,1.4IN
WRITE   'SYSTAT'/HEIGHT=.5IN,WIDTH=.5IN
DRAW  BOX/HEIGHT=.11IN,WIDTH=2.9IN,Y=.62IN,FILL=1
DRAW  BOX/HEIGHT=.11IN,WIDTH=2.9IN,Y=-.23IN,FILL=1
DRAW  BOX/HEIGHT=.11IN,WIDTH=1.93IN,Y=.86IN,FILL=1
DRAW  BOX/HEIGHT=.11IN,WIDTH=1.93IN,X=.97IN,Y=-.47IN,FILL=1
```

References

Akima, H. (1978). A method of bivariate interpolation and smooth surface fitting for irregularly distributed data points. *ACM Transactions on Mathematical Software*, *4*, 148-159.

Andrews, D.F. (1972). Plots of high-dimensional data. *Biometrics*, *28*, 125-136.

Baird, J.C. (1970). *Psychophysical Analysis of Visual Space*. New York: Pergamon Press.

Bertin, J. (1983). *Semiology of Graphics*. Madison, Wisconsin: University of Wisconsin Press. (English translation of *Semiologie Graphique*, Paris: Gauthier-Villars, 1967).

Bickel, P.J., Hammel, E.A., O'Connell, J.W. (1975). Sex bias in graduate admissions: Data from Berkeley. *Science*, *187*, 398-404.

Bornstein, M.H., Kessen, W., and Weiskopf, S. (1976). Color vision and hue categorization in young human infants. *Journal of Experimental Psychology: Human Perception and Performance*, *2*, 115-129.

Brodlie, K.W. (1980). A review of methods for curve and function drawing. In K.W. Brodlie (Ed.), *Mathematical Methods in Computer Graphics and Design*. London: Academic Press, Inc.

Chambers, J.M., Cleveland, W.S., Kleiner, B., and Tukey, P.A. (1983). *Graphical Methods for Data Analysis*. Boston: Duxbury Press.

Chernoff, H. (1973). Using faces to represent points in k-dimensional space graphically. *Journal of the American Statistical Association*, *68*, 361-368.

Chernoff, H., and Rizvi, M.H. (1975). Effect on classificaion error of random permutations of features in representing multivariate data by faces. *Journal of the American Statistical Association*, *70*, 548-554.

Cleveland, W.S. (1979). Robust locally weight regression and smoothing scatterplots. *Journal of the American Statistical Association*, *74*, 829-836.

Cleveland, W.S. (1981). LOWESS: A program for smoothing scatterplots by robust locally weighted regression. *The American Statistician*, *35*, 54.

Cleveland, W.S. (1984). Graphs in scientific publications. *The American Statistician, 38*, 261-269.

Cleveland, W.S. (1984). Graphical methods for data presentation: Full scale breaks, dot charts, and multibased logging. *The American Statistician, 38* 270-280.

Cleveland, W.S. (1985). *The Elements of Graphing Data.* Monterey, CA: Wadsworth Advanced Books.

Cleveland, W.S., Kleiner, B., McRae, and Warner (1976). Photochemical Air Pollution: Transport from the New York City Area into Conn. and Mass. *Science, 191*, 179-181.

Cleveland, W.S., Diaconis, P., and McGill, R. (1982). Variables on scatterplots look more highly correlated when the scales are increased. *Science, 216*, 1138-1141.

Cleveland, W.S., Harris, C.S., and McGill, R. (1982). Judgments of circle sizes on statistical maps. *Journal of the American Statistical Association, 77*, 541-547.

Cleveland, W.S. and McGill, R. (1983). A color caused optical illusion on a statistical graph. *American Statistician , 37*, 101-105.

Cleveland, W.S. and McGill, R. (1984). Graphical perception: theory, experimentation, and application to the development of graphical methods. *Journal of the American Statistical Association, 79*, 531-554.

Cleveland, W.S. and McGill, R. (1985). The many faces of a scatterplot. *Journal of the American Statistical Association, 79*, 807-822.

Cleveland, W.S. and McGill, R. (1987). Graphical perception: The visual decoding of quantitative information on graphical displays of data. Unpublished paper. AT&T Bell Laboratories.

Cleveland, W.S., McGill, R., and McGill, M.E. (1988). The shape parameter of a two-variable graph. *Journal of the American Statistical Association*, in press.

Coombs, C.H. (1964). *A Theory of Data.* New York: John Wiley and Sons.

Coren, S. and Girgus, J.S. (1978). *Seeing is Deceiving: The Psychology of Visual Illusions.* Hillsdale, NJ: Lawrence Erlbaum Associates.

Croley, T.E. and Hartmann, H.C. (1985). Resolving Thiessen polygons. *Journal of Hydrology, 76*, 363-379.

Croxton, F.E. and Struker, R.E. (1927). Bar charts versus circle diagrams. *Journal of the American Statistical Association*, *22*, 473-482.

Curtis, D.B., Burton, R.P. , and Campbell, D.M. (1987). An alternative to Cartesian graphics. *Computer Graphics World* , *40* , 95-98.

Daniel, C., and Wood, F.S. (1971). *Fitting equations to data.* New York: John Wiley & Sons.

Diamond, W.J. (1981). *Practical Experiment Designs for Engineers and Scientists.* Belmont, CA: Wadsworth.

Doane, D.P. (1976). Aesthetic frequency classifications. *The American Statistician, 30*, 181-183.

Dunn, R. (1987). Variable-width framed rectangle charts for statistical mapping. *The American Statistician*, *41*, 153-156.

Durrett, H.J. (Ed.) (1987). *Color and the Computer.* New York: Academic Press.

Eels, W.C. (1926). The relative merits of circles and bars for representing component parts. *Journal of the American Statistical Association*, *21*, 119-132.

Everitt, B. (1978). *Graphical Techniques for Multivariate Data.* London: Heinemann Educational Books.

Fienberg, S.E. (1979). Graphical methods in statistics. *The American Statistician*, *33*, 165-177.

Freedman, D., Pisani, and Purves (1980). *Statistics.* New York: W.W. Norton & Co.

Freni-Titulaer, L.W.J. and Louv, W.C. (1984). Comparisons of some graphical methods for exploratory multivariate data analysis. *The American Statistician*, *38*, 184-188.

Frisby, J.P. (1980). *Seeing: Illusion, Brain and Mind.* Oxford: Oxford University Press.

Gale, N . and Halperin, W.C. (1982). A case for better graphics: the unclassified choropleth map. *The American Statistician*, *36*, 330-336.

Garner, W.R. (1974). *The Processing of Information and Structure. Hillsdale*, N .J.: Lawrence Erlbaum.

Garner, W.R. and Felfoldy, G.L. (1970). Integrality of stimulus dimensions in various types of information processing. *Cognitive Psychology*, *1*, 225-241.

Gilbert, E.N. (1962). Random subdivisions of space into crystals. *Annals of Mathematical Statistics*, *33*, 958-972.

Giloh, H. and Sadat, J.W. (1982). Fluorescence microscopy: Reduced photobleaching of rhodamine and flourescein protein conjugates by *n*-propyl gallate. *Science*, *217*, 1252-1255.

Gnanadesikan, R. (1977). *Methods for Statistical Data Analysis of Multivariate Observations*. New York: John Wiley & Sons.

Green, P.J. and Sibson, R. (1978). Computing Dirichlet tesselations in the plane. *Computer Journal*, *21*, 168-173.

Gregory, R.L. (1969). *Eye and Brain*. New York: McGraw-Hill.

Haber, R.N . and Hershenson, M. (1980). *The Psychology of Visual Perception*. 2nd. Ed. New York: Holt, Rinehart and Winston.

Haber, R.N . and Wilkinson, L. (1982). Perceptual components of computer displays. *IEEE Computer Graphics and Applications*, *2*, 23-36.

Harris, J.E. (1987). "Who should profit from cigarettes?" *The New York Times*. Sunday, March 15, Section C, 3.

Hartigan, J.H. (1975a). Printer graphics for clustering. *Journal of Statistical Computation and Simulation*, *4*, 187-213.

Hartigan, J.H. (1975b). *Clustering Algorithms*. New York: John Wiley & Sons.

Hershey, A.V. (1972). A computer system for scientific typography. *Computer Graphics and Image Processing*, *1*, 373-385.

Inselberg, A. (1985). The plane with parallel coordinates. *The Visual Computer*, *1*, 69-91.

Jacob, R.J.K. (1983). Investigating the space of Chernoff faces. In M.H. Rizvi, J.S. Rustaqi, and D. Siegmund (Eds.), *Recent Advances in Statistics: A Festschrift in Honor of Herman Chernoff's Sixtieth Birthday*. New York: Academic Press.

Kosslyn, S.M. (1980). *Image and Mind*. Cambridge, MA: Harvard University Press.

Krumhansl, C.L., and Shepard, R.N. (1979). Quantification of the hierarchy of tonal functions within a diatonic context. *Journal of Experimental Psychology: Human Perception and Performance*, *5*, 579-594.

Kruskal, W.H. (1982). Criteria for judging statistical graphics. *Utilitas Mathematica*, *21B*, 283-310.

Levine, M.W. and Shefner, J.M. (1981). *Fundamentals of Sensation and Perception.* Reading, MA: Addison-Wesley.

Lodwick, G.D. and Whittle, J. (1970). A technique for automatic contouring field survey data. *Australian Computer Journal* , *2* , 104-109.

Long, L.H. (Ed.) (1971). *The World Almanac and Book of Facts.* New York: Doubleday and Co., Inc.

Maltz, M.D. (1984). *Recidivism.* New York: Academic Press.

McGill, R., Tukey, J.W., and Larsen, W.A. (1978). Variations of box plots. *The American Statistician, 32,* 12-16.

McLain, D.H. (1974). Drawing contours from arbitrary data points. *The Computer Journal, 17,* 318-324.

Michalske, T.A., and Bunker, B.C. (1987). The fracturing of glass. *Scientific American, 257* (December), 122-129.

Miles, R.E. (1974). A synopsis of "Poisson flats in Euclidean spaces." In E.F. Harding and D.G. Kendall, Eds., *Stochastic Geometry.* New York: John Wiley & Sons, 202-227.

Miller, G.A. (1956). The magical number seven, plus or minus two. *Psychological Review, 63,* 81-97.

Nelson, S.L. (1987). Plotting investment profitability. *Lotus,* April, 1987, 61-68.

Preparata, F.P. and Shamos, M.I. (1985). *Computational Geometry: An Introduction.* New York: Springer Verlag.

Rhynsburger, D. (1973). Analytic delineation of Thiessen Polygons. *Geographical Analysis,* 5, 133-144.

Richardus, P. and Adler, R.K. (1972) *Map Projections for Geodesists, Cartographers, and Geographers.* New York: North-Holland/American Elsevier.

Ripley, B.D. (1981). Spatial Statistics. New York: John Wiley & Sons.

Rudnick, J. and Gaspari, G. (1987). The shapes of random walks. *Science, 237,* 384-389.

SAS Institute Inc. (1986) *SAS/GRAPH.* Cary, NC: SAS Institute Inc.

Scott, D.W. (1979). Optimal and data-based histograms. *Biometrika,* a, 605-610.

Shepard, R.N. (1978). The mental image. *American Psychologist, 33,* 125-137.

Simken, D. and Hastie, R. (1987). An information-processing analysis of graph perception. *Journal of the American Statistical Association*, *82*, 454-465.

Spoehr, K.T. and Lehmkuhle, S.W. (1982). *Visual Information Processing.* San Francisco: W.H. Freeman.

Sturges, H.A. (1926). The choice of a class interval. *Journal of the American Statistical Association*, *21*, 65.

Trumbo, B.E. (1981). A theory for coloring bivariate statistical maps. *The American Statistician, 35*, 220-226.

Tufte, E.R. (1983). *The Visual Display of Quantitative Information.* Cheshire, CT: Graphics Press.

Tukey, J.W. (1977). *Exploratory Data Analysis.* Reading, Mass: Addison-Wesley.

U.S. Bureau of the Census (1986). *State and Metropolitan Area Data Book.* U.S. Government Printing Office.

Velleman, P.F. and Hoaglin, D.C. (1981). *Applications, Basics, and Computing of Exploratory Data Analysis.* Boston: Duxbury Press.

Wainer, H. and Francolini, C.M. (1980). An empirical inquiry concerning human understanding of two-variable color maps. *The American Statistician*, *34*, 81-93.

Wainer, H. and Thissen, D. (1981). Graphical data analysis. *Annual Review of Psychology*, *32*, 191-241.

Wang, P.C.C. (Ed.) (1978). *Graphical Representation of Multivariate Data.* New York: Academic Press.

Warner, B.G., Mathewes, R.W., and Clague, J.J. (1982). Ice-free conditions on the Queen Charlotte Islands, British Columbia, at the height of late Wisconsin glaciation. *Science*, *218*, 675-677.

Wegman, E.J. (1982). Density estimation. In S. Kotz and N .L. Johnson (Eds.), *Encyclopedia of Statistical Sciences.* Vol. 2. New York: John Wiley & Sons, 309-315.

Wegman, E.J. (1986). Hyperdimensional data analysis using parallel coordinates. *George Mason University Center for Computational Statistics and Probability Technical Report No. 1.*

Wilkinson, L. (1982). An experimental evaluation of multivariate graphical point representations. Human Factors in Computer Systems: Proceedings. Gaithersburg, Maryland, 202-209.

Wilkinson, L. (1983). *Fuzzygrams*. Cambridge, MA: Harvard Computer Graphics Week.

Winer, B.J. (1971). *Statistical principles in experimental design*, 2nd. ed. New York: McGraw-Hill.

Appendix A

TYPE FACES

SYGRAPH contains five type faces: STROKE, SWISS, BRITISH, HERSHEY, and GREEK. Allen V. Hershey (Hershey, 1972) digitized the HERSHEY font and I digitized the others. Their size is infinitely variable with the **HEIGHT** and **WIDTH** options of the **WRITE** and other commands. The following figures contain the faces with height equal to width.

Figure 1

TYPE=STROKE

!"#$%&'(

)*+,-./0

12345678

9:;<=>?@

ABCDEFGH

IJKLMNOP

QRSTUVWX

YZ[\]^_

abcdefgh

ijklmnop

qrstuvwx

yz{|}~

Figure 2

TYPE=STROKE/ITALIC

!"#$%&'(
)*+,-./0
12345678
9:;<=>?@
ABCDEFGH
IJKLMNOP
QRSTUVWX
YZ[\]^_
abcdefgh
ijklmnop
qrstuvwx
yz{|}~

Figure 3

TYPE=SWISS

!"#$%&'(

)*+,-./0

12345678

9:;<=>?@

ABCDEFGH

IJKLMNOP

QRSTUVWX

YZ[\]^_'

abcdefgh

ijklmnop

qrstuvwx

yz{|}~

Figure 4

TYPE=SWISS/ITALIC

!"#$%&'(
)+,-./0*
12345678
9:;<=>?@
ABCDEFGH
IJKLMNOP
QRSTUVWX
YZ[\]^_'
abcdefgh
ijklmnop
qrstuvwx
yz{|}~

Figure 5

TYPE=BRITISH

!” #$%&`(

)*+,−./0

12345678

9:;<=>?@

ABCDEFGH

IJKLMNOP

QRSTUVWX

YZ[\]^_

abcdefgh

ijklmnop

qrstuvwx

yz{|}~

Figure 6

TYPE=BRITISH/ITALIC

!" #$%&'(

)+,-./0*

12345678

9:;<=>?@

ABCDEFGH

IJKLMNOP

QRSTUVWX

YZ[\]^_

abcdefgh

ijklmnop

qrstuvwx

yz{|}~

Figure 7

TYPE=HERSHEY

!"#$%&'(
)*+,-./0
12345678
9:;<=>?@
ABCDEFGH
IJKLMNOP
QRSTUVWX
YZ[\]^_'
abcdefgh
ijklmnop
qrstuvwx
yz{|}~

Figure 8

TYPE=HERSHEY/ITALIC

!"#$%&'(
)+,-./0*
12345678
9:;<=>?@
ABCDEFGH
IJKLMNOP
QRSTUVWX
YZ[\]^_'
abcdefgh
ijklmnop
qrstuvwx
yz{|}~

Figure 9

TYPE=GREEK

!∀#∃%&∍(

)*+,−./0

12345678

9:;<=>?≅

ΑΒΧΔΕΦΓΗ

ΙϑΚΛΜΝΟΠ

ΘΡΣΤΥςΩΞ

ΨΖ[∴]⊥_‾

αβχδεφγη

ιφκλμνοπ

θρστυϖωξ

ψζ{|}~

Figure 10

`TYPE=GREEK/ITALIC`

!∀#∃%&∋(

)+,−./0*

12345678

9:;<=>?≅

ΑΒΧΔΕΦΓΗ

ΙϑΚΛΜΝΟΠ

ΘΡΣΤΥςΩΞ

ΨΖ[∴]⊥_‾

αβχδεφγη

ιϕκλμνοπ

θρστυϖωξ

ψζ{|}~

Appendix B

MAP BOUNDARY FILES

SYGRAPH plots maps using two files at the same time. One has a .MAP extension and contains the coordinates of the boundaries of each polygon (state, precinct, etc.) in the file. The other has a .SYS extension and contains data about each polygon. Both files are binary. The MAP file has a special format that cannot be read by the DATA module. The SYS file is an ordinary SYSTAT or SYGRAPH file and can be edited or created with the DATA editor.

The MAP File

The IMPORT command in the DATA module will convert an ASCII (character) file containing latitude and longitude coordinates to a MAP file. This file must have a structure like the following:

```
ID   NP   X    Y    X    Y    X    Y
ID   NP   X    Y    X    Y    ID   NP   X    Y
X    Y    ID   NP   X    Y    X    Y    X    Y...
```

and so on. ID is an ID number for each polygon. NP is the number of points in the polygon (X,Y pairs). X and Y are the longitude and latitude, respectively, of each point on the boundary of the polygon. SYGRAPH will plot a "map" for any arbitrary polygon with X,Y coordinates in any units, but most geographical data files use longitude and latitude in decimal degrees.

The records in this file can be unequal lengths (up to 999 characters) and the data may be integer or real or exponential. Any numerical format readable by the SYSTAT DATA module can be read by the IMPORT facility. If you are uncertain about a format, the simplest is one with two numbers per record, separated by a blank or comma:

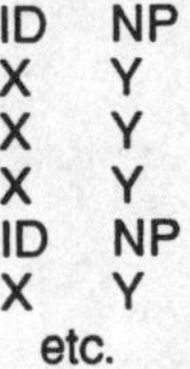

```
ID   NP
X    Y
X    Y
X    Y
ID   NP
X    Y
 etc.
```

The ID variable should be sorted in ascending order of absolute values in the file (early ID's smaller than later). Several polygons may have the same ID. The Massachusets map in the US.MAP file, for example, has three polygons for the mainland, Nantucket, and Martha's Vineyard, respectively. ID's need not be sequential numbers (i.e. you can skip a number), but they must be integers or they will be truncated to integers (decimals discarded).

If an ID is negative, then its associated polygon will not be filled with color or fill pattern. This is a useful device for representing rivers or roads within a state or polygon. A Massachusetts map, for example could have the following ID's: 4 (mainland), 4 (Martha's Vineyard), 4 (Nantucket), 4 (Cape Cod), -4 (Mass Turnpike), -4 (Concord River), -4 (Route 128). All of the points following these ID's would be plotted as Massachusetts.

Islands are represented as part of their surrounding polygon. The following figure shows an example of an island surrounded by an irregular polygon. If you trace the numbers, you can see that the filled area will exclude the triangular island in the center. The path from 6 to 7 and 10 to 11 is called a "zero width corridor." To represent this polygon and its island, you should enter 11 X,Y coordinates into the map file. The corridor will show on maps drawn with SYGRAPH unless you use the **FILL** option to conceal it. Otherwise, you should represent the island and the outer polygon as two separate polygons.

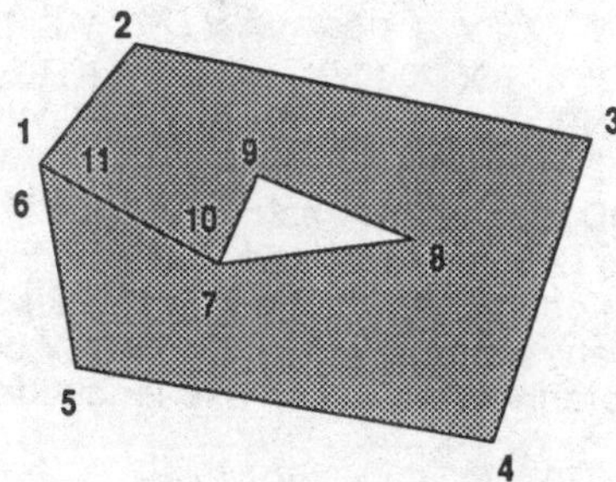

The SYS File

The DATA module can be used to create and modify SYS files containing information used to plot and fill polygons. SYS files have the following variables:

```
MAPNUM    MINLAT    MAXLAT    MINLON    MAXLON    LABLAT    LABLON
```

where the above names represent the following:

`MAPNUM` : ID number of each polygon
`MINLAT` : Minimum latitude of polygon
`MAXLAT` : Maximum latitude of polygon
`MINLON` : Minimum longitude of polygon
`MAXLON` : Maximum longitude of polygon
`LABLAT` : Latitude of label for polygon
`LABLON` : Longitude of label for polygon

These variables may be in any order in the file, but if they are missing, the MAP command in SYGRAPH will not work. The SYS file may contain additional variables on each record. The variable names must be spelled exactly as they appear above.

How SYGRAPH Plots a Map

To plot a map, an ID for a polygon is selected by reading the MAPNUM variable in the first record of the SYS file or the first appropriate record selected with the `BY` or `SELECT` command. Next, the MAP file is read until a matching ID variable absolute value is found. The subsequent NP points of the polygon corresponding to that ID are plotted and, possibly, filled with color and fill pattern and labeled. Next, the MAP file is read further to check for remaining ID's which match the current MAPNUM. Any polygons with ID's corresponding in absolute value to the current value of MAPNUM are similarly plotted. If an ID is negative and its absolute value corresponds to the current value of MAPNUM, its associated polygon is plotted but not filled. When no further ID's are found corresponding to MAPNUM's value, the next appropriate record in the SYS file is selected. Polygon(s) for this ID are plotted and the process continues until no further appropriate records are available in the SYS file. The MINLAT, MAXLAT, MINLON, and MAXLON variables are used for scaling maps in the viewing window and the LABLAT and LABLON variables are used for labeling polygons. Up to 200 polygons can be labeled in a single MAP command.

Drawing Other Stuff

You may have figured out that the MAP file is a way to plot *any* filled or empty shape in SYGRAPH. You can take a digitizer tablet, for example, and trace letters, figures, and symbols from published material or laboratory data. Most CAD programs convert these digitized tracings into X,Y coordinate ASCII files. If you IMPORT these files into a MAP file, you can plot irregular shapes with SYGRAPH.

Sources of Map Files

Contact SYSTAT Inc. for information on map files. The following companies distribute ASCII map files and associated information which can be plotted in SYGRAPH.

Geographic Data Technology, Inc.
13 Dartmouth College Highway
Lyme, NH 03768
(603)-795-2183

National Planning Data Corporation
P.O. Box 610
Ithaca, New York 14851
(607)-273-8208

Rand McNally & Company
8255 Central Park Avenue
Skokie, IL 60076
(312)-673-9100

Appendix C

Common Devices and SYGRAPH Compatible Emulation Modes

A number of devices do not have specific SYGRAPH drivers. Many of these devices, however, emulate a different device which *is* supported by one or our drivers. Here is a list of such devices under the following categories:

- Printers
- Laser Printers
- PostScript Printers
- Plotters
- Cameras

Printers

This section lists many common printers which do not have a specific SYGRAPH driver. Each of these devices emulates a printer which is supported by one of our drivers. However, we do not guarantee that all of the devices here will work with SYGRAPH since 'perfect' emulation is required. If you have one of the printers listed below, we recommend that you try the driver referred to by the emulation code.

Emulation code	*Printer*	*Driver name*
1	Epson FX80	EPSONX.SYS
1	FX100	EPSONX.SYS
2	IBM Proprinter	IBMPRO.SYS
3	Epson LQ series	EPSONLQ.SYS

Device	*Emulation code*
Facit B3100	2
Facit B3150	2
Facit B3350	2
Fortis DM1310	1
Fujitsu DL2600	1
Fujitsu DL3400	2
Fujitsu DX2300	1
Fujitsu DX2400	2
Genicom Centronics Printstation 220	1
Honeywell Bull 4/66	1
Mannesmann Tally 87	1
Mannesmann Tally 90	2
Mannesmann Tally 330	2
Nissho NP-2405	3
Okidata Microline 393	3

Olympia NP30	2
Olympia NP80	2
Olympia NP136	1
OTC TriMatrix 850XL	2
Panasonic KX-P1080i	1
Panasonic KX-P1091i	1
Panasonic KX-P1092i	2
Panasonic KX-P1524	3
Panasonic KX-P1592	1
Printronix S-7024	2
Sanyo PR-241	3
Seikosha MP-5300AI	1
Seikosha SK-3000AI	1
Seikosha SK-3005AI	1
Seikosha SL-80AI	1
Seikosha SP-180AI	1
Seikosha SP-1200AI	1
Star NB24-15	1
Star NR-15	1
Star NX-15	1

Laser Printers

The following laser printers offer compatibility with the HP LaserJet. This is not a complete list. Only laser printers having 100% compatibility with the HP LaserJet driver will work with our LaserJet driver.

BlaserStar
CIE LIPS 10 Plus
C. Itoh Jet-Setter
Dataproducts LZR-1230
Data Technology CrystalPrint VIII
Destiny Laser Act I
Kyocera F-1010
Kyocera F-2010
Kyocera F-3010
Oasys LaserPro Express Series II
Okidata Laserline 6
Personal Computer Products LaserImage 2000
Personal Computer Products LaserImage 3000
Printronix L1012
QMS SmartWriter 80 Plus
Ricoh PC Laser 6000
Texas Instruments OmniLaser 2115

PostScript Printers

This is a partial list of the laser printers supported by the SYGRAPH PostScript driver. This is not a complete list; any PostScript laser printer is supported by the PostScript driver.

Agfa-Gevaert P400PS
Apollo Domain/Laser 26
AST Turbo Laser /PS
DataProducts LZR 2665
DEC PrintServer 40
DEC ScriptPrinter
Diconix Dijit 1/PS
IBM 4216-020 Personal Pageprinter
Laser Connection PS Jet
LaserWriter, LaserWriter+
Linotype Linotronic 100
Linotype Linotronic 300
NBI Model 908
NEC SilentWriter LC-890
QMS-PS 2400
QMS-PS800, PS-800+, PS-800 II
Qume Corporation ScirpTEN
Texas Instruments OmniLaser 2108
Texas Instruments OmniLaser 2115
The Laser Connection PS Jet/ PS Jet+
Varityper VT-600
Wang LCS15

Appendix D

Driver Files Listed By Disk

Disk#	*File*	*Device*
1	CGITEST.EXE	Driver test program
1	DRIVERS.EXE	Program to load and initialize CGI
1	ADAGE30.SYS	Adage/Lexidata PG 90 Model 30 display
1	CGI6300B.SYS	AT&T 6300/6310 monochrome display
1	CGI6300C.SYS	AT&T 6300/6310 color display
1	CGIDGIS.SYS	DGIS High Performance Displays
1	CGIPOST.SYS	PostScript printers
1	CGIPREP	PostScript driver data file
1	COMPAQ3.SYS	Compaq Portable III display
1	DIAB150.SYS	Diablo C150 / Xerox 4020 printer
2	DICONIXH.SYS	Diconix 150 printer—high resolution
2	DICONIXL.SYS	Diconix 150 printer—low resolution
2	EPSONLQ.SYS	Epson printer—LQ series
2	EPSONX.SYS	Epson printer—MX, FX and EX series
2	GSSCGI.SYS	Required by all output devices
2	HERCBW.SYS	Hercules monochrome display
2	HERCINCO.SYS	Hercules InColor display
2	HIRESEGA.SYS	Hi resolution EGA displays
3	HPGLPLTR.SYS	HP, IBM and Roland plotters
3	IBMAFH.SYS	IBM 8514/a 1024X768 display
3	IBMAFL.SYS	IBM 8514/a 640X480 display
3	IBMBW.SYS	IBM CGA mono/COMPAQ mono
3	IBMCO.SYS	IBM CGA 320X200 4 color display
3	IBMEGA.SYS	IBM EGA display
3	IBMGPR.SYS	IBM graphics printer
3	IBMPRCOL.SYS	IBM Color Graphics printer
4	IBMPRO.SYS	IBM Proprinter II/XL
4	IBMQW2.SYS	IBM Quietwriter II printer
4	IBMQW3.SYS	IBM Quietwriter III printer
4	IBMVGA11.SYS	IBM Personal System/2—Mode 11
4	IBMVGA12.SYS	IBM Personal System/2—Mode 12
4	IBMVGA13.SYS	IBM Personal System/2—Mode 13,MCGA
4	IBMX124.SYS	IBM Proprinter X24 and XL24
4	LASERJET.SYS	HP LaserJet Plus/Series II printer
5	NECP5.SYS	NEC P5, P6, P7 and P9XL (mono),P2200
5	PALETTE.SYS	Polaroid Palette
5	QUIETJET.SYS	HP Quiet Jet/QuietJet+ printer
5	T3100.SYS	Toshiba 3100 Lap Top display
5	TEK4695.SYS	Tektronix 4695/4696 printer
5	THINKJET.SYS	HP ThinkJet printer
5	TOSHIBA.SYS	Toshiba P351 printer
5	VERSATEC.SYS	Versatec printers/plotters

Appendix E

Driver Files Listed by Hardware

If you cannot find your hardware in this appendix refer to Appendix A.

Device	*File*	*Disk #*
Adage PG 90 Model 30 display	ADAGE30.SYS	1
Apple Laserwriter	CGIPOST.SYS	1
	CGIPREP	1
AT&T 6300/6310 color display	CGI6300C.SYS	1
AT&T 6300/6310 monochrome display	CGI6300B.SYS	1
ATI EGA Wonder	HIRESEGA.SYS	2
ATI VIP	HIRESEGA.SYS	2
Aurealis Graphics Accelerator	CGIDGIS.SYS	1
COMPAQ monochrome display	IBMBW.SYS	3
Compaq Portable III display	COMPAQ3.SYS	1
DGIS High Performance displays	CGIDGIS.SYS	1
Diablo C150 printer	DIAB150.SYS	1
Diconix 150 printer—high resolution	DICONIXH.SYS	2
Diconix 150 printer—low resolution	DICONIXL.SYS	2
Epson printer—LQ series: 500,800,1000,2500	EPSONLQ.SYS	2
Epson printer—MX, FX and EX series	EPSONX.SYS	2
Genoa Super EGA	HIRESEGA.SYS	2
Hercules InColor display	HERCINCO.SYS	2
Hercules monochrome display	HERCBW.SYS	2
High resolution EGA displays	HIRESEGA.SYS	2
HP LaserJet Plus/Series II printer	LASERJET.SYS	4
HP Quiet Jet/QuietJet+ printer	QUIETJET.SYS	5
HP ThinkJet printer	THINKJET.SYS	5
HP plotters	HPGLPLTR.SYS	3
IBM 8514/a display		
640X480 resolution	IBMAFL.SYS	3
1024X768 resolution	IBMAFH.SYS	3
IBM Color Graphics Adapter		
640X200 monochrome/higher resolution	IBMBW.SYS	3
320X200 4 color/lower resolution	IBMCO.SYS	3
IBM Color Graphics Printer	IBMPRCOL.SYS	3
IBM EGA display	IBMEGA.SYS	3
IBM Graphics printer	IBMGPR.SYS	3
IBM Personal System/2		
Mode 11—640X480 2 color	IBMVGA11.SYS	4
Mode 12—640X480 16 color	IBMVGA12.SYS	4
Mode 13—320X200 256 color,MCGA	IBMVGA13.SYS	4
IBM plotters	HPGLPLTR.SYS	3
IBM Proprinter II/XL	IBMPRO.SYS	4
IBM Proprinter X24 and XL24	IBMXL24.SYS	4
IBM Quietwriter II printer	IBMQW2.SYS	4
IBM Quietwriter III printer	IBMQW3.SYS	4
Lexidata PG 90 Model 30 display	ADAGE30.SYS	1
NEC P5, P6, P7 and P9XL (mono)	NECP5.SYS	5
Paradise AutoSwitch EGA 480	HIRESEGA.SYS	2
Polaroid Palette	PALETTE.SYS	5
PostScript printers	CGIPOST.SYS	1
	CGIPREP	1
Quadram ProSync	HIRESEGA.SYS	2

Roland plotters—980, 990, 2000 and 3300	HPGLPLTR.SYS	5
Tecmar EGA Master 800	HIRESEGA.SYS	2
Tektronix 4695/4696 printer	TEK4695.SYS	5
Toshiba 3100 Lap Top display	T3100.SYS	5
Toshiba P351 printer (*not* P321 or P341)	TOSHIBA.SYS	5
Versatec printers/plotters Ve-80 C2552 C2558 CE3224 CE3236 CE3224 CE3444 CE3436 CE3444 7222 7224 7236 7244 7422 7424 7436 7444 ECP-42 Versacolor	VERSATEC.SYS	5
Video Seven VEGA Deluxe	HIRESEGA.SYS	2
Video Seven VGA	HIRESEGA.SYS	2
Xerox 4020 printer	DIAB150.SYS	1

Appendix F

Supplemental Drivers Listing

Drivers for the following items are available from SYSTAT for a processing fee:

Printers

IDS Prism 80, 132
IDS Microprism 480
Okidata Microline 84
Okidata Microline 92, 93
Datasouth DS180
Qume Sprint 11
Seikosha GP-700A
Texas Instruments 855
Toshiba P1350
Anadex 9501A
Genicom Multicolor
NEC 3350
QMS Lasergrafix

Plotters

Amdek Amplott II
Houston Instruments Hiplot
Nicolet Zeta 8

Camera Film Recorders

CalComp Samurai
Magi Slide System

Appendix G

Hardware Specific Operation Notes

Here is a reference for required and optional AUTOEXEC.BAT commands for various display, printers and plotters.

Displays (Monitors and Graphics Cards)

■ Adage PG 90 Model 30

Required AUTOEXEC.BAT command:

```
SET DISPLAY=ADAGE30
```

Optional AUTOEXEC.BAT commands:

`SET LEXIDATA=1300`	Default address as supplied by Lexidata
`SET LEXIDATA=<Addr>`	Address of monitor if different from default.

LEXIDATA: You probably will not have to worry about this command. It allows you to identify an 'address' which SYGRAPH uses to 'talk' with the printer. Lexidata uses 1300 (hexidecimal) as the default address and so we use the same. If you have changed this address then identify the new address with the SET command as indicated above.

■ ATI EGA Wonder

Required AUTOEXEC.BAT command:

```
SET DISPLAY=HIRESEGA
```

Optional AUTOEXEC.BAT commands:

`SET EGA=MR3`	Specifies 320X200 resolution.
`SET EGA=HR3`	Specifies 640X200 resolution.
`SET EGA=HR4`	Specifies 640X350 resolution.
`SET EGA=640X480`	Specifies 640X480 resolution.
`SET EGA=800X600`	Specifies 800X800 resolution. The default.

Note: You must have at least 256kb of display memory and a Multi-Sync type display.

■ ATI VIP

Required AUTOEXEC.BAT command:

SET DISPLAY=HIRESEGA

Optional AUTOEXEC.BAT commands:

SET EGA=MR3	Specifies 320X200 resolution.
SET EGA=HR3	Specifies 640X200 resolution.
SET EGA=HR4	Specifies 640X350 resolution.
SET EGA=800X560	Specifies 800X800 resolution. The default.

Note: You must have at least 256kb of display memory and a Multi-Sync type display.

■ AT&T 6300/6310 Monochrome (640X400)

Required AUTOEXEC.BAT command:

SET DISPLAY=CGI6300B

Optional AUTOEXEC.BAT commands:

None available

■ AT&T 6300/6310 Color (640X400)

Required AUTOEXEC.BAT command:

SET DISPLAY=CGI6300C

Optional AUTOEXEC.BAT commands:

None available

■ COMPAQ Monochrome (except COMPAQ Portable III)

Required AUTOEXEC.BAT command:

SET DISPLAY=IBMBW

Optional AUTOEXEC.BAT commands:

None available

■ COMPAQ Portable III

Required AUTOEXEC.BAT command:

SET DISPLAY=COMPAQ3

Optional AUTOEXEC.BAT commands:

None available

■ Genoa Super EGA

Required AUTOEXEC.BAT command:

SET DISPLAY=HIRESEGA

Optional AUTOEXEC.BAT commands:

SET EGA=MR3	Specifies 320X200 resolution.
SET EGA=HR3	Specifies 640X200 resolution.
SET EGA=HR4	Specifies 640X350 resolution.
SET EGA=640X480	Specifies 640X480 resolution.
SET EGA=800X600	Specifies 800X600 resolution. The default.

Note: You must have at least 256kb of display memory and a Multi-Sync type display.

■ Hercules InColor DISPLAY

Required AUTOEXEC.BAT command:

```
SET DISPLAY=HERCINCO
```

Optional AUTOEXEC.BAT commands:

None available

■ Hercules Monochrome Adapter

Required AUTOEXEC.BAT command:

```
SET DISPLAY=HERCBW
```

Optional AUTOEXEC.BAT commands:

None available

■ IBM 8514/a—Low Resolution

Required AUTOEXEC.BAT command:

```
SET DISPLAY=IBMAFL
```

Optional AUTOEXEC.BAT commands:

None available

Note: You must load the IBM adapter interface software, HDILOAD.EXE, prior to using SYGRAPH. Please refer to your IBM 8514/A reference manual for more information about HDILOAD.EXE. The IBM Color Display requires the higher resolution driver (640x480).

■ IBM 8514/a—High Resolution

Required AUTOEXEC.BAT command:

```
SET DISPLAY=IBMAFH
```

Optional AUTOEXEC.BAT commands:

None available

Note: You must load the IBM adapter interface software, HDILOAD.EXE, prior to using SYGRAPH. Please refer to your IBM 8514/A reference manual for more information about HDILOAD.EXE. The IBM Color Display requires this higher resolution driver (1024x768).

- **IBM Color Graphics Adapter—High Resolution Monochrome**
  Required AUTOEXEC.BAT command:
  ```
  SET DISPLAY=IBMBW
  ```
  Optional AUTOEXEC.BAT commands:
  ```
  None available
  ```

Note: This graphics card supports either low or high resolution. With lower resolution, multiple colors are supported. With higher resolution, only monochrome graphics are supported. If you want to swap between these two modes, install each of the drivers IBMBW.SYS and IBMCO.SYS onto your system and make the appropriate addition to CONFIG.SYS. Then, when you want to graph in higher resolution, enter the command

```
SET DISPLAY=IBMBW
```

at the DOS prompt. Or, to graph with colors, type the command

```
SET DISPLAY=IBMCO
```

at the DOS prompt.

- **IBM Color Graphics Adapter—Medium Resolution Color**
  Required AUTOEXEC.BAT command:
  ```
  SET DISPLAY=IBMCO
  ```
  Optional AUTOEXEC.BAT commands:
  ```
  None available
  ```

Note: This graphics card supports either low or high resolution. With lower resolution, multiple colors are supported. With higher resolution, only monochrome graphics are supported. If you want to swap between these two modes, INSTALL each of the drivers IBMBW.SYS and IBMCO.SYS onto your system and make the appropriate addition to the CONFIG.SYS file which appears in the root directory of your boot disk. Then, when you want to graph in higher resolution, enter the command

```
SET DISPLAY=IBMBW
```

at the DOS prompt. Or, to graph with colors, type the command

```
SET DISPLAY=IBMCO
```

at the DOS prompt. The lower resolution color mode supports up to four colors.

■ IBM Enhanced Graphics Adapter

Required AUTOEXEC.BAT command:

`SET DISPLAY=IBMEGA`

Optional AUTOEXEC.BAT commands:

`SET EGA=MR3`	320X200 resolution. Maximum of sixteen colors.
`SET EGA=HR3`	640X200 resolution. Maximum of sixteen colors.
`SET EGA=HR4`	640X350 resolution. Maximum of either four or sixteen colors (default).
`SET EGA=MONO`	640X350 monochrome resolution.

MR3 supports 320X200 resolution with a maximum of sixteen colors on the screen in one plot.

HR3 supports 640X200 resolution with a maximum of sixteen colors on the screen in one plot.

HR4 supports 640X350 resolution with a maximum either four or sixteen colors depending on the amount of memory available on your graphics card. 64K of memory allows 4 colors, 128 or 256K allows 16 colors.

MONO produces 640X350 resolution with a with a monochrome monitor. If you have a monochrome system you must use this SET option.

■ IBM PS/2 VGA Mode 11 (640x480 2 color)

Required AUTOEXEC.BAT command:

`SET DISPLAY=IBMVGA11`

Optional AUTOEXEC.BAT commands:

None available

■ IBM PS/2 VGA Mode 12 (640x480 16 color)

Required AUTOEXEC.BAT command:

`SET DISPLAY=IBMVGA12`

Optional AUTOEXEC.BAT commands:

None available

■ IBM PS/2 VGA Mode 13 (320x200 256 color) and PS/2 MCGA

Required AUTOEXEC.BAT command:

`SET DISPLAY=IBMVGA13`

Optional AUTOEXEC.BAT commands:

None available

■ Lexidata PG 90 Model 30

Required AUTOEXEC.BAT command:

```
SET DISPLAY=ADAGE30
```

Optional AUTOEXEC.BAT commands:

`SET LEXIDATA=1300`	Default address as supplied by Lexidata.
`SET LEXIDATA=<Addr>`	Address of monitor if different from default.

LEXIDATA: You probably will not have to worry about this command. It allows you to identify an 'address' which SYGRAPH uses to 'talk' with the printer. Lexidata uses 1300 (hexidecimal) as the default address and so we use the same. If you have changed this address then identify the new address with the SET command as indicated above.

■ Paradise AutoSwitch EGA 480

Required AUTOEXEC.BAT command:

```
SET DISPLAY=HIRESEGA
```

Optional AUTOEXEC.BAT commands:

`SET EGA=MR3`	Specifies 320X200 resolution.
`SET EGA=HR3`	Specifies 640X200 resolution.
`SET EGA=HR4`	Specifies 640X350 resolution.
`SET EGA=640X480`	Specifies 640X480 resolution. The default.

Note: You must have at least 256kb of display memory and a Multi-Sync type display.

■ Quadram ProSync

Required AUTOEXEC.BAT command:

```
SET DISPLAY=HIRESEGA
```

Optional AUTOEXEC.BAT commands:

`SET EGA=MR3`	Specifies 320X200 resolution.
`SET EGA=HR3`	Specifies 640X200 resolution.
`SET EGA=HR4`	Specifies 640X350 resolution.
`SET EGA=640X480`	Specifies 640X480 resolution. The default.

Note: You must have at least 256kb of display memory and a Multi-Sync type display.

■ Tecmar EGA Master 800

Required AUTOEXEC.BAT command:

```
SET DISPLAY=HIRESEGA
```

Optional AUTOEXEC.BAT commands:

`SET EGA=MR3`	Specifies 320X200 resolution.
`SET EGA=HR3`	Specifies 640X200 resolution.
`SET EGA=HR4`	Specifies 640X350 resolution.
`SET EGA=640X480`	Specifies 640X480 resolution.
`SET EGA=800X600`	Specifies 800X600 resolution. The default.

Note: You must have at least 256kb of display memory and a Multi-Sync type display.

■ Toshiba 3100 Lap Top

Required AUTOEXEC.BAT command:

```
SET DISPLAY=T3100
```

Optional AUTOEXEC.BAT commands:

```
None available
```

■ Video 7 Vega Deluxe

Required AUTOEXEC.BAT command:

```
SET DISPLAY=HIRESEGA
```

Optional AUTOEXEC.BAT commands:

`SET EGA=MR3`	Specifies 320X200 resolution.
`SET EGA=HR3`	Specifies 640X200 resolution.
`SET EGA=HR4`	Specifies 640X350 resolution.
`SET EGA=640X480`	Specifies 640X480 resolution. The default.

Note: You must have at least 256kb of display memory and a Multi-Sync type display.

■ Video 7 Vega VGA

Required AUTOEXEC.BAT command:

```
SET DISPLAY=HIRESEGA
```

Optional AUTOEXEC.BAT commands:

`SET EGA=MR3`	Specifies 320X200 resolution.
`SET EGA=HR3`	Specifies 640X200 resolution.
`SET EGA=HR4`	Specifies 640X350 resolution.
`SET EGA=800X600`	Specifies 800X600 resolution. The default.

Note: You must have at least 256kb of display memory and a Multi-Sync type display. For 640X480 resolution use the IBM PS/2 MODE 12 driver.

Printers

- Diablo C-150 Color Printer

  Required AUTOEXEC.BAT command:

  ```
  SET PRINTER=DIAB150
  ```

  Optional AUTOEXEC.BAT commands:

`SET ORIENTATION=<mode>`	In PORTRAIT mode output is not rotated (the default). In LANDSCAPE mode the output is rotated 270 degrees.
`SET ORIENTATION=LANDSCAPE`	Output rotated 270 degrees counterclockwise.
`SET TEMPDIR=<path>`	Specifies directory in which to write temporary files.
`SET PLISTSIZE=<buffer size>`	Specifies number of bytes for the printer buffer The default is 512 bytes.
`SET DIAB150=<port>`	Specifies the port in which the printer is connected. The default is LPT1.

DIAB150 specifies the port in which the printer is connected. COM1, COM2, LPT1 and LPT2 are valid options. Note that you cannot include the colon associated with the port. For example, COM1: is not valid and will be ignored by the system.

TEMPDIR See the last page of this document for a description.

PLISTSIZE See the last page of this document for a description.

■ Diconix Inkjet Printer—High Resolution Mode

Required AUTOEXEC.BAT command:

```
SET PRINTER=DICONIXH
```

Optional AUTOEXEC.BAT commands:

`SET ORIENTATION=<mode>`	In PORTRAIT mode output is not rotated (the default). In LANDSCAPE mode the output is rotated 270 degrees.
`SET TEMPDIR=<path>`	Specifies directory in which to write temporary files.
`SET PLISTSIZE=<buffer size>`	Specifies number of bytes for the printer buffer The default is 512 bytes.
`SET DICONIXH=<port>`	Specifies the port in which the printer is connected. The default is LPT1.

DICONIXH specifies the port in which the printer is connected. COM1, COM2, LPT1 and LPT2 are among valid options. Note that you cannot include the colon associated with the port; for example, COM1: is not valid and will be ignored by the system.
TEMPDIR See the last page of this document for a description.
PLISTSIZE See the last page of this document for a description.

Note: This printer can print in either low or high resolution. With lower resolution, printing speed is significantly faster. With higher resolution, printing speed is reduced but with a significant increase in clarity. If you want to swap between these two modes, install each of the drivers DICONIXL.SYS and DICONIXH.SYS onto your system and make the appropriate addition to your CONFIG.SYS file. Then, when you want to print in higher resolution, enter the command

```
SET PRINTER=DICONIXH
```

at the DOS prompt. Or, to print faster, type the command

```
SET PRINTER=DICONIXL
```

at the DOS prompt.

■ Diconix Inkjet Printer—Low Resolution Mode

Required AUTOEXEC.BAT command:

```
SET PRINTER=DICONIXH
```

Optional AUTOEXEC.BAT commands:

`SET ORIENTATION=<mode>`	In PORTRAIT mode output is not rotated (the default). In LANDSCAPE mode the output is rotated 270 degrees.
`SET TEMPDIR=<path>`	Specifies directory in which to write temporary files.
`SET PLISTSIZE=<buffer size>`	Specifies number of bytes for the printer buffer. The default is 512 bytes.
`SET DICONIXH=<port>`	Specifies the port in which the printer is connected. The default is LPT1.

DICONIXH specifies the port in which the printer is connected. COM1, COM2, LPT1 and LPT2 are among valid options. Note that you cannot include the colon associated with the port; for example, COM1: is not valid and will be ignored by the system.
TEMPDIR See the last page of this document for a description.
PLISTSIZE See the last page of this document for a description.

Note: This printer can print in either low or high resolution. With lower resolution, printing speed is significantly faster. With higher resolution, printing speed is reduced but with a significant increase in clarity. If you want to swap between these two modes, install each of the drivers DICONIXL.SYS and DICONIXH.SYS onto your system and make the appropriate addition to your CONFIG.SYS file. Then, when you want to print in higher resolution, enter the command

```
SET PRINTER=DICONIXH
```

at the DOS prompt. Or, to print faster, type the command

```
SET PRINTER=DICONIXL
```

at the DOS prompt.

■ Epson LQ Printers (500, 800, 1000, 2500)

Required AUTOEXEC.BAT command:

```
SET PRINTER=EPSONLQ
```

Optional AUTOEXEC.BAT commands:

`SET ORIENTATION=<mode>`	In PORTRAIT mode output is not rotated (the default). In LANDSCAPE mode the output is rotated 270 degrees.
`SET TEMPDIR=<path>`	Specifies directory in which to write temporary files.
`SET PLISTSIZE=<buffer size>`	Specifies number of bytes for the printer buffer. Default is 512 bytes.
`SET PAPER=ISOA4`	Requires European (210mmX297mm)paper.
`SET PAPER=NARROW`	Requires narrow (8.5"x11") paper (default).
`SET PAPER=WIDE`	Requires wide (14"x11") paper.
`SET SHEETFEEDER=<mode>`	OFF (default) has top and bottom margins of 1/2 an inch. ON has a 1 inch top margin and a 1/2 inch bottom margin.
`SET EPSONLQ=<port>`	Specifies port to which the printer is connected. Default is LPT1.

EPSONLQ specifies the port in which the printer is connected. COM1, COM2, LPT1 and LPT2 are among valid options. Note that you cannot include the colon associated with the port; for example, COM1: will be ignored by the system.
PAPER specifies the type of paper in th printer. Use **NARROW** for 8.5"x11" paper, **WIDE** with 11"x14" paper, **ISOA4** with European paper (210mmX297mm).
SHEETFEEDER informs the printer driver that the cut sheet feeder is being used. Under the default case of OFF, output assumes top and bottom margins of 1/2 of an inch. If it is set ON, output assumes a top margin of one inch and a bottom margin of 1/2 of an inch. If you are running the cut feeder insure that DIP switch 1-8 is set to the on position. Otherwise, set the DIP switch to the off position.
TEMPDIR See the last page of this document for a description.
PLISTSIZE See the last page of this document for a description.

■ Epson EX-80, EX-800, EX-1000, FX-85, FX-86, FX-185, FX-186, FX-286, MX-80F/T, MX-100 III Printers

Required AUTOEXEC.BAT command:

```
SET PRINTER=EPSONX
```

Optional AUTOEXEC.BAT commands:

`SET ORIENTATION=<mode>`	In PORTRAIT mode output is not rotated (the default). In LANDSCAPE mode the output is rotated 270 degrees.
`SET PAPER=NARROW`	Requires narrow (8.5"x11") paper (default).
`SET PAPER=WIDE`	Requires wide (14"x11") paper
`SET PAPER=ISOA4`	Requires European (210mmX297mm)paper.
`SET FF=ON`	Form feeds after each graph (default).
`SET FF=OFF`	Does not form feed after each graph.
`SET TEMPDIR=<path>`	Specifies directory in which to write temporary files.
`SET PLISTSIZE=<buffer size>`	Specifies number of bytes for the display buffer. Default is 512 bytes.
`SET EPSONX=<port>`	Specifies port to which the printer is connected. The default is LPT1.

EPSONX specifies the port in which the printer is connected. COM1, COM2, LPT1 and LPT2 are among valid options. Note that you cannot include the colon associated with the port; for example, COM1: will be ignored by the system.
PAPER specifies the type of paper in th printer. Use **NARROW** for 8.5"x11" paper, **WIDE** with 11"x14" paper, **ISOA4** with European paper (210mmX297mm).
FF See the last page of this document for a description.
WIDE with 11"x14" paper, **ISOA4** with European paper (210mmX297mm).
TEMPDIR See the last page of this document for a description.
PLISTSIZE See the last page of this document for a description.

Hardware installation:

The printer must be in **EPSON** mode.

■ Hewlett Packard LaserJet /LaserJet+ Printers

Required AUTOEXEC.BAT command:

```
SET PRINTER=LASERJET
```

Optional AUTOEXEC.BAT commands:

`SET ORIENTATION=<mode>`	In PORTRAIT mode output is not rotated (the default). In LANDSCAPE mode the output is rotated 270 degrees.
`SET RESOLUTION=<resolution>`	75, 100, 150 (default) or 300 dpi (see note below).
`SET PLISTSIZE=<buffer size>`	Specifies number of bytes for the display buffer. The default is 512 bytes.
`SET TEMPDIR=<path>`	Specifies directory in which to write temporary files.
`SET LASERJET=<port>`	Identifies in which port the printer is connected LASERJET=COM1 is the default.

RESOLUTION specifies the output resolution to be used by the printer. The lower resolution (75) provides faster output with some loss of output quality. The higest resolution (300) requires 2 Megabytes of RAM in your LaserJet for proper operation. 150 dpi resolution is the default.
LASERJET specifies the port to which the printer is connected. COM1, COM2, LPT1 and LPT2 are among the valid options. Note that you cannot include the colon associated with the port; for example, COM1: is not valid and will be ignored by the system.
TEMPDIR See the last page of this document for a description.
PLISTSIZE See the last page of this document for a description.

Note: Some LaserJet (not the LaserJet+) printers have a maximum of one-half page of graphics memory. If your graphs are not printing completely, you have this limitation. In the event that this occurs, you will have to print smaller graphs using the SYGRAPH commands SCALE or HEIGHT and WIDTH to control the size of your graphs.

■ Hewlett Packard QuietJet Printer

Required AUTOEXEC.BAT command:

```
SET PRINTER=QUIETJET
```

Optional AUTOEXEC.BAT commands:

`SET ORIENTATION=<mode>`	In PORTRAIT mode output is not rotated (the default). In LANDSCAPE mode the output is rotated 270 degrees.
`SET PAPER=NARROW`	Requires narrow (8.5"x11") paper (default).
`SET PAPER=WIDE`	Requires wide (14"x11") paper
`SET PLISTSIZE=<buffer size>`	Specifies number of bytes for the display buffer. Default is 512 bytes.
`SET TEMPDIR=<path>`	Specifies directory in which to write temporary files.
`SET QUIETJET=<port>`	Specifies port to which the printer is connected. The default is LPT1.

QUIETJET specifies the port to which the printer is connected. COM1, COM2, LPT1 and LPT2 are among valid options. Note that you cannot include the colon associated with the port; for example, COM1: is not valid and will be ignored by the system.

PAPER specifies the type of paper in th printer. Use **NARROW** for 8.5"x11" paper, and **WIDE** with 11"x14" paper.

TEMPDIR See the last page of this document for a description.

PLISTSIZE See the last page of this document for a description.

■ Hewlett Packard Thinkjet

Required AUTOEXEC.BAT command:

```
SET PRINTER=THINKJET
```

Optional AUTOEXEC.BAT commands:

`SET ORIENTATION=<mode>`	In PORTRAIT mode output is not rotated (the default). In LANDSCAPE mode the output is rotated 270 degrees.
`SET PAPER=ISOA4`	Requires European (210mmX297mm)paper.
`SET FF=ON`	Form feeds after each graph (default).
`SET FF=OFF`	Does not form feed after each graph.
`SET TEMPDIR=<path>`	Specifies directory in which to write temporary files.
`SET PLISTSIZE=<buffer size>`	Specifies number of bytes for the display buffer. Default is 512 bytes.
`SET RESOLUITION=96`	Sets horizontal dpi to 96 (default).
`SET RESOLUITION=192`	Sets horizontal dpi to 192.
`SET THINKJET=<port>`	Specifies port to which the printer is connected. The default is LPT1.

THINKJET specifies the port to which the printer is connected. COM1, COM2, LPT1 and LPT2 are among valid options. Note that you cannot include the colon associated with the port; for example, COM1: is not valid and will be ignored by the system.
PAPER specifies the type of paper in th printer. Use **ISOA4** with European paper (210mmX297mm).
RESOLUTION specifies the horizontal resolution of output.
FF See the last page of this document for a description.
TEMPDIR See the last page of this document for a description.
PLISTSIZE See the last page of this document for a description.

■ IBM Color Graphics Printer

Required AUTOEXEC.BAT command:

```
SET PRINTER=IBMPRCOL
```

Optional AUTOEXEC.BAT commands:

`SET ORIENTATION=<mode>`	In PORTRAIT mode output is not rotated (the default). In LANDSCAPE mode the output is rotated 270 degrees.
`SET PAPER=NARROW`	Requires narrow (8.5"x11") paper (default).
`SET PAPER=WIDE`	Requires wide (14"x11") paper.
`SET RIBBON=BLACK`	Requires black ribbon.
`SET RIBBON=RGB`	Requires RGB ribbon.
`SET RIBBON=PROCESS`	Requires process ribbon (default).
`SET IBMPRCOL=<port>`	Specifies the port to which the printer is connected. The default is LPT1.

IBMPRCOL specifies the port to which the printer is connected. COM1, COM2, LPT1 and LPT2 are among valid options. Note that you cannot include the colon associated with the port; for example, COM1: is not valid and will be ignored by the system.
PAPER specifies the type of paper in th printer. Use **NARROW** for 8.5"x11" paper, and **WIDE** with 11"x14" paper.
RIBBON informs the printer driver of the type of ribbon installed in your printer. PROCESS is the default.

■ IBM Graphics Printer

Required AUTOEXEC.BAT command:

```
SET PRINTER=IBMGPR
```

Optional AUTOEXEC.BAT commands:

`SET ORIENTATION=<mode>`	In PORTRAIT mode output is not rotated (the default). In LANDSCAPE mode the output is rotated 270 degrees.
`SET TEMPDIR=<path>`	Specifies directory in which to write temporary files.
`SET PLISTSIZE=<buffer size>`	Specifies number of bytes for the display buffer. The default is 512 bytes.
`SET IBMGPR=<port>`	Specifies the port to which the printer is connected. The default is LPT1.

IBMGPR specifies the port to which the printer is connected. COM1, COM2, LPT1 and LPT2 are among valid options. Note that you cannot include the colon associated with the port; for example, COM1: is not valid and will be ignored by the system.
TEMPDIR See the last page of this document for a description.
PLISTSIZE See the last page of this document for a description.

■ IBM ProPrinter, ProPrinter II and ProPrinter XL

Required AUTOEXEC.BAT command:

```
SET PRINTER=IBMPRO
```

Optional AUTOEXEC.BAT commands:

`SET ORIENTATION=<mode>`	In PORTRAIT mode output is not rotated (the default). In LANDSCAPE mode the output is rotated 270 degrees.
`SET PAPER=ISOA4`	Requires European (210mmX297mm) paper.
`SET PAPER=NARROW`	Requires narrow (8.5"x11") paper (default).
`SET PAPER=WIDE`	Requires wide (14"x11") paper.
`SET RESOLUTION=<resolution>`	60 or 120 (120 default).
`SET FF=ON`	Ends each page with a formfeed (default).
`SET FF=OFF`	Does not end page with a formfeed.
`SET TEMPDIR=<directory>`	Specifies directory in which to write temporary files
`SET PLISTSIZE=<buffer size>`	Specifies number of bytes for the display buffer. The default is 512 bytes.
`SET IBMPRO=<port>`	Specifies the port to which the printer is connected. The default is LPT1.

IBMPRO specifies the port to which the printer is connected. COM1, COM2, LPT1 and LPT2 are among valid options. Note that you cannot include the colon associated with the port; for example, LPT1: is not valid and will be ignored by the system.
PAPER specifies the type of paper in th printer. Use **NARROW** for 8.5"x11" paper, **WIDE** with 11"x14" paper, **ISOA4** with European paper (210mmX297mm).
RESOLUTION specifies the output resolution to be used by the printer. The lower resolution provides faster output with some loss of output quality.
FF See the last page of this document for a description.
TEMPDIR See the last page of this document for a description.
PLISTSIZE See the last page of this document for a description.

■ IBM ProPrinter XL24 and X24

Required AUTOEXEC.BAT command:

```
SET PRINTER=IBMXL24
```

Optional AUTOEXEC.BAT commands:

SET ORIENTATION=<mode>	In PORTRAIT mode output is not rotated (the default). In LANDSCAPE mode the output is rotated 270 degrees.
SET PAPER=ISOA4	Requires European (210mmX297mm) paper.
SET PAPER=NARROW	Requires narrow (8.5"x11") paper (default).
SET PAPER=WIDE	Requires wide (14"x11") paper.
SET RESOLUTION=<resolution>	120 or 180 (180 default).
SET FF=ON	Ends each page with a formfeed (default).
SET FF=OFF	Does not end page with a formfeed.
SET TEMPDIR=<directory>	Specifies directory in which to write temporary files
SET PLISTSIZE=<buffer size>	Specifies number of bytes for the display buffer. The default is 512 bytes.
SET IBMXL24=<port>	Specifies the port to which the printer is connected. The default is LPT1.

IBMXL24 specifies the port to which the printer is connected. COM1, COM2, LPT1 and LPT2 are among valid options. Note that you cannot include the colon associated with the port; for example, LPT1: is not valid and will be ignored by the system.
PAPER specifies the type of paper in th printer. Use **NARROW** for 8.5"x11" paper, **WIDE** with 11"x14" paper, **ISOA4** with European paper (210mmX297mm).
RESOLUTION specifies the output resolution to be used by the printer. The lower resolution provides faster output with some loss of output quality.
FF See the last page of this document for a description.
TEMPDIR See the last page of this document for a description.
PLISTSIZE See the last page of this document for a description.

■ IBM Quietwriter II

Required AUTOEXEC.BAT command:

```
SET PRINTER=IBMQW2
```

Optional AUTOEXEC.BAT commands:

`SET ORIENTATION=<mode>`	In PORTRAIT mode output is not rotated (the default). In LANDSCAPE mode the output is rotated 270 degrees.
`SET PAPER=ISOA4`	Requires European (210mmX297mm) paper.
`SET PAPER=NARROW`	Requires narrow (8.5"x11") paper (default).
`SET PAPER=WIDE`	Requires wide (14"x11") paper.
`SET RESOLUTION=<resolution>`	60 or 120 (120 default).
`SET FF=ON`	Ends each page with a formfeed (default).
`SET FF=OFF`	Does not end page with a formfeed.
`SET TEMPDIR=<directory>`	Specifies directory in which to write temporary files
`SET PLISTSIZE=<buffer size>`	Specifies number of bytes for the display buffer. The default is 512 bytes.
`SET IBMQW2=<port>`	Specifies the port to which the printer is connected. The default is LPT1.

IBMQW2 specifies the port to which the printer is connected. COM1, COM2, LPT1 and LPT2 are among valid options. Note that you cannot include the colon associated with the port; for example, COM1: will be ignored by the system.
PAPER specifies the type of paper in th printer. Use **NARROW** for 8.5"x11" paper, **WIDE** with 11"x14" paper, **ISOA4** with European paper (210mmX297mm).
RESOLUTION specifies the output resolution to be used by the printer. The lower resolution provides faster output with some loss of output quality.
FF See the last page of this document for a description.
TEMPDIR See the last page of this document for a description.
PLISTSIZE See the last page of this document for a description.

■ IBM Quietwriter III

Required AUTOEXEC.BAT command:

```
SET PRINTER=IBMQW3
```

Optional AUTOEXEC.BAT commands:

`SET ORIENTATION=<mode>`	In PORTRAIT mode output is not rotated (the default). In LANDSCAPE mode the output is rotated 270 degrees.
`SET PAPER=NARROW`	Requires narrow (8.5"x11") paper (default).
`SET PAPER=WIDE`	Requires wide (14"x11") paper.
`SET TEMPDIR=<directory>`	Specifies directory in which to write temporary files.
`SET PLISTSIZE=<buffer size>`	Specifies number of bytes for the display buffer. The default is 512 bytes.
`SET IBMQW3=<port>`	Specifies the port to which the printer is connected. The default is LPT1.

IBMQW3 specifies the port to which the printer is connected. COM1, COM2, LPT1 and LPT2 are among valid options. Note that you cannot include the colon associated with the port; for example, COM1: will be ignored by the system.
PAPER specifies the type of paper in th printer. Use **NARROW** for 8.5"x11" paper, and **WIDE** with 11"x14" paper.
FORMEED specifies whether a formfeed is to be issued at the end of an output page. The default (ON) will issue a formfeed at the end of each output page. When FORMFEED=OFF no formfeed is issued. This allows consecutive output pages to appear to be continuous graphics output with no page breaks.
TEMPDIR See the last page of this document for a description.
PLISTSIZE See the last page of this document for a description.

■ NEC P-5, P-6, P-7, P9XL (mono), P2200 Printers

Required AUTOEXEC.BAT command:

```
SET PRINTER=NECP5
```

Optional AUTOEXEC.BAT commands:

`SET ORIENTATION=<mode>`	In PORTRAIT mode output is not rotated (the default). In LANDSCAPE mode the output is rotated 270 degrees.
`SET PAPER=NARROW`	Requires narrow (8.5"x11") paper (default).
`SET PAPER=WIDE`	Requires wide (14"x11") paper
`SET PAPER=ISOA4`	Requires European (210mmX297mm)paper.
`SET TEMPDIR=<path>`	Specifies directory in which to write temporary files.
`SET PLISTSIZE=<buffer size>`	Specifies number of bytes for the display buffer. Default is 512 bytes.
`SET RESOLUTION=<resolution>`	120 or 180 (180 default).
`SET NECP5=<port>`	Specifies port to which the printer is connected. The default is LPT1.

NECP5 specifies the port in which the printer is connected. COM1, COM2, LPT1 and LPT2 are among valid options. Note that you cannot include the colon associated with the port; for example, COM1: will be ignored by the system.
PAPER specifies the type of paper in th printer. Use **NARROW** for 8.5"x11" paper, **WIDE** with 11"x14" paper, **ISOA4** with European paper (210mmX297mm).
WIDE with 11"x14" paper, **ISOA4** with European paper (210mmX297mm).
RESOLUTION specifies the output resolution to be used by the printer. The lower resolution provides faster output with some loss of output quality.
TEMPDIR See the last page of this document for a description.
PLISTSIZE See the last page of this document for a description.

■ Postscript Printers

Required AUTOEXEC.BAT command:

`SET PRINTER=CGIPOST`	
`MODE COMn:9600,N,8,1,P`	where COMn is the communications port used with the post script printer.

Optional AUTOEXEC.BAT commands:

`SET ORIENTATION=<mode>`	In PORTRAIT mode output is not rotated (the default). In LANDSCAPE mode the output is rotated 270 degrees.
`SET CGIPOST=<port>`	Specifies the port to which the printer is connected. The default is LPT1.

CGIPOST specifies the port to which the printer is connected. COM1, COM2, LPT1 and LPT2 are among valid options. Note that you cannot include the colon associated with the port; for example, COM1: is not valid and will be ignored by the system.

Note: A required configuration file, CGIPREP, is provided on the disk with the driver. CGIPREP must reside in the same directory as CGIPOST.SYS. The output from the PostScript driver cannot be redirected to a file. This is because the driver must communicate with the printer at the time of printing.

Hardware installation:

The Apple LaserWriter and QMP PS 800 require that the 9600 baud and Post Script batch mode switch be set by the user. These settings are labeled as follows (on both printers the switch is located next to the interface connector):

Printer	*Switch and Setting*
Apple LaserWriter	Switch 4 Setting 9600
QMS PS 800	Switch 4 Setting 1

All PostScript printers must have correct configuration for the 25 pin RS232 connector for the printer. The configuration must be:

Pin	*Function*
2	Transmit data
3	Receive data
4	Request to send (optional)
7	Signal Ground
20	Data Terminal Ready (optional)

■ Tektronix 4695/4696 Color Printer

Required AUTOEXEC.BAT command:

SET PRINTER=TEK4695

Optional AUTOEXEC.BAT commands:

SET ORIENTATION=<mode>	In PORTRAIT mode output is not rotated (the default). In LANDSCAPE mode the output is rotated 270 degrees.
SET TEMPDIR=<directory>	Specifies directory in which to write temporary files.
SET PLISTSIZE=<buffer size>	Specifies number of bytes for the display buffer. The default is 512 bytes.
SET TEK4695=<port>	Specifies the port to which the printer is connected. The default is LPT1.

TEK4695 specifies the port to which the printer is connected. COM1, COM2, LPT1 and LPT2 are among valid options. Note that you cannot include the colon associated with the port; for example, COM1: is not valid and will be ignored by the system.
TEMPDIR See the last page of this document for a description.
PLISTSIZE See the last page of this document for a description.

■ Toshiba Printers

Required AUTOEXEC.BAT command:

SET PRINTER=TOSHIBA

Optional AUTOEXEC.BAT commands:

SET ORIENTATION=PORTRAIT	Output is not rotated (default).
SET ORIENTATION=LANDSCAPE	Output rotated 270 degrees counterclockwise.
SET PAPER=NARROW	Requires narrow (8.5"x11") paper (default).
SET PAPER=WIDE	Requires wide (14"x11") paper.
SET TEMPDIR=<directory>	Specifies directory in which to write temporary files.
SET PLISTSIZE=<buffer size>	Specifies number of bytes for the display buffer. The default is 512 bytes.
SET TOSHIBA=<port>	Specifies the port to which the printer is connected. The default is LPT1.

TOSHIBA specifies the port to which the printer is connected. COM1, COM2, LPT1 and LPT2 are among valid options. Note that you cannot include the colon associated with the port; for example, COM1: is not valid and will be ignored by the system.
PAPER specifies the type of paper in th printer. Use **NARROW** for 8.5"x11" paper, and **WIDE** with 11"x14" paper.
TEMPDIR See the last page of this document for a description.
PLISTSIZE See the last page of this document for a description.

Plotters

■ HP, IBM and Roland Plotters

Required AUTOEXEC.BAT command:

`SET PLOTTER=HPGLPLTR`	
`MODE COMn:9600,N,8,1,P`	where COMn is the communications port used with the plotter.

Optional AUTOEXEC.BAT commands:

`SET ORIENTATION=<mode>`	In PORTRAIT mode output is rotated. In LANDSCAPE mode (the default) the output is not rotated.
`SET HP_TYPE=<class,page size, #pens>`	See description below.
`SET HPGLPLTR=<COM port>`	Identifies port to which the plotter is connected. HPGLPLTR=COM1 is the default.

HPGLPLTR Identifies the port to which the plotter is connected. If your plotter is connected to COM2, you must specify HPGLPLTR=COM2.

HP_TYPE

Class Identifies the type of plotter being used and default characteristics. Valid classes are:

Class	Model	Pagesize	Number of pens
980	Roland DG 980	ANSI A	8 pens.
990	Roland DG 990	ANSI B	8 pens.
2000	Roland DG 2000	ANSI C	8 pens.
3300	Roland DG 3300	ANSI D	8 pens.
7440	HP 7440 and 6180, 7370	ANSI A	8 pens.
7470	HP 7470 and 7371	ANSI A	2 pens.
7475	HP 7475 and 7372	ANSI B	6 pens.
7550	HP 7550	ANSI B	8 pens.
7580	HP 7580 and 6184, 7374, 7375, 7570, 7585, 7586, 7595, 7596	ANSI D	6 pens.
6180	IBM 6180	ANSI A	8 pens.
6184	IBM 6184	ANSI A	8 pens.
7370	IBM 7370	ANSI A	8 pens.
7371	IBM 7371	ANSI A	8 pens.
7372	IBM 7372	ANSI A	8 pens.
7374	IBM 7374	ANSI A	8 pens.
7375	IBM 7375	ANSI A	8 pens.

Page size This optional field overrides the default page size setting from the device class field. Valid page sizes are:

- A specifies ANSI A paper.
- B specifies ANSI B paper.
- C specifies ANSI C paper.
- D specifies ANSI D paper.
- E specifies ANSI E paper.

#Pens This optional field overrides the default number of pens.

Examples:

```
SET   HP_TYPE=980,A,4
SET   HP_TYPE=980
```

You can redirect output to a file instead of the plotter. To do so enter the following command at the DOS prompt:

```
>SET   HPGLPLTR=<filename>
```

where **<filename>** is the name of the text file for output.

To redirect output back to the plotter just reset your computer or enter the following command at the DOS prompt:

```
>SET   HPGLPLTR=<port>
```

where **<port>** is the port in which your plotter is connected.

■ VERSATEC Plotters

Required AUTOEXEC.BAT command:

`SET PLOTTER=VERSATEC`	
`MODE COMn:9600,N,8,1,P`	where COMn is the communications port used with the plotter.

Optional AUTOEXEC.BAT commands:

`SET VERSA=<model>`	Identifies your output device, see list below.
`SET ORIENTATION=<mode>`	In PORTRAIT mode output is not rotated (the default). In LANDSCAPE mode the output is rotated 270 degrees.
`SET PAPER=<paper size>`	Specifies size of paper loaded in device .
`SET VERSATEC=<port>`	Specifies the port to which the printer is connected. The default is LPT1.

VERSATEC specifies the port to which the printer is connected. COM1, COM2, LPT1 and LPT2 are among valid options. Note that you cannot include the colon associated with the port; for example, COM1: is not valid and will be ignored by the system.

PAPER specifies the type of paper in your plotter. The default and valid options depend on your output device. The following table lists valid paper sizes for each plotter. The first paper size listed next to each printer type is the default for that plotter.

VERSA specifies the model of VersaTec used as an output device.

MODEL	*SET Command*	*Valid Paper Sizes*
V-80	SET VERSA=V80	A, B
C2552	SET VERSA=2552	A, B
C2558	SET VERSA=2558	A, B
CE3224	SET VERSA=3224	C, D
CE3236	SET VERSA=3236	D, E
CE3244	SET VERSA=3244	E, F
CE3424	SET VERSA=3424	C, D
CE3436	SET VERSA=3436	D, E
CE3444	SET VERSA=3444	E, F
7222	SET VERSA=7222	C, D
7224	SET VERSA=7224	C, D
7236	SET VERSA=7224	D, E
7244	SET VERSA=7244	E, F
7422	SET VERSA=7422	C, D
7436	SET VERSA=7436	D, E
7444	SET VERSA=7444	E, F
ECP-42	SET VERSA=9242	D, E
VERSACOLORSET	VERSA=VERSACOLOR	A, B

Cameras

■ Polaroid Palette

Required AUTOEXEC.BAT command:

```
SET CAMERA=PALETTE
```

Optional AUTOEXEC.BAT commands:

`SET PALETTE=<COM port>`	Identifies port to which the camera is connected. PALETTE=COM1 is the default.

PALETTE Identifies the port to which the camera is connected. If your camera is connected to COM2, you must specify PALETTE=COM2.

■ Common SET options for SYGRAPH drivers.

TEMPDIR specifies the directory in which the printer drivers writes any temporary files. The default directory is the directory from which you started SYGRAPH.

PLISTSIZE informs the printer driver of the maximum number of bytes for the display buffer. The default is 512 bytes and maximum is 64000. Although you can allocate up to 64000 for the buffer, this will most often slow graphics processing. You should allocate either 1024 or 2048 for a reduction of disk operations by 50 and 75 percent, respectively.

FF specifies whether a formfeed is to be issued at the end of an output page. The default (ON) will issue a formfeed at the end of each output page. When FORMFEED=OFF no formfeed is issued. This allows consecutive output pages to appear to be continuous graphics output with no page breaks.

Appendix H

Saving SYGRAPH Graphs to a File

SYGRAPH allows you to write graphics to an output file and store them until you want to print them. This means you can create a graph at one computer and print it from another. This is done using an intermediary text file to which a graph is written. You can save only one graph to a text file.

NOTE: To save a PostScript graph, you must have a PostScript printer connected to the computer where you are saving the graph.

Here are the basic steps for saving a graph to a file:

- Select a printer driver
- Create a text file for storing the graph
- Issue the appropriate SET commands
- Enter SYGRAPH
- Issue the OUTPUT PRINTER command
- Plot your graph

Select a Printer Driver

The first thing you must do is to select the appropriate driver for the output device you will be printing from. Appendix C lists output devices, their device drivers, and the DRIVERS DISKs on which the drivers are located. If your specific device is not listed in Appendix C, look to Appendix A. This lists emulation modes of common printers and plotters. Your device may emulate another for which SYGRAPH provides a driver. When you have located the proper driver, do the following:

- If you do not have a \DRIVERS subdirectory, make one by typing from the C (hard disk) prompt:

```
>MD\DRIVERS
```

- Insert the appropriate DRIVERS DISK into the A: drive and type:

```
>CD\DRIVERS
>COPY  A:<file  name>
```

  where <file name> is the name of the driver file.

- Enter the appropriate SET command in your AUTOEXEC.BAT file. AUTOEXEC.BAT is a text file located in the root directory of your C drive. You can edit it (or create it if you do not already have one) in any word processor or text editor. The SET command has the format:

```
SET  PRINTER=<driver  name>
```

or

```
SET  PLOTTER=<driver  name>
```

For example, if you are using a LaserJet printer, the command reads:

```
SET  PRINTER=LASERJET
```

If you are unsure what your SET command should be, Appendix E gives them for every device supported by SYGRAPH.

- Create a text file to which you will save the graphics. You can create the file in any word processor or text editor. *The file must contain at least one character.* SYGRAPH cannot write graphics to an empty file. Save the file into the subdirectory from which you will call SYGRAPH.

- Reboot your machine. In order for the changes you have made to AUTOEXEC.BAT, you must restart your computer by pressing the Ctrl, Alt, and Delete keys simultaneously.

- Go to the directory containing the text file to which you are saving the graph.

- Issue a SET command specifying the text file as follows:

```
>SET  <driver  name>=<text  file  name>
```

For example, if you are using a LaserJet and your text file name is GRAPHICS.DAT, the command would be:

```
>SET  LASERJET=GRAPHICS.DAT
```

- Enter SYGRAPH and direct output to the printer with the command:

```
>OUTPUT  PRINTER
```

- Issue your plot command. Note that the text file will hold only one graph or plot! The file will contain the most recent graph that you plot.

■ To print the graph, copy the file to the printer on LPT1 with the command:

```
COPY <text file name> LPT1
```

or to the the printer on LPT2 with the command:

```
COPY <text file name> LPT1
```

The printer must be compatible with the driver that you used to save the file.

Appendix I

Saving Metafiles

SYGRAPH can generate computer graphics metafiles, otherwise known as CGM files. A metafiles will store a SYGRAPH graphic. Because many graphics programs read metafiles, you can create a graph in SYGRAPH, read it into another program, edit it, and print it from that program.

To use metafiles, do the following:

- Install the driver META.SYS. META.SYS is on DRIVERS DISK 3. Copy it to the subdirectory where you keep your drivers (most likely the \DRIVERS subdirectory).

- Add a DEVICE statement to CONFIG.SYS telling the computer where to find META.SYS:

  ```
  DEVICE=C:\<directory>\META.SYS
  ```

  For example, if you put the driver in your \DRIVERS subdirectory, the DEVICE command would read:

  ```
  DEVICE=C:\DRIVERS\META.SYS
  ```

  No modification to AUTOEXEC.BAT is necessary.

- Reboot your machine by pressing the Ctrl, Alt, and Delete keys simultaneously.

- Now enter the SYGRAPH module. To save a plot to a metafile, first type:

  ```
  >OUTPUT  METAFIL
  ```

  Then give your plotting command. SYGRAPH directs the plot into a metafile called METAFILE.DAT. You can only use this name to direct output to a metafile and you can only save one graph to a metafile. Therefore, if you wish to save more metafiles, rename the one you have just created by typing (from within SYGRAPH):

  ```
  >DOS  'RENAME  METAFIL.DAT  META1'
  ```

  This renames your first metafile to META1. METAFILE.DAT is now open to receive the next graph you want to save. When you are done saving files and no longer want output sent to a metafile, type OUTPUT * to return output to the display.

INDEX

SYSTAT

O

P

SYSTAT

Z

Suggestions and Problem Report

Name______________________________ Date____________________

Organization____

Street____

City, State, Zip____

Telephone____

Machine____

Operating System____

SYSTAT Command____

SYSTAT Registration Number___________________________________

Problem or Suggestion:

If possible, enclose a printout of the commands and data which caused your problem.

New features desired in SYSTAT:

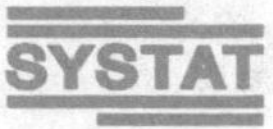

SYSTAT, Inc.

SYSTAT, Inc.

SYSTAT, Inc.

SYSTAT, Inc.

SYSTAT, Inc.

SYSTAT, Inc.

SYSTAT, Inc.